Kaplan Publishing are constantly fin… difference to your studies and our e… ally do offer something different to students looking for exam success.

This book comes with free MyKaplan online resources so that you can study anytime, anywhere. **This free online resource is not sold separately and is included in the price of the book.**

Having purchased this book, you have access to the following online study materials:

| CONTENT | AAT | |
|---|---|---|
| | Text | Kit |
| Electronic version of the book | ✓ | ✓ |
| Progress tests with instant answers | ✓ | |
| Mock assessments online | ✓ | ✓ |
| Material updates | ✓ | ✓ |

## How to access your online resources

Kaplan Financial students will already have a MyKaplan account and these extra resources will be available to you online. You do not need to register again, as this process was completed when you enrolled. If you are having problems accessing online materials, please ask your course administrator.

If you are not studying with Kaplan and did not purchase your book via a Kaplan website, to unlock your extra online resources please go to www.mykaplan.co.uk/addabook (even if you have set up an account and registered books previously). You will then need to enter the ISBN number (on the title page and back cover) and the unique pass key number contained in the scratch panel below to gain access. You will also be required to enter additional information during this process to set up or confirm your account details.

If you purchased through the Kaplan Publishing website you will automatically receive an e-mail invitation to MyKaplan. Please register your details using this email to gain access to your content. If you do not receive the e-mail or book content, please contact Kaplan Publishing.

## Your Code and Information

This code can only be used once for the registration of one book online. This registration and your online content will expire when the final sittings for the examinations covered by this book have taken place. Please allow one hour from the time you submit your book details for us to process your request.

**Please scratch the film to access your unique code.**

Please be aware that this code is case-sensitive and you will need to include the dashes within the passcode, but not when entering the ISBN.

# ADVANCED DIPLOMA IN ACCOUNTING

# SYNOPTIC ASSESSMENT

# STUDY TEXT

**Qualifications and Credit Framework**

**AQ2016**

This Study Text supports study for the following AAT qualifications:

AAT Advanced Diploma in Accounting – Level 3

AAT Advanced Certificate in Bookkeeping – Level 3

AAT Advanced Diploma in Accounting at SCQF – Level 6

**British Library Cataloguing-in-Publication Data**

A catalogue record for this book is available from the British Library.

Published by
Kaplan Publishing UK
Unit 2, The Business Centre
Molly Millars Lane
Wokingham
Berkshire
RG41 2QZ

ISBN: 978-1-78740-784-8



Printed and bound in Great Britain.

We are grateful to the Association of Accounting Technicians for permission to reproduce past assessment materials and example tasks based on the new syllabus. The solutions to past answers and similar activities in the style of the new syllabus have been prepared by Kaplan Publishing.

# CONTENTS

# INTRODUCTION

## HOW TO USE THESE MATERIALS

These Kaplan Publishing learning materials have been carefully designed to make your learning experience as easy as possible and to give you the best chance of success in your AAT assessments.

They contain a number of features to help you in the study process.

The sections on the Unit Guide, the Assessment and Study Skills should be read before you commence your studies.

They are designed to familiarise you with the nature and content of the assessment and to give you tips on how best to approach your studies.

## STUDY TEXT

This study text has been specially prepared for the revised AAT qualification introduced in September 2016.

It is written in a practical and interactive style:

- key terms and concepts are clearly defined
- all topics are illustrated with practical examples with clearly worked solutions based on sample tasks provided by the AAT in the new examining style
- frequent activities throughout the chapters ensure that what you have learnt is regularly reinforced
- 'pitfalls' and 'examination tips' help you avoid commonly made mistakes and help you focus on what is required to perform well in your examination.

## SPREADSHEETS CHAPTERS

The spreadsheet chapters in this text use a slightly different format to other chapters and Kaplan study texts at this level due to the nature of the syllabus content.

The screen shots for this text are based around Excel 2010. However, the techniques explained should also be applicable to other versions of spreadsheet software, although the screens will look slightly different.

There are also 'tips and shortcuts' that will highlight quick ways in Excel to navigate to the correct function.

Throughout these chapters, there will be opportunities to test your knowledge through the activities. For some of these activities you will need to access pre-populated spreadsheets that you can view inside your MyKaplan account. The login details for this account can be found on the insert contained within the study text.

**Please note that suggested answers to all the activities in these chapters can be accessed through your MyKaplan account**.

## ICONS

The chapters include the following icons throughout.

They are designed to assist you in your studies by identifying key definitions and the points at which you can test yourself on the knowledge gained.

### Definition

These sections explain important areas of Knowledge which must be understood and reproduced in an assessment

### Example

The illustrative examples can be used to help develop an understanding of topics before attempting the activity exercises

### Test your understanding

These are exercises which give the opportunity to assess your understanding of all the assessment areas.

Quality and accuracy are of the utmost importance to us so if you spot an error in any of our products, please send an email to mykaplanreporting@kaplan.com with full details.

Our Quality Co-ordinator will work with our technical team to verify the error and take action to ensure it is corrected in future editions.

## Progression

There are two elements of progression that we can measure: first how quickly students move through individual topics within a subject; and second how quickly they move from one course to the next. We know that there is an optimum for both, but it can vary from subject to subject and from student to student. However, using data and our experience of student performance over many years, we can make some generalisations.

A fixed period of study set out at the start of a course with key milestones is important. This can be within a subject, for example 'I will finish this topic by 30 June', or for overall achievement, such as 'I want to be qualified by the end of next year'.

Your qualification is cumulative, as earlier papers provide a foundation for your subsequent studies, so do not allow there to be too big a gap between one subject and another.

We know that exams encourage techniques that lead to some degree of short term retention, the result being that you will simply forget much of what you have already learned unless it is refreshed (look up Ebbinghaus Forgetting Curve for more details on this). This makes it more difficult as you move from one subject to another: not only will you have to learn the new subject, you will also have to relearn all the underpinning knowledge as well. This is very inefficient and slows down your overall progression which makes it more likely you may not succeed at all.

In addition, delaying your studies slows your path to qualification which can have negative impacts on your career, postponing the opportunity to apply for higher level positions and therefore higher pay.

You can use the following diagram showing the whole structure of your qualification to help you keep track of your progress.

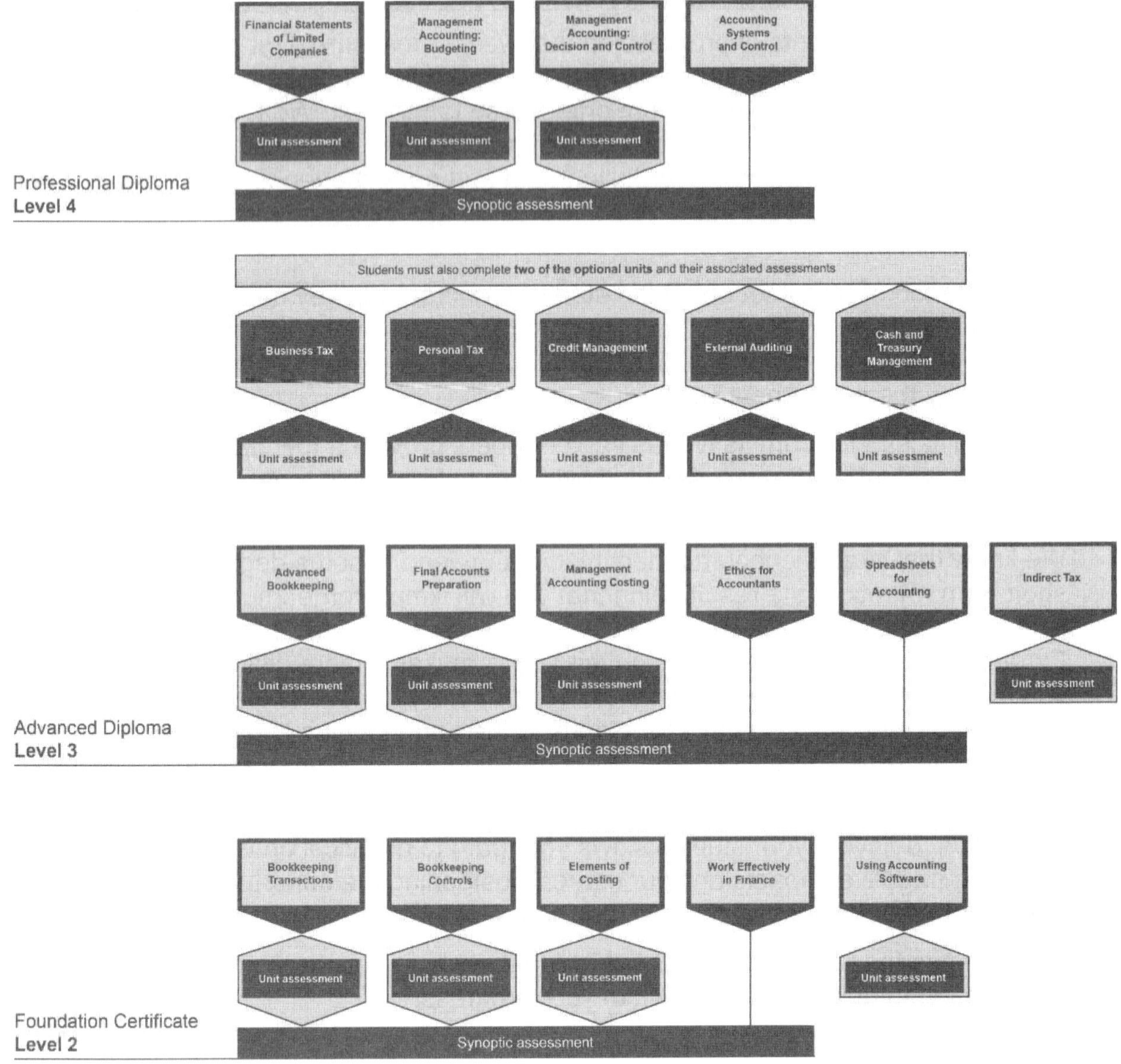
Financial Statements of Limited Companies
Management Accounting: Budgeting
Management Accounting: Decision and Control
Accounting Systems and Control
Unit assessment
Unit assessment
Unit assessment
Professional Diploma
Level 4
Synoptic assessment
Students must also complete two of the optional units and their associated assessments
Business Tax
Personal Tax
Credit Management
External Auditing
Cash and Treasury Management
Unit assessment
Unit assessment
Unit assessment
Unit assessment
Unit assessment
Advanced Bookkeeping
Final Accounts Preparation
Management Accounting Costing
Ethics for Accountants
Spreadsheets for Accounting
Indirect Tax
Unit assessment
Unit assessment
Unit assessment
Unit assessment
Advanced Diploma
Level 3
Synoptic assessment
Bookkeeping Transactions
Bookkeeping Controls
Elements of Costing
Work Effectively in Finance
Using Accounting Software
Unit assessment
Unit assessment
Unit assessment
Unit assessment
Foundation Certificate
Level 2
Synoptic assessment

# SYNOPTIC GUIDE

## Introduction

AAT AQ16 introduces a Synoptic Assessment, which students must complete if they are to achieve the appropriate qualification upon completion of a qualification. In the case of the Advanced Diploma in Accounting, students must pass all of the mandatory assessments and the Synoptic Assessment to achieve the qualification.

As a Synoptic Assessment is attempted following completion of individual units, it draws upon knowledge and understanding from those units. It may be appropriate for students to retain their study materials for individual units until they have successfully completed the Synoptic Assessment for that qualification.

All units within the Advanced Diploma in Accounting are mandatory. Four units are assessed individually in end of unit assessments, but this qualification also includes a synoptic assessment, sat towards the end of the qualification, which draws on and assesses knowledge and understanding from across the qualification:

- Advanced Bookkeeping – end of unit assessment
- Final Accounts Preparation – end of unit assessment
- Management Accounting: Costing – end of unit assessment
- Ethics for accountants – assessed within the synoptic assessment only
- Spreadsheets for Accounting – assessed within the synoptic assessment only

## Scope of content

To perform this synoptic test effectively you will need to know and understand the following:

| | |
|---|---|
| Assessment objective 1 | Demonstrate an understanding of the relevance of the ethical code for accountants, the need to act ethically in a given situation and the appropriate action to take in reporting questionable behaviour |
| Related learning objectives | **Ethics for Accountants**<br>LO1 Understand the need to act ethically<br>LO2 Understand the relevance to the accountant's work of the ethical code for professional accountants<br>LO4 Identify action to take in relation to unethical behaviour or illegal acts. |
| Assessment objective 2 | Prepare accounting records and respond to errors, omissions and other concerns, in accordance with accounting and ethical principles and relevant regulations |
| Related learning objectives | **Ethics for Accountants**<br>LO3 Recognise how to act ethically in an accounting role<br>LO4 Identify action to take in relation to unethical behaviour or illegal acts<br>**Advanced Bookkeeping**<br>LO1 Apply the principles of advanced double-entry bookkeeping<br>LO2 Implement procedures for the acquisition and disposal of non-current assets LO3 Prepare and record depreciation calculations<br>LO4 Record period end adjustments<br>**Final Accounts Preparation**<br>LO2 Explain the need for final accounts and the accounting and ethical principles underlying their preparation<br>LO3 Prepare accounting records from incomplete information |

| Assessment objective 3 | Apply ethical and accounting principles when preparing final accounts for different types of organisation, develop ethical courses of action and communicate relevant information effectively. |
|---|---|
| Related learning objectives | **Ethics for Accountants**<br><br>LO3 Recognise how to act ethically in an accounting role<br><br>**Final Accounts Preparation**<br><br>LO1 Distinguish between the financial recording and reporting requirements of different types of organisation<br><br>LO2 Explain the need for final accounts and the accounting and ethical principles underlying their preparation<br><br>LO3 Prepare accounting records from incomplete information LO4 Produce accounts for sole traders<br><br>LO5 Produce accounts for partnerships<br><br>LO6 Recognise the key differences between preparing accounts for a limited company and a sole trader |
| Assessment objective 4 | Use relevant spreadsheet skills to analyse, interpret and report management accounting data |
| Related learning objectives | **Management Accounting: Costing**<br><br>LO1 Understand the purpose and use of management accounting within an organisation<br><br>LO3 Apportion costs according to organisational requirements<br><br>LO4 Analyse and review deviations from budget and report these to management<br><br>LO5 Apply management accounting techniques to support decision making<br><br>**Spreadsheets for Accounting**<br><br>LO1 Design and structure appropriate spreadsheets to meet customer needs<br><br>LO2 Use spreadsheet software to record, format and organise data |

| Assessment objective 5 | Prepare financial accounting information, comprising extended trial balances and final accounts for sole traders and partnerships, using spreadsheets. |
| --- | --- |
| Related learning objectives | **Final Accounts Preparation**<br><br>LO4 Produce accounts for sole traders<br><br>LO5 Produce accounts for partnerships<br><br>**Advanced Bookkeeping**<br><br>LO5 Produce and extend the trial balance<br><br>**Spreadsheets for Accounting**<br><br>LO1 Design and structure appropriate spreadsheets to meet customer needs<br><br>LO2 Use spreadsheet software to record, format and organise data<br><br>LO3 Use relevant tools to manipulate and analyse data<br><br>LO4 Use software tools to verify accuracy and protect data<br><br>LO5 Use tools and techniques to prepare and report accounting information |

## Summary

| *Underlying paper* | ***LOs required*** |
| --- | --- |
| Advanced Bookkeeping | LO1, LO2, LO3, LO4, LO5 |
| Final Accounts Preparation | LO1, LO2, LO3, LO4, LO5, LO6 |
| Management Accounting: Costing | LO1, LO2, LO3, LO4, LO5 |
| Ethics for accountants | LO1, LO2, LO3, LO4, LO5 |
| Spreadsheets for Accounting | LO1, LO2, LO3, LO4, LO5 |

# THE ASSESSMENT

## Test specification for this synoptic assessment

| Assessment type | Marking type | Duration of exam |
|---|---|---|
| Computer based synoptic assessment | Partially computer/ partially human marked | 2 hours 45 minutes, composed of two components (plus an additional 15 minutes to upload evidence) |

| Assessment objective | Weighting |
|---|---|
| **A01** | |
| Demonstrate an understanding of the relevance of the ethical code for accountants, the need to act ethically in a given situation, and the appropriate action to take in reporting questionable behaviour | 15% |
| **A02** | |
| Prepare accounting records and respond to errors, omissions and other concerns, in accordance with accounting and ethical principles and relevant regulations | 15% |
| **A03** | |
| Apply ethical and accounting principles when preparing final accounts for different types of organisation, develop ethical courses of action and communicate relevant information effectively | 15% |
| **A04** | |
| Use relevant spreadsheet skills to analyse, interpret and report management accounting data | 25% |
| **A05** | |
| Prepare financial accounting information, comprising extended trial balances and final accounts for sole traders and partnerships, using spreadsheets | 30% |
| **Total** | **100%** |

# UNIT GUIDE FOR SPREADSHEETS ASPECTS

## Introduction

This Advanced level unit is about using spreadsheets to accurately enter, analyse and present information so that informed accountancy judgements can be made. The skills and knowledge from this unit integrate spreadsheet use within the other Advanced level accountancy subjects.

Accounting technicians need to use spreadsheets as it is important that financial information is accurately analysed and presented in an unambiguous way. Spreadsheets are widely used within industry, commerce and practice, and a variety of spreadsheet packages are available specifically to assist with accounting roles (routine and one-off): Features of spreadsheet packages allow calculations, manipulation of data, analysis, budgeting, preparing financial statements, reporting, forecasting and decision making.

The student will add value to their organisation if they are familiar with the underlying principles of such software and can use it competently within their workplace. Completing this unit will allow the student to apply these important skills to Advanced Bookkeeping, Final Accounts Preparation and Management Accounting: Costing.

The student will be able to analyse data using their spreadsheet skills and then communicate the most important information to enable appropriate judgements to be made. This means that the information presented needs to be accurate and easily understood by the recipient.

The objective of this unit is to equip students with sufficient skills and knowledge to enable them to select the correct information and then accurately input raw data into a spreadsheet. The student may need to use spreadsheets developed by others or to produce their own. The student will then be able to demonstrate their use of a range of skills to analyse this data in line with accountancy conventions. Skills such as the use of formulas, functions, data analysis tools, sorting and filtering will be vital within accountancy to enable students to perform complex calculations quickly and accurately. After analysis, the data needs to be comprehensively checked and then presented using a range of methods, for example as a structured spreadsheet with pivot tables and charts. The responsibility for checking accuracy of information at Advanced level remains with the student.

Students need to demonstrate their spreadsheet skills across the whole range of accountancy topics at Advanced level. Therefore, this unit can only be examined when the knowledge and skills of the other Advanced level units are understood.

Students must have access to a suitable spreadsheet software package as part of their study for this unit and for the assessment. The program selected by learning providers must be capable of producing reports in at least one of the following formats at various stages of the process: XLS, XLSX. Assessment evidence submitted in alternative file formats will not be marked.

Spreadsheets for Accounting is a mandatory unit in this qualification. This unit links to Advanced Bookkeeping, Final Accounts Preparation, Indirect Tax and Management Accounting: Costing at Advanced level.

## Learning outcomes

On completion of these units the learner will be able to:

- Design and structure appropriate spreadsheets to meet customer needs
- Use spreadsheet software to record, format and organise data
- Use relevant tools to manipulate and analyse data
- Use software tools to verify accuracy and protect data
- Use tools and techniques to prepare and report accounting information

## Scope of content

To perform this unit effectively you will need to know and understand the following:

| | | Chapter |
|---|---|---|
| **1** | **Design and structure appropriate spreadsheets to meet customer needs** | |
| **1.1** | **Organise data in a timely manner**<br>Students need to be able to:<br>• Identify all customer requirements, including deadlines<br>• Consider the use of a template or design a bespoke spreadsheet<br>• Plan and design the spreadsheet to meet customer needs<br>• Develop a spreadsheet for specific accountancy purposes | 1, 2, 3, 16, 18 |
| **1.2** | **Securely store and retrieve relevant information**<br>Students need to be able to:<br>• Securely store, backup, archive and retrieve data and information in line with local policies<br>• Rename files in line with local conventions | 1, 16, 17 |
| **2** | **Use spreadsheet software to record, format and organise data** | |
| **2.1** | **Select relevant data**<br>Students need to know:<br>• When they have sufficient data and information<br>Student need to be able to:<br>• Select valid, reliable and accurate data<br>• Select relevant raw data from different sources<br>• Differentiate between what information is required and what is not required | 1, 2, 3, 15 |

| | | Chapter |
|---|---|---|
| **2.2** | **Accurately enter data**<br>Students need to know:<br>• Why their own data input needs to be accurate<br>• Why they may need to select relevant data from different sources and where to paste that data in their spreadsheet<br>Students need to be able to:<br>• Manually enter data accurately<br>• Link data from different sources and across different worksheets<br>• Remove duplications in data<br>• Import data | 2, 7, 11, 21 |
| **2.3** | **Format data**<br>Students need to be able to:<br>• Use a range of appropriate formatting tools to aid understanding and present the data effectively (see Skills list) | 3, 8, 9, 10, 19 |
| **3** | **Use relevant tools to manipulate and analyse data** | |
| **3.1** | **Select and use a range of appropriate formulas and functions to perform calculations**<br>Students need to be able to:<br>• Plan, select and use a range of formulas to manipulate and analyse the data (see Skills list)<br>• Plan, select and use appropriate mathematical and logical functions (for example, IF, Subtotal, Lookup and so on), and statistical techniques (for example, Goal Seek, Forecast), to perform calculations (see Skills list) | 4, 6, 7, 9, 12, 21, 22 |

| | | Chapter |
|---|---|---|
| 3.2 | **Select and use relevant tools to analyse and interpret data**<br>Students need to be able to:<br>• Assess and select the correct analysis tool for a given task<br>• Analyse data using multiple sorting criteria<br>• Analyse data using multiple filtering criteria<br>• Use Conditional Formatting to enhance decisions<br>• Analyse data using pivot tables and charts<br>• Remove duplicates<br>• Use lookup tables<br>• Select and use appropriate forecasting tools<br>• Summarise data using sub totals | 4, 8, 9, 12, 19, 20, 21, 23 |
| 3.3 | **Select and use appropriate tools to generate and format charts**<br>Students need to be able to:<br>• Critically select and use a range of charts to summarise and present information<br>• Develop and format charts appropriately to aid understanding<br>– Altering scales<br>– Altering and formatting axes<br>– Labelling charts<br>– Change data series colour/format<br>• Produce an output in a format suitable to ensure equality of opportunity | 14, 20 |
| 3.4 | **Edit and update data**<br>Students need to be able to:<br>• Change existing data<br>• Include relevant new data in a spreadsheet<br>• Identify and remove any further duplicates<br>• Update relevant new data in a chart | 1, 2, 3, 14 |

| | | Chapter |
|---|---|---|
| **4** | **Use software tools to verify accuracy and protect data** | |
| **4.1** | **Use appropriate tools to identify and resolve errors**<br>Students need to be able to:<br>• Use formula auditing tools<br>• Select and use error checking tools<br>• Show the formulas within a spreadsheet | 7, 13, 23, |
| **4.2** | **Assess that new data has been accurately added**<br>Students need to be able to:<br>• Consider if any new data added to the spreadsheet is included in the analysis<br>• Check new data is fully included in an existing chart | 1, 2, 3, 14 |
| **4.3** | **Protect integrity of data**<br>Students need to know:<br>• Why protection if the integrity of their data is important<br>• Why they may need to use and share spreadsheet passwords<br>• With whom they can share spreadsheet passwords<br>Students need to be able to:<br>• Use data validation to restrict editing<br>• Protect cells and worksheets<br>• Use passwords<br>• Keep data secure from unauthorised use | 13, 15, 17, 18 |

| | | Chapter |
|---|---|---|
| **5** | **Use tools and techniques to prepare and report accounting information** | |
| **5.1** | **Prepare reports**<br>Students need to be able to:<br>• Insert headers and footers<br>• Hide rows and or columns<br>• Format column, rows and outputs to enhance understanding of relevant data<br>• Adjust margins, orientation and print area<br>• Produce a summary sheet linking to other data and/or worksheets | 3, 5, 8, 9, 11 |
| **5.2** | **Report accounting information**<br>Students need to know:<br>• Why is it important to confirm that the result meets customer requirements<br>Students need to be able to:<br>• Ensure that data produced is suitable for publication, using the appropriate house style<br>• Show all worksheet formulas in a format suitable for publication<br>• Communicate the completed information to the customer appropriately | 5, 9, 11, 13 |

## Skills list

### SPREADSHEET DESIGN AND FORMATTING

- Adjusting/setting column width and row height
- Advanced formatting e.g. negative figures are coloured green
- Clearing cells
- Changing cell fill colour
- Comments box: show and hide
- Conditional formatting
- Copying and pasting: including special (values, linking etc.)
- Currency formatting
- Custom formatting: e.g. dates/times/contents
- Decimal formatting, including 1000 separator
- Find and replace
- Formatting text and cells: font type and colour, size, bold, italics
- Freezing rows and columns
- Headers and footers
- Hiding and unhiding rows and columns
- Hiding and showing formulas
- Inserting data, rows and columns
- Inserting fields in header/footer: page number, no. of pages, date, time, filename
- Locking and unlocking cells
- Merging cells
- Naming and renaming worksheets
- Naming cells and ranges
- Password protecting a worksheet/range of cells
- Page orientation: landscape, portrait
- Page setup: adjust margins, print area
- Print scaling
- Print screen/snipping tool
- Renaming files
- Saving as (CSV, PDF, XLSX)

## DATA

- Cell referencing: absolute and direct
- Custom sorting
- Filtering data using multiple criteria, including number filter
- Importing data
- Linking data across several worksheets
- Percentages
- Sorting data using multiple criteria
- Scaling information for publication
- Spell checking
- Wrapping text

## VALIDITY AND ACCURACY

- Checking validity of results
- Checking links
- Data validation
- Error checking

## CHARTS

- Changing chart type
- Changing data series colour and/or format
- Chart labelling: axis scale, titles, legend
- Chart production and alteration: bar, column, line, pie, in stacked, 3D, exploded formats where appropriate
- Moving and resizing chart
- Pivot tables (simple) and pivot charts
- Trend lines

## FORMULAS AND FUNCTIONS

- Auditing formulas
- Formulas: now, sum, today
- Formulas (logical): Count, Counta, Countif, IF (simple and nested), Lookup
- Formulas (mathematical): add, minus, divide, multiply, average, maximum, minimum, Roundup and Rounddown
- Statistical techniques: Goal Seek and Forecast
- Removal of duplicates
- Subtotalling a range
- Subtotalling formulas: sum, average, maximum, minimum

# STUDY SKILLS

## Preparing to study

### Devise a study plan

Determine which times of the week you will study.

Split these times into sessions of at least one hour for study of new material. Any shorter periods could be used for revision or practice.

Put the times you plan to study onto a study plan for the weeks from now until the assessment and set yourself targets for each period of study – in your sessions make sure you cover the whole course, activities and the associated Test your knowledge activities.

If you are studying more than one unit at a time, try to vary your subjects as this can help to keep you interested and see subjects as part of wider knowledge.

When working through your course, compare your progress with your plan and, if necessary, re-plan your work (perhaps including extra sessions) or, if you are ahead, do some extra revision/practice questions.

## Effective studying

### Active reading

You are not expected to learn the text by rote, rather, you must understand what you are reading and be able to use it to pass the assessment and develop good practice.

A good technique is to use SQ3Rs – Survey, Question, Read, Recall, Review:

1 **Survey the chapter**

   Look at the headings and read the introduction, knowledge, skills and content, so as to get an overview of what the chapter deals with.

2 **Question**

   Whilst undertaking the survey ask yourself the questions you hope the chapter will answer for you.

3 **Read**

   Read through the chapter thoroughly working through the activities and, at the end, making sure that you can meet the learning objectives highlighted on the first page.

4 **Recall**

At the end of each section and at the end of the chapter, try to recall the main ideas of the section/chapter without referring to the text. This is best done after short break of a couple of minutes after the reading stage.

5 **Review**

Check that your recall notes are correct.

You may also find it helpful to re-read the chapter to try and see the topic(s) it deals with as a whole.

### Note taking

Taking notes is a useful way of learning, but do not simply copy out the text.

The notes must:

- be in your own words
- be concise
- cover the key points
- be well organised
- be modified as you study further chapters in this text or in related ones.

Trying to summarise a chapter without referring to the text can be a useful way of determining which areas you know and which you don't.

**Three ways of taking notes**

1 **Summarise the key points of a chapter**

2 **Make linear notes**

A list of headings, subdivided with sub-headings, listing the key points.

If you use linear notes, you can use different colours to highlight key points and keep topic areas together.

Use plenty of space to make your notes easy to use.

**3 Try a diagrammatic form**

The most common of which is a mind map.

To make a mind map, put the main heading in the centre of the paper and put a circle around it.

Draw lines radiating from this to the main sub-headings which again have circles around them.

Continue the process from the sub-headings to sub-sub-headings.

### Highlighting and underlining

You may find it useful to underline or highlight key points in your study text – but do be selective.

You may also wish to make notes in the margins.

## Revision phase

Kaplan has produced material specifically designed for your final examination preparation for this unit.

These include pocket revision notes and a bank of revision questions specifically in the style of the new syllabus.

Further guidance on how to approach the final stage of your studies is given in these materials.

## Further reading

In addition to this text, you should also read the 'Accounting Technician' magazine every month to keep abreast of any guidance from the examiners.

# Introduction to spreadsheet basics

1

## Introduction

This chapter will guide you through how to open and close spreadsheets, guide you how to change names of workbooks/worksheets, and also how to save your work.

### ASSESSMENT CRITERIA

Organise data in a timely manner (1.1)

Securely store and retrieve relevant information (1.2)

Select relevant data (2.1)

Edit and update data (3.4)

Assess that new data has been accurately added (4.2)

### CONTENTS

# 1 Different spreadsheet software applications

## 1.1 Introduction

There are many different spreadsheet applications available. Microsoft Excel is by far the most commonly used, and this guide is written specifically for Microsoft Excel 2010. There are 3 other versions of Excel in common use – the key differences between these and Excel 2010 are explained below, along with Open Office, a spreadsheet application which is freely available online:

**Excel 2003**

This looks very different to 2010 – a major overhaul to the menu system was introduced in 2007. As a result, many of the explanations for methods in this text will not apply. However, all of the formulas and techniques are the same.

Conditional Formatting has also been updated since 2003, although the basics required for this course are the same in 2003.

**Excel 2007**

This version, as mentioned earlier, underwent a huge cosmetic change from Excel 2003. Many features were improved in terms of functionality, although the underlying basics remained the same.

The number of rows and columns available were greatly increased, however from a practical point of view this will make no difference to your studies – no spreadsheet example would ever be big enough to fill up all the space on either version!

There are actually very few differences between Excel 2007 and 2010 – the only important one is that 2007 has the 'Office button' in the top-left of the spreadsheet, which is the equivalent of the 'File tab' in 2010. The File tab is discussed later.

The Excel 2007 'Office button'.

**Excel 2013**

The newest version of Excel. Again, some cosmetic changes have been made, meaning that the menu layout may not be the same as the examples shown. However, the functionality has not changed significantly enough for this to pose too much of a problem.

**Open Office**

As mentioned earlier, this software has the enormous advantage of being free. Its appearance is closer to Excel 2003, with a less visual menu system. The formulas are largely the same, although there are slight differences in the way some formulas are entered.

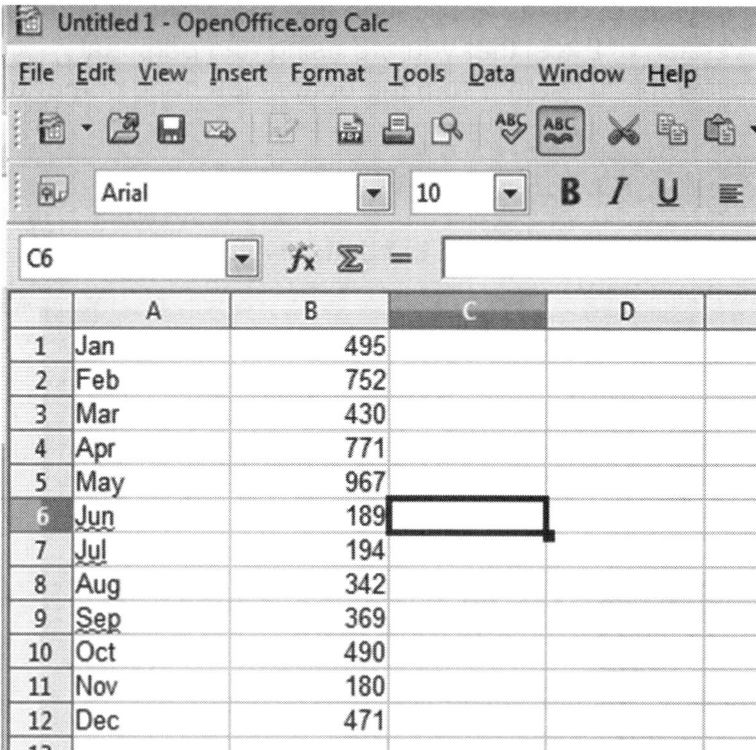


Most of the features are the same, although the appearance is different.

If you are having any problems with any spreadsheet software other than Excel 2010, the internet contains vast resources on all available software, and a quick search should be able to find the correct method.

# 2 Basic navigation

## 2.1 Opening the application

There are numerous ways to open the application and the way that you do it will depend on the version of Excel that you are using and personal preference. We will follow the full path. From the bottom left hand corner of the screen:

- Click the Windows button in the bottom left of the screen (or the Start Menu)
- Select (left click) 'All Programs'
- Select 'Microsoft Office'
- Select 'Microsoft Excel 2010'

Excel will open.

## 2.2 Opening a new workbook

If you wish to open a new workbook:

- Select the **File** tab
- Select '**New**'
- Select '**Blank workbook**' from Available Templates.

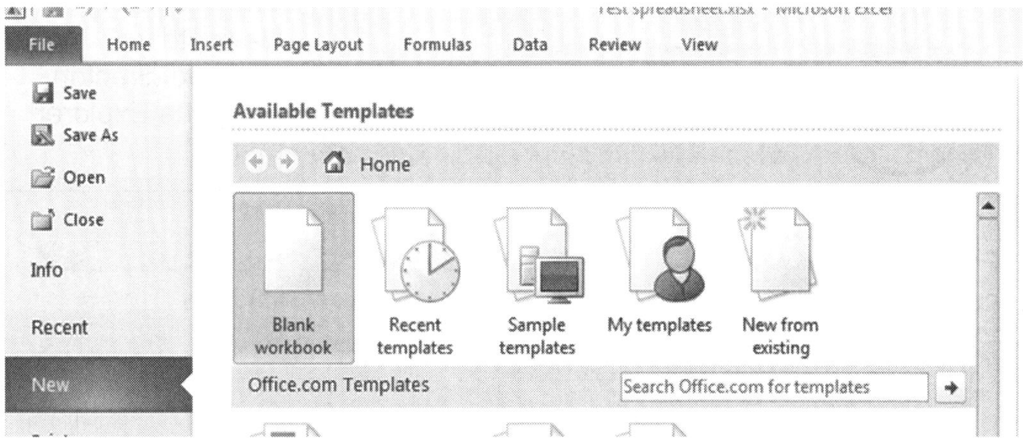


**Shortcut**

**Ctrl-n**

Opens a new workbook automatically.

## 2.3 Saving the workbook

Saving the workbook allows you to give it a more appropriate name, as well as keeping it for future use. To save a file:

- Select the File tab
- Select Save to save the file as it is, or Save As to give it a new name
- The 'Save As' Dialogue Box will open. Navigate to the directory in which you wish to save the file
- Type the name of the spreadsheet in the File name box
- Click 'Save'.

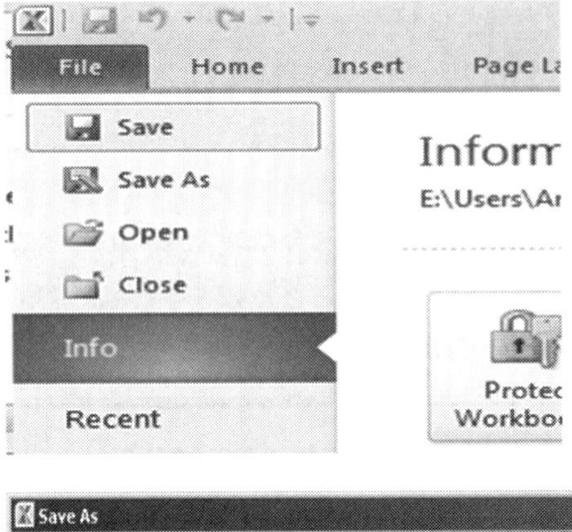


The File tab allows you to save (as well as open and close files).

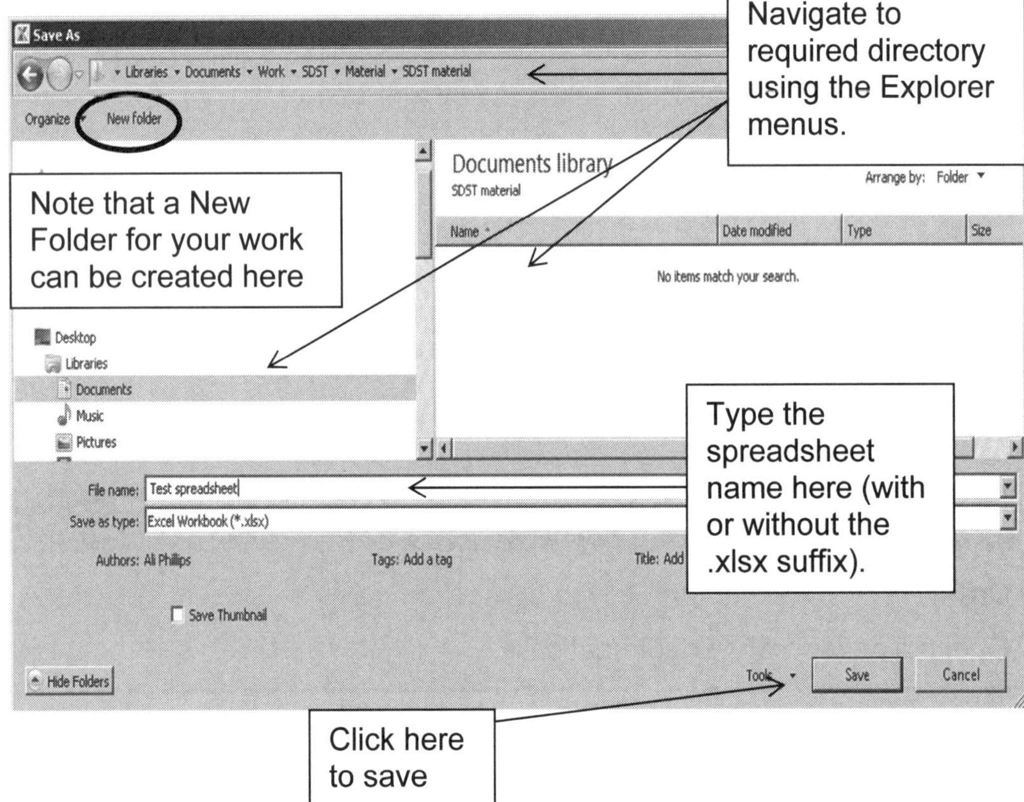


## Shortcut

**Ctrl-s**

Will reveal the 'Save' dialogue box if a file hasn't been saved yet. It will save a file that already has a name.

## 2.4 Opening an existing workbook

To work on a spreadsheet that has been previously saved, open Excel as before, then:

- Click the 'File' tab in the top left of the screen
- Click the 'Open' button
- Navigate to the file you wish to open
- Click the 'Open' button, or double click on the file.

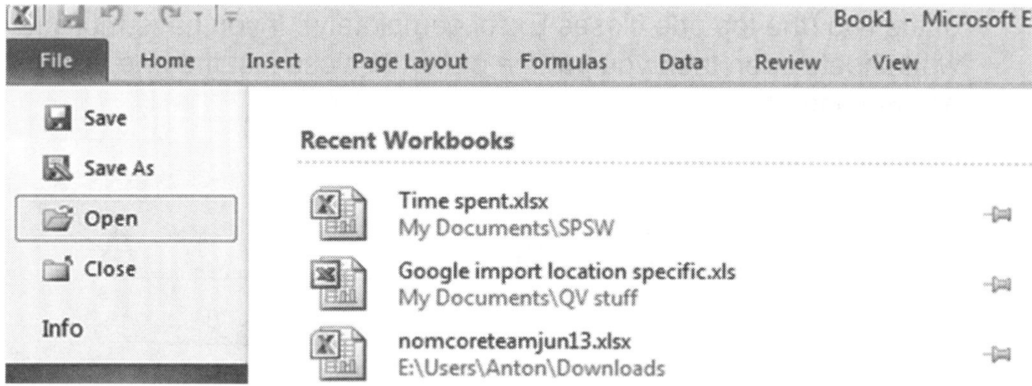


Notice that recently used workbooks can also be selected without having to use the 'Open' button.

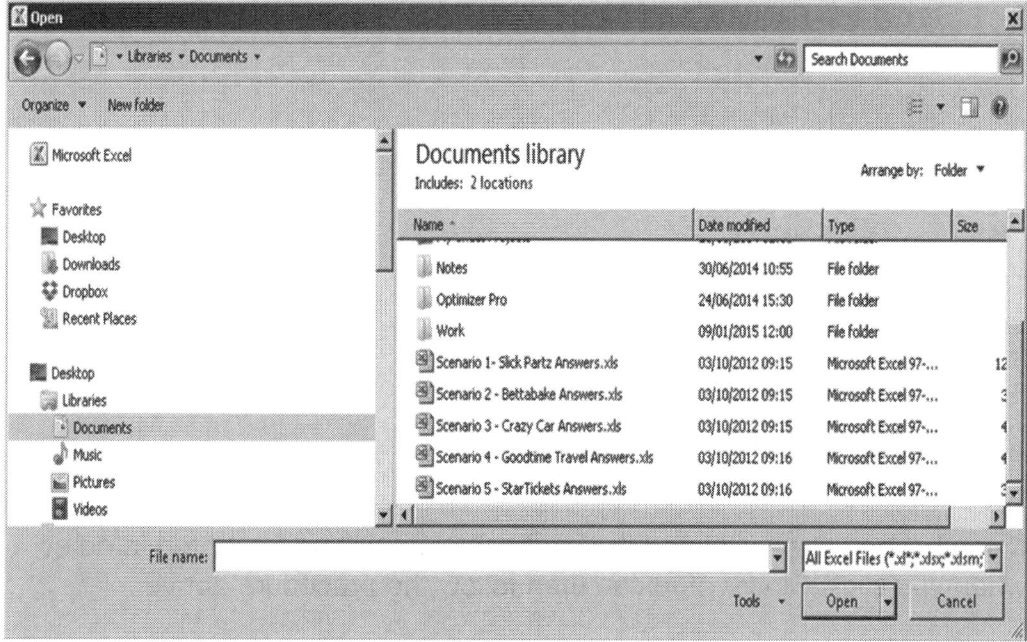


You can navigate to the folder/file you need by selecting the appropriate directory from the dialogue box shown.

**Shortcut**

**Ctrl-o**

Will reveal the 'Open' dialogue box.

## 2.5 Closing the workbook

Having saved your workbook you can then close it. There are 2 basic options:

1 Click the 'X' in the top right hand corner of the screen – the lower one of the two (the top one closes Excel completely). If you have multiple worksheets open then you get the option to close just the one you are working on.

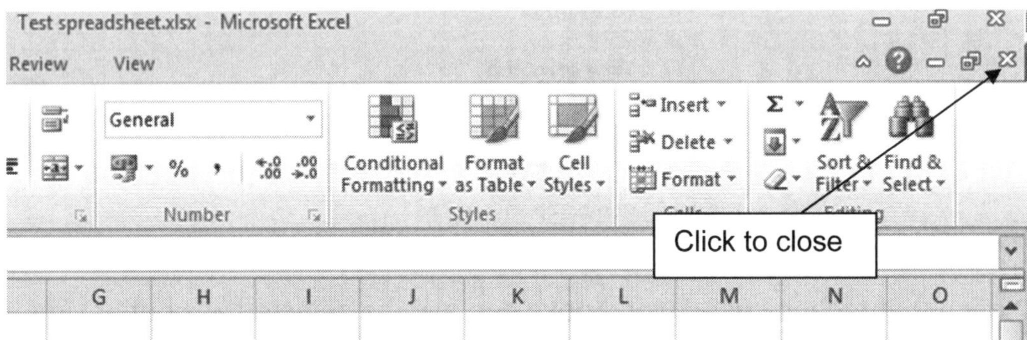


2 Select the File tab, and then Close.

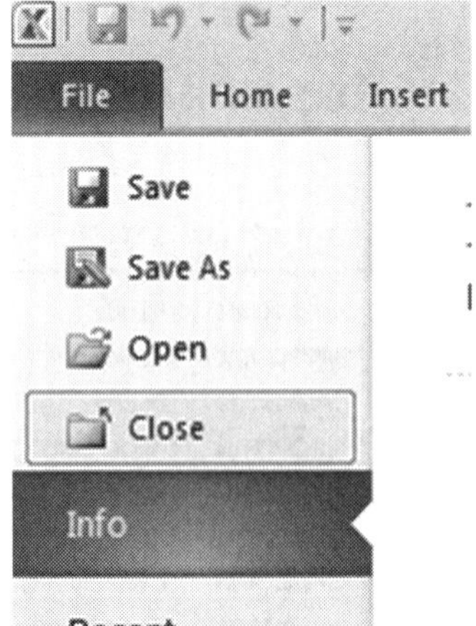


If you haven't already saved the workbook you will be prompted to do so when you click 'Close'. You can then follow the procedure above.

## 2.6 Renaming the workbook

To 'Rename' your workbook you could:

(a) Save the file using a different name, using Save As (note that this will keep a copy of the original file)

(b) Or with the workbook closed

- Locate the File using Windows Explorer (or My Computer)
- Right Click on the file and select 'Rename'
- Type the new name
- Press Enter.

**Shortcut**

**F2**

Renames a file in Windows Explorer.

**Shortcut**

On your keyboard you have a key with the 'Windows' icon

Press '**Windows-e**' to open Windows Explorer.

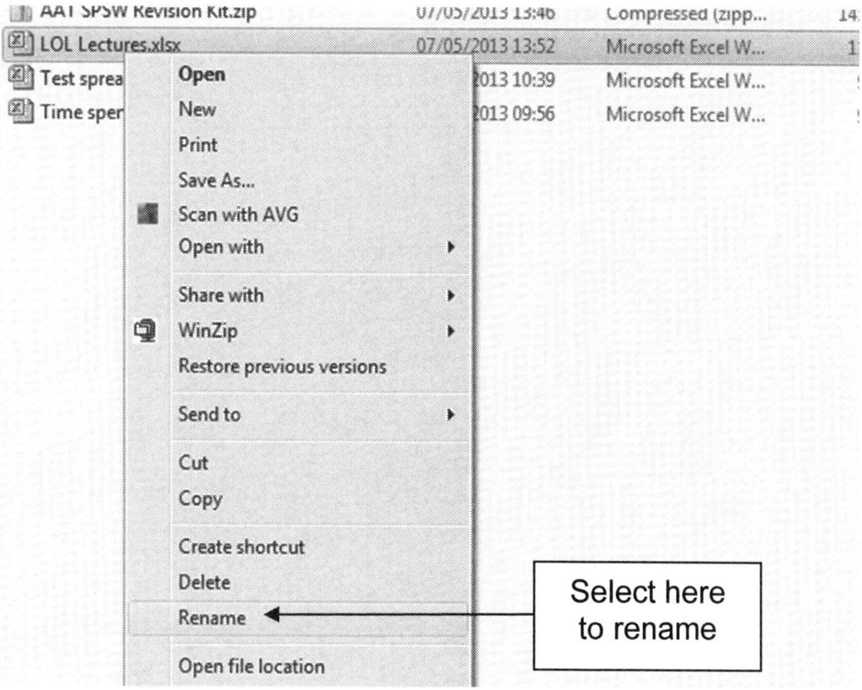

## 2.7 Renaming a worksheet

To 'Rename' a particular **worksheet** within a **workbook** you should do the following:

- Select the Home tab
- Select Format
- Select Rename Sheet
- The Sheet name will then be highlighted. Type the new name to overwrite it.

**OR**

- Right click on the worksheet name at the bottom of the page
- Select rename
- The Sheet name will then be highlighted. Type the new name to overwrite it.

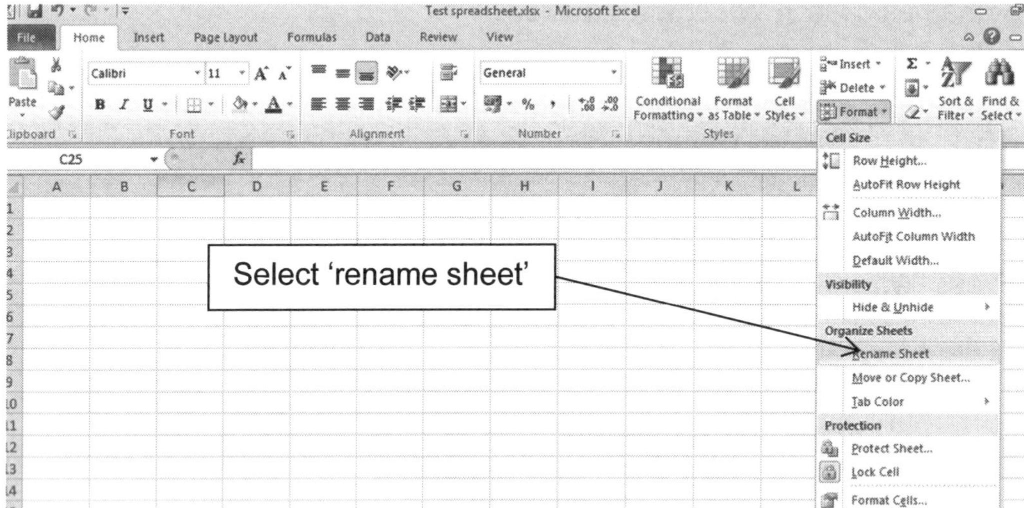

Or

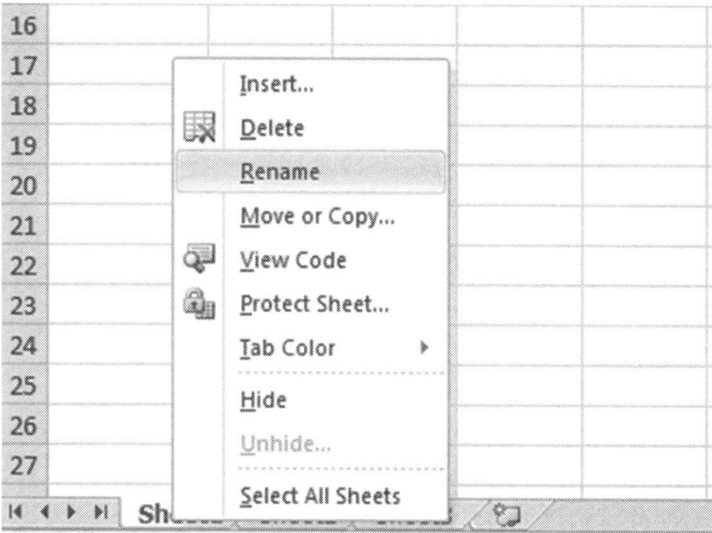


The quickest way is just to **DOUBLE CLICK** on the sheet name to edit it.

## 2.8 Adding worksheets

There are two ways to achieve this, as with renaming a worksheet:

- Select the Home tab
- Select Insert
- Select Insert Sheet
- A new sheet will be added

**OR**

- Right click on the worksheet name at the bottom of the page
- Select Insert
- Select Worksheet
- A new sheet will be added

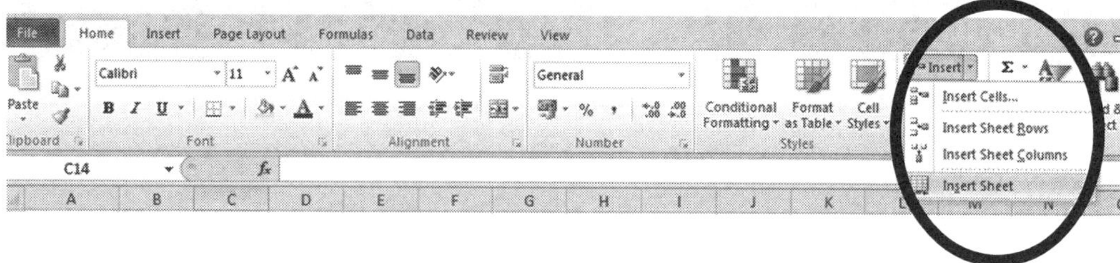

OR

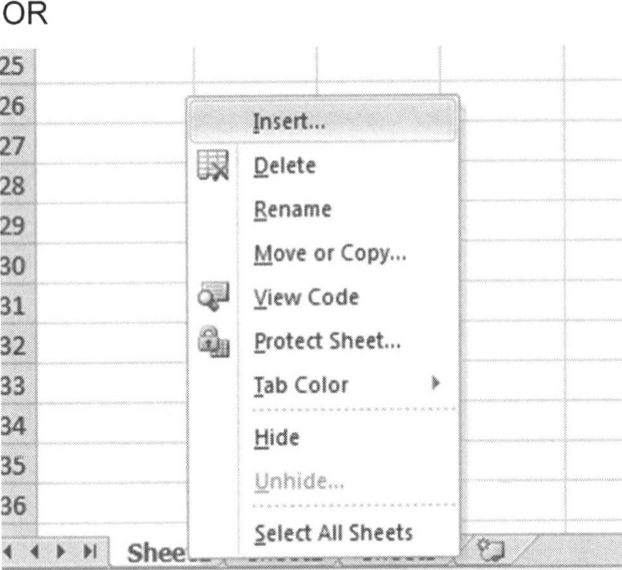


Then select Worksheet to add one.

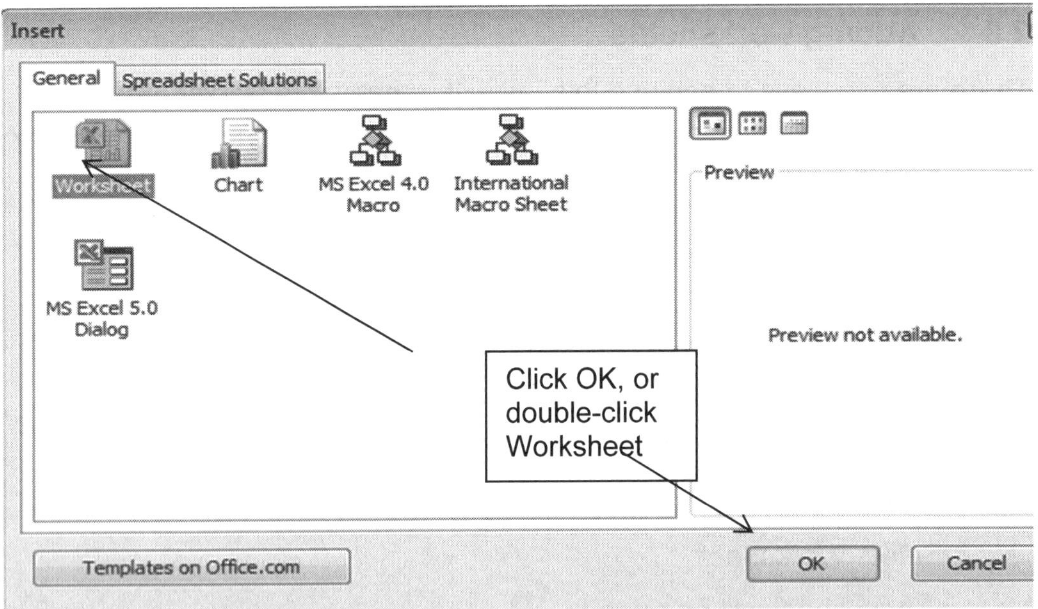

**Shortcut**

**Shift+F11**

Inserts a new worksheet

Or

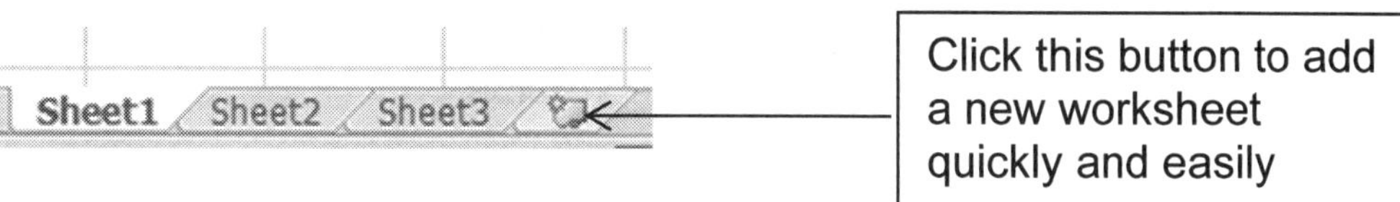


Click this button to add a new worksheet quickly and easily

## 2.9 Deleting worksheets

Similar method to adding worksheets:

- Select the Home tab
- Select Delete
- Select Delete Sheet
- A warning will show – click Delete
- The current sheet will be deleted.

**OR**

- Right click on the worksheet name at the bottom of the page
- Select Delete
- A warning will show – click Delete
- The current sheet will be deleted.

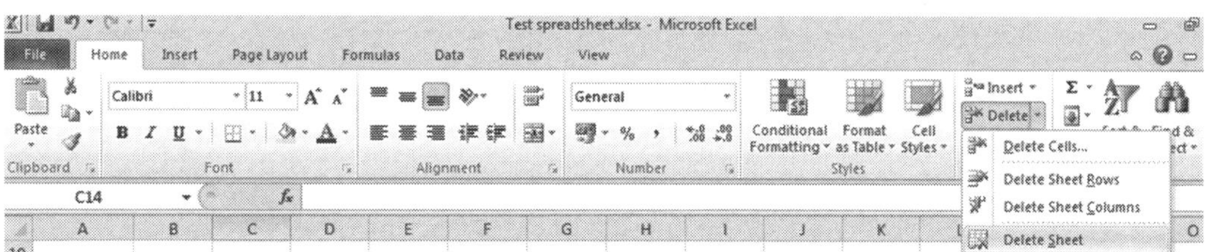

Warning message – take note, once a sheet has been deleted this action **CANNOT** be undone.

## 2.10 Moving/Copying worksheets

The order of your worksheets can easily be changed in Excel, and you can also quickly copy a sheet to get a duplicate version.

- Select the Home tab
- Select Format
- Select Move or Copy Sheet
- A Dialogue box will open – select where you want the current sheet to be located
- Click OK when complete.

**OR**

- Right click on the worksheet name at the bottom of the page
- Select Move or Copy
- The same dialogue box will be displayed.

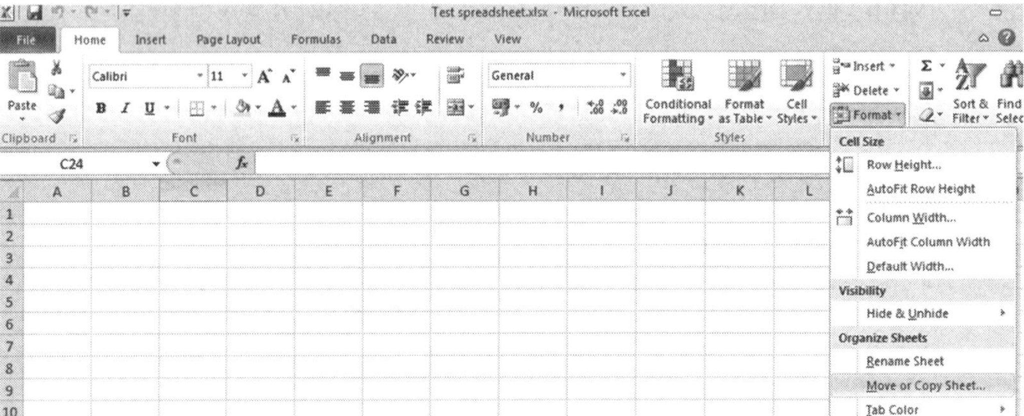


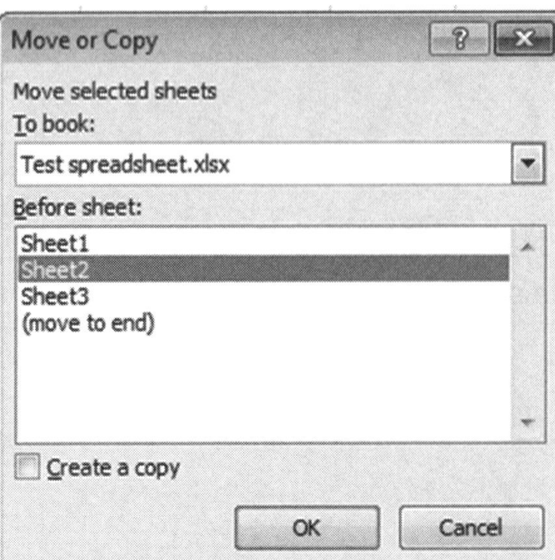

**Shortcut**

Simply **LEFT CLICK** and **HOLD** the button down while pointing at the sheet name – then **DRAG** the sheet to the position you require

Note that a worksheet can be moved within the existing workbook, or to another workbook you have open.

To copy a worksheet, follow exactly the same steps, but tick the 'Create a copy' box before clicking OK.

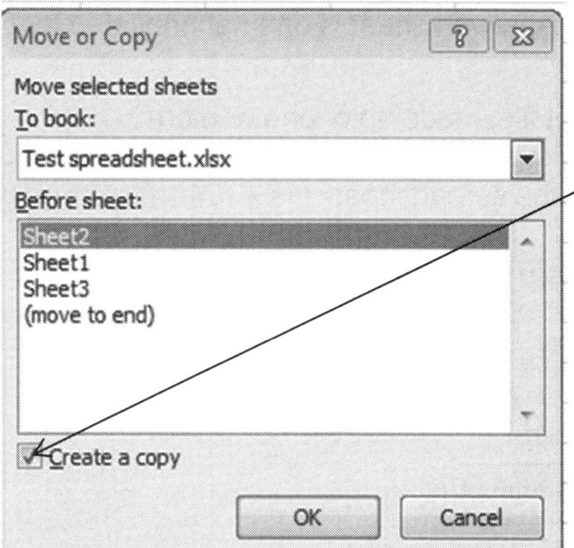


Tick this box (left click) to create a copy

**Shortcut**

If using the **LEFT-CLICK** and **DRAG** approach above, hold down **Ctrl** before releasing the mouse button. A + will appear by the mouse pointer, and a copy made of the worksheet.

# 3 Workbooks and worksheets

## 3.1 Workbooks and worksheets

When Excel opens, a new, blank spreadsheet will be shown. The following terms will be used throughout this material:

A **WORKSHEET** is a single page or sheet in the spreadsheet. A new spreadsheet will have 3 of these by default (called 'Sheet1', 'Sheet2', 'Sheet3'), but this can be changed, and worksheets can be added or deleted, as well as renamed. The term worksheet is often abbreviated to **SHEET**.

A **WORKBOOK** is the spreadsheet file, made up of one or more worksheets. The default blank workbook is made up of 3 worksheets. The workbook name is the filename of the spreadsheet.

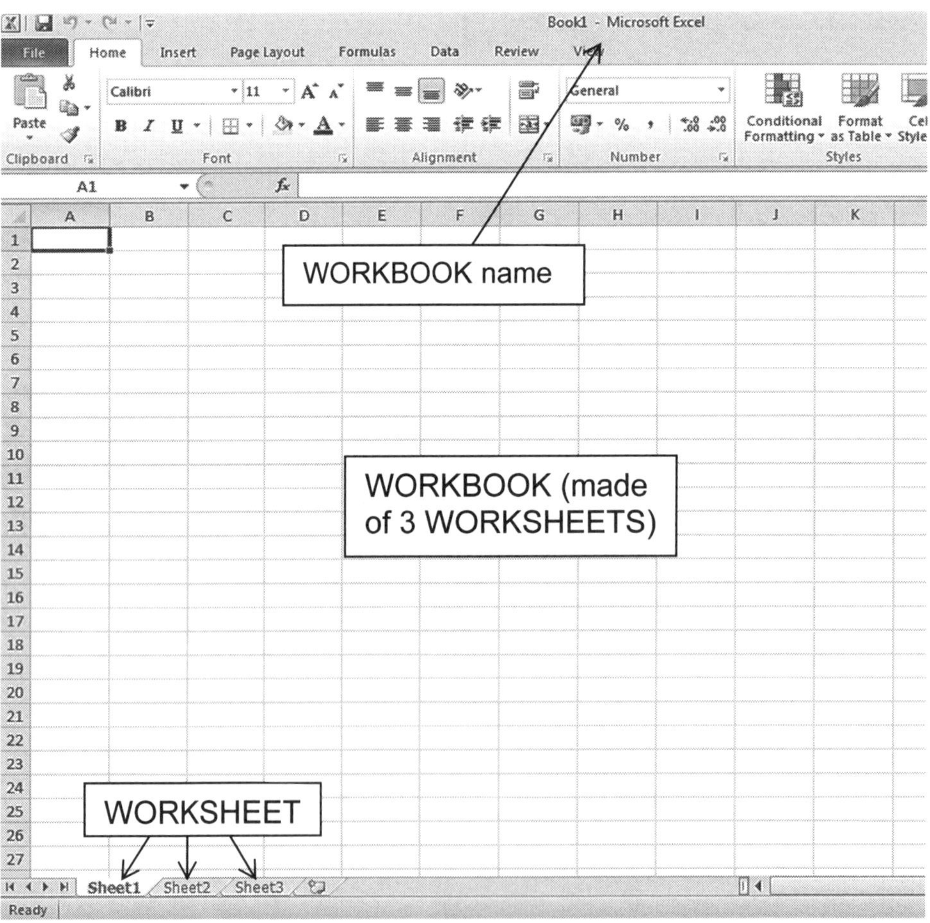

## 3.2 The Ribbon

The 'Ribbon' is Excel's menu system. It is made up of various tabs and buttons, allowing you access to all of Excel's features. There are many, many options within the Ribbon – the good news is that most people only use a few of them. This guide will concentrate on the key features only.

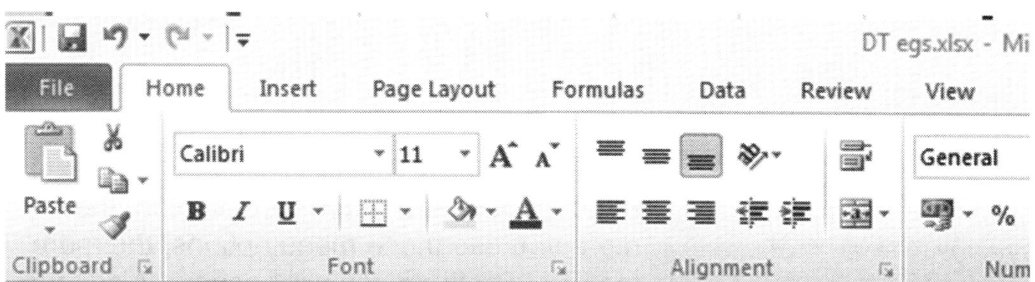


### Tabs

There are usually 8 **tabs** across the top of the Ribbon – File, Home, Insert etc. and clicking on these offers different options. Sometimes more tabs appear depending on context – for example if you are editing a graph, the Chart Tools tabs appear.

Click on the name of the tab to change it, and see the different options.

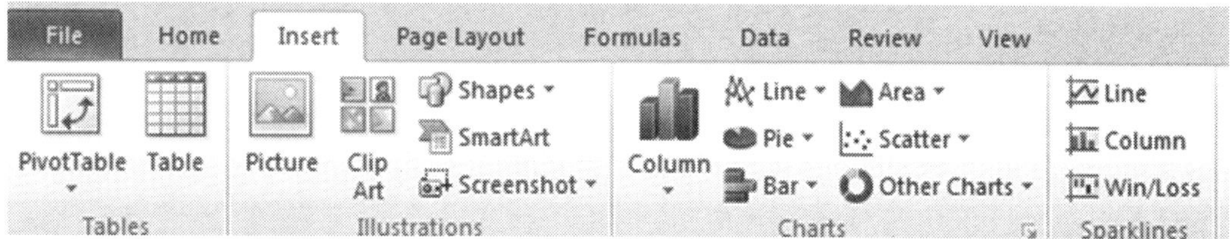


This is the Insert Tab.

### Buttons

The buttons on each tab perform a series of tasks – formatting, spreadsheet appearance, analysis etc. Some of them open up a new menu.

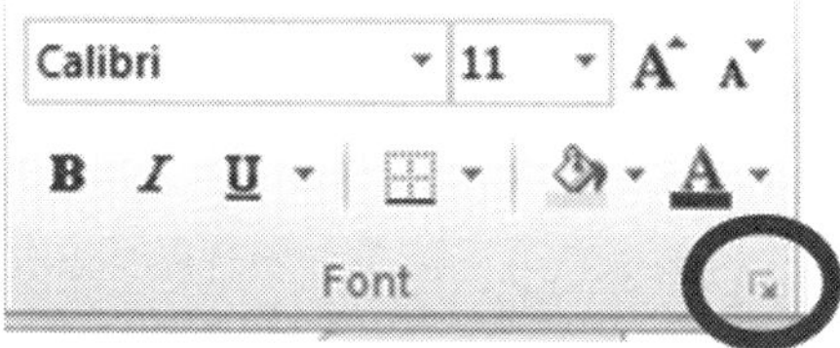


Many of the menu items on the ribbon have the above button. This opens up a specific menu – usually the 'classic' menu from previous versions of Excel, which some people are more used to.

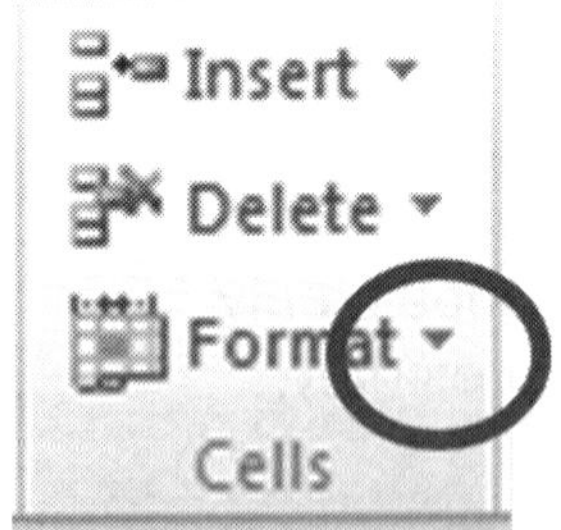


Other buttons have a small down arrow next to the name. Clicking on this opens brings up more options.

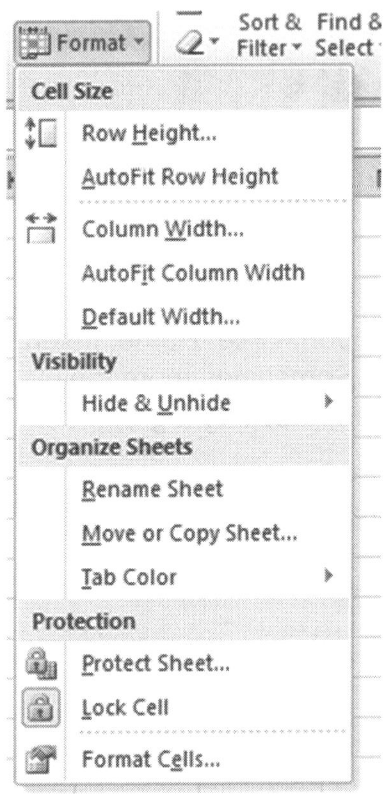


Although it seems like a lot to take in, the more you use these menu options, the more familiar with them you will become. Also, due to the way they are grouped with similar commands, you can often find what you need by looking in these menus.

Note that if you are not sure what a particular option does, hover the mouse pointer over it for a second or two and more information will be shown.

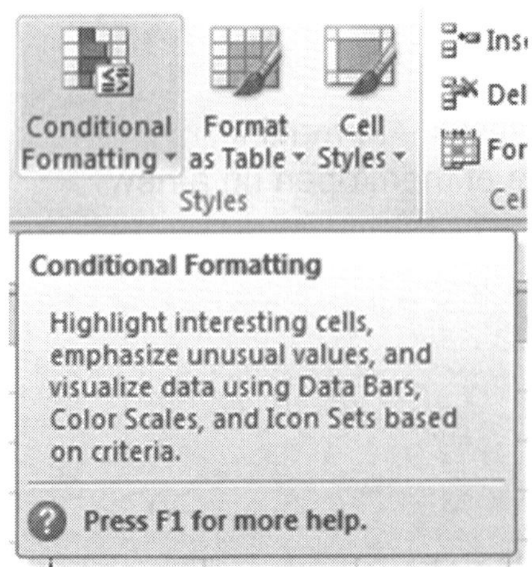


Further information about Conditional Formatting is shown by hovering over the button.

# 4 Help

## 4.1 The Help function

If you are not used to dealing with spreadsheets, they can be quite daunting – there are often lots of numbers and many options for how to deal with your data. Fortunately, Excel has an excellent in-built help function to help you.

The  Help Function is in the **File** tab – click on **File**, then select **Help** or click on

**Shortcut**

Press **F1** to bring up the Help menu

**Important note –** the help function is automatically connected to the Internet. You are not allowed to use the Internet during your AAT assessment. However if you click '?' during the exam a limited help function will be launched.

## 4.2 Right-click

Using the right mouse button within Excel (and most other Windows based programs) is very useful. Context-sensitive menus will appear depending on where you click.

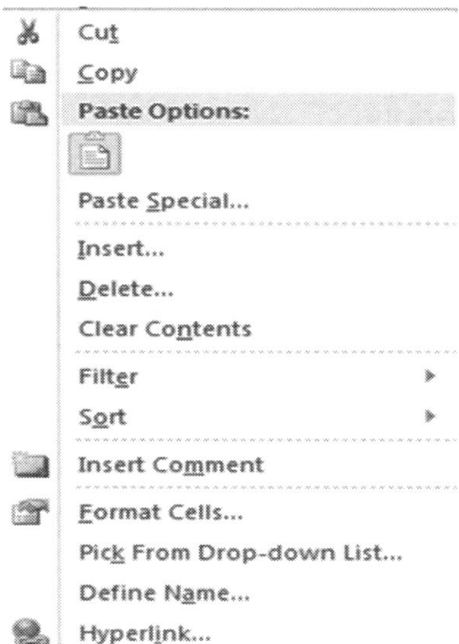


Right-clicking on an individual cell brings up several useful options, and is often the quickest way of completing a task.

## 4.3 Undo and Redo

Probably the most frequently used command within Excel. Undo, as the name suggests, cancels the last thing you did. The most useful thing about this is that it means you should not be afraid to experiment – if you are not sure what something does, try it. If it did not do what you wanted, undo.

Redo allows you to cancel an undo, if you decide that is what you did want!

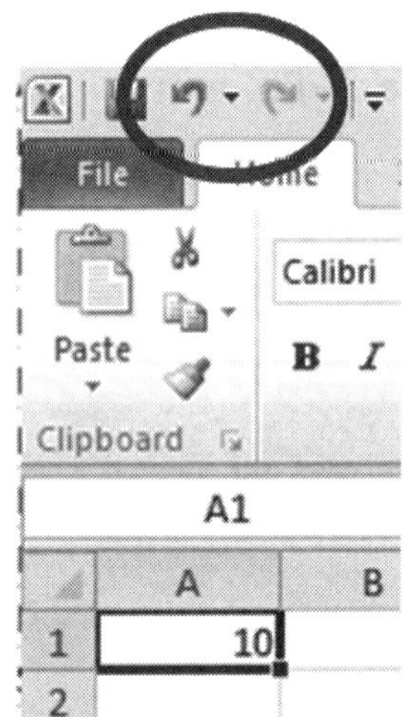


The Undo button (the left arrow) is located in the top-left corner of the file. It is always visible, whichever tab you have clicked on in the ribbon.

The Redo button (the right arrow) is greyed out as there are currently no commands to redo.

Clicking on the blue arrow will undo the last command. Clicking on the small triangle will allow you to undo more than one recent command.

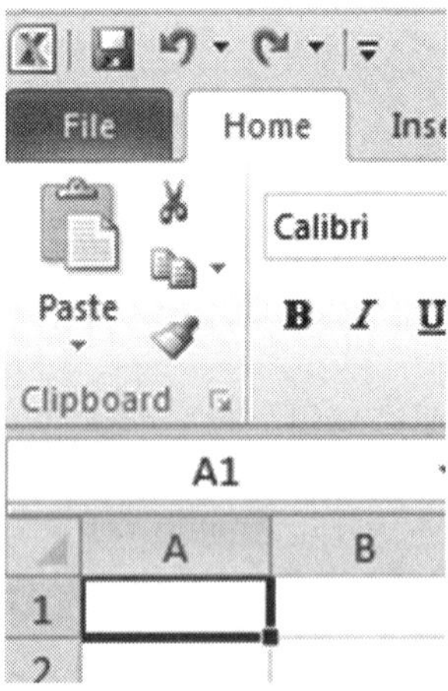


After clicking Undo, the 10 which had been typed in has gone – this has been 'undone'. Note that the redo button has now turned blue – if we click on that, the command (typing 10 into cell A1) will be 'redone'.

Remember, formatting, data entry and formula entry can all be 'undone', so if things start to look wrong, undo what you have done. If you realise you were right, simply redo!

**Shortcut**

- **Ctrl-z** (hold Ctrl, then press z) will undo the last command
- **Ctrl-y** will redo the last undone command

# 5 Test your understanding

The activities in this guide are designed to test your knowledge on the techniques shown in this chapter. They may also use techniques used in previous chapters, to build on your knowledge. Suggested answers are available on MyKaplan, although it is better to refer to the notes and try to understand the methods than look straight at the answers.

## Test your understanding 1-1

**Aim** – to practice opening, closing and saving spreadsheets, as well as renaming worksheets.

(a) **Open** your spreadsheet application.

(b) If no spreadsheet is open, **Open** a blank workbook.

(c) **Rename** the worksheet **Sheet1** – call it **Data**.

(d) **Delete Sheet2** and **Sheet3**.

(e) **Save** the file in a **New Folder** called **Solutions**, filename **Test**.

(f) **Close** the file.

(g) **Rename** the file **Activity 1-1**.

(h) **Open Activity 1-1**.

(i) **Add** a new **worksheet**.

(g) **Rename** the worksheet – call it **Analysis**.

(k) **Move** the Analysis worksheet to the **left** of the Data worksheet.

(l) **Save** and **Close** Activity 1-1.

# Getting started on your worksheet

## Introduction

This chapter will guide you through the structure of the worksheet and how to enter and amend data. You will also learn how to copy, paste, and merge data and how to insert and delete rows and columns.

### ASSESSMENT CRITERIA

Organise data in a timely manner (1.1)

Select relevant data (2.1)

Accurately enter data (2.2)

Edit and update data (3.4)

Assess that new data has been accurately added (4.2)

### CONTENTS

# 1 Spreadsheet structure

## 1.1 Spreadsheet structure

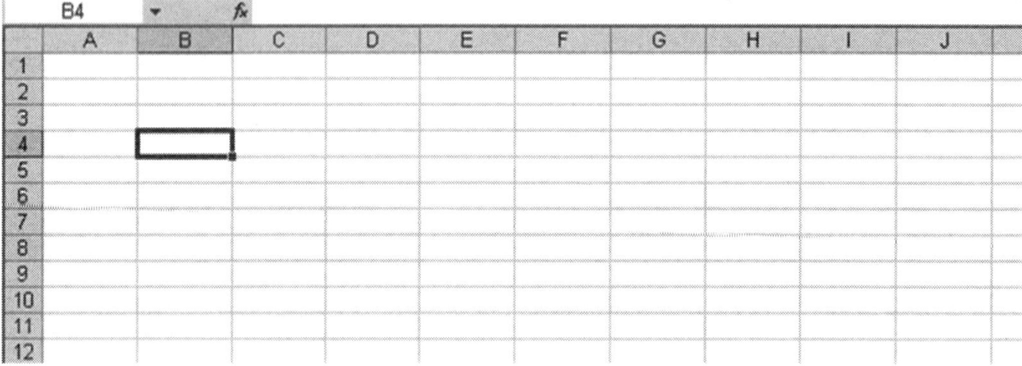

The spreadsheet (worksheet) shown above is made up of 'Rows', 'Columns' and 'Cells:

- The 'Rows' are numbered down the left hand-side from 1 onwards.
- The 'Columns' are lettered along the top from A onwards.
- The 'Cells' are the junction of columns and rows [example cell A1 is the junction of Column A and Row 1].
- The 'Active' cell is where you are be able to enter data and is highlighted with a bold border [See B4 above]. Both the column letter and the row number are also highlighted.

**Shortcut**

Ctrl-Home takes you to cell A1.

Ctrl-End takes you to the cell furthest into the worksheet that has been active (even if the content has been removed).

# 2 Entering data

## 2.1 Selecting cells

To select a cell, left-click on the cell you wish to select. This is now the Active Cell. The value or formula in the Active Cell will be shown in the Formula Bar, and the Cell Reference will be shown in the Name Box.

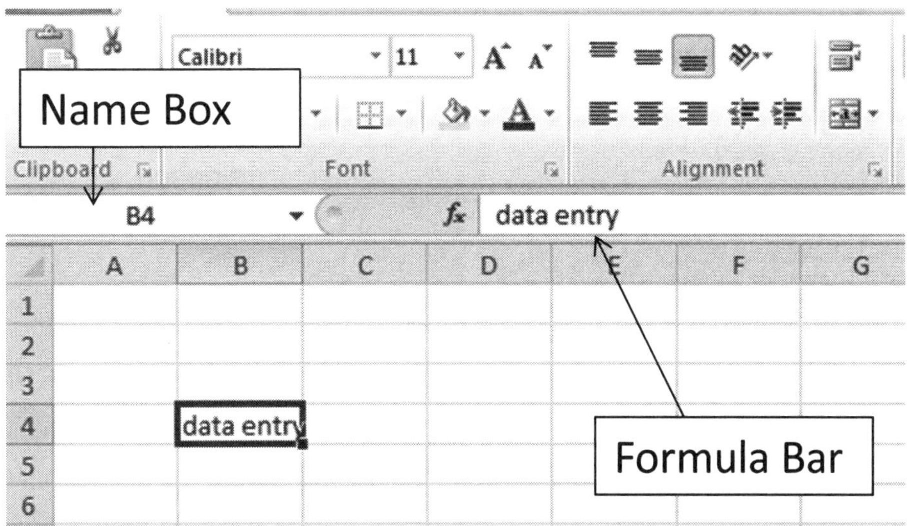


You can also change the selection by using the arrow keys to move the Active Cell Box around the screen until you reach the cell you require, or by typing the cell reference you require into the Name Box, and pressing 'Enter'.

## 2.2 Selecting multiple cells

Selecting several cells at once is easiest using the mouse.

- Using the mouse, **Left-Click** on a cell to select it, but **HOLD DOWN** the mouse button
- **DRAG** the mouse pointer to select neighbouring cells.

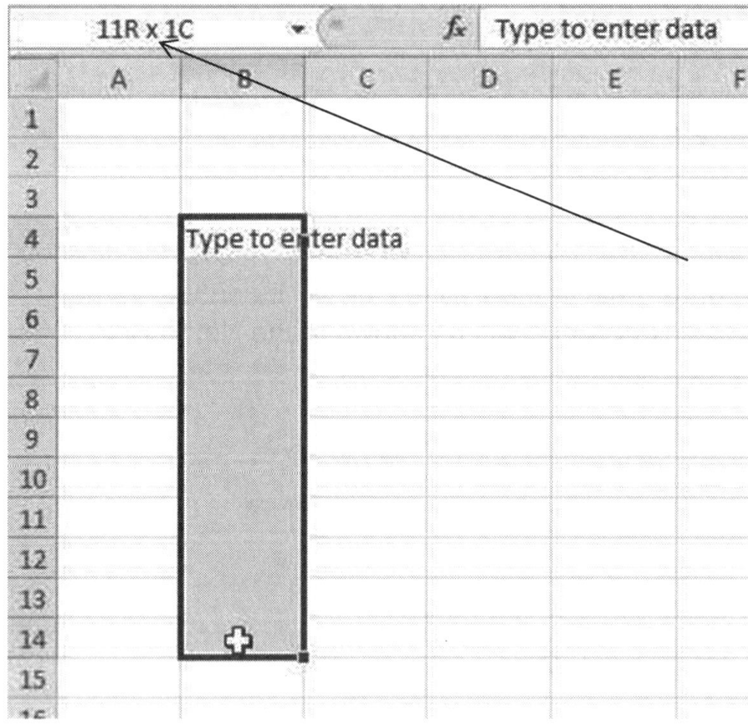


While the mouse button is held down, the dimensions of the box chosen will be shown in the Name Box – this will disappear when the mouse button is released.

If you wish to select non-contiguous (not neighbouring) cells, press the Ctrl key while selecting individual cells.

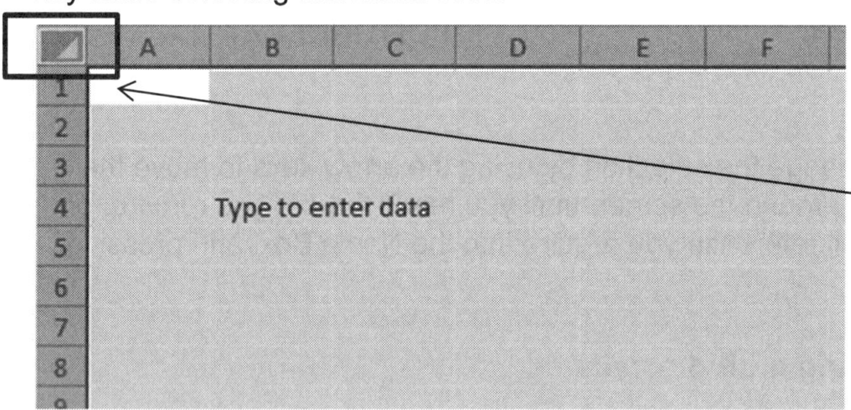


To select **ALL** cells in a worksheet, click on the box in the top-left of the sheet.

## 2.3 Cell ranges

As we have seen, each cell in Excel has a name for example A1, B7. If you select multiple cells, this is a **RANGE** of cells. If you select 2 separate cells, for example C2 and E5, the cells would be separated by a comma, so this would be displayed as **(C2, E5)**. If, as is more common, a **BLOCK** of cells is selected, these are displayed as:

**(Top left cell:Bottom right cell)**

For example:

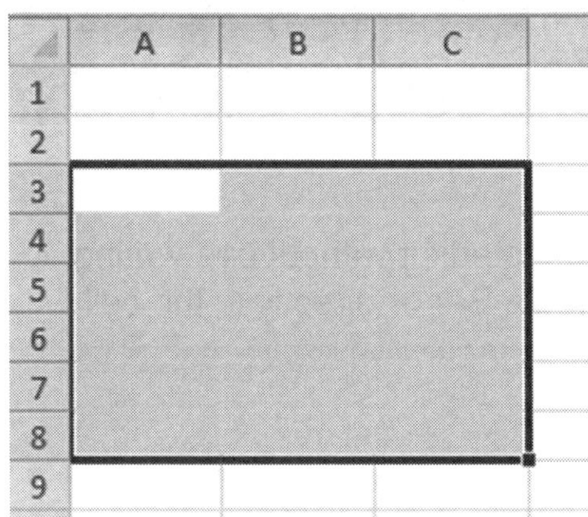


To refer to the cells selected, we would enter **(A3:C8)**.

This notation becomes important when we deal with functions later.

## 2.4 Entering data

To enter data into the active cell, simply type the data required into the cell – either numeric or text. This will overwrite any existing data.

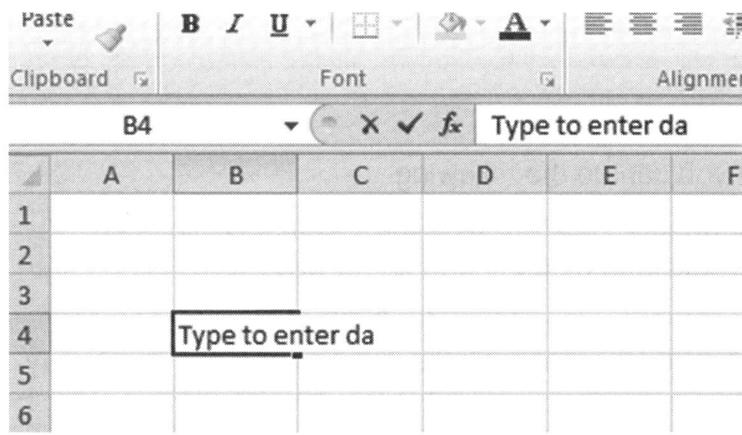


As you type, the data will be displayed on the spreadsheet itself and within the Formula Bar.

# 3 Editing and deleting cell content

## 3.1 Editing existing data

If a cell already contains data and you wish to edit it without overwriting, there are two ways to do this, via the Formula Bar or directly in the cell:

- **Double Click** on a cell to edit it

Or

- With the cell selected, **Left-click** in the **Formula Bar** to edit its contents.

**Shortcut**

Press **F2** to edit the Active Cell

## 3.2 Deleting data

To **delete** cell content you can do the following

1 Go to the cell you wish to delete. Press the delete key. You can highlight multiple cells and delete in the same way.

2 'Right-Click' in the active cell and then 'Left-Click' **clear contents.** You can highlight multiple adjacent cells and delete in the same way.

**CAUTION!!!**

If you 'Right-Click' a cell (or cells) and then click 'delete' Excel thinks you want to delete the cells completely. You will be offered a dialogue box asking you which way you want to shift the cells. This is a useful tool if it is your intention to shift data, but proceed with caution. You can always click 'Edit, Undo' or the undo icon on the toolbar if you change your mind.

# 4 Inserting and deleting rows and columns

## 4.1 Introduction

You can insert both rows and columns into your 'Worksheet'. Doing so will not increase or decrease the number of rows and columns in your worksheet. Excel will merely insert a blank row(s) or column(s) where it is told to do so and shift the other rows or columns down/right. Excel cannot insert when all rows or columns are in use – a very unlikely event – and it cannot insert if the last row or column are in use. You would need to delete a row or column from elsewhere first.

## 4.2 To add a row to your worksheet

- Select the **'Home'** tab
- Select **'Insert'**
- Select **'Insert Sheet Rows'**

A row will be inserted, and the row with the Active Cell in it will be shifted **DOWN**.

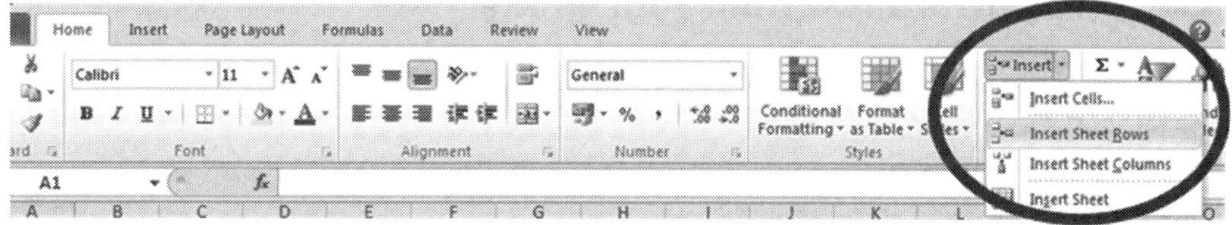


## 4.3 To add a column to your worksheet

- Select the **'Home'** tab
- Select **'Insert'**
- Select **'Insert Sheet Columns'**

A column will be inserted, and the column with the Active Cell in it will be shifted **RIGHT**.

**Shortcut**

**'Right-Click'** the row number or column letter where you wish to insert, then click **'Insert'**

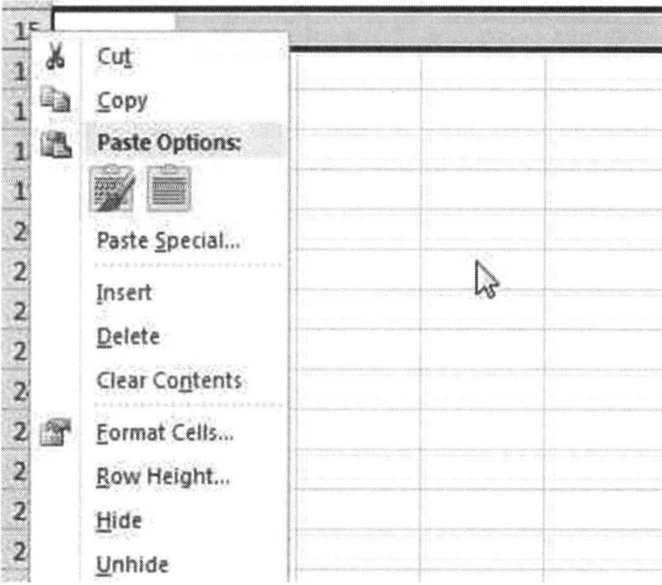


Right clicking on the **'15'** brings up this menu – select Insert to insert a row here.

### 4.4 To delete a row from your worksheet

- Select the **'Home'** tab
- Select **'Delete'**
- Select **'Delete Sheet Rows'**

The data in the row will be deleted, and the rows underneath shifted **UP**

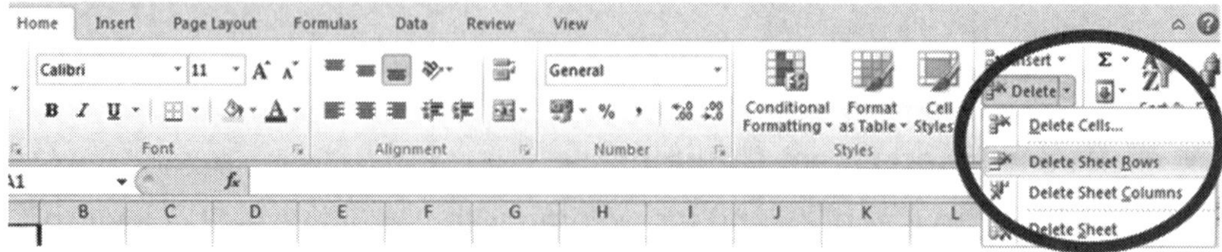

### 4.5 To delete a column from your worksheet

- Select the **'Home'** tab
- Select **'Delete'**
- Select **'Delete Sheet Columns'**

The data in the column will be deleted, and the columns underneath shifted **UP**

**Shortcut**

'Right-Click' the row number(s) or column letter(s) you wish to delete, then click **'Delete'**

## 5 Copy, cut, paste and autofill

### 5.1 Copy and paste

Excel allows you to copy data from the 'Active Cell(s)' to other cells.

- Click in the active cell(s)
- Select the **'Home'** tab
- Press the **'Copy'** button 
- Select the cell (or cells) where you wish to copy to
- Press the **'Paste'** button

Copy and paste are together on the Ribbon

**Shortcut**

'**Right-Click**' the 'Active Cell(s)'. Click '**Copy**'.

Select the cell(s) where you wish to copy to.

'**Right-Click**' and then click '**Paste**'.

**Shortcut**

Highlight the active cells.

**Ctrl-c** will copy the selected cell(s)

**Ctrl-v** will paste the copied cell(s) to the location you have selected

## 5.2 Cut and paste

Excel allows you to move data from the 'Active Cell(s)' to other cells.

- Click in the active cell(s)
- Select the **'Home'** tab
- Press the **'Cut'** button
- Select the cell (or cells) where you wish to move to
- Press the **'Paste'** button 

Cut and paste are together on the Ribbon

**Shortcut**

'**Right-Click**' the 'Active Cell(s)'. Click '**Cut'**.

Select the cell(s) where you wish to copy to.

'**Right-Click**' and then click '**Paste'**.

**Shortcut**

Highlight the active cells.

**Ctrl-x** will copy the selected cell(s)

**Ctrl-v** will paste the copied cell(s) to the location you have selected

## 5.3 AutoFill

The AutoFill tool is an incredibly useful feature within Excel. In the main it is used to quickly copy data into neighbouring cells, but it has several other uses that can save time and effort.

To copy a cell's contents into adjacent cells, hover the mouse pointer over the **bottom right** of the cell. The mouse pointer should change from a fat cross ( ) to a normal cross:

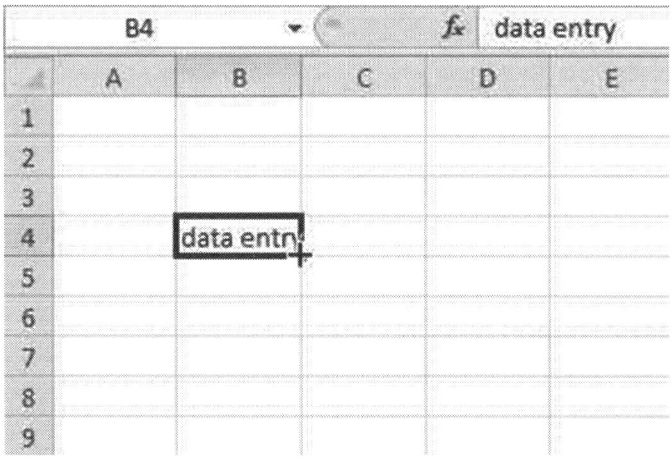

Once the pointer has changed as shown, **left click** and **drag** the mouse in the direction you wish to copy the information.

Release the mouse button to complete the fill.

Autofill becomes especially useful when copying formulas (see later), and can also be used to save time when typing out common lists, such as days of the week, or repetitive sequences.

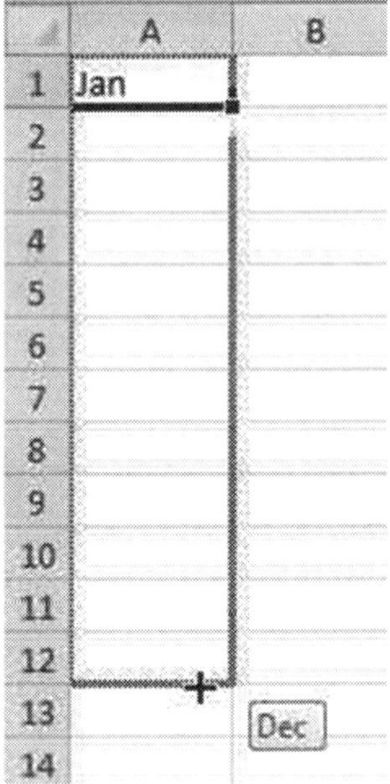


Here, 'Jan' has been typed into cell A1. Autofill has been used to 'drag' the cell down for 12 rows. You can see a pop up over B13 there's a box saying 'Dec' – this is telling us that the Autofill is going to put 'Dec' in cell A12 – the last cell in the fill.

The Autofill is complete. Note that if cell A1 was 'January', the other cells would be populated with the full month name too.

Days of the week are another common autofill.

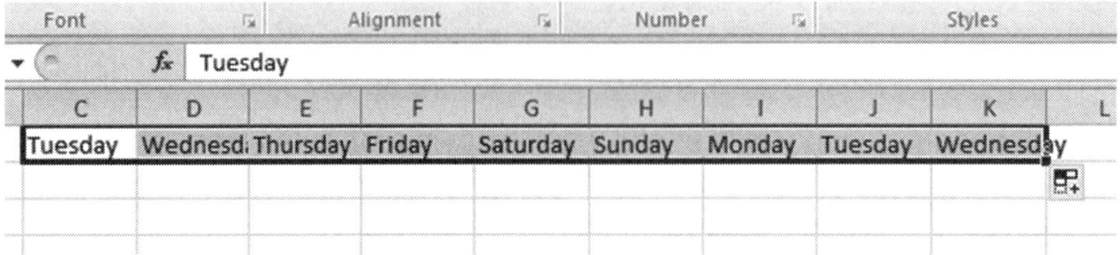

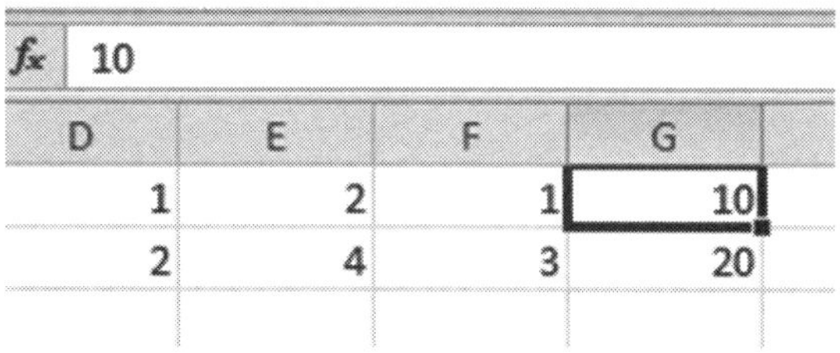

fx 10

| D | E | F | G |
|---|---|---|---|
| 1 | 2 | 1 | 10 |
| 2 | 4 | 3 | 20 |

You can also autofill sequences of numbers – 4 examples shown here. To do this you need to have at least the first 2 numbers of the sequence. Highlight both cells and then 'drag' the cells down.

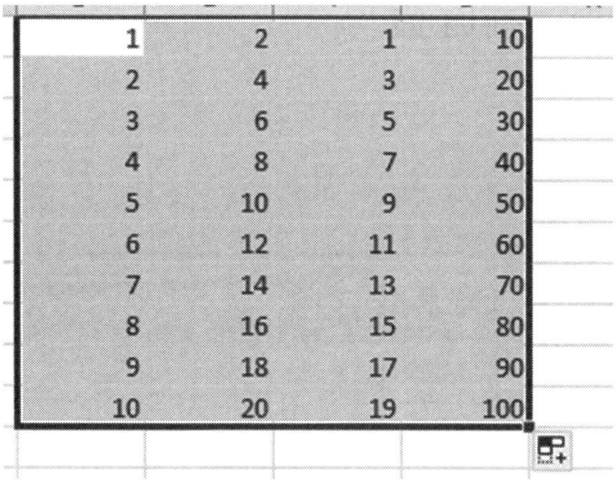

| | | | |
|---|---|---|---|
| 1 | 2 | 1 | 10 |
| 2 | 4 | 3 | 20 |
| 3 | 6 | 5 | 30 |
| 4 | 8 | 7 | 40 |
| 5 | 10 | 9 | 50 |
| 6 | 12 | 11 | 60 |
| 7 | 14 | 13 | 70 |
| 8 | 16 | 15 | 80 |
| 9 | 18 | 17 | 90 |
| 10 | 20 | 19 | 100 |

AutoFill completes the sequence.

## 5.4 Paste Special

There is another function 'Paste Special'. This function allows you to paste different aspects of what could be contained in a cell. Certain parts of these will be covered in later sessions.

- **Copy** the cell(s) you wish to Paste
- **Select** the destination cell(s)
- **Left-click** the down arrow underneath the **Paste** button on the **Home** tab
- Select **Paste Special**

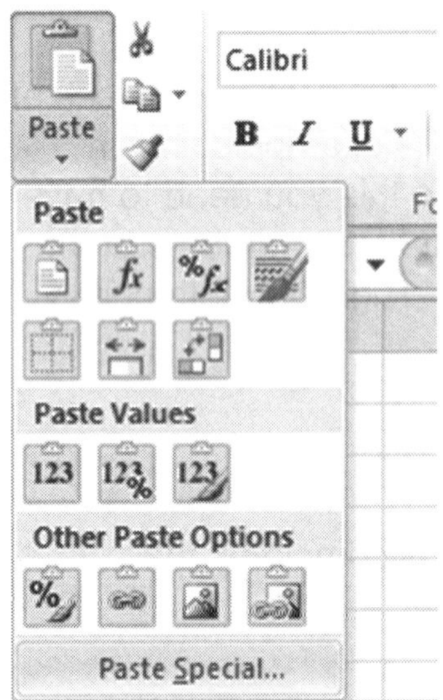


Here you can either select Paste Special, or one of the buttons shown to paste certain features only. Hover over each button to see what they do – a very commonly used one in Paste Values, which removes any formulas and just pastes the cell values.

## Shortcut

**Ctrl-c** to copy the cells

**Ctrl-Alt-v** to paste special

The Paste Special menu gives all of the options available:

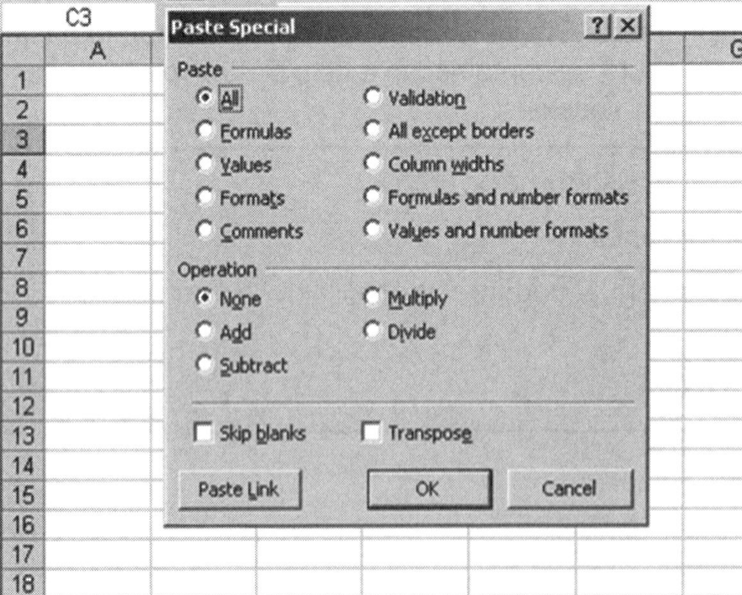

(i) **'All'** pastes content, formula and formatting but it will not alter column width.

(ii) **'Formulas'** pastes the formula from the cell(s) to the new location, without affecting the formatting of the destination cell.

(iii) **'Values'** pastes the value of a cell and not the formula that may have created the value.

(iv) **'Formats'** pastes any formatting that you might have carried out to the new cell(s). This includes cell shading, borders and number formats, but not column width.

(v) **'Comments'** pastes any comments that have been entered into a cell to the new location. '**Comments'** allow you to write a note about a particular cell for you – and others – to see.

Once you have written your comment you will be able to delete and/or hide it by 'Right-Clicking' again in the 'Active Cell'.

(vi) **'Validation'** pastes any data validation rules that you might have created. This will be covered in a later session.

(vii) **'All except borders', 'Column widths', 'Formulas and number formats' and 'Values and number formats'** are derivatives of the above and are self-explanatory.

You will also note that part of the 'Paste-Special' dialogue box allows you to carry out operations. For example the **'add'** operation will add the value of the 'Active Cell' to the value of the cell(s) that you are pasting to. It will add formula outcomes to values and it will also add formulas to formulas.

The last part of the 'Paste-Special' dialogue box allows two other actions.

(i) **'Skip Blanks'** ignores the content – formatting etc – of a cell with no data in it. However, it does maintain the gaps between non-adjacent cells.

(ii) **'Transpose'** is a useful tool for pasting the content of a column into a row, and vice-versa.

# 6 Test your understanding

The activities in this guide are designed to test your knowledge on the techniques shown in this chapter. They may also use techniques used in previous chapters, to build up your knowledge. Suggested answers are available on MyKaplan, although it is better to refer to the notes and try to understand the methods than look straight at the answers.

## Test your understanding 2-1

This activity allows you to practice navigating a workbook, and entering simple data.

(a) Open the file **Simple Report** in the **Activities** folder. The aim is to create a simple report showing just sales and profits for each month. The layout of the report will be:

| | *Jan* | *Feb* | *Mar* |
|---|---|---|---|
| Sales | | | |
| Profit | | | |

(b) First, the **Summary Report** worksheet needs a heading. **Copy** the Heading from the **Existing Data** worksheet and **Paste** it into cell A1 on the summary report worksheet.

(c) In cells A3 and A4 on the **Summary Report** worksheet, type 'Sales' and 'Profit' respectively.

(d) In cells B2:I2, we need the months of the year. You can either type these manually, or (quicker) use Autofill. Type January in B2, and AutoFill to the right to create the months.

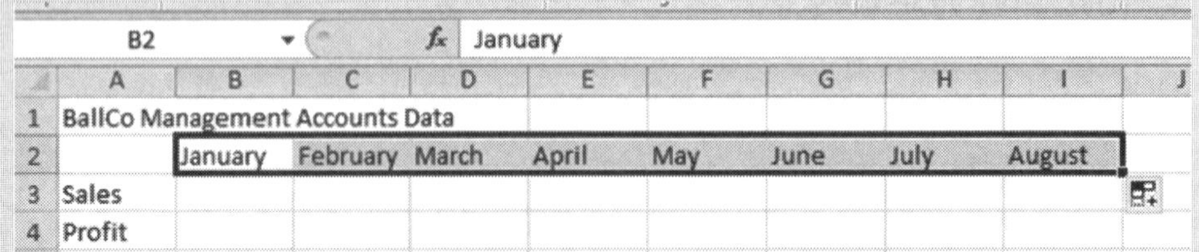


(e) It has now been pointed out that the August sales figure in the **Existing Data** is incorrect, and should be 7,223. Edit the August sales to reflect this. The profit will update automatically.

(f) We now need to put the sales and profit data in the report. We could just type it in, but it's much quicker to **copy** the information. Unfortunately, a straight copy/paste won't work – the existing data has months as rows, the summary has months as columns.

Use **Paste Special** to copy the data. **Select** cells B3:B10 and **copy** them.

(g)

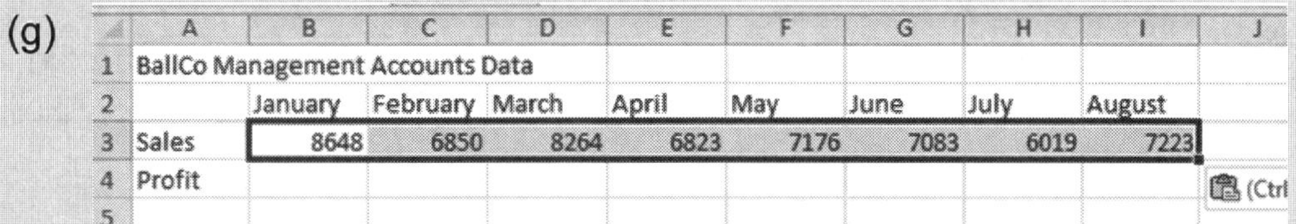

| | A | B | C | D | E | F | G | H | I | J |
|---|---|---|---|---|---|---|---|---|---|---|
| 1 | BallCo Management Accounts Data | | | | | | | | | |
| 2 | | January | February | March | April | May | June | July | August | |
| 3 | Sales | 8648 | 6850 | 8264 | 6823 | 7176 | 7083 | 6019 | 7223 | |
| 4 | Profit | | | | | | | | | (Ctrl |
| 5 | | | | | | | | | | |

On the **Summary report** worksheet, use **Paste special** in cell B3, and select **Transpose**.

(h) Repeat for profits. However, the profits are worked out by using a **formula**. We only want the values of the profits, as the formulas won't work. Using **Paste Special**, select **transpose** and **values.**

(i) The September figures have been received. On the **Summary report** worksheet, add the following data for September in column:

Sales – 7579

Profit – 3444

(j) It has now been decided to enter a half-year total after June's figures. **Insert** a column between June and July, and in row 2, type 'Half Year'.

The half year values are:

Sales – 44844

Profit – 23739

(k) Save the file as **Activity 2-1** in the **Solutions** folder. Close the file.

# 3 Formatting your worksheet

## Introduction

In this chapter you will learn how to change the visual appearance of a spreadsheet so that relevant data is shown. You will also learn how to use the correct formatting.

### ASSESSMENT CRITERIA

Organise data in a timely manner (1.1)

Select relevant data (2.1)

Format data (2.3)

Edit and update data (3.4)

Assess that new data has been accurately added (4.2)

Prepare reports (5.1)

### CONTENTS

# 1 Formatting

## 1.1 Introduction

**Formatting** is a process whereby you change the visual aspects of your worksheet. Under the terms of the Equality Act we need to provide an appropriate format for any person viewing the data. For example:

- Someone with limited eye sight may want a graph in high contrasting colours – using patterns rather than colours.
- Do not produce a graph in say red/green as 6% of males are red/green colour blind.
- A partially sighted person may require the font type and size to be adapted for aid viewing.

The person viewing the data needs to request it in such a format and the spreadsheet needs to be altered to suit the demands of the individual.

The types of formatting you are required to be able to do are:

1 Adjust row height and column width.

2 Add borders and shading to cells and cell ranges.

3 Formatting text and numbers.

4 Hide columns and rows.

## 1.2 The format cells menu

Most formatting options can be found within the Format Cells menu, and if you are unsure this should be the first place to look. To view the Format Cells menu:

- Select the cell(s) you wish to format
- In the **Home** menu, select **Format Cells**

**OR**

- **Right-Click** on the cell(s) to format
- Select Format Cells

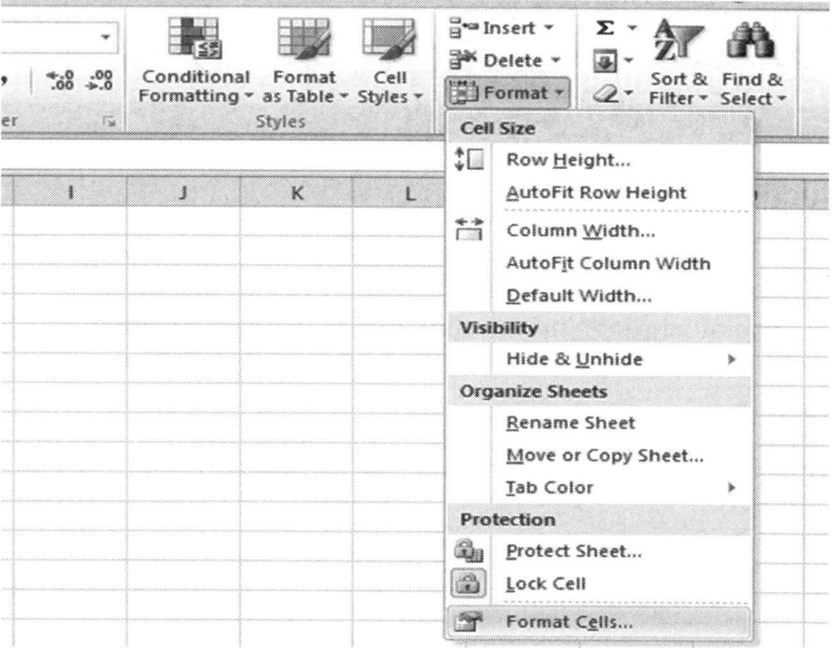


**Shortcut**

Press **Ctrl-1** to bring up the format cells menu.

The **Format Cells** menu has several options, as summarised below:

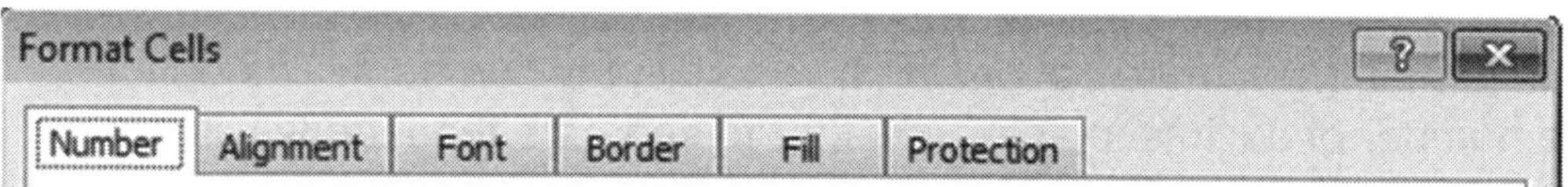


**Number** Changes number formats, for example the number of decimal places, currency type or percentages.

**Alignment** Allows adjustment of where data is shown within a cell for example left or right alignment, and merging cells together.

**Font** Appearance and size of text, along with special features like bold and underline.

**Border** Affects the cell itself, rather than the data within – place lines of varying size and colours around the cell.

**Fill** Colour the cell in various shades and patterns.

**Protection** Affects whether a cell can be edited (dealt with later).

To Exit the menu, click OK to accept any changes, or Cancel to reject them.

The above options will be discussed in turn.

# 2 Number formats

## 2.1 Introduction

Although the name implies that this affects numbers, this option will change the way information within all selected cells will be displayed. Its primary use is to display numeric information in a user-friendly fashion.

## 2.2 General

The default format is 'General', where no special formatting will apply.

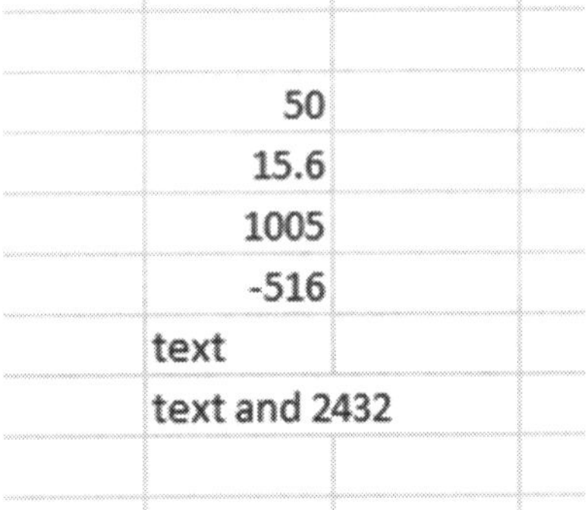

| 50 |
|---|
| 15.6 |
| 1005 |
| -516 |
| text |
| text and 2432 |

This sample data shows how Excel displays numbers and text by default – with no special formatting.

## 2.3 Number

This format gives more options on how to display numbers. The options are number of decimal places, whether to separate thousands with a comma, and how to display negative numbers:

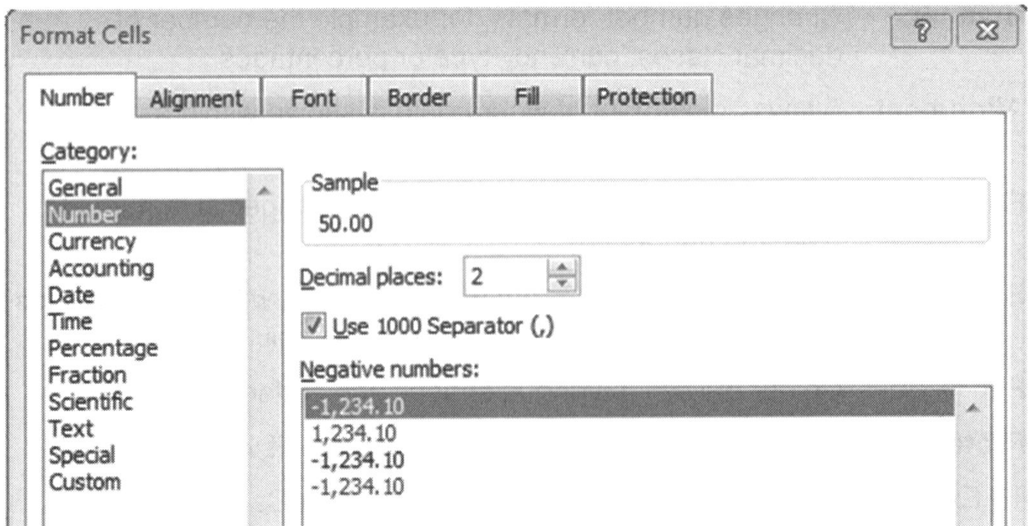

The Sample window shows what the cell will look like with the current options selected. The 1000 separator is an excellent way of making numeric data easier to read. The negative number option can be used to display negative numbers as red, with or without a minus sign.

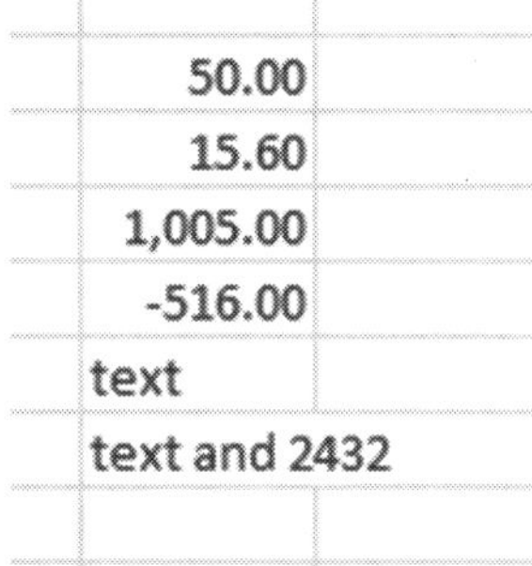

| |
|---|
| 50.00 |
| 15.60 |
| 1,005.00 |
| -516.00 |
| text |
| text and 2432 |

The same information now formatted as a Number. Note that the text information in the bottom two cells is unchanged – even though there is a number in the final cell, Excel recognises it as text only, and will not format the number separately (this can be done, but is beyond the scope of the syllabus).

## 2.4 Currency

This is very similar to **Number**, with the added option of putting a currency symbol at the front of the number:

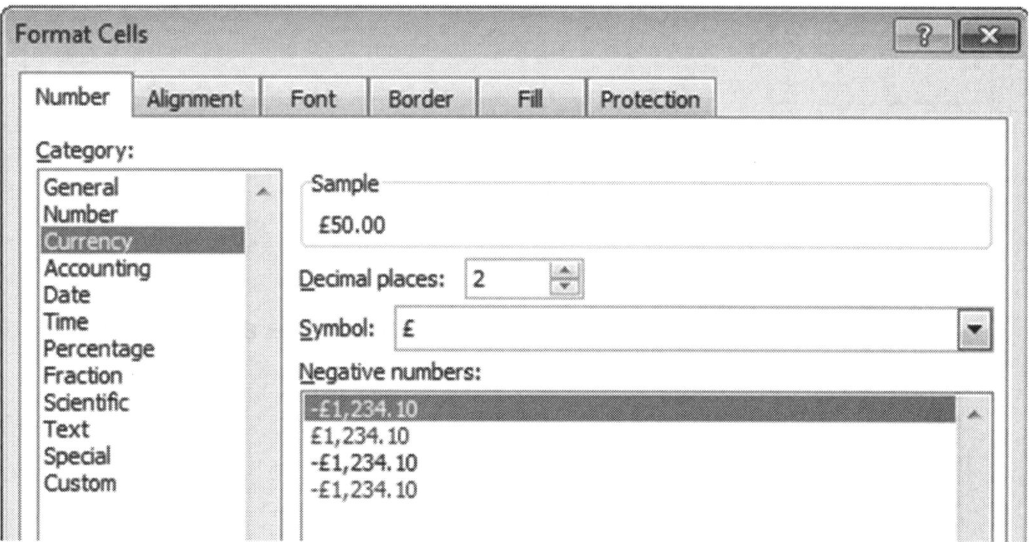


| |
|---|
| £50.00 |
| £15.60 |
| £1,005.00 |
| -£516.00 |
| text |
| text and 2432 |

The only difference is the "£" sign at the front of the numbers.

## 2.5 Accounting

This is very similar to **Currency**, but decimal points and currency symbols will be lined up in a column, potentially making it easier to interpret data:

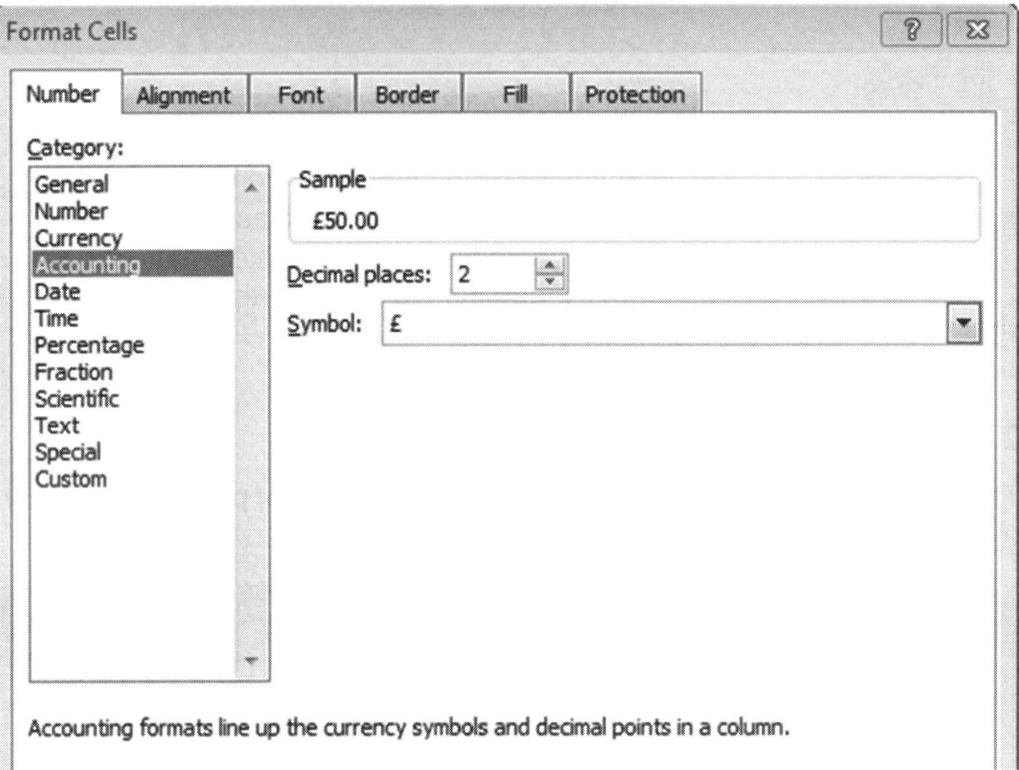


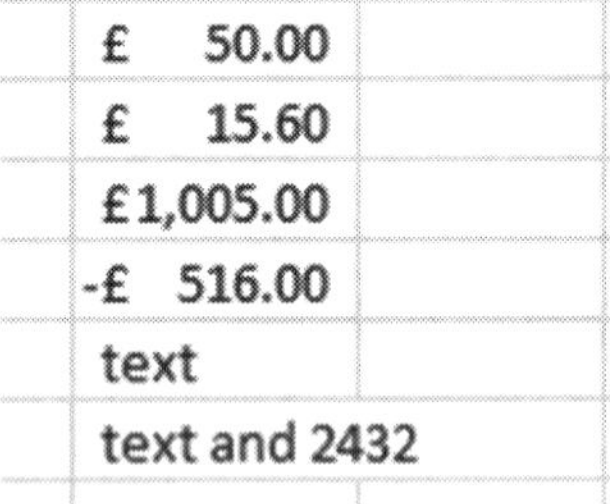


It's a matter of personal choice as to which you prefer.

## 2.6 Percentage

This enables numbers to be displayed with a '**%**' symbol at the end, and also multiplies the value in the cell by 100 – this will be covered in more detail later.

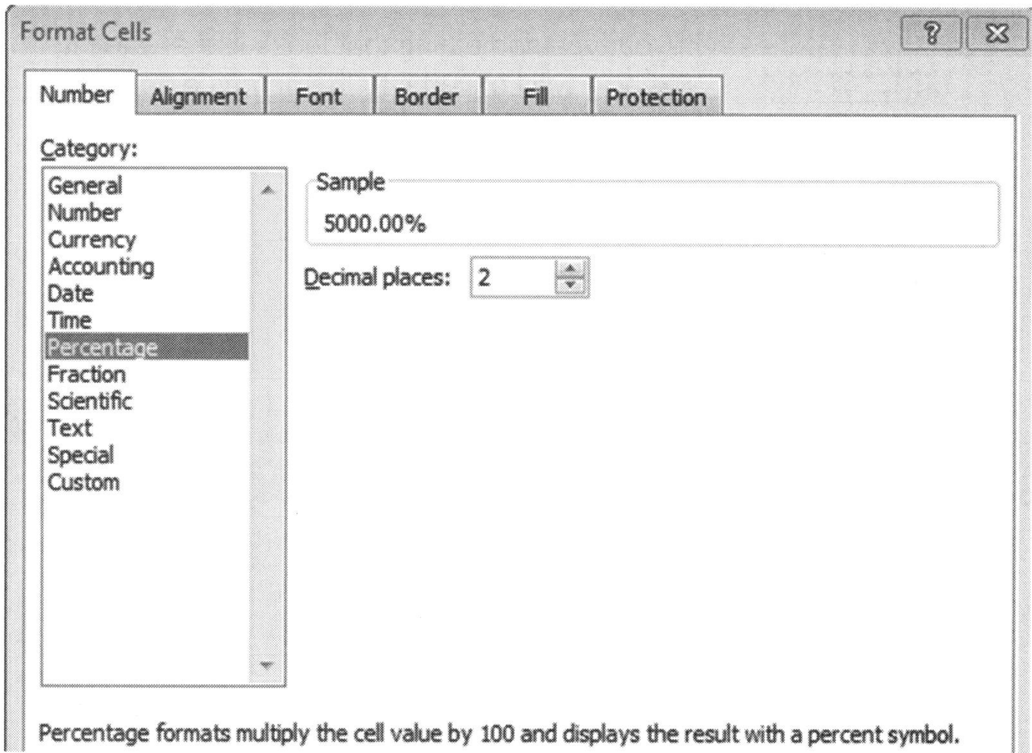


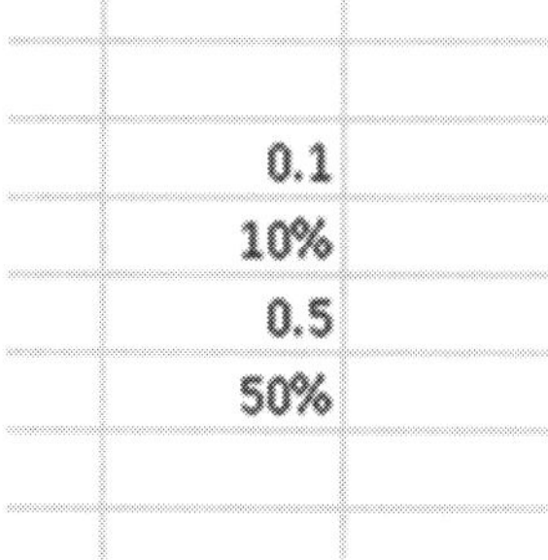


If 0.1 is typed in a cell and percentage formatting is applied then this will be changed to 10%. 0.5 will be changed to 50%. The % format will come in very useful later on.

## 2.7 Date

The **Date** format is used to display dates in various different ways. The best thing to do is type the date in you wish to use, and then select the different options until you find the one you want:

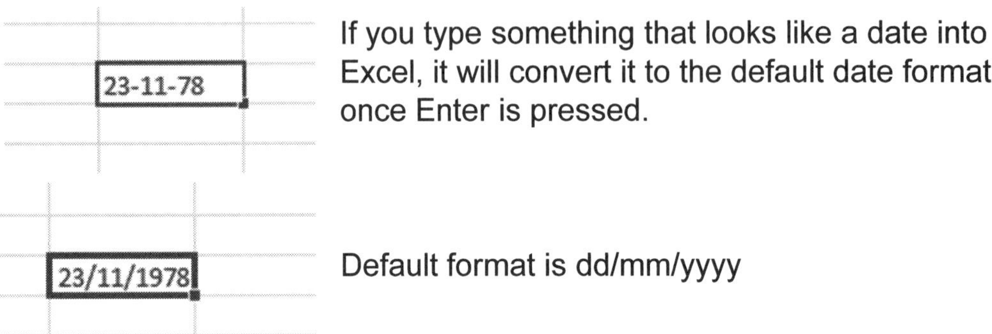


If you type something that looks like a date into Excel, it will convert it to the default date format once Enter is pressed.

Default format is dd/mm/yyyy

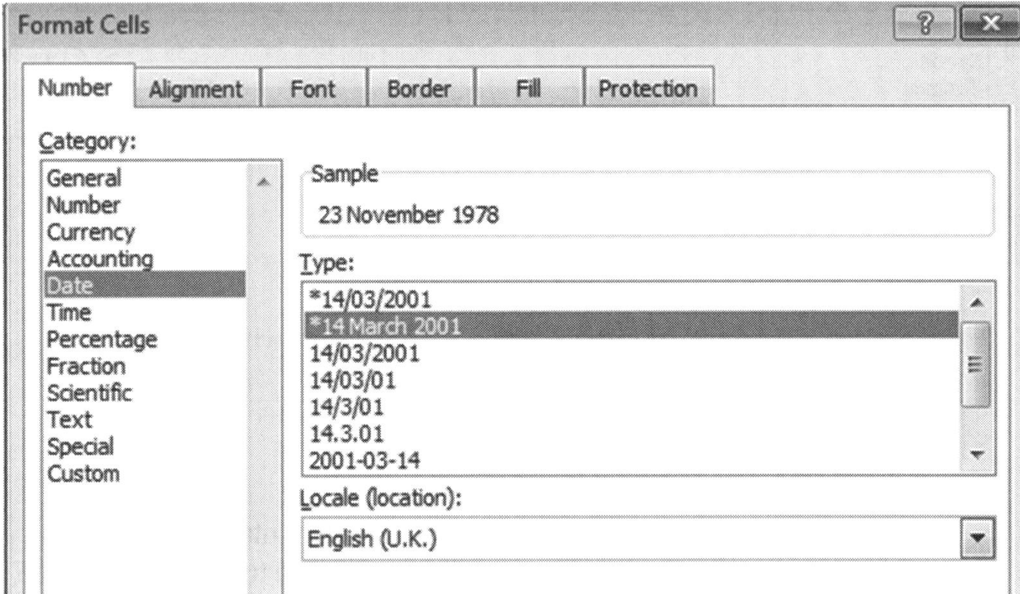


Choosing the appropriate option will display the date as required.

## 2.8 Custom

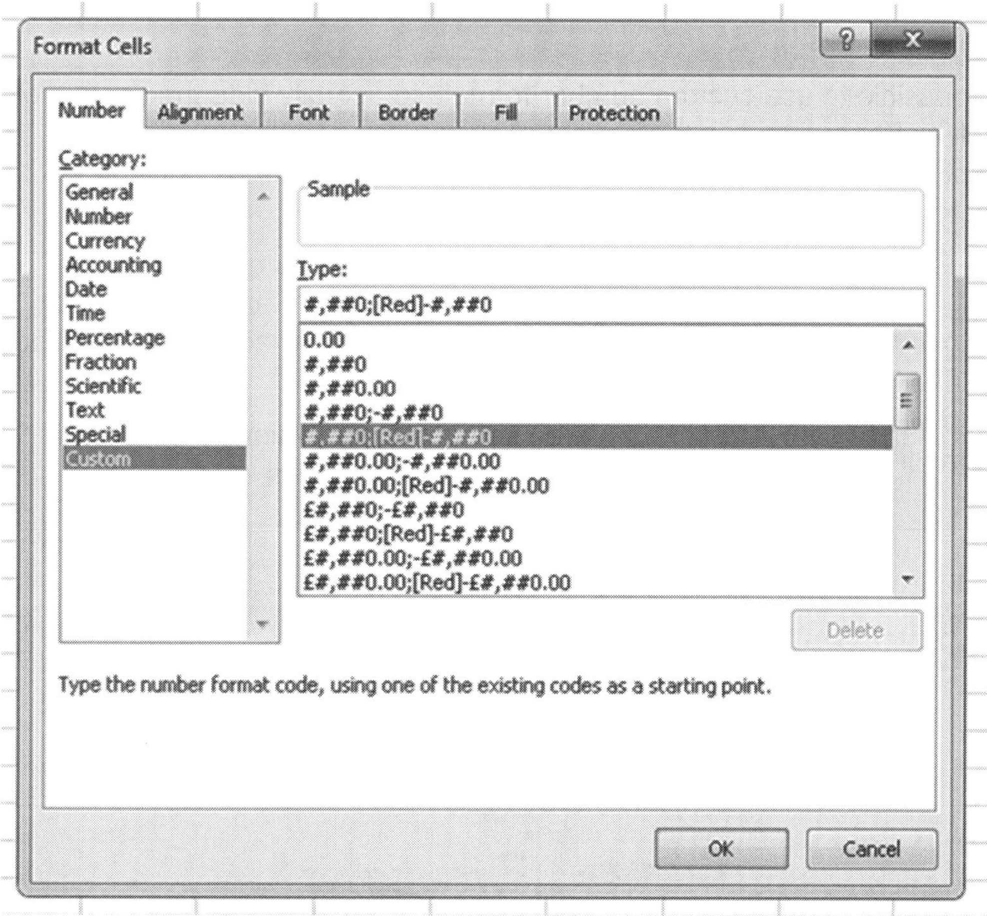


In the **custom** number list there are a number of formats that can be adapted to create the formatting required.

If chose the option highlighted in blue above -2345.68 would become:

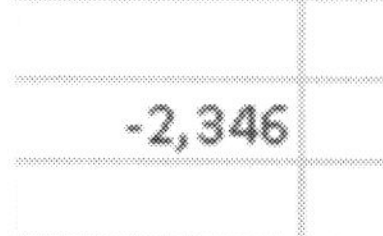


#,##0;[Red]-#,##0, formats numbers to have no decimal places and negative numbers shown in red with a minus sign in front.

You can change this to use brackets instead of the minus sign:

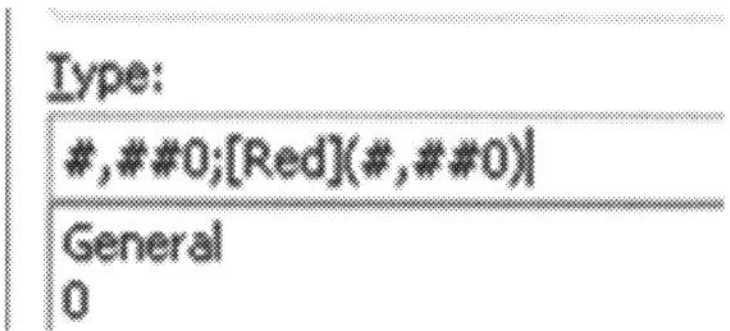


The value now looks like: (2,346)

You can also change the colour if required to Black, Green, White, Blue, Magenta, Yellow, or Cyan or keep it as Red, by changing the word in square brackets [ ].

It is possible to use custom number formats to actually hide the content of a cell[s]. For example in the sheet below you can see the salaries of Directors P, Q and R. To maintain confidentiality it might be considered best to hide individual figures but keep the total visible.

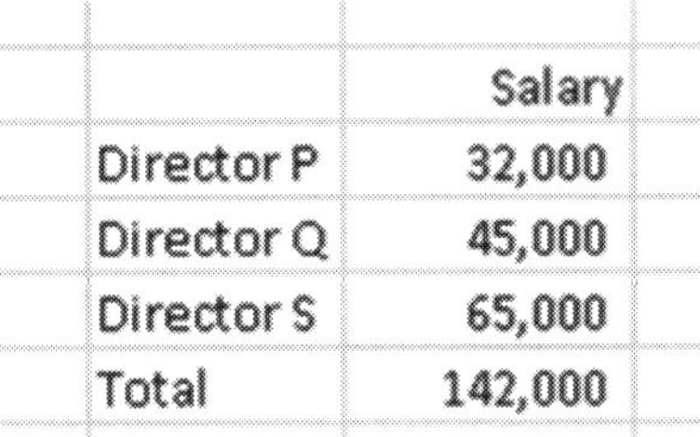

| | Salary |
|---|---|
| Director P | 32,000 |
| Director Q | 45,000 |
| Director S | 65,000 |
| Total | 142,000 |

This can be achieved by highlighting the figures you want to hide and then creating the custom number format as below to hide the content.

Three semi-colons ;;; followed by OK will hide the contents of cells

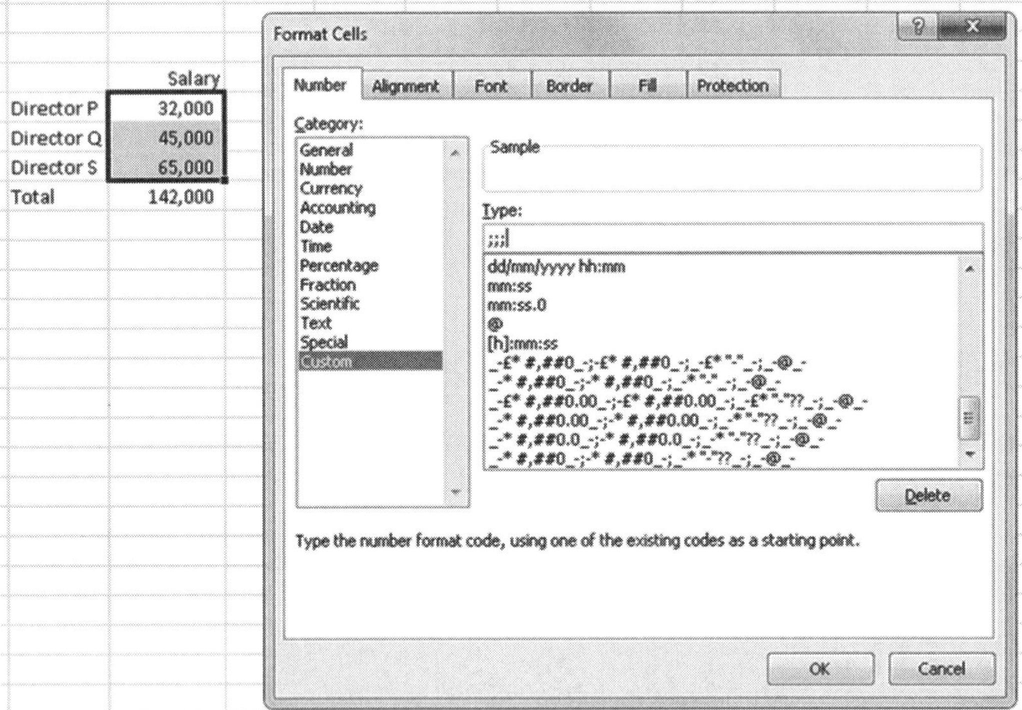


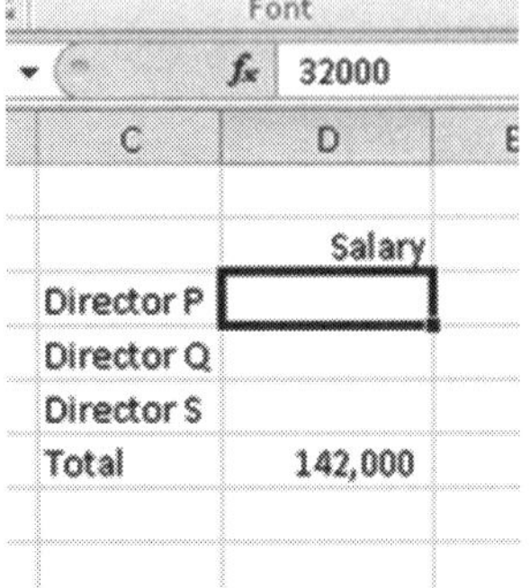


The individual salaries are now hidden from view on the worksheet but if the individual cells are clicked into the values still show in the formula bar.

## 2.9 Other formats

The other formats are not usually required, but can be experimented with – if something goes wrong, just Undo what you did, or select a different number format.

**IMPORTANT NOTE ON FORMATTING!**

It is worth noting that changing the number format of a cell HAS NO EFFECT on the actual number within the cell. For example, if the cell contains the value 15.6, and you change the format to zero decimal places, the value of the cell used in calculations will still be 15.6, even though 16 will be displayed.

This is dealt with in more detail when discussing the ROUND function.

**Shortcuts**

There are several shortcuts available to change the Number Format on the **Home menu**.

Number formats can be chosen directly, or percentage symbols, 1000 separators and number of decimal points changed.

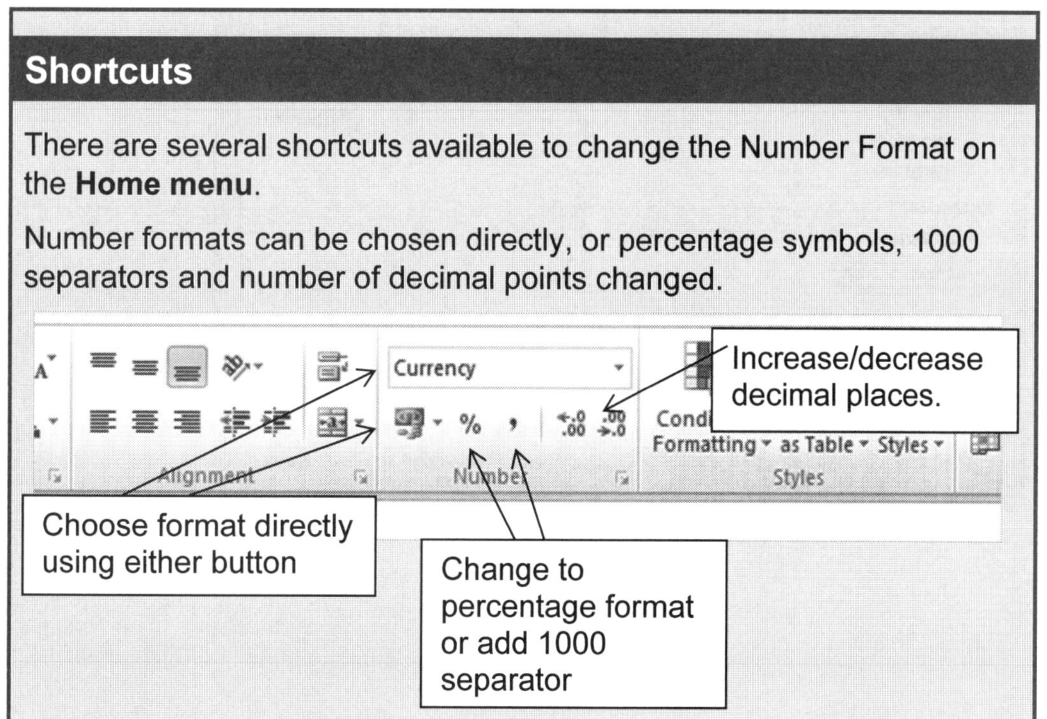

# 3 Alignment

## 3.1 Introduction

The **Alignment** tab allows you to choose where in a cell text will be displayed, as well as the options to wrap text, merge cells, shrink text to fit in cells and also adjust orientation of the text in a cell:

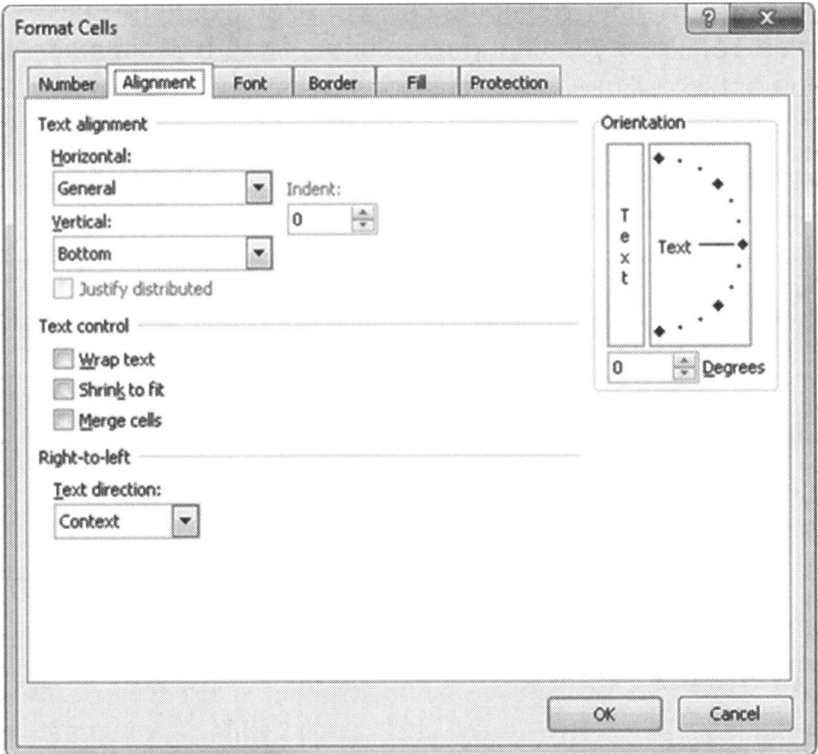

## 3.2 Text alignment

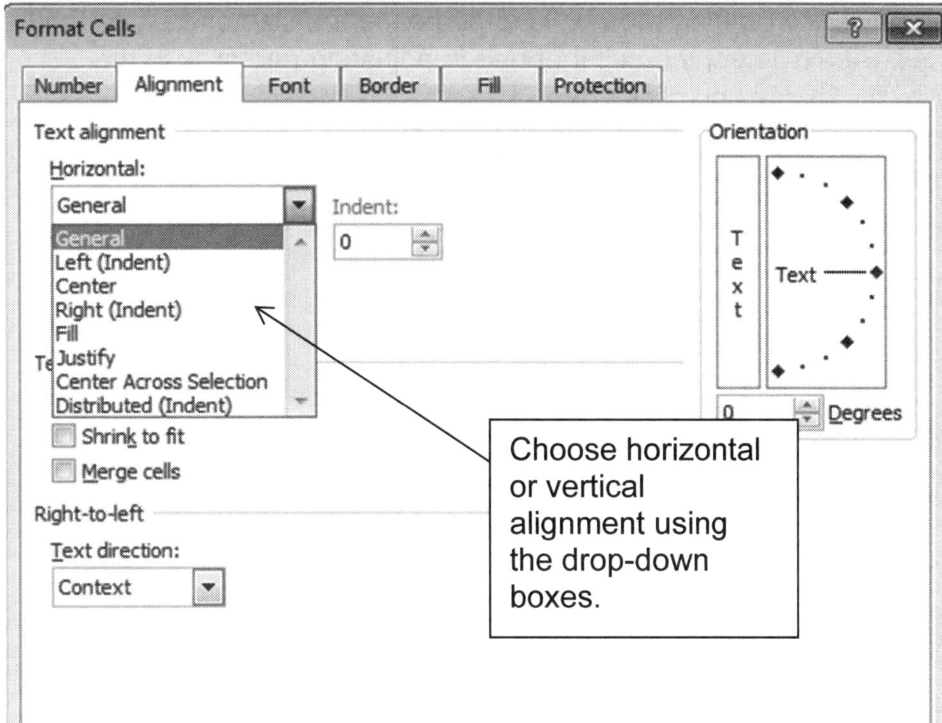


## 3.3 Wrap text

This allows all contents of a cell to be displayed on multiple lines within the one cell.

Select the cells that need to the text to be wrapped in and then in the **Alignment** menu, tick the **Wrap text** tickbox, and click **OK**.

The contents of the cell will now appear over 2 or more rows within the single cell.

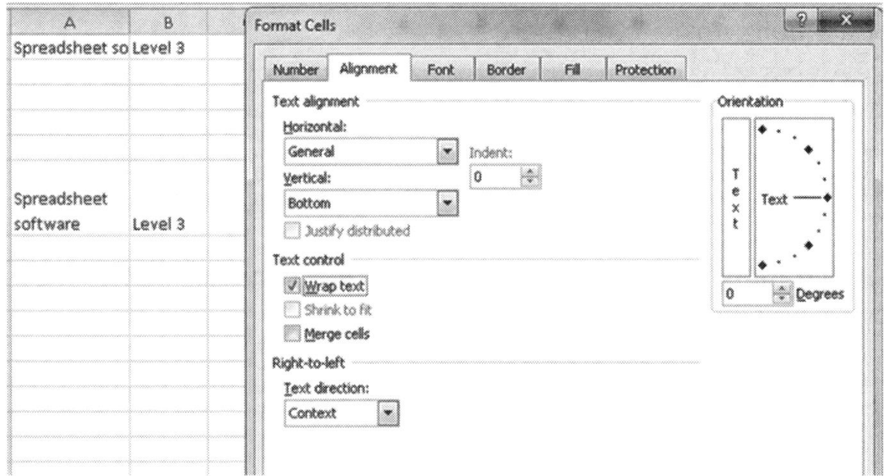

## 3.4 Shrink to fit

An alternative to wrapping the text is to decrease the size of the text to fit in the cell. Again select the cell that needs adjusting and click in the **Shrink to fit** tickbox and click **OK**.

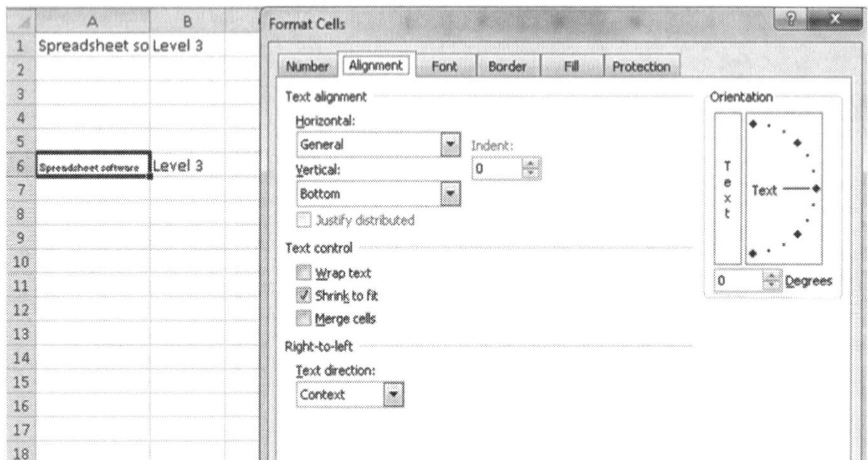


## 3.5 Merge cells

Merging cells joins them together so Excel treats them as one cell. This can be useful for headings that run over more than one column, for example, or if you wish to create a heading across a whole page.

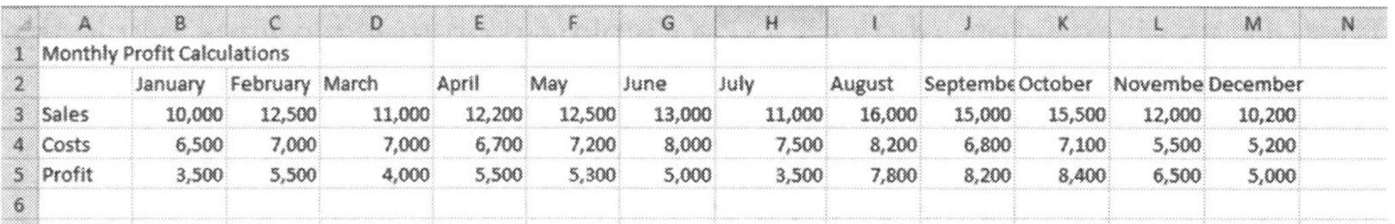

| | A | B | C | D | E | F | G | H | I | J | K | L | M | N |
|---|---|---|---|---|---|---|---|---|---|---|---|---|---|---|
| 1 | Monthly Profit Calculations | | | | | | | | | | | | | |
| 2 | | January | February | March | April | May | June | July | August | Septembe | October | Novembe | December | |
| 3 | Sales | 10,000 | 12,500 | 11,000 | 12,200 | 12,500 | 13,000 | 11,000 | 16,000 | 15,000 | 15,500 | 12,000 | 10,200 | |
| 4 | Costs | 6,500 | 7,000 | 7,000 | 6,700 | 7,200 | 8,000 | 7,500 | 8,200 | 6,800 | 7,100 | 5,500 | 5,200 | |
| 5 | Profit | 3,500 | 5,500 | 4,000 | 5,500 | 5,300 | 5,000 | 3,500 | 7,800 | 8,200 | 8,400 | 6,500 | 5,000 | |
| 6 | | | | | | | | | | | | | | |

The heading for this data would look nicer if it was centred across the columns. This can be done firstly by merging the cells, then by centering.

First, **select** the **cells** you wish to merge:

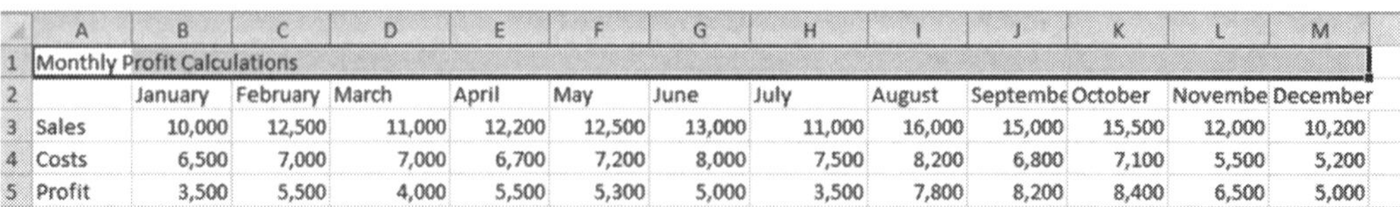

| | A | B | C | D | E | F | G | H | I | J | K | L | M |
|---|---|---|---|---|---|---|---|---|---|---|---|---|---|
| 1 | Monthly Profit Calculations | | | | | | | | | | | | |
| 2 | | January | February | March | April | May | June | July | August | Septembe | October | Novembe | December |
| 3 | Sales | 10,000 | 12,500 | 11,000 | 12,200 | 12,500 | 13,000 | 11,000 | 16,000 | 15,000 | 15,500 | 12,000 | 10,200 |
| 4 | Costs | 6,500 | 7,000 | 7,000 | 6,700 | 7,200 | 8,000 | 7,500 | 8,200 | 6,800 | 7,100 | 5,500 | 5,200 |
| 5 | Profit | 3,500 | 5,500 | 4,000 | 5,500 | 5,300 | 5,000 | 3,500 | 7,800 | 8,200 | 8,400 | 6,500 | 5,000 |

In the **Alignment** menu, tick the **Merge Cells** tickbox, and click **OK**. The cells will now be treated as one big cell.

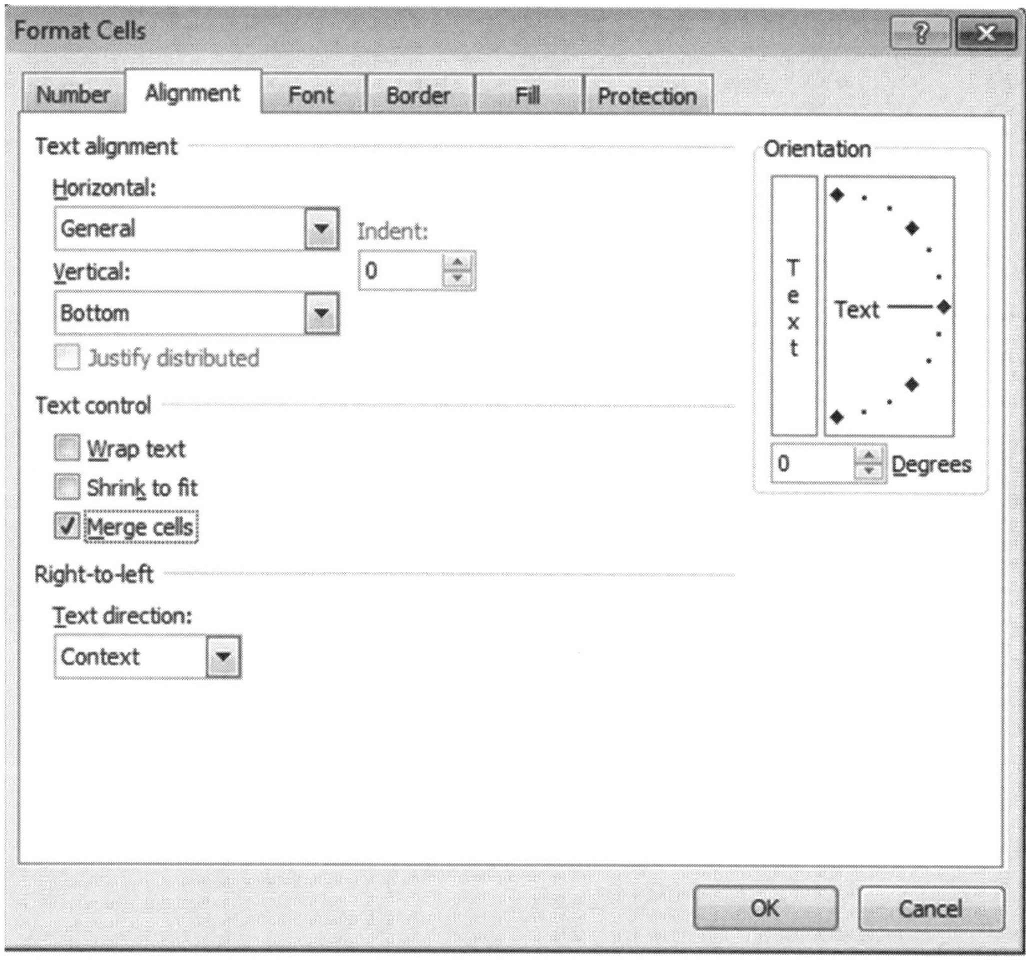


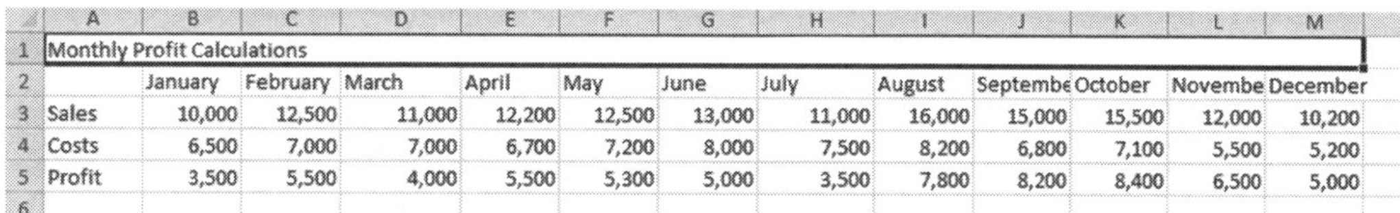

| | A | B | C | D | E | F | G | H | I | J | K | L | M |
|---|---|---|---|---|---|---|---|---|---|---|---|---|---|
| 1 | Monthly Profit Calculations | | | | | | | | | | | | |
| 2 | | January | February | March | April | May | June | July | August | Septembe | October | Novembe | December |
| 3 | Sales | 10,000 | 12,500 | 11,000 | 12,200 | 12,500 | 13,000 | 11,000 | 16,000 | 15,000 | 15,500 | 12,000 | 10,200 |
| 4 | Costs | 6,500 | 7,000 | 7,000 | 6,700 | 7,200 | 8,000 | 7,500 | 8,200 | 6,800 | 7,100 | 5,500 | 5,200 |
| 5 | Profit | 3,500 | 5,500 | 4,000 | 5,500 | 5,300 | 5,000 | 3,500 | 7,800 | 8,200 | 8,400 | 6,500 | 5,000 |
| 6 | | | | | | | | | | | | | |

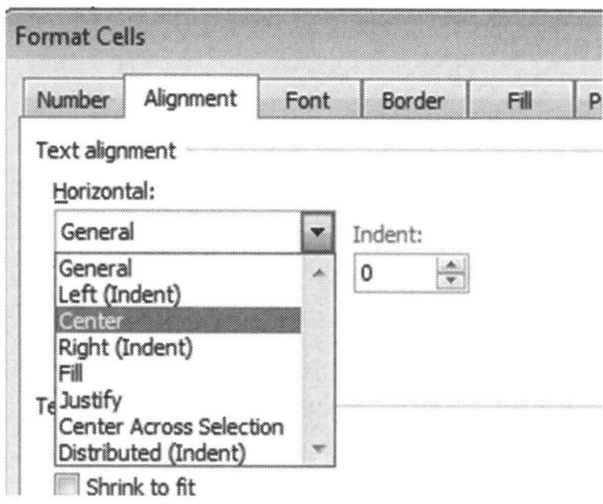


In the Alignment menu then select **Horizontal Alignment** as **Center** to show your heading in the centre of the data.

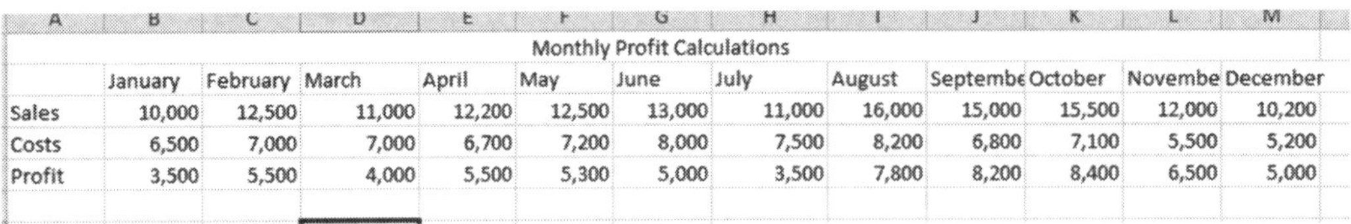

| | | | | | | | | | | | | |
|---|---|---|---|---|---|---|---|---|---|---|---|---|
| | | | | | | Monthly Profit Calculations | | | | | | |
| | January | February | March | April | May | June | July | August | Septembe | October | Novembe | December |
| Sales | 10,000 | 12,500 | 11,000 | 12,200 | 12,500 | 13,000 | 11,000 | 16,000 | 15,000 | 15,500 | 12,000 | 10,200 |
| Costs | 6,500 | 7,000 | 7,000 | 6,700 | 7,200 | 8,000 | 7,500 | 8,200 | 6,800 | 7,100 | 5,500 | 5,200 |
| Profit | 3,500 | 5,500 | 4,000 | 5,500 | 5,300 | 5,000 | 3,500 | 7,800 | 8,200 | 8,400 | 6,500 | 5,000 |

## 3.6 Orientation

Using orientation allow you to rotate the text in a cell to a diagonal angle or vertical orientation. This is often useful for labelling columns that are narrow.

As with the other alignment formatting, highlight the text that needs the orientation changed and choose the degree of angle you require:

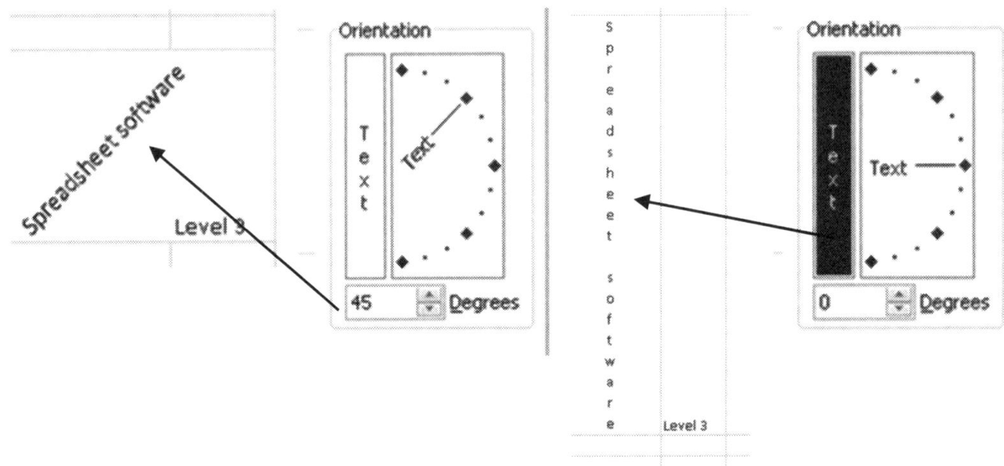


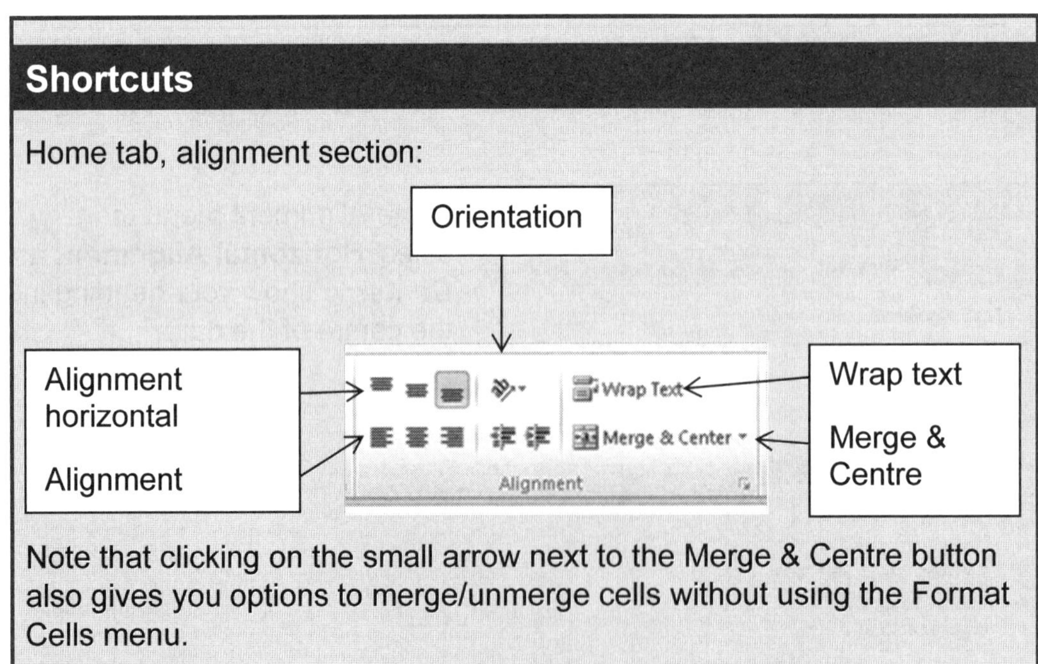

Shortcuts
Home tab, alignment section:
Orientation
Alignment horizontal
Alignment
Wrap Text
Merge & Center
Alignment
Wrap text
Merge & Centre
Note that clicking on the small arrow next to the Merge & Centre button also gives you options to merge/unmerge cells without using the Format Cells menu.

# 4 Font

## 4.1 Introduction

This is used to change the font type, size, and colour and to add effects to the text – the options are fairly self-explanatory:

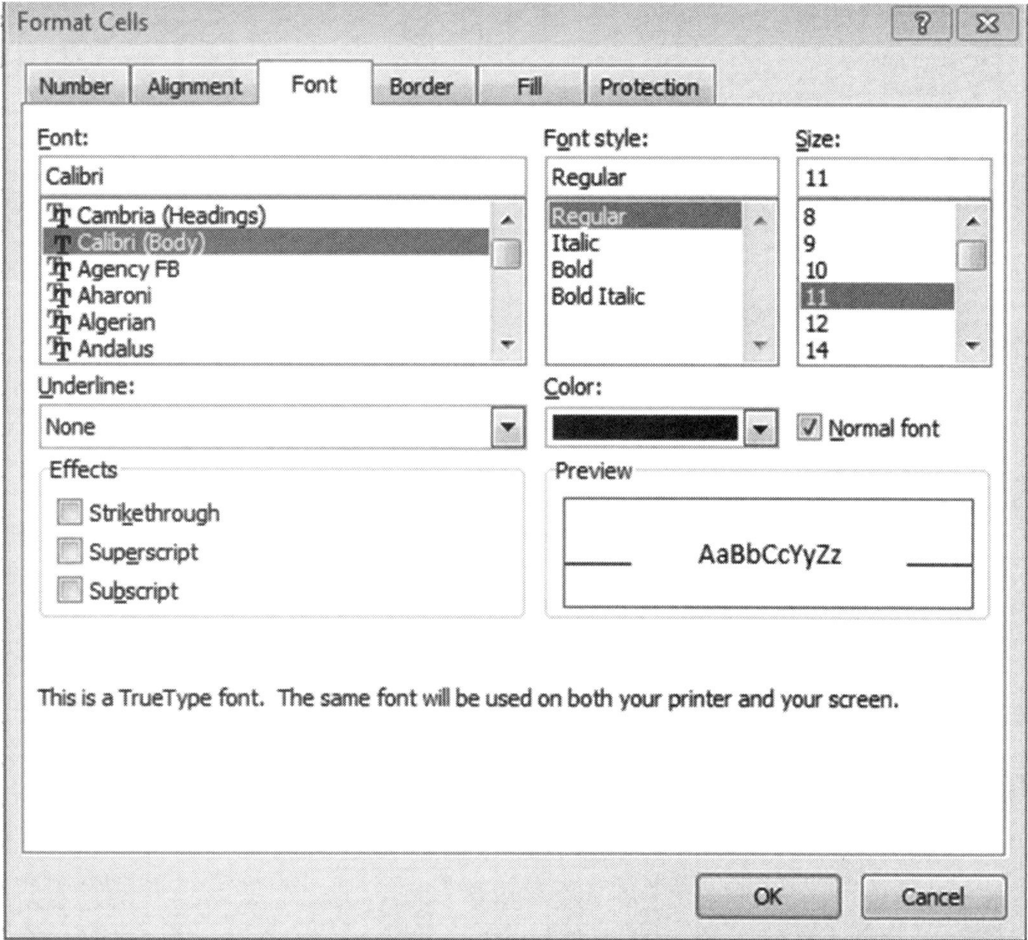

## 4.2 Underline

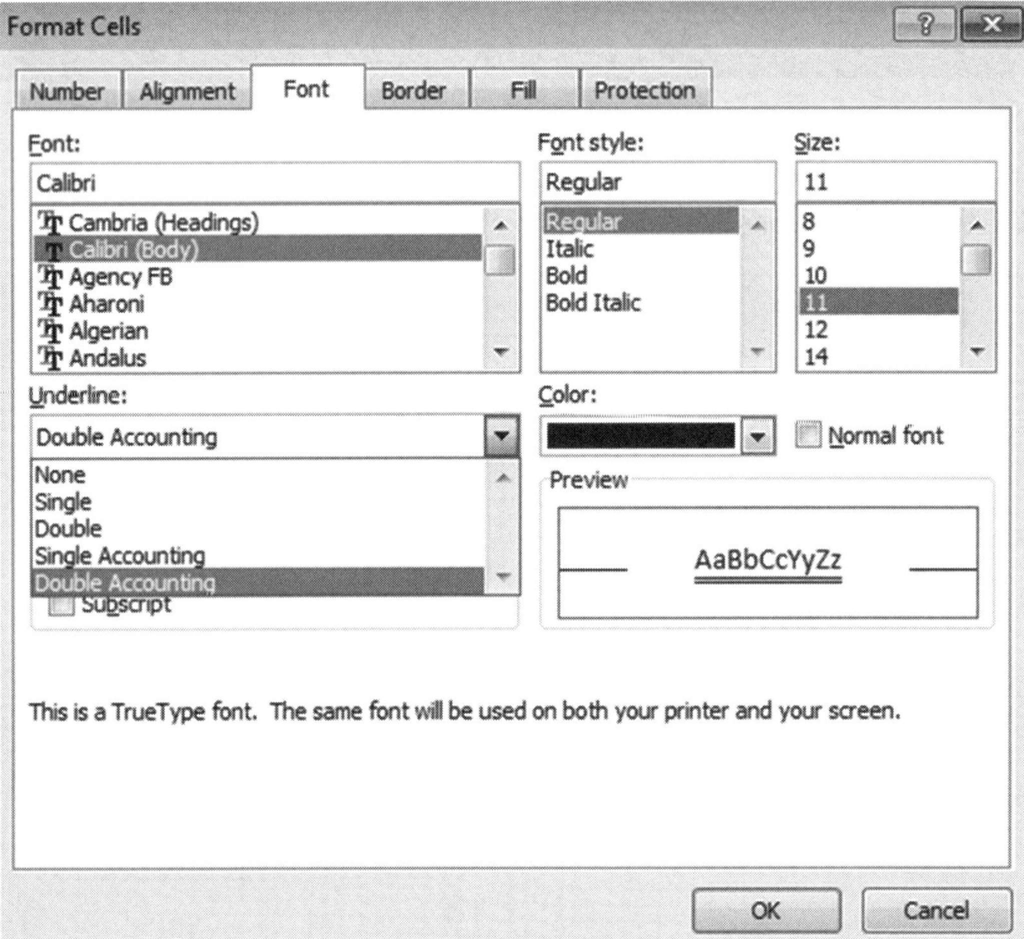


The Underline option allows you to use the Double Accounting Underline.

**Double Accounting Underline** shown under the Profit calculations.

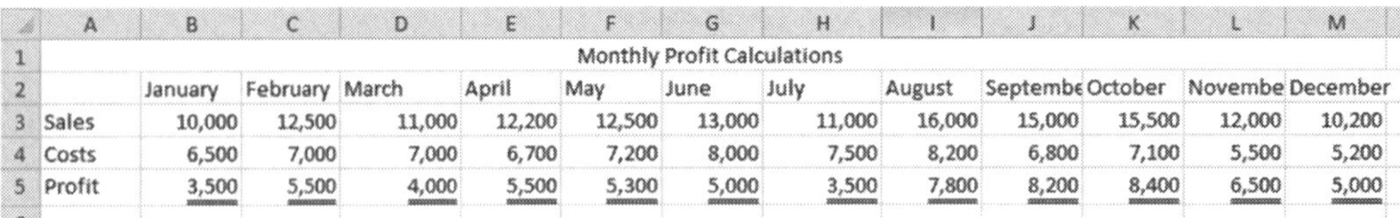

| | A | B | C | D | E | F | G | H | I | J | K | L | M |
|---|---|---|---|---|---|---|---|---|---|---|---|---|---|
| 1 | | | | | | Monthly Profit Calculations | | | | | | | |
| 2 | | January | February | March | April | May | June | July | August | Septembe | October | Novembe | December |
| 3 | Sales | 10,000 | 12,500 | 11,000 | 12,200 | 12,500 | 13,000 | 11,000 | 16,000 | 15,000 | 15,500 | 12,000 | 10,200 |
| 4 | Costs | 6,500 | 7,000 | 7,000 | 6,700 | 7,200 | 8,000 | 7,500 | 8,200 | 6,800 | 7,100 | 5,500 | 5,200 |
| 5 | Profit | 3,500 | 5,500 | 4,000 | 5,500 | 5,300 | 5,000 | 3,500 | 7,800 | 8,200 | 8,400 | 6,500 | 5,000 |

The title of this information could also be made bold, by selecting the bold option in Font Style:

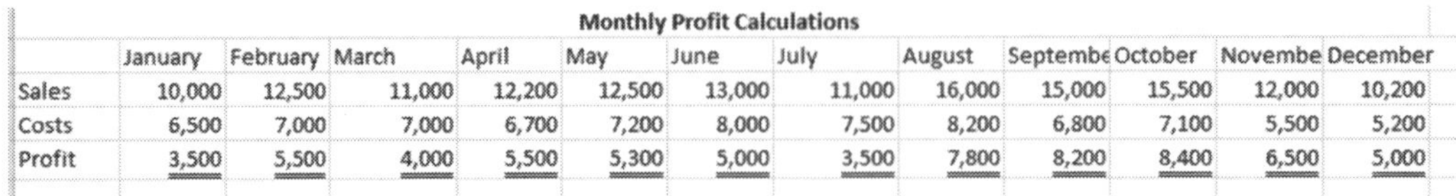

| | | | | | **Monthly Profit Calculations** | | | | | | | |
|---|---|---|---|---|---|---|---|---|---|---|---|---|
| | January | February | March | April | May | June | July | August | Septembe | October | Novembe | December |
| Sales | 10,000 | 12,500 | 11,000 | 12,200 | 12,500 | 13,000 | 11,000 | 16,000 | 15,000 | 15,500 | 12,000 | 10,200 |
| Costs | 6,500 | 7,000 | 7,000 | 6,700 | 7,200 | 8,000 | 7,500 | 8,200 | 6,800 | 7,100 | 5,500 | 5,200 |
| Profit | 3,500 | 5,500 | 4,000 | 5,500 | 5,300 | 5,000 | 3,500 | 7,800 | 8,200 | 8,400 | 6,500 | 5,000 |

## Shortcuts

The Font options can also be selected from the font section of the **Home Menu**, in the same way as alignment and Number formats.

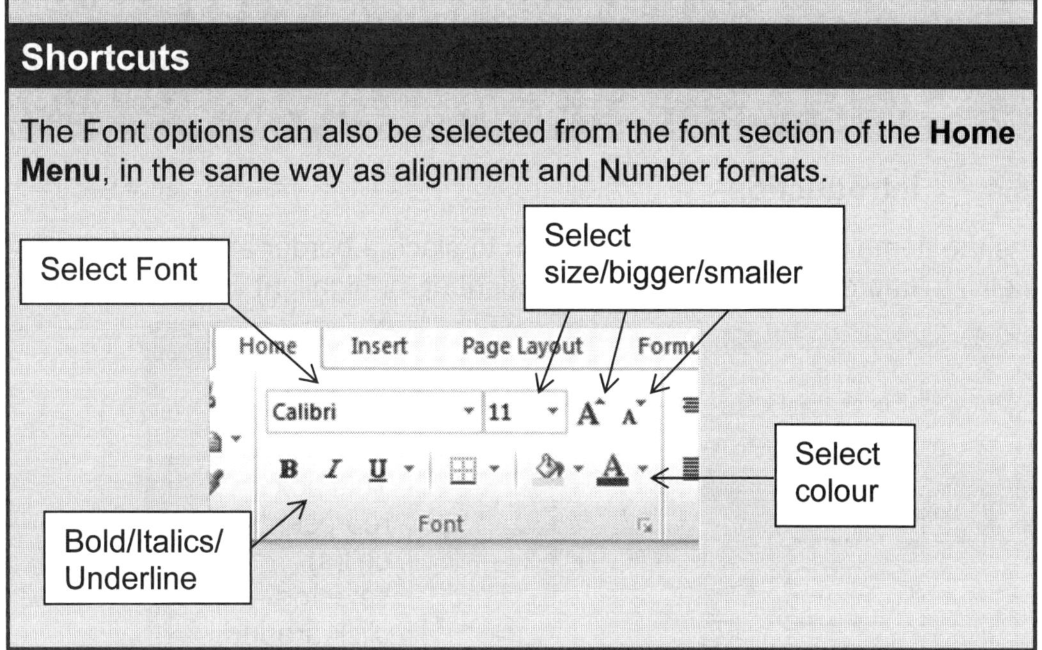

# 5 Border

## 5.1 Introduction

As the name suggests, this allows you to place a border around a cell or cells, to improve the look of the spreadsheet, or highlight important cells.

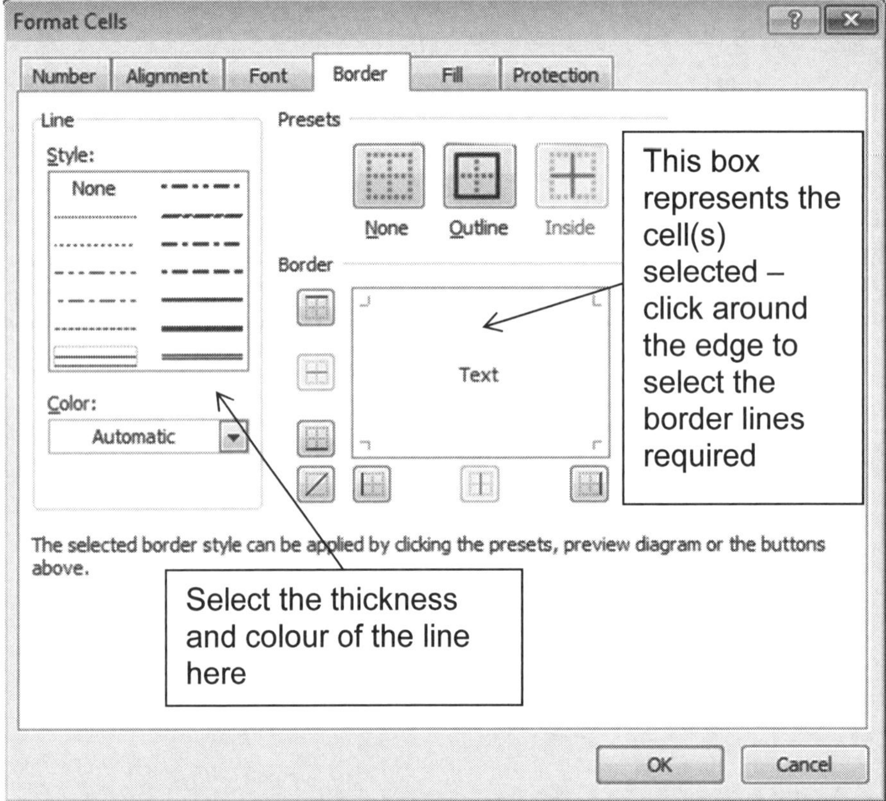

For example, a thick red border can be applied.

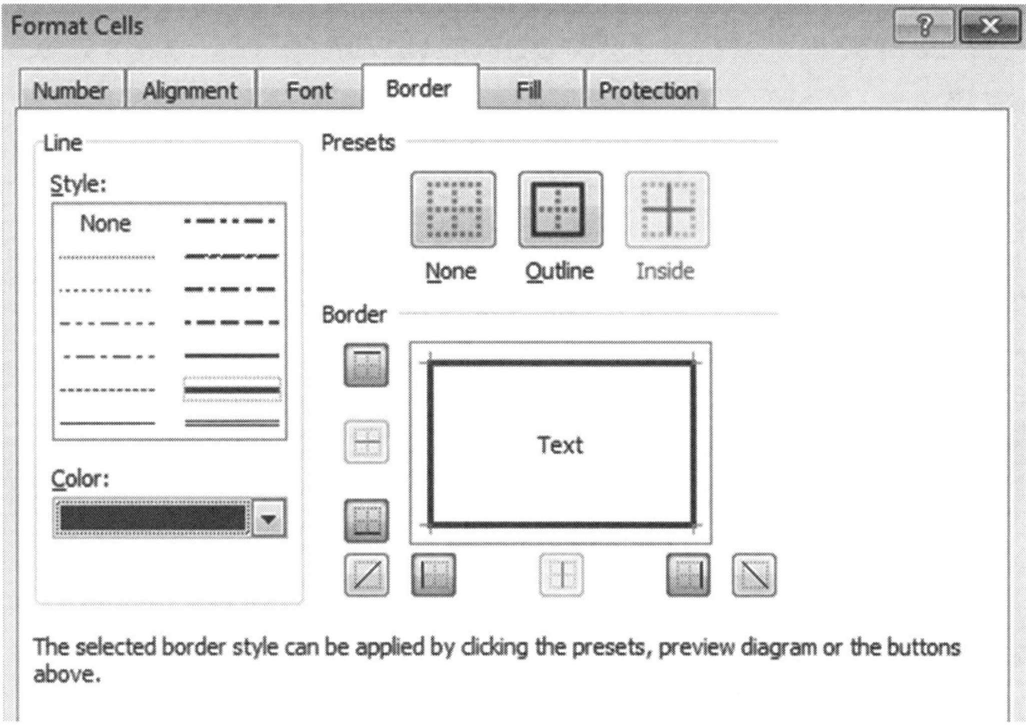


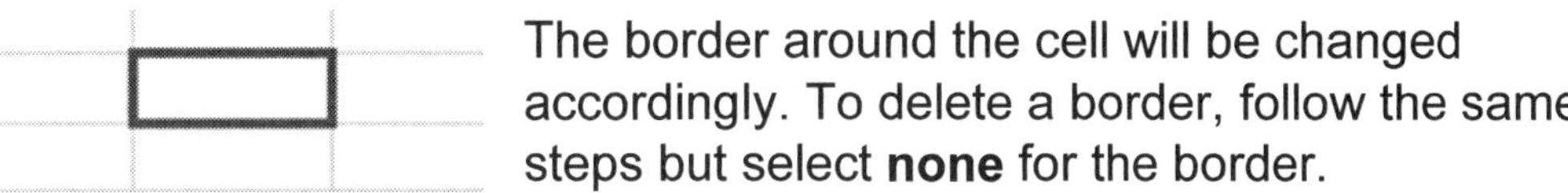

The border around the cell will be changed accordingly. To delete a border, follow the same steps but select **none** for the border.

If several cells are selected, the same borders will be applied to each:

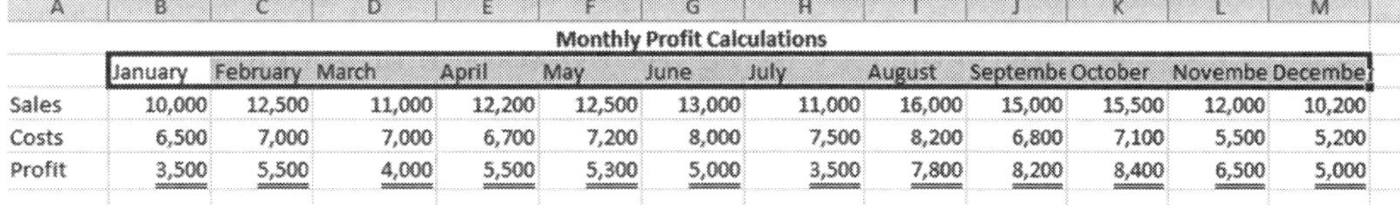

| A | B | C | D | E | F | G | H | I | J | K | L | M |
|---|---|---|---|---|---|---|---|---|---|---|---|---|
| | | | | | Monthly Profit Calculations | | | | | | | |
| | January | February | March | April | May | June | July | August | Septembe | October | Novembe | Decembe |
| Sales | 10,000 | 12,500 | 11,000 | 12,200 | 12,500 | 13,000 | 11,000 | 16,000 | 15,000 | 15,500 | 12,000 | 10,200 |
| Costs | 6,500 | 7,000 | 7,000 | 6,700 | 7,200 | 8,000 | 7,500 | 8,200 | 6,800 | 7,100 | 5,500 | 5,200 |
| Profit | 3,500 | 5,500 | 4,000 | 5,500 | 5,300 | 5,000 | 3,500 | 7,800 | 8,200 | 8,400 | 6,500 | 5,000 |

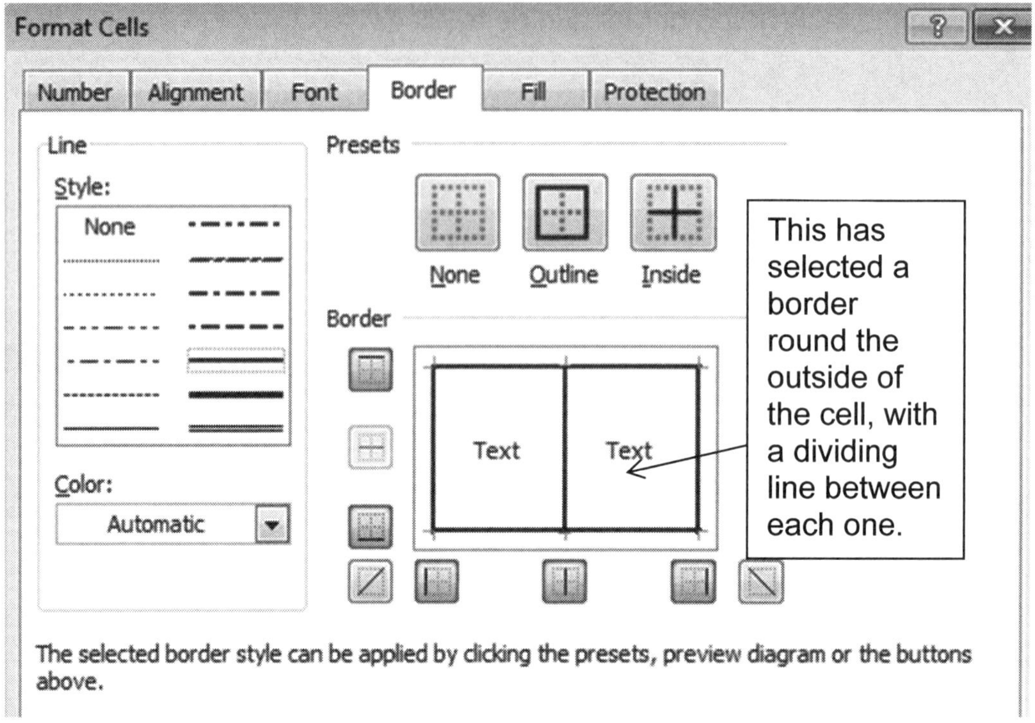


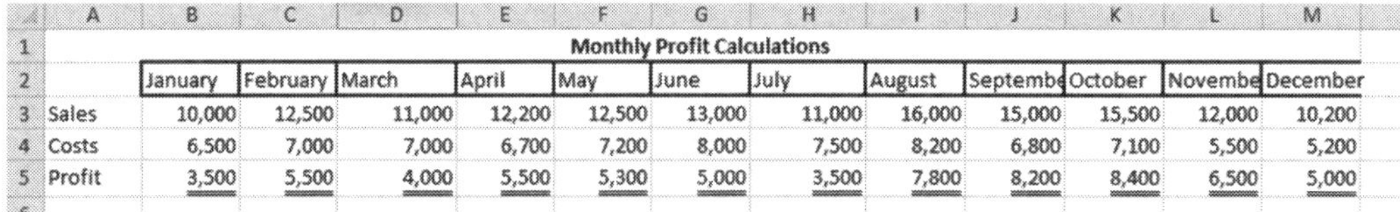

| | A | B | C | D | E | F | G | H | I | J | K | L | M |
|---|---|---|---|---|---|---|---|---|---|---|---|---|---|
| 1 | | | | | | Monthly Profit Calculations | | | | | | | |
| 2 | | January | February | March | April | May | June | July | August | Septembe | October | Novembe | December |
| 3 | Sales | 10,000 | 12,500 | 11,000 | 12,200 | 12,500 | 13,000 | 11,000 | 16,000 | 15,000 | 15,500 | 12,000 | 10,200 |
| 4 | Costs | 6,500 | 7,000 | 7,000 | 6,700 | 7,200 | 8,000 | 7,500 | 8,200 | 6,800 | 7,100 | 5,500 | 5,200 |
| 5 | Profit | 3,500 | 5,500 | 4,000 | 5,500 | 5,300 | 5,000 | 3,500 | 7,800 | 8,200 | 8,400 | 6,500 | 5,000 |

## Shortcut

Borders can be applied directly using the **borders** button in the **Home Menu**

The appropriate border can be selected directly from here.

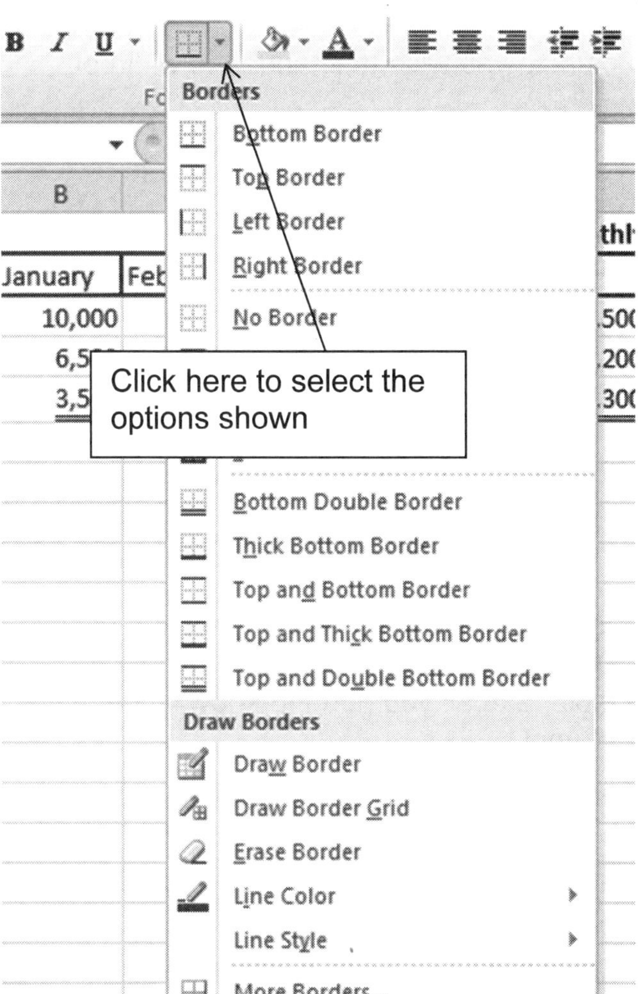


# 6 Adjusting row and column widths

## 6.1 Adjusting column width

You may need to adjust column widths so that all of your data is shown. For example in the screenshot below, columns J, L and M are not wide enough to display the month properly.

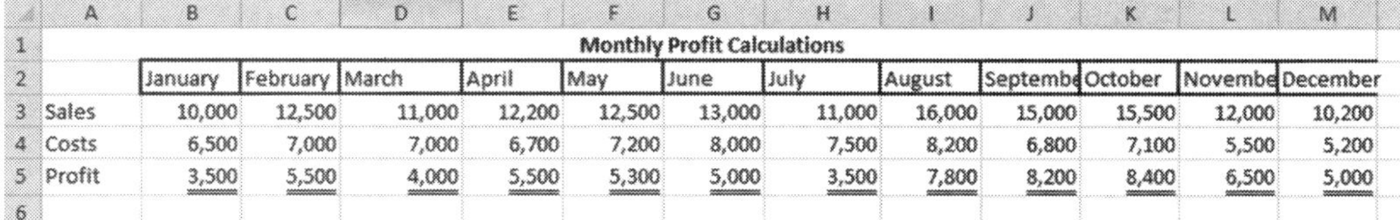

| | A | B | C | D | E | F | G | H | I | J | K | L | M |
|---|---|---|---|---|---|---|---|---|---|---|---|---|---|
| 1 | | | | | | | Monthly Profit Calculations | | | | | | |
| 2 | | January | February | March | April | May | June | July | August | Septembe | October | Novembe | December |
| 3 | Sales | 10,000 | 12,500 | 11,000 | 12,200 | 12,500 | 13,000 | 11,000 | 16,000 | 15,000 | 15,500 | 12,000 | 10,200 |
| 4 | Costs | 6,500 | 7,000 | 7,000 | 6,700 | 7,200 | 8,000 | 7,500 | 8,200 | 6,800 | 7,100 | 5,500 | 5,200 |
| 5 | Profit | 3,500 | 5,500 | 4,000 | 5,500 | 5,300 | 5,000 | 3,500 | 7,800 | 8,200 | 8,400 | 6,500 | 5,000 |
| 6 | | | | | | | | | | | | | |

There are several ways to adjust the column width.

- Select the Column or Columns you wish to change the width of
- In the **'Home Menu'**, select **Format** (in the **Cells** section)
- Select Column Width
- Type in the numeric value of the width required.

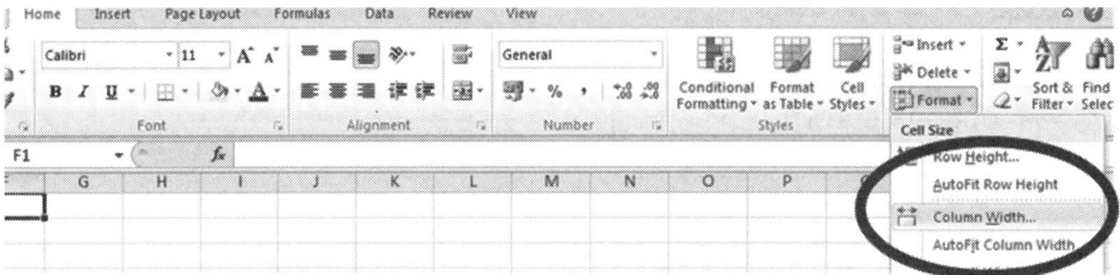


**Note** – column widths are measured in characters. For example a column width of 10 would be wide enough for 10 characters of text in the font being used. This is not examinable, and all you need to know is that a bigger number gives a wider column!

Alternatively (and usually easier), adjust the columns visually as follows:

- Hover the mouse over the dividing line between two columns. The mouse pointer will change to
- **Left click** and **drag** to the left or right to adjust the width as required
- Release the mouse button to accept the new width.

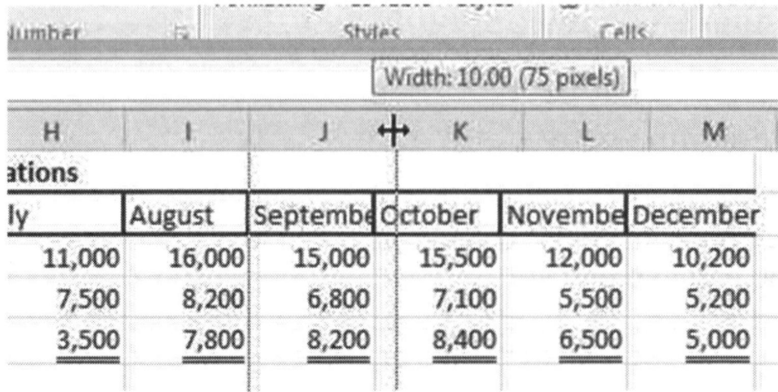


Drag the mouse to the left or right to adjust the column width.

| H | I | J | K | L | M |
|---|---|---|---|---|---|
| lations | | | | | |
| ly | August | September | October | Novembe | December |
| 11,000 | 16,000 | 15,000 | 15,500 | 12,000 | 10,200 |
| 7,500 | 8,200 | 6,800 | 7,100 | 5,500 | 5,200 |
| 3,500 | 7,800 | 8,200 | 8,400 | 6,500 | 5,000 |

Once the mouse button is released, the column will be the correct width.

## 6.2 Adjusting row height

This works in exactly the same way as adjusting column widths.

- Select the Row or Rows you wish to change the height of
- In the **'Home Menu'**, select **Format** (in the **Cells** section)
- Select Row Height
- Type in the numeric value of the width required.

**Or**

- Hover the mouse over the dividing line between two rows. The mouse pointer will change to
- **Left click** and **drag** up or down to adjust the height as required
- Release the mouse button to accept the new height.

## 6.3 AutoFit

A very useful feature for setting column widths/row heights is **AutoFit**. You may have seen this option when selecting a column width:

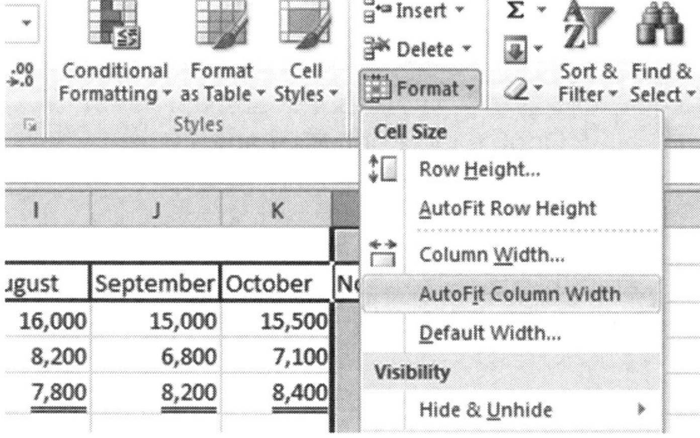

Selecting AutoFit will set the column width or row height to match the largest cell in the column. This way you know that all of your data will be visible.

**Shortcut**

Hover the mouse pointer over the dividing line between two columns/rows and **DOUBLE CLICK** to AutoFit.

### 6.4 AutoFit all rows/columns

After your work is finished, it is sensible to AutoFit all rows/columns to ensure that everything is visible. This is quickly and easily achieved as follows:

- Click the **Select All Cells** button in the top left of the spreadsheet
- AutoFit **ANY** column
- AutoFit **Any** row

All columns and rows will be correctly adjusted.

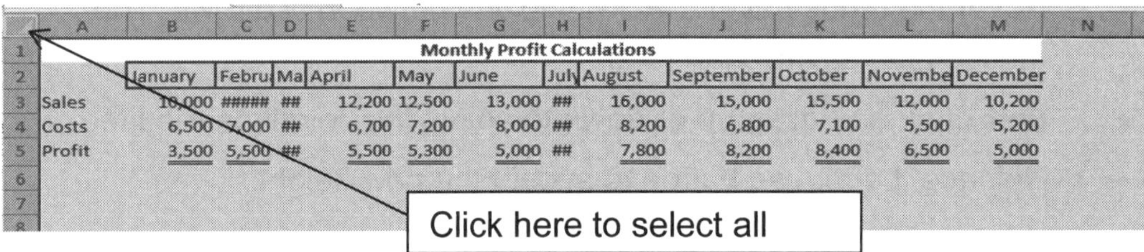
Click here to select all

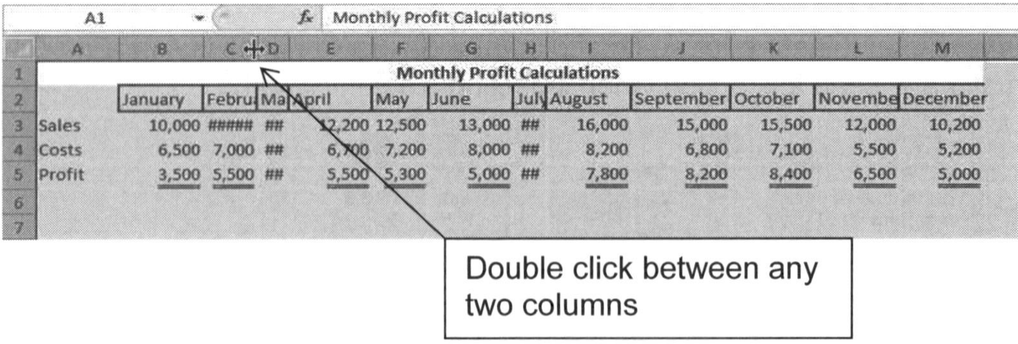
Double click between any two columns

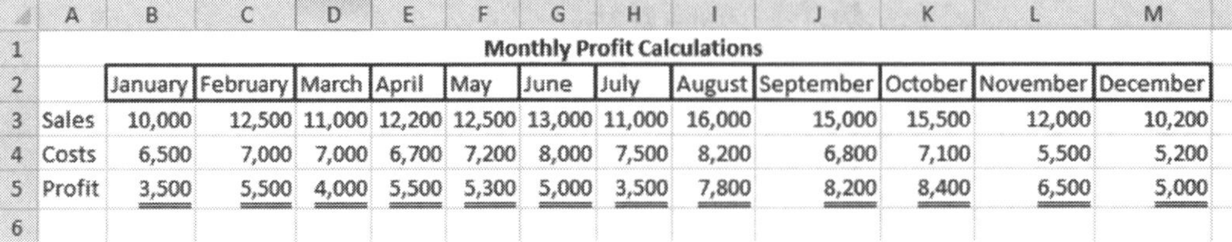

| | A | B | C | D | E | F | G | H | I | J | K | L | M |
|---|---|---|---|---|---|---|---|---|---|---|---|---|---|
| 1 | | | | | | | Monthly Profit Calculations | | | | | | |
| 2 | | January | February | March | April | May | June | July | August | September | October | November | December |
| 3 | Sales | 10,000 | 12,500 | 11,000 | 12,200 | 12,500 | 13,000 | 11,000 | 16,000 | 15,000 | 15,500 | 12,000 | 10,200 |
| 4 | Costs | 6,500 | 7,000 | 7,000 | 6,700 | 7,200 | 8,000 | 7,500 | 8,200 | 6,800 | 7,100 | 5,500 | 5,200 |
| 5 | Profit | 3,500 | 5,500 | 4,000 | 5,500 | 5,300 | 5,000 | 3,500 | 7,800 | 8,200 | 8,400 | 6,500 | 5,000 |
| 6 | | | | | | | | | | | | | |

All columns are now wide enough to display their data.

## 6.5 Hide and unhide columns and rows

It is possible to hide columns or rows on a worksheet. Select the column(s) or row(s) that need to be hidden and on the **Home** tab in the **Cells** section you will find **Format**. Click on the down arrow and choose **Hide & unhide** and select the option you want.

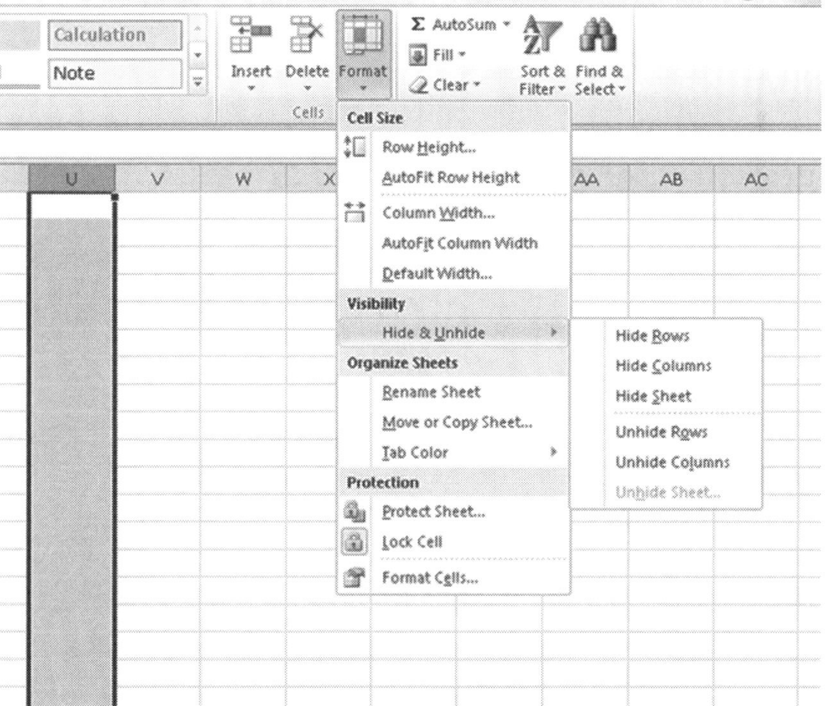


This can also be done by right clicking on the mouse:

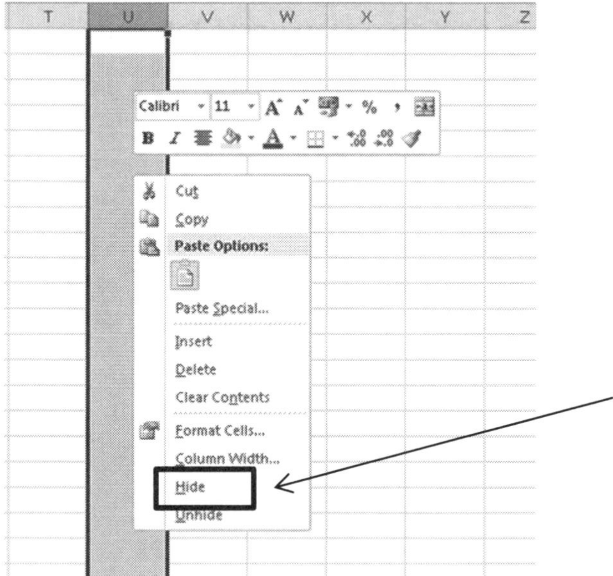

You can see if a column or row is hidden as the letter or number representing the column or row is missing.

Column U is hidden:

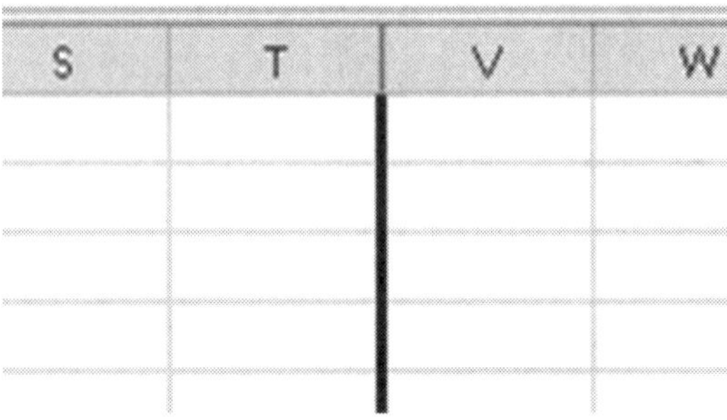


Row 10 is hidden:

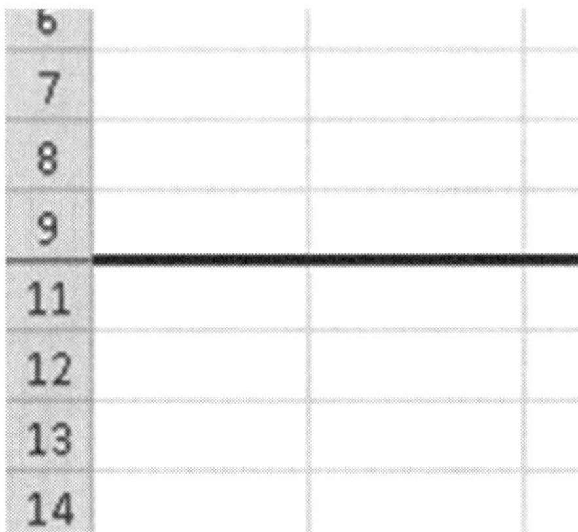


To unhide a row or column highlight the rows or columns on either side of the hidden row or column, right click on the mouse and choose unhide. You can also unhide by using the Cells section on the home tab and Format.

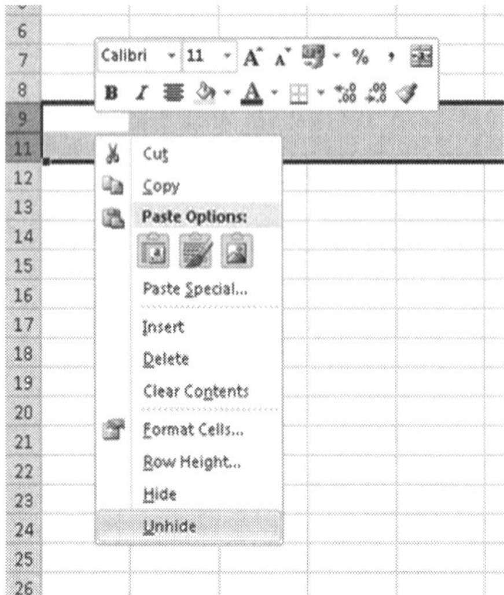

# 7 Test your understanding

The activities in this guide are designed to test your knowledge on the techniques shown in this chapter. They may also use techniques used in previous chapters, to build up your knowledge. Suggested answers are available on MyKaplan, although it is better to refer to the notes and try to understand the methods than look straight at the answers.

## Test your understanding 3-1

This activity allows you to practice essential formatting techniques which are required as part of the SPSH syllabus.

(a) Open the **Unformatted Report** file from the **Activities** folder.

(b) **Merge** and **Center** the title on the **Summary report** sheet across the data. **Bold** and **Underline** the title, and change the **font size** to **16**.

(c) Change the **number format** of the numbers to **Number**, with **0 decimal places** and **1000 separator**.

(d) Apply a **double accounting underline** to the profit figures.

(e) **Fill** the Half year information in cells H2:H4 using **yellow**. Place a single line **border** around the edge of cells H2:H4 and **remove** the **double underline** from cell H4.

(f) **Insert** a row between the title and Months.

(g) **Autofit** all column widths.

(h) **Save** the file in the **Solutions** folder as **Activity 3-1**.

# Simple calculations and data analysis

## Introduction

This chapter will explain how to create simple functions and to understand how Excel performs calculations:

### ASSESSMENT CRITERIA

Select and use a range of formulas and functions to perform calculations (3.1)

Select and use relevant tolls to analyse and interpret data (3.2)

### CONTENTS

# 1 Simple calculations

## 1.1 Simple calculations

Excel's primary purpose is to manipulate raw data through calculations and formulas. One of the main things you will use Excel for is simple calculations. The most basic calculations are the mathematical functions addition +, subtraction -, multiplication * and divide /.

To use these, you need to tell Excel that you are using a **FUNCTION**. To do this, enter an equals sign, '**=**', before the calculation you require.

So, to find the answer to 3+5, type in any cell

**=3+5** and press **Enter**.

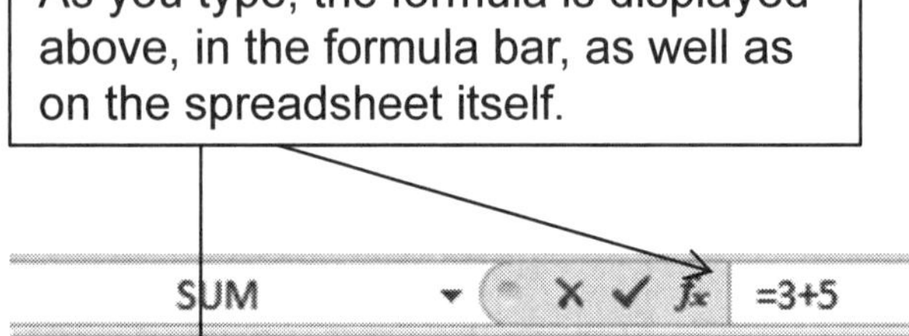

As you type, the formula is displayed above, in the formula bar, as well as on the spreadsheet itself.


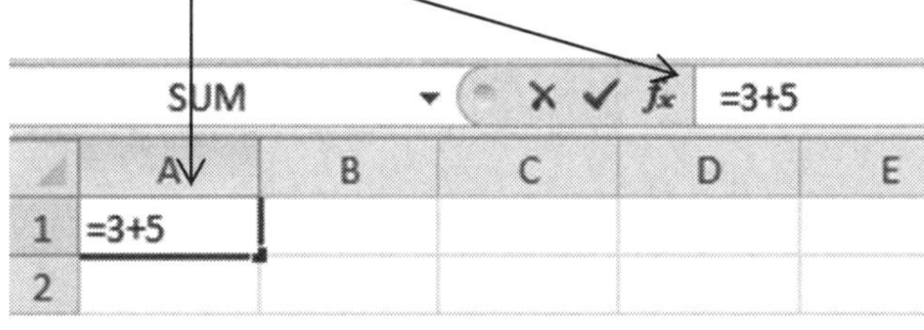


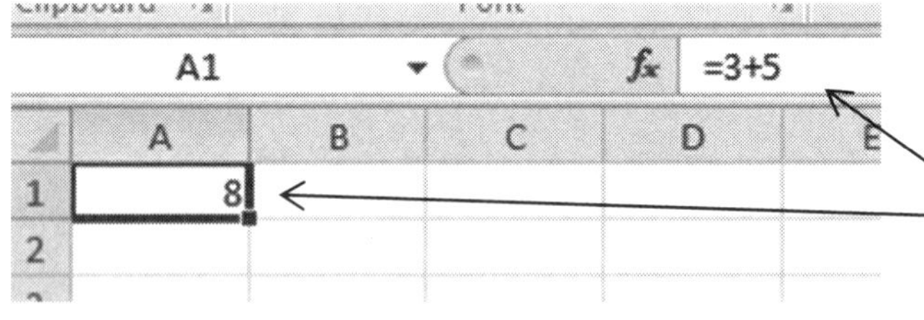


Once enter is pressed, the result of the calculation is shown on the spreadsheet, but the calculation itself is still shown in the formula bar.

Excel can be used in this way as a simple calculator by entering the calculation required, using +, -, * or /.

## 1.2 Calculations using existing values

The real power of Excel comes to the fore when using the values in other cells as part of your calculations. Take the following example:

| | A | B | C | D |
|---|---|---|---|---|
| 1 | Name | Hourly Rate | Hours Worked | Pay |
| 2 | Srnicek | £8.60 | 30 | |
| 3 | Watson | £8.60 | 20 | |
| 4 | Peacock | £9.00 | 20 | |
| 5 | Albert | £11.50 | 25 | |
| 6 | Beresford | £10.50 | 30 | |
| 7 | Batty | £12.00 | 40 | |
| 8 | Lee | £13.00 | 42 | |
| 9 | Beardsley | £14.00 | 35 | |
| 10 | Ginola | £16.00 | 15 | |
| 11 | Shearer | £18.00 | 35 | |
| 12 | Ferdinand | £16.00 | 32 | |
| 13 | | | | |

We need to find each person's pay – as the hourly rate * hours worked. You could simply type each one in, for example **'=8.60*30'** for Srnicek. This is time consuming and not much better than using pen and paper.
We can instead tell Excel to 'take the value in cell B2 and multiply by the value in cell C2'

| | A | B | C | D | E |
|---|---|---|---|---|---|
| 1 | Name | Hourly Rate | Hours Worked | Pay | |
| 2 | Srnicek | £8.60 | 30 | =b2 | |
| 3 | Watson | £8.60 | 20 | | |
| 4 | Peacock | £9.00 | 20 | | |
| 5 | Albert | £11.50 | 25 | | |
| 6 | Beresford | £10.50 | 30 | | |
| 7 | Batty | £12.00 | 40 | | |
| 8 | Lee | £13.00 | 42 | | |
| 9 | Beardsley | £14.00 | 35 | | |
| 10 | Ginola | £16.00 | 15 | | |
| 11 | Shearer | £18.00 | 35 | | |
| 12 | Ferdinand | £16.00 | 32 | | |
| 13 | | | | | |

Each cell is referred to by its column and row reference. To perform the calculation, start with the **'='** sign to show that you want to perform a calculation. Then type the cell reference of the cell you wish to use. A box will appear around the cell.

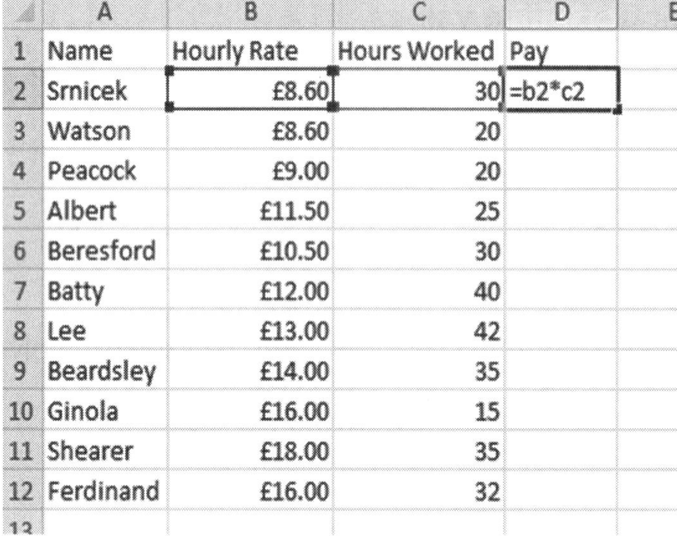

| | A | B | C | D | E |
|---|---|---|---|---|---|
| 1 | Name | Hourly Rate | Hours Worked | Pay | |
| 2 | Srnicek | £8.60 | 30 | =b2*c2 | |
| 3 | Watson | £8.60 | 20 | | |
| 4 | Peacock | £9.00 | 20 | | |
| 5 | Albert | £11.50 | 25 | | |
| 6 | Beresford | £10.50 | 30 | | |
| 7 | Batty | £12.00 | 40 | | |
| 8 | Lee | £13.00 | 42 | | |
| 9 | Beardsley | £14.00 | 35 | | |
| 10 | Ginola | £16.00 | 15 | | |
| 11 | Shearer | £18.00 | 35 | | |
| 12 | Ferdinand | £16.00 | 32 | | |

Finish off the calculation as required – the cell references are just saying "use whatever number is in this cell".

Note that although the column letters are always displayed in capitals, if you enter them in lower case it does not matter.

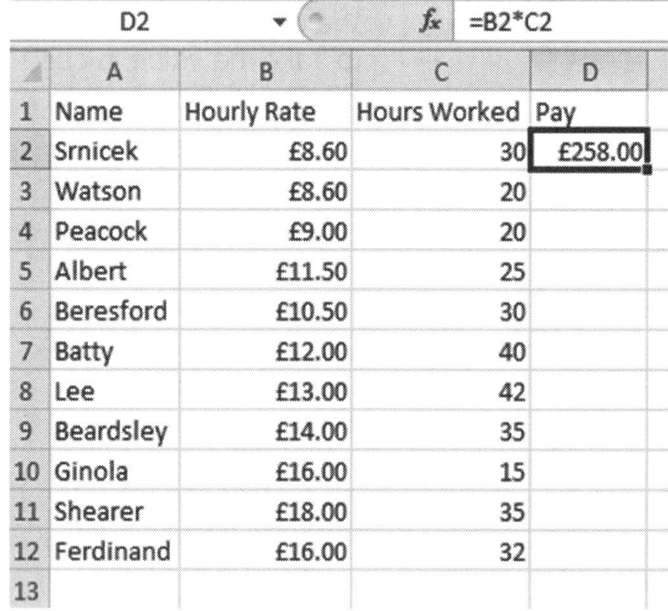

D2 | $f_x$ | =B2*C2

| | A | B | C | D |
|---|---|---|---|---|
| 1 | Name | Hourly Rate | Hours Worked | Pay |
| 2 | Srnicek | £8.60 | 30 | £258.00 |
| 3 | Watson | £8.60 | 20 | |
| 4 | Peacock | £9.00 | 20 | |
| 5 | Albert | £11.50 | 25 | |
| 6 | Beresford | £10.50 | 30 | |
| 7 | Batty | £12.00 | 40 | |
| 8 | Lee | £13.00 | 42 | |
| 9 | Beardsley | £14.00 | 35 | |
| 10 | Ginola | £16.00 | 15 | |
| 11 | Shearer | £18.00 | 35 | |
| 12 | Ferdinand | £16.00 | 32 | |
| 13 | | | | |

The result of the calculation is shown – note that the actual calculation being performed is shown in the formula bar above.

Any calculation can be performed using existing information in cells – this allows complex analysis to be undertaken relatively easily.

One huge benefit of this is that if the numbers in the data cells change, then the calculation will be updated to reflect this.

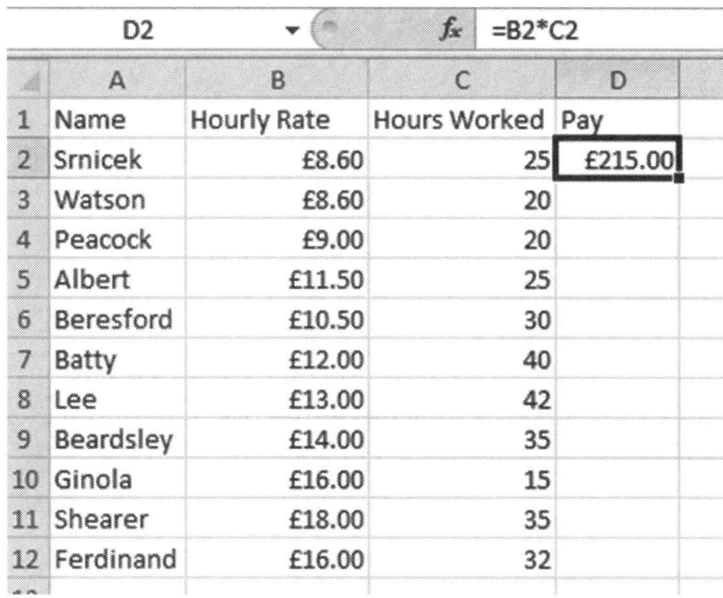

D2 | $f_x$ =B2*C2

| | A | B | C | D |
|---|---|---|---|---|
| 1 | Name | Hourly Rate | Hours Worked | Pay |
| 2 | Srnicek | £8.60 | 25 | £215.00 |
| 3 | Watson | £8.60 | 20 | |
| 4 | Peacock | £9.00 | 20 | |
| 5 | Albert | £11.50 | 25 | |
| 6 | Beresford | £10.50 | 30 | |
| 7 | Batty | £12.00 | 40 | |
| 8 | Lee | £13.00 | 42 | |
| 9 | Beardsley | £14.00 | 35 | |
| 10 | Ginola | £16.00 | 15 | |
| 11 | Shearer | £18.00 | 35 | |
| 12 | Ferdinand | £16.00 | 32 | |

Changing the hours worked to 25 has given an updated value in the pay column.

You can use any cell within your formulas, in the same way.

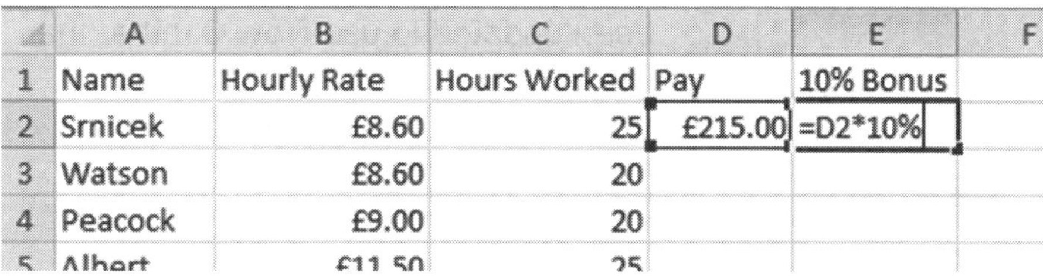

| | A | B | C | D | E | F |
|---|---|---|---|---|---|---|
| 1 | Name | Hourly Rate | Hours Worked | Pay | 10% Bonus | |
| 2 | Srnicek | £8.60 | 25 | £215.00 | =D2*10% | |
| 3 | Watson | £8.60 | 20 | | | |
| 4 | Peacock | £9.00 | 20 | | | |

Will give

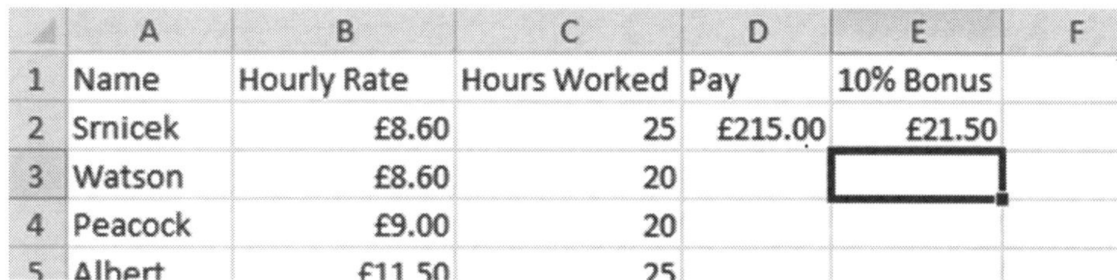

| | A | B | C | D | E | F |
|---|---|---|---|---|---|---|
| 1 | Name | Hourly Rate | Hours Worked | Pay | 10% Bonus | |
| 2 | Srnicek | £8.60 | 25 | £215.00 | £21.50 | |
| 3 | Watson | £8.60 | 20 | | | |
| 4 | Peacock | £9.00 | 20 | | | |

**IMPORTANT NOTE –** when entering cell references into a formula, rather than typing the reference **'B2'**, you can **LEFT-CLICK** on the cell you wish to use. This way you are less likely to type the wrong cell reference.

# 2 Copying formulas

## 2.1 Copying formulas

A formula has been entered into cells D2 and E2 to calculate staff pay and we need to perform the same calculation for the other 10 staff.

Using the same copy and paste feature seen in chapter 2, we can duplicate formulas used to speed up calculations.

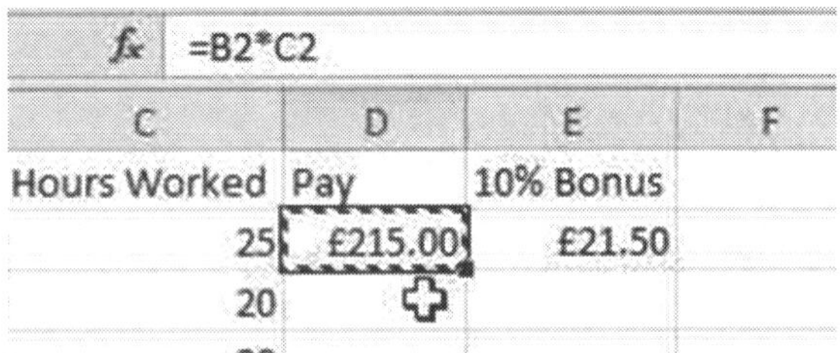


**Ctrl-C** to copy the formula (or whichever method you prefer)

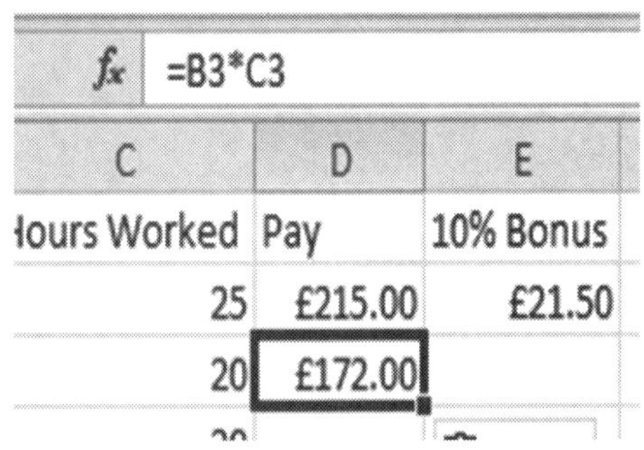


**Ctrl-V** can be used to paste the formula. Notice how the formula has been updated to use **Row 3** rather than Row 2. This is due to 'relative' referencing (covered in chapter 7)

You can paste the formula to more than one cell, as required:

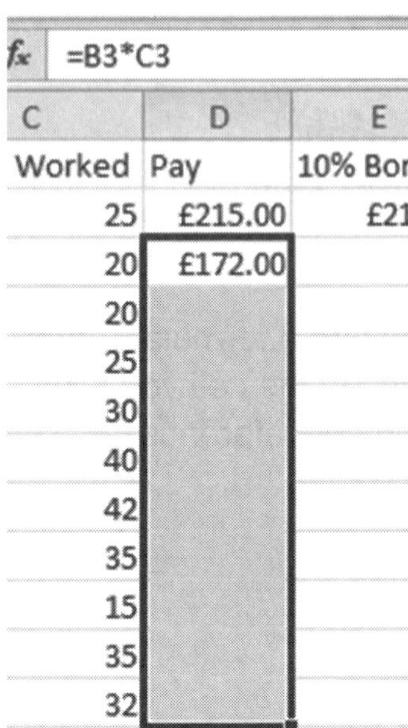


Select all the cells the formula is required in, before pasting.

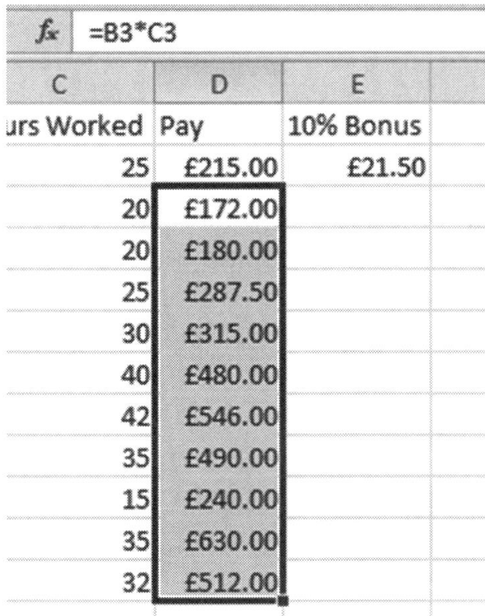

fx =B3*C3

| C | D | E |
|---|---|---|
| urs Worked | Pay | 10% Bonus |
| 25 | £215.00 | £21.50 |
| 20 | £172.00 | |
| 20 | £180.00 | |
| 25 | £287.50 | |
| 30 | £315.00 | |
| 40 | £480.00 | |
| 42 | £546.00 | |
| 35 | £490.00 | |
| 15 | £240.00 | |
| 35 | £630.00 | |
| 32 | £512.00 | |

The formula has been successfully copied.

If you find that the values do not change then your spreadsheet may not be set up to perform calculations automatically. Go to the Formula tab and check **Calculation Options** – click **Automatic**.

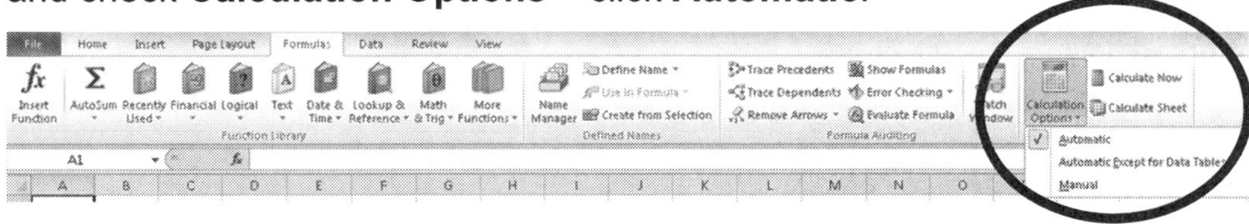


## 2.2 Using Autofill

Another quick way to copy formulas is to use the Autofill function explained in chapter 2. Formulas can be "dragged" up, down, left or right to copy them:

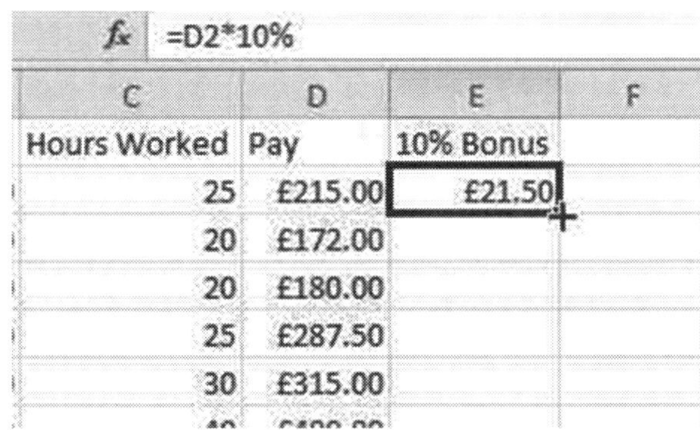

fx =D2*10%

| C | D | E | F |
|---|---|---|---|
| Hours Worked | Pay | 10% Bonus | |
| 25 | £215.00 | £21.50 | |
| 20 | £172.00 | | |
| 20 | £180.00 | | |
| 25 | £287.50 | | |
| 30 | £315.00 | | |

Hover the mouse over the bottom-right corner of the cell until the cursor changes.

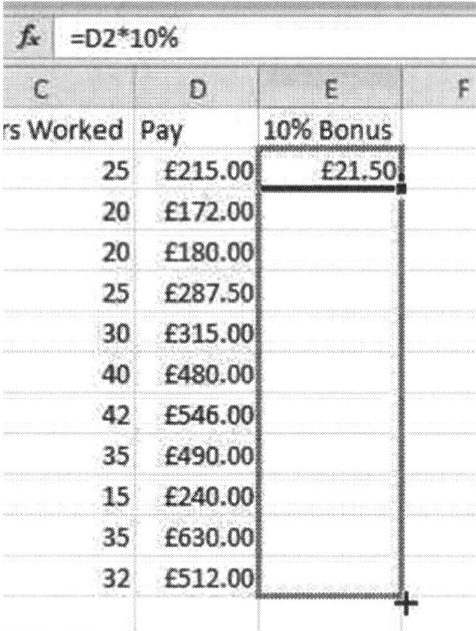

=D2*10%

| C | D | E | F |
|---|---|---|---|
| rs Worked | Pay | 10% Bonus | |
| 25 | £215.00 | £21.50 | |
| 20 | £172.00 | | |
| 20 | £180.00 | | |
| 25 | £287.50 | | |
| 30 | £315.00 | | |
| 40 | £480.00 | | |
| 42 | £546.00 | | |
| 35 | £490.00 | | |
| 15 | £240.00 | | |
| 35 | £630.00 | | |
| 32 | £512.00 | | |

Drag the mouse in the direction you want the formulas copied, and let go of the mouse button.

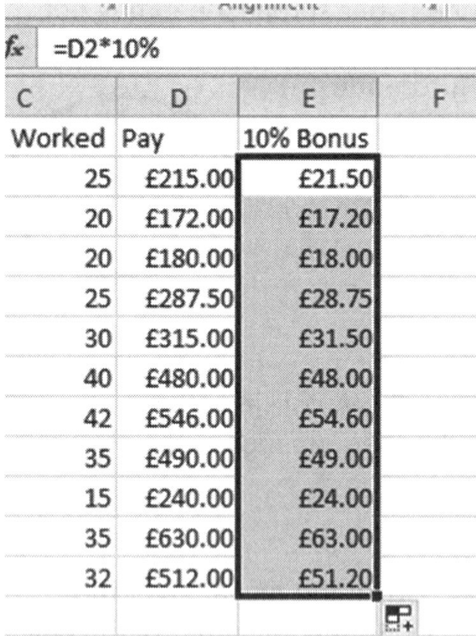

=D2*10%

| C | D | E | F |
|---|---|---|---|
| Worked | Pay | 10% Bonus | |
| 25 | £215.00 | £21.50 | |
| 20 | £172.00 | £17.20 | |
| 20 | £180.00 | £18.00 | |
| 25 | £287.50 | £28.75 | |
| 30 | £315.00 | £31.50 | |
| 40 | £480.00 | £48.00 | |
| 42 | £546.00 | £54.60 | |
| 35 | £490.00 | £49.00 | |
| 15 | £240.00 | £24.00 | |
| 35 | £630.00 | £63.00 | |
| 32 | £512.00 | £51.20 | |

### Shortcut

Instead of dragging the Autofill box down, **DOUBLE CLICK** to automatically copy formulas down to the bottom of a block of cells.

# 3 Operators and order of precedence

## 3.1 Introduction

The order of precedence determines which operators Excel will use first in its calculations. It can be seen below that Excel will calculate a formula that contains multiplication or division before it calculates and addition or subtraction. By inserting brackets around part of a formula it forces Excel to calculate the content of the brackets first, followed by the remainder of the formula. You can have multiple sets of brackets in a formula as you will see in later chapters when you deal with more complex calculations.

| Operator | Symbol | Order of Precedence |
|---|---|---|
| Brackets | () | 1 |
| Multiplication | * | 2 |
| Division | / | 2 |
| Addition | + | 3 |
| Subtraction | - | 3 |

### Important

You may have come across the phrase BODMAS during a maths class. This stands for Brackets Off, Divide, Multiply, Add, Subtract – the order of precedence.

Continuing with the same example, we can demonstrate the order of precedence. We need to calculate the tax each person will pay, as 20% of their total pay.

To calculate this using one formula we need to add up two cells, and then multiply the total by 20%. However, due to the order of operations, care must be taken.

SUM =D2+E2*20%

| A | B | C | D | E | F | G |
|---|---|---|---|---|---|---|
| ne | Hourly Rate | Hours Worked | Pay | 10% Bonus | Tax @ 20% | |
| icek | £8.60 | 25 | £215.00 | £21.50 | =D2+E2*20% | |
| tson | £8.60 | 20 | £172.00 | £17.20 | | |
| cock | £9.00 | 20 | £180.00 | £18.00 | | |

It would be tempting to type the above, as this is what we are trying to do – add up the two cells then multiply by 20%. However, Excel reads this as:

Multiply E2 by 20%, and then add on D2.

So the answer comes out as £219.30

To get round this problem, you must use brackets – put the calculation you want to happen first in brackets, to force the order as required. So:

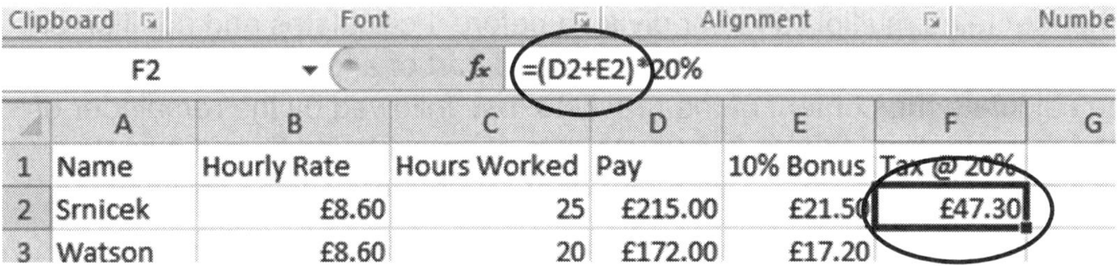


## 3.2 Calculation of percentage

To calculate percentages you can use:

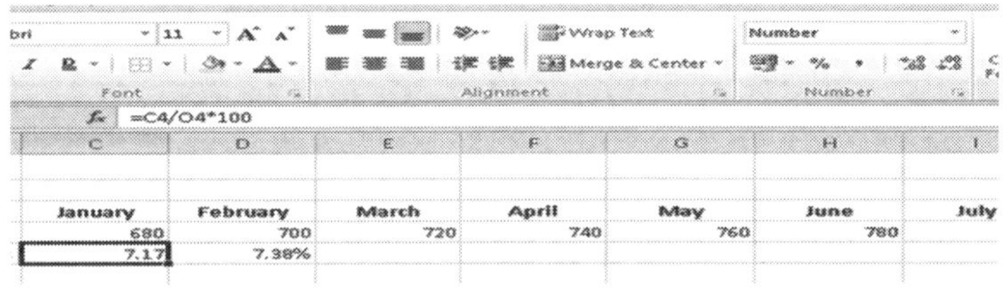


Simple mathematical formula (note formula bar)

or

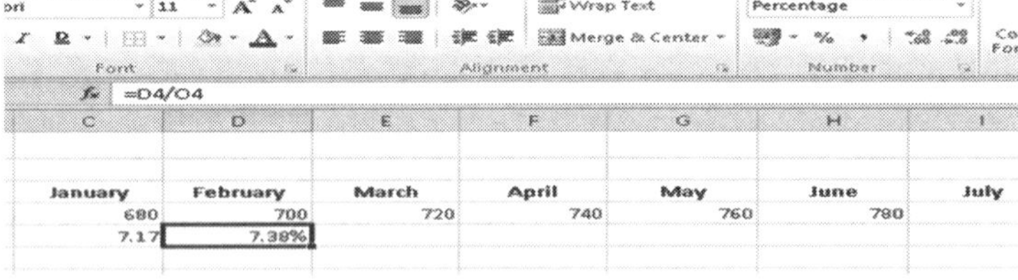


format the cells as percentages. The percentage format can be found on the numbers tab of 'Format Cells'.

Alternatively it can be found on the format toolbar as a **%** icon.

# 4 Sorting data

## 4.1 Sorting data

Sometimes you will need to change the order of your data so that it is sorted according to your requirements. This can be performed quickly and easily, using the Sort function, located in both the **Home** tab and the **Data** tab.

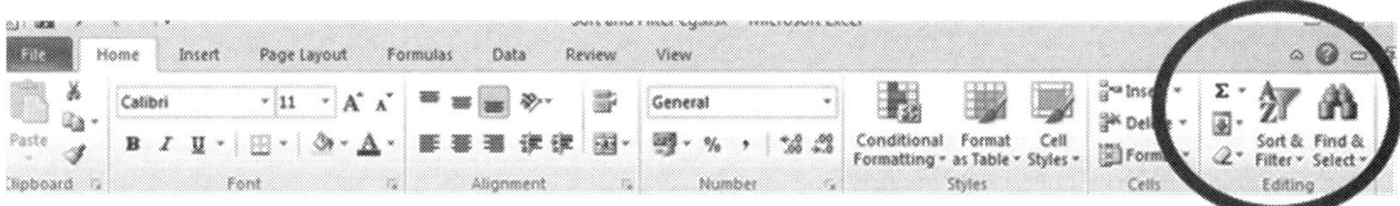


To sort, select the data you wish to sort, and click on the **Sort** button.

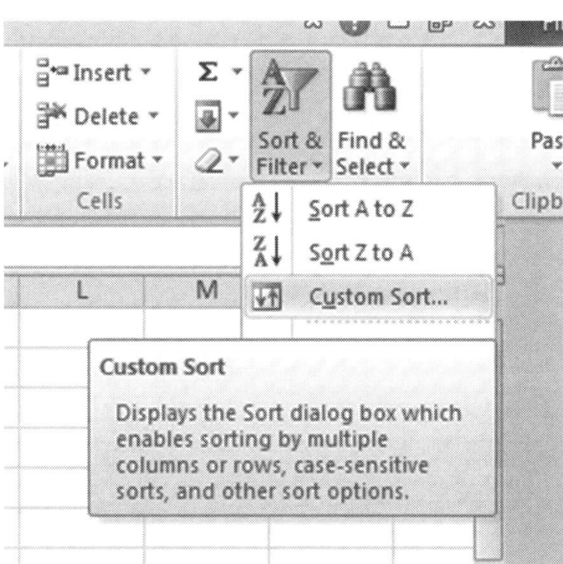


Sort A to Z and Z to A will sort data into either ascending order or descending order. This may not be what you need, so Custom Sort is usually what is required.

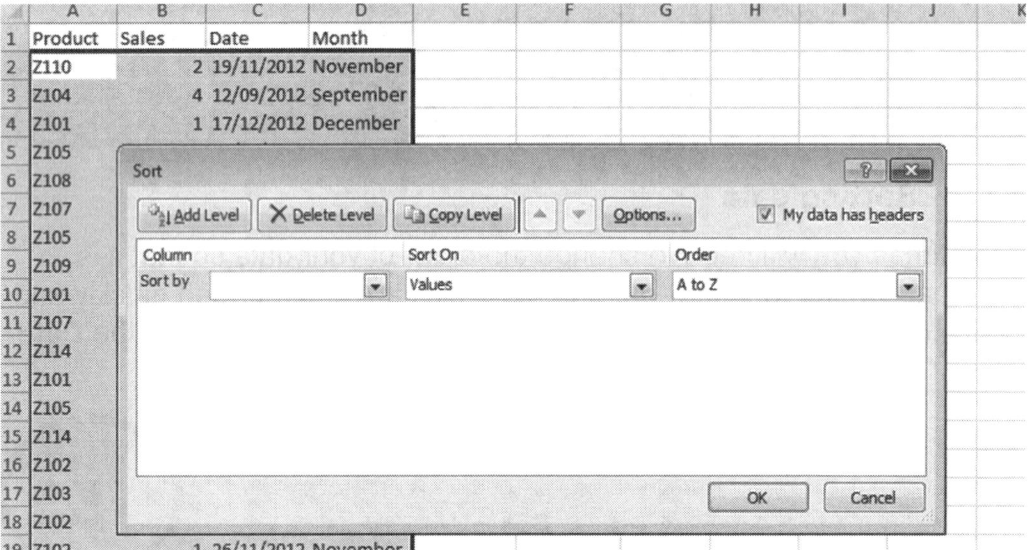

The Sort menu is displayed. Your data should have headers (titles), but if it does not, uncheck the check box.

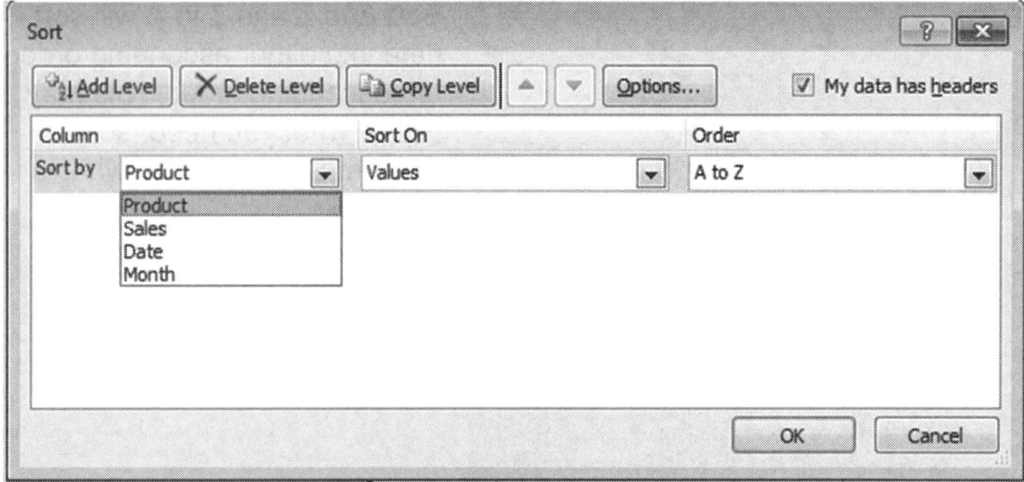

Select the column you wish to sort by, and click OK. The data will be sorted.

You may wish to sort by one column, and then another. For example, with this data set, we might want to have the transactions grouped by product, then by sales volume. This is also done with a custom sort:

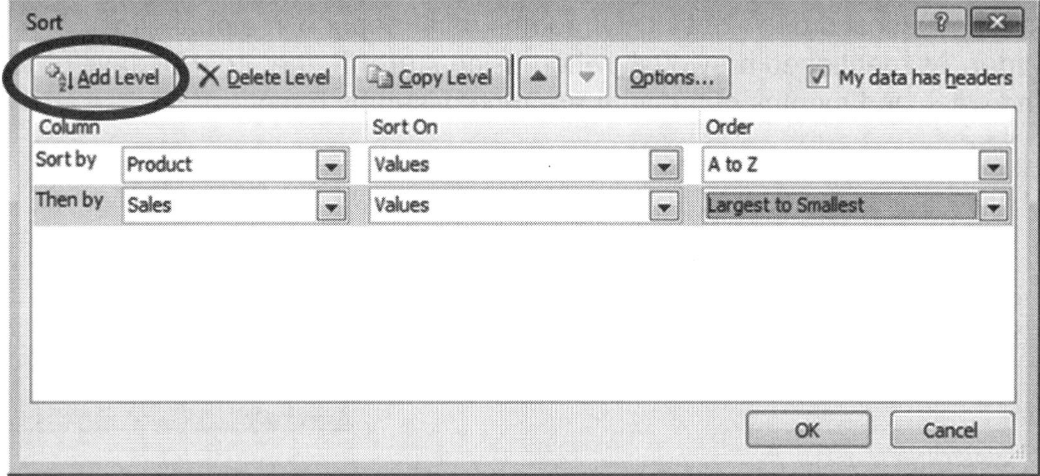


Clicking on **Add Level** will allow you to add more sort criteria. Delete Level will remove any unwanted levels.

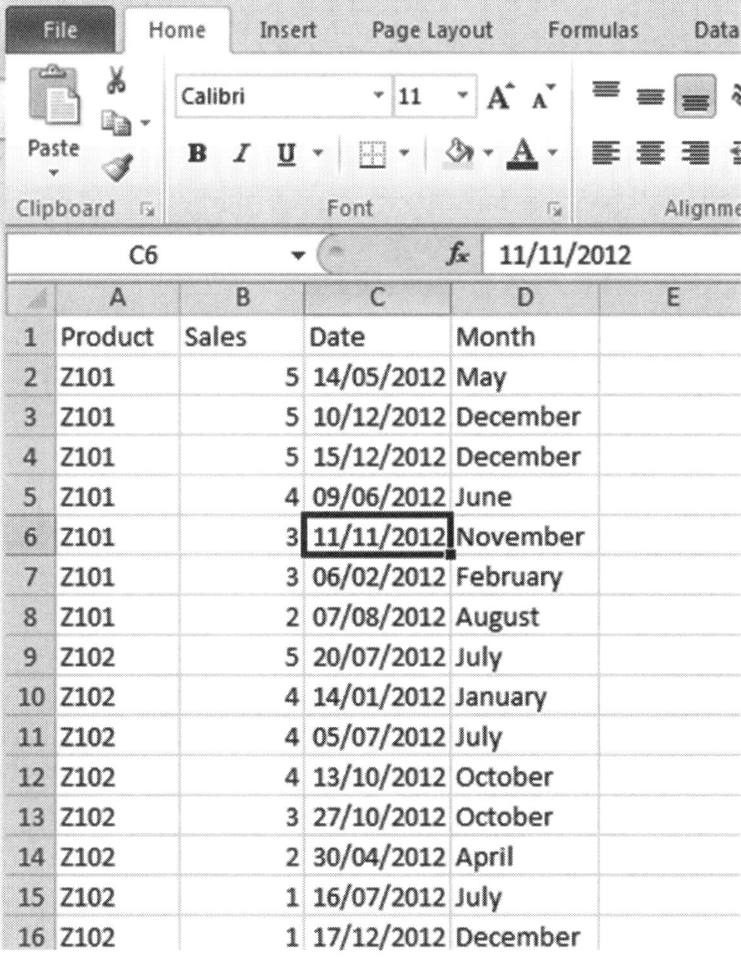

| | A | B | C | D | E |
|---|---|---|---|---|---|
| 1 | Product | Sales | Date | Month | |
| 2 | Z101 | 5 | 14/05/2012 | May | |
| 3 | Z101 | 5 | 10/12/2012 | December | |
| 4 | Z101 | 5 | 15/12/2012 | December | |
| 5 | Z101 | 4 | 09/06/2012 | June | |
| 6 | Z101 | 3 | 11/11/2012 | November | |
| 7 | Z101 | 3 | 06/02/2012 | February | |
| 8 | Z101 | 2 | 07/08/2012 | August | |
| 9 | Z102 | 5 | 20/07/2012 | July | |
| 10 | Z102 | 4 | 14/01/2012 | January | |
| 11 | Z102 | 4 | 05/07/2012 | July | |
| 12 | Z102 | 4 | 13/10/2012 | October | |
| 13 | Z102 | 3 | 27/10/2012 | October | |
| 14 | Z102 | 2 | 30/04/2012 | April | |
| 15 | Z102 | 1 | 16/07/2012 | July | |
| 16 | Z102 | 1 | 17/12/2012 | December | |

The data is now sorted in the order required.

## 4.2 Sorting by date

It is very common to want to sort by day/date. This could cause trouble – if we sort on a column containing months, for example, these will be sorted in alphabetical order – obviously months don't happen in alphabetical order. As mentioned previously when using **Autofill**, the order of days of the week and months of the year are recognised by Excel:

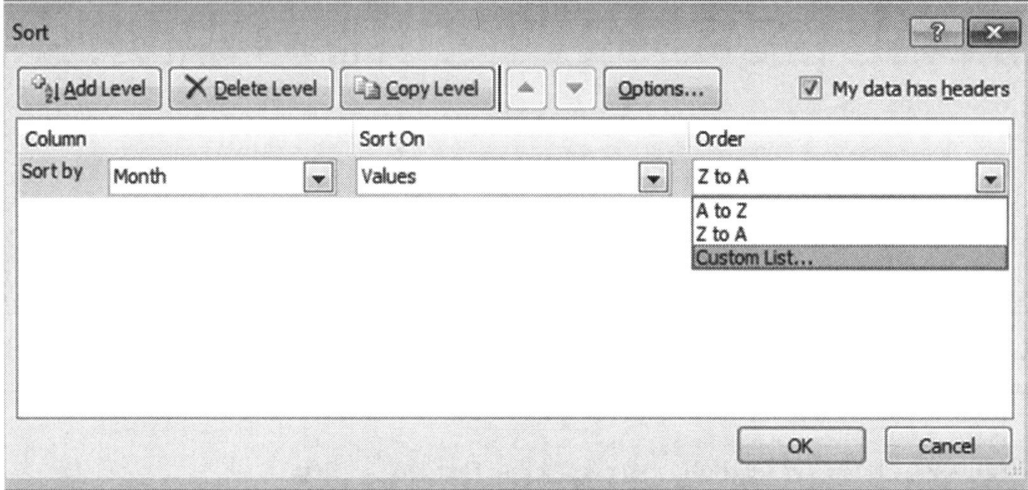


Choose custom list when sorting by month or days, and select the relevant list required.

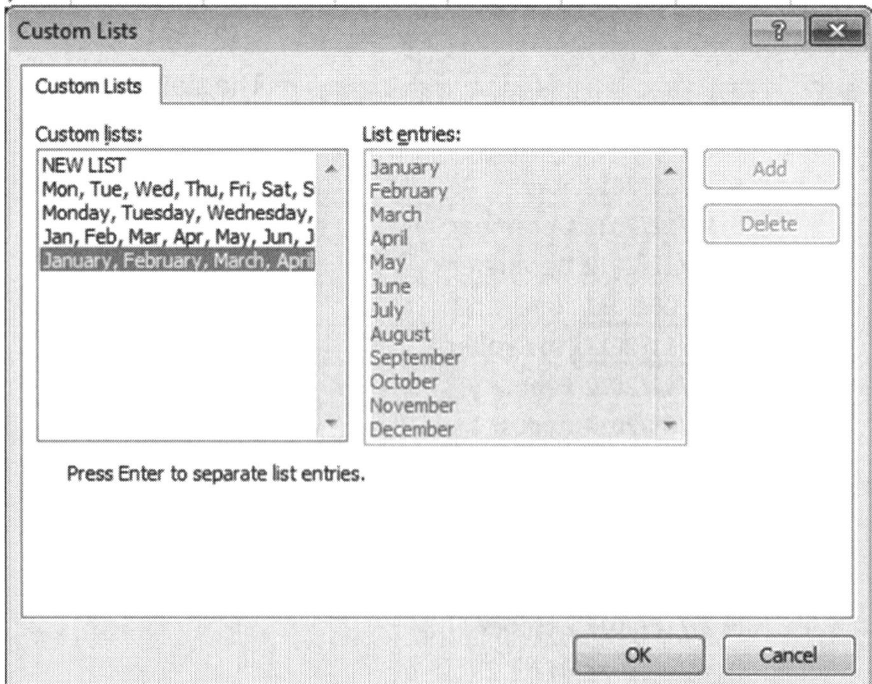

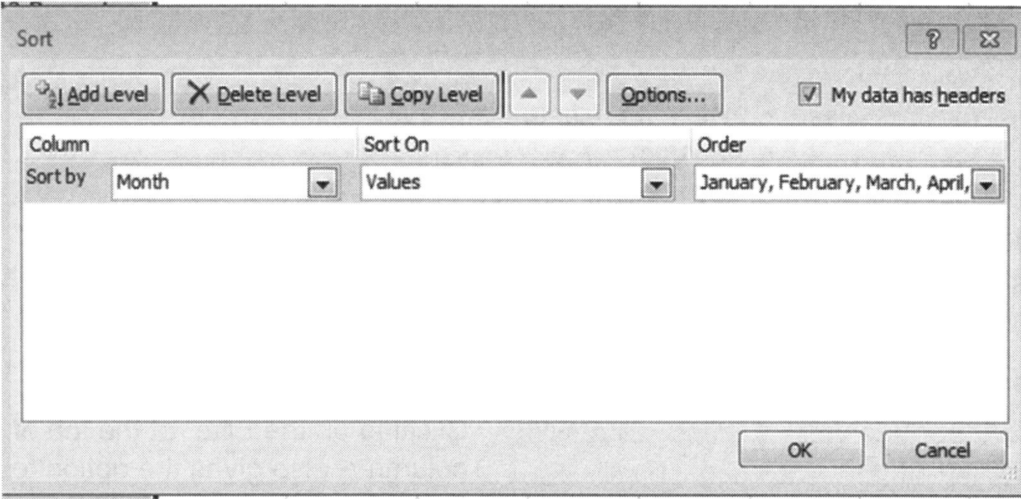


The data will then be sorted as required.

## 4.3 Filtering data

Filtering Data is a powerful way of quickly analysing large data sets to find the information you need. There are two types of filter – **Autofilter** and **Advanced Filter**. AutoFilter is all that is covered here, and should be all that is required – Advanced Filter is only required very rarely and not as part of the SPSH syllabus.

To apply **AutoFilter**, select the data you wish to analyse, and click the Filter button.

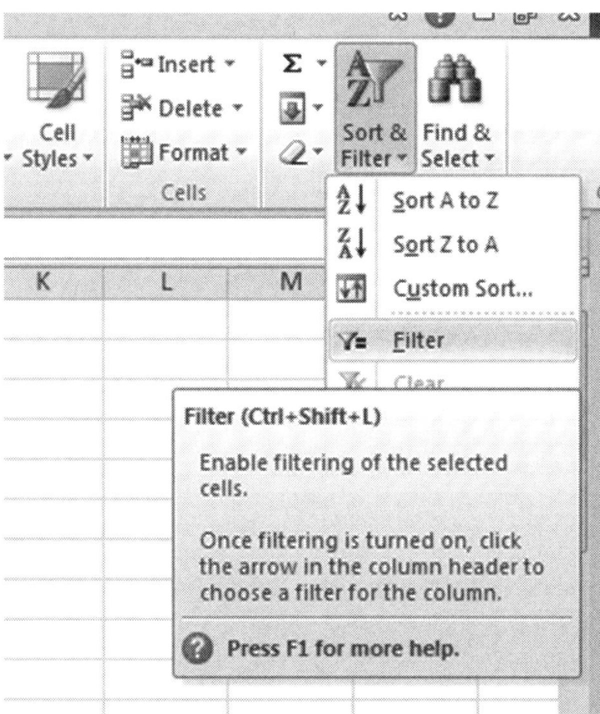

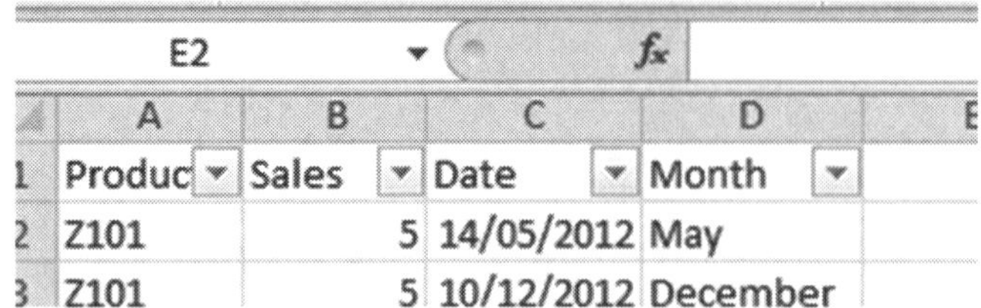

The arrows at the top of each column are the Filters – click on one to apply a Filter. Once the filter is in place, rows which do not meet the criteria applied will be hidden.

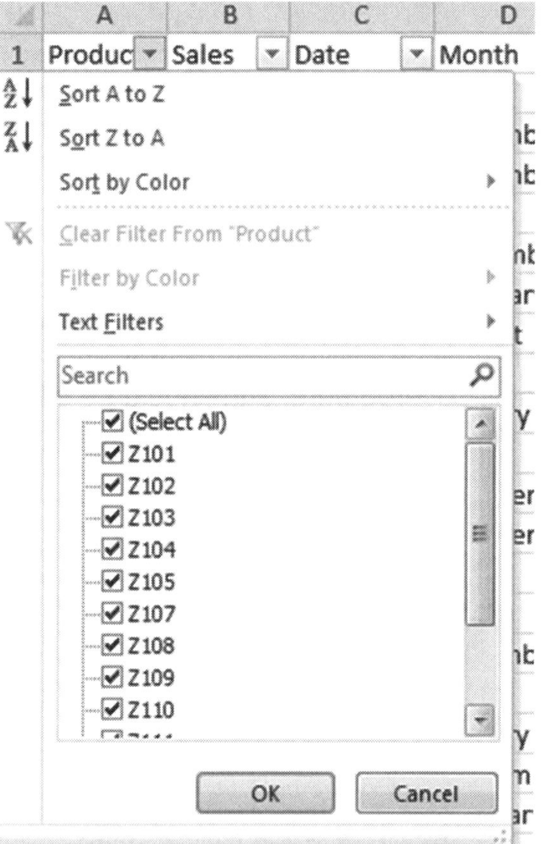


Clicking on the Filter at the top of column A also gives the option to Sort your data.

You can simply check/uncheck the items you wish to see/not see. Clicking the (Select All) box will also deselect all items if they are all selected.

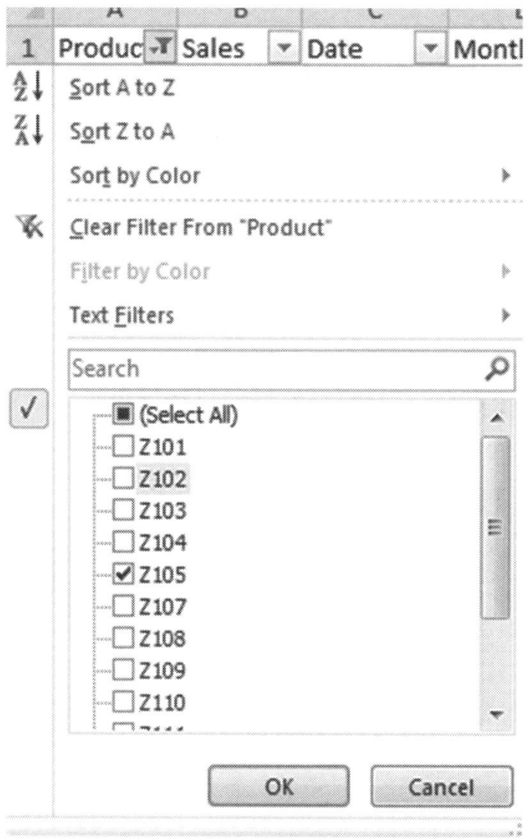


Select the item(s) you wish to see and click **OK**.

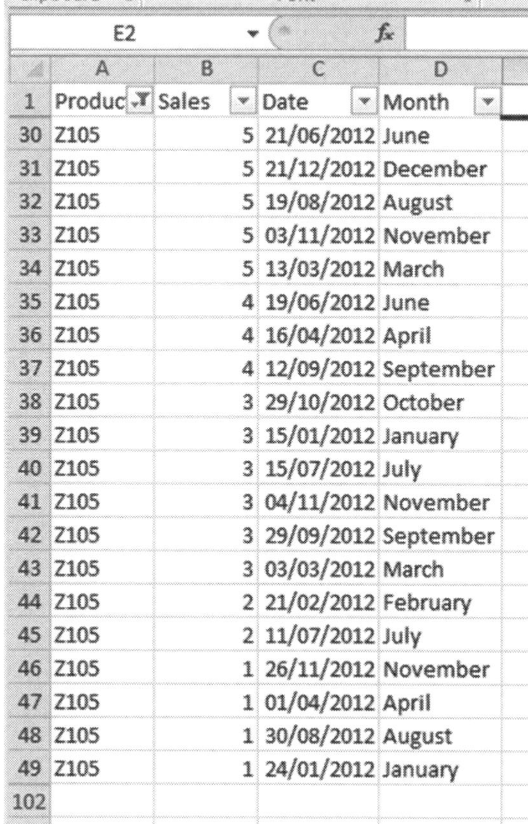

| | A | B | C | D |
|---|---|---|---|---|
| 1 | Produc | Sales | Date | Month |
| 30 | Z105 | 5 | 21/06/2012 | June |
| 31 | Z105 | 5 | 21/12/2012 | December |
| 32 | Z105 | 5 | 19/08/2012 | August |
| 33 | Z105 | 5 | 03/11/2012 | November |
| 34 | Z105 | 5 | 13/03/2012 | March |
| 35 | Z105 | 4 | 19/06/2012 | June |
| 36 | Z105 | 4 | 16/04/2012 | April |
| 37 | Z105 | 4 | 12/09/2012 | September |
| 38 | Z105 | 3 | 29/10/2012 | October |
| 39 | Z105 | 3 | 15/01/2012 | January |
| 40 | Z105 | 3 | 15/07/2012 | July |
| 41 | Z105 | 3 | 04/11/2012 | November |
| 42 | Z105 | 3 | 29/09/2012 | September |
| 43 | Z105 | 3 | 03/03/2012 | March |
| 44 | Z105 | 2 | 21/02/2012 | February |
| 45 | Z105 | 2 | 11/07/2012 | July |
| 46 | Z105 | 1 | 26/11/2012 | November |
| 47 | Z105 | 1 | 01/04/2012 | April |
| 48 | Z105 | 1 | 30/08/2012 | August |
| 49 | Z105 | 1 | 24/01/2012 | January |
| 102 | | | | |

You can see that all the rows not required are hidden. The rows have also turned blue – this is a useful visual indication that a filter has been applied.

As well as this, the filter at the top of the column has changed to show that a filter is in place.

You can continue to apply filters to other columns as required.

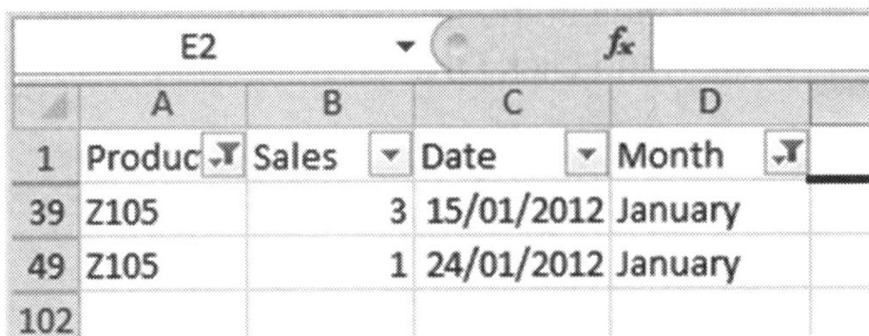


For example – Z105 sales in January filtered by product and month.

## 4.4 Removing Filters

Either click back in the filter and **Select All**, or within the **Sort & Filter** button, click the **Clear** option.

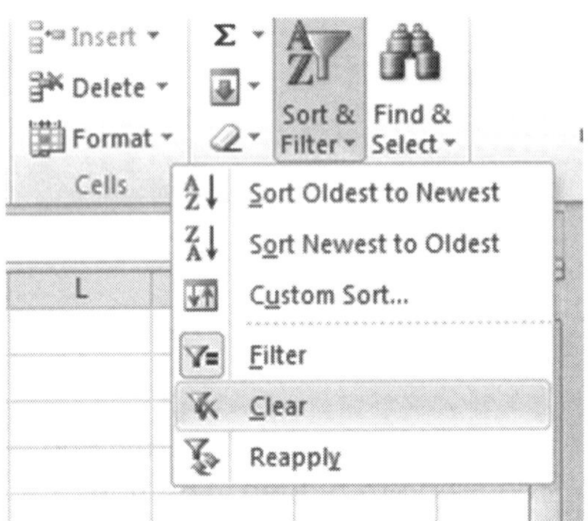


This will clear all current Filters.

# 5 Other filtering options

## 5.1 Other options

Depending on the data in the row you are applying the filter to, different options will be available.

## 5.2 Text Filters

If the column contains text, the following options are available.

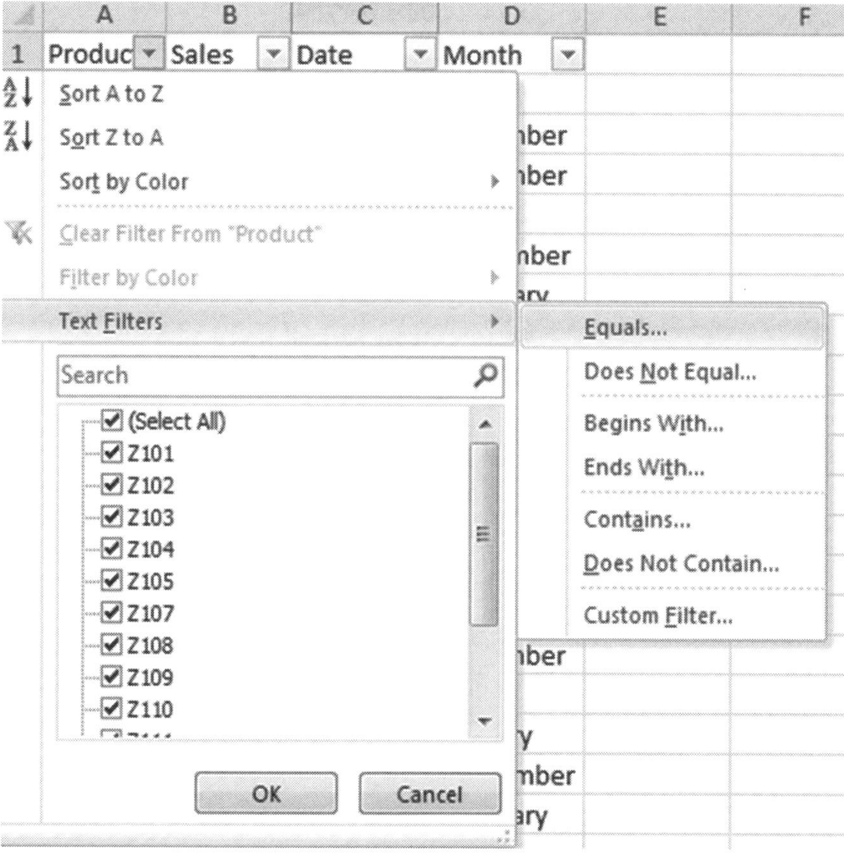


These should be self-explanatory. Custom Filter allows you to apply two constraints in your filter.

## 5.3 Numeric Filters

For purely numeric data, the following options are available:

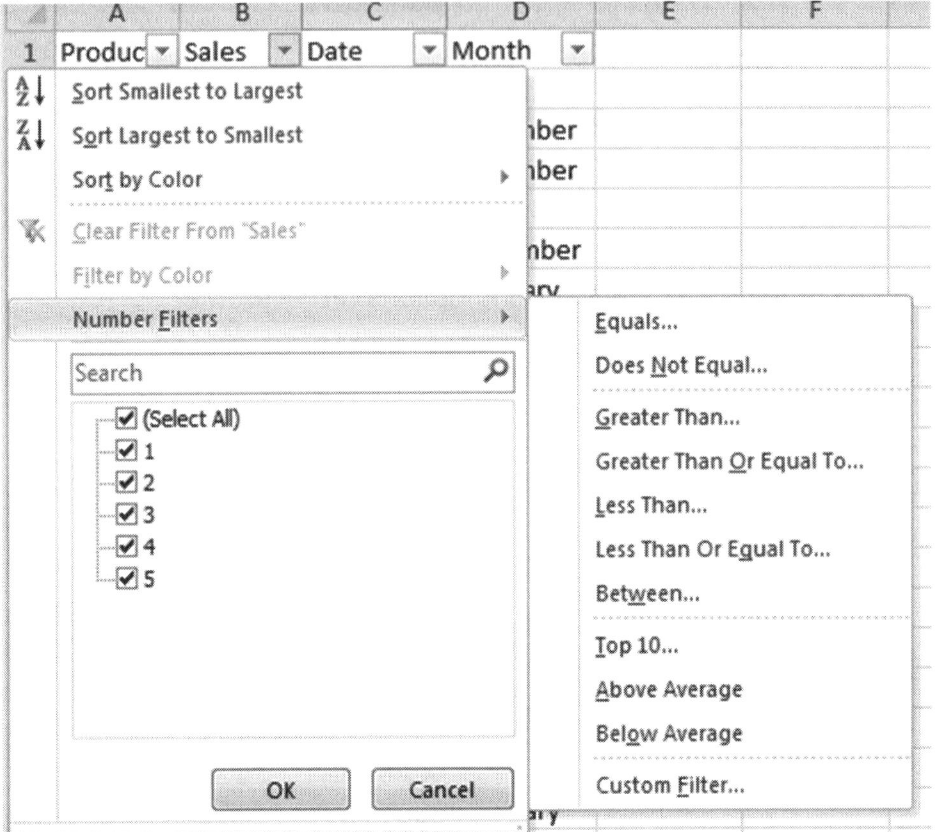

## 5.4 Date Filters

If the column contains dates only, there are many options available for your filter.

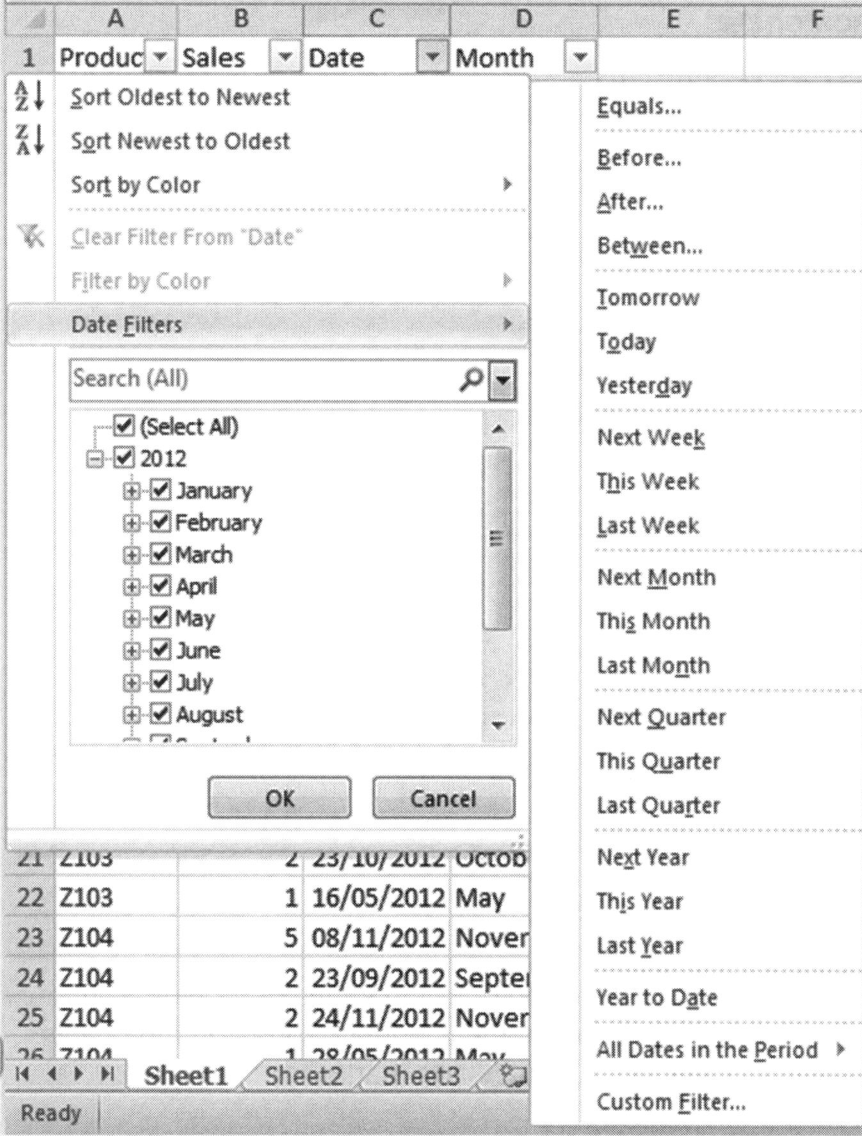

# 6 Concatenate

## 6.1 Concatenate

The **CONCATENATE** function can be used to join items such as text, numbers, cell references, or a combination of those items.

For example, if your worksheet contains a person's first name in cell A1 and the person's last name in cell B1, you can combine the two values in another cell by using the following formula:

=CONCATENATE(A1," ",B1)

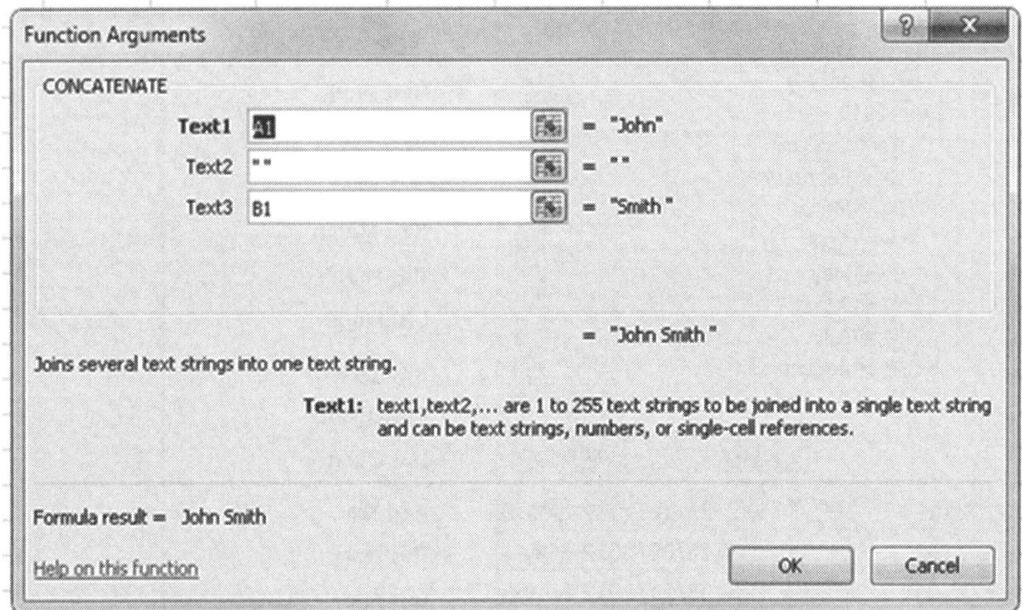


The second argument in this example (**" "**) is a space character. You must specify any spaces or punctuation that you want to appear in the results as an argument that is enclosed in quotation marks.

# 7 Test your understanding

The activities in this guide are designed to test your knowledge on the techniques shown in this chapter. They may also use techniques used in previous chapters, to build up your knowledge. Suggested answers are available on MyKaplan, although it is better to refer to the notes and try to understand the methods than look straight at the answers.

## Test your understanding 4-1

This activity tests some simple calculations, including percentages, along with some basic data entry.

(a) Open the **Formatted Report** file from the **Activities** folder.

(b) Select the **Summary Report** worksheet.

(c) Look at the Half Year data in cells H4 and H5 – this is hard coded in. Enter a **formula** in cell H4 to add the numbers in cells B4 to G4.

(d) **Copy** the formula into cell H5. You may notice that the border around H5 is changed. This can be avoided by using **Paste Special**, and only pasting formulas. Alternatively, it's probably easier to just put the border back on.

(e) In row 6, you need to calculate **Profit Margin**. This is the profit figure as a percentage of sales. The calculation for this is:

Profit/Sales*100%

However, using the percentage format, the *100 is not required.

Enter 'Profit Margin' in A6, and add a formula to divide profit by sales in columns B-K.

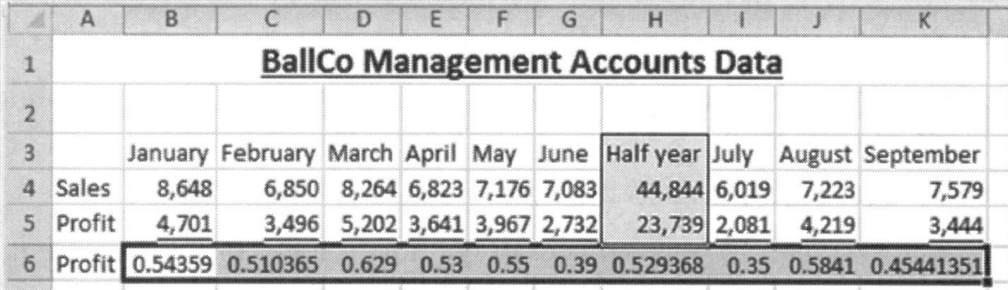

|  | A | B | C | D | E | F | G | H | I | J | K |
|---|---|---|---|---|---|---|---|---|---|---|---|
| 1 | BallCo Management Accounts Data | | | | | | | | | | |
| 2 | | | | | | | | | | | |
| 3 | | January | February | March | April | May | June | Half year | July | August | September |
| 4 | Sales | 8,648 | 6,850 | 8,264 | 6,823 | 7,176 | 7,083 | 44,844 | 6,019 | 7,223 | 7,579 |
| 5 | Profit | 4,701 | 3,496 | 5,202 | 3,641 | 3,967 | 2,732 | 23,739 | 2,081 | 4,219 | 3,444 |
| 6 | Profit | 0.54359 | 0.510365 | 0.629 | 0.53 | 0.55 | 0.39 | 0.529368 | 0.35 | 0.5841 | 0.45441351 |

(f) Now change the format of these numbers to **percentage**, 1 decimal place

(g) The final quarter's results are:

Oct – Sales 8243, Profit 4343

Nov – Sales 8496, Profit 4611

Dec – Sales 7199, Profit 3290

Add this information to the report, along with the Profit Margin calculations.

(h) Add a total in column O for the second half of the year. Either enter this manually, or (better), copy and paste the Half year formulas and formatting – they will add up the previous 6 months' data.

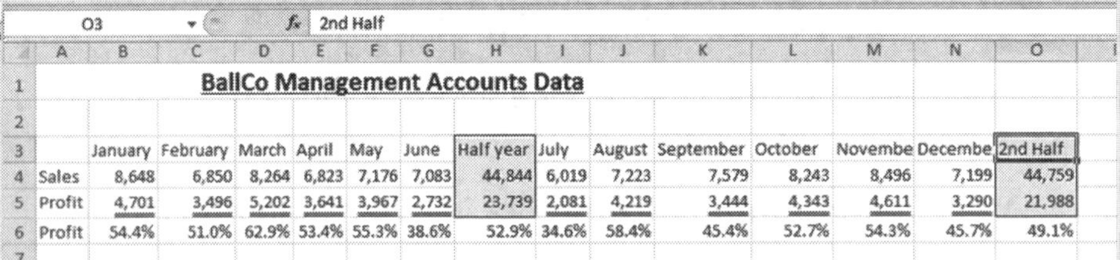
O3 | 2nd Half

**BallCo Management Accounts Data**

| | January | February | March | April | May | June | Half year | July | August | September | October | Novembe | Decembe | 2nd Half |
|---|---|---|---|---|---|---|---|---|---|---|---|---|---|---|
| Sales | 8,648 | 6,850 | 8,264 | 6,823 | 7,176 | 7,083 | 44,844 | 6,019 | 7,223 | 7,579 | 8,243 | 8,496 | 7,199 | 44,759 |
| Profit | 4,701 | 3,496 | 5,202 | 3,641 | 3,967 | 2,732 | 23,739 | 2,081 | 4,219 | 3,444 | 4,343 | 4,611 | 3,290 | 21,988 |
| Profit | 54.4% | 51.0% | 62.9% | 53.4% | 55.3% | 38.6% | 52.9% | 34.6% | 58.4% | 45.4% | 52.7% | 54.3% | 45.7% | 49.1% |

Change the column title to 2nd Half.

(i) **Autofit** Columns, and **Save** the file as **Activity 4-1** in the **Solutions** folder.

## Test your understanding 4-2

This activity allows you to practice Sorting and Filtering Data. It is important that after each step you check that the data is in the correct order.

(a) Open the **Eastern Region** file in the **Activities** folder.

(b) Autofit the Column Widths so the data can be viewed.

(c) **Sort** the data by Salesperson (A to Z) (remove sort).

(d) **Sort** the data by Month – January-December (remove sort).

(e) **Sort** the data by Month (January – December), then by Product code (add level).

(f) Add an **AutoFilter** to the data.

(g) Apply a filter to column A to only show sales from June and July.

(h) Apply a filter to column F to only show James Beardsley's data.

(i) Apply a filter to column C to only show amounts greater than or equal to 100.

(j) Save the file as **Activity 4-2** in the **Solutions** folder.

# Page setup, presentation and printing 5

## Introduction

This chapter will ensure that you are able to provide a document that is ready to publish and print showing only the necessary information that needs printing.

### ASSESSMENT CRITERIA

Prepare reports (5.1)

Report accounting information (5.2)

### CONTENTS

# 1 Headers and Footers

## 1.1 Headers and Footers

Headers and Footers are used to provide information in a document such as document titles, data owner, version numbers, page numbers, dates etc.

To add them, use the **Insert** tab, then **Header & Footer**.

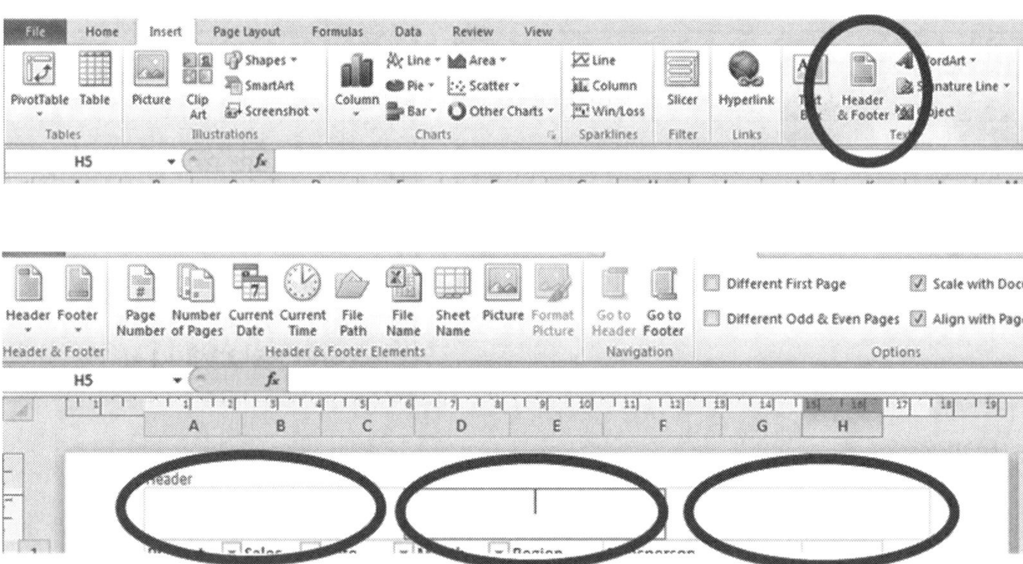


You will be taken to the Header – the page is split into three sections, where you can type in the header required. You can also select from the **Header & Footer Elements** in the Ribbon.

To edit the **Footer**, either navigate to the bottom of the page and click in the footer, or click the **Go to Footer** button.

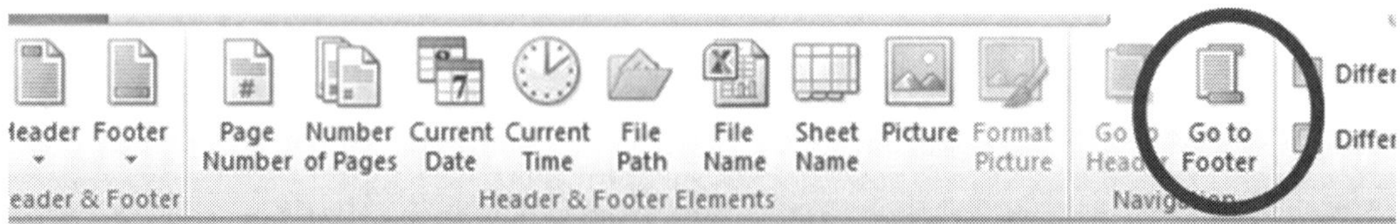

# 2 Page margins, breaks and orientation

## 2.1 Introduction

All three of these options can be adjusted from the **Page Layout** tab.

## 2.2 Margins

To prepare documents so that they are visually pleasing – especially for printing – you need to set the page margins. Select the **Margins** button.

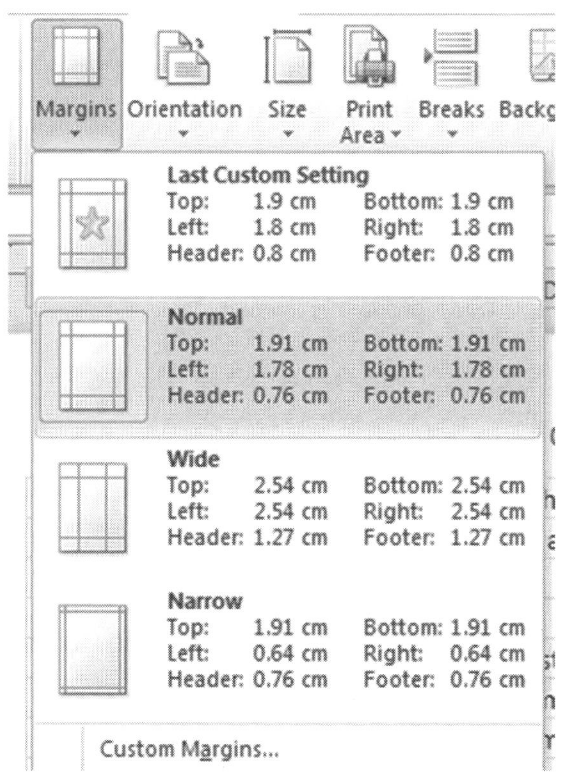


A few standard options are shown.

For more flexibility select the **Custom Margins** option.

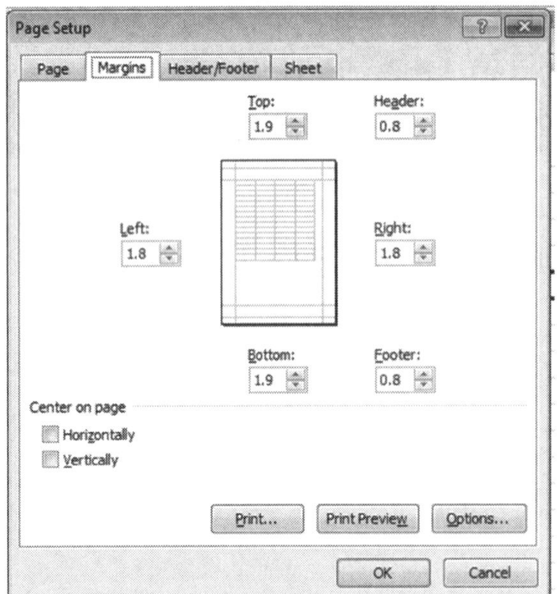


Each individual margin can be adjusted as required.

Once you have selected your margins these will be indicated on your worksheet by broken dashed lines.

## 2.3 Page Breaks

With your margins set, Excel will automatically insert a break in the data so that the right amount of data is displayed on a page. However, you will find that sometimes a natural break in the data is apparent and that you want to insert your own 'Page Break'. Select the **Breaks** button.

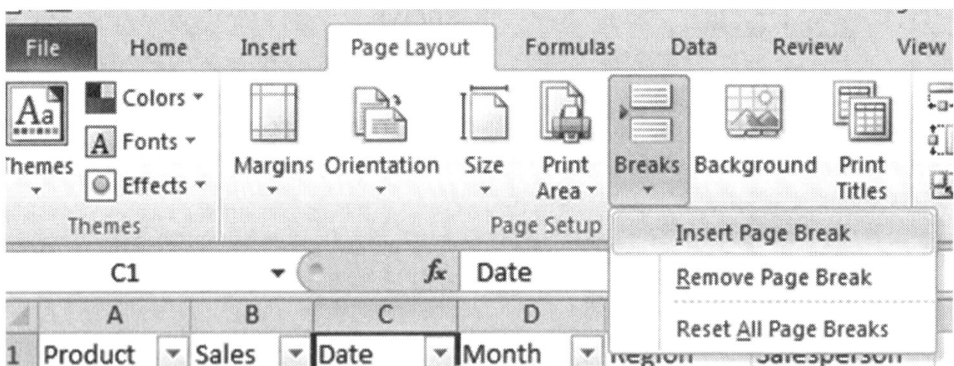


Use this to add or remove breaks as required – select the area on the sheet you would like the new page to start, and **Insert Page Break**. You can also view (and edit) page breaks in **Page Break Preview** mode. In the **View** tab, select **Page Break Preview**.

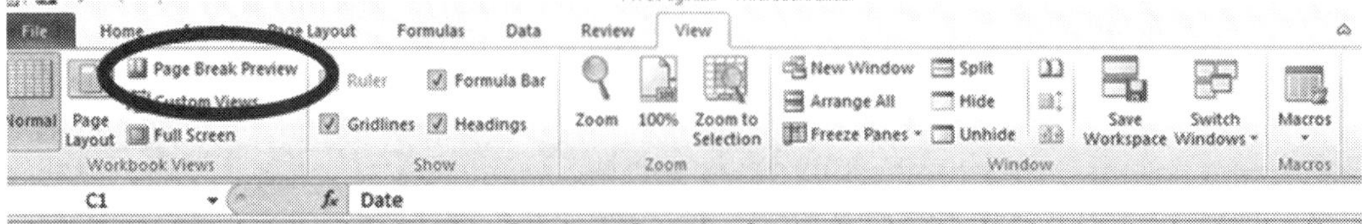


To return to normal view at any stage, select the **Normal** button just to the left of Page Break Preview.

### 2.4 Orientation

There are 2 ways to orientate your worksheet portrait or landscape.

Excel defaults to 'Portrait', but sometimes it is better to view your document in 'Landscape'. Viewing in this way allows you to view more columns [but fewer rows] on a page.

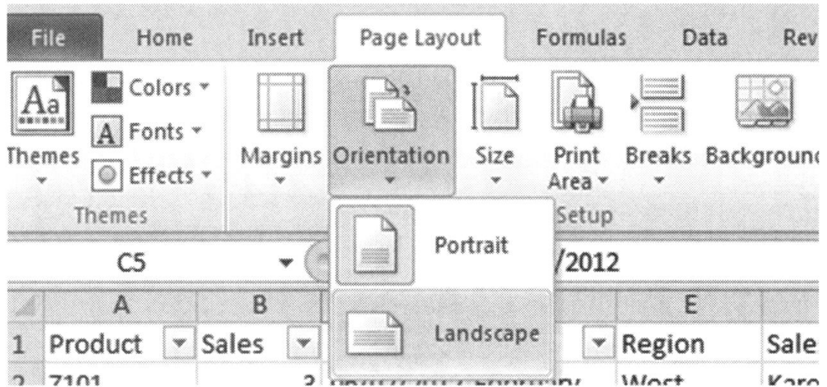


Select the orientation required.

## 3 Printing

### 3.1 Print Area

Sometimes you may want to print only part of a document. This is quite easy to do. Simply highlight the cells you wish to print, and click the **Set Print Area** button on the **Page Layout** tab.

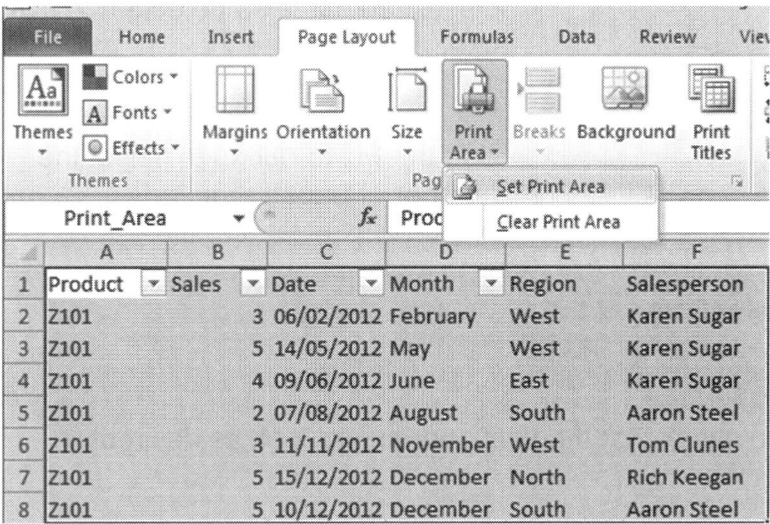


| | A | B | C | D | E | F |
|---|---|---|---|---|---|---|
| 1 | Product | Sales | Date | Month | Region | Salesperson |
| 2 | Z101 | 3 | 06/02/2012 | February | West | Karen Sugar |
| 3 | Z101 | 5 | 14/05/2012 | May | West | Karen Sugar |
| 4 | Z101 | 4 | 09/06/2012 | June | East | Karen Sugar |
| 5 | Z101 | 2 | 07/08/2012 | August | South | Aaron Steel |
| 6 | Z101 | 3 | 11/11/2012 | November | West | Tom Clunes |
| 7 | Z101 | 5 | 15/12/2012 | December | North | Rich Keegan |
| 8 | Z101 | 5 | 10/12/2012 | December | South | Aaron Steel |

Choose **Clear Print Area** to remove this setting.

## 3.2 Fitting the data onto one or more sheets

One of the most useful features regarding printing is the ability to specify how many pages you want your data to appear on. Excel will then change the size of the font accordingly. Obviously this has practical limits – if you try and squeeze 1,000 lines of data onto one page, it will be impossible to read! However, it is invaluable for making your work look professional and user-friendly.

One way to do this is using the **Page Setup** menu. This is accessed by clicking on the arrow in the bottom corner of the Page Setup section of the **Page Layout** menu.

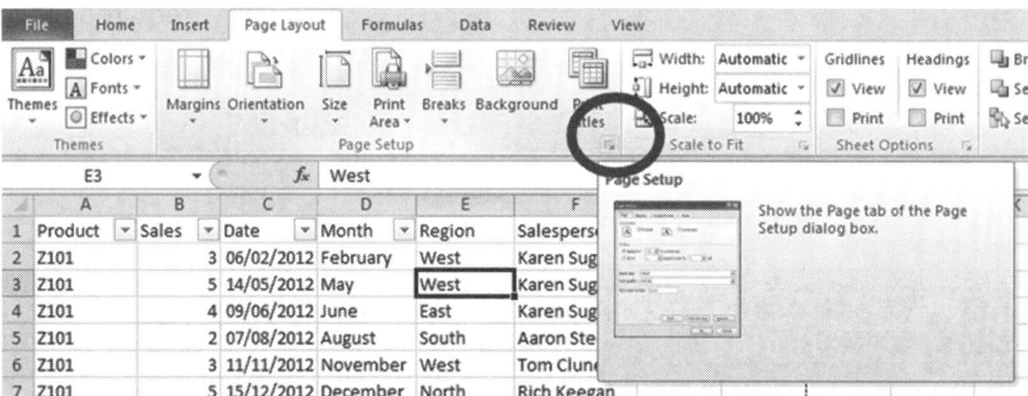


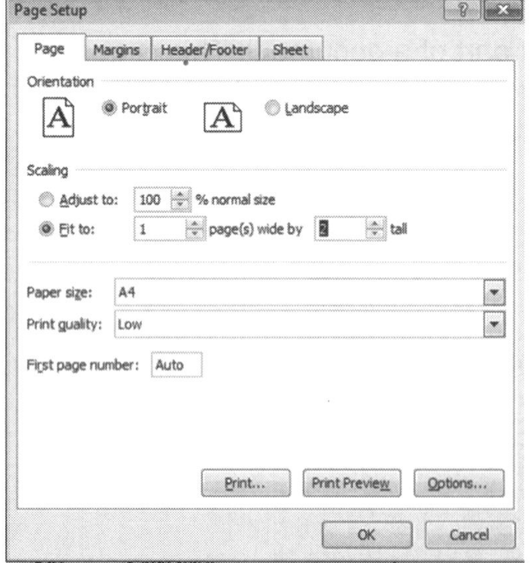


Several of the options already discussed can also be edited in this useful menu.

Use the **Fit to** option to select the number of pages required.

Use Print Preview to check that the final printout will look as desired.

## 3.3 Print preview and printing

Print preview has changed since Excel 2007. Rather than being a separate window view, Print Preview is found within the **File** tab, by clicking **Print**.

Having made all the adjustments to the data, format etc you will be in a position to print your document. Before you do this you should review it one more time – just to make sure. This is 'Print Preview'. When you are happy that your document is in the condition that you want it to be then you are in a position to 'Print'.

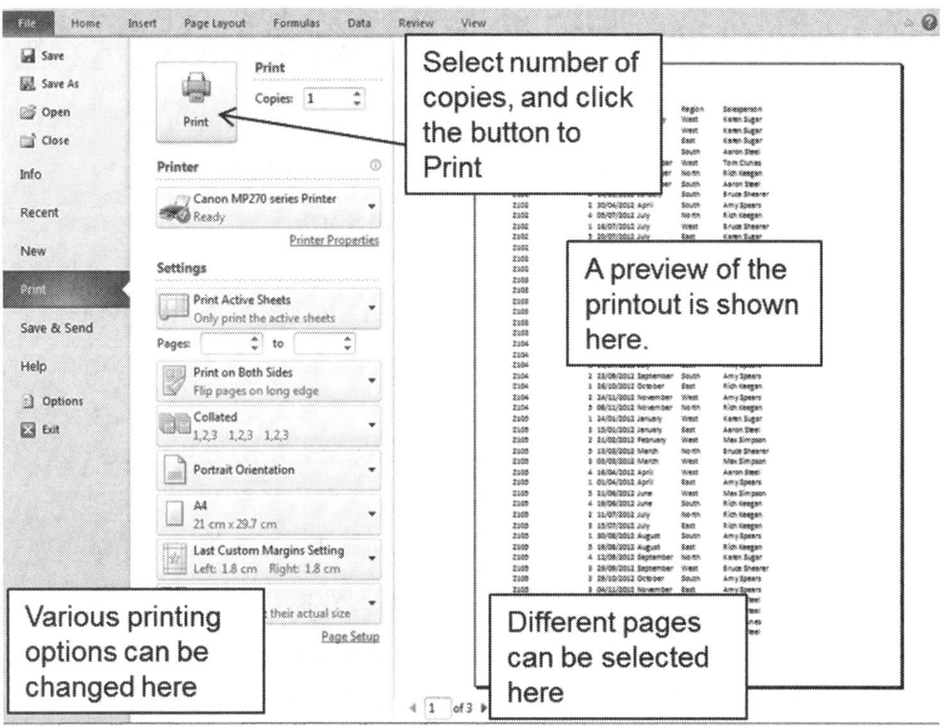

# 4 Test your understanding

It is essential that before you submit any document you check that the print setup has been performed correctly – these techniques can be applied to any document. The following activities give you the chance to practice some of the more important ones specifically, but try the other techniques yourself on any document.

## Test your understanding 5-1

This activity requires you to setup a document ready for printing.

(a) Open the **Report for Printing** file in the **Activities** folder.

(b) Add a Footer to the document – with your name in the left section, and today's date in the right.

Note you can use the **Design** tab to insert the date, or just type it in.

(c) Return to Normal view (use the **View** tab).

(d) Change the **Orientation** to **Landscape**. Notice how the page breaks move.

(e) Go to **Print Preview.** Notice that the report requires two pages.

(f) Use **Page Setup** to fit the report to 1 page wide by 1 page tall.

(g) Note that the Print Preview shows the whole report.

(h) Save the file as **Activity 5-1** in the **Solutions** folder.

## Test your understanding 5-2

This activity is again centred on Printing a document, but also highlighting the use of Filters to find the information you need.

(a) Open the **Eastern Region** file in the **Activities** folder.

(b) **AutoFit** Column widths.

(c) Go to **Print Preview** – notice that the data spans 2 pages.

(d) Use **Page Setup** to fit the printout to 1 page wide by 1 page tall.

(e) Note that while this is possible, it will be hard to read. Exit print preview (click the **home** tab).

(f) Apply an **Autofilter** to the data.

(g) Sort the data by month – January-December, then by product, A-Z.

(h) Apply a filter so that only James Beardsley's sales are shown.

(i) Go to **Print Preview** – see that the data is visible!

(j) **Save** the file as **Activity 5-2-1** in the **Solutions** folder.

(k) Go back to the data – Filter so that Eva Nasri's sales are visible.

(l) **Save** the file as **Activity 5-2-2** in the **Solutions** folder.

# Using Excel Functions

## Introduction

This chapter will explain to you how to use some of the most commonly used and useful functions within Excel.

### ASSESSMENT CRITERIA

Select and use a range of formulae and functions to perform calculations (3.1)

### CONTENTS

# 1 Functions

## 1.1 Functions

In the chapter 4, we started to perform simple calculations. This is very useful, but more flexibility and speed comes from **Functions**.

These are specific words which tell Excel to perform much more than just adding up a couple of cell values. They range from the relatively simple functions to more complicated tools.

## 1.2 Using a function

To enter a function into a cell, always start with an **EQUALS SIGN** first.

You then type the **NAME** of the function, followed by an **OPEN BRACKET** '**(**'.

The **ARGUMENTS** of the function are then required. These tell Excel exactly what to do, and depend on the function required. If more than one argument is needed, they must be separated by a **COMMA**.

The function is ended with a **CLOSE BRACKET** '**)**'.

This will become more important as we look at different functions.

## 1.3 The Insert Function button

A great way of getting used to functions within Excel is the **Insert Function** button *fx* located just above the column names.

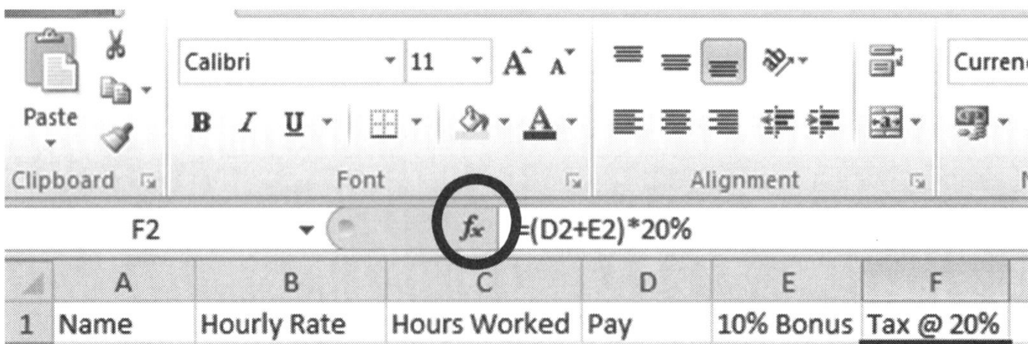


Clicking this button brings up the **Insert Function** menu, which can help work out which function is required.

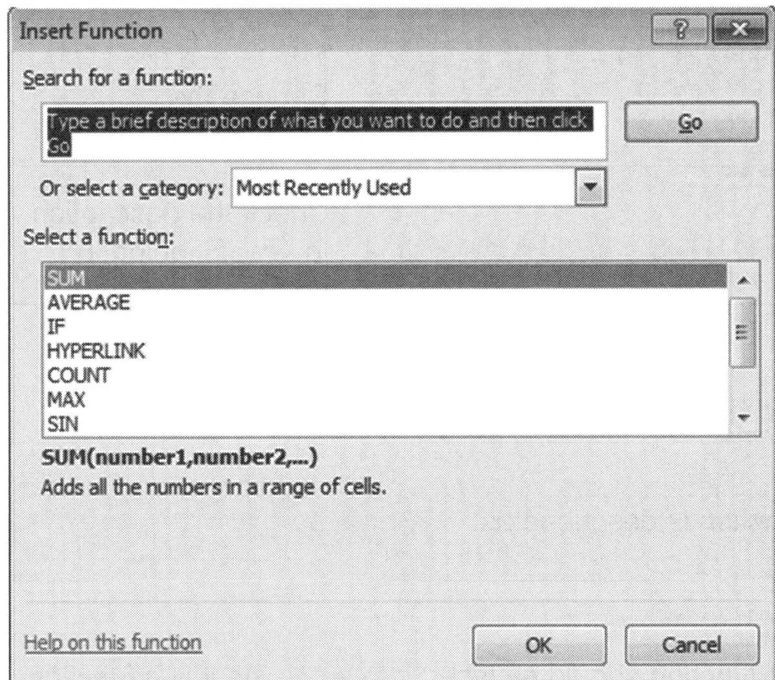


This allows you to type in – in plain English, what you require, and several options will be provided based on your search.

Using **Insert Function** also provides a more user-friendly way of entering the calculation you require, as we shall see.

# 2 SUM

## 2.1 SUM

**SUM** is probably the most commonly used function in Excel. As the name suggests, it is used to add up a selection of numbers. As discussed previously, you could use the **Insert Function** button:

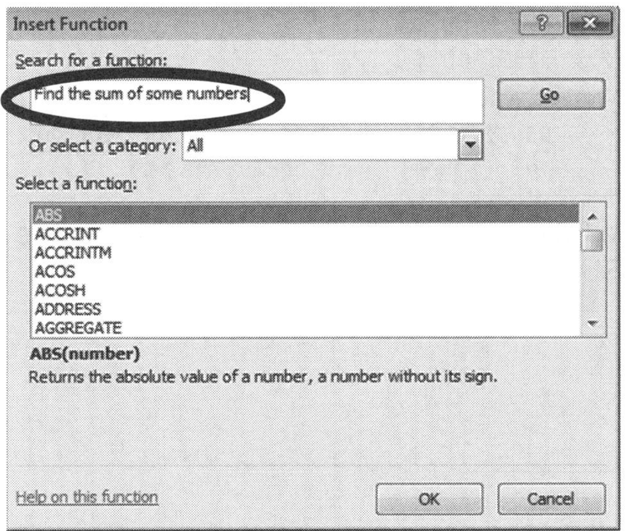


Type in what you require and click the **Go** button.

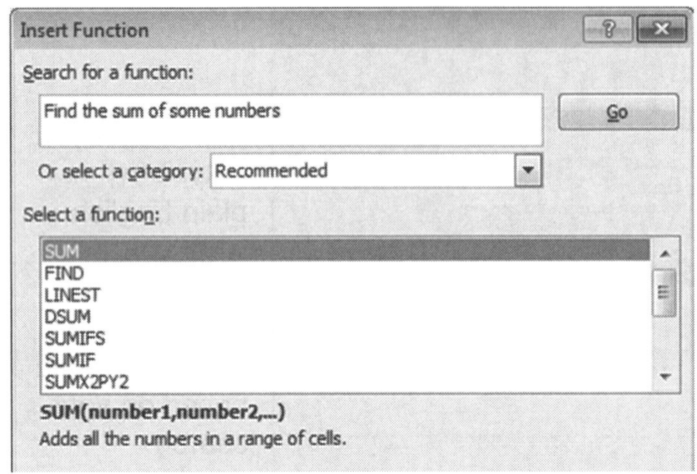


Choose the appropriate formula.

Check the description to see if it going to perform the correct function.

To use the **SUM** function is described as:

**SUM(number1,number2,...)**
Adds all the numbers in a range of cells.

This shows how the function should be typed into a cell. As it is a function, you start with an '**=**' first, even though this is omitted in the description.

**Number1, number2,...** are the **ARGUMENTS**. In the case of SUM, these are the numbers (or cells) you wish to add. Each number you wish to add should be separated by a **comma**. For example, typing

**=SUM(3,5)**

will return the value 8. You can do this for any number of additions, and it is no different to using **+**, as in chapter 4.

Just like using **+**, you can also subtract cell values. In the example below, we want to find Net Pay as the sum of Pay and Bonus, less Tax; this can be done using SUM:

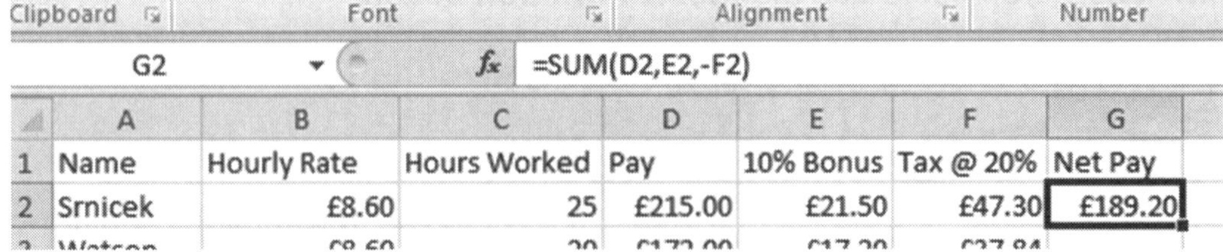


| | A | B | C | D | E | F | G |
|---|---|---|---|---|---|---|---|
| 1 | Name | Hourly Rate | Hours Worked | Pay | 10% Bonus | Tax @ 20% | Net Pay |
| 2 | Srnicek | £8.60 | 25 | £215.00 | £21.50 | £47.30 | £189.20 |

Note the minus sign before the F2 reference to indicate a subtraction. We could have done this without SUM, by typing

**=D2+E2-F2**

**SUM** is really useful when you have many numbers to add up – take the following example:

| | A | B | C | D | E | F | G |
|---|---|---|---|---|---|---|---|
| 1 | Name | Hourly Rate | Hours Worked | Pay | 10% Bonus | Tax @ 20% | Net Pay |
| 2 | Srnicek | £8.60 | 25 | £215.00 | £21.50 | £47.30 | £189.20 |
| 3 | Watson | £8.60 | 20 | £172.00 | £17.20 | £37.84 | £151.36 |
| 4 | Peacock | £9.00 | 20 | £180.00 | £18.00 | £39.60 | £158.40 |
| 5 | Albert | £11.50 | 25 | £287.50 | £28.75 | £63.25 | £253.00 |
| 6 | Beresford | £10.50 | 30 | £315.00 | £31.50 | £69.30 | £277.20 |
| 7 | Batty | £12.00 | 40 | £480.00 | £48.00 | £105.60 | £422.40 |
| 8 | Lee | £13.00 | 42 | £546.00 | £54.60 | £120.12 | £480.48 |
| 9 | Beardsley | £14.00 | 35 | £490.00 | £49.00 | £107.80 | £431.20 |
| 10 | Ginola | £16.00 | 15 | £240.00 | £24.00 | £52.80 | £211.20 |
| 11 | Shearer | £18.00 | 35 | £630.00 | £63.00 | £138.60 | £554.40 |
| 12 | Ferdinand | £16.00 | 32 | £512.00 | £51.20 | £112.64 | £450.56 |
| 13 | Total | | | | | | |
| 14 | | | | | | | |

We now wish to put Total figures into columns C, D, E, F and G. Using the methods already discussed, we would either type:

**=C2+C3+C4….+C12**

Or

**=SUM(C2,C3,C4,…,C12)**

Neither of which is ideal – nor would it be practical if we had a list of hundreds of numbers to add up. Fortunately, Excel has an easy solution – rather than referring to an individual cell, we can refer to a **RANGE** of cells. We want to add the block of cells from C2 to C12, and would write that as **C2:C12** (the **:** indicating a range). Our **SUM** would be:

=**SUM(C2:C12)**

However, it is worth looking at how to enter this into a cell.

## 2.2 Direct cell entry

If you know the function required (as we do here), you can just type it in to the cell directly, as follows:

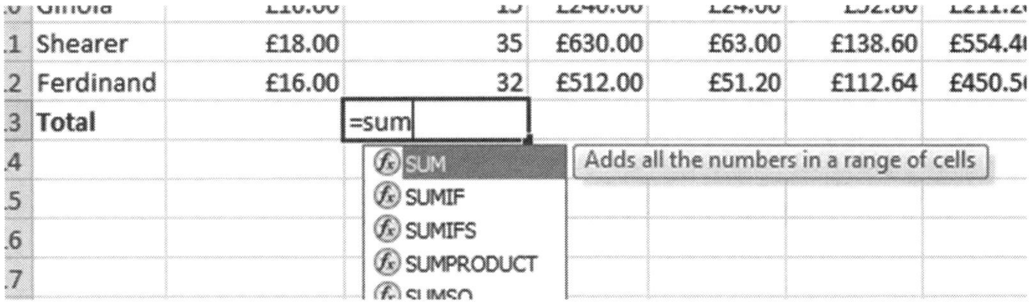

As you type, Excel will suggest possible functions. Note again the equals sign to start the function.

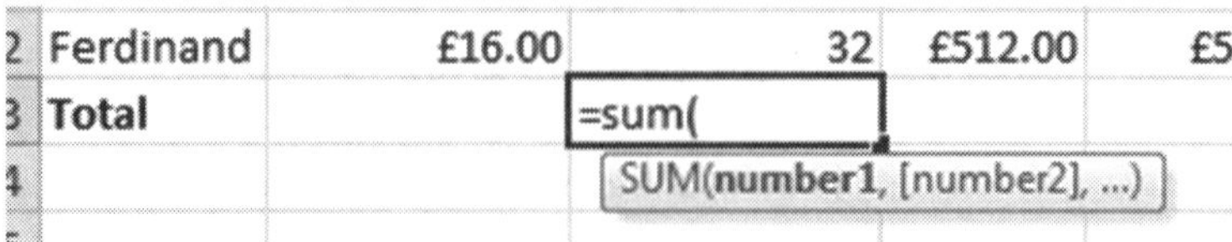


Open a bracket to enter the arguments. Note that the required format for the function is shown – **number1** is highlighted in bold showing that Excel is expecting you to enter the first number here. This becomes especially useful with more complex functions, as it helps you work out which part of the function you are on.

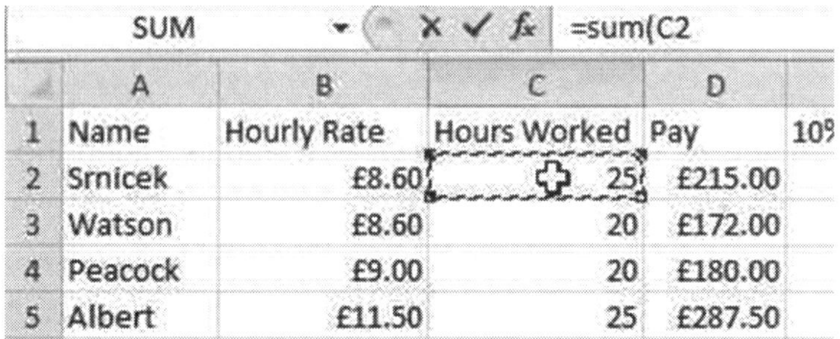
SUM =sum(C2

| | A | B | C | D |
|---|---|---|---|---|
| 1 | Name | Hourly Rate | Hours Worked | Pay |
| 2 | Srnicek | £8.60 | 25 | £215.00 |
| 3 | Watson | £8.60 | 20 | £172.00 |
| 4 | Peacock | £9.00 | 20 | £180.00 |
| 5 | Albert | £11.50 | 25 | £287.50 |

Left-click (and hold) on the first cell you wish to include. Note the formula is updated.

=sum(C2:C12

| | C | D | E |
|---|---|---|---|
| e | Hours Worked | Pay | 10% Bonus |
| 8.60 | 25 | £215.00 | £21.50 |
| 8.60 | 20 | £172.00 | £17.20 |
| 9.00 | 20 | £180.00 | £18.00 |
| 1.50 | 25 | £287.50 | £28.75 |
| 0.50 | 30 | £315.00 | £31.50 |
| 2.00 | 40 | £480.00 | £48.00 |
| 3.00 | 42 | £546.00 | £54.60 |
| 4.00 | 35 | £490.00 | £49.00 |
| 6.00 | 15 | £240.00 | £24.00 |
| 8.00 | 35 | £630.00 | £63.00 |
| 6.00 | 32 | £512.00 | £51.20 |
| | =sum(C2:C12 | 11R x 1C | |

SUM(**number1**, [number2], ...)

Drag the mouse down to the last cell you wish to include – the formula is automatically updated with the correct syntax. This saves you having to remember how to type the cell reference.

The box around the cells gives a visual display of the cells selected.

Release the mouse button to continue.

Close the bracket and press **Enter** to finish the formula. The correct answer will be shown.

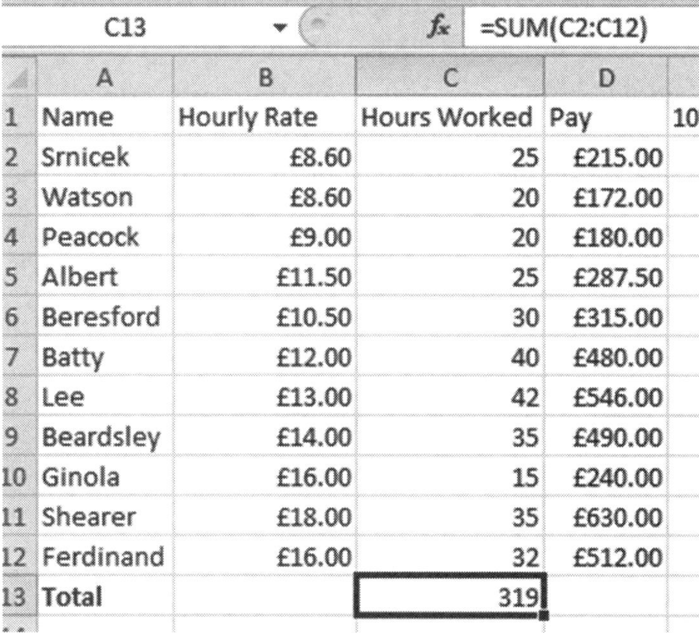

C13 =SUM(C2:C12)

| | A | B | C | D |
|---|---|---|---|---|
| 1 | Name | Hourly Rate | Hours Worked | Pay |
| 2 | Srnicek | £8.60 | 25 | £215.00 |
| 3 | Watson | £8.60 | 20 | £172.00 |
| 4 | Peacock | £9.00 | 20 | £180.00 |
| 5 | Albert | £11.50 | 25 | £287.50 |
| 6 | Beresford | £10.50 | 30 | £315.00 |
| 7 | Batty | £12.00 | 40 | £480.00 |
| 8 | Lee | £13.00 | 42 | £546.00 |
| 9 | Beardsley | £14.00 | 35 | £490.00 |
| 10 | Ginola | £16.00 | 15 | £240.00 |
| 11 | Shearer | £18.00 | 35 | £630.00 |
| 12 | Ferdinand | £16.00 | 32 | £512.00 |
| 13 | **Total** | | 319 | |

## 2.3 Using Insert Function

Although **SUM** is relatively straightforward to use, it's worth seeing how using **Insert Function** gives a different way of entering formulae.

To enter the sum into cell D13, after selecting the **SUM** function from the **Insert Function** menu:

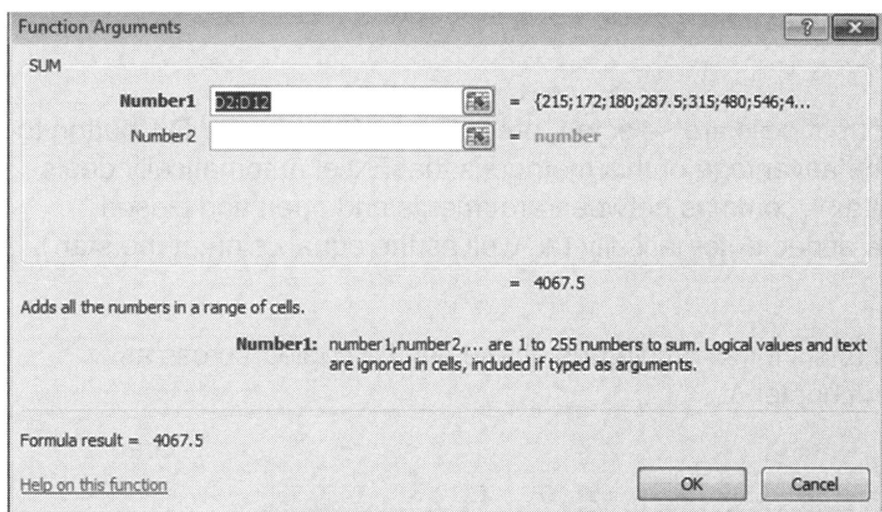


The Function Arguments dialogue box is displayed. This shows the arguments required – note that although only 2 are shown here, if more numbers are required then they will be added automatically.

**Number1** has already been populated with the required range – D2:D12.

Clicking **OK** would give the required answer. This is because Excel "guesses" which numbers you're likely to be adding up – it's not always correct, but it is here. It's a feature discussed later under the **Autosum** function.

If this wasn't correct, you could simply type in the numbers or range required into the Number1 box. However, you may prefer to use the method just shown, and select the cells visually – this is also possible. The button at the end of the box is a **REFERENCE BUTTON**, which appears throughout Excel. If you click on this, you can then select the cells required as before:

=SUM(D2:D8)

| C | D | E | F | G | H | I |
|---|---|---|---|---|---|---|
| rs Worked | Pay | 10% Bonus | Tax @ 20% | Net Pay | | |
| 25 | £215.00 | £21.50 | £47.30 | £189.20 | | |
| 20 | £172.00 | £17. | | | | |
| 20 | £180.00 | £18. | | | | |
| 25 | £287.50 | £28.75 | £63.25 | £253.00 | | |
| 30 | £315.00 | £31.50 | £69.30 | £277.20 | | |
| 40 | £480.00 | £48.00 | £105.60 | £422.40 | | |
| 42 | £546.00 | £54.60 | £120.12 | £480.48 | | |
| 35 | £490.00 | £49.00 | £107.80 | £431.20 | | |
| 15 | £240.00 | £24.00 | £52.80 | £211.20 | | |
| 35 | £630.00 | £63.00 | £138.60 | £554.40 | | |
| 32 | £512.00 | £51.20 | £112.64 | £450.56 | | |
| 319 | (D2:D8) | | | | | |

Function Arguments

D2:D8

Once the correct cells are selected, press Enter. Click on the **OK** button to continue. The advantage of this method is that Excel automatically deals with the syntax – commas between arguments and open and closed brackets are added automatically (as well as the equals sign at the start).

**Reminder**

As we need totals for all 5 columns, these can be copied across as discussed in chapter 4.

| | | | | | |
|---|---|---|---|---|---|
| 5.00 | 32 | £512.00 | £51.20 | £112.64 | £450.56 |
| | 319 | 4067.5 | 406.75 | 894.85 | 3579.4 |

Drag across

Note that the formatting is not consistent with the numbers above it – this would need to be adjusted.

# 3 Average

## 3.1 Average

Another commonly used function is **AVERAGE**. This takes the average of a selection of numbers by adding them all up and dividing by how many numbers there are (arithmetic mean). It works in exactly the same way as SUM – the arguments are all the numbers or cells you wish to take the average of.

SUM | =average(C2:C12

| | A | B | C | D | E |
|---|---|---|---|---|---|
| 1 | Name | Hourly Rate | Hours Worked | Pay | 10% Bonus |
| 2 | Srnicek | £8.60 | 25 | £215.00 | £21.50 |
| 3 | Watson | £8.60 | 20 | £172.00 | £17.20 |
| 4 | Peacock | £9.00 | 20 | £180.00 | £18.00 |
| 5 | Albert | £11.50 | 25 | £287.50 | £28.75 |
| 6 | Beresford | £10.50 | 30 | £315.00 | £31.50 |
| 7 | Batty | £12.00 | 40 | £480.00 | £48.00 |
| 8 | Lee | £13.00 | 42 | £546.00 | £54.60 |
| 9 | Beardsley | £14.00 | 35 | £490.00 | £49.00 |
| 10 | Ginola | £16.00 | 15 | £240.00 | £24.00 |
| 11 | Shearer | £18.00 | 35 | £630.00 | £63.00 |
| 12 | Ferdinand | £16.00 | 32 | £512.00 | £51.20 |
| 13 | Total | | 319 | £4,067.50 | £406.75 |
| 14 | Average | | =average(C2:C12 | | |
| 15 | | | AVERAGE(**number1**, [number2], ...) | | |

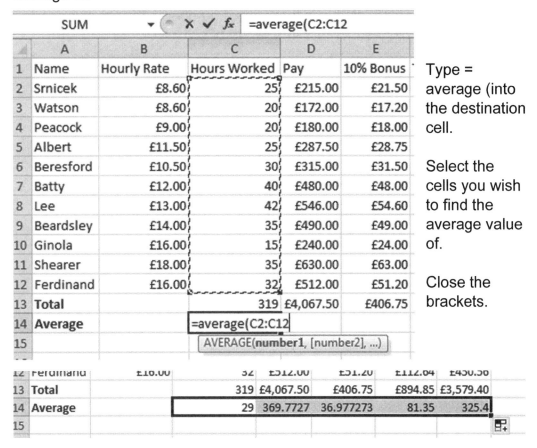

Type = average (into the destination cell.

Select the cells you wish to find the average value of.

Close the brackets.

| | | | | | | | |
|---|---|---|---|---|---|---|---|
| 12 | Ferdinand | £16.00 | 32 | £512.00 | £51.20 | £112.04 | £450.56 |
| 13 | Total | | 319 | £4,067.50 | £406.75 | £894.85 | £3,579.40 |
| 14 | Average | | 29 | 369.7727 | 36.977273 | 81.35 | 325.4 |
| 15 | | | | | | | |

The formula can then be copied across as before.

**Note –** the results can be checked – whenever cells are selected, the **Status Bar** at the bottom of the screen gives information, including the average, about those cells.

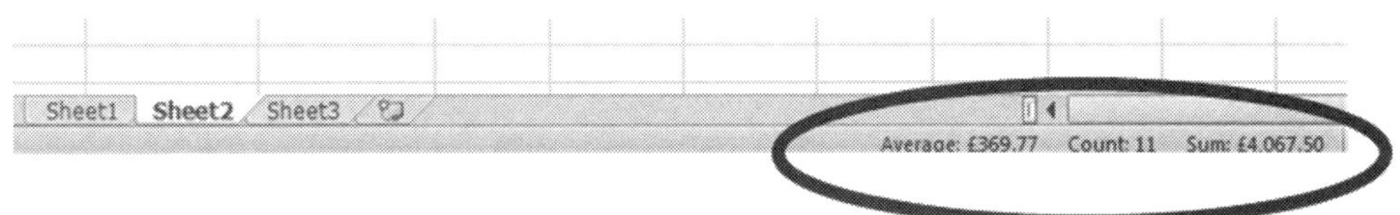


The average and sum are shown. Count is the number of cells with a value in.

# 4 Max and Min

## 4.1 MAX and MIN

You may be asked to find the biggest or smallest number in a list – use the **MAX** and **MIN** functions to do this. The format is again the same as **SUM**, for example:

**=MAX(3,2,6,15,12,9)**

will return the value 15, as this is the biggest number in the list. It is more useful to find the biggest number in a range of cells:

C15 =MAX(C2:C12)

| | A | B | C | D | E | F | G |
|---|---|---|---|---|---|---|---|
| 1 | Name | Hourly Rate | Hours Worked | Pay | 10% Bonus | Tax @ 20% | Net Pay |
| 2 | Srnicek | £8.60 | 25 | £215.00 | £21.50 | £47.30 | £189.20 |
| 3 | Watson | £8.60 | 20 | £172.00 | £17.20 | £37.84 | £151.36 |
| 4 | Peacock | £9.00 | 20 | £180.00 | £18.00 | £39.60 | £158.40 |
| 5 | Albert | £11.50 | 25 | £287.50 | £28.75 | £63.25 | £253.00 |
| 6 | Beresford | £10.50 | 30 | £315.00 | £31.50 | £69.30 | £277.20 |
| 7 | Batty | £12.00 | 40 | £480.00 | £48.00 | £105.60 | £422.40 |
| 8 | Lee | £13.00 | 42 | £546.00 | £54.60 | £120.12 | £480.48 |
| 9 | Beardsley | £14.00 | 35 | £490.00 | £49.00 | £107.80 | £431.20 |
| 10 | Ginola | £16.00 | 15 | £240.00 | £24.00 | £52.80 | £211.20 |
| 11 | Shearer | £18.00 | 35 | £630.00 | £63.00 | £138.60 | £554.40 |
| 12 | Ferdinand | £16.00 | 32 | £512.00 | £51.20 | £112.64 | £450.56 |
| 13 | **Total** | | 319 | £4,067.50 | £406.75 | £894.85 | £3,579.40 |
| 14 | **Average** | | 29 | £369.77 | £36.98 | £81.35 | £325.40 |
| 15 | **Max** | | 42 | | | | |

So you can easily see in this case the most hours worked in the period.

Using **MIN** will show the smallest:

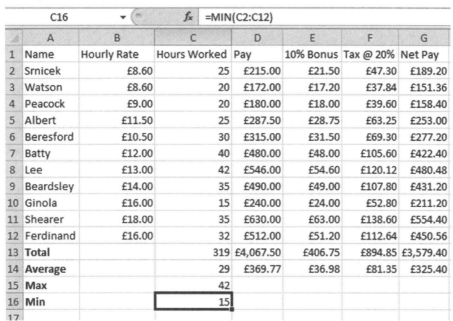

C16 | fx | =MIN(C2:C12)

| | A | B | C | D | E | F | G |
|---|---|---|---|---|---|---|---|
| 1 | Name | Hourly Rate | Hours Worked | Pay | 10% Bonus | Tax @ 20% | Net Pay |
| 2 | Srnicek | £8.60 | 25 | £215.00 | £21.50 | £47.30 | £189.20 |
| 3 | Watson | £8.60 | 20 | £172.00 | £17.20 | £37.84 | £151.36 |
| 4 | Peacock | £9.00 | 20 | £180.00 | £18.00 | £39.60 | £158.40 |
| 5 | Albert | £11.50 | 25 | £287.50 | £28.75 | £63.25 | £253.00 |
| 6 | Beresford | £10.50 | 30 | £315.00 | £31.50 | £69.30 | £277.20 |
| 7 | Batty | £12.00 | 40 | £480.00 | £48.00 | £105.60 | £422.40 |
| 8 | Lee | £13.00 | 42 | £546.00 | £54.60 | £120.12 | £480.48 |
| 9 | Beardsley | £14.00 | 35 | £490.00 | £49.00 | £107.80 | £431.20 |
| 10 | Ginola | £16.00 | 15 | £240.00 | £24.00 | £52.80 | £211.20 |
| 11 | Shearer | £18.00 | 35 | £630.00 | £63.00 | £138.60 | £554.40 |
| 12 | Ferdinand | £16.00 | 32 | £512.00 | £51.20 | £112.64 | £450.56 |
| 13 | **Total** | | 319 | £4,067.50 | £406.75 | £894.85 | £3,579.40 |
| 14 | **Average** | | 29 | £369.77 | £36.98 | £81.35 | £325.40 |
| 15 | **Max** | | 42 | | | | |
| 16 | **Min** | | 15 | | | | |
| 17 | | | | | | | |

# 5 AutoSum

## 5.1 AutoSum

**AutoSum** is a useful shortcut to perform any of the above functions (and a few others) quickly and easily. The **AutoSum** button can be found in the top right of the **Home** menu.

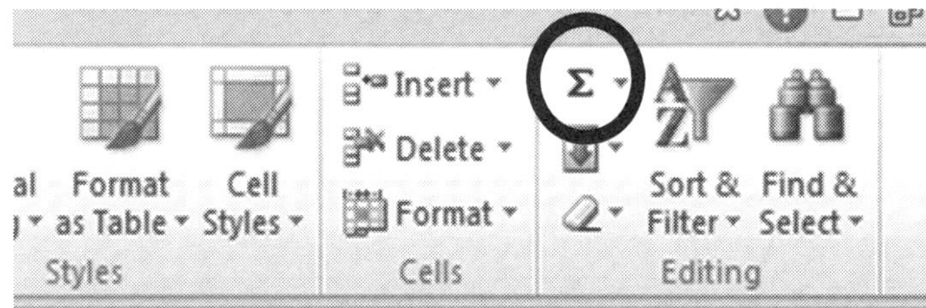

Instead of entering the function in the normal way, click in the destination cell and click the AutoSum button:

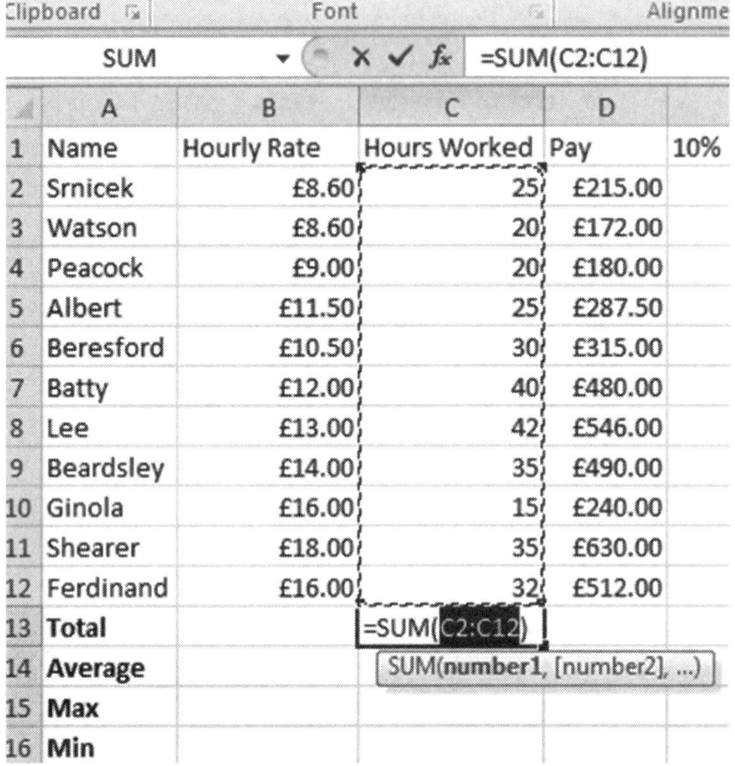


| | A | B | C | D | |
|---|---|---|---|---|---|
| 1 | Name | Hourly Rate | Hours Worked | Pay | 10% |
| 2 | Srnicek | £8.60 | 25 | £215.00 | |
| 3 | Watson | £8.60 | 20 | £172.00 | |
| 4 | Peacock | £9.00 | 20 | £180.00 | |
| 5 | Albert | £11.50 | 25 | £287.50 | |
| 6 | Beresford | £10.50 | 30 | £315.00 | |
| 7 | Batty | £12.00 | 40 | £480.00 | |
| 8 | Lee | £13.00 | 42 | £546.00 | |
| 9 | Beardsley | £14.00 | 35 | £490.00 | |
| 10 | Ginola | £16.00 | 15 | £240.00 | |
| 11 | Shearer | £18.00 | 35 | £630.00 | |
| 12 | Ferdinand | £16.00 | 32 | £512.00 | |
| 13 | **Total** | | =SUM(C2:C12) | | |
| 14 | **Average** | | | | |
| 15 | **Max** | | | | |
| 16 | **Min** | | | | |

Excel will put in a SUM function, and guess at the cells required.

If these are incorrect, you can reselect the cells needed in the normal way.

To insert a function other than sum, click on the small triangle to the right of the AutoSum button, and select the function required.

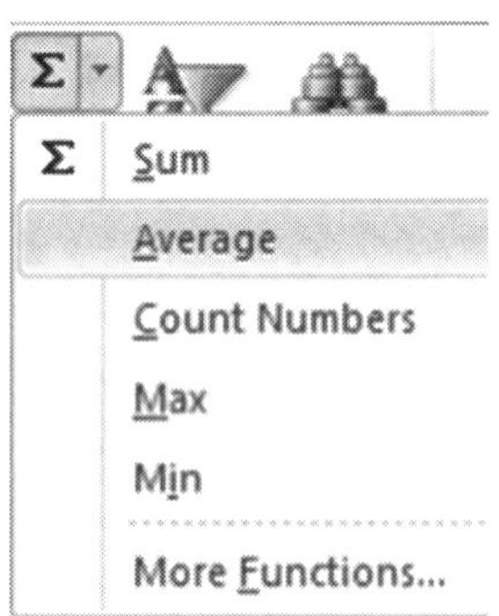


These are the most commonly required functions, although selecting the 'More Functions' option actually allows you to select any function available within Excel.

# 6 Test your understanding

The activities in this guide are designed to test your knowledge on the techniques shown in this chapter. They may also use techniques used in previous chapters, to build up your knowledge. Suggested answers are available on MyKaplan, although it is better to refer to the notes and try to understand the methods than look straight at the answers.

## Test your understanding 6-1

This activity uses some of the important functions within excel – AVERAGE, MIN and MAX.

(a) Open the **Report needing summary** file in the **Activities** folder, and select the **Summary Report** worksheet.

(b) We need to create a summary of the information underneath the report. This will show the monthly averages, as well as best and worst performance.

(c) In cell A9, type 'Biggest sales'. Use a formula in cell B9 to return the largest monthly sales figure.

(d) In cell A10, type 'Lowest sales', and use the MIN function in B10 to find the worst monthly sales.

| | A | B | C | D |
|---|---|---|---|---|
| 1 | | | BallCo Man | |
| 2 | | | | |
| 3 | | January | February | March |
| 4 | Sales | 8,648 | 6,850 | 8,264 |
| 5 | Profit | 4,701 | 3,496 | 5,202 |
| 6 | Profit Margin | 54.4% | 51.0% | 62.9% |
| 7 | | | | |
| 8 | | | | |
| 9 | Biggest Sales | 8,648 | | |
| 10 | Lowest sales | 6,019 | | |
| 11 | | | | |

(e) Change the value in C4 to 1000 – check that the value in B10 alters to reflect this.

(f) **Undo** the last command to restore February's sales.

(g) In A12, type 'Average Profit', and use a formula in B12 to calculate the **average monthly profit figure**.

(h) **Merge** and **Center** the title so that it is centered across all of the information.

(j) **Autofit** Column widths and **save** the file as **Activity 6-1** in the **Solutions** folder.

## Test your understanding 6-2

This activity is primarily included to allow more practice with percentage calculations, and use of brackets in a calculation. It also reinforces the functions already introduced.

(a) Open the **Southern Sales data** workbook in the **Activities** folder. This contains sales by month for 5 salespeople. We need to populate the Annual Statistics 2012 table.

(b) The **Sales** row is already populated. Use a similar approach to find the Average, Maximum and Minimum for each salesperson, and the totals on the right hand side.

**Annual Statistics 2012**

| | [illegible] | [illegible] | [illegible] | [illegible] | [illegible] | | [illegible] |
|---|---|---|---|---|---|---|---|
| Average | 155 | 130 | 155 | 164 | 187 | | 158 |
| Maximum | 210 | 140 | 220 | 180 | 205 | | 220 |
| Minimum | 100 | 120 | 100 | 142 | 150 | | 100 |
| Sales | 1,860 | 1,560 | 1,860 | 1,969 | 2,245 | | 9,494 |
| Percentage Increase | | | | | | | |
| Percentage of Total Sales | | | | | | | |

(c) We now need the percentage increase. This is the percentage increase in sales from January to December.

(d) If you are struggling to get the percentages to work, remember that you need to put the increase in sales calculation in **brackets** so that is calculated before dividing by January sales.

**Annual Statistics 2012**

| | [illegible] | [illegible] | [illegible] | [illegible] | [illegible] | | [illegible] |
|---|---|---|---|---|---|---|---|
| Average | 155 | 130 | 155 | 164 | 187 | | 158 |
| Maximum | 210 | 140 | 220 | 180 | 205 | | 220 |
| Minimum | 100 | 120 | 100 | 142 | 150 | | 100 |
| Sales | 1,860 | 1,560 | 1,860 | 1,969 | 2,245 | | 9,494 |
| Percentage Increase | 110.0% | 7.7% | 120.0% | -6.5% | 7.9% | | 35.4% |
| Percentage of Total Sales | | | | | | | |

(e) Calculate each salesperson's sales as a percentage of the total (K21) to 1 decimal place.

(f) **Save** the file as **Activity 6-2** and close it.

# Cell referencing

7

## Introduction

This chapter will guide you through the importance of referencing cells and how to create various types of cell referencing – including referencing to different workbooks or worksheets. You will also learn how to switch between viewing the results of our formulas and the formulas themselves.

### ASSESSMENT CRITERIA

Accurately enter data (2.2)

Select and use a range of formulas and functions to perform calculations (3.1)

Use appropriate tools to identify and resolve errors (4.1)

### CONTENTS

# 1 Cell referencing

## 1.1 Introduction

In chapter 4, simple formulas were introduced into your worksheet. These formulas were based on looking at the content of the individual cells and producing a mathematical answer.

You can create different types of formulas that use cell references to create the solution that you are looking for. This is particularly useful when you are using a particular number in a calculation that is used in different places and is also prone to change – such as tax rates.

There are three types of cell referencing that you have to be able to use for your assessment.

1 Relative cell referencing

2 Absolute cell referencing

3 Mixed cell referencing.

**Note** – the type of cell referencing used only matters when you COPY the formulas to other cells within the spreadsheet.

You may also need to refer to cells on another workbook or worksheet. This is relatively straightforward, but can create complicated looking formulas.

## 1.2 Viewing formulas

Viewing formulas is very useful to be able to check what has been used and where. In the **Formulas** tab, select **Show Formulas**.

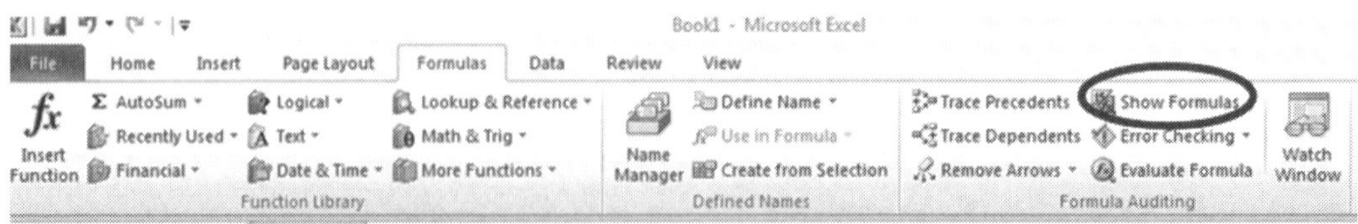


**Shortcut**

**Ctrl +** ` [control and grave] will do the same as above. The same routine will also return you to the normal view.

# 2 Relative cell referencing

## 2.1 Relative cell referencing

This has already been introduced when dealing with functions. We have already seen that if you copy a formula down, the row number is updated. Likewise, if you copy a formula across, the column is updated. This is the type of referencing most people are used to.

C4 | =B2

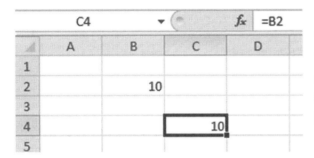

|   | A | B | C | D |
|---|---|---|---|---|
| 1 |   |   |   |   |
| 2 |   | 10 |   |   |
| 3 |   |   |   |   |
| 4 |   |   | 10 |   |
| 5 |   |   |   |   |

The formula in cell C4 is **=B2**. This means that when the value in cell B2 is changed, C4 will be updated to show this (C4 is **LINKED** to B2).

With relative referencing like this, if you **Copy** and **Paste** the formula in cell C4 into another cell, the reference to B2 will change. The way it works is as follows:

- If you copy the formula **UP**, the row number decreases.
- If you copy the formula **DOWN**, the row number increases.
- If you copy the formula **RIGHT**, the column letter increases.
- If you copy the formula **LEFT**, the column letter decreases.

It is easiest to see this in action. If we copy the formula into cell D3:

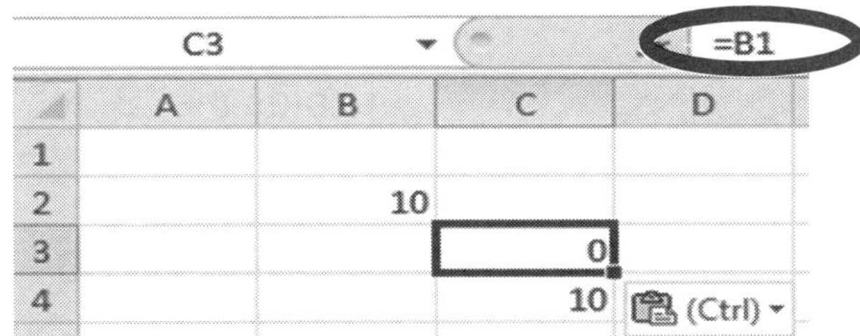


Here you can see the formula has been copied **UP** a row, so the row number in the reference has reduced by one. As there is no entry in cell B1, the result is shown as zero.

Similarly, we can copy the formula down, say three rows:

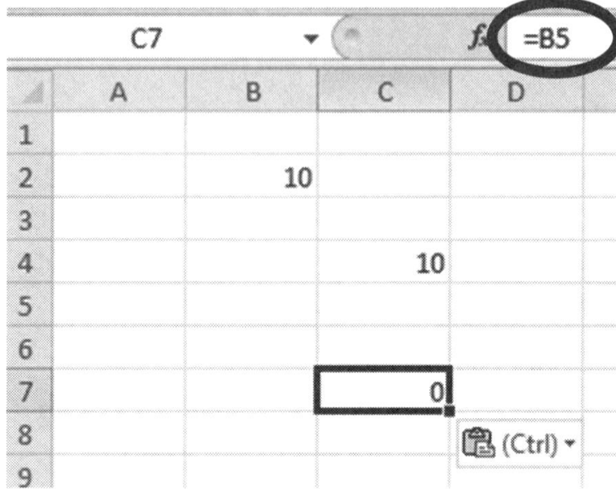


Copying the formula down three rows increases the row number by three.

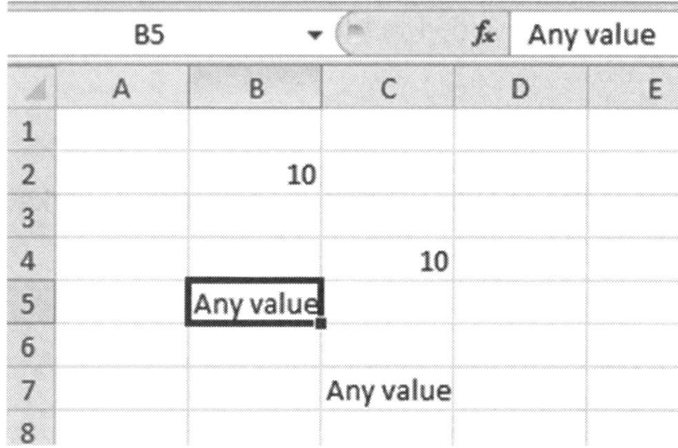


As you can see, typing any value in to B5 means that cell C7 is updated to reflect this.

Copying the formula across works in the same way:

E4 | $f_x$ =D2

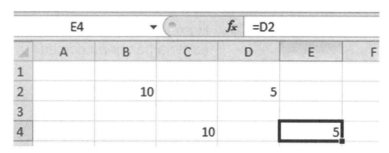

| | A | B | C | D | E | F |
|---|---|---|---|---|---|---|
| 1 | | | | | | |
| 2 | | 10 | | 5 | | |
| 3 | | | | | | |
| 4 | | | 10 | | 5 | |

Copying across two columns updates the "B" to a "D" in the formula, as D is two letters after B in the alphabet.

**NOTE** – this can lead to errors! If you copy the formula two columns to the left, the "B" should be reduced by two, but there is no letter two before B, so an error is shown:

A4 $f_x$ =#REF!

| | A | B | C | D | E |
|---|---|---|---|---|---|
| 1 | | | | | |
| 2 | | 10 | | 5 | |
| 3 | | | | | |
| 4 | #REF! | | 10 | | 5 |

The way relative referencing really works is as the name suggests – the cell reference is relative to the current cell. For example the formula **=B2** shown in cell C4 is really saying "return the value in the cell one column to the left and two rows up from this one".

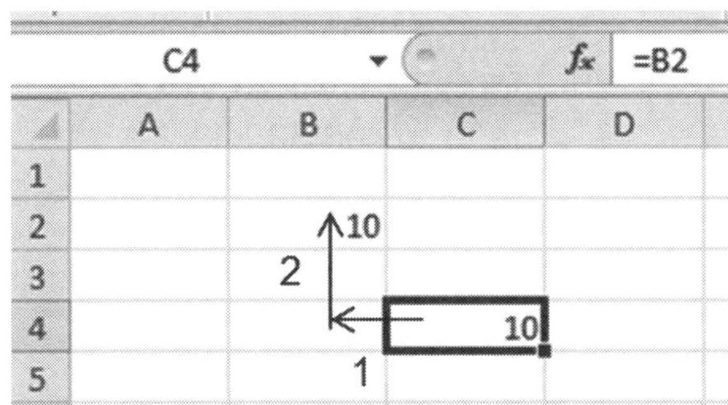


The reference **B2** is relative to the cell the formula is in, C4.

E779 $f_x$ =D777

| | A | B | C | D | E |
|---|---|---|---|---|---|
| 772 | | | | | |
| 773 | | | | | |
| 774 | | | | | |
| 775 | | | | | |
| 776 | | | | | |
| 777 | | | | Random cell | |
| 778 | | | | 2 | |
| 779 | | | | | Random cell |
| 780 | | | | 1 | |

Whichever cell the formula is copied to, it will show the value in the cell one column to the left and two up from it.

# 3 Absolute cell referencing

## 3.1 Absolute cell referencing

This is used to ensure that a formula always looks at the content of a particular cell. This means that if you were to drag or place a formula to/in a different cell – or range of cells – that Excel would continue to use that cell to calculate the solution. This is very useful for 'what-if' analysis when you are looking at particular scenarios.

To create an **Absolute** reference we use a **$** sign before the letter and the number in the cell reference:

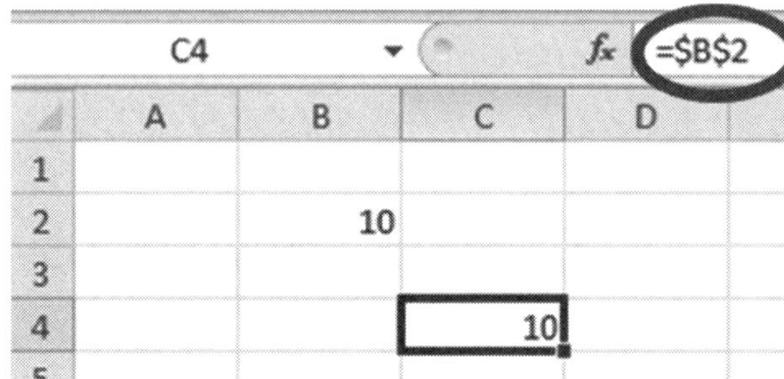


Although the result is the same at first, if you copy this formula, it will **ALWAYS** refer to cell B2.

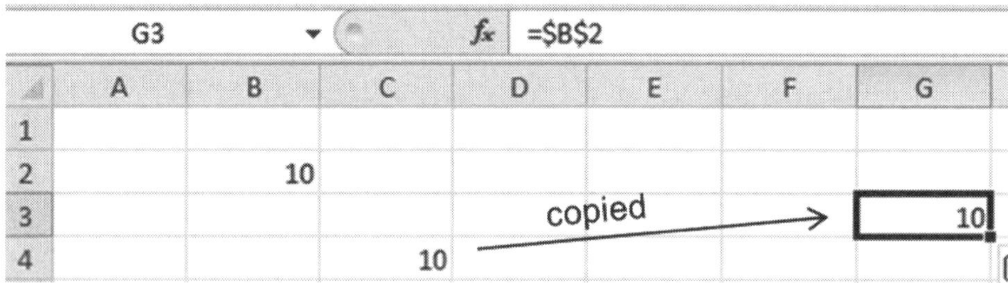


**Absolute** cell referencing can save lots of time when using formulas.

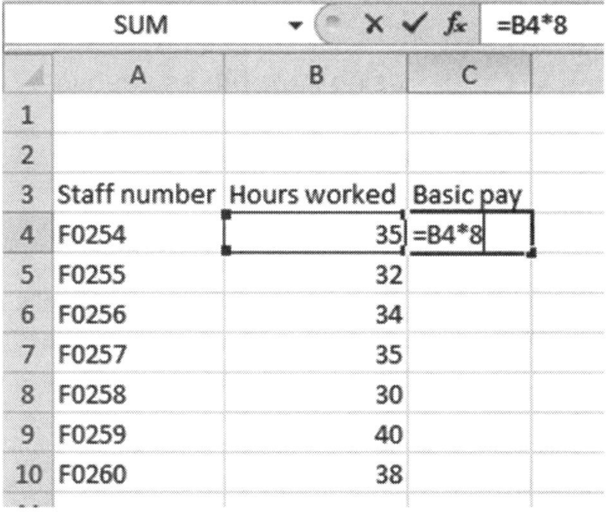

SUM | =B4*8

| | A | B | C |
|---|---|---|---|
| 1 | | | |
| 2 | | | |
| 3 | Staff number | Hours worked | Basic pay |
| 4 | F0254 | 35 | =B4*8 |
| 5 | F0255 | 32 | |
| 6 | F0256 | 34 | |
| 7 | F0257 | 35 | |
| 8 | F0258 | 30 | |
| 9 | F0259 | 40 | |
| 10 | F0260 | 38 | |

Here, we need to work out basic pay for each staff member. If each member of staff is paid £8 per hour, the formula shown would work.

However, every time the labour rate changed, we would have to update all the formulas. Much better would be to enter the labour rate in one cell, and only update that when the rate changes. This also makes the spreadsheet easier to follow:

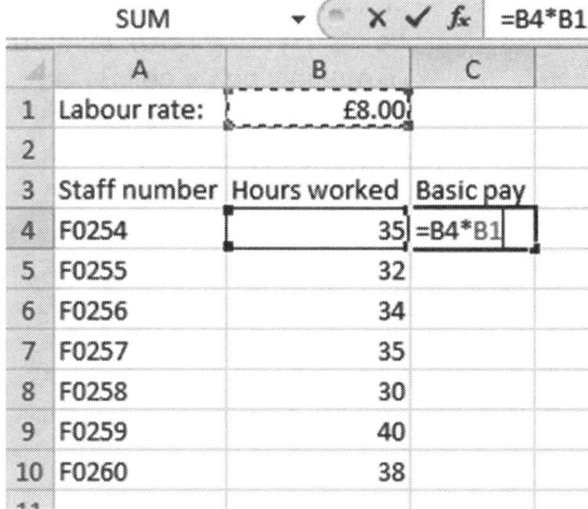

SUM | =B4*B1

| | A | B | C |
|---|---|---|---|
| 1 | Labour rate: | £8.00 | |
| 2 | | | |
| 3 | Staff number | Hours worked | Basic pay |
| 4 | F0254 | 35 | =B4*B1 |
| 5 | F0255 | 32 | |
| 6 | F0256 | 34 | |
| 7 | F0257 | 35 | |
| 8 | F0258 | 30 | |
| 9 | F0259 | 40 | |
| 10 | F0260 | 38 | |

The formula refers to the labour rate in cell B1 (formatted as currency), and will update with a new labour rate. We would like to copy this formula down to the rows below.

C4 | $f_x$ | =B4*B1

| | A | B | C |
|---|---|---|---|
| 1 | Labour rate: | £8.00 | |
| 2 | | | |
| 3 | Staff number | Hours worked | Basic pay |
| 4 | F0254 | 35 | £280.00 |
| 5 | F0255 | 32 | £0.00 |
| 6 | F0256 | 34 | #VALUE! |
| 7 | F0257 | 35 | £1,225.00 |
| 8 | F0258 | 30 | £960.00 |
| 9 | F0259 | 40 | £1,360.00 |
| 10 | F0260 | 38 | £1,330.00 |
| 11 | | | |

Using **Autofill**, as seen in the last chapter, gives disastrous results!

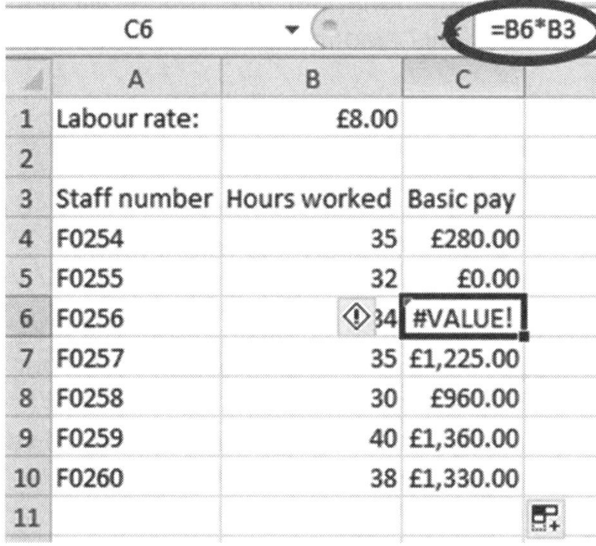

C6 | $f_x$ | =B6*B3

| | A | B | C |
|---|---|---|---|
| 1 | Labour rate: | £8.00 | |
| 2 | | | |
| 3 | Staff number | Hours worked | Basic pay |
| 4 | F0254 | 35 | £280.00 |
| 5 | F0255 | 32 | £0.00 |
| 6 | F0256 | 34 | #VALUE! |
| 7 | F0257 | 35 | £1,225.00 |
| 8 | F0258 | 30 | £960.00 |
| 9 | F0259 | 40 | £1,360.00 |
| 10 | F0260 | 38 | £1,330.00 |
| 11 | | | |

Further investigation reveals the problem, while the correct hours worked are being used (cell B6), instead of multiplying by cell B1 as required, the reference has been updated to B3 – because a **RELATIVE** reference has been used.

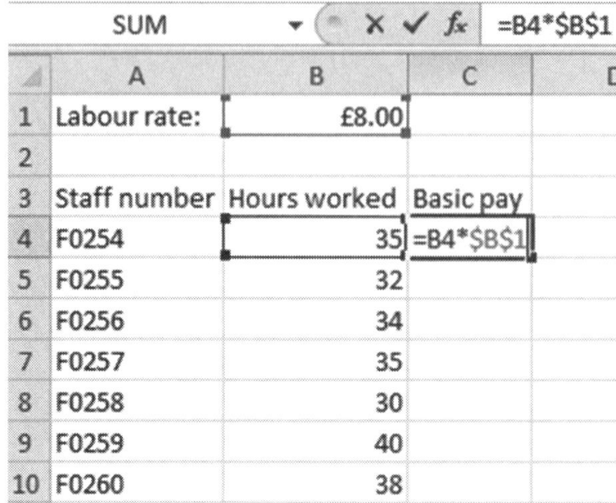

SUM | $f_x$ | =B4*$B$1

| | A | B | C | D |
|---|---|---|---|---|
| 1 | Labour rate: | £8.00 | | |
| 2 | | | | |
| 3 | Staff number | Hours worked | Basic pay | |
| 4 | F0254 | 35 | =B4*$B$1 | |
| 5 | F0255 | 32 | | |
| 6 | F0256 | 34 | | |
| 7 | F0257 | 35 | | |
| 8 | F0258 | 30 | | |
| 9 | F0259 | 40 | | |
| 10 | F0260 | 38 | | |

The **$** signs in the reference indicate an **ABSOLUTE** reference.

C4 | $f_x$ | =B4*$B$1

| | A | B | C | D |
|---|---|---|---|---|
| 1 | Labour rate: | £8.00 | | |
| 2 | | | | |
| 3 | Staff number | Hours worked | Basic pay | |
| 4 | F0254 | 35 | £280.00 | |
| 5 | F0255 | 32 | £256.00 | |
| 6 | F0256 | 34 | £272.00 | |
| 7 | F0257 | 35 | £280.00 | |
| 8 | F0258 | 30 | £240.00 | |
| 9 | F0259 | 40 | £320.00 | |
| 10 | F0260 | 38 | £304.00 | |

The formulas all now refer to cell **B1**, as required.

# 4 Mixed cell referencing

## 4.1 Mixed cell referencing

This is a combination of both **Absolute** and **Relative** referencing. Remember, the type of referencing is only relevant when you copy a formula. You might want the row number to be relative (i.e. change when you copy), but the column to remain fixed.

The **$** sign used in absolute referencing above is key here. When we used the absolute reference **$B$1**, what we really said was "keep the column and the row fixed." It can be broken up as **$B** – keep the column fixed, and **$1**, keep the row fixed.

D2 | $f_x$ |

| | A | B | C | D |
|---|---|---|---|---|
| 1 | Labour rate: | Bonus % | | |
| 2 | £8.00 | 10% | | |
| 3 | | | | |
| 4 | Staff number | Hours worked | Basic pay | Bonus |
| 5 | F0254 | 35 | | |
| 6 | F0255 | 32 | | |
| 7 | F0256 | 34 | | |
| 8 | F0257 | 35 | | |
| 9 | F0258 | 30 | | |
| 10 | F0259 | 40 | | |
| 11 | F0260 | 38 | | |
| 12 | | | | |

Let's take a similar example:

We need to calculate basic pay in the same way. We can use an absolute reference like before, but a mixed reference is actually better.

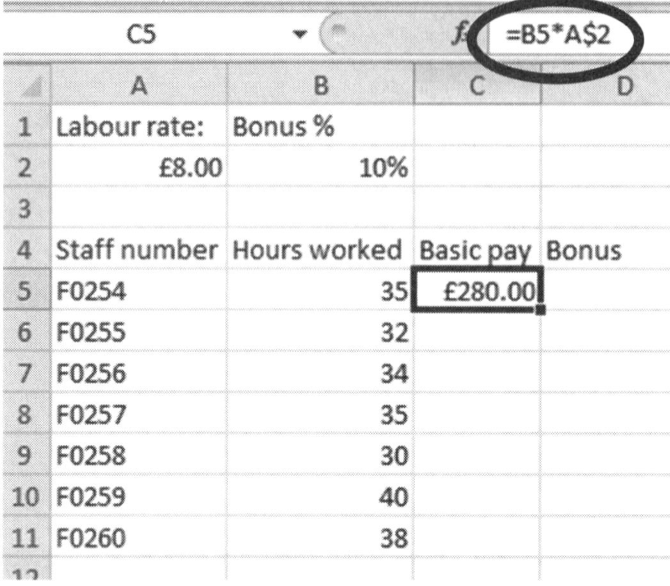

C5 | =B5*A$2

| | A | B | C | D |
|---|---|---|---|---|
| 1 | Labour rate: | Bonus % | | |
| 2 | £8.00 | 10% | | |
| 3 | | | | |
| 4 | Staff number | Hours worked | Basic pay | Bonus |
| 5 | F0254 | 35 | £280.00 | |
| 6 | F0255 | 32 | | |
| 7 | F0256 | 34 | | |
| 8 | F0257 | 35 | | |
| 9 | F0258 | 30 | | |
| 10 | F0259 | 40 | | |
| 11 | F0260 | 38 | | |

This formula gives the same result as before. However, when copied down, the **$2** in the reference to cell A2 means that the row will remain fixed as before.

C10 | =B10*A$2

| | A | B | C | D |
|---|---|---|---|---|
| 1 | Labour rate: | Bonus % | | |
| 2 | £8.00 | 10% | | |
| 3 | | | | |
| 4 | Staff number | Hours worked | Basic pay | Bonus |
| 5 | F0254 | 35 | £280.00 | |
| 6 | F0255 | 32 | £256.00 | |
| 7 | F0256 | 34 | £272.00 | |
| 8 | F0257 | 35 | £280.00 | |
| 9 | F0258 | 30 | £240.00 | |
| 10 | F0259 | 40 | £320.00 | |
| 11 | F0260 | 38 | £304.00 | |

As the formula has been copied down, the column does not change anyway. The $2 means that cell A2 is still referred to correctly.

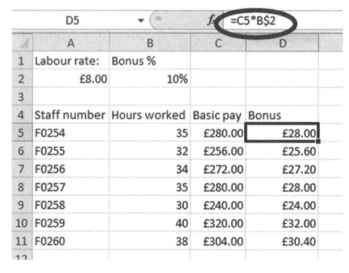

D5 | =C5*B$2

| | A | B | C | D |
|---|---|---|---|---|
| 1 | Labour rate: | Bonus % | | |
| 2 | £8.00 | 10% | | |
| 3 | | | | |
| 4 | Staff number | Hours worked | Basic pay | Bonus |
| 5 | F0254 | 35 | £280.00 | £28.00 |
| 6 | F0255 | 32 | £256.00 | £25.60 |
| 7 | F0256 | 34 | £272.00 | £27.20 |
| 8 | F0257 | 35 | £280.00 | £28.00 |
| 9 | F0258 | 30 | £240.00 | £24.00 |
| 10 | F0259 | 40 | £320.00 | £32.00 |
| 11 | F0260 | 38 | £304.00 | £30.40 |

You can copy the formula across though, and the bonus is correctly calculated based on cell **B2** – because there is no $ before the A in the original formula, the column is not fixed.

**Shortcut**

When entering a cell reference in a formula, pressing **F4** repeatedly will cycle through the different types of referencing by adding/removing $ signs as required.

# 5 Referencing worksheets and workbooks

## 5.1 Referencing other worksheets

We have dealt with cell referencing within a worksheet. It is very common that a calculation will need to refer to a cell on another worksheet within the same workbook. This works in the same way, but now instead of saying "Use the value in cell A1", we need to say "Use the value in Cell A1 on Sheet 2" (for example). The format for this would be:

**='Sheet 2'!A1**

The 'A1' part of the formula is referring to cell A1 – to specify the sheet name, use the quote marks, followed by an exclamation mark.

This is fairly cumbersome, and prone to typing errors. Fortunately, Excel makes this referencing fairly straightforward to achieve. Remember that when entering a formula, you can click on the cell you wish to use rather than typing its reference. This is true whether the cell is on the current worksheet or not.

**NOTE:** the use of quote marks is only required if the worksheet name contains two or more items and there are spaces between the items e.g. *worksheet* would not require quote marks but *work sheet* would. The exclamation mark is always required.

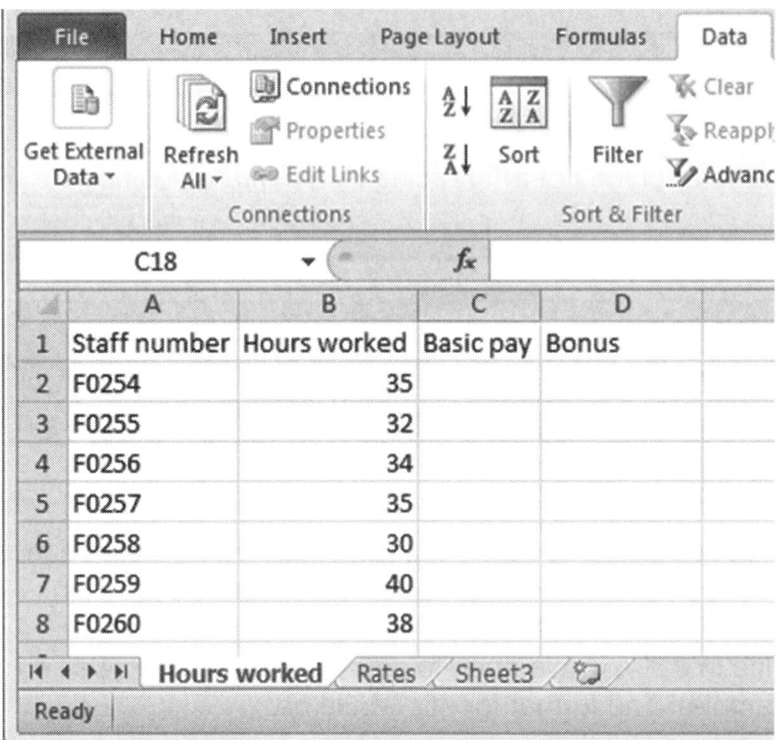


| | A | B | C | D |
|---|---|---|---|---|
| 1 | Staff number | Hours worked | Basic pay | Bonus |
| 2 | F0254 | 35 | | |
| 3 | F0255 | 32 | | |
| 4 | F0256 | 34 | | |
| 5 | F0257 | 35 | | |
| 6 | F0258 | 30 | | |
| 7 | F0259 | 40 | | |
| 8 | F0260 | 38 | | |

Using the same example, the basic rate of pay and bonus rate are now on the 'Rates' worksheet.

To calculate 'Basic pay', select cell C2 and press '=' to start entering a formula:

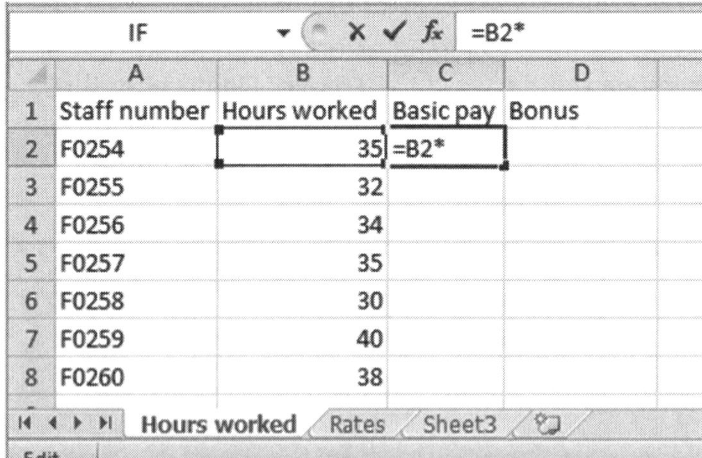


| | A | B | C | D |
|---|---|---|---|---|
| 1 | Staff number | Hours worked | Basic pay | Bonus |
| 2 | F0254 | 35 | =B2* | |
| 3 | F0255 | 32 | | |
| 4 | F0256 | 34 | | |
| 5 | F0257 | 35 | | |
| 6 | F0258 | 30 | | |
| 7 | F0259 | 40 | | |
| 8 | F0260 | 38 | | |

Select the hours worked cell in the usual way (or just type 'B2'). We wish to multiply this by the labour rate, so use '*'. You can now select the labour rate from the Rates worksheet.

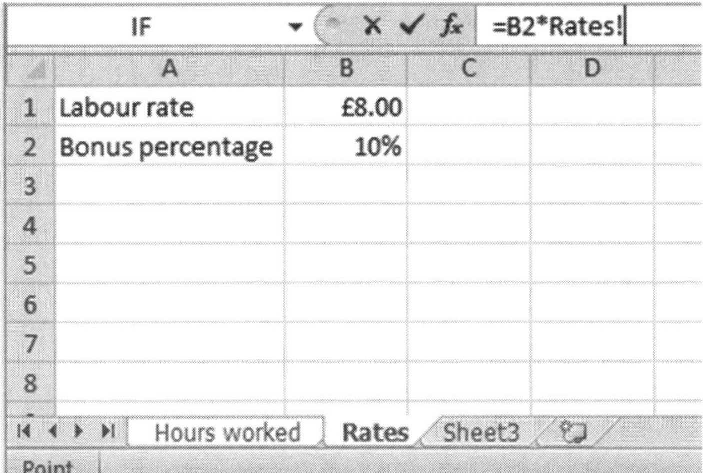

IF | =B2*Rates!

| | A | B | C | D |
|---|---|---|---|---|
| 1 | Labour rate | £8.00 | | |
| 2 | Bonus percentage | 10% | | |
| 3 | | | | |
| 4 | | | | |
| 5 | | | | |
| 6 | | | | |
| 7 | | | | |
| 8 | | | | |

Hours worked | Rates | Sheet3

Point

When the Rates sheet is selected, the first part of the reference is automatically filled in. Note that there are no quote marks around the name here as it is one word with no space.

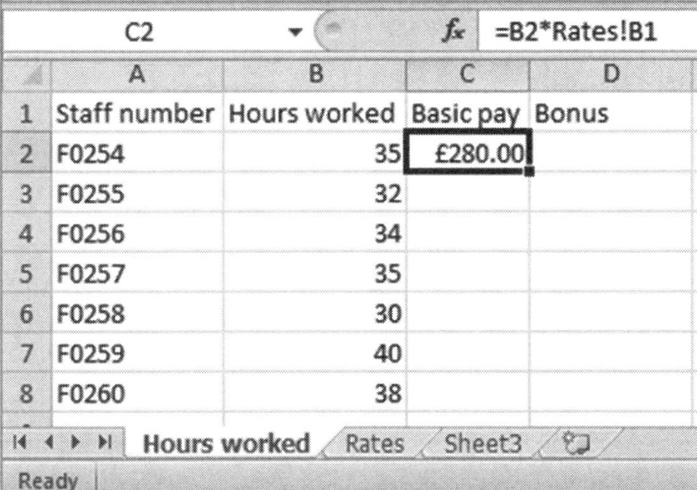

C2 | =B2*Rates!B1

| | A | B | C | D |
|---|---|---|---|---|
| 1 | Staff number | Hours worked | Basic pay | Bonus |
| 2 | F0254 | 35 | £280.00 | |
| 3 | F0255 | 32 | | |
| 4 | F0256 | 34 | | |
| 5 | F0257 | 35 | | |
| 6 | F0258 | 30 | | |
| 7 | F0259 | 40 | | |
| 8 | F0260 | 38 | | |

Hours worked | Rates | Sheet3

Ready

Select the cell, and press **Enter** to complete the formula. This can then be copied in the normal way – the usual referencing rules apply, so we need to use $ signs for an **absolute** reference.

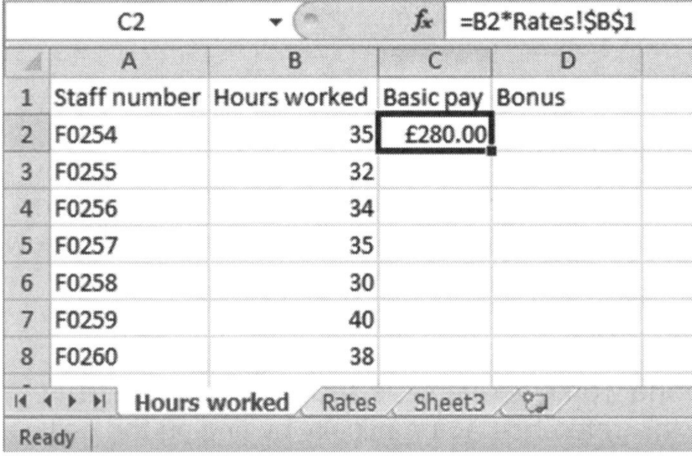

C2 | =B2*Rates!$B$1

| | A | B | C | D |
|---|---|---|---|---|
| 1 | Staff number | Hours worked | Basic pay | Bonus |
| 2 | F0254 | 35 | £280.00 | |
| 3 | F0255 | 32 | | |
| 4 | F0256 | 34 | | |
| 5 | F0257 | 35 | | |
| 6 | F0258 | 30 | | |
| 7 | F0259 | 40 | | |
| 8 | F0260 | 38 | | |

Hours worked | Rates | Sheet3

Ready

Now the formula can be copied down effectively to achieve the desired result.

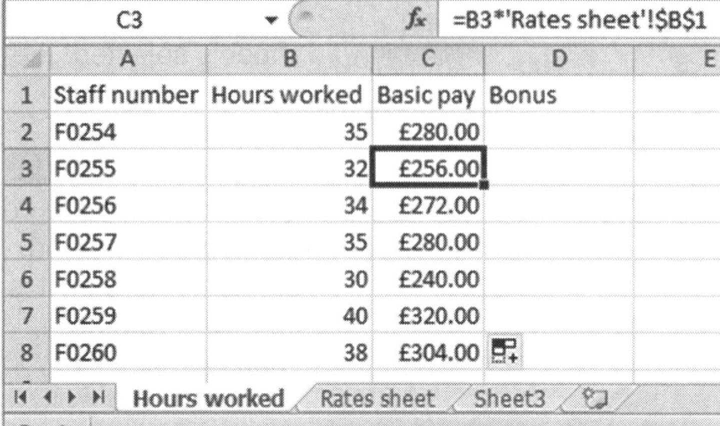

C3 =B3*'Rates sheet'!$B$1

| | A | B | C | D | E |
|---|---|---|---|---|---|
| 1 | Staff number | Hours worked | Basic pay | Bonus | |
| 2 | F0254 | 35 | £280.00 | | |
| 3 | F0255 | 32 | £256.00 | | |
| 4 | F0256 | 34 | £272.00 | | |
| 5 | F0257 | 35 | £280.00 | | |
| 6 | F0258 | 30 | £240.00 | | |
| 7 | F0259 | 40 | £320.00 | | |
| 8 | F0260 | 38 | £304.00 | | |

Hours worked / Rates sheet / Sheet3

Note that if the sheet name is changed, the formulas update automatically. Now the name has a space, the quote marks are added too.

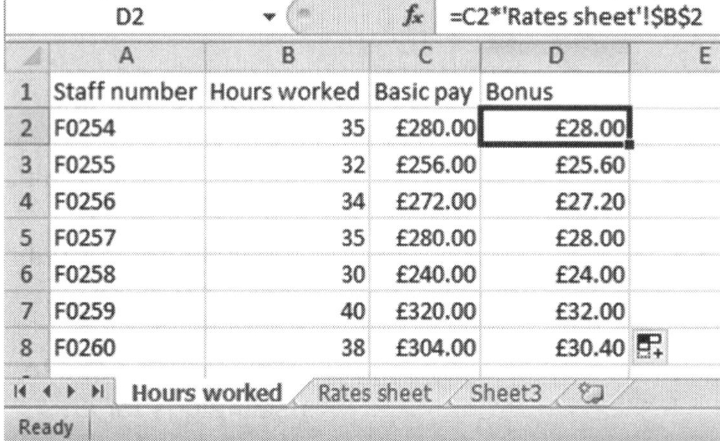

D2 =C2*'Rates sheet'!$B$2

| | A | B | C | D | E |
|---|---|---|---|---|---|
| 1 | Staff number | Hours worked | Basic pay | Bonus | |
| 2 | F0254 | 35 | £280.00 | £28.00 | |
| 3 | F0255 | 32 | £256.00 | £25.60 | |
| 4 | F0256 | 34 | £272.00 | £27.20 | |
| 5 | F0257 | 35 | £280.00 | £28.00 | |
| 6 | F0258 | 30 | £240.00 | £24.00 | |
| 7 | F0259 | 40 | £320.00 | £32.00 | |
| 8 | F0260 | 38 | £304.00 | £30.40 | |

Hours worked / Rates sheet / Sheet3

Ready

The final formula can be added in the same way.

**Shortcut**

**Ctrl-Page Up** and **Ctrl-Page Down** will switch between worksheets on the active workbook.

### 5.2 Referencing other workbooks

Again, you may wish to refer to another workbook within your calculations. This works in exactly the same way as referring to other worksheets – now our reference would be 'Cell A1 on Sheet 1 of Workbook 1'.

**='[Workbook 1.xlsx]Sheet 1'!A1**

The only difference being the workbook name is shown within square brackets. You can create this reference automatically by finding the cell you need and clicking on it.

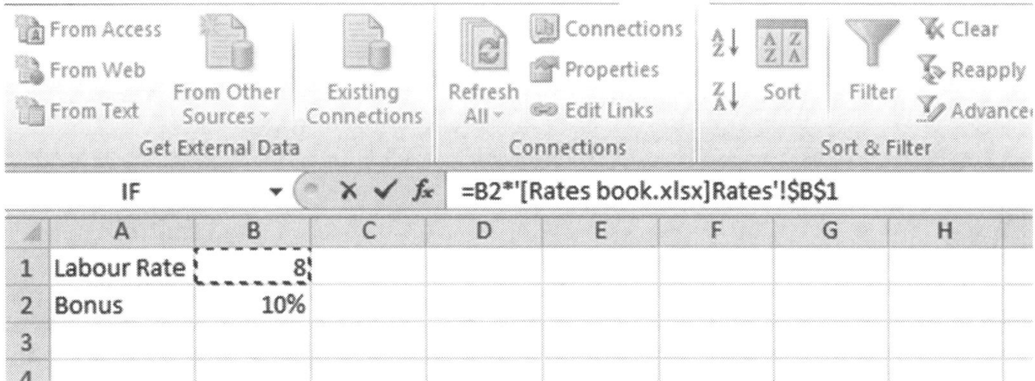


As you select the cell, the formula is populated automatically. Note that by default, **absolute** cell referencing is used – the dollar signs can be removed/added by pressing **F4** as you enter the formula, or manually.

> **Shortcut**
>
> **Ctrl-Tab** and **Ctrl-Shift-Tab** will switch between open workbooks.

## 5.3 Links

Once a formula is set up referencing another workbook, a **link** has been created. These can be managed using the **Edit links** option in the **Data** tab.

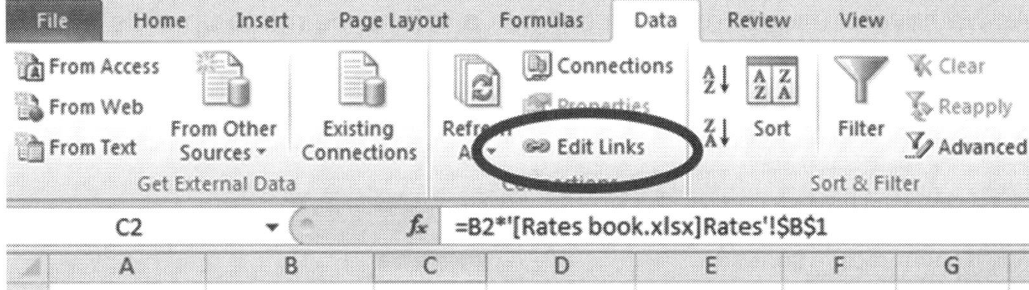

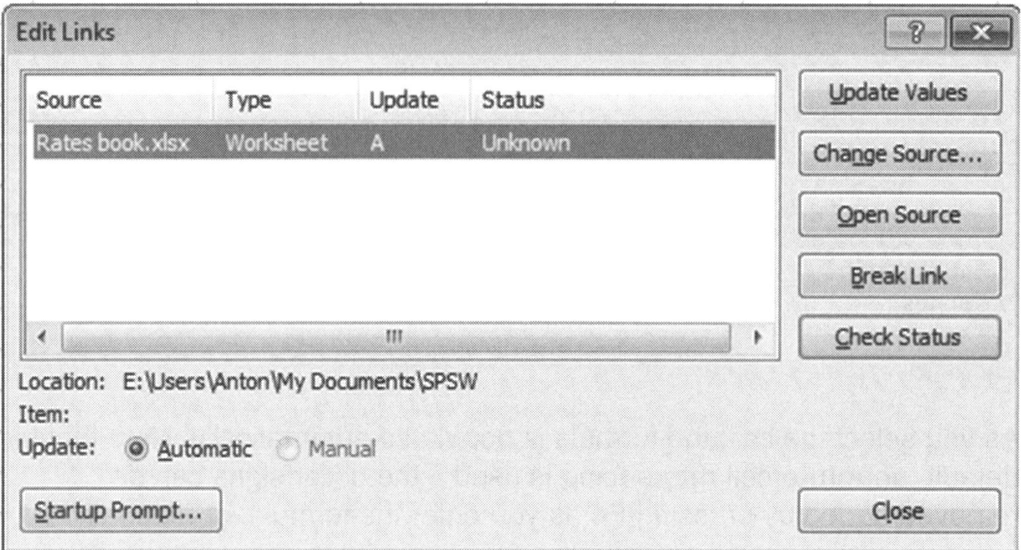


Here, links can be managed if necessary. **Break link** removes the link from the formula – the current value of the formula will be retained.

# 6 Naming cells

## 6.1 Naming cells

Naming cells and ranges of cells can make formulas easier to understand. As we have already seen, each cell has a **reference** made up of its column and row position. Instead of this, it can be given a name. The simplest way to do this is by using the **Name Box**.

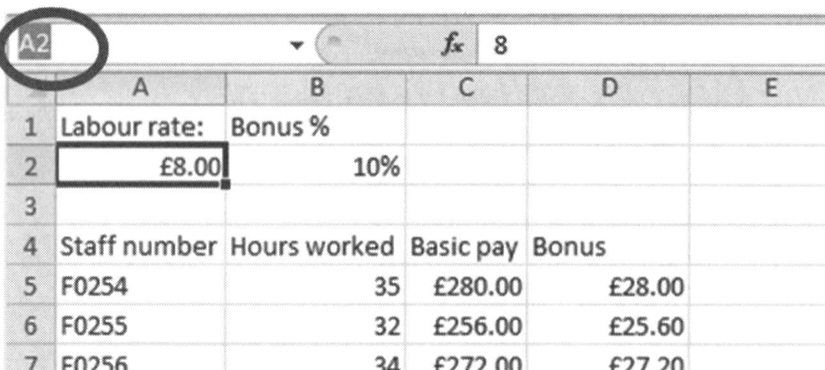

A2 | fx 8

| | A | B | C | D | E |
|---|---|---|---|---|---|
| 1 | Labour rate: | Bonus % | | | |
| 2 | £8.00 | 10% | | | |
| 3 | | | | | |
| 4 | Staff number | Hours worked | Basic pay | Bonus | |
| 5 | F0254 | 35 | £280.00 | £28.00 | |
| 6 | F0255 | 32 | £256.00 | £25.60 | |
| 7 | F0256 | 34 | £272.00 | £27.20 | |

The **Name Box**, showing that Cell **A2** is selected.

To give this cell a **name**, simply type the name in the **Name Box**. There are a few rules for cell names:

- No spaces (underscore is often used instead).
- Your name cannot be a valid cell reference (e.g. AB123).
- The name must be less than 256 characters.
- The name must start with a letter, an underscore or a backslash (\).
- Other valid characters after the first letter are letters, numbers, backslash, full stop and underscore, £ signs should NOT be used.
- Names are not case sensitive.

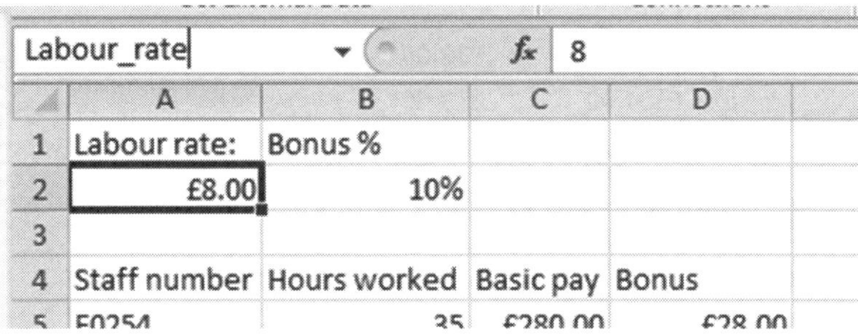

Labour_rate | fx 8

| | A | B | C | D |
|---|---|---|---|---|
| 1 | Labour rate: | Bonus % | | |
| 2 | £8.00 | 10% | | |
| 3 | | | | |
| 4 | Staff number | Hours worked | Basic pay | Bonus |
| 5 | F0254 | 35 | £280.00 | £28.00 |

Cell A2 has been named '**Labour_rate**'

This means we can now refer to the cell 'Labour rate', instead of A2, which can make things easier to understand.

IF | fx =B5*Labour_rate

| | A | B | C | D | E |
|---|---|---|---|---|---|
| 1 | Labour rate: | Bonus % | | | |
| 2 | £8.00 | 10% | | | |
| 3 | | | | | |
| 4 | Staff number | Hours worked | Basic pay | Bonus | |
| 5 | F0254 | 35 | =B5*Labour_rate | | |
| 6 | F0255 | 32 | | £0.00 | |
| 7 | F0256 | 34 | | £0.00 | |
| 8 | F0257 | 35 | | £0.00 | |
| 9 | F0258 | 30 | | £0.00 | |
| 10 | F0259 | 40 | | £0.00 | |
| 11 | F0260 | 38 | | £0.00 | |

When entering the formula, clicking on the cell enters its name rather than its cell reference.

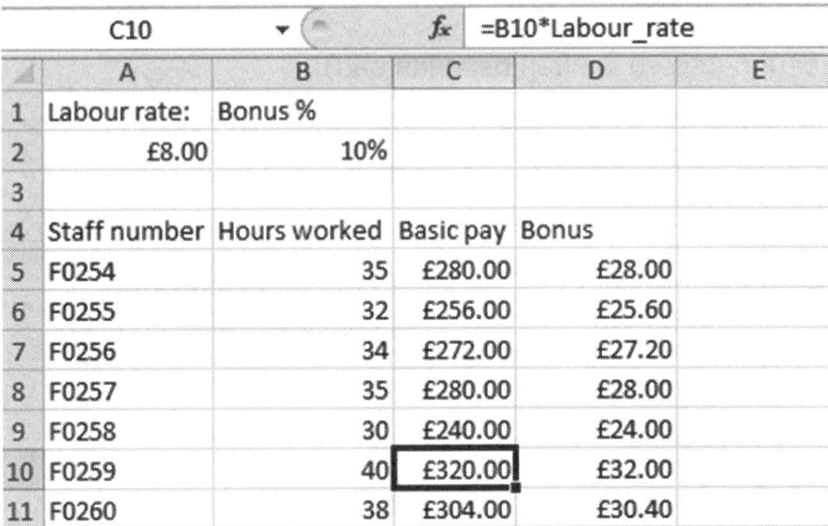

C10 =B10*Labour_rate

| | A | B | C | D | E |
|---|---|---|---|---|---|
| 1 | Labour rate: | Bonus % | | | |
| 2 | £8.00 | 10% | | | |
| 3 | | | | | |
| 4 | Staff number | Hours worked | Basic pay | Bonus | |
| 5 | F0254 | 35 | £280.00 | £28.00 | |
| 6 | F0255 | 32 | £256.00 | £25.60 | |
| 7 | F0256 | 34 | £272.00 | £27.20 | |
| 8 | F0257 | 35 | £280.00 | £28.00 | |
| 9 | F0258 | 30 | £240.00 | £24.00 | |
| 10 | F0259 | 40 | £320.00 | £32.00 | |
| 11 | F0260 | 38 | £304.00 | £30.40 | |

This also has the advantage of automatically making the cell reference **absolute**, when it is copied down.

The same thing can be done for the bonus percentage – name the cell 'Bonus'.

If you are entering a formula and cannot remember a cells name, press **F5** to navigate to **named cells**.

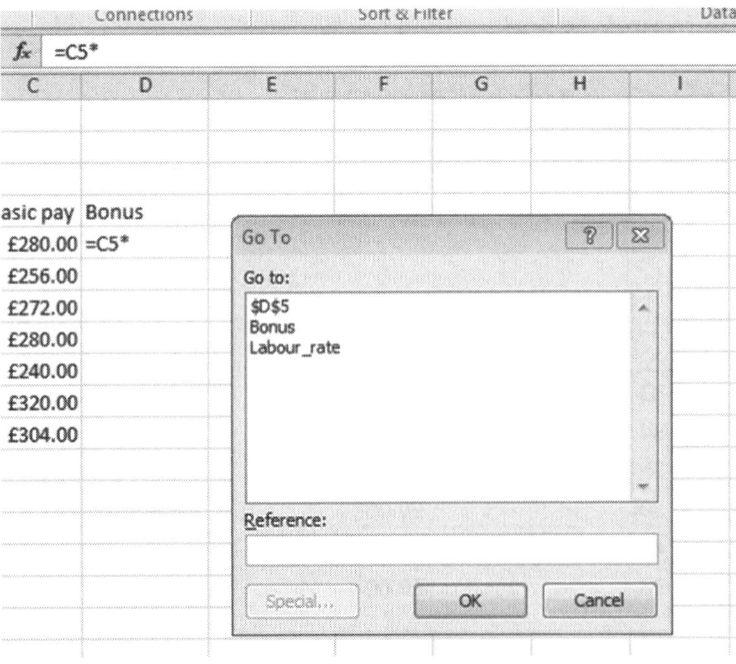


Select the Name you wish to use, and click **OK**.

Other commands to do with Naming Cells can be found in the **Formulas** tab, in the **Defined Names** section.

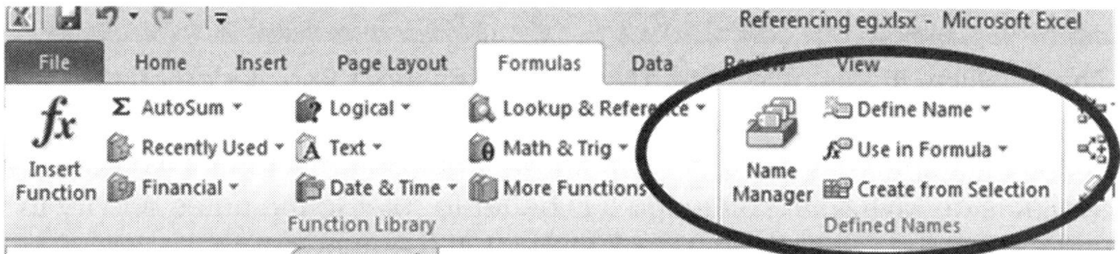

You can use **Define Name** as an alternative way of creating a name. **Use in Formula** is another way of inserting names into a formula, and **Create from Selection** is a way of automatically creating names.

The **Name Manager** is used to Add, Edit and

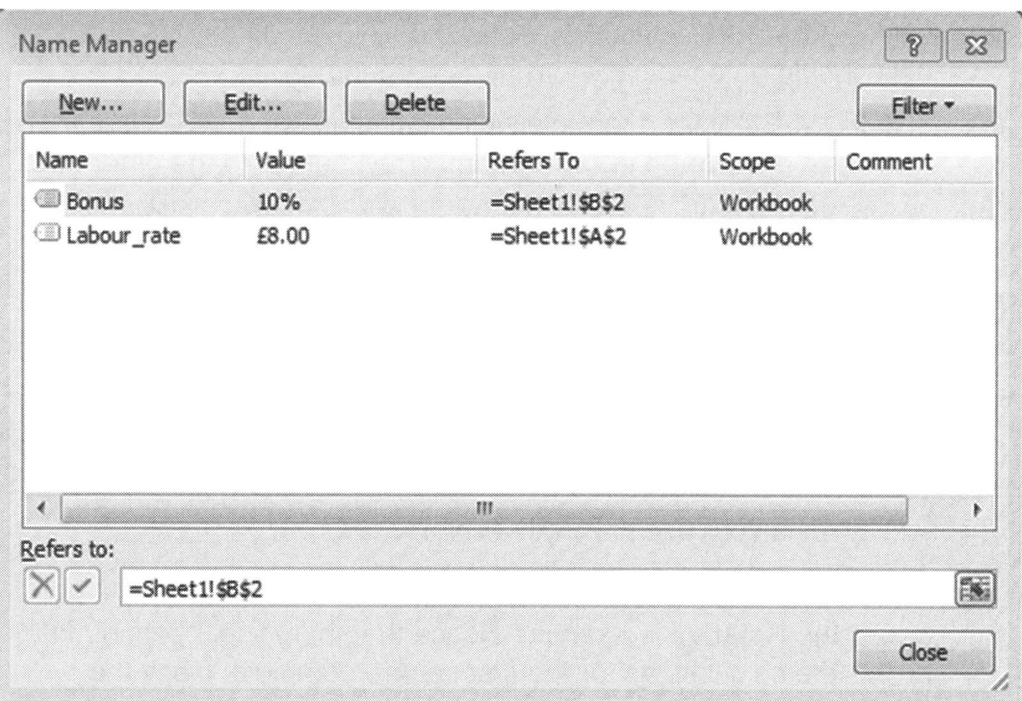

Delete names.

# 7 Test your understanding

The activities in this guide are designed to test your knowledge on the techniques shown in this chapter. They may also use techniques used in previous chapters, to build up your knowledge. Suggested answers are available on MyKaplan, although it is better to refer to the notes and try to understand the methods than look straight at the answers.

## Test your understanding 7-1

This activity tests your use of **absolute** references.

(a) Open the **Referencing** workbook in the **Activities** folder.

(b) On the **Absolute** worksheet, enter the VAT rate in cell B1 as 20% (this should automatically format as percentage).

(c) In cells B4-B8 enter a formula which calculates the VAT. Use an **Absolute Reference** in cell B4, and copy it down to the other cells.

(d) Complete the table by using a formula in column C to add up sales and VAT (there is more than one correct formula).

(e) Save the file as **Activity 7-1** in the **Solutions** folder.

## Test your understanding 7-2

This activity tests your use of **relative** references.

(a) Open the **Referencing** workbook in the **Activities** folder.

(b) Select the **Relative** worksheet. Notice that there are 3 sets of data here – the calculations for the first set are complete. Copy the formulas from C4:E8 into Cells I4:K8 – the references will update to use the correct sales figures.

(c) Repeat this to copy the formulas into cells O4:Q4.

(d) **Show Formulas** on this worksheet.

(e) Save the file as **Activity 7-2** in the **Solutions** folder.

## Test your understanding 7-3

This activity tests your use of **mixed** referencing.

(a) Open the **Referencing** workbook in the **Activities** folder.

(b) Select the **Mixed Referencing** worksheet. The table will show how our sales will change with varying volume, and with different percentage increases added. Firstly, calculate forecast sales in column B. An **absolute** reference should be used on B1.

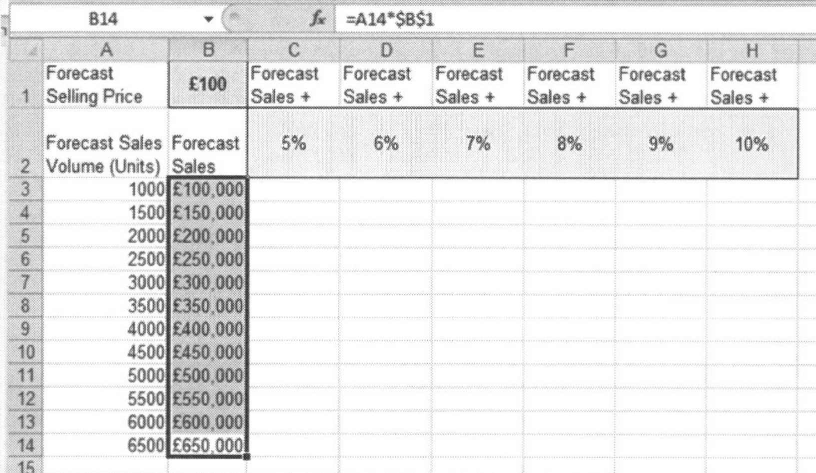

B14 =A14*$B$1

| | A | B | C | D | E | F | G | H |
|---|---|---|---|---|---|---|---|---|
| 1 | Forecast Selling Price | £100 | Forecast Sales + | Forecast Sales + | Forecast Sales + | Forecast Sales + | Forecast Sales + | Forecast Sales + |
| 2 | Forecast Sales Volume (Units) | Forecast Sales | 5% | 6% | 7% | 8% | 9% | 10% |
| 3 | 1000 | £100,000 | | | | | | |
| 4 | 1500 | £150,000 | | | | | | |
| 5 | 2000 | £200,000 | | | | | | |
| 6 | 2500 | £250,000 | | | | | | |
| 7 | 3000 | £300,000 | | | | | | |
| 8 | 3500 | £350,000 | | | | | | |
| 9 | 4000 | £400,000 | | | | | | |
| 10 | 4500 | £450,000 | | | | | | |
| 11 | 5000 | £500,000 | | | | | | |
| 12 | 5500 | £550,000 | | | | | | |
| 13 | 6000 | £600,000 | | | | | | |
| 14 | 6500 | £650,000 | | | | | | |
| 15 | | | | | | | | |

(c) We now need to calculate the forecast sales plus the percentage increase. This calculation could be:

**Forecast sales*(1+percentage increase)**

We need to be careful with the referencing. If we start in cell C3, the calculation is **=B3*(1+C2)**. This will give the correct answer of £105,000.

However, when we copy the formula across to the other columns, it will not work. If we copy across into column D, the formula will become **=C3*(1+D2)**. This is not correct, as we need to always refer to column B for the Forecast sales.

So, the formula becomes **=$B3*(1+C2)**. If this is copied across, the top row will be correct.

We also have to consider the reference to C2. If we copy this **down** a row, the formula will become **=$B4*(1+C3)** which is no longer multiplying by the correct percentage. We need to always refer to the row in this part of the formula, which becomes **=$B4*(1+C$2)**

**Note:** There are different formulas that can be used to calculate the forecast sale plus the percentage increase. The formula could also be =$B3+$B3*C$2

The final result looks like this:

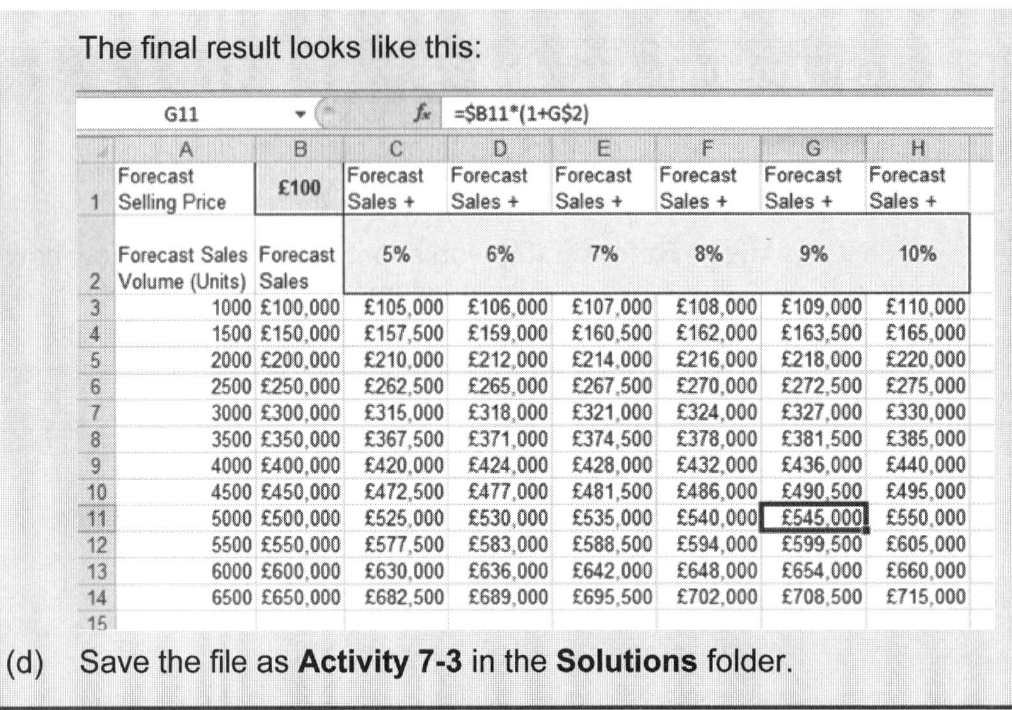

G11 =$B11*(1+G$2)

| | A | B | C | D | E | F | G | H |
|---|---|---|---|---|---|---|---|---|
| 1 | Forecast Selling Price | £100 | Forecast Sales + | Forecast Sales + | Forecast Sales + | Forecast Sales + | Forecast Sales + | Forecast Sales + |
| 2 | Forecast Sales Volume (Units) | Forecast Sales | 5% | 6% | 7% | 8% | 9% | 10% |
| 3 | 1000 | £100,000 | £105,000 | £106,000 | £107,000 | £108,000 | £109,000 | £110,000 |
| 4 | 1500 | £150,000 | £157,500 | £159,000 | £160,500 | £162,000 | £163,500 | £165,000 |
| 5 | 2000 | £200,000 | £210,000 | £212,000 | £214,000 | £216,000 | £218,000 | £220,000 |
| 6 | 2500 | £250,000 | £262,500 | £265,000 | £267,500 | £270,000 | £272,500 | £275,000 |
| 7 | 3000 | £300,000 | £315,000 | £318,000 | £321,000 | £324,000 | £327,000 | £330,000 |
| 8 | 3500 | £350,000 | £367,500 | £371,000 | £374,500 | £378,000 | £381,500 | £385,000 |
| 9 | 4000 | £400,000 | £420,000 | £424,000 | £428,000 | £432,000 | £436,000 | £440,000 |
| 10 | 4500 | £450,000 | £472,500 | £477,000 | £481,500 | £486,000 | £490,500 | £495,000 |
| 11 | 5000 | £500,000 | £525,000 | £530,000 | £535,000 | £540,000 | £545,000 | £550,000 |
| 12 | 5500 | £550,000 | £577,500 | £583,000 | £588,500 | £594,000 | £599,500 | £605,000 |
| 13 | 6000 | £600,000 | £630,000 | £636,000 | £642,000 | £648,000 | £654,000 | £660,000 |
| 14 | 6500 | £650,000 | £682,500 | £689,000 | £695,500 | £702,000 | £708,500 | £715,000 |
| 15 | | | | | | | | |

(d) Save the file as **Activity 7-3** in the **Solutions** folder.

## Test your understanding 7-4

This activity uses a named range to calculate values.

(a) Open the **Referencing** workbook from the **Activities** folder.

(b) Enter the VAT rate in cell A1 of the **Absolute** folder as 20%.

(c) **Name** cell B1 vat_rate.

(d) Calculate the VAT in cells B4:B8 using the name vat_rate.

(e) Complete the Total column.

(f) Show Formulas.

(g) Save the file as **Activity 7-4** in the **Activities** folder.

## Test your understanding 7-5

This activity tests your use of formulas referencing different worksheets.

(a) Open the **Regional Combined** workbook from the **Activities** folder.

(b) The **Regional Combined Sales** worksheet needs populating with the sum of the values on **District 1** and **District 2** worksheets.

(c) Enter a formula in cell B2 on the totals worksheet which adds cell B2 from District 1 to B2 from District 2.

(d) Copy the formula down and across into the other cells.

(e) Format the numbers in **Number** format, to zero decimal places with a 1000 separator comma.

(f) Save the file as **Activity 7-5** in the **Activities** folder.

## Test your understanding 7-6

This activity tests your use of formulas referring to cells in other workbooks, along with some basic formatting and some simple functions.

(a) Open the **District Totals, Northern** and **Southern** workbooks from the **Activities** folder.

(b) The **District Totals** workbook needs populating with the sum of the values on **Northern** and **Southern** workbooks.

(c) Enter a formula in cell B2 on the Totals workbook which adds cell B2 from Northern to Southern.

(d) Copy the formula down and across into the other cells so that all the cells populate with the correct totals (check the referencing in the formula).

(e) Populate the **Total** row with a formula to add the figures.

(f) Place a **Border** around the Total figures – single line on the top of the cell, double line on the bottom.

(g) Calculate the monthly average sales in cell B8.

(h) Format the numbers in **Number** format, to zero decimal places with a 1000 separator comma.

(i) Save the file as **Activity 7-6** in the **Activities** folder.

# Conditional formatting

## Introduction

This chapter will guide you on how to apply conditional formatting to cells based upon pre-determined criteria. You will also learn the different ways in which conditional formatting can be applied.

### ASSESSMENT CRITERIA

Format data (2.3)

Select and use relevant tools to analyse and interpret data (3.2)

Prepare reports (5.1)

### CONTENTS

# 1 Conditional formatting

## 1.1 Introduction

Formatting cells has already been discussed in chapter 3 – changing the appearance of cells or the text within them. **Conditional Formatting** is where you can change the format of a cell based on certain conditions.

For example you could want to colour a cell in red if its value is less than a certain number, or make the font bold if its value is equal to a number. In the example below, we might want to highlight any staff member who has worked more than a standard 35 hour week.

| | A | B | C | D |
|---|---|---|---|---|
| 1 | Labour rate: | Bonus % | | |
| 2 | £8.00 | 10% | | |
| 3 | | | | |
| 4 | Staff number | Hours worked | Basic pay | Bonus |
| 5 | F0254 | 35 | £280.00 | £28.00 |
| 6 | F0255 | 32 | £256.00 | £25.60 |
| 7 | F0256 | 34 | £272.00 | £27.20 |
| 8 | F0257 | 35 | £280.00 | £28.00 |
| 9 | F0258 | 30 | £240.00 | £24.00 |
| 10 | F0259 | 40 | £320.00 | £32.00 |
| 11 | F0260 | 38 | £304.00 | £30.40 |

## 1.2 Managing Conditional Formatting Rules

To see any conditional formatting already in place, or to create a conditional format, select the cell(s) you wish to format, and in the **Home Menu**, select **Conditional Formatting**. Several options appear.

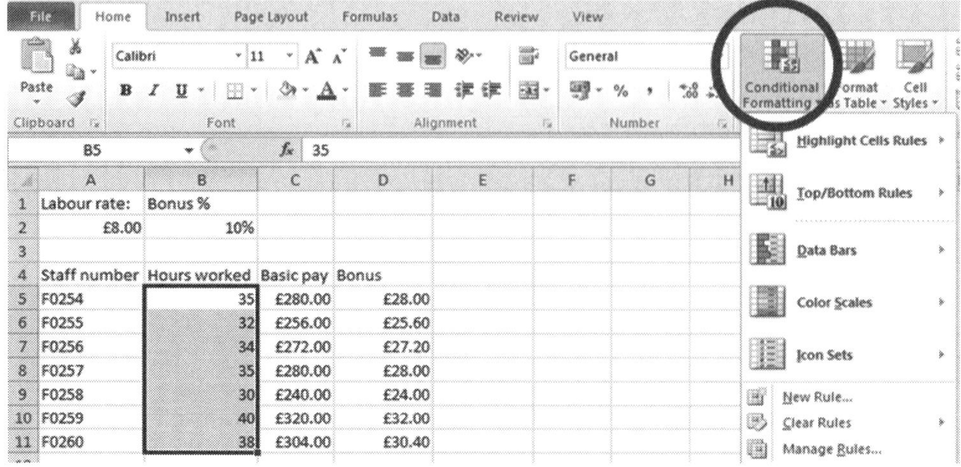

Select **Manage Rules** to bring up the Conditional Formatting Rules Manager.

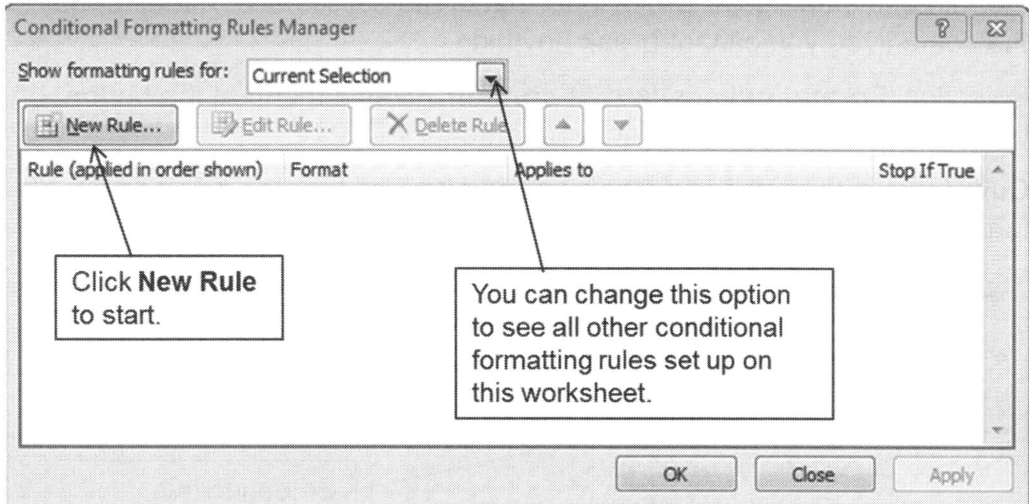


From here you can **Edit** or **Delete** any existing conditional formatting, or create new formatting rules.

# 2 Creating rules

## 2.1 Creating a New Rule

Clicking **New Rule** from the **Rules Manager** menu brings up the following options:

The most frequently used rule is 'Format only cells that contain', circled in red below so we shall focus on how this rule works.

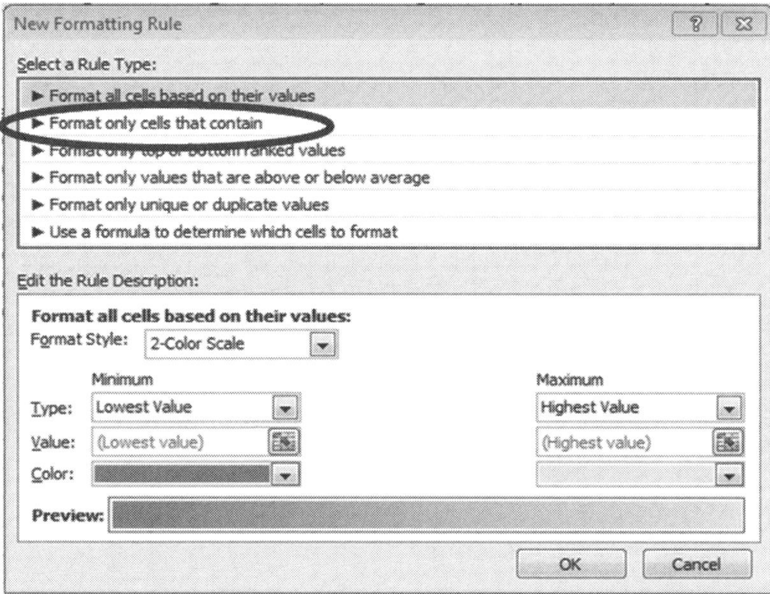

The other rules are useful and reasonably self-explanatory – the trick is to try them, and see what happens. Remember, if it goes wrong, just delete the rule and start again. Only the format of the cells is ever affected, not the content, so you cannot break anything

Selecting '**Format only cells that contain**' gives a menu at the bottom of the page, allowing you to select your criteria.

**Cell Value** is the most commonly used option, as this can be used to format cells based on numerical values.

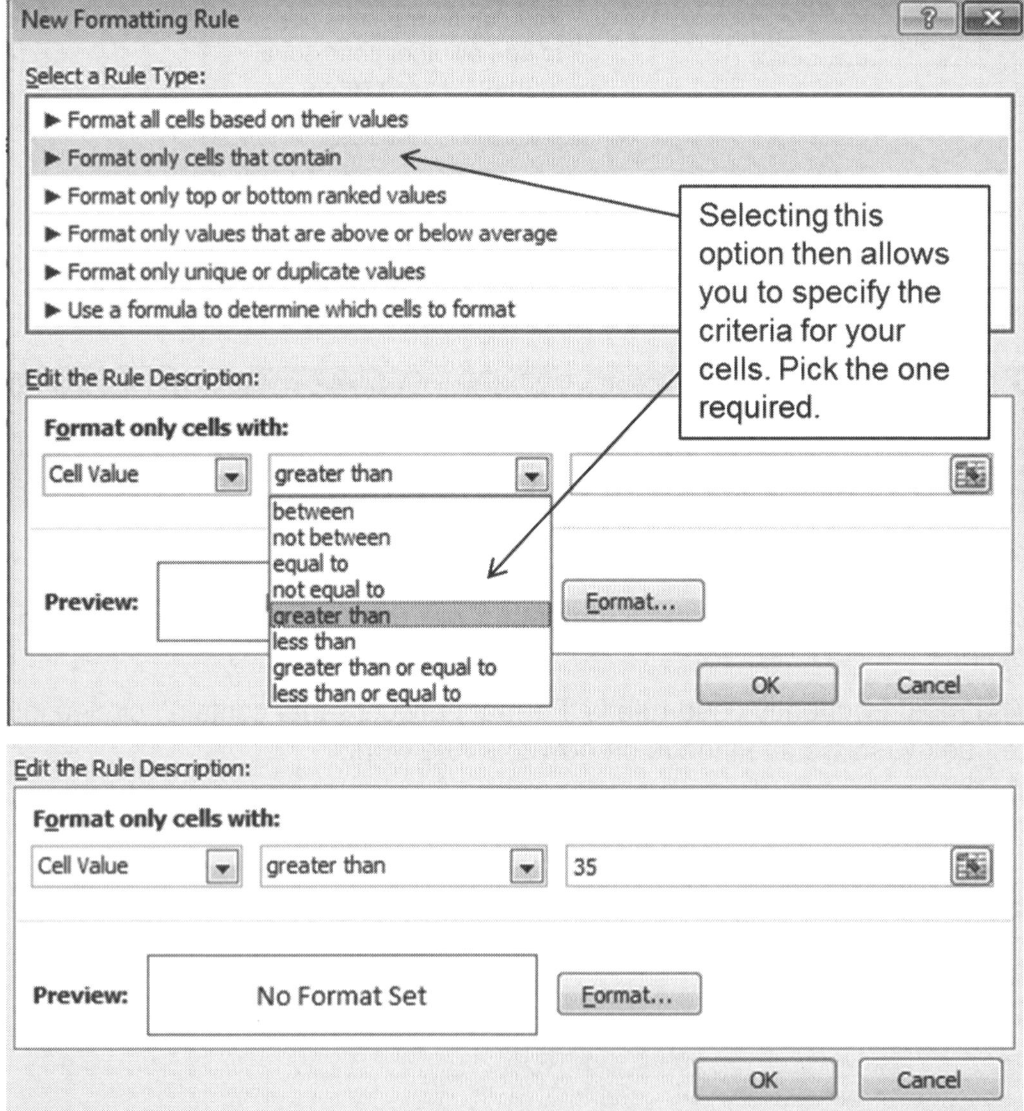


The rule is set up – the formatting will change for any cell (out of the ones selected) whose value is greater than 35. However, no special format has been set. To do this, click the **Format** button.

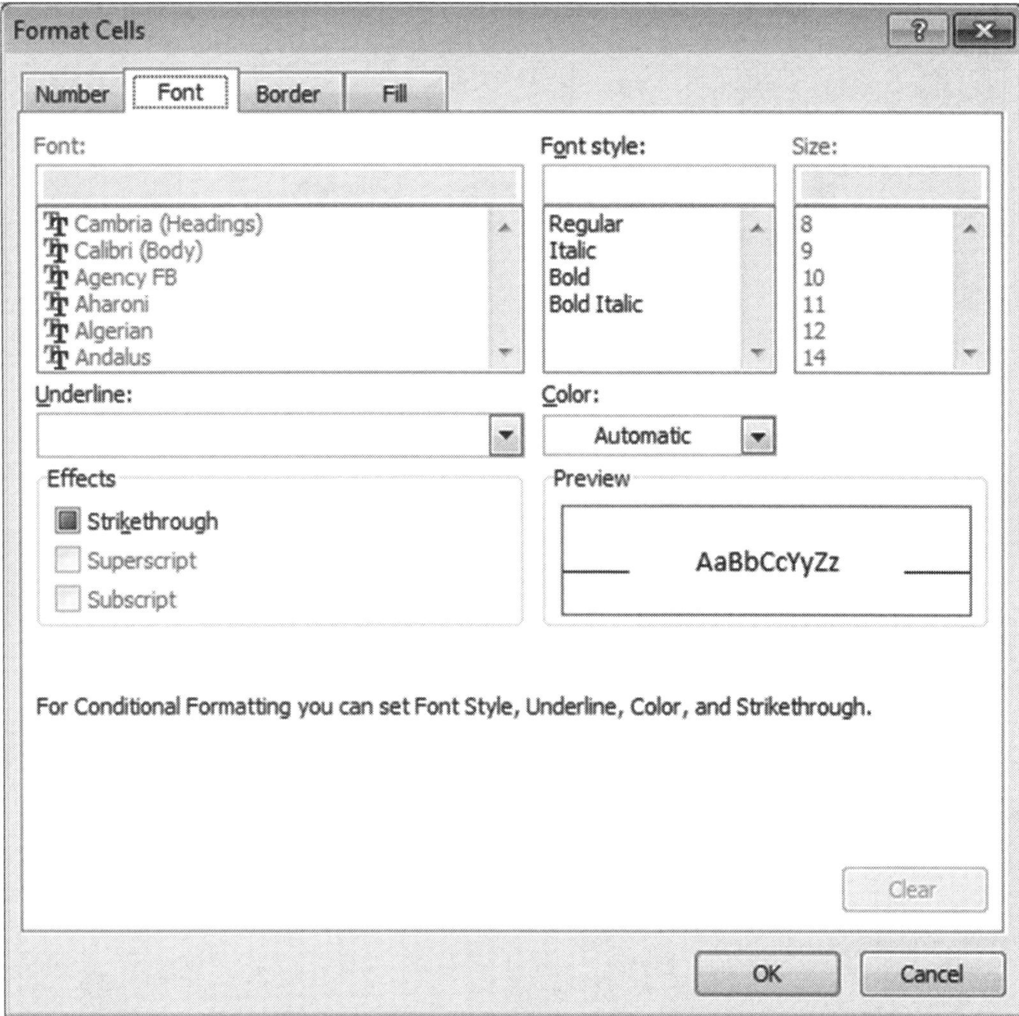


The normal **Format Cells** dialogue box opens – use this to set how you would like the cell to be formatted, if the value is over 35.

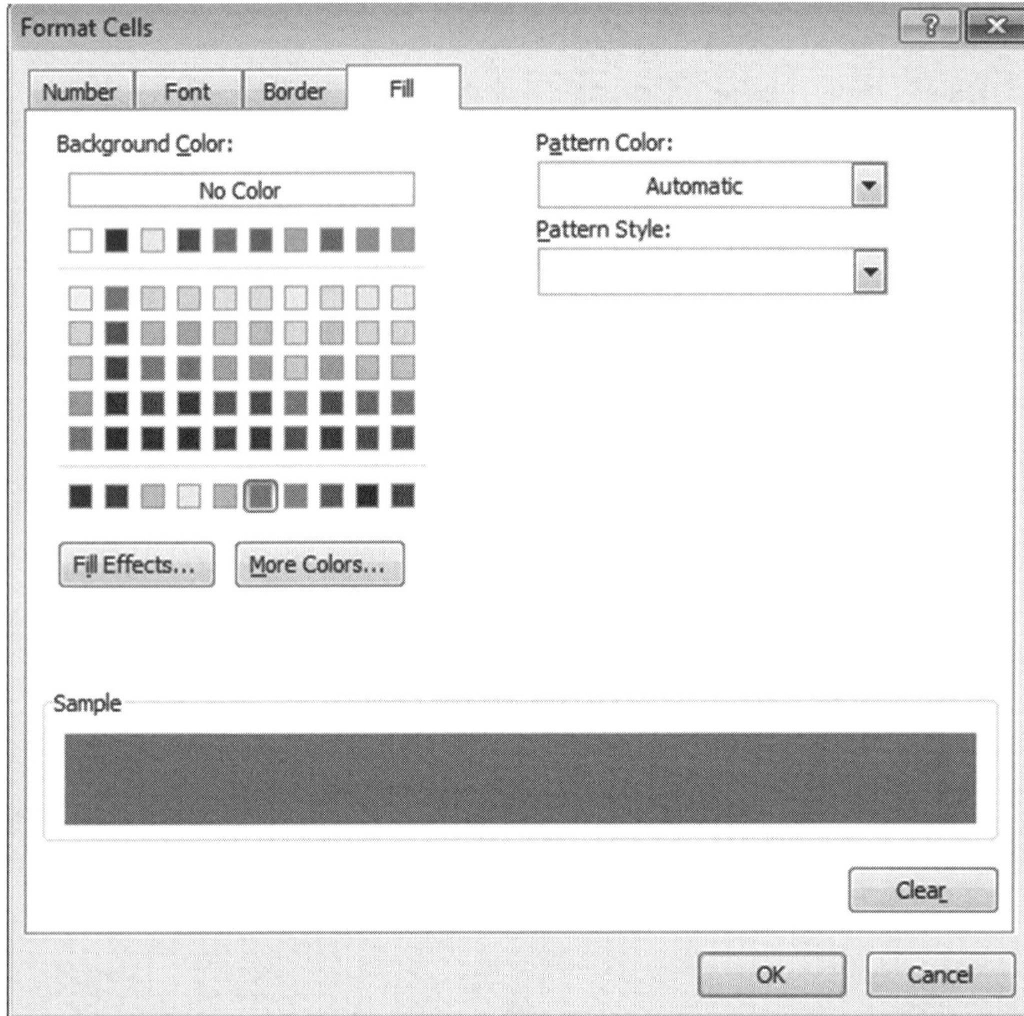


A common use of conditional formatting is to highlight unusual values by colouring the cell – green in this case.

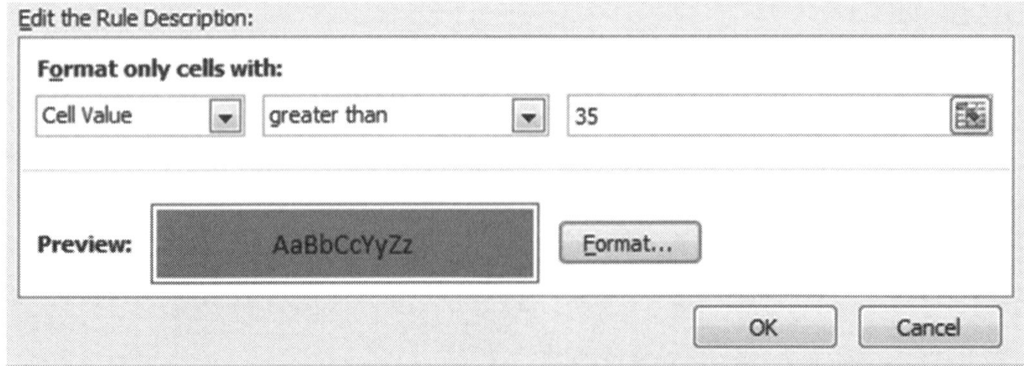


The final rule is shown – any cell with a value greater than 35 will be coloured green.

| | A | B | C | D |
|---|---|---|---|---|
| 1 | Labour rate: | Bonus % | | |
| 2 | £8.00 | 10% | | |
| 3 | | | | |
| 4 | Staff number | Hours worked | Basic pay | Bonus |
| 5 | F0254 | 35 | £280.00 | £28.00 |
| 6 | F0255 | 32 | £256.00 | £25.60 |
| 7 | F0256 | 34 | £272.00 | £27.20 |
| 8 | F0257 | 35 | £280.00 | £28.00 |
| 9 | F0258 | 30 | £240.00 | £24.00 |
| 10 | F0259 | 40 | £320.00 | £32.00 |
| 11 | F0260 | 38 | £304.00 | £30.40 |

The final result shows that the two cells with values above 35 are coloured green.

Note that the cell with value 35 is not coloured – the 'greater than or equal to' option would need to be used.

## 2.2 Multiple Rules

It is possible to have up to 64 conditional formatting rules for any cell.

Extra rules are added in the same way as a new rule – select the cells required and create a new rule. For example a rule to highlight in red any cells with a value below 32 can be used:

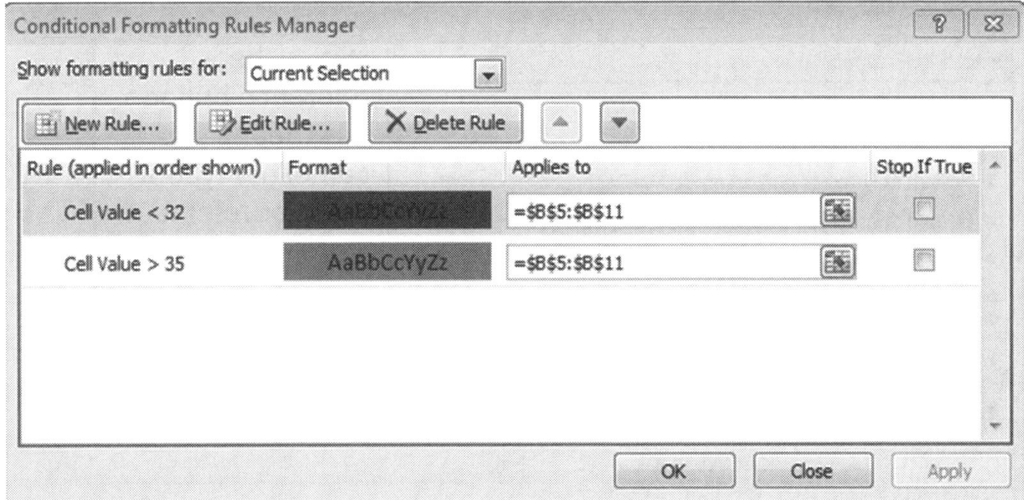


Note that if any of the rules conflict with each other, they will be applied in the order shown. The order of priority can be changed with the arrows next to the Delete Rule box.

## 2.3 Rules depending on another cell

Excel is designed to be flexible, and the conditional formatting rules can be designed to refer to the values in other cells. For example, rather than having to change the conditional formatting if the weekly hours changed, we could show them in a separate cell:

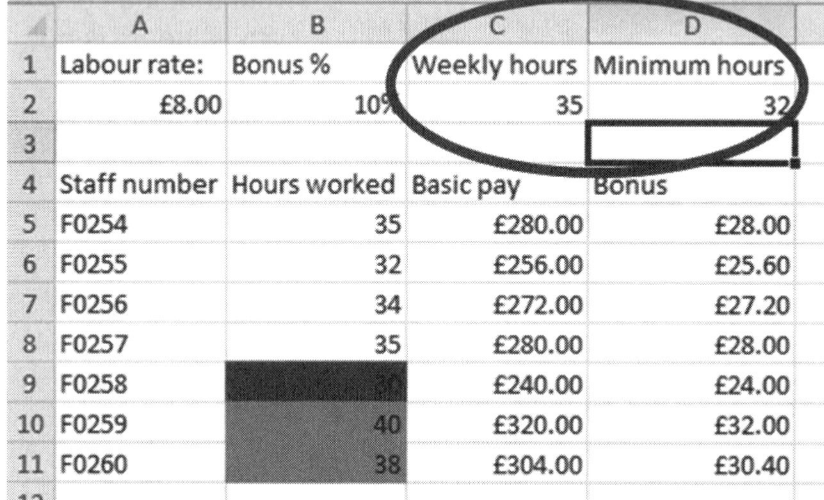

| | A | B | C | D |
|---|---|---|---|---|
| 1 | Labour rate: | Bonus % | Weekly hours | Minimum hours |
| 2 | £8.00 | 10% | 35 | 32 |
| 3 | | | | |
| 4 | Staff number | Hours worked | Basic pay | Bonus |
| 5 | F0254 | 35 | £280.00 | £28.00 |
| 6 | F0255 | 32 | £256.00 | £25.60 |
| 7 | F0256 | 34 | £272.00 | £27.20 |
| 8 | F0257 | 35 | £280.00 | £28.00 |
| 9 | F0258 | 30 | £240.00 | £24.00 |
| 10 | F0259 | 40 | £320.00 | £32.00 |
| 11 | F0260 | 38 | £304.00 | £30.40 |

We would like the conditional formatting to be based on these figures.

Deleting the existing formats and starting again:

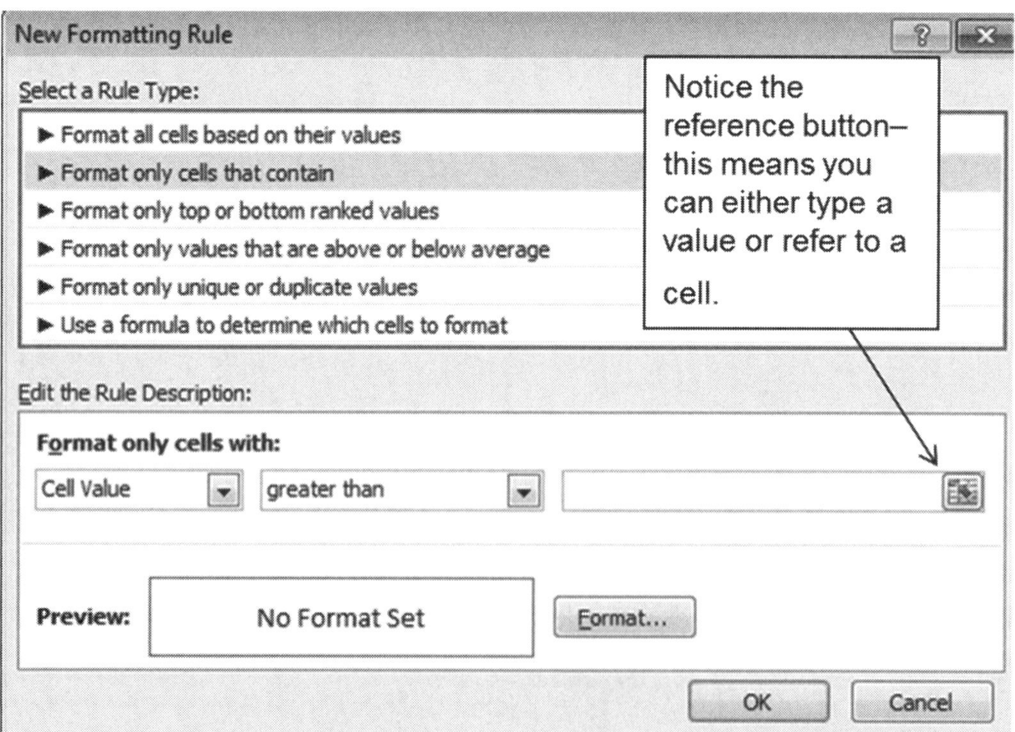


A new rule needs to be set up – formatting all cells with a value greater than that in cell C2.

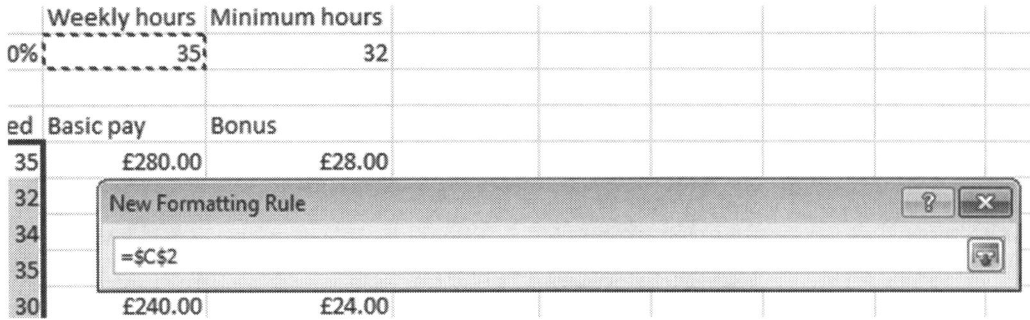


Click on the **Reference** Button and select C2. Note that **Absolute** referencing is used by default (remove the $ signs if you wish to use relative referencing).

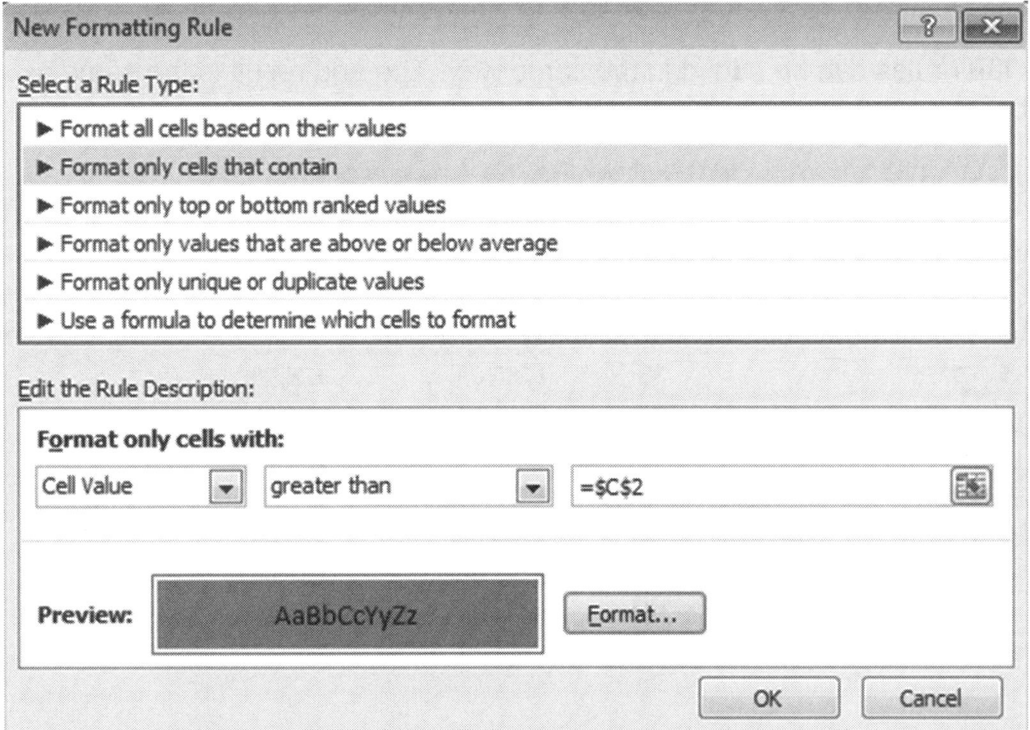


The final rule is shown. **Note** – the **'='** is required – if you click on the cell it will automatically be put in. Without this, the rule will not work.

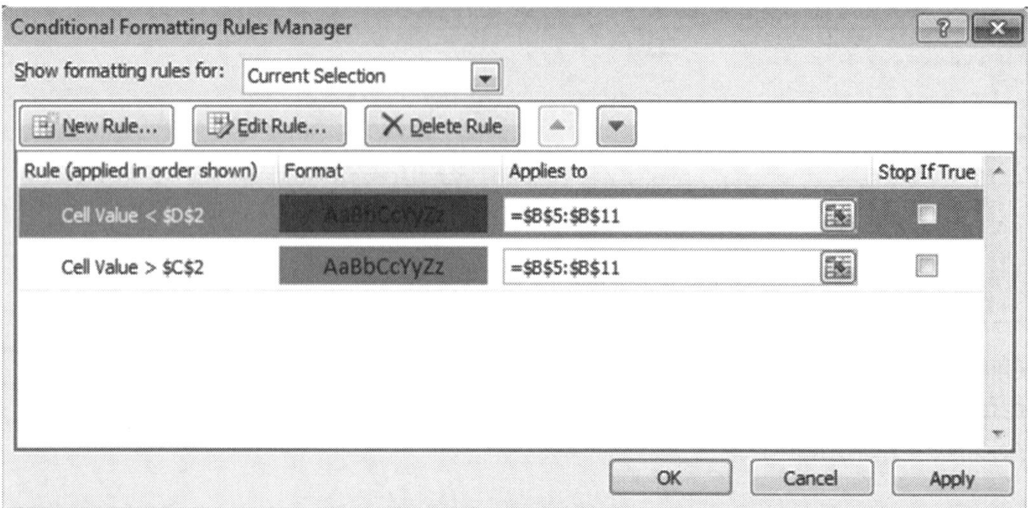


Other rules can be added in the same way. The end result is the same as before:

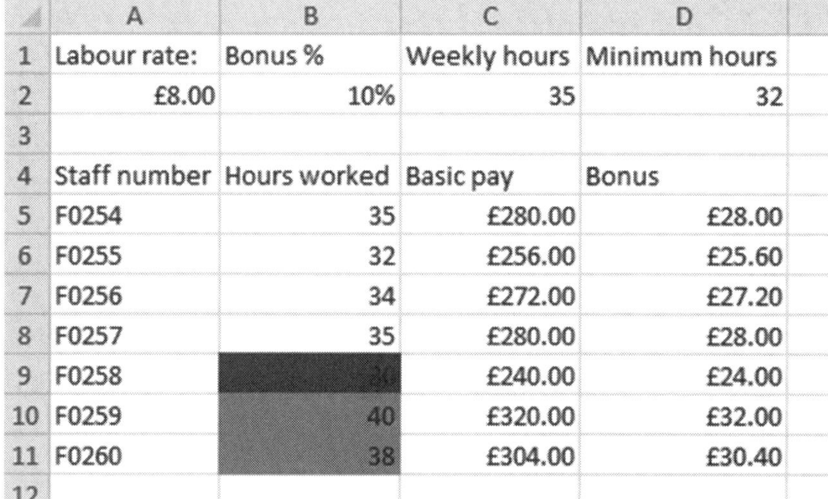

| | A | B | C | D |
|---|---|---|---|---|
| 1 | Labour rate: | Bonus % | Weekly hours | Minimum hours |
| 2 | £8.00 | 10% | 35 | 32 |
| 3 | | | | |
| 4 | Staff number | Hours worked | Basic pay | Bonus |
| 5 | F0254 | 35 | £280.00 | £28.00 |
| 6 | F0255 | 32 | £256.00 | £25.60 |
| 7 | F0256 | 34 | £272.00 | £27.20 |
| 8 | F0257 | 35 | £280.00 | £28.00 |
| 9 | F0258 | 30 | £240.00 | £24.00 |
| 10 | F0259 | 40 | £320.00 | £32.00 |
| 11 | F0260 | 38 | £304.00 | £30.40 |
| 12 | | | | |

The extra flexibility of this method can be seen if we change the minimum hours to 33 (say):

| | A | B | C | D |
|---|---|---|---|---|
| 1 | Labour rate: | Bonus % | Weekly hours | Minimum hours |
| 2 | £8.00 | 10% | 35 | 33 |
| 3 | | | | |
| 4 | Staff number | Hours worked | Basic pay | Bonus |
| 5 | F0254 | 35 | £280.00 | £28.00 |
| 6 | F0255 | 32 | £256.00 | £25.60 |
| 7 | F0256 | 34 | £272.00 | £27.20 |
| 8 | F0257 | 35 | £280.00 | £28.00 |
| 9 | F0258 | 30 | £240.00 | £24.00 |
| 10 | F0259 | 40 | £320.00 | £32.00 |
| 11 | F0260 | 38 | £304.00 | £30.40 |
| 12 | | | | |

The extra figure is now highlighted.

**NOTE ON CONDITIONAL FORMATTING**

Conditional formatting overwrites any existing formatting. If, for example, you try to highlight cells B5:B11 above in yellow, the four already highlighted **WILL NOT CHANGE COLOUR**. This can lead to confusion – if a cell's formatting will not change, check to see if there is conditional formatting in place. This is the most likely reason.

# 3 Editing and Deleting Rules

## 3.1 Editing Rules

**Edit** rules from within the **Rules Manager** box.

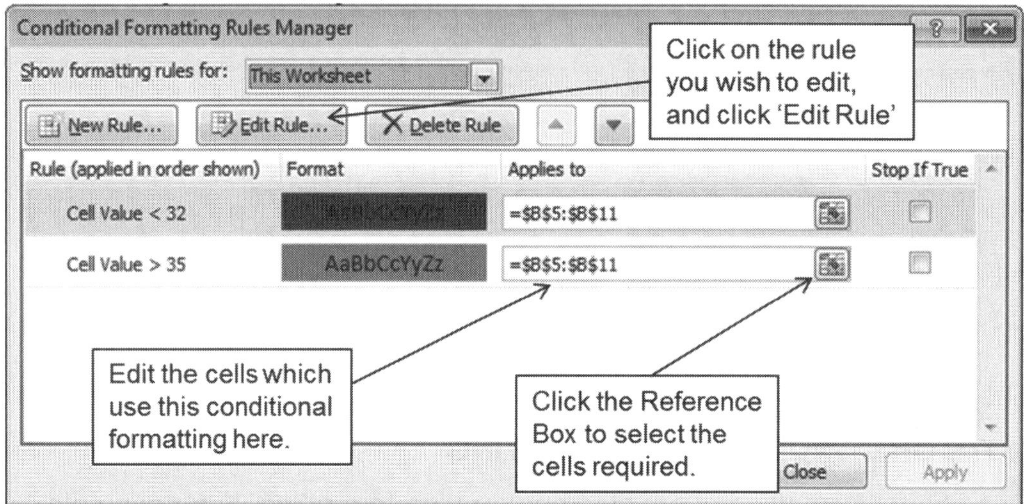


Clicking on **Edit Rule** brings up the same menu as for a New Rule, so make the changes as required.

## 3.2 Deleting Rules

Use the **Rules Manager** to delete a rule in the same way. Alternatively, all rules can be deleted through the **Conditional Formatting** button in the **Home Menu**.

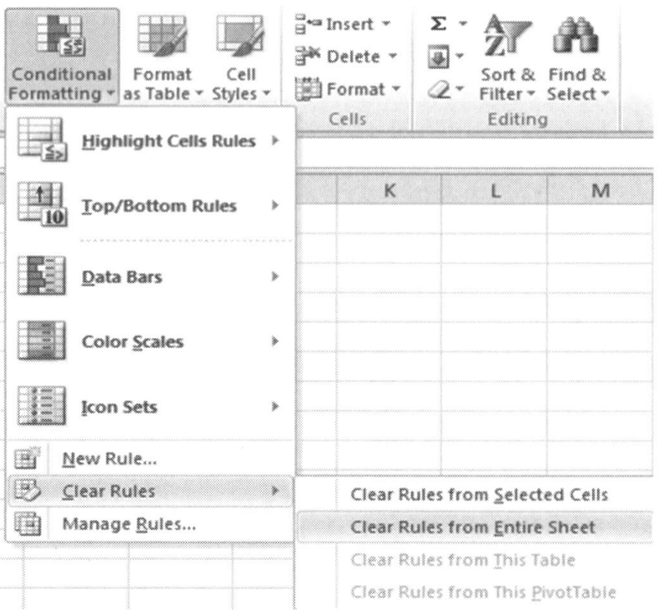


Select to delete all conditional formats either from the selected cell(s) or the whole sheet.

# 4 Test your understanding

The activities in this guide are designed to test your knowledge on the techniques shown in this chapter. They may also use techniques used in previous chapters, to build up your knowledge. Suggested answers are available on MyKaplan, although it is better to refer to the notes and try to understand the methods than look straight at the answers.

## Test your understanding 8-1

This activity tests several aspects of **conditional formatting**, along with some simple calculations and referencing.

(a) Open the **Conditional** workbook in the **Activities** folder.

(b) The values in cells B6:G13 need to be populated. Column B is **revenue** – calculated as the sales price (column A) multiplied by the sales volume. The sales volume needs to be used in each row, so the row number in cell G1 must be fixed – you can either use an **absolute** reference, $G$1, or mixed, G$1, it doesn't matter as long as the '1' is held.

(c) The **variable costs** in column C is just the sales volume * variable cost/unit. Again, this will be the same in rows 6-13, so make sure the row numbers in the calculation are fixed.

(d) **Revenue- Variable costs** (contribution) is simply column B minus column C.

(e) **Fixed costs** will be the same whatever the sales price – use an **absolute** reference to refer to the value in G2.

(f) **Total Cost** is column C plus column E.

(g) **Profit** can be calculated a few ways – column D minus column E is one.

C6 =$G$1*$G$3

| | A | B | C | D | E | F | G |
|---|---|---|---|---|---|---|---|
| 1 | Forecast Profit Calculations | | | | | Sales Volume | 25,000 |
| 2 | | | | | | Fixed Costs | £600,000 |
| 3 | | | | | | Variable Costs/unit | £14 |
| 4 | | | | | | | |
| 5 | Sales Price | Forecast Revenue | Variable Costs | Revenue minus Variable Costs | Fixed Costs | Total Cost | Profit |
| 6 | £38 | £950,000 | £350,000 | £600,000 | £600,000 | £950,000 | £0 |
| 7 | £39 | £975,000 | £350,000 | £625,000 | £600,000 | £950,000 | £25,000 |
| 8 | £40 | £1,000,000 | £350,000 | £650,000 | £600,000 | £950,000 | £50,000 |
| 9 | £41 | £1,025,000 | £350,000 | £675,000 | £600,000 | £950,000 | £75,000 |
| 10 | £42 | £1,050,000 | £350,000 | £700,000 | £600,000 | £950,000 | £100,000 |
| 11 | £43 | £1,075,000 | £350,000 | £725,000 | £600,000 | £950,000 | £125,000 |
| 12 | £44 | £1,100,000 | £350,000 | £750,000 | £600,000 | £950,000 | £150,000 |
| 13 | £45 | £1,125,000 | £350,000 | £775,000 | £600,000 | £950,000 | £175,000 |

(h) Now the figures are populated, we can add some conditional formats.

Select cell G6, and using the **Manage Rules** menu, apply the following conditional formats:

Cell value<0 – Fill Red

Cell value=0 – Fill Yellow

Cell value>0 – Fill Green

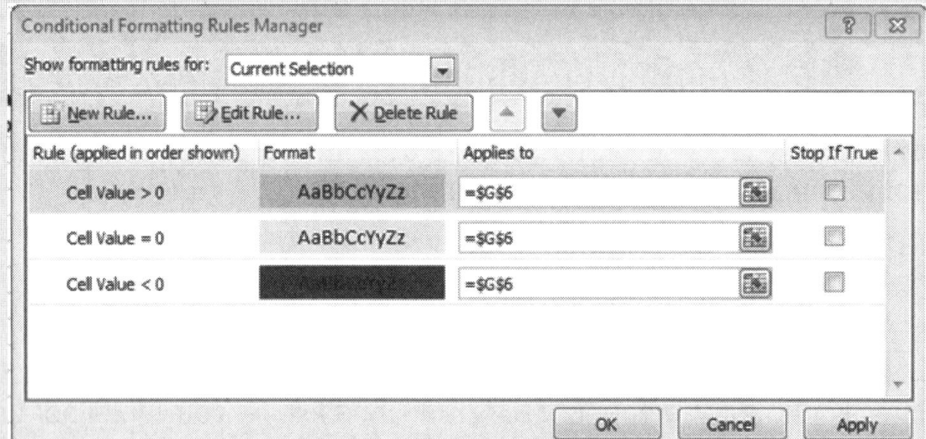


The cell should turn yellow, as profit is zero.

(i) Copy the format down onto cells G7:G13 (use paste special, or just drag). The remaining cells will turn green, as their values are all greater than zero.

(j) Change the **sales volume** in cell **G1** to 20000. Note the change in colour of the formatted cells.

(k) Save the file as **Activity 8-1** in the **solutions** folder.

## Test your understanding 8-2

This activity uses slightly more difficult **conditional formatting**, based on the value in another cell.

(a) Open the **CF Report** file in the **Activities** folder.

(b) We want to highlight the largest sales figure in the data – use **conditional formatting** to fill this cell as green. Select cells B4:M4, and set up a new conditional formatting rule. The largest sales figure in cell B9 so we want to format the cell which is equal to this.

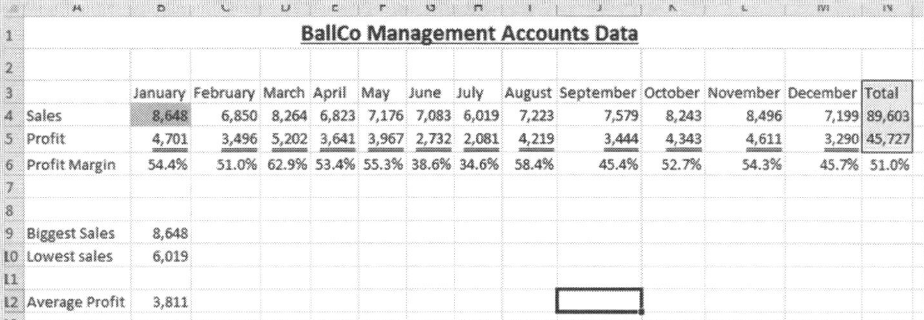

**BallCo Management Accounts Data**

| | January | February | March | April | May | June | July | August | September | October | November | December | Total |
|---|---|---|---|---|---|---|---|---|---|---|---|---|---|
| Sales | 8,648 | 6,850 | 8,264 | 6,823 | 7,176 | 7,083 | 6,019 | 7,223 | 7,579 | 8,243 | 8,496 | 7,199 | 89,603 |
| Profit | 4,701 | 3,496 | 5,202 | 3,641 | 3,967 | 2,732 | 2,081 | 4,219 | 3,444 | 4,343 | 4,611 | 3,290 | 45,727 |
| Profit Margin | 54.4% | 51.0% | 62.9% | 53.4% | 55.3% | 38.6% | 34.6% | 58.4% | 45.4% | 52.7% | 54.3% | 45.7% | 51.0% |
| | | | | | | | | | | | | | |
| | | | | | | | | | | | | | |
| Biggest Sales | 8,648 | | | | | | | | | | | | |
| Lowest sales | 6,019 | | | | | | | | | | | | |
| | | | | | | | | | | | | | |
| Average Profit | 3,811 | | | | | | | | | | | | |

(c) Change the value in cell J4 to 10,000. The value in B9 will change, and cell J4 will be coloured green.

(d) Undo the last command to return September sales to 7,579.

(e) Apply a similar conditional format to the sales figures to colour the lowest value red. July will be highlighted.

(f) Apply conditional formatting to cells B5:M5 to **bold** any profits lower than average, and fill the cell blue.

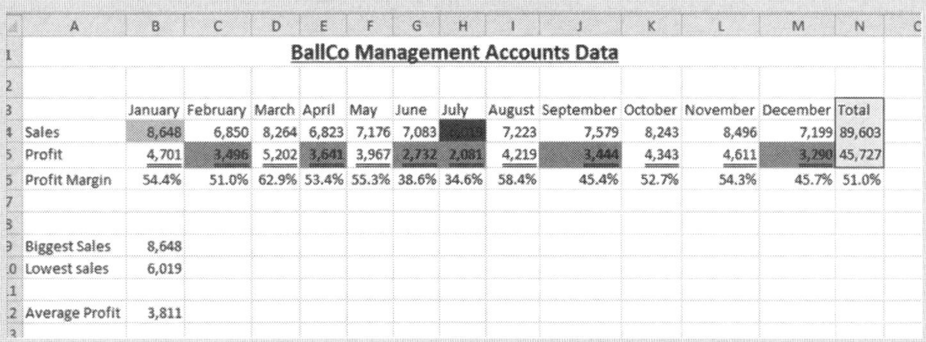

**BallCo Management Accounts Data**

| | January | February | March | April | May | June | July | August | September | October | November | December | Total |
|---|---|---|---|---|---|---|---|---|---|---|---|---|---|
| Sales | 8,648 | 6,850 | 8,264 | 6,823 | 7,176 | 7,083 | 6,019 | 7,223 | 7,579 | 8,243 | 8,496 | 7,199 | 89,603 |
| Profit | 4,701 | 3,496 | 5,202 | 3,641 | 3,967 | 2,732 | 2,081 | 4,219 | 3,444 | 4,343 | 4,611 | 3,290 | 45,727 |
| Profit Margin | 54.4% | 51.0% | 62.9% | 53.4% | 55.3% | 38.6% | 34.6% | 58.4% | 45.4% | 52.7% | 54.3% | 45.7% | 51.0% |
| | | | | | | | | | | | | | |
| | | | | | | | | | | | | | |
| Biggest Sales | 8,648 | | | | | | | | | | | | |
| Lowest sales | 6,019 | | | | | | | | | | | | |
| | | | | | | | | | | | | | |
| Average Profit | 3,811 | | | | | | | | | | | | |

(g) Save the file as **Activity 8-2** in the **Solutions** folder.

# Subtotalling

## Introduction

This chapter will guide you on how to apply Excel's subtotalling tool to provide a quick and convenient method of data analysis.

### ASSESSMENT CRITERIA

Format data (2.3)

Select and use a range of appropriate formulas and functions to perform calculations (3.1)

Select and use relevant tools to analyse and interpret data (3.2)

Prepare reports (5.1)

Report accounting information (5.2)

### CONTENTS

# 1 Subtotalling

## 1.1 Introduction

Excel has a tool that allows you to do insert subtotals quickly and easily.

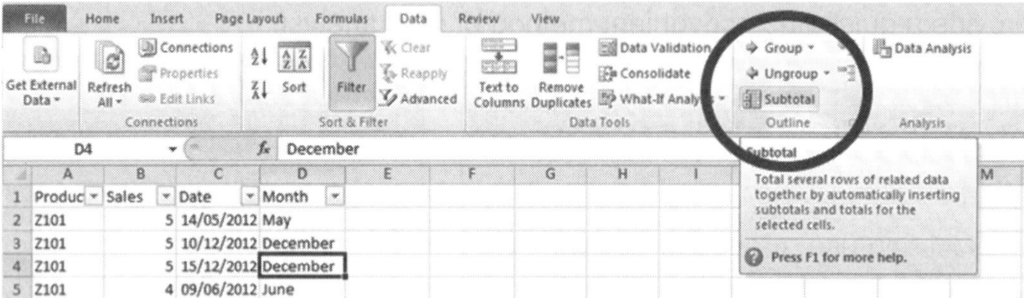


| | A | B | C | D |
|---|---|---|---|---|
| 1 | Produc | Sales | Date | Month |
| 2 | Z101 | 5 | 14/05/2012 | May |
| 3 | Z101 | 5 | 10/12/2012 | December |
| 4 | Z101 | 5 | 15/12/2012 | December |
| 5 | Z101 | 4 | 09/06/2012 | June |

## 1.2 Creating subtotals

The Subtotal function is found in the **Data** tab, in the **Outline** menu.

**Important note** – in order for the subtotal to work, the data **MUST** be **sorted** first, in order of the column you wish to subtotal by.

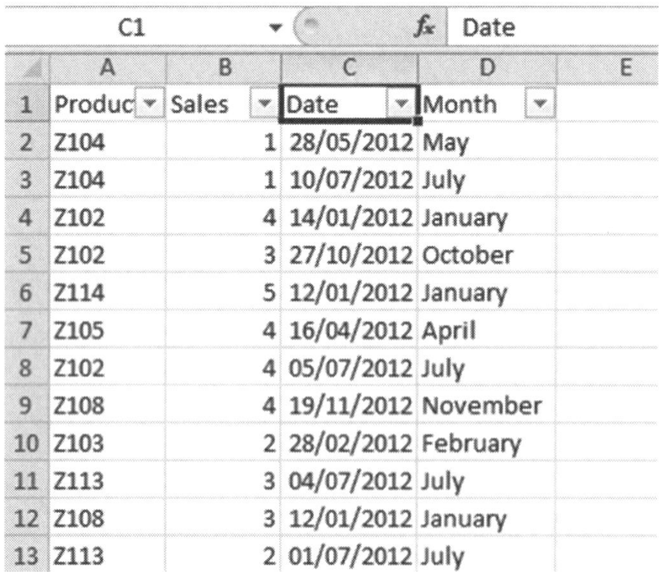

C1 | Date

| | A | B | C | D |
|---|---|---|---|---|
| 1 | Produc | Sales | Date | Month |
| 2 | Z104 | 1 | 28/05/2012 | May |
| 3 | Z104 | 1 | 10/07/2012 | July |
| 4 | Z102 | 4 | 14/01/2012 | January |
| 5 | Z102 | 3 | 27/10/2012 | October |
| 6 | Z114 | 5 | 12/01/2012 | January |
| 7 | Z105 | 4 | 16/04/2012 | April |
| 8 | Z102 | 4 | 05/07/2012 | July |
| 9 | Z108 | 4 | 19/11/2012 | November |
| 10 | Z103 | 2 | 28/02/2012 | February |
| 11 | Z113 | 3 | 04/07/2012 | July |
| 12 | Z108 | 3 | 12/01/2012 | January |
| 13 | Z113 | 2 | 01/07/2012 | July |

Here, we may wish to add a subtotal to show the total sales by each product. To do this, we must sort by product first.

See **chapter 4** for more detail on sorting data.

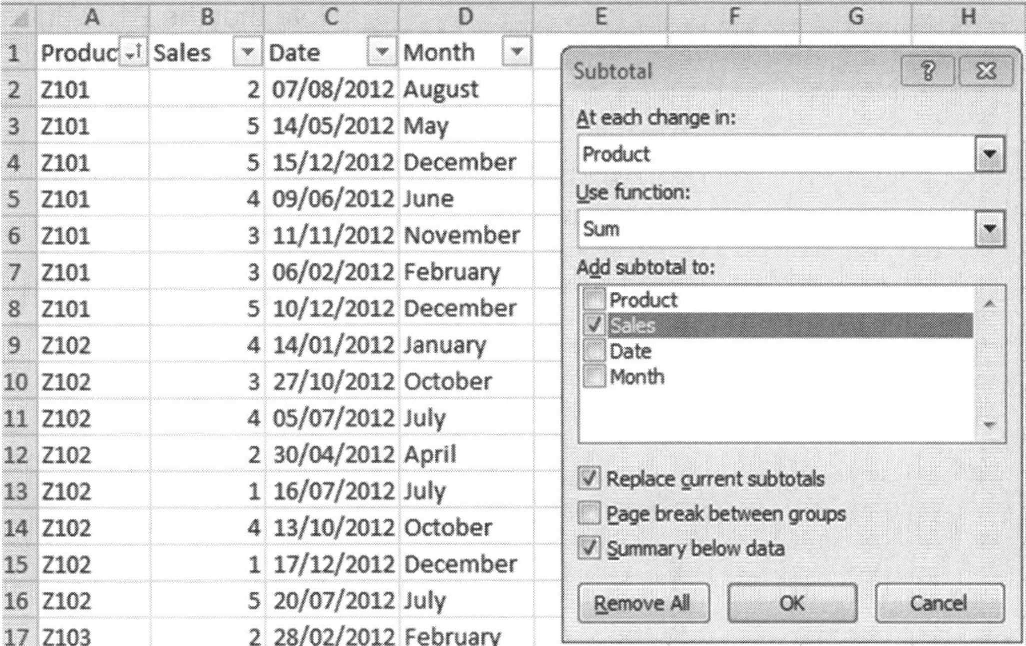

| | Product | Sales | Date | Month |
|---|---|---|---|---|
| 2 | Z101 | 2 | 07/08/2012 | August |
| 3 | Z101 | 5 | 14/05/2012 | May |
| 4 | Z101 | 5 | 15/12/2012 | December |
| 5 | Z101 | 4 | 09/06/2012 | June |
| 6 | Z101 | 3 | 11/11/2012 | November |
| 7 | Z101 | 3 | 06/02/2012 | February |
| 8 | Z101 | 5 | 10/12/2012 | December |
| 9 | Z102 | 4 | 14/01/2012 | January |
| 10 | Z102 | 3 | 27/10/2012 | October |
| 11 | Z102 | 4 | 05/07/2012 | July |
| 12 | Z102 | 2 | 30/04/2012 | April |
| 13 | Z102 | 1 | 16/07/2012 | July |
| 14 | Z102 | 4 | 13/10/2012 | October |
| 15 | Z102 | 1 | 17/12/2012 | December |
| 16 | Z102 | 5 | 20/07/2012 | July |
| 17 | Z103 | 2 | 28/02/2012 | February |



Once the data is sorted, select it, and click the **subtotal** button.

The Subtotal dialogue box will appear. Choose the column you wish to subtotal by – we wish to add a subtotal at each change in product.

The function depends on the information you need. We want a total of the sales, so use **SUM**.

As we want to find the total sales, this is the column we need a subtotal for – note that more than one column can be chosen.

The options at the bottom can be checked or unchecked depending on what you need. Click OK to complete the subtotals.

## 1.3 Grouping

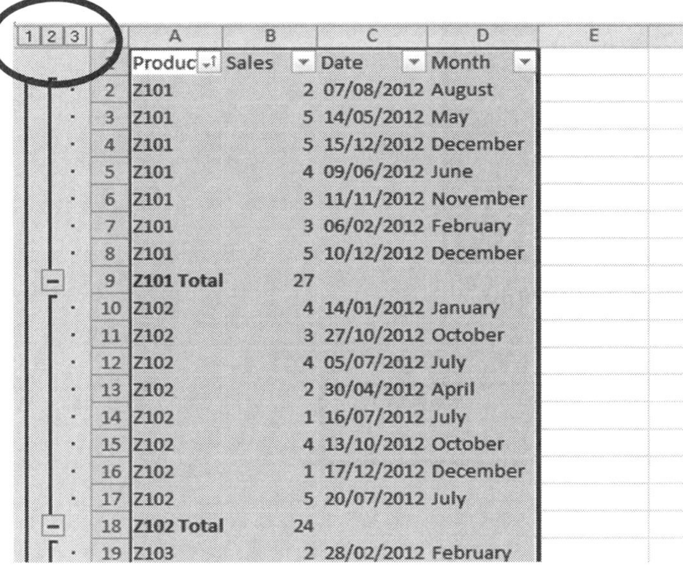

| | Product | Sales | Date | Month |
|---|---|---|---|---|
| 2 | Z101 | 2 | 07/08/2012 | August |
| 3 | Z101 | 5 | 14/05/2012 | May |
| 4 | Z101 | 5 | 15/12/2012 | December |
| 5 | Z101 | 4 | 09/06/2012 | June |
| 6 | Z101 | 3 | 11/11/2012 | November |
| 7 | Z101 | 3 | 06/02/2012 | February |
| 8 | Z101 | 5 | 10/12/2012 | December |
| 9 | **Z101 Total** | 27 | | |
| 10 | Z102 | 4 | 14/01/2012 | January |
| 11 | Z102 | 3 | 27/10/2012 | October |
| 12 | Z102 | 4 | 05/07/2012 | July |
| 13 | Z102 | 2 | 30/04/2012 | April |
| 14 | Z102 | 1 | 16/07/2012 | July |
| 15 | Z102 | 4 | 13/10/2012 | October |
| 16 | Z102 | 1 | 17/12/2012 | December |
| 17 | Z102 | 5 | 20/07/2012 | July |
| 18 | **Z102 Total** | 24 | | |
| 19 | Z103 | 2 | 28/02/2012 | February |

The subtotals are added below each set of data, as required. Note that some extra buttons have appeared on the left of the sheet too – these allow you to quickly hide and show data. Clicking on the **[–]** boxes will hide the data concerned.

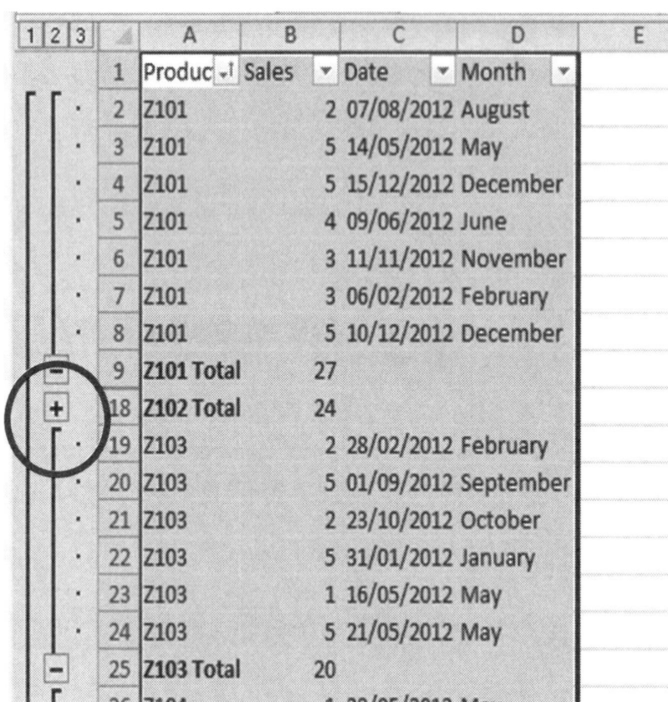

| | A | B | C | D |
|---|---|---|---|---|
| 1 | Product | Sales | Date | Month |
| 2 | Z101 | 2 | 07/08/2012 | August |
| 3 | Z101 | 5 | 14/05/2012 | May |
| 4 | Z101 | 5 | 15/12/2012 | December |
| 5 | Z101 | 4 | 09/06/2012 | June |
| 6 | Z101 | 3 | 11/11/2012 | November |
| 7 | Z101 | 3 | 06/02/2012 | February |
| 8 | Z101 | 5 | 10/12/2012 | December |
| 9 | **Z101 Total** | 27 | | |
| 18 | **Z102 Total** | 24 | | |
| 19 | Z103 | 2 | 28/02/2012 | February |
| 20 | Z103 | 5 | 01/09/2012 | September |
| 21 | Z103 | 2 | 23/10/2012 | October |
| 22 | Z103 | 5 | 31/01/2012 | January |
| 23 | Z103 | 1 | 16/05/2012 | May |
| 24 | Z103 | 5 | 21/05/2012 | May |
| 25 | **Z103 Total** | 20 | | |

Note that the Z102 data is summarised. Clicking on the + will show it again. This is an example of Grouping.

You can also specify what level of data is shown with the 1, 2, 3 buttons in the top left of the screen. The higher the number the more data is shown – clicking **3** will show all data. **2** will hide the lowest level of data:

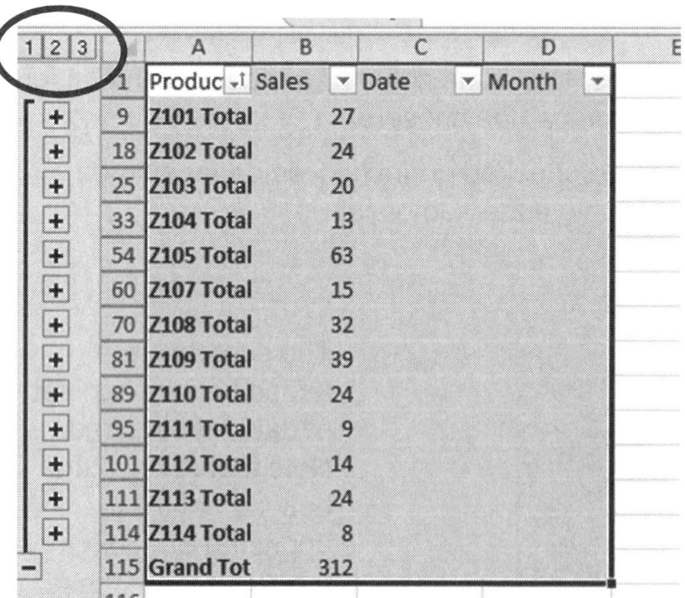

| | A | B | C | D |
|---|---|---|---|---|
| 1 | Product | Sales | Date | Month |
| 9 | **Z101 Total** | 27 | | |
| 18 | **Z102 Total** | 24 | | |
| 25 | **Z103 Total** | 20 | | |
| 33 | **Z104 Total** | 13 | | |
| 54 | **Z105 Total** | 63 | | |
| 60 | **Z107 Total** | 15 | | |
| 70 | **Z108 Total** | 32 | | |
| 81 | **Z109 Total** | 39 | | |
| 89 | **Z110 Total** | 24 | | |
| 95 | **Z111 Total** | 9 | | |
| 101 | **Z112 Total** | 14 | | |
| 111 | **Z113 Total** | 24 | | |
| 114 | **Z114 Total** | 8 | | |
| 115 | **Grand Tot** | 312 | | |

Clicking 1 will show the Grand Total only.

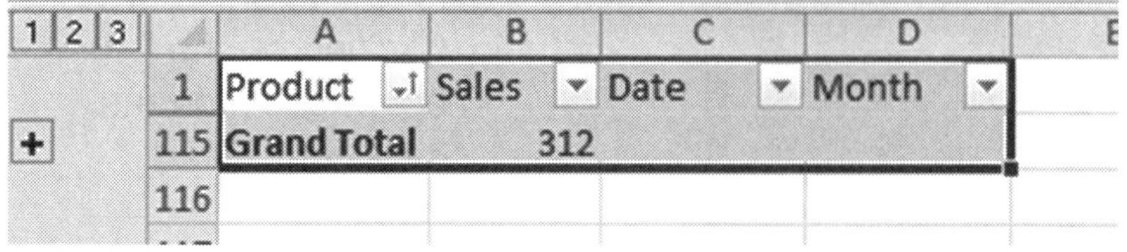

| | A | B | C | D |
|---|---|---|---|---|
| 1 | Product | Sales | Date | Month |
| 115 | **Grand Total** | 312 | | |
| 116 | | | | |

## 1.4 Removing subtotals

Removing subtotals is done in a similar way to adding subtotals – select the data with the subtotals on, and click the **Subtotal** button.

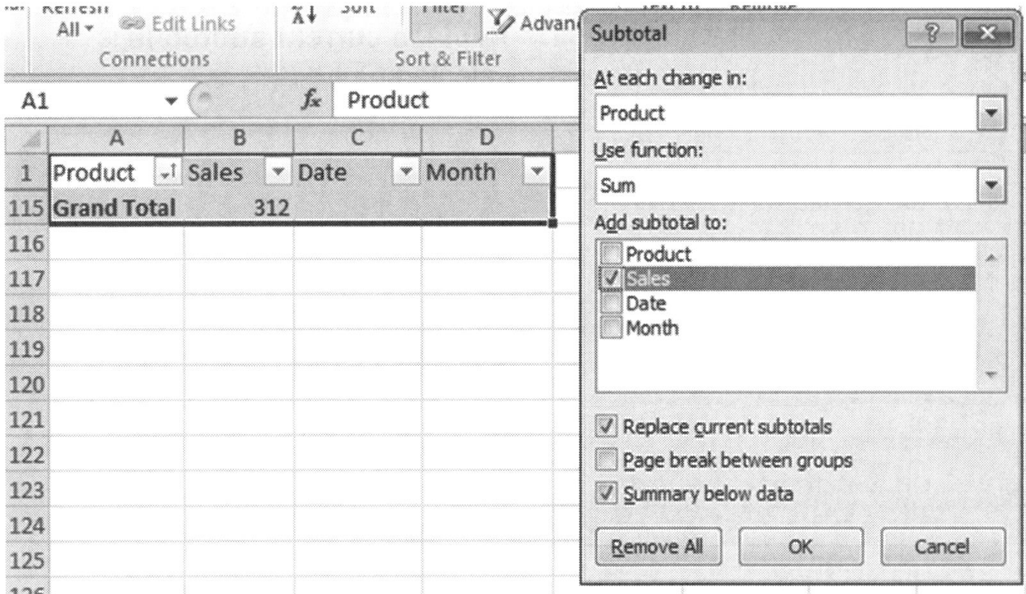


Click the **Remove All** button the remove the subtotals.

## 1.5 Multiple subtotals

It is possible to have more than one subtotal on a data set. For example we may wish to show sales by product, but then summarised by month within each product.

As with normal subtotalling, the data must be sorted accordingly – if we need to subtotal on 2 bases, we must sort by the column we are subtotalling on first, then by the second subtotal column.

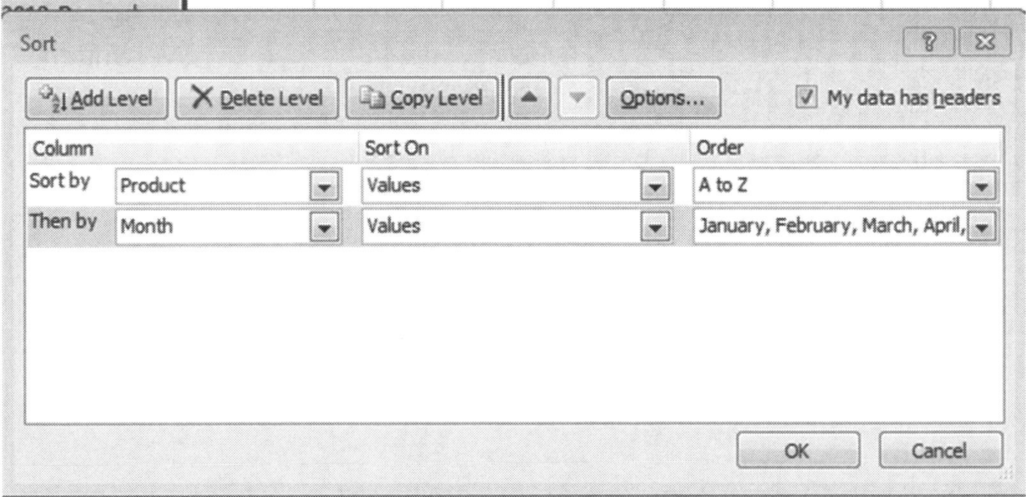

Add the first subtotal in the normal way:

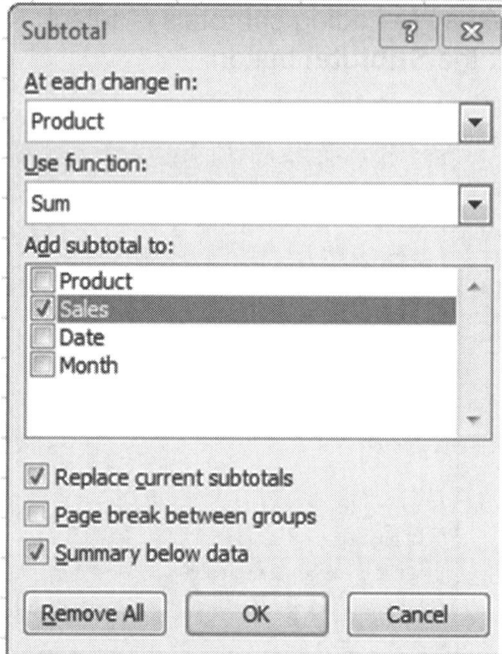


If you already have a subtotal in place, it will be overwritten as **Replace current subtotals** is selected.

To add the second subtotal, simply select the data again (although it should still be selected), and click subtotal again.

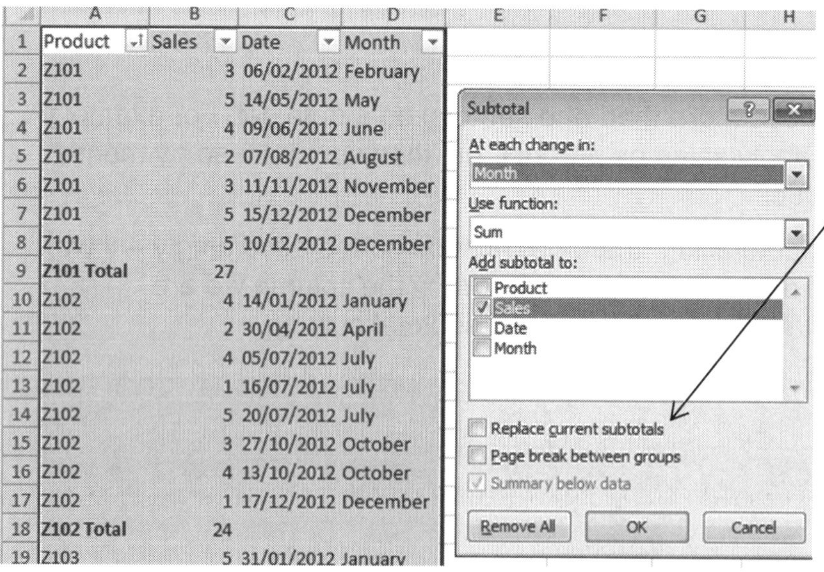


It is essential here that **Replace current subtotals** is unchecked, otherwise the first subtotal will be overwritten.

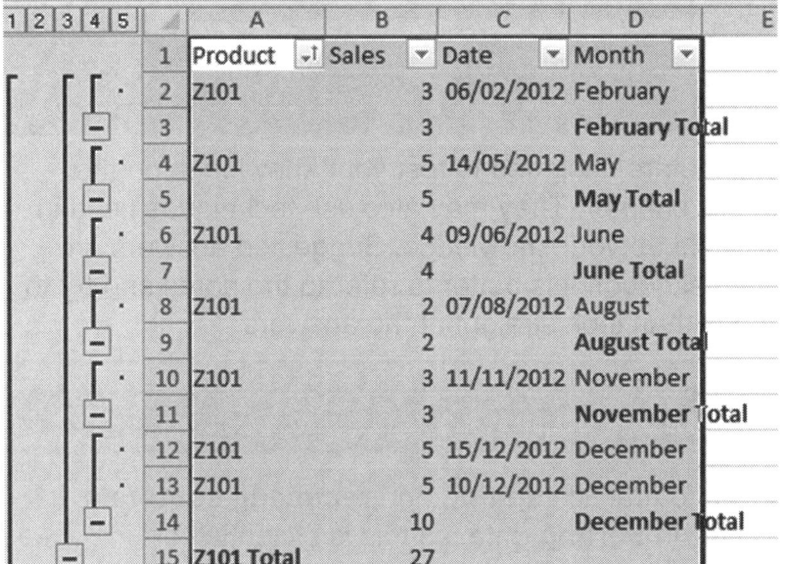

The second subtotals will be inserted. You can see there are now five levels of data to display, and these can be used to quickly show what we need to see.

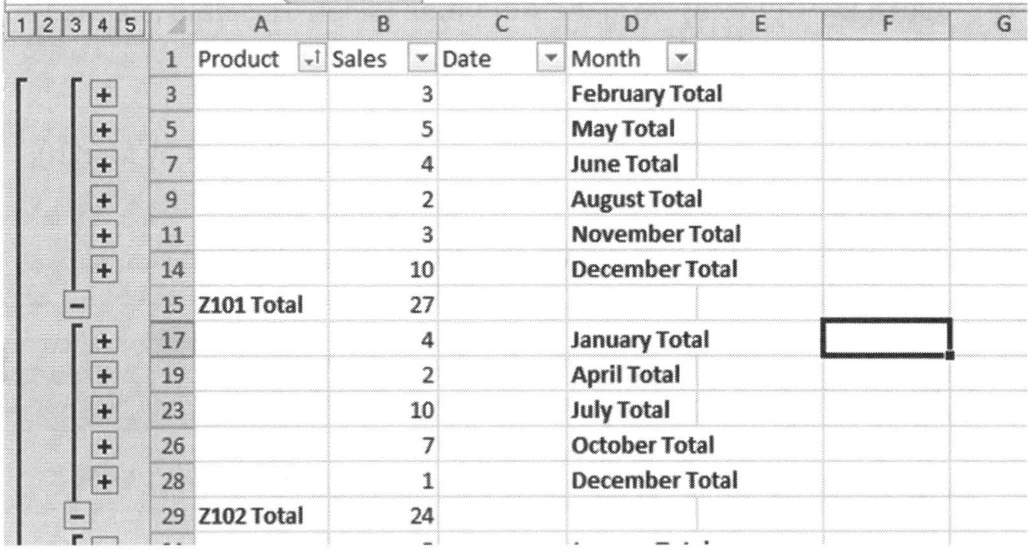

Level 4 shows the totals for each product and month.

# 2 Test your understanding

The activities in this guide are designed to test your knowledge on the techniques shown in this chapter. They may also use techniques used in previous chapters, to build up your knowledge. Suggested answers are available on MyKaplan, although it is better to refer to the notes and try to understand the methods than look straight at the answers.

## Test your understanding 9-1

This activity allows you to practice **adding** and **removing subtotals**. It also acts as a reminder on **Sorting** data, as this is essential for subtotalling.

(a) Open the **Subtotal** file in the **Activities** folder. This data is already subtotalled by Product.

(b) Remove the subtotals.

(c) Add subtotals for Quantity and Revenue by month (sort by Month).

(d) Select grouping level 2 – to show the monthly totals.

(e) Save the file as **Activity 9-1** in the **Solutions** folder.

## Test your understanding 9-2

This activity allows you to practice **adding** and **removing subtotals**. It also acts as a reminder on **Sorting** data, as this is essential for subtotalling.

(a) Open the **Subtotal** file in the **Activities** folder. This data is already subtotalled by Product.

(b) Remove the subtotals.

(c) Sort the data by Month and by Product Code.

(d) Add a subtotal of Sales Quantity and Revenue by month.

(d) Add another subtotal by Product Code (keeping the other subtotals).

(e) Select grouping level 3 – to show the monthly and product subtotals.

(f) Save the file as **Activity 9-2** in the **Solutions** folder.

# Panes, windows and split

10

## Introduction

This chapter will explain to you how to freeze panes and show you how to view two or more worksheets side by side.

### ASSESSMENT CRITERIA

Format data (2.3)

### CONTENTS

# 1 Panes, windows and split

## 1.1 Introduction

Each of the options required are found on the **View** tab, in the **Window** menu.

# 2 Freeze panes

## 2.1 Freeze panes

When you have a lot of data in a spreadsheet and you want to scroll down or across, it is very handy to be able to 'Freeze Panes'. When you do this Excel will 'freeze' in position all rows above the 'Active Cell' and all columns to the left of the 'Active Cell'.

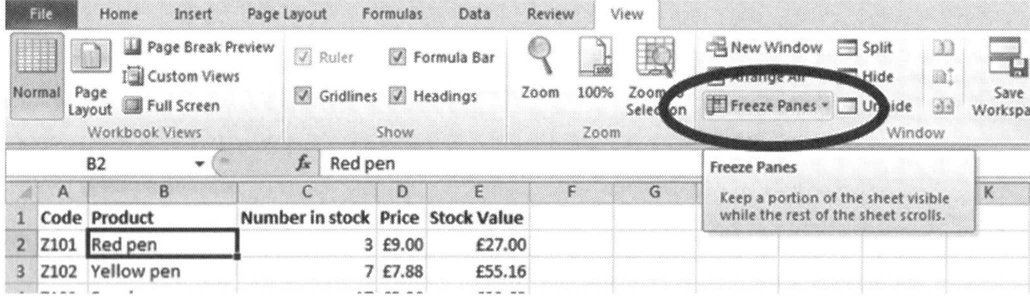


Click on the **Freeze Panes** button within the **View** tab to turn freeze on or off.

This is very useful for large spreadsheets where you want the header row(s) to stay visible, and possibly the first column(s).

# 3 Windows

## 3.1 Windows

It is possible to view 2 or more workbooks at the same time. You need to open the workbooks that you want to view first, and then select the **Arrange All** button.

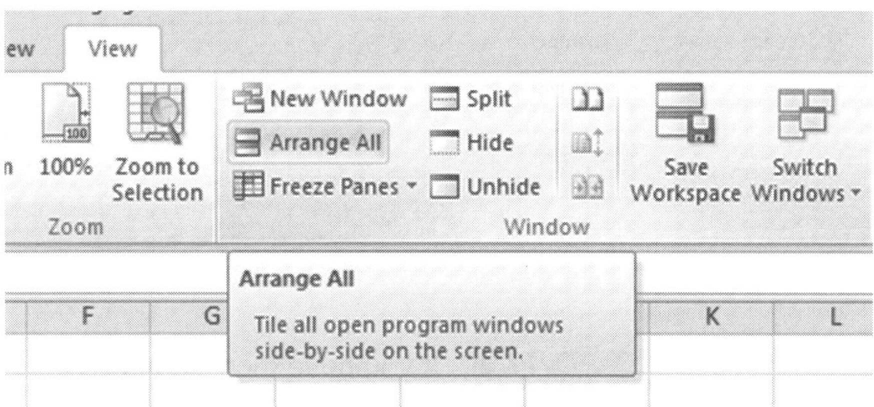


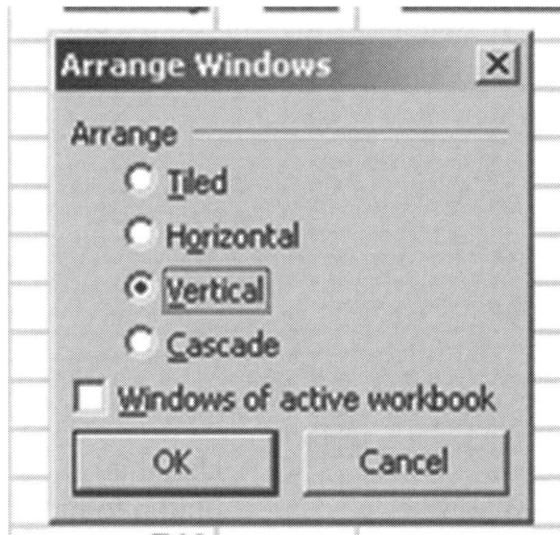


Horizontal and Vertical are often the best options. Using this method you get the opportunity to have one or the other of the workbooks as 'Active', and you can work and move around in it. It would be useful to do this if you were using data from one worksheet to create formulas in another.

### 3.2 View side-by-side

This is an extension of the Arrange option. You can compare two workbooks side by side. Using this option you can enable **synchronous scrolling** – in effect both workbooks are 'active', so if you scroll down in one, the other scrolls down too.

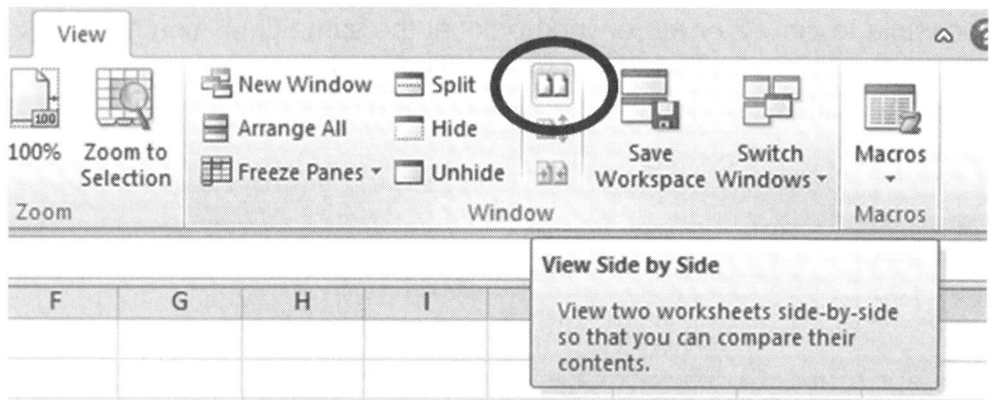


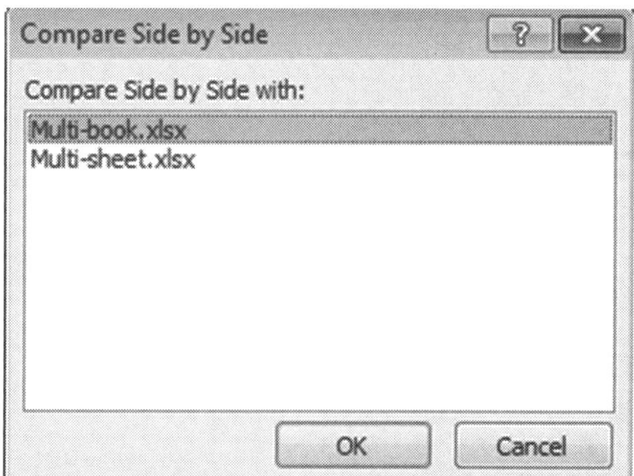


If you have more than two workbooks open, you will be asked which one you wish to compare with the active book.

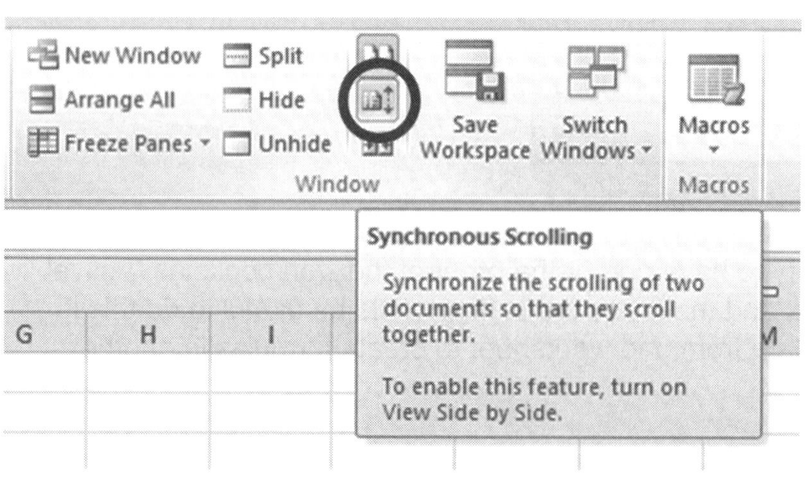


Use this button to turn synchronous scrolling on or off when in this view.

# 4 Split

## 4.1 Splitting a worksheet

This tool is used when you have a great deal of similar data in a worksheet and you wish to make a comparison to 2 different parts.

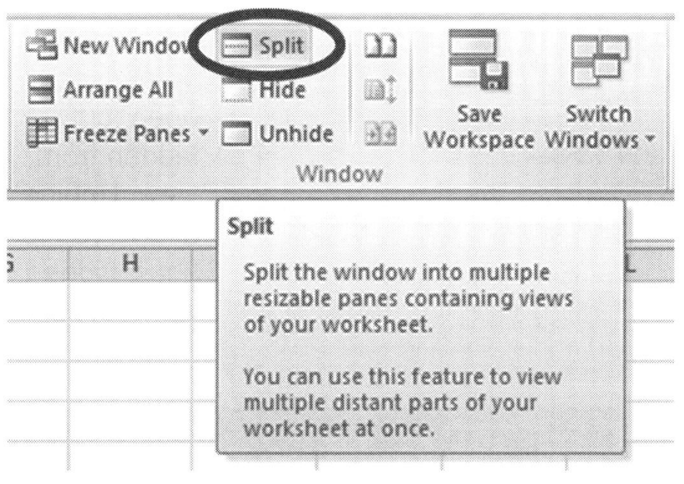


Select this option to split the worksheet into different 'panes'.

The split will occur above and to the left of the active cell.

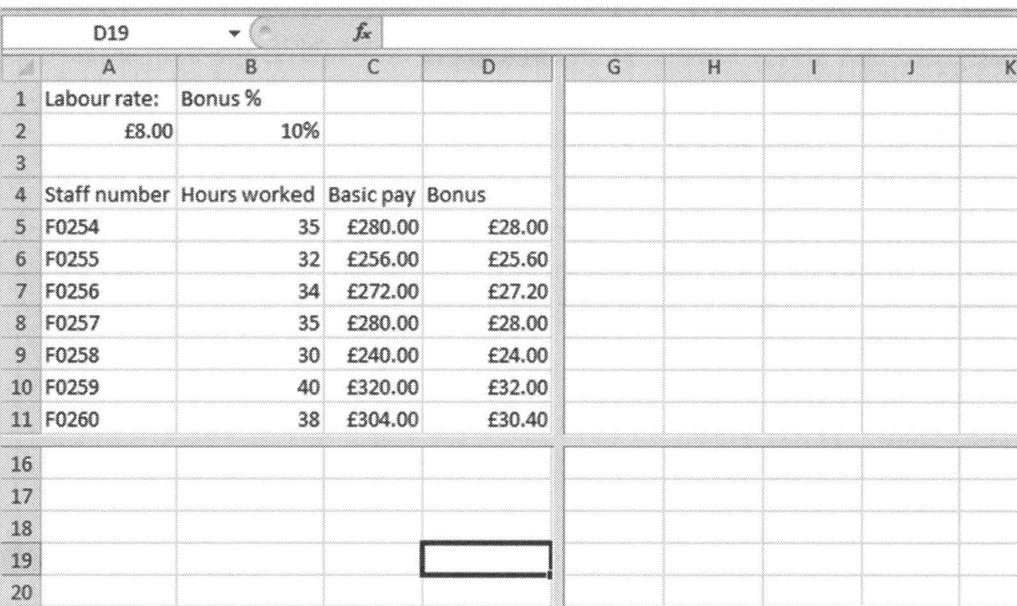

D19

| | A | B | C | D | G | H | I | J | K |
|---|---|---|---|---|---|---|---|---|---|
| 1 | Labour rate: | Bonus % | | | | | | | |
| 2 | £8.00 | 10% | | | | | | | |
| 3 | | | | | | | | | |
| 4 | Staff number | Hours worked | Basic pay | Bonus | | | | | |
| 5 | F0254 | 35 | £280.00 | £28.00 | | | | | |
| 6 | F0255 | 32 | £256.00 | £25.60 | | | | | |
| 7 | F0256 | 34 | £272.00 | £27.20 | | | | | |
| 8 | F0257 | 35 | £280.00 | £28.00 | | | | | |
| 9 | F0258 | 30 | £240.00 | £24.00 | | | | | |
| 10 | F0259 | 40 | £320.00 | £32.00 | | | | | |
| 11 | F0260 | 38 | £304.00 | £30.40 | | | | | |
| 16 | | | | | | | | | |
| 17 | | | | | | | | | |
| 18 | | | | | | | | | |
| 19 | | | | | | | | | |
| 20 | | | | | | | | | |

The panes can be resized by dragging on the borders as required. Click on the **Split** button again to remove the split.

# 5 Hide and unhide

## 5.1 Hide and unhide

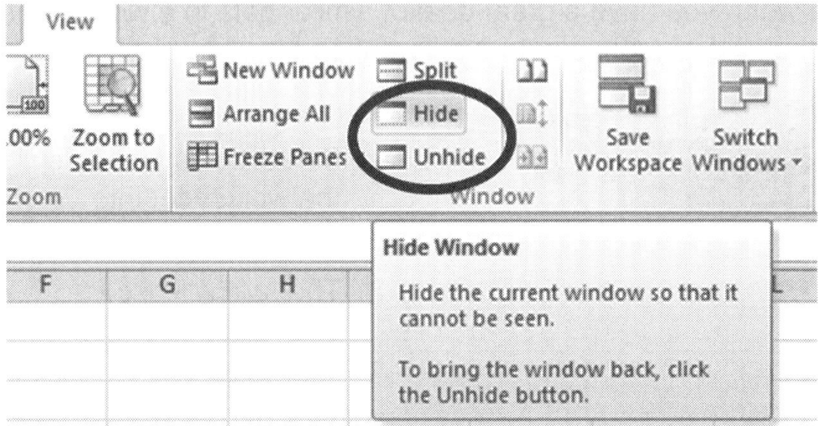


The Hide option can be used to keep a spreadsheet open, but hidden from view. Unhide allows you to show hidden workbooks.

# 6 Test your understanding

These techniques can be used with any spreadsheet – try them out. Have another go at populating the District Totals workbook in Test your understanding 7-6 with the workbooks arranged vertically.

These techniques relate to the appearance of the workbook on the screen, the underlying data will not be affected anyway, so there is no need to worry about accidentally deleting anything important.

# Sharing data

11

## Introduction

This chapter will explain how to import data into different formats, how to link data to other applications, and how to embed data.

### ASSESSMENT CRITERIA

Accurately enter data (2.2)

Prepare reports (5.1)

Report accounting information (5.2)

### CONTENTS

# 1 Types of data formats

## 1.1 Types of data formats

Sometimes we are given data that is not in spreadsheet format and will therefore not open up in Excel within the rows and columns that are provided. This data can be in a number of different formats. In this session we are going to look at data that comes in a **delimited format**. Common types of format could be **Text** [.txt] or **CSV** [.csv] files. These are often 'data dumps' from other systems within an organisation, so this technique is very useful in many practical circumstances.

Delimited data comes with characters such as commas or tabs separating each field. Excel will open these data formats but we need to do some work on them first before they are easily viewed.

## 1.2 CSV files

CSV are probably the most commonly used type of import file. The name means **Comma Separated Values** – each data item is separated by a comma. They can be viewed using programmes such as Microsoft Word or Notepad, and would look something like this.

Stock download.csv - Notepad

File Edit Format View Help

```
Code,Product,Number in stock,Price
Z101,Red pen,3,£9.00
Z102,Yellow pen,7,£7.88
Z103,Purple pen,17,£5.86
Z104,Green pen,13,£1.19
Z105,Red crayon,20,£9.56
Z105,Yellow crayon,4,£7.27
Z107,Purple crayon,9,£1.86
Z108,Green crayon,17,£0.86
Z109,Red ruler,17,£4.55
Z110,Yellow ruler,20,£0.56
Z111,Green ruler,12,£5.35
Z112,Purple ruler,4,£4.88
Z113,Blue calculator,12,£3.53
Z114,Orange calculator,6,£7.16
```

Notice how the rows appear as we would expect to see them, but there are no columns within Notepad, so each data item is separated by a comma. If we copy this into Excel then all the commas would make data manipulation difficult.

While CSV is the most common, any character can be used to separate data items, such as **space**, **semi-colon**, or **tab**.

# 2 Importing data

## 2.1 Importing CSV or other text files

This is performed using the **Get External Data** menu on the **Data** tab.

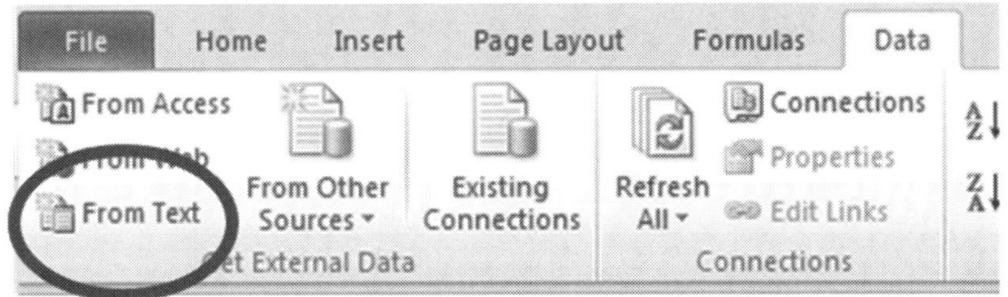


There are a few options here, but the most commonly required is the **From Text** option circled. This allows you to import any type of text file.

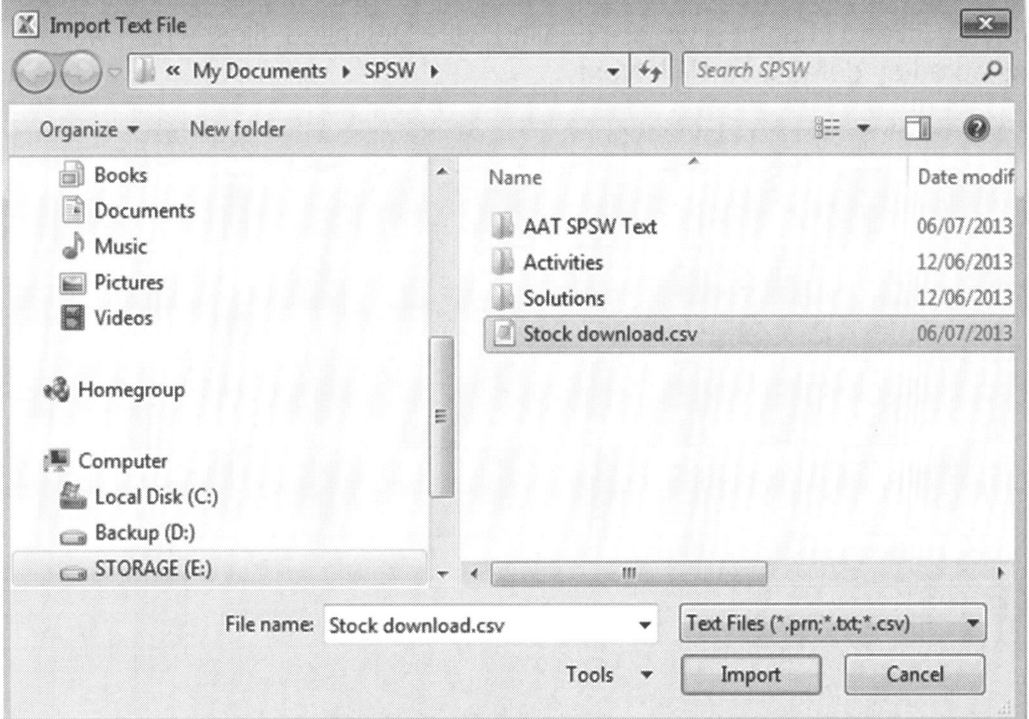


After clicking the **From Text** button, find the file required in the same way as you would when opening a normal Excel file.

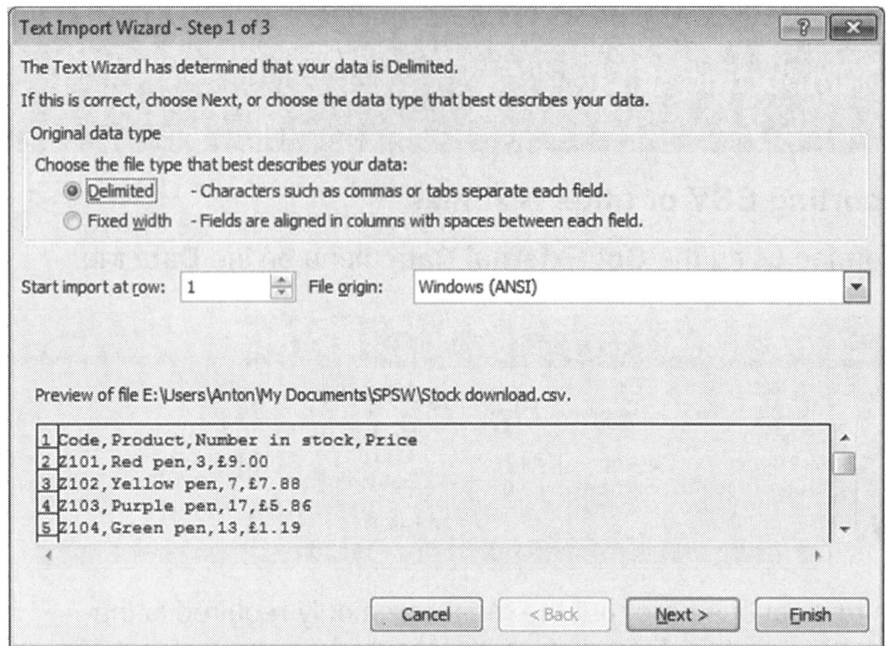


The **Text Import Wizard** will then open. This looks complicated, but there is very little to change – we are dealing with 'Delimited' files, which will be selected by default, so click **Next**.

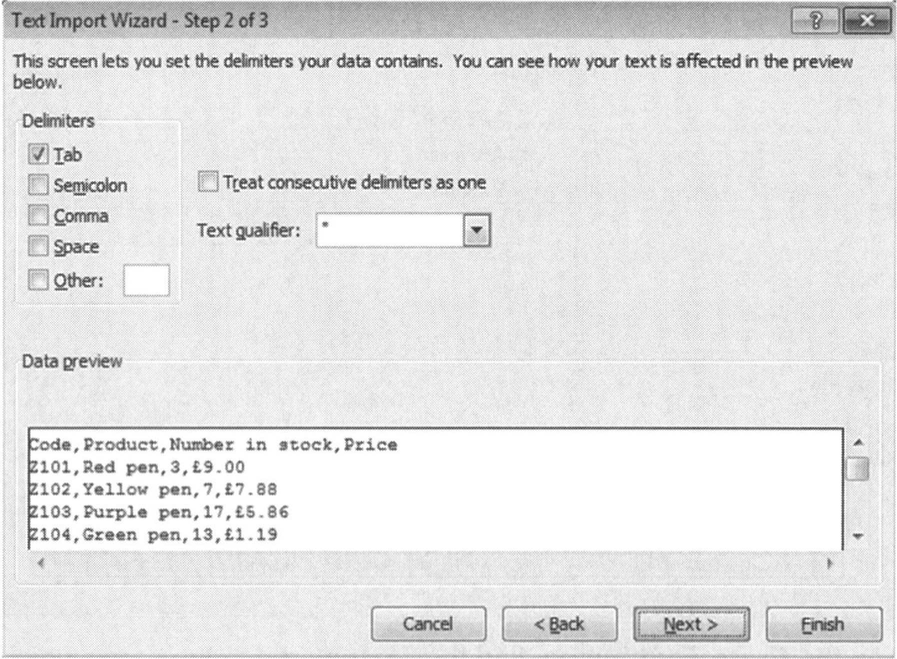


The second step is the most important – choosing the delimiter. We are using a comma delimited file as you see in the data preview box, so select that and unselect tab. It should be fairly clear which character is being used, but if you are not sure try clicking on the different options and see how the preview changes – you will not affect the original data.

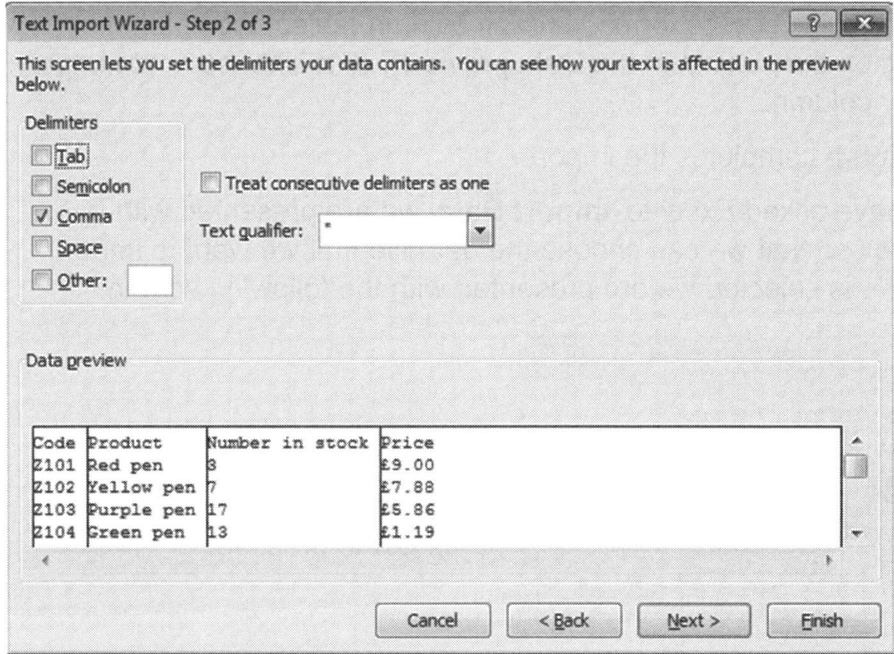


You can see once the correct delimiter is chosen, the commas in the preview are removed and replaced with column breaks, which is exactly what is required. The next step allows each column of data to be formatted or ignored in the import but as we can do that within Excel we could click on **Finish** now. For reference let us look at the final step.

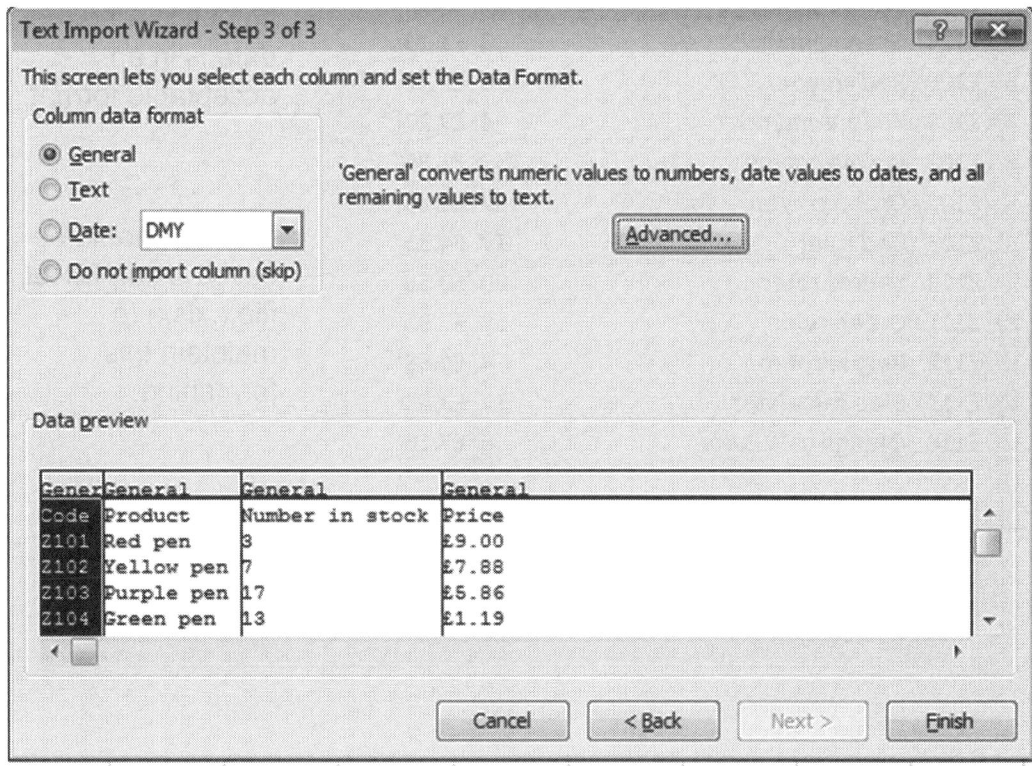

This allows you to set the format of each column (select the column by left-clicking on the column in the Data preview), or to choose not to import a particular column.

Clicking **Finish** completes the import.

Once we have asked Excel to '**Import Data**' we are presented with a dialogue box so that we can choose the data file that we want to import. Once the file is selected we are presented with the following screen.

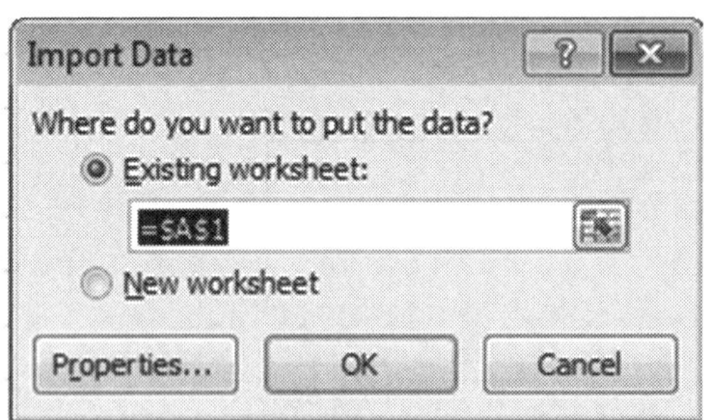


You can then select where you would like the data to be placed. The default is usually acceptable. Click **OK** to proceed.

| | A | B | C | D | E |
|---|---|---|---|---|---|
| 1 | Code | Product | Number in stock | Price | |
| 2 | Z101 | Red pen | 3 | £9.00 | |
| 3 | Z102 | Yellow pen | 7 | £7.88 | |
| 4 | Z103 | Purple pen | 17 | £5.86 | |
| 5 | Z104 | Green pen | 13 | £1.19 | |
| 6 | Z105 | Red crayon | 20 | £9.56 | |
| 7 | Z105 | Yellow crayon | 4 | £7.27 | |
| 8 | Z107 | Purple crayon | 9 | £1.86 | |
| 9 | Z108 | Green crayon | 17 | £0.86 | |
| 10 | Z109 | Red ruler | 17 | £4.55 | |
| 11 | Z110 | Yellow ruler | 20 | £0.56 | |
| 12 | Z111 | Green ruler | 12 | £5.35 | |
| 13 | Z112 | Purple ruler | 4 | £4.88 | |
| 14 | Z113 | Blue calculator | 12 | £3.53 | |
| 15 | Z114 | Orange calculator | 6 | £7.16 | |
| 16 | | | | | |
| 17 | | | | | |

The import is complete, and the data is in an acceptable format.

The file should be saved as an Excel file (.xlsx) to maintain this formatting.

# 3 Copying data

## 3.1 Embedding data

Embedding data is effectively a copy and paste from Excel to another Microsoft Office application such as Word.

To **embed** the data:

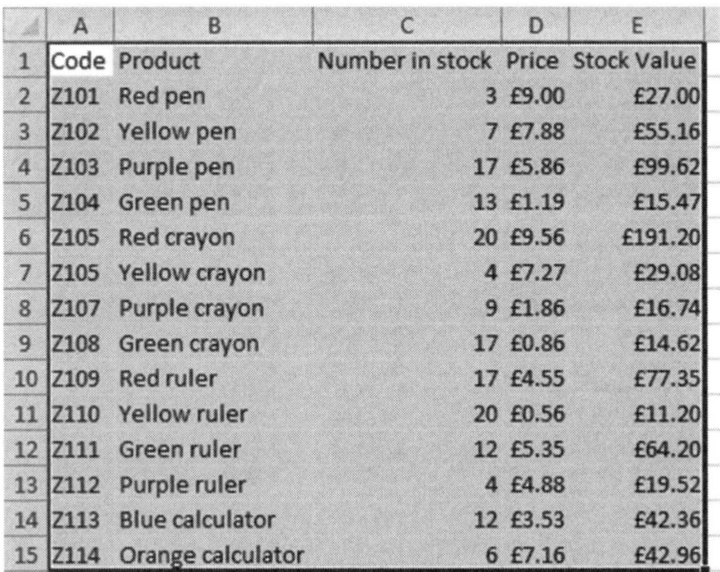

| | A | B | C | D | E |
|---|---|---|---|---|---|
| 1 | Code | Product | Number in stock | Price | Stock Value |
| 2 | Z101 | Red pen | 3 | £9.00 | £27.00 |
| 3 | Z102 | Yellow pen | 7 | £7.88 | £55.16 |
| 4 | Z103 | Purple pen | 17 | £5.86 | £99.62 |
| 5 | Z104 | Green pen | 13 | £1.19 | £15.47 |
| 6 | Z105 | Red crayon | 20 | £9.56 | £191.20 |
| 7 | Z105 | Yellow crayon | 4 | £7.27 | £29.08 |
| 8 | Z107 | Purple crayon | 9 | £1.86 | £16.74 |
| 9 | Z108 | Green crayon | 17 | £0.86 | £14.62 |
| 10 | Z109 | Red ruler | 17 | £4.55 | £77.35 |
| 11 | Z110 | Yellow ruler | 20 | £0.56 | £11.20 |
| 12 | Z111 | Green ruler | 12 | £5.35 | £64.20 |
| 13 | Z112 | Purple ruler | 4 | £4.88 | £19.52 |
| 14 | Z113 | Blue calculator | 12 | £3.53 | £42.36 |
| 15 | Z114 | Orange calculator | 6 | £7.16 | £42.96 |

**Copy** the data in the usual way – highlight and **Ctrl-C** is usually quickest.

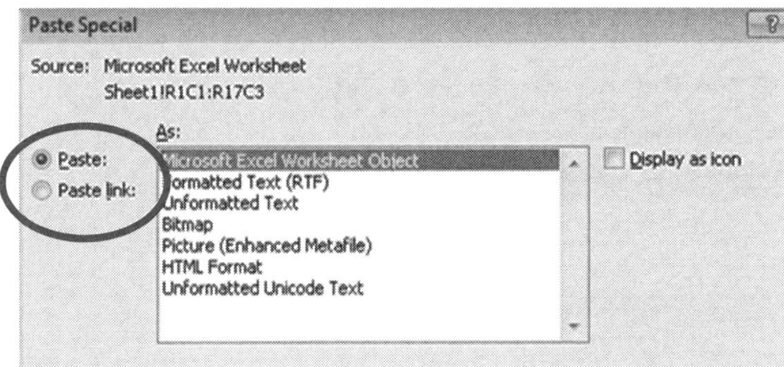


In Word, or whichever application you wish to paste the data into, select Paste Special and choose Paste.

The data is embedded in Word. It can be edited by double-clicking within the data.

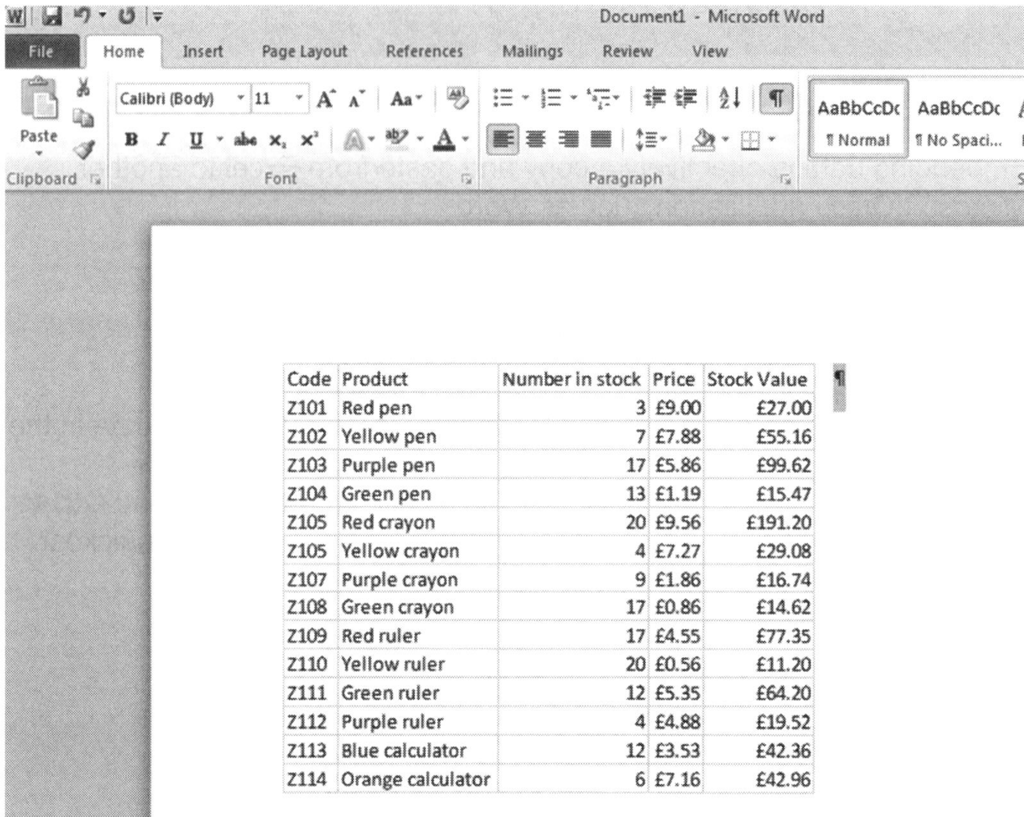


| Code | Product | Number in stock | Price | Stock Value |
|---|---|---|---|---|
| Z101 | Red pen | 3 | £9.00 | £27.00 |
| Z102 | Yellow pen | 7 | £7.88 | £55.16 |
| Z103 | Purple pen | 17 | £5.86 | £99.62 |
| Z104 | Green pen | 13 | £1.19 | £15.47 |
| Z105 | Red crayon | 20 | £9.56 | £191.20 |
| Z105 | Yellow crayon | 4 | £7.27 | £29.08 |
| Z107 | Purple crayon | 9 | £1.86 | £16.74 |
| Z108 | Green crayon | 17 | £0.86 | £14.62 |
| Z109 | Red ruler | 17 | £4.55 | £77.35 |
| Z110 | Yellow ruler | 20 | £0.56 | £11.20 |
| Z111 | Green ruler | 12 | £5.35 | £64.20 |
| Z112 | Purple ruler | 4 | £4.88 | £19.52 |
| Z113 | Blue calculator | 12 | £3.53 | £42.36 |
| Z114 | Orange calculator | 6 | £7.16 | £42.96 |

This will effectively open Excel within Word, and allow you to edit as required.

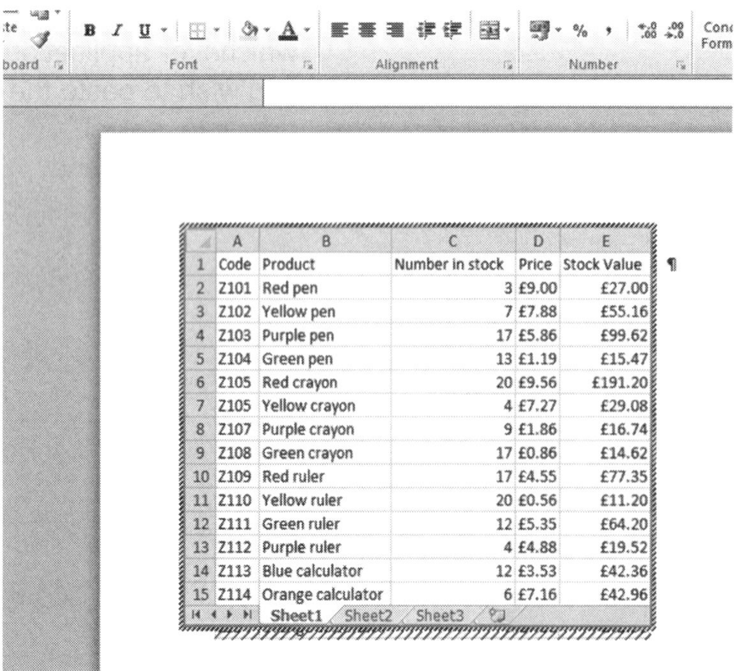


| | A | B | C | D | E |
|---|---|---|---|---|---|
| 1 | Code | Product | Number in stock | Price | Stock Value |
| 2 | Z101 | Red pen | 3 | £9.00 | £27.00 |
| 3 | Z102 | Yellow pen | 7 | £7.88 | £55.16 |
| 4 | Z103 | Purple pen | 17 | £5.86 | £99.62 |
| 5 | Z104 | Green pen | 13 | £1.19 | £15.47 |
| 6 | Z105 | Red crayon | 20 | £9.56 | £191.20 |
| 7 | Z105 | Yellow crayon | 4 | £7.27 | £29.08 |
| 8 | Z107 | Purple crayon | 9 | £1.86 | £16.74 |
| 9 | Z108 | Green crayon | 17 | £0.86 | £14.62 |
| 10 | Z109 | Red ruler | 17 | £4.55 | £77.35 |
| 11 | Z110 | Yellow ruler | 20 | £0.56 | £11.20 |
| 12 | Z111 | Green ruler | 12 | £5.35 | £64.20 |
| 13 | Z112 | Purple ruler | 4 | £4.88 | £19.52 |
| 14 | Z113 | Blue calculator | 12 | £3.53 | £42.36 |
| 15 | Z114 | Orange calculator | 6 | £7.16 | £42.96 |

## 3.2 Linking data

It is also possible to link a spreadsheet to another Microsoft Office application such as Word. The advantage of doing this is, should you update the spreadsheet then the Word document will also update – once you have told it to do so. This makes it a very useful tool when writing reports that use the same data frequently.

The drawback with linking is that the link can be easily broken by:

- moving the spreadsheet to another place or
- renaming the spreadsheet.

If you break the link you will have to establish the link once again.

To **link** the data to the original Excel file, select Paste Special and then **Paste Link**.

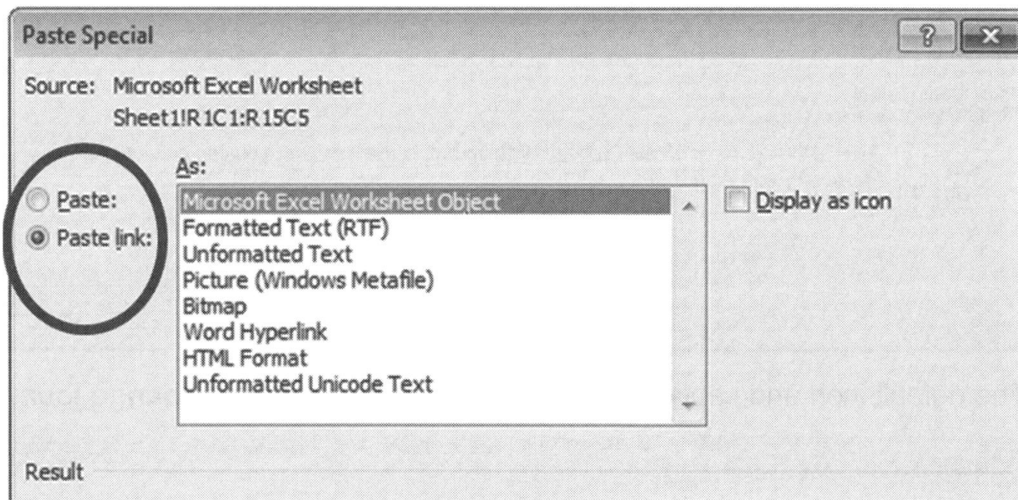


The data will appear in the same way in Word.

If data is updated in the Excel file the Word document will also update once you have told word to do so by right-clicking in the word document and clicking **Update link**.

If you double-click on the data in Word to edit it you will be taken to the original workbook within Excel, rather than editing within Word.

### Display as Icon

Another option you may need is the **Display as Icon** checkbox. Rather than showing the data itself, an icon (picture) of your choice will be shown. This can prevent your document being cluttered with lots of data, and allow users to click on the icon to see the data as required.

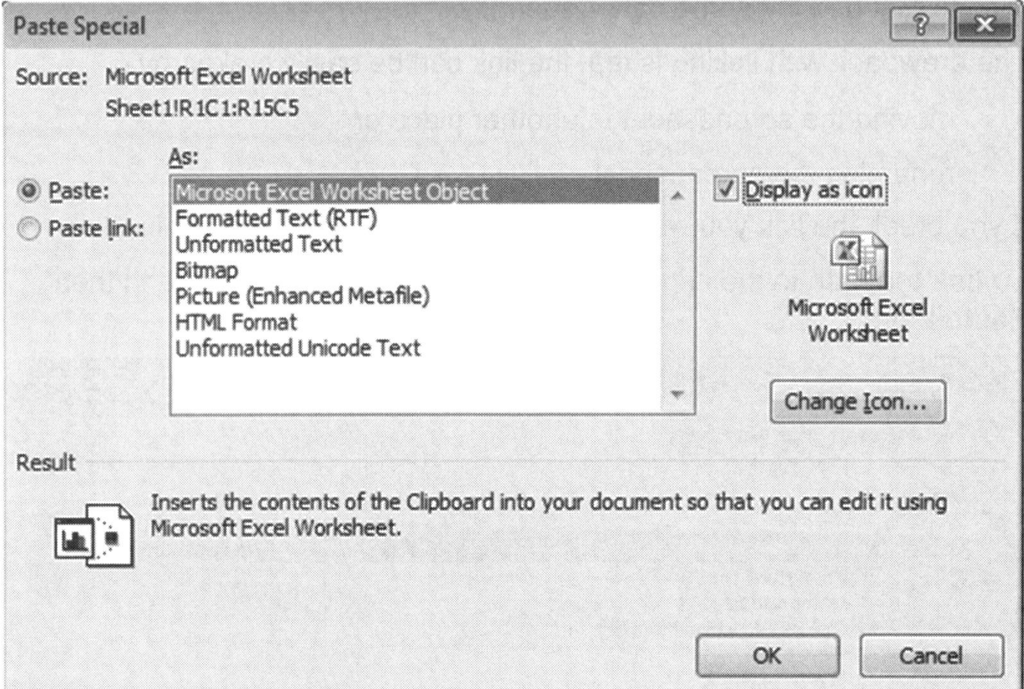


The default icon and caption can be changed by clicking on **Change Icon**.

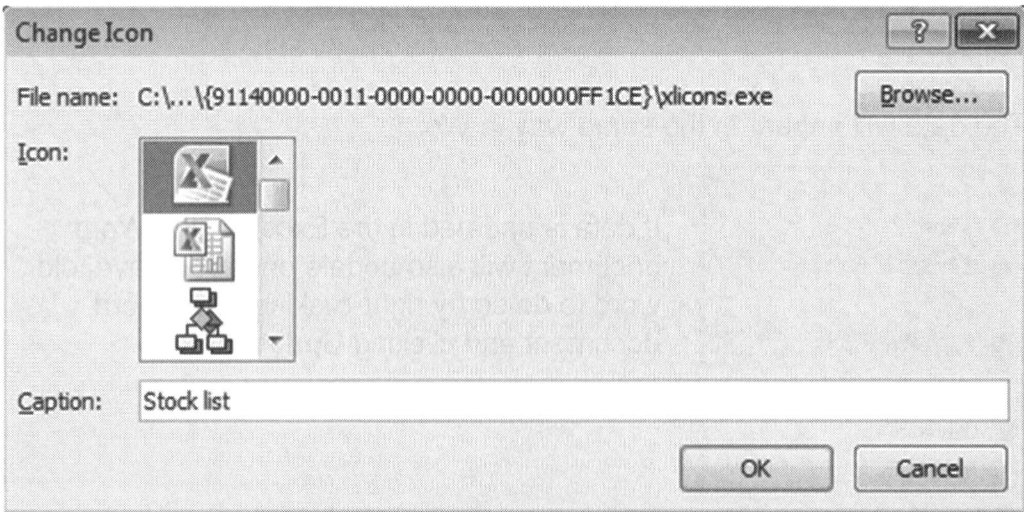

The icon will be shown within the report. This method is the same for both linked and embedded data.

## 3.3 Embedding objects into Excel

It is possible to paste objects such as pictures and word documents into Excel. This is useful if you want to put a logo or picture into a spreadsheet. If you embed a Word document into a spreadsheet you have the facility to use the Word formatting tools. You can either import a blank word document or one that has been previously saved.

This works in the same way as exporting data from Excel – copy the data, and use the **Paste Special** option to embed or link the data.

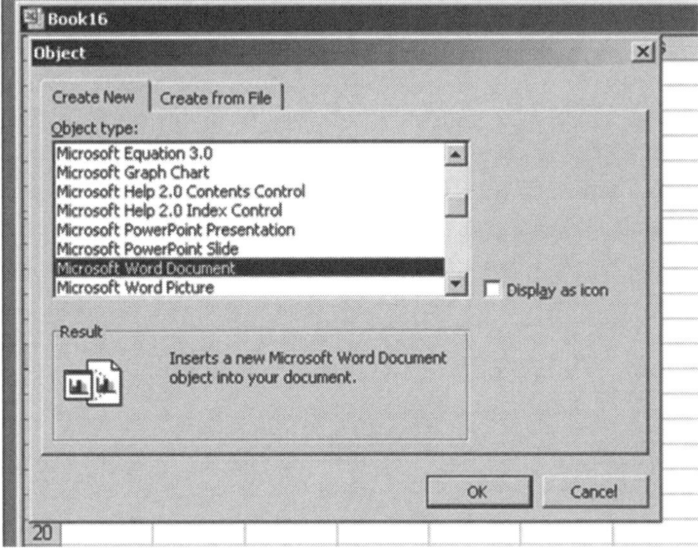

Select the required options to **paste** the information into Excel.

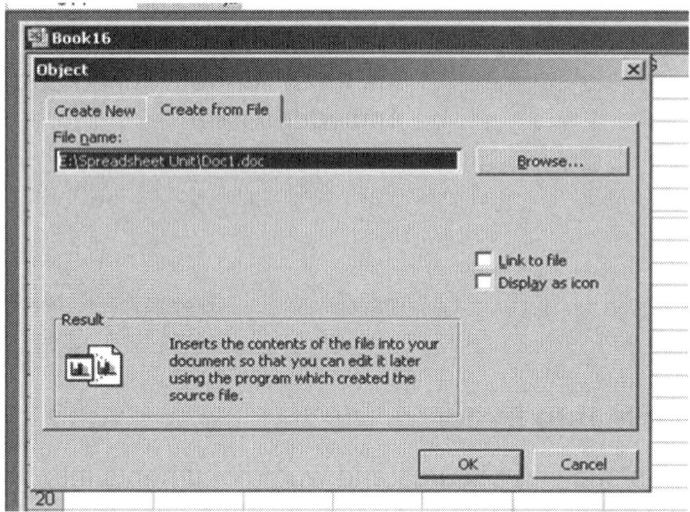

## 4 Test your understanding

The activities in this guide are designed to test your knowledge on the techniques shown in this chapter. They may also use techniques used in previous chapters, to build up your knowledge. Suggested answers are available on MyKaplan, although it is better to refer to the notes and try to understand the methods than look straight at the answers.

### Test your understanding 11-1

This activity allows you to practise importing a text file into Excel.

(a) Open a **New** Excel workbook.

(b) In the **Activities** folder, there is a text file called **exam results**. (you may need to save the text file to be able to access it to import it).

(c) Use the **Get External Data** tool in the **Data** tab to import the text file.

(d) When importing, note that the file is **comma delimited**.

(e) Once the file is imported, save the Excel file as **Activity 11-1** in the **Solutions** folder.

### Test your understanding 11-2

This activity allows you to practise exporting data from Excel into Microsoft Word.

(a) Open a **New Word document** (in the same way you would open a New Excel Document, but from within Word).

(b) In Excel, open the **Eastern Region3** workbook in the **Activities** folder.

(c) Copy all of the data from the Excel Spreadsheet.

(d) Use **Paste Special** within word to **Embed** the Excel information into Word (no link).

(e) Save the Word Document as **Activity 11-2** in the **Solutions** folder, and close it.

## Test your understanding 11-3

This activity allows you to practise exporting data from Excel into Microsoft Word.

(a) Open a **New Word document** (in the same way you would open a New Excel Document, but from within Word).

(b) In Excel, open the **Eastern Region3** workbook in the **Activities** folder.

(c) Copy all of the data from the Excel Spreadsheet.

(d) Use **Paste Special** within word to **Link** the Excel information into Word.

(e) Change the value in cell C2 of the Excel worksheet to 9999. In the word document right click and update the link. Check that the value in the Word document is also changed.

(f) Save the Word Document as **Activity 11-3** in the **Solutions** folder, and close it.

(g) Close the Excel file without saving.

# Formulas and functions

12

## Introduction

This chapter will look at the various formulas and functions that are used in Excel and you will learn how to evaluate and write complex formulas.

It is common for these functions to be used together to get formulas to work effectively.

### ASSESSMENT CRITERIA

Select and use a range of appropriate formulas and functions to perform calculations (3.1)

Select and use relevant tools to analyse and interpret data (3.2)

### CONTENTS

# 1 ROUND

## 1.1 ROUND

We have seen how to change the format of cells so that values can be shown with different amounts of decimal places are shown. One important feature of formatting that is often overlooked is that changing the format does not affect the number used.

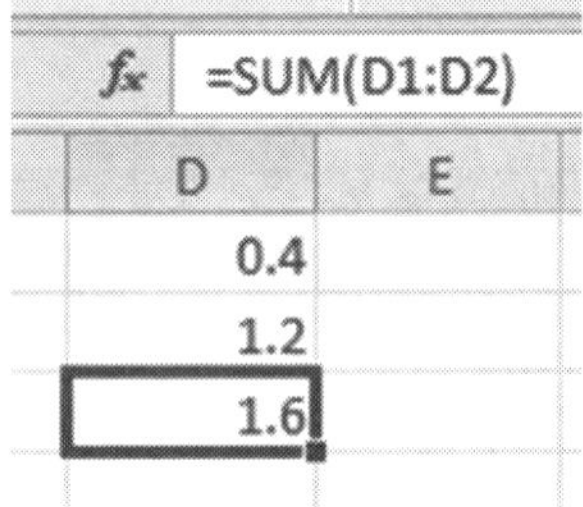


Taking a simple example, 0.4 + 1.2 = 1.6

If we change the formatting to show these numbers to 0 decimal places, the result looks odd:

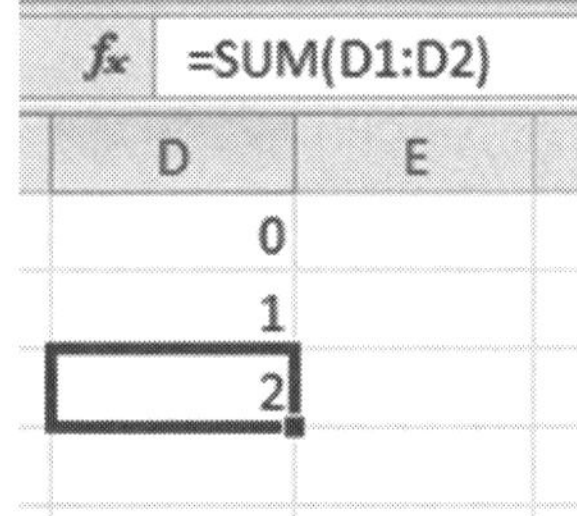


According to this, 0 + 1 = 2!

This is because Excel uses the value in the cell, not the displayed format to perform the calculation – it is still calculating 0.4 + 1.2, then rounding to 0 decimal places.

Instead of changing the format, you may wish to instruct Excel to round the numbers to a certain number of decimal places – this is often useful when dealing with currency – round to 2 decimal places. To do this, use the **ROUND** function. Like all functions in Excel, it has a set format:

**=ROUND(number,num_digits)**

- 'number' and 'num_digits' are the ARGUMENTS
- **number** is the number or cell reference which needs rounding
- **num_digits** is the number of decimal places you wish to round to.

For example, if you type =ROUND(4.5682,3), the value shown will be 4.568 – rounded to 3 decimal places:

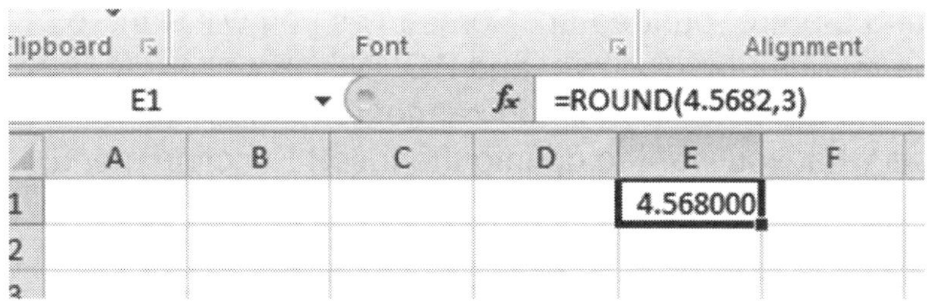

The formatting is shown to 6 decimal places, but the number has been rounded to 3.

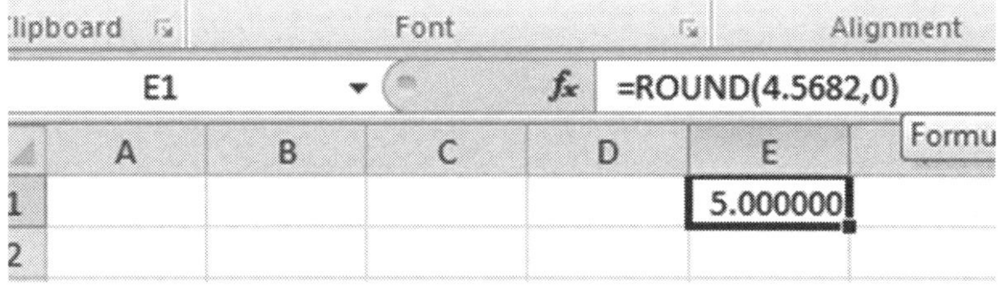

To round to the nearest number, use 0 for **num_digits**.

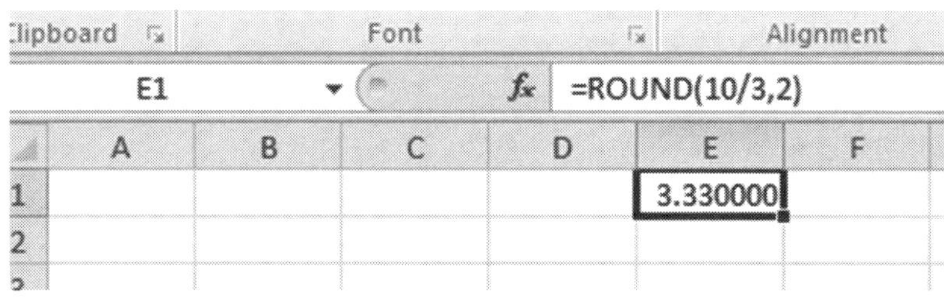

You can also use round to round calculations:

10/3=3.333333 but here it has been rounded to 2 decimal places.

Most usefully though, ROUND can be used to round cell values, by referring to them in the usual way:

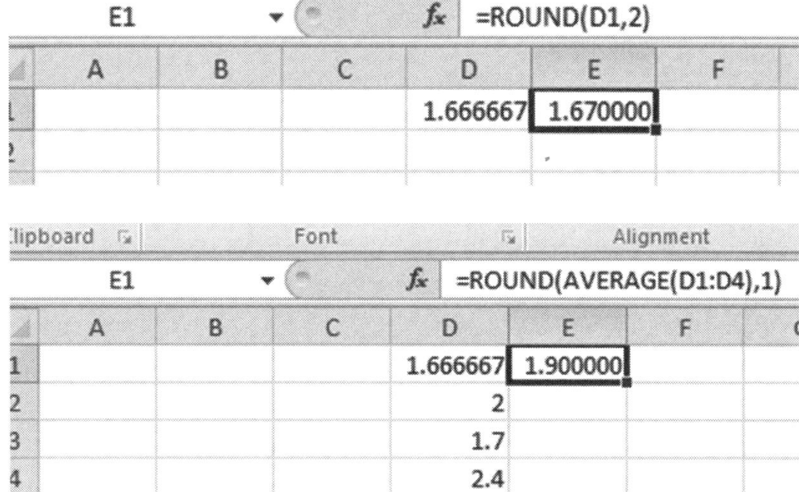

You can combine cell references, calculations and functions when using ROUND.

For example using **ROUND** with **AVERAGE**.

## 1.2 ROUNDUP and ROUNDDOWN

The ROUND function follows normal mathematical rounding rules – 0-4 are rounded down and 5-9 are rounded up. Sometimes you will want to force a number to be rounded up or down, and ROUNDUP or ROUNDDOWN will do this (remember, if you cannot remember the function's name, type what you want to do into the Insert Function menu.

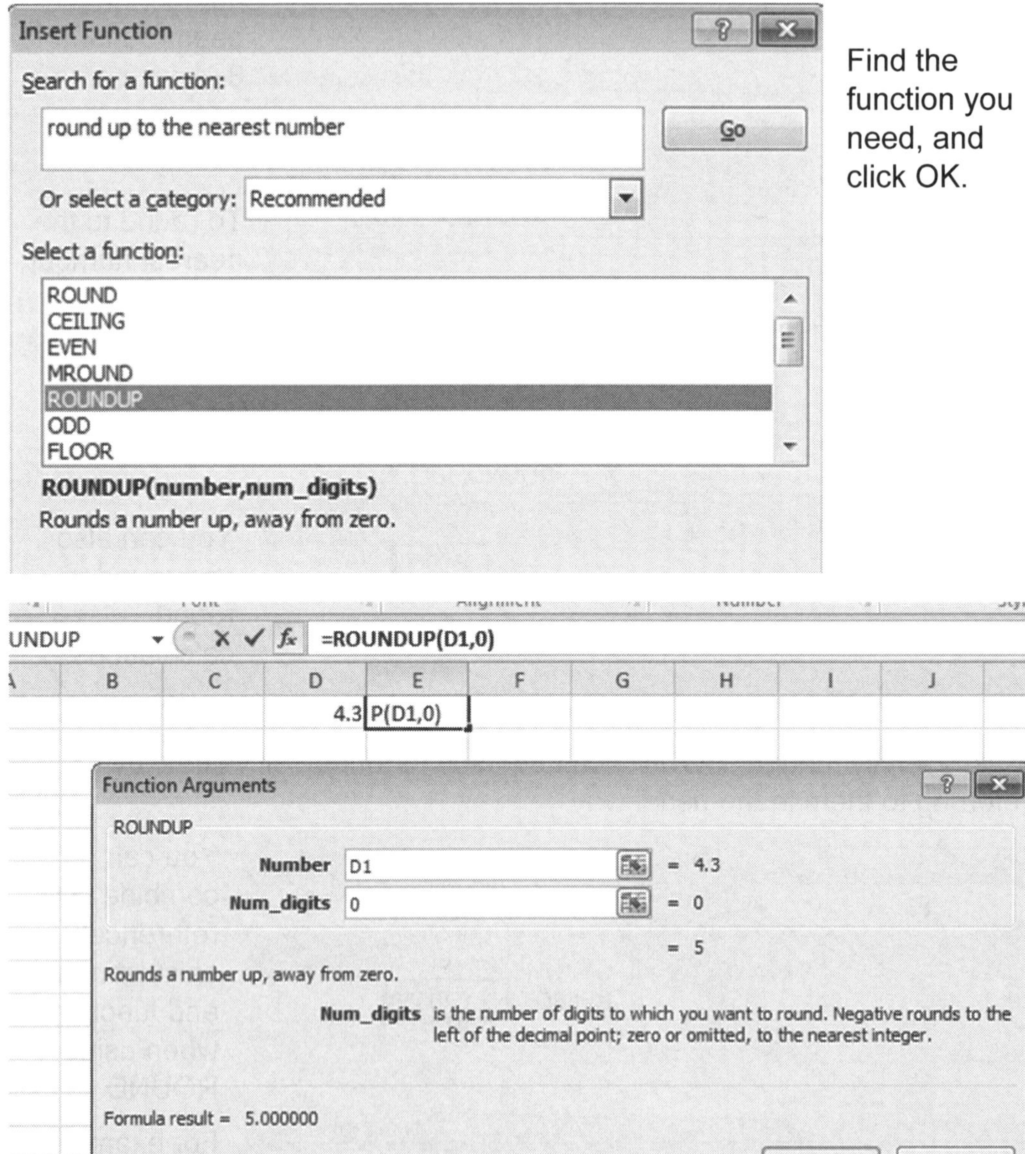


Find the function you need, and click OK.

ROUNDUP has exactly the same arguments as ROUND – using the Insert Function option here allows you to enter them in a more user-friendly way – when you click in the argument box help is displayed explaining what is required. The result is also shown before you click OK.

ROUNDDOWN works in exactly the same way:

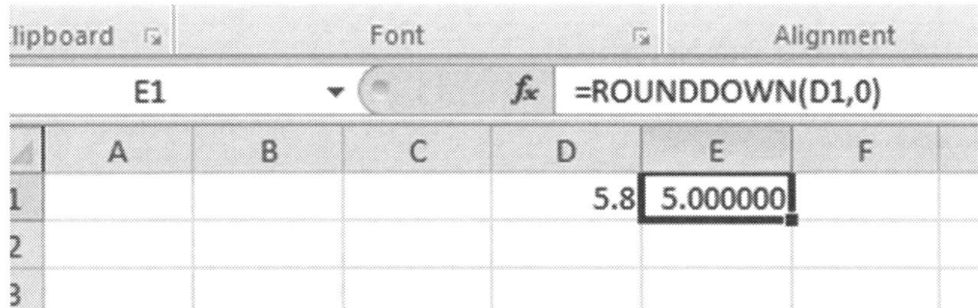


# 2 LOOKUPS – VLOOKUPS

## 2.1 VLOOKUP

VLOOKUP is a useful function in Excel. As an accounting tool it is absolutely invaluable.

Often, data is held in one location (spreadsheet) – this is important as if there are several different spreadsheets with the same data, they must all be updated when the data changes, which is time consuming and may lead to errors. VLOOKUP can be used to interrogate large 'blocks' of data, and find the information required – linking the two together, so if the original is edited, the other spreadsheet will be too.

Let us take a simple data set:

| | A | B | C |
|---|---|---|---|
| 1 | Product | Number in stock | Price |
| 2 | Z101 | 3 | £9.00 |
| 3 | Z102 | 7 | £7.88 |
| 4 | Z103 | 17 | £5.86 |
| 5 | Z104 | 13 | £1.19 |
| 6 | Z105 | 20 | £9.56 |
| 7 | Z106 | 4 | £7.27 |
| 8 | Z107 | 9 | £1.86 |
| 9 | Z108 | 17 | £0.86 |
| 10 | Z109 | 17 | £4.55 |
| 11 | Z110 | 20 | £0.56 |
| 12 | Z111 | 12 | £5.35 |
| 13 | Z112 | 4 | £4.88 |
| 14 | Z113 | 12 | £3.53 |
| 15 | Z114 | 6 | £7.16 |

We might have another spreadsheet used to calculate an invoice price. It would be time consuming to have to find each product's price to enter it onto the invoice – imagine if there were thousands of products. This is where VLOOKUP comes in.

If we set up the Invoice on the same sheet, for simplicity:

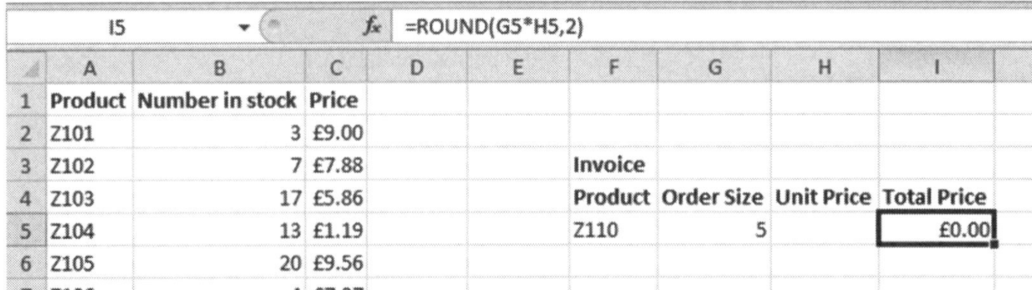

I5 =ROUND(G5*H5,2)

| | A | B | C | D | E | F | G | H | I |
|---|---|---|---|---|---|---|---|---|---|
| 1 | Product | Number in stock | Price | | | | | | |
| 2 | Z101 | 3 | £9.00 | | | | | | |
| 3 | Z102 | 7 | £7.88 | | | Invoice | | | |
| 4 | Z103 | 17 | £5.86 | | | Product | Order Size | Unit Price | Total Price |
| 5 | Z104 | 13 | £1.19 | | | Z110 | 5 | | £0.00 |
| 6 | Z105 | 20 | £9.56 | | | | | | |

We need the unit price of Z110 to calculate the price VLOOKUP can be used to automatically 'find' the price. VLOOKUP looks more complicated as it has four arguments, so using Insert Function is a good way to deal with this. The arguments are as follows:

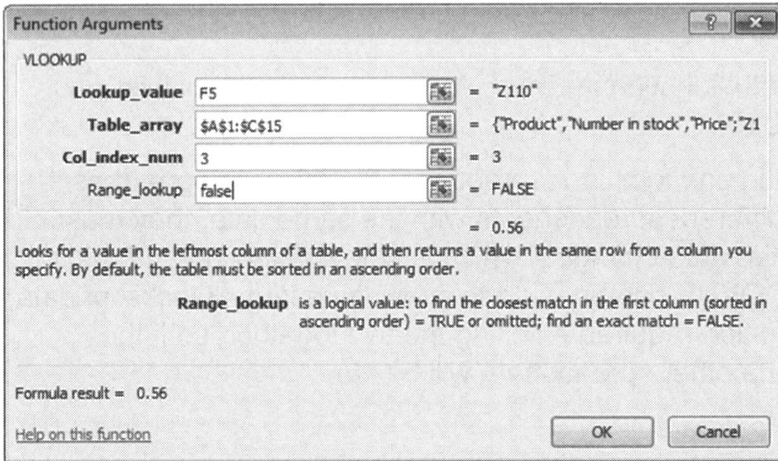
Function Arguments
VLOOKUP
Lookup_value F5 = "Z110"
Table_array $A$1:$C$15 = {"Product","Number in stock","Price";"Z1
Col_index_num 3 = 3
Range_lookup false = FALSE
= 0.56
Looks for a value in the leftmost column of a table, and then returns a value in the same row from a column you specify. By default, the table must be sorted in an ascending order.
Range_lookup is a logical value: to find the closest match in the first column (sorted in ascending order) = TRUE or omitted; find an exact match = FALSE.
Formula result = 0.56
Help on this function
OK
Cancel

- **lookup_value** – this is the data item you are looking for – in our case the product number.
- **table_array** – this is the range the data is in – i.e. where you are looking.

  The first column should contain the item being looked up and absolute referencing needs to be added to ensure that Excel continues to look at the correct data if the vlookup is being used in more than one cell.
- **col_index_number** – this is the column number we want to use from the table_array. We need the price of the product – this is the third column in the table.
- **[range lookup]** – this should either be TRUE or FALSE. The square brackets indicate that this is an optional argument. If you leave it out then Excel will assume its value is TRUE.

- FALSE means that an exact match to the lookup_value must be found – useful for looking up specific items in a list.
- TRUE means the nearest value to the lookup_value will be found – useful if there is a range of values that the lookup_value lies between.

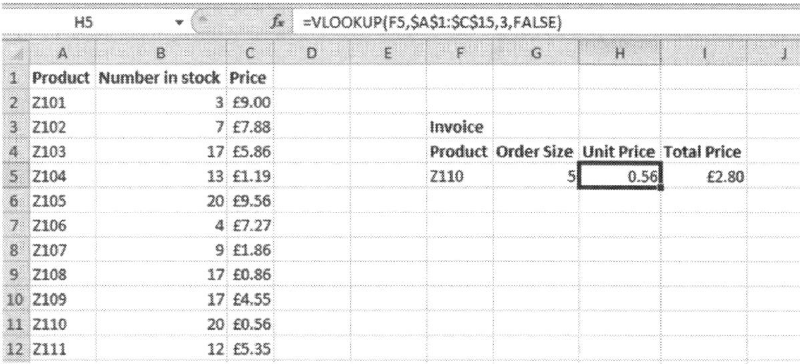

H5 =VLOOKUP(F5,$A$1:$C$15,3,FALSE)

| | A | B | C | D | E | F | G | H | I |
|---|---|---|---|---|---|---|---|---|---|
| 1 | Product | Number in stock | Price | | | | | | |
| 2 | Z101 | 3 | £9.00 | | | | | | |
| 3 | Z102 | 7 | £7.88 | | | Invoice | | | |
| 4 | Z103 | 17 | £5.86 | | | Product | Order Size | Unit Price | Total Price |
| 5 | Z104 | 13 | £1.19 | | | Z110 | 5 | 0.56 | £2.80 |
| 6 | Z105 | 20 | £9.56 | | | | | | |
| 7 | Z106 | 4 | £7.27 | | | | | | |
| 8 | Z107 | 9 | £1.86 | | | | | | |
| 9 | Z108 | 17 | £0.86 | | | | | | |
| 10 | Z109 | 17 | £4.55 | | | | | | |
| 11 | Z110 | 20 | £0.56 | | | | | | |
| 12 | Z111 | 12 | £5.35 | | | | | | |

The correct price is shown, and the total price calculated.

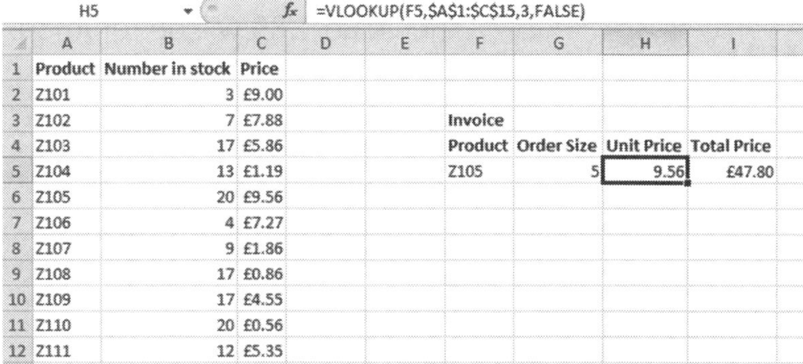

H5 =VLOOKUP(F5,$A$1:$C$15,3,FALSE)

| | A | B | C | D | E | F | G | H | I |
|---|---|---|---|---|---|---|---|---|---|
| 1 | Product | Number in stock | Price | | | | | | |
| 2 | Z101 | 3 | £9.00 | | | | | | |
| 3 | Z102 | 7 | £7.88 | | | Invoice | | | |
| 4 | Z103 | 17 | £5.86 | | | Product | Order Size | Unit Price | Total Price |
| 5 | Z104 | 13 | £1.19 | | | Z105 | 5 | 9.56 | £47.80 |
| 6 | Z105 | 20 | £9.56 | | | | | | |
| 7 | Z106 | 4 | £7.27 | | | | | | |
| 8 | Z107 | 9 | £1.86 | | | | | | |
| 9 | Z108 | 17 | £0.86 | | | | | | |
| 10 | Z109 | 17 | £4.55 | | | | | | |
| 11 | Z110 | 20 | £0.56 | | | | | | |
| 12 | Z111 | 12 | £5.35 | | | | | | |

If the Product Number in F5 is changed, the price changes accordingly:

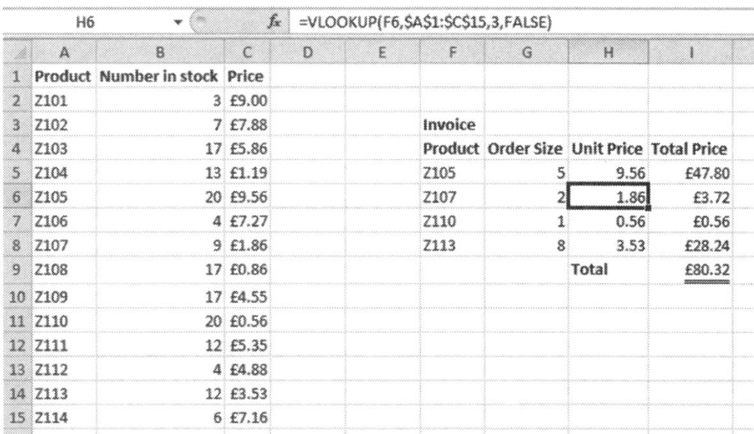

H6 =VLOOKUP(F6,$A$1:$C$15,3,FALSE)

| | A | B | C | D | E | F | G | H | I |
|---|---|---|---|---|---|---|---|---|---|
| 1 | Product | Number in stock | Price | | | | | | |
| 2 | Z101 | 3 | £9.00 | | | | | | |
| 3 | Z102 | 7 | £7.88 | | | Invoice | | | |
| 4 | Z103 | 17 | £5.86 | | | Product | Order Size | Unit Price | Total Price |
| 5 | Z104 | 13 | £1.19 | | | Z105 | 5 | 9.56 | £47.80 |
| 6 | Z105 | 20 | £9.56 | | | Z107 | 2 | 1.86 | £3.72 |
| 7 | Z106 | 4 | £7.27 | | | Z110 | 1 | 0.56 | £0.56 |
| 8 | Z107 | 9 | £1.86 | | | Z113 | 8 | 3.53 | £28.24 |
| 9 | Z108 | 17 | £0.86 | | | | | Total | £80.32 |
| 10 | Z109 | 17 | £4.55 | | | | | | |
| 11 | Z110 | 20 | £0.56 | | | | | | |
| 12 | Z111 | 12 | £5.35 | | | | | | |
| 13 | Z112 | 4 | £4.88 | | | | | | |
| 14 | Z113 | 12 | £3.53 | | | | | | |
| 15 | Z114 | 6 | £7.16 | | | | | | |

You can copy this formula down, and use it for each line of the Invoice – using an absolute reference on the table_array means that this will not be changed:

### 2.2 How does it work?

It is easier to use VLOOKUP if you understand what it is doing. If we use the above example, we are looking for the value of the product in cell **F6**, in the cells from A1-C15, and want the value in the 3rd column.

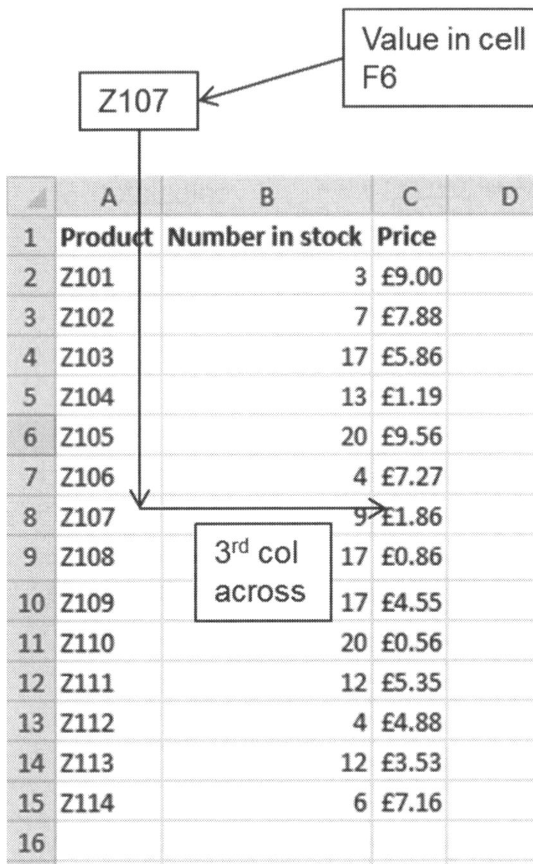


| | A | B | C | D |
|---|---|---|---|---|
| 1 | Product | Number in stock | Price | |
| 2 | Z101 | 3 | £9.00 | |
| 3 | Z102 | 7 | £7.88 | |
| 4 | Z103 | 17 | £5.86 | |
| 5 | Z104 | 13 | £1.19 | |
| 6 | Z105 | 20 | £9.56 | |
| 7 | Z106 | 4 | £7.27 | |
| 8 | Z107 | 9 | £1.86 | |
| 9 | Z108 | 17 | £0.86 | |
| 10 | Z109 | 17 | £4.55 | |
| 11 | Z110 | 20 | £0.56 | |
| 12 | Z111 | 12 | £5.35 | |
| 13 | Z112 | 4 | £4.88 | |
| 14 | Z113 | 12 | £3.53 | |
| 15 | Z114 | 6 | £7.16 | |
| 16 | | | | |

Excel 'looks' down the 1st column until it finds a match, then returns the value in the 3rd column of the table.

The value 1.86 will be returned.

Note that only the **FIRST COLUMN IN THE TABLE** is used to search. If the value is not there, an error will be given.

### 2.3 Errors

As mentioned above, if the **lookup_value** cannot be found in the first column of the table, an error will be shown. The cell value will show **#N/A** to indicate the value could not be found.

| Invoice | | | |
|---|---|---|---|
| **Product** | **Order Size** | **Unit Price** | **Total Price** |
| Y105 | 5 | #N/A | #N/A |
| Z107 | 2 | 1.86 | £3.72 |
| Z110 | 1 | 0.56 | £0.56 |
| Z113 | 8 | 3.53 | £28.24 |
| | | **Total** | #N/A |

Incorrect product code gives this error – all formulas following on will also show an error. This will be dealt with later.

The other common error with VLOOKUP is **#REF!**. This is a referencing error and will occur if the **col_index_number** is too big. For example, our table is 3 columns wide – if you use **col_index_number** greater than 3, the error will show:

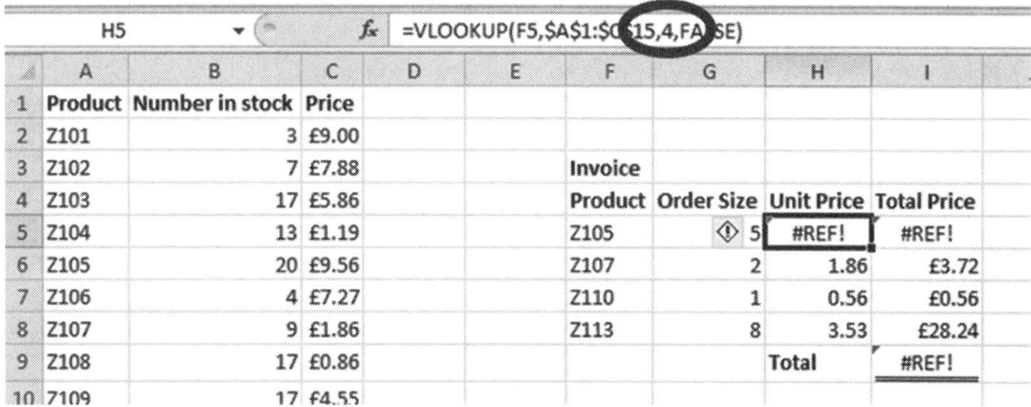
H5 | =VLOOKUP(F5,$A$1:$C$15,4,FALSE)

| | A | B | C | D | E | F | G | H | I |
|---|---|---|---|---|---|---|---|---|---|
| 1 | Product | Number in stock | Price | | | | | | |
| 2 | Z101 | 3 | £9.00 | | | | | | |
| 3 | Z102 | 7 | £7.88 | | | Invoice | | | |
| 4 | Z103 | 17 | £5.86 | | | Product | Order Size | Unit Price | Total Price |
| 5 | Z104 | 13 | £1.19 | | | Z105 | 5 | #REF! | #REF! |
| 6 | Z105 | 20 | £9.56 | | | Z107 | 2 | 1.86 | £3.72 |
| 7 | Z106 | 4 | £7.27 | | | Z110 | 1 | 0.56 | £0.56 |
| 8 | Z107 | 9 | £1.86 | | | Z113 | 8 | 3.53 | £28.24 |
| 9 | Z108 | 17 | £0.86 | | | | | Total | #REF! |
| 10 | Z109 | 17 | £4.55 | | | | | | |

## 2.4 Limitations of VLOOKUP

### Duplicates

One big limitation of **VLOOKUP** is that it is not suitable for searching data with duplicate items. The reason for this is that as explained above, Excel looks down each row of the first column until it finds a match – any matches below this will be ignored.

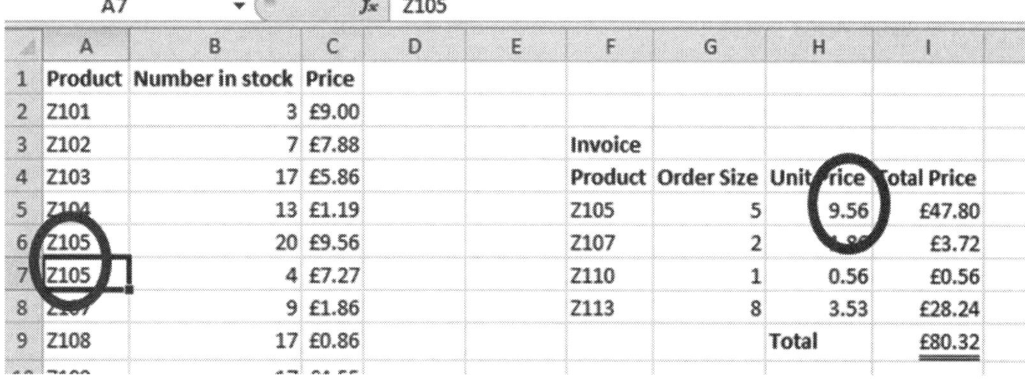
A7 | Z105

| | A | B | C | D | E | F | G | H | I |
|---|---|---|---|---|---|---|---|---|---|
| 1 | Product | Number in stock | Price | | | | | | |
| 2 | Z101 | 3 | £9.00 | | | | | | |
| 3 | Z102 | 7 | £7.88 | | | Invoice | | | |
| 4 | Z103 | 17 | £5.86 | | | Product | Order Size | Unit Price | Total Price |
| 5 | Z104 | 13 | £1.19 | | | Z105 | 5 | 9.56 | £47.80 |
| 6 | Z105 | 20 | £9.56 | | | Z107 | 2 | 1.86 | £3.72 |
| 7 | Z105 | 4 | £7.27 | | | Z110 | 1 | 0.56 | £0.56 |
| 8 | Z107 | 9 | £1.86 | | | Z113 | 8 | 3.53 | £28.24 |
| 9 | Z108 | 17 | £0.86 | | | | | Total | £80.32 |

To demonstrate, if there were two product Z105, only the price for the first one will be shown.

**First column only**

As already mentioned, only the first column of the table is 'searched' for the **lookup_value**, if we extend the example:

| | A | B | C | D | E | F | G | H | I | J |
|---|---|---|---|---|---|---|---|---|---|---|
| 1 | **Product** | **Code** | **Number in stock** | **Price** | | | | | | |
| 2 | Red pen | Z101 | 3 | £9.00 | | | | | | |
| 3 | Yellow pen | Z102 | 7 | £7.88 | | | **Invoice** | | | |
| 4 | Purple pen | Z103 | 17 | £5.86 | | | **Code** | **Order Size** | **Unit Price** | **Total Price** |
| 5 | Green pen | Z104 | 13 | £1.19 | | | Z105 | 5 | | £0.00 |
| 6 | Red crayon | Z105 | 20 | £9.56 | | | Z107 | 2 | | £0.00 |
| 7 | Yellow crayon | Z105 | 4 | £7.27 | | | Z110 | 1 | | £0.00 |
| 8 | Purple crayon | Z107 | 9 | £1.86 | | | Z113 | 8 | | £0.00 |
| 9 | Green crayon | Z108 | 17 | £0.86 | | | | | **Total** | £0.00 |
| 10 | Red ruler | Z109 | 17 | £4.55 | | | | | | |
| 11 | Yellow ruler | Z110 | 20 | £0.56 | | | | | | |
| 12 | Green ruler | Z111 | 12 | £5.35 | | | | | | |
| 13 | Purple ruler | Z112 | 4 | £4.88 | | | | | | |
| 14 | Blue calculator | Z113 | 12 | £3.53 | | | | | | |
| 15 | Orange calculator | Z114 | 6 | £7.16 | | | | | | |

The idea is the same – we need to know the price of each one. If you use the following arguments:

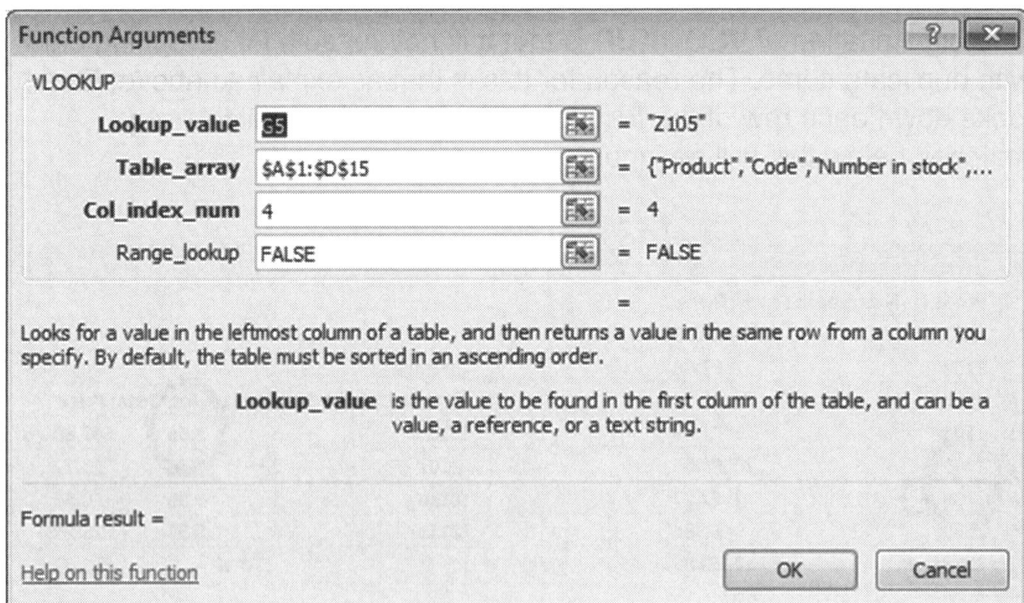
Function Arguments
VLOOKUP
Lookup_value G5 = "Z105"
Table_array $A$1:$D$15 = {"Product","Code","Number in stock",...
Col_index_num 4 = 4
Range_lookup FALSE = FALSE
=
Looks for a value in the leftmost column of a table, and then returns a value in the same row from a column you specify. By default, the table must be sorted in an ascending order.
Lookup_value is the value to be found in the first column of the table, and can be a value, a reference, or a text string.
Formula result =
Help on this function
OK
Cancel

A #N/A error is given. The Col_index_num of 4 is correct, as the price is the 4th column in our table. The problem is that "Z105" cannot be found in the first column:

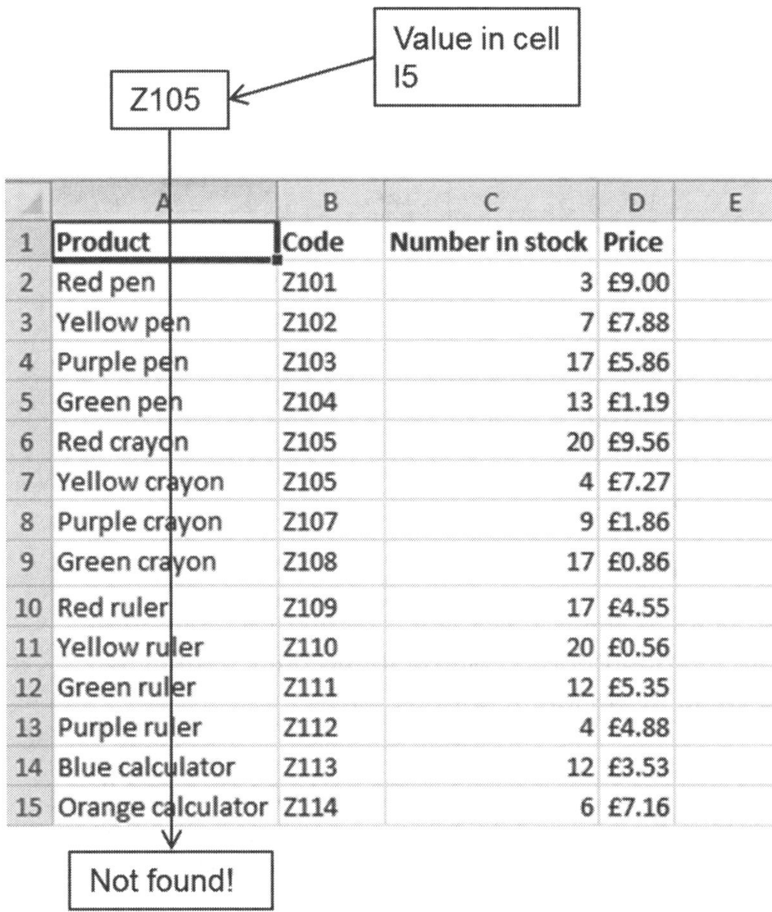


| | A | B | C | D | E |
|---|---|---|---|---|---|
| 1 | **Product** | **Code** | **Number in stock** | **Price** | |
| 2 | Red pen | Z101 | 3 | £9.00 | |
| 3 | Yellow pen | Z102 | 7 | £7.88 | |
| 4 | Purple pen | Z103 | 17 | £5.86 | |
| 5 | Green pen | Z104 | 13 | £1.19 | |
| 6 | Red crayon | Z105 | 20 | £9.56 | |
| 7 | Yellow crayon | Z105 | 4 | £7.27 | |
| 8 | Purple crayon | Z107 | 9 | £1.86 | |
| 9 | Green crayon | Z108 | 17 | £0.86 | |
| 10 | Red ruler | Z109 | 17 | £4.55 | |
| 11 | Yellow ruler | Z110 | 20 | £0.56 | |
| 12 | Green ruler | Z111 | 12 | £5.35 | |
| 13 | Purple ruler | Z112 | 4 | £4.88 | |
| 14 | Blue calculator | Z113 | 12 | £3.53 | |
| 15 | Orange calculator | Z114 | 6 | £7.16 | |

The table MUST start in column B, where the product codes are.

To edit the formula, click in the cell and then press the **Insert Function** button to display the arguments. These can then be changed:

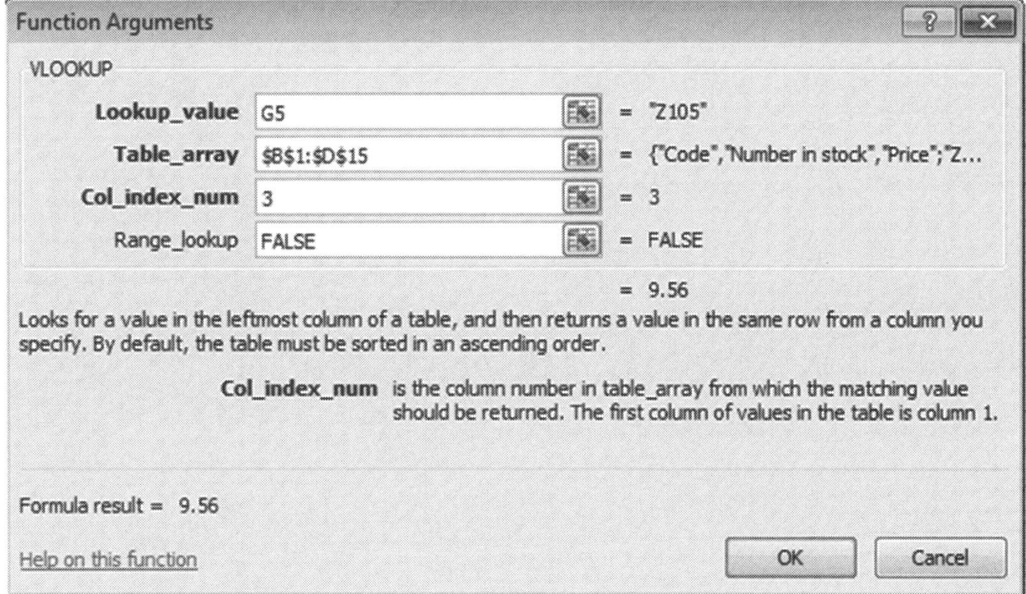

Note that **Table_array** has been altered to start with column B. **Col_index_num** has also been changed – this is because our table starts with column B – the Price column is the third column in our table.

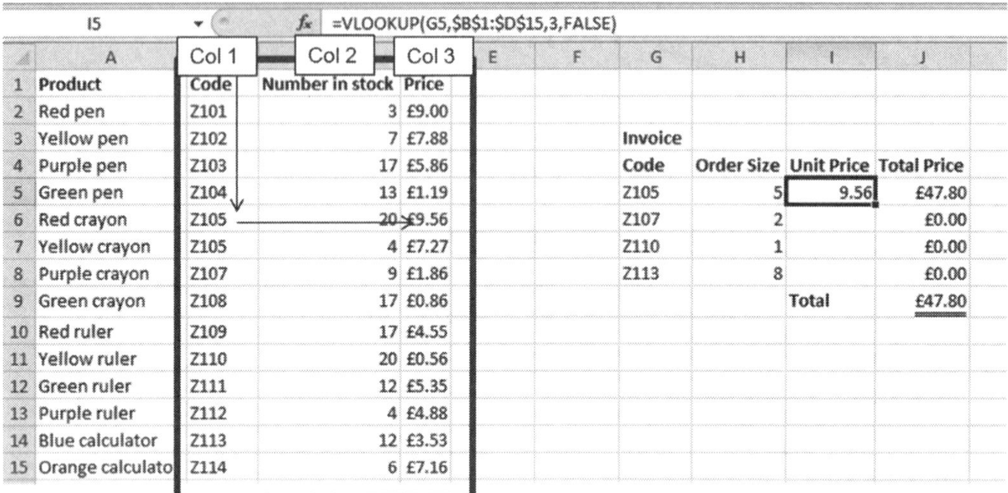

I5 =VLOOKUP(G5,$B$1:$D$15,3,FALSE)

| | A | B | C | D | E | F | G | H | I | J |
|---|---|---|---|---|---|---|---|---|---|---|
| 1 | Product | Code | Number in stock | Price | | | | | | |
| 2 | Red pen | Z101 | 3 | £9.00 | | | | | | |
| 3 | Yellow pen | Z102 | 7 | £7.88 | | | Invoice | | | |
| 4 | Purple pen | Z103 | 17 | £5.86 | | | Code | Order Size | Unit Price | Total Price |
| 5 | Green pen | Z104 | 13 | £1.19 | | | Z105 | 5 | 9.56 | £47.80 |
| 6 | Red crayon | Z105 | 20 | £9.56 | | | Z107 | 2 | | £0.00 |
| 7 | Yellow crayon | Z105 | 4 | £7.27 | | | Z110 | 1 | | £0.00 |
| 8 | Purple crayon | Z107 | 9 | £1.86 | | | Z113 | 8 | | £0.00 |
| 9 | Green crayon | Z108 | 17 | £0.86 | | | | | Total | £47.80 |
| 10 | Red ruler | Z109 | 17 | £4.55 | | | | | | |
| 11 | Yellow ruler | Z110 | 20 | £0.56 | | | | | | |
| 12 | Green ruler | Z111 | 12 | £5.35 | | | | | | |
| 13 | Purple ruler | Z112 | 4 | £4.88 | | | | | | |
| 14 | Blue calculator | Z113 | 12 | £3.53 | | | | | | |
| 15 | Orange calculato | Z114 | 6 | £7.16 | | | | | | |



### Cannot Look 'Backwards'

As seen, **VLOOKUP** 'finds' a value in the first column of a table, then returns the value from the appropriate column to the right. What if we wanted to return the value to the left of our column?

| | Invoice | | | |
|---|---|---|---|---|
| **Code** | **Product** | **Order Size** | **Unit Price** | **Total Price** |
| Z105 | | 5 | 9.56 | £47.80 |
| Z107 | | 2 | 1.86 | £3.72 |
| Z110 | | 1 | 0.56 | £0.56 |
| Z113 | | 8 | 3.53 | £28.24 |
| | | | **Total** | £80.32 |

We want to find the product name based on the product code.

| | A | B | C | D |
|---|---|---|---|---|
| 1 | **Product** | **Code** | **Number in stock** | **Price** |
| 2 | Red pen | Z101 | 3 | £9.00 |
| 3 | Yellow pen | Z102 | 7 | £7.88 |
| 4 | Purple pen | Z103 | 17 | £5.86 |
| 5 | Green pen | Z104 | 13 | £1.19 |
| 6 | Red crayon | Z105 | 20 | £9.56 |
| 7 | Yellow crayon | Z105 | 4 | £7.27 |
| 8 | Purple crayon | Z107 | 9 | £1.86 |
| 9 | Green crayon | Z108 | 17 | £0.86 |
| 10 | Red ruler | Z109 | 17 | £4.55 |
| 11 | Yellow ruler | Z110 | 20 | £0.56 |
| 12 | Green ruler | Z111 | 12 | £5.35 |
| 13 | Purple ruler | Z112 | 4 | £4.88 |
| 14 | Blue calculator | Z113 | 12 | £3.53 |
| 15 | Orange calculator | Z114 | 6 | £7.16 |
| 16 | | | | |

This is not possible here using VLOOKUP, as the Product Code is to the right of the Product column.

One way round this problem is to swap the columns over in the original data, as shown below.

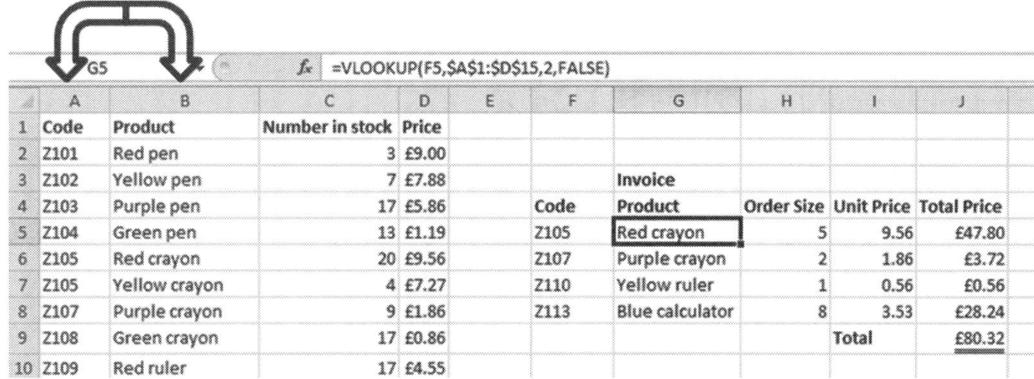

G5 =VLOOKUP(F5,$A$1:$D$15,2,FALSE)

| | A | B | C | D | E | F | G | H | I | J |
|---|---|---|---|---|---|---|---|---|---|---|
| 1 | **Code** | **Product** | **Number in stock** | **Price** | | | | | | |
| 2 | Z101 | Red pen | 3 | £9.00 | | | | | | |
| 3 | Z102 | Yellow pen | 7 | £7.88 | | | **Invoice** | | | |
| 4 | Z103 | Purple pen | 17 | £5.86 | | **Code** | **Product** | **Order Size** | **Unit Price** | **Total Price** |
| 5 | Z104 | Green pen | 13 | £1.19 | | Z105 | Red crayon | 5 | 9.56 | £47.80 |
| 6 | Z105 | Red crayon | 20 | £9.56 | | Z107 | Purple crayon | 2 | 1.86 | £3.72 |
| 7 | Z105 | Yellow crayon | 4 | £7.27 | | Z110 | Yellow ruler | 1 | 0.56 | £0.56 |
| 8 | Z107 | Purple crayon | 9 | £1.86 | | Z113 | Blue calculator | 8 | 3.53 | £28.24 |
| 9 | Z108 | Green crayon | 17 | £0.86 | | | | | **Total** | £80.32 |
| 10 | Z109 | Red ruler | 17 | £4.55 | | | | | | |

# 3 LOOKUPS – HLOOKUPS

## 3.1 HLOOKUP

**HLOOKUP** works in a very similar way to **VLOOKUP**. In **VLOOKUP**, we searched **DOWN** a column to find the value we needed. The 'V' in **VLOOKUP** stands for '**Vertical**' to show this.

Likewise, **HLOOKUP** is a Horizontal Lookup. We will search **ALONG** a row to find the value we need, and then return the value in the n$^{th}$ row of the table:

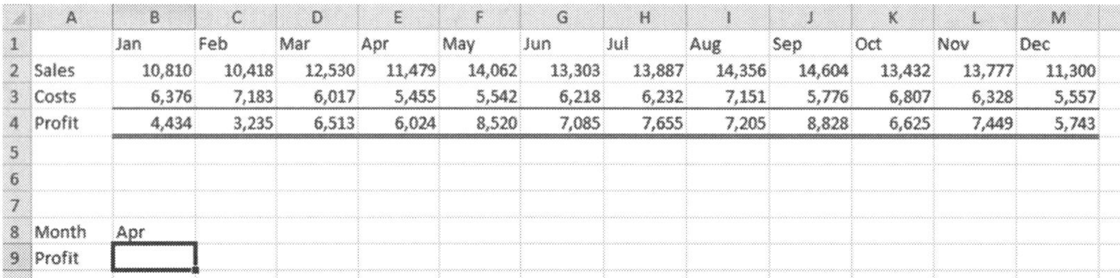

| | A | B | C | D | E | F | G | H | I | J | K | L | M |
|---|---|---|---|---|---|---|---|---|---|---|---|---|---|
| 1 | | Jan | Feb | Mar | Apr | May | Jun | Jul | Aug | Sep | Oct | Nov | Dec |
| 2 | Sales | 10,810 | 10,418 | 12,530 | 11,479 | 14,062 | 13,303 | 13,887 | 14,356 | 14,604 | 13,432 | 13,777 | 11,300 |
| 3 | Costs | 6,376 | 7,183 | 6,017 | 5,455 | 5,542 | 6,218 | 6,232 | 7,151 | 5,776 | 6,807 | 6,328 | 5,557 |
| 4 | Profit | 4,434 | 3,235 | 6,513 | 6,024 | 8,520 | 7,085 | 7,655 | 7,205 | 8,828 | 6,625 | 7,449 | 5,743 |
| 5 | | | | | | | | | | | | | |
| 6 | | | | | | | | | | | | | |
| 7 | | | | | | | | | | | | | |
| 8 | Month | Apr | | | | | | | | | | | |
| 9 | Profit | | | | | | | | | | | | |

If we wanted to automatically return the correct profit figure depending on the month input into B8, use **HLOOKUP**.

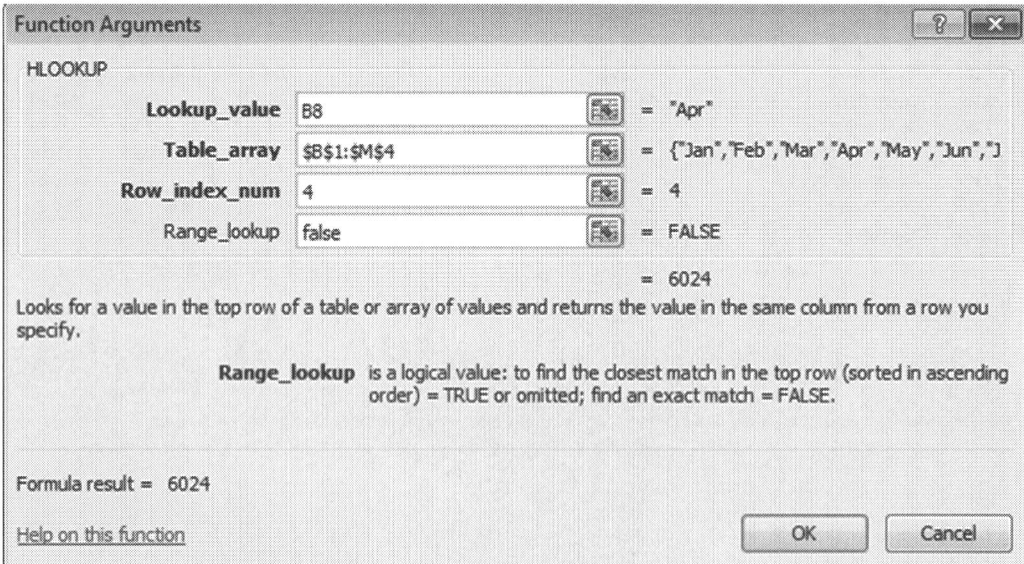


- **Lookup_value** – B8, the month we choose.
- **Table_array** – the table of data – note that only the **FIRST ROW** will be searched, so that must contain the data we are looking for.
- **Row_index_num** – we want profit, the 4th row in our table.
- **Range_lookup** – FALSE, for an exact match.

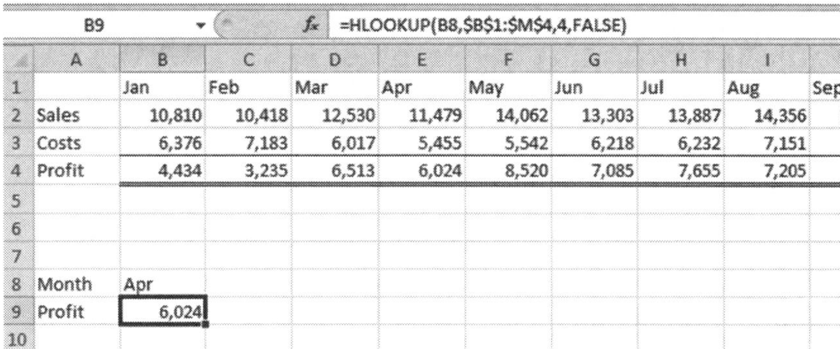

B9 =HLOOKUP(B8,$B$1:$M$4,4,FALSE)

| | A | B | C | D | E | F | G | H | I | |
|---|---|---|---|---|---|---|---|---|---|---|
| 1 | | Jan | Feb | Mar | Apr | May | Jun | Jul | Aug | Sep |
| 2 | Sales | 10,810 | 10,418 | 12,530 | 11,479 | 14,062 | 13,303 | 13,887 | 14,356 | |
| 3 | Costs | 6,376 | 7,183 | 6,017 | 5,455 | 5,542 | 6,218 | 6,232 | 7,151 | |
| 4 | Profit | 4,434 | 3,235 | 6,513 | 6,024 | 8,520 | 7,085 | 7,655 | 7,205 | |
| 5 | | | | | | | | | | |
| 6 | | | | | | | | | | |
| 7 | | | | | | | | | | |
| 8 | Month | Apr | | | | | | | | |
| 9 | Profit | 6,024 | | | | | | | | |
| 10 | | | | | | | | | | |

The lookup is complete.

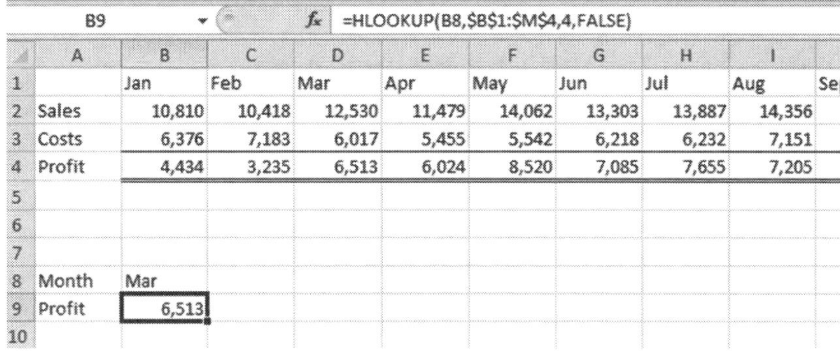

B9 =HLOOKUP(B8,$B$1:$M$4,4,FALSE)

| | A | B | C | D | E | F | G | H | I | |
|---|---|---|---|---|---|---|---|---|---|---|
| 1 | | Jan | Feb | Mar | Apr | May | Jun | Jul | Aug | Sep |
| 2 | Sales | 10,810 | 10,418 | 12,530 | 11,479 | 14,062 | 13,303 | 13,887 | 14,356 | |
| 3 | Costs | 6,376 | 7,183 | 6,017 | 5,455 | 5,542 | 6,218 | 6,232 | 7,151 | |
| 4 | Profit | 4,434 | 3,235 | 6,513 | 6,024 | 8,520 | 7,085 | 7,655 | 7,205 | |
| 5 | | | | | | | | | | |
| 6 | | | | | | | | | | |
| 7 | | | | | | | | | | |
| 8 | Month | Mar | | | | | | | | |
| 9 | Profit | 6,513 | | | | | | | | |
| 10 | | | | | | | | | | |

If the month is changed, the profit will update accordingly

**Note** – **VLOOKUP** is far more commonly used than **HLOOKUP**, as most spreadsheets are set up with the data arranged in columns.

# 4 Logical functions

## 4.1 Introduction

Logical functions are very useful for What-If analysis within Excel. They can be used to check whether certain criteria have been met (like conditional formatting), and changing the calculation required as a result.

Logical functions give an answer of either **TRUE** or **FALSE**. A very simple logical function would be:

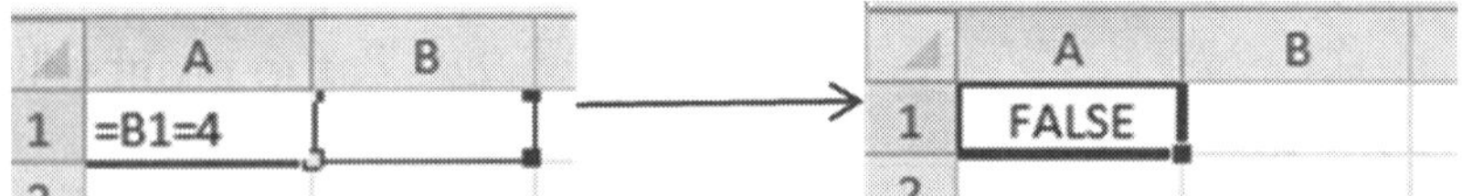


The first '=' is just there to tell Excel that this is a formula. The logical test is **B1=4**. This can either be TRUE – if B1 does equal 4, or FALSE, if it does not. As there is no value in cell B1, the answer is FALSE.

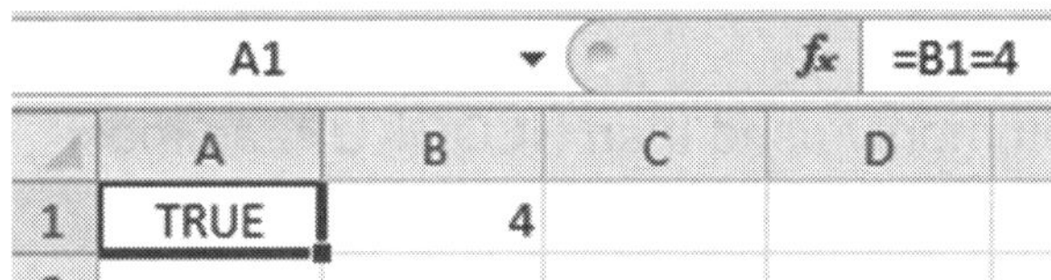


If you enter 4 into B1, the answer changes to TRUE.

This is very useful for checking if two cells which should have the same value do have the same value!

The full list of logical checks is as follows:

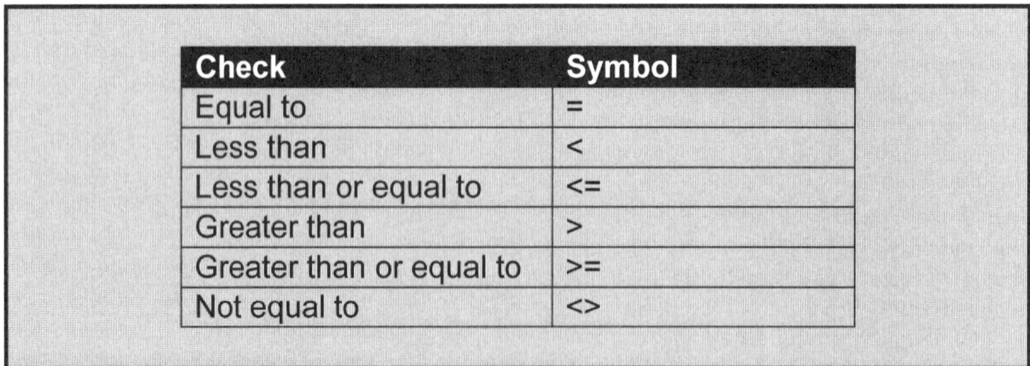

| Check | Symbol |
|---|---|
| Equal to | = |
| Less than | < |
| Less than or equal to | <= |
| Greater than | > |
| Greater than or equal to | >= |
| Not equal to | <> |

Note the 'Not equal to' and 'Less/greater than or equal to' – the order of the symbols is important.

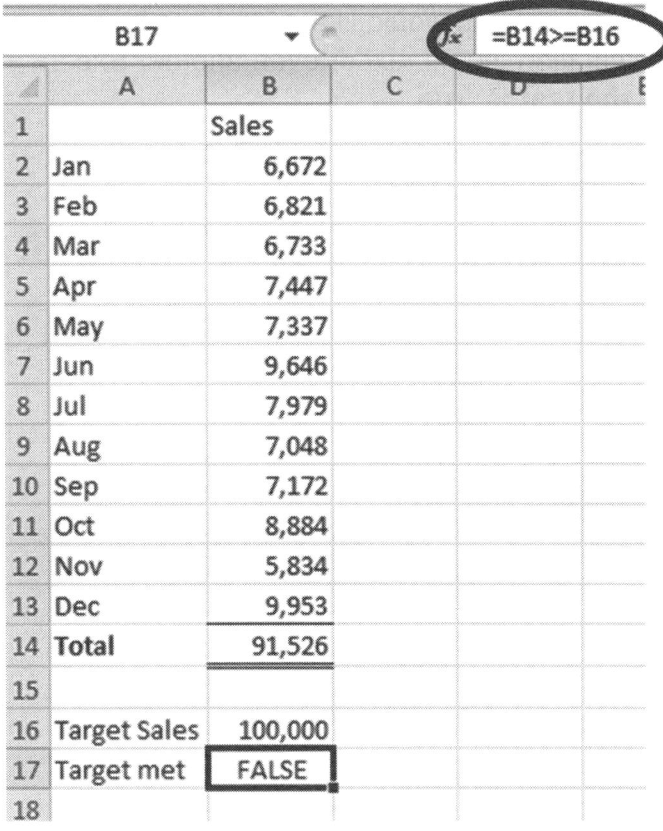

B17 fx =B14>=B16

| | A | B |
|---|---|---|
| 1 | | Sales |
| 2 | Jan | 6,672 |
| 3 | Feb | 6,821 |
| 4 | Mar | 6,733 |
| 5 | Apr | 7,447 |
| 6 | May | 7,337 |
| 7 | Jun | 9,646 |
| 8 | Jul | 7,979 |
| 9 | Aug | 7,048 |
| 10 | Sep | 7,172 |
| 11 | Oct | 8,884 |
| 12 | Nov | 5,834 |
| 13 | Dec | 9,953 |
| 14 | Total | 91,526 |
| 15 | | |
| 16 | Target Sales | 100,000 |
| 17 | Target met | FALSE |
| 18 | | |

Here, we are checking whether a target has been met – is the value in B14, total sales, at least as big as the target.

It is not, so the value is FALSE.

## 4.2 IF

Logical checks are very useful, but it may be more appropriate to have something other than TRUE or FALSE as a response, an IF function can do this.

The **IF** function has 3 arguments, as follows:

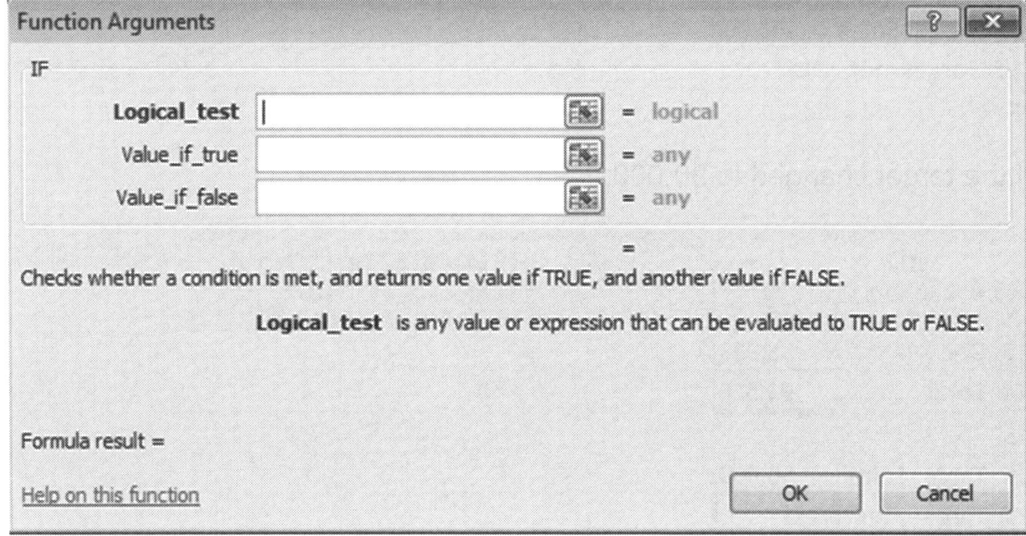


- **Logical_test** – as above, a logical test is a test that will have the value TRUE or FALSE. **What are we testing?**

- **Value_if_true** – enter here what you would like to do if the test is true – this could be a calculation, some text or even another Excel function. **What to do if the test is true.**
- **Value_if_false** – enter here what to do if the test is false, in the same way. **What to do if the test is false**.

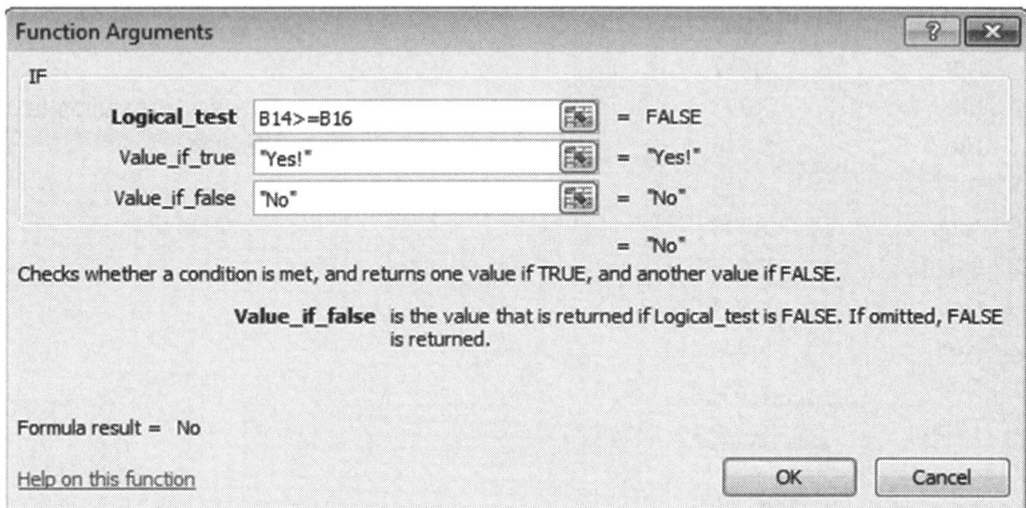


The logical test is as it was in the previous example – have the target sales been met? If they have, we want text saying "Yes!", otherwise "No". Note that the quote marks ("") are required to tell Excel to show text.

B17 =IF(B14>=B16,"Yes!","No")

| | A | B | C | D | E | F |
|---|---|---|---|---|---|---|
| 13 | Dec | 9,953 | | | | |
| 14 | **Total** | 91,526 | | | | |
| 15 | | | | | | |
| 16 | Target Sales | 100,000 | | | | |
| 17 | Target met | No | | | | |

If the target changed to 90,000:

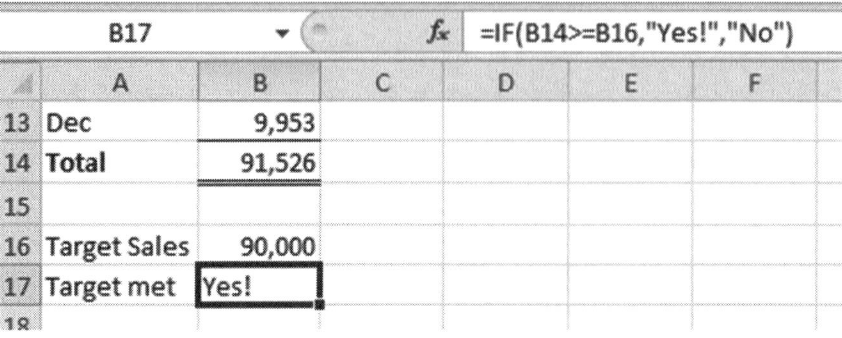

B17 =IF(B14>=B16,"Yes!","No")

| | A | B | C | D | E | F |
|---|---|---|---|---|---|---|
| 13 | Dec | 9,953 | | | | |
| 14 | **Total** | 91,526 | | | | |
| 15 | | | | | | |
| 16 | Target Sales | 90,000 | | | | |
| 17 | Target met | Yes! | | | | |

You can then bring in more complicated calculations:

B18 | $f_x$ | =IF(B17="Yes!",B14*10%,0)

| | A | B | C | D | E | F |
|---|---|---|---|---|---|---|
| 10 | Sep | 7,172 | | | | |
| 11 | Oct | 8,884 | | | | |
| 12 | Nov | 5,834 | | | | |
| 13 | Dec | 9,953 | | | | |
| 14 | **Total** | 91,526 | | | | |
| 15 | | | | | | |
| 16 | Target Sales | 90,000 | | | | |
| 17 | Target met | Yes! | | | | |
| 18 | 10% Bonus | 9,153 | | | | |
| 19 | | | | | | |

So here, if B17 equals "Yes!", multiply B14 by 10%, otherwise the bonus is zero.

Going back to the **VLOOKUP** example, we might want to check that we have enough stock.

| | A | B | C | D | E | F | G | H | I | J | K |
|---|---|---|---|---|---|---|---|---|---|---|---|
| 1 | **Code** | **Product** | **Number in stock** | **Price** | | | | | | | |
| 2 | Z101 | Red pen | 3 | £9.00 | | | | | | | |
| 3 | Z102 | Yellow pen | 7 | £7.88 | | | **Invoice** | | | | |
| 4 | Z103 | Purple pen | 17 | £5.86 | | **Code** | **Product** | **Order Size** | **Unit Price** | **Total Price** | **Stock check** |
| 5 | Z104 | Green pen | 13 | £1.19 | | Z105 | Red crayon | 5 | 9.56 | £47.80 | |
| 6 | Z105 | Red crayon | 20 | £9.56 | | Z107 | Purple crayon | 2 | 1.86 | £3.72 | |
| 7 | Z105 | Yellow crayon | 4 | £7.27 | | Z110 | Yellow ruler | 1 | 0.56 | £0.56 | |
| 8 | Z107 | Purple crayon | 9 | £1.86 | | Z113 | Blue calculator | 8 | 3.53 | £28.24 | |
| 9 | Z108 | Green crayon | 17 | £0.86 | | | | | **Total** | £80.32 | |
| 10 | Z109 | Red ruler | 17 | £4.55 | | | | | | | |
| 11 | Z110 | Yellow ruler | 20 | £0.56 | | | | | | | |
| 12 | Z111 | Green ruler | 12 | £5.35 | | | | | | | |
| 13 | Z112 | Purple ruler | 4 | £4.88 | | | | | | | |
| 14 | Z113 | Blue calculator | 12 | £3.53 | | | | | | | |
| 15 | Z114 | Orange calculator | 6 | £7.16 | | | | | | | |

To start an IF formula, think "What do I need to compare or check?" Here, we need to see if the order size is less than or equal to the number in stock (note that you could check the other way round – is the number in stock greater than or equal to the order size – it does not matter). The order size is easy – cell H5. The number in stock depends on the product code in cell F5 though – we need to do a **VLOOKUP** to find this. This leads to a very big formula, but if you break it down step by step it is things we have already used. One way to go about this is to do the logical test first, and build the IF formula around it.

We need a **VLOOKUP** to find the stock levels:

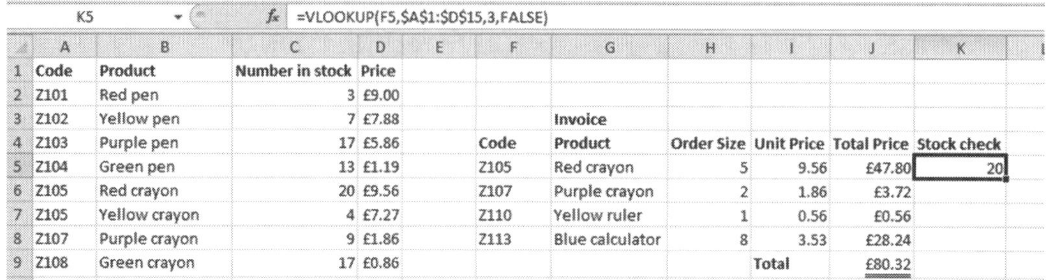

K5 =VLOOKUP(F5,$A$1:$D$15,3,FALSE)

| | A | B | C | D | E | F | G | H | I | J | K |
|---|---|---|---|---|---|---|---|---|---|---|---|
| 1 | Code | Product | Number in stock | Price | | | | | | | |
| 2 | Z101 | Red pen | 3 | £9.00 | | | | | | | |
| 3 | Z102 | Yellow pen | 7 | £7.88 | | | Invoice | | | | |
| 4 | Z103 | Purple pen | 17 | £5.86 | | Code | Product | Order Size | Unit Price | Total Price | Stock check |
| 5 | Z104 | Green pen | 13 | £1.19 | | Z105 | Red crayon | 5 | 9.56 | £47.80 | 20 |
| 6 | Z105 | Red crayon | 20 | £9.56 | | Z107 | Purple crayon | 2 | 1.86 | £3.72 | |
| 7 | Z105 | Yellow crayon | 4 | £7.27 | | Z110 | Yellow ruler | 1 | 0.56 | £0.56 | |
| 8 | Z107 | Purple crayon | 9 | £1.86 | | Z113 | Blue calculator | 8 | 3.53 | £28.24 | |
| 9 | Z108 | Green crayon | 17 | £0.86 | | | | | Total | £80.32 | |

Similar to the earlier price example; we need to compare this to cell H5 – either click in the formula bar at the top, or press F2 to edit the cell.

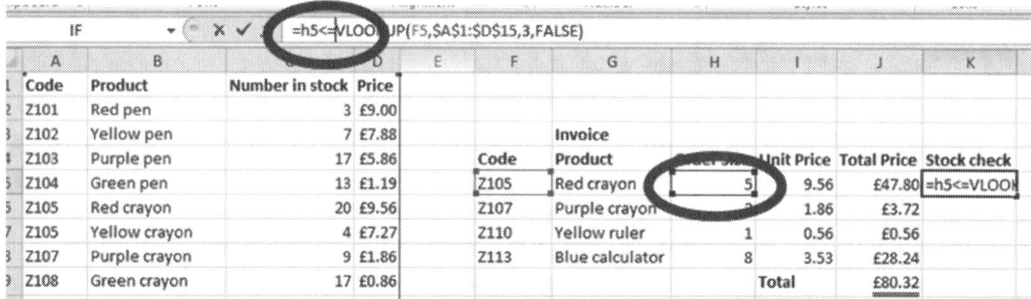

IF =h5<=VLOOKUP(F5,$A$1:$D$15,3,FALSE)

| | A | B | C | D | E | F | G | H | I | J | K |
|---|---|---|---|---|---|---|---|---|---|---|---|
| 1 | Code | Product | Number in stock | Price | | | | | | | |
| 2 | Z101 | Red pen | 3 | £9.00 | | | | | | | |
| 3 | Z102 | Yellow pen | 7 | £7.88 | | | Invoice | | | | |
| 4 | Z103 | Purple pen | 17 | £5.86 | | Code | Product | | Unit Price | Total Price | Stock check |
| 5 | Z104 | Green pen | 13 | £1.19 | | Z105 | Red crayon | 5 | 9.56 | £47.80 | =h5<=VLOOK |
| 6 | Z105 | Red crayon | 20 | £9.56 | | Z107 | Purple crayon | | 1.86 | £3.72 | |
| 7 | Z105 | Yellow crayon | 4 | £7.27 | | Z110 | Yellow ruler | 1 | 0.56 | £0.56 | |
| 8 | Z107 | Purple crayon | 9 | £1.86 | | Z113 | Blue calculator | 8 | 3.53 | £28.24 | |
| 9 | Z108 | Green crayon | 17 | £0.86 | | | | | Total | £80.32 | |

A box appears around the cell to show which one is being used.

| | Invoice | | | | |
|---|---|---|---|---|---|
| **Code** | **Product** | **Order Size** | **Unit Price** | **Total Price** | **Stock check** |
| Z105 | Red crayon | 5 | 9.56 | £47.80 | TRUE |
| Z107 | Purple crayon | 2 | 1.86 | £3.72 | TRUE |
| Z110 | Yellow ruler | 1 | 0.56 | £0.56 | TRUE |
| Z113 | Blue calculator | 8 | 3.53 | £28.24 | TRUE |
| | | | **Total** | £80.32 | |

All the logical checks are TRUE – we have enough of each product. Changing one of the product codes shows how this will update:

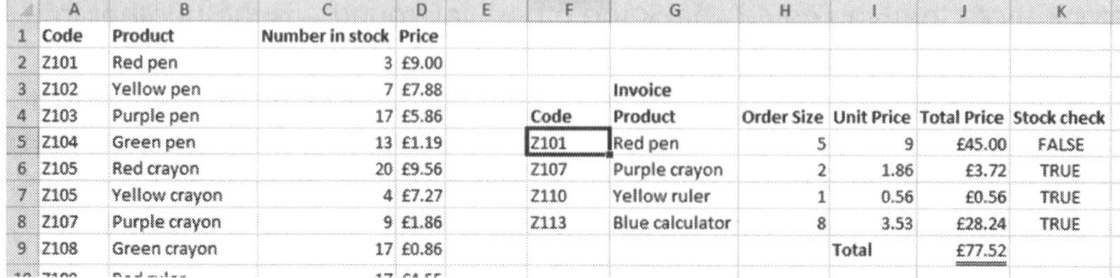

| | A | B | C | D | E | F | G | H | I | J | K |
|---|---|---|---|---|---|---|---|---|---|---|---|
| 1 | Code | Product | Number in stock | Price | | | | | | | |
| 2 | Z101 | Red pen | 3 | £9.00 | | | | | | | |
| 3 | Z102 | Yellow pen | 7 | £7.88 | | | Invoice | | | | |
| 4 | Z103 | Purple pen | 17 | £5.86 | | Code | Product | Order Size | Unit Price | Total Price | Stock check |
| 5 | Z104 | Green pen | 13 | £1.19 | | Z101 | Red pen | 5 | 9 | £45.00 | FALSE |
| 6 | Z105 | Red crayon | 20 | £9.56 | | Z107 | Purple crayon | 2 | 1.86 | £3.72 | TRUE |
| 7 | Z105 | Yellow crayon | 4 | £7.27 | | Z110 | Yellow ruler | 1 | 0.56 | £0.56 | TRUE |
| 8 | Z107 | Purple crayon | 9 | £1.86 | | Z113 | Blue calculator | 8 | 3.53 | £28.24 | TRUE |
| 9 | Z108 | Green crayon | 17 | £0.86 | | | | | Total | £77.52 | |

There are only 3 red pens in stock, so the order size is too big.

Now we have the logical check, the IF function can be built around it. Remember how the IF function works =IF(logical test, value_if_true, value_if_false), if we edit the formula, and type **"IF("** in front of the logical test (but after the first equals sign).

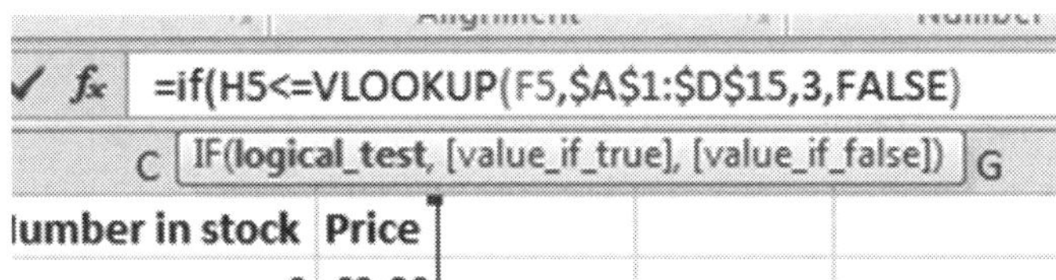


Notice how **logical_test** is in bold – Excel is showing which argument is being entered.

You can then either manually enter the comma after the logical test and enter the other arguments; or click the **Insert Function** button to bring up the appropriate menu:

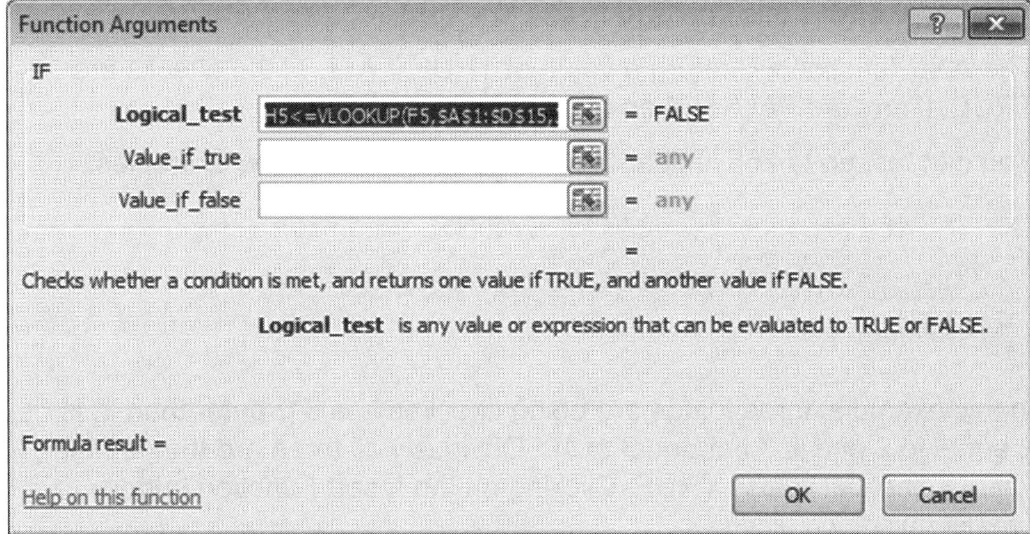


Enter the other two arguments as required:

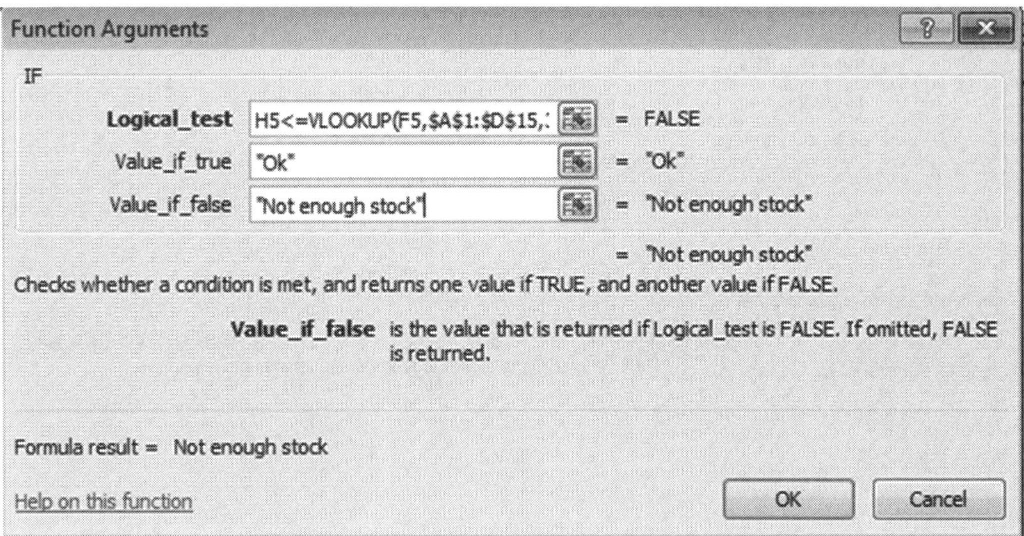

| | Invoice | | | | |
|---|---|---|---|---|---|
| **Code** | **Product** | **Order Size** | **Unit Price** | **Total Price** | **Stock check** |
| Z101 | Red pen | 5 | 9 | £45.00 | Not enough stock |
| Z107 | Purple crayon | 2 | 1.86 | £3.72 | Ok |
| Z110 | Yellow ruler | 1 | 0.56 | £0.56 | Ok |
| Z113 | Blue calculator | 8 | 3.53 | £28.24 | Ok |
| | | | **Total** | £77.52 | |

## 4.3 AND

**AND** is used when you want to check more than one thing is true. As it is a logical function, the result of an **AND** function will be TRUE or FALSE. The basic idea is to say:

Is this true **and** is this true **and** is this true **and**…

The **AND** function will return a value of TRUE if **ALL** of the checks are TRUE. If any are FALSE, then the answer will be FALSE.

You can test up to 255 logical checks. Let us look at a few examples:

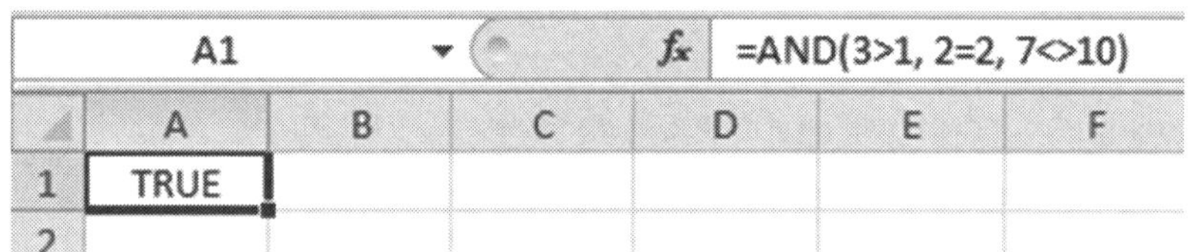


In this example, three things are being checked – is 3 greater than 1, is 2 equal to 2 and is 7 not equal to 10. Obviously all three are true, so the value in the cell is also TRUE. Clicking on the Insert Function button breaks this down nicely:

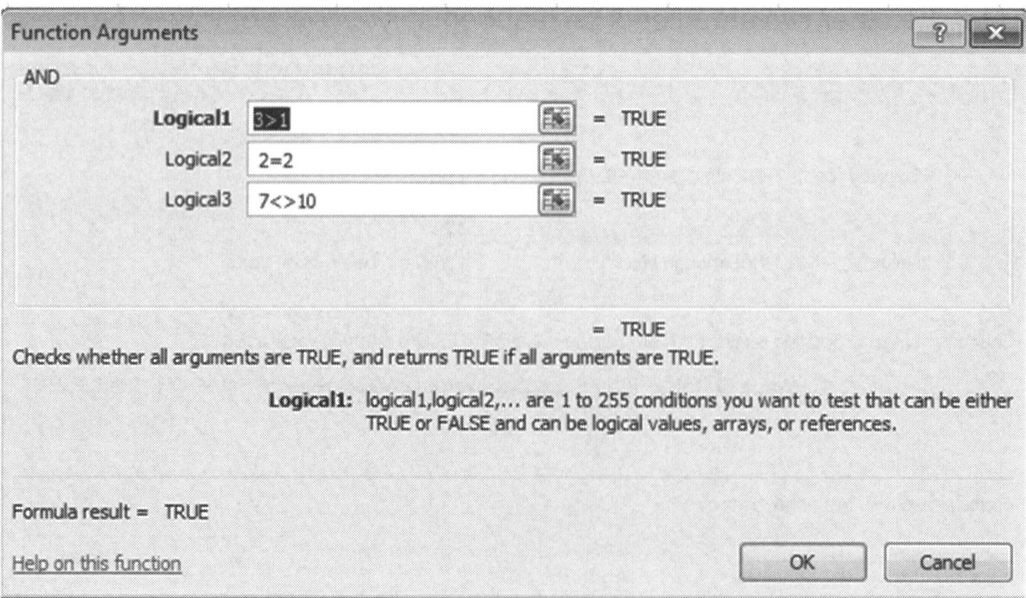

If we change the arguments so that only one is false, this will affect the outcome:

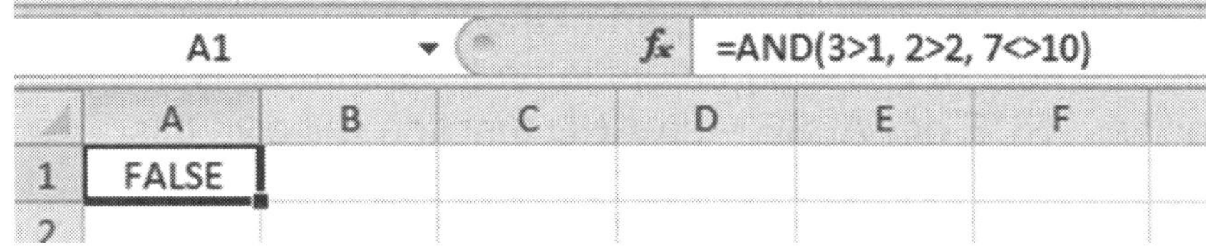


2 is not greater than 2, so the value is FALSE!

## 4.4 OR

**OR** works in a similar way to **AND**, but this time we are checking:

Is this true **OR** is this true **OR** is this true….

As a result only ONE of the logical checks needs to be true for the value to be TRUE.

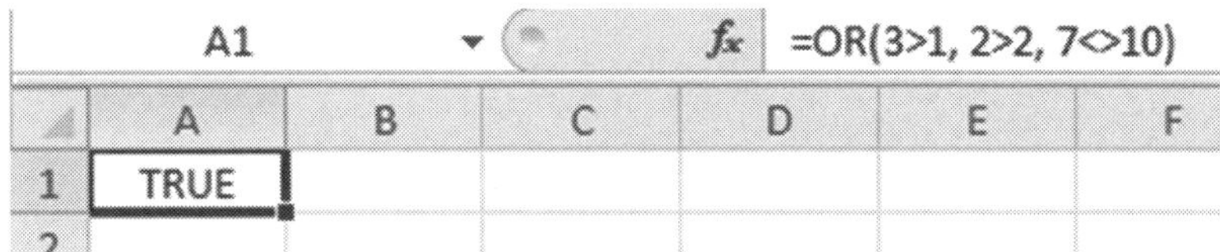


Taking the same checks as the previous example, as at least one is TRUE, the value returned is TRUE.

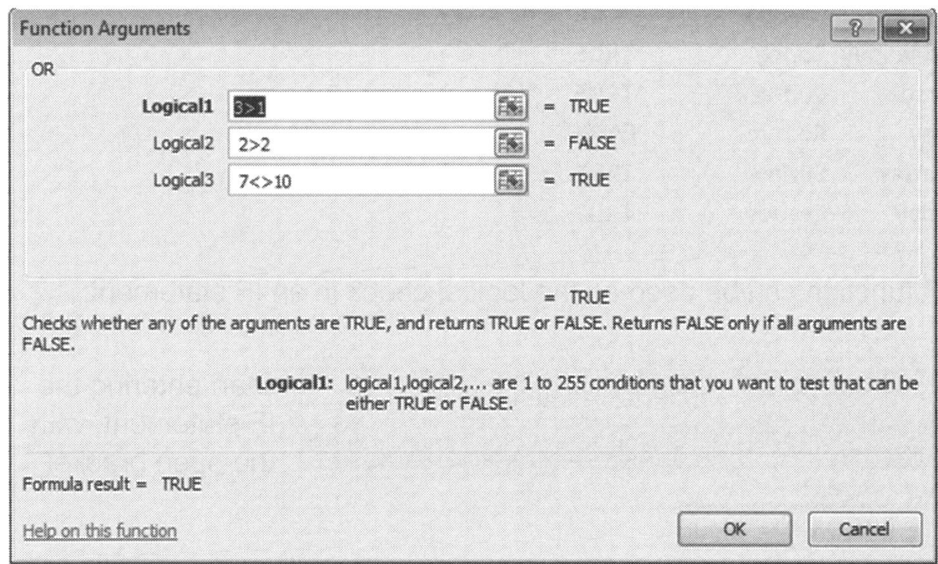


As explained in the function box, OR will only give a FALSE answer if ALL of the checks are FALSE.

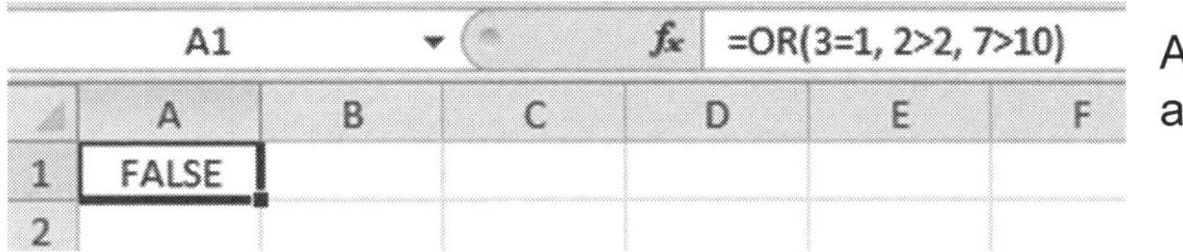


All three checks are FALSE.

## 4.5 Using AND OR

The main use of these will be within an **IF** statement. If, for example, you wish to check two things, the logical test part of the **IF** formula would be an **AND** function. Remember, the first argument in an **IF** statement is a logical test with the answer TRUE or FALSE – an **AND** function will give this.

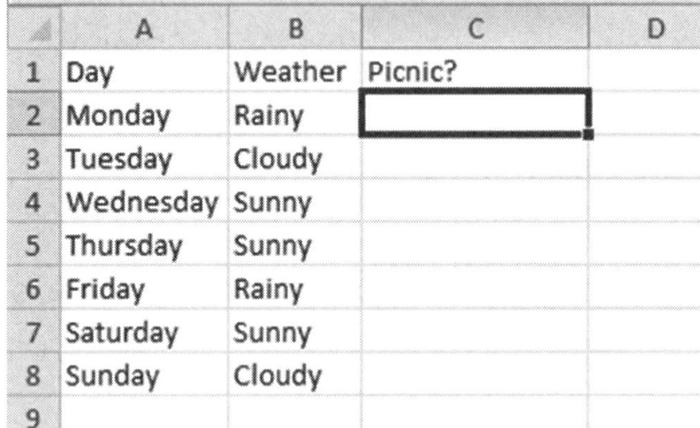

| | A | B | C | D |
|---|---|---|---|---|
| 1 | Day | Weather | Picnic? | |
| 2 | Monday | Rainy | | |
| 3 | Tuesday | Cloudy | | |
| 4 | Wednesday | Sunny | | |
| 5 | Thursday | Sunny | | |
| 6 | Friday | Rainy | | |
| 7 | Saturday | Sunny | | |
| 8 | Sunday | Cloudy | | |
| 9 | | | | |

We might want to check that the weather is going to be sunny or cloudy for our picnic.

Set up the logical check first.

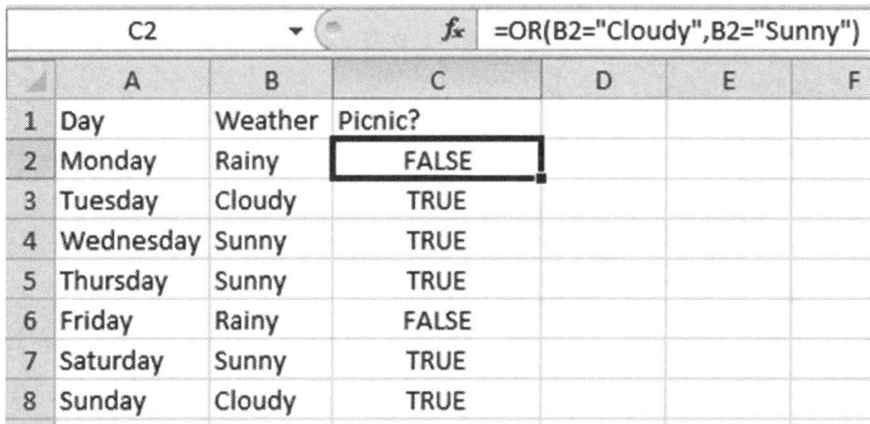

C2 =OR(B2="Cloudy",B2="Sunny")

| | A | B | C | D | E | F |
|---|---|---|---|---|---|---|
| 1 | Day | Weather | Picnic? | | | |
| 2 | Monday | Rainy | FALSE | | | |
| 3 | Tuesday | Cloudy | TRUE | | | |
| 4 | Wednesday | Sunny | TRUE | | | |
| 5 | Thursday | Sunny | TRUE | | | |
| 6 | Friday | Rainy | FALSE | | | |
| 7 | Saturday | Sunny | TRUE | | | |
| 8 | Sunday | Cloudy | TRUE | | | |

This OR function can be used as the logical check in an IF statement:

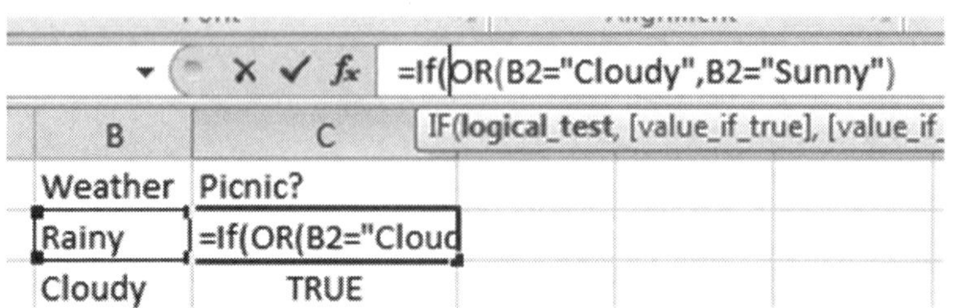


Start entering the IF statement, with the open bracket.

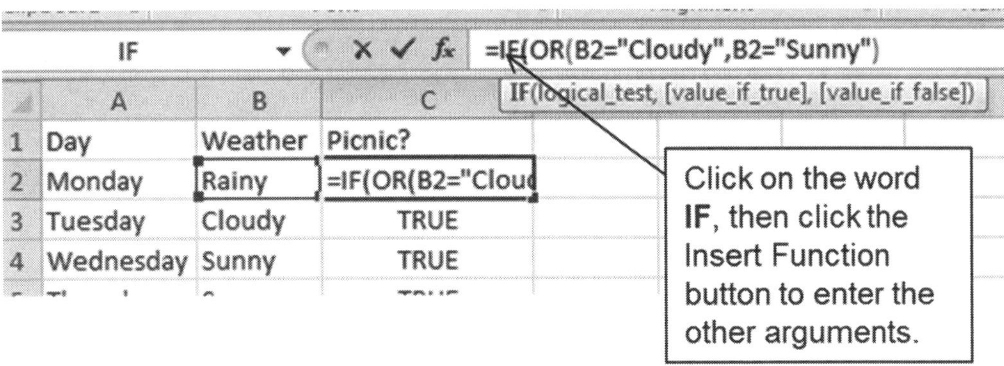


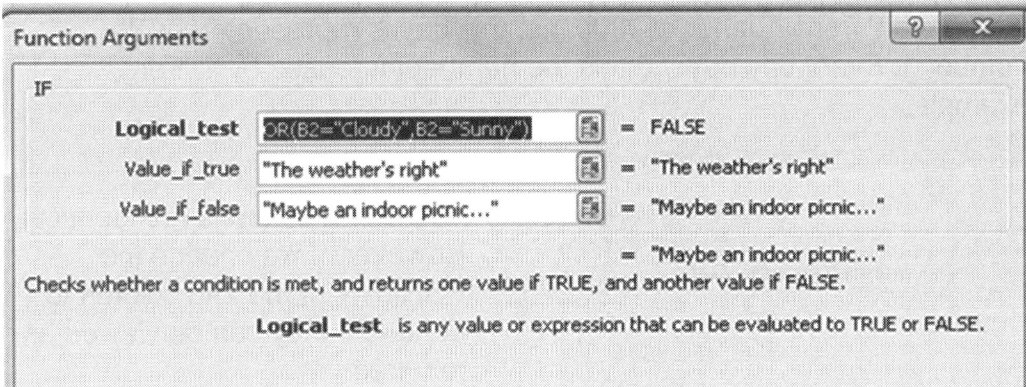


This is easier to understand than TRUE/FALSE and although it creates a long formula, it is no more complicated than any of the previous examples.

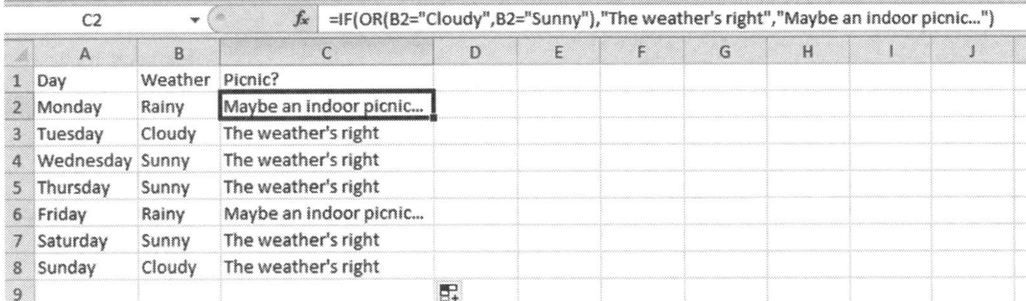


We might only want to go for a picnic on a sunny Saturday, for example. The idea is exactly the same – our logical test is "Is the day Saturday **AND** is the weather sunny?"

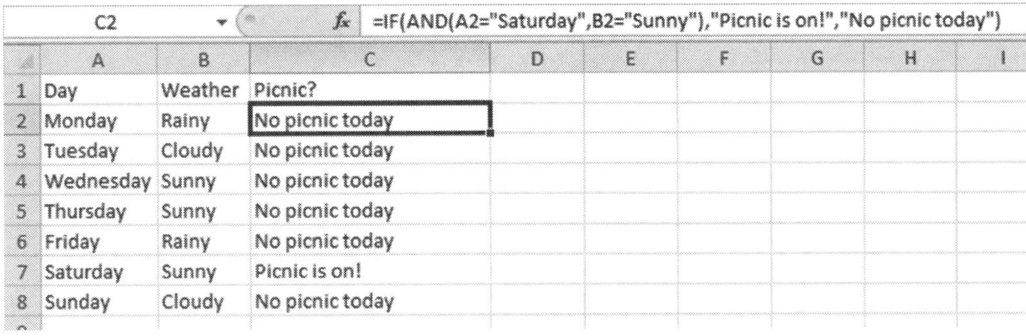

# 5 Date functions

## 5.1 Introduction

Date functions can be used to insert dates into worksheets so that they are always current or they can be used in formulas to help calculations.

To deal with dates, Excel treats every date as a number – how it is displayed is based on the format you choose in the Format Cells menu.

Dates 'start' from 1 January 1900, i.e. this day is represented by the number 1. Every day beyond this the number increases by 1. For example:

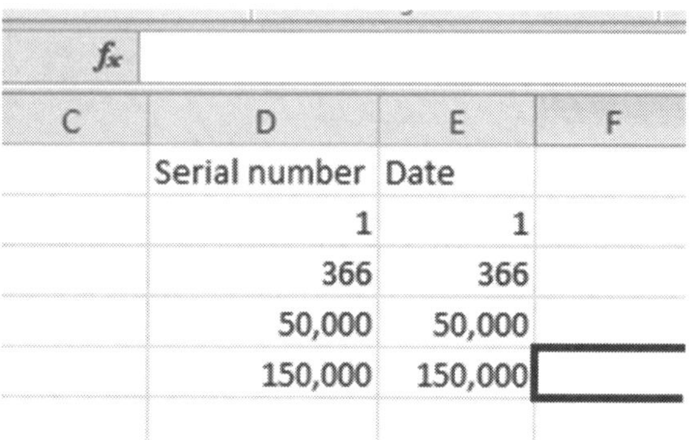

These two columns are identical. However, if we change the FORMAT of the 2nd column to be dates, they can be viewed as required.

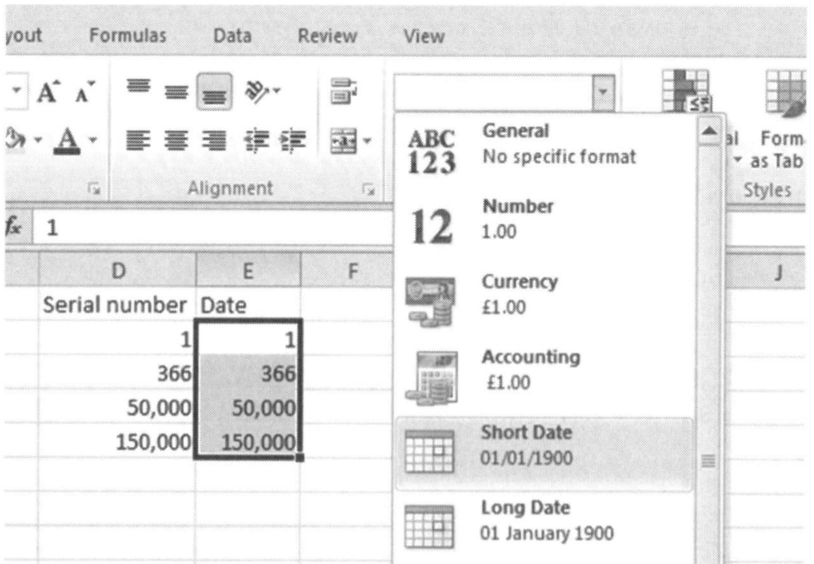

Select the cells, then either use the format cells option, or the drop down box in the **Home Menu**, under **Number**.

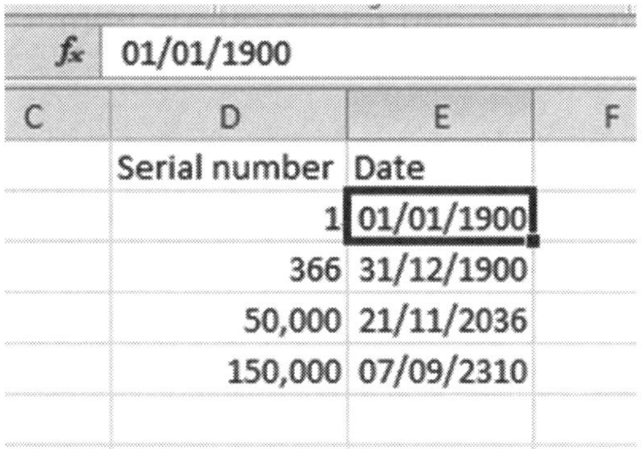

fx 01/01/1900

| C | D | E | F |
|---|---|---|---|
| | Serial number | Date | |
| | 1 | 01/01/1900 | |
| | 366 | 31/12/1900 | |
| | 50,000 | 21/11/2036 | |
| | 150,000 | 07/09/2310 | |

The dates are shown as required. Notice that they have been updated in the formula bar too.

## 5.2 NOW

The **NOW** function returns the current date and time.

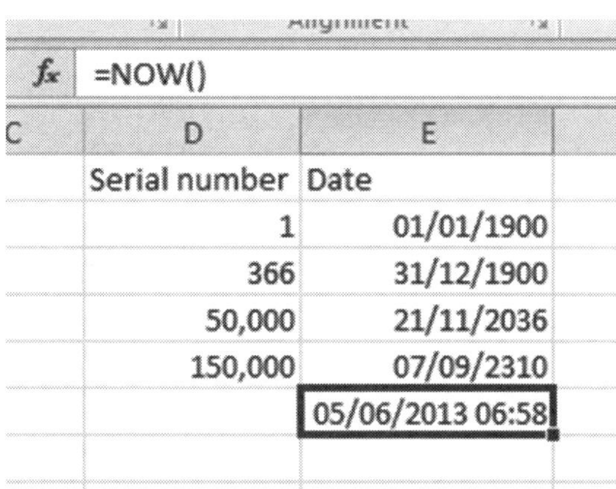

fx =NOW()

| C | D | E |
|---|---|---|
| | Serial number | Date |
| | 1 | 01/01/1900 |
| | 366 | 31/12/1900 |
| | 50,000 | 21/11/2036 |
| | 150,000 | 07/09/2310 |
| | | 05/06/2013 06:58 |

Notice the brackets – remember ALL functions in Excel take the form **=Function(arguments)**. NOW does not have any arguments, but still requires the brackets.

The cell is automatically formatted to show the date and time.

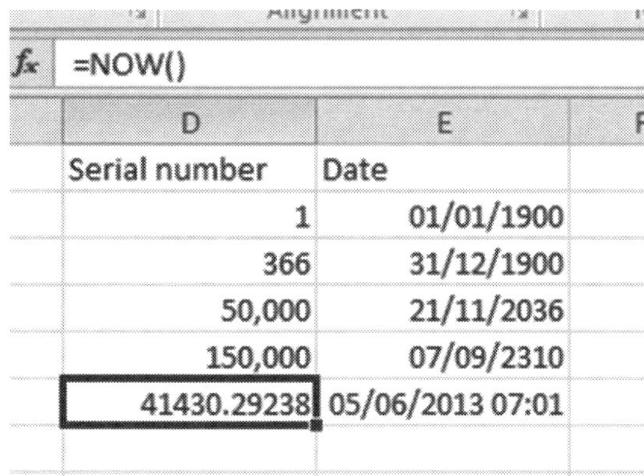

fx =NOW()

| D | E | F |
|---|---|---|
| Serial number | Date | |
| 1 | 01/01/1900 | |
| 366 | 31/12/1900 | |
| 50,000 | 21/11/2036 | |
| 150,000 | 07/09/2310 | |
| 41430.29238 | 05/06/2013 07:01 | |

Note that the format can be changed if required to show the serial number.

(also note the time changes – NOW shows the **current** time and date)

If you wish to 'fix' the value in the cell, use **copy** and **paste values** from the **Paste Special** menu.

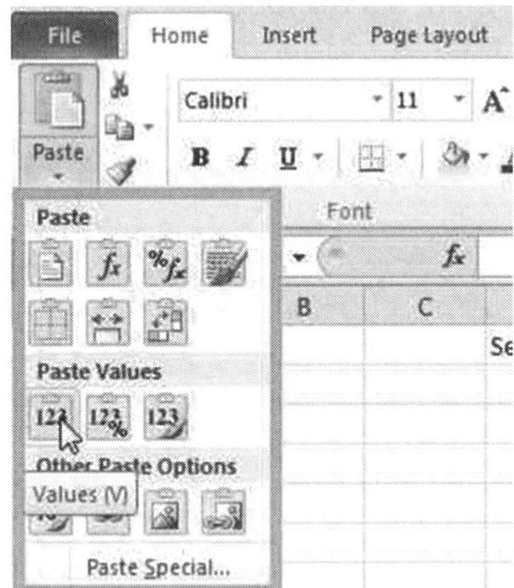


Paste values will remove the formulas from the cells.

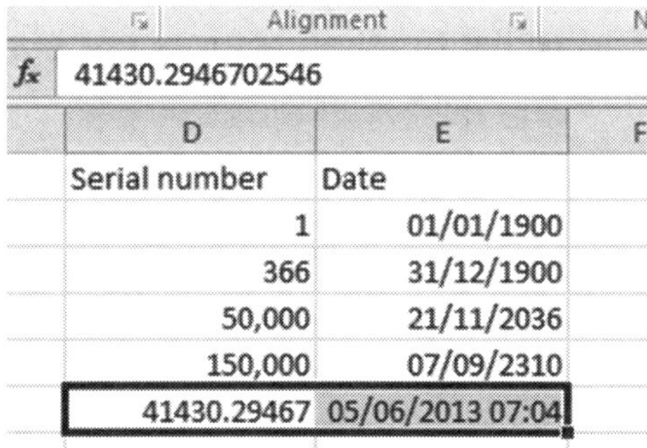

$f_x$ 41430.2946702546

| D | E |
|---|---|
| Serial number | Date |
| 1 | 01/01/1900 |
| 366 | 31/12/1900 |
| 50,000 | 21/11/2036 |
| 150,000 | 07/09/2310 |
| 41430.29467 | 05/06/2013 07:04 |

Now the date/time is fixed.

## 5.3 TODAY

**TODAY** is very similar to **NOW**, except that only todays date is shown, not the time.

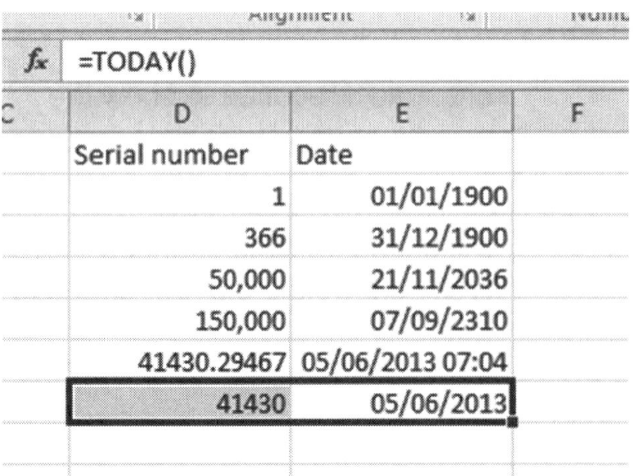

$f_x$ =TODAY()

| D | E |
|---|---|
| Serial number | Date |
| 1 | 01/01/1900 |
| 366 | 31/12/1900 |
| 50,000 | 21/11/2036 |
| 150,000 | 07/09/2310 |
| 41430.29467 | 05/06/2013 07:04 |
| 41430 | 05/06/2013 |

The format is set as a date, but can be changed if necessary.

## 5.4 DAY

The **DAY** function returns the day in the month of a given date or serial number.

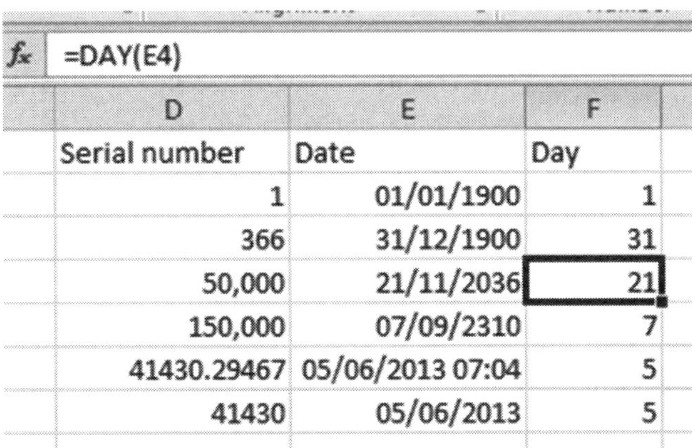

| Serial number | Date | Day |
|---|---|---|
| 1 | 01/01/1900 | 1 |
| 366 | 31/12/1900 | 31 |
| 50,000 | 21/11/2036 | 21 |
| 150,000 | 07/09/2310 | 7 |
| 41430.29467 | 05/06/2013 07:04 | 5 |
| 41430 | 05/06/2013 | 5 |

Just the day is shown. Note that **=DAY(D4)** would give the same result.

## 5.5 MONTH

Similar to **DAY**, this function returns the month (from 1-12) of a given date or serial number.

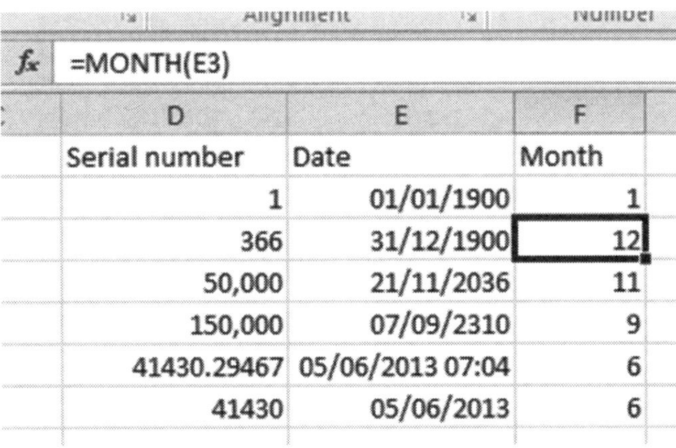

| Serial number | Date | Month |
|---|---|---|
| 1 | 01/01/1900 | 1 |
| 366 | 31/12/1900 | 12 |
| 50,000 | 21/11/2036 | 11 |
| 150,000 | 07/09/2310 | 9 |
| 41430.29467 | 05/06/2013 07:04 | 6 |
| 41430 | 05/06/2013 | 6 |

If you wanted to show this as "January", rather than 1, you could use **VLOOKUP**.

| | A | B | C | D | E | F |
|---|---|---|---|---|---|---|
| 1 | Number | Month | | Serial number | Date | Month |
| 2 | 1 | January | | 1 | 01/01/1900 | 1 |
| 3 | 2 | February | | 366 | 31/12/1900 | 12 |
| 4 | 3 | March | | 50,000 | 21/11/2036 | 11 |
| 5 | 4 | April | | 150,000 | 07/09/2310 | 9 |
| 6 | 5 | May | | 41430.29467 | 05/06/2013 07:04 | 6 |
| 7 | 6 | June | | 41430 | 05/06/2013 | 6 |
| 8 | 7 | July | | | | |
| 9 | 8 | August | | | | |
| 10 | 9 | September | | | | |
| 11 | 10 | October | | | | |
| 12 | 11 | November | | | | |
| 13 | 12 | December | | | | |

The VLOOKUP formula would then be:

F2 =VLOOKUP(MONTH(E2),$A$1:$B$13,2,FALSE)

| | A | B | C | D | E | F |
|---|---|---|---|---|---|---|
| 1 | Number | Month | | Serial number | Date | Month |
| 2 | 1 | January | | 1 | 01/01/1900 | January |
| 3 | 2 | February | | 366 | 31/12/1900 | December |
| 4 | 3 | March | | 50,000 | 21/11/2036 | November |
| 5 | 4 | April | | 150,000 | 07/09/2310 | September |
| 6 | 5 | May | | 41430.29467 | 05/06/2013 07:04 | June |
| 7 | 6 | June | | 41430 | 05/06/2013 | June |
| 8 | 7 | July | | | | |
| 9 | 8 | August | | | | |
| 10 | 9 | September | | | | |
| 11 | 10 | October | | | | |
| 12 | 11 | November | | | | |
| 13 | 12 | December | | | | |

Our **lookup_value** is MONTH(E2) – i.e. a number from 1-12. The formula will then search for this number is cells A1:A13, and give the value in the corresponding row of column B (the second column).

Note that this is not the only way to achieve this result – in Excel there is usually more than one way to achieve a desired result (for example using **SUM** or +) – if it works, it is correct!

## 5.6 YEAR

This function returns the year of a given date or serial number.

fx =YEAR(E4)

| C | D | E | F |
|---|---|---|---|
| | Serial number | Date | Year |
| | 1 | 01/01/1900 | 1900 |
| | 366 | 31/12/1900 | 1900 |
| | 50,000 | 21/11/2036 | 2036 |
| | 150,000 | 07/09/2310 | 2310 |
| | 41430.29467 | 05/06/2013 07:04 | 2013 |
| | 41430 | 05/06/2013 | 2013 |

Again, it does not matter whether column D or E is used – the same result would be given.

## 5.7 DATE

The DATE function converts numbers into a date. It is written as follows:

**=DATE(Year,Month,Day)**

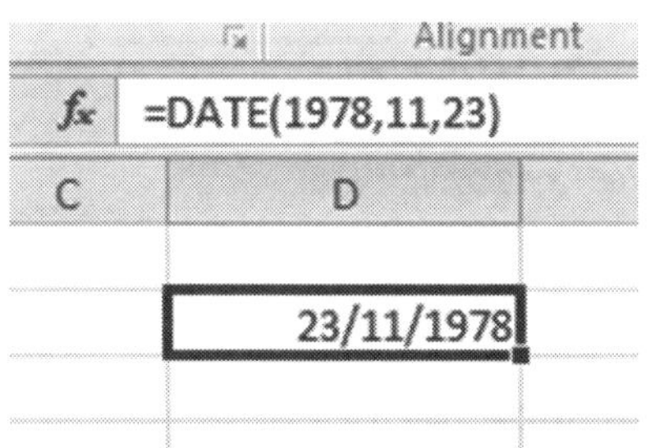

fx =DATE(1978,11,23)

| C | D |
|---|---|
| | |
| | 23/11/1978 |

Each argument can be a number, cell reference or calculation, as usual.

For example, you might want to find the first day of the month of a given date:

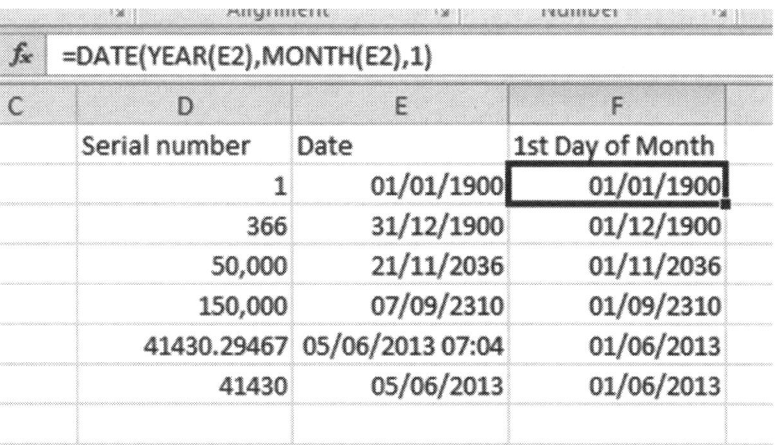

fx =DATE(YEAR(E2),MONTH(E2),1)

| C | D | E | F |
|---|---|---|---|
| | Serial number | Date | 1st Day of Month |
| | 1 | 01/01/1900 | 01/01/1900 |
| | 366 | 31/12/1900 | 01/12/1900 |
| | 50,000 | 21/11/2036 | 01/11/2036 |
| | 150,000 | 07/09/2310 | 01/09/2310 |
| | 41430.29467 | 05/06/2013 07:04 | 01/06/2013 |
| | 41430 | 05/06/2013 | 01/06/2013 |

## 5.8 WEEKDAY

This useful function returns the day of the week of a given date – from 1-7, with 1 being Sunday, 2 Monday, etc.

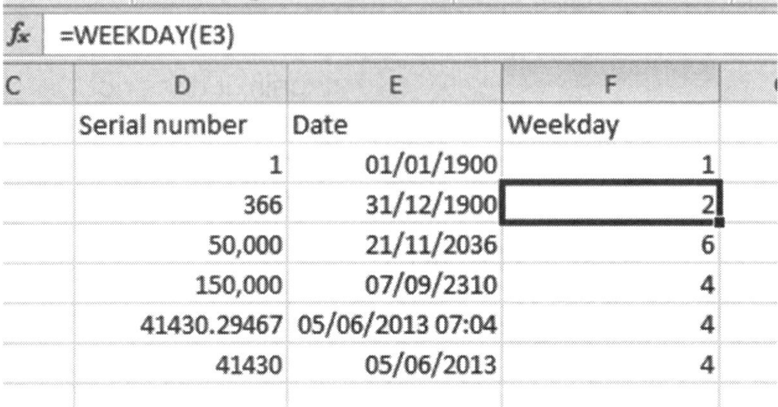

=WEEKDAY(E3)

| C | D | E | F |
|---|---|---|---|
| | Serial number | Date | Weekday |
| | 1 | 01/01/1900 | 1 |
| | 366 | 31/12/1900 | 2 |
| | 50,000 | 21/11/2036 | 6 |
| | 150,000 | 07/09/2310 | 4 |
| | 41430.29467 | 05/06/2013 07:04 | 4 |
| | 41430 | 05/06/2013 | 4 |

Again, it would be more use to see "Saturday" etc.

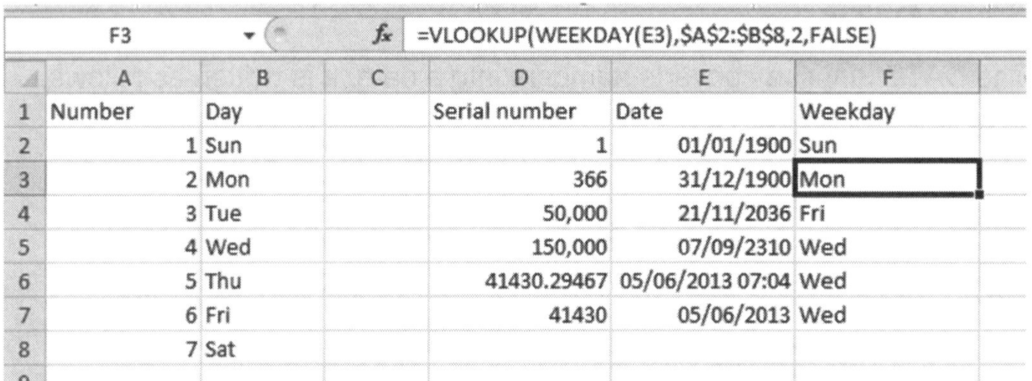

F3 =VLOOKUP(WEEKDAY(E3),$A$2:$B$8,2,FALSE)

| | A | B | C | D | E | F |
|---|---|---|---|---|---|---|
| 1 | Number | Day | | Serial number | Date | Weekday |
| 2 | 1 | Sun | | 1 | 01/01/1900 | Sun |
| 3 | 2 | Mon | | 366 | 31/12/1900 | Mon |
| 4 | 3 | Tue | | 50,000 | 21/11/2036 | Fri |
| 5 | 4 | Wed | | 150,000 | 07/09/2310 | Wed |
| 6 | 5 | Thu | | 41430.29467 | 05/06/2013 07:04 | Wed |
| 7 | 6 | Fri | | 41430 | 05/06/2013 | Wed |
| 8 | 7 | Sat | | | | |
| 9 | | | | | | |

Note in this example the **table_array** does not include the headers (row 1). It does not matter whether these are included or not.

# 6 Forecasting functions

## 6.1 Introduction

Excel contains a number of functions that allow you to forecast future figures based on current and historic data. The key one that you need to be familiar with is the FORECAST function.

## 6.2 The formula

The FORECAST formula is written as

**=FORECAST(x, known_y's, known_x's)**

- "x" is the independent variable for the forecast – e.g. the future month you want
- "known_y's" are the known dependent variables – e.g. sales figures we already have
- "known_x's" are the known independent variables – e.g. the months for which we already have sales figures

It is best to use absolute referencing for known_y's and known_x's in order to move the formula around.

## 6.3 Example

Suppose you are given sales for the first 9 months of the year and want to forecast sales for the six months after that.

| | A | B | C |
|---|---|---|---|
| 1 | Month | Sales | Forecast |
| 2 | "x" | "y" | |
| 3 | 1 | 10 | |
| 4 | 2 | 11 | |
| 5 | 3 | 13 | |
| 6 | 4 | 9 | |
| 7 | 5 | 12 | |
| 8 | 6 | 13 | |
| 9 | 7 | 15 | |
| 10 | 8 | 10 | |
| 11 | 9 | 14 | |
| 12 | 10 | | |
| 13 | 11 | | |
| 14 | 12 | | |
| 15 | 13 | | |
| 16 | 14 | | |
| 17 | 15 | | |
| 18 | | | |

In cell C12 we would enter **=FORECAST(A12,$B$3:$B$11,$A$3:$A$11)**

- The first element, **A12**, gives the "x" value of the month for which we need a forecast (month 10)
- The second, **$B$3:$B$11**, gives the range of sales figures ("y" values) we know (B3 to B11)
- Finally, **$A$3:$A$11** gives the range of months ("x" values) for which we know sales figures (A3 to A11)

This gives the forecast:

| | A | B | C |
|---|---|---|---|
| 1 | Month | Sales | Forecast |
| 2 | "x" | "y" | |
| 3 | 1 | 10 | |
| 4 | 2 | 11 | |
| 5 | 3 | 13 | |
| 6 | 4 | 9 | |
| 7 | 5 | 12 | |
| 8 | 6 | 13 | |
| 9 | 7 | 15 | |
| 10 | 8 | 10 | |
| 11 | 9 | 14 | |
| 12 | 10 | | 13.63889 |
| 13 | 11 | | |
| 14 | 12 | | |
| 15 | 13 | | |
| 16 | 14 | | |
| 17 | 15 | | |

Because we set up the references for known sales and months as absolute cell references, we can now drag the formula down for other months to give:

| | A | B | C |
|---|---|---|---|
| 1 | Month | Sales | Forecast |
| 2 | "x" | "y" | |
| 3 | 1 | 10 | |
| 4 | 2 | 11 | |
| 5 | 3 | 13 | |
| 6 | 4 | 9 | |
| 7 | 5 | 12 | |
| 8 | 6 | 13 | |
| 9 | 7 | 15 | |
| 10 | 8 | 10 | |
| 11 | 9 | 14 | |
| 12 | 10 | | 13.63889 |
| 13 | 11 | | 13.98889 |
| 14 | 12 | | 14.33889 |
| 15 | 13 | | 14.68889 |
| 16 | 14 | | 15.03889 |
| 17 | 15 | | 15.38889 |

We can then reformat column C and use the forecast in any other way we need.

## 7 Test your understanding

The activities in this guide are designed to test your knowledge on the techniques shown in this chapter. They may also use techniques used in previous chapters, to build up your knowledge. Suggested answers are available on MyKaplan, although it is better to refer to the notes and try to understand the methods than look straight at the answers.

### Test your understanding 12-1

This activity mainly tests use of the **ROUND** function, along with some conditional formatting and simple functions.

(a) Open the **Stock list** file in the **Activities** folder.

(b) Note the information – we have a list of stock items, the amount in stock and the total value of the stock. In column E, we need to calculate the cost per unit.

(c) In column E, calculate the **cost per unit**, rounded to **2 decimal places**.

(d) Format the figures in column E showing the figures to **3 decimal places**, with a **£** sign in front of the numbers (currency format).

(e) In cells E16, E17 and E18, enter formulas to show the **average**, **smallest** and **largest** cost per unit respectively.

(f) Label these as Average, Lowest and Highest in cells D16-D18.

(g) Use conditional formatting to fill the largest value in cells E2:E15 in yellow.

(h) Change the value in cell **C3** to **5** – Note that this should change the value in D18 to £45.60 and the E3 should fill yellow.

(i) Save the file in the **Solutions** folder as **Activity 12-1** and close it.

## Test your understanding 12-2

This is a normal **VLOOKUP**, with a date function.

(a) Open the **Stock Checker** workbook from the **Activities** folder.

(b) This is a simple stock checker – the product can be selected from a drop down menu in Cell A3. We need the number in stock to be returned from column D on the stock sheet.

(c) Use a **VLOOKUP** formula in **B3** to find the stock level based on the value in **A3**).

(d) Change the product in **A3** to '**Doodad 2**'. Click in A3 and select the drop down menu to change the product.

(e) The value in **B3** should change to **99**.

(f) Enter a formula to put **today's date** into **B1**.

(g) **Left-Align** and **Bold** cell **B1**.

(h) Save the file as **Activity 12-2** in the **Solutions** folder and close it.

## Test your understanding 12-3

This exercise requires the use of an **IF** function to check whether a target profit margin has been met.

(a) **Open** the **Target GP** file from the **Activities** folder.

(b) We need to calculate the Gross Profit in column D, and then GP % in column E. GP% is Gross Profit as a percentage of sales.

(c) **Format** the values in column E as **percentage** format to **1 decimal place**.

(d)

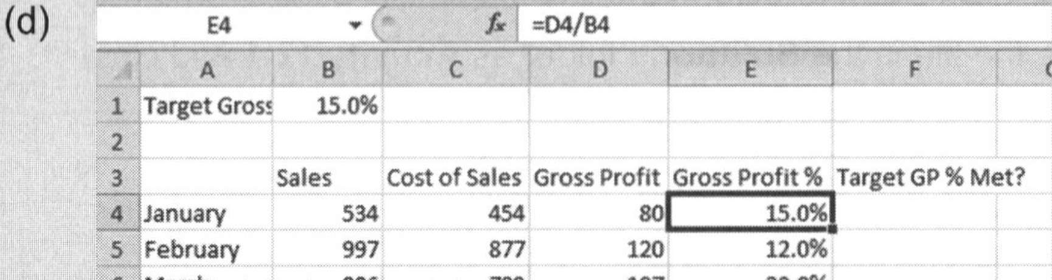

E4 =D4/B4

| | A | B | C | D | E | F |
|---|---|---|---|---|---|---|
| 1 | Target Gross | 15.0% | | | | |
| 2 | | | | | | |
| 3 | | Sales | Cost of Sales | Gross Profit | Gross Profit % | Target GP % Met? |
| 4 | January | 534 | 454 | 80 | 15.0% | |
| 5 | February | 997 | 877 | 120 | 12.0% | |

Your spreadsheet should look like this.

(e) Using an **IF** statement, return 'Yes' if the GP% is greater than or equal to the target in B1 and 'No' if it is not.

(f) Sense check your results – are you getting the results you expect?

(g)

| | A | B | C | D | E | F |
|---|---|---|---|---|---|---|
| 1 | Target Gross | 15.0% | | | | |
| 2 | | | | | | |
| 3 | | Sales | Cost of Sales | Gross Profit | Gross Profit % | Target GP % Met? |
| 4 | January | 534 | 454 | 80 | 15.0% | No |

You may find you get the above – this should be Yes – the target has been met! Let us see why it is not working.

(h) Change the **format** in column E to **2 decimal places**.

(i)

| Gross Profit % | Target GP % Met? |
|---|---|
| 14.98% | No |

As this calculation is unrounded, the target has not been met.

(j) Use the **ROUND** function in column E to round the calculation to 3 **decimal places.** Note that for percentages, 14.98% is equivalent to 0.1498, so we need to round to 3 decimal places.

(k) Your Formulas should now work. If you are not getting the results you expect, check the formula that is not working – see which cells are being used. It is usually a problem with absolute/relative references.

(l) **Change** the value in **B1** to 20% – see how column F changes.

(m) **AutoFit** the column widths and save as **Activity 12-3** in the Solutions folder. Close the file.

## Test your understanding 12-4

This example uses calculations across worksheets, as well as requiring an **IF** formula.

(a) **Open** the **Boat sales** file from the **Activities** folder.

(b) This workbook contains four worksheets:

**Sales Volume** – shows the sales to four customers of four different products.

**Pricing** – shows the price of the four products.

**Discounting** – shows the discount offered to each customer if target sales are met.

**Monthly sales** – calculates revenue, and any discount offered.

The calculations are required on the **Monthly Sales** worksheet.

(c) On the Monthly Sales sheet, in cells **C4:F7**, calculate the sales revenue from each product by customer. Note that a combination of relative and mixed referencing is required.

(d) Calculate the totals by product and customer in cells **G4:G7** and **C9:G9**.

(e) In cells **H4:H7** we need to calculate the value of the discount. A discount is given **IF** the actual sales (from the Sales Volume sheet) are greater than or equal to the volume target for each customer – in cells B4:B7.

The discount offered will be the total sales figure multiplied by the discount on the Discounting sheet.

(f) Calculate the **discounted sales in column I** and **copy the totals across** in row 9.

(g) In **J4:J7** you need a formula to say 'Yes' if a discount has been given and 'No' if it has not. There are several ways to achieve this.

(h) Save the file as **Activity 12-4** in the **Solutions** folder and close it.

## Test your understanding 12-5

This example builds on the last example, but requires the use of an AND formula.

(a) **Open** the **Boat sales Two** file from the **Activities** folder.

(b) This workbook contains four worksheets:

**Sales Volume** – shows the sales to four customers of four different products.

**Pricing** – shows the price of the four products.

**Discounting** – shows the discount offered to each customer if target sales are met.

**Monthly sales** – calculates revenue, and any discount offered.

The calculations are required on the **Monthly Sales** worksheet.

(c) On the Monthly Sales sheet, in cells **C4:D7**, calculate the sales revenue from each product by customer. Note that a combination of relative and mixed referencing is required.

(d) Calculate the totals by product and customer in cells **E4:E7** and **C9:E9**.

(e) In cells **F4:F7** we need to calculate the value of the discount. A discount is now given **IF** the actual sales (from the Sales Volume sheet) **FOR EACH PRODUCT** are greater than or equal to the volume target for each customer – in cells B4:B7. So the sales for SuperCruise AND the sales for Windrush must be bigger than target – this will form your logical test.

The discount offered will be the total sales figure multiplied by the discount on the Discounting sheet.

(f) Calculate the discounted sales in column I, and copy the totals across in row 9.

(g) In **H4:H7** you need a formula to say 'Yes' if a discount has been given and 'No' if it has not. There are several ways to achieve this.

(h) Save the file as **Activity 12-5** in the **Solutions** folder and close it.

## Test your understanding 12-6

This example builds on the last example, but requires the use of an **OR** formula.

(a) **Open** the **Boat sales Three** file from the **Activities** folder.

(b) This workbook contains four worksheets:

**Sales Volume** – shows the sales to four customers of four different products.

**Pricing** – shows the price of the four products.

**Discounting** – shows the discount offered to each customer if target sales are met.

**Monthly sales** – calculates revenue, and any discount offered.

The calculations are required on the **Monthly Sales** worksheet.

(c) On the Monthly Sales sheet, in cells **C4:D7**, calculate the sales revenue from each product by customer. Note that a combination of relative and mixed referencing is required.

(d) Calculate the totals by product and customer in cells **E4:E7** and **C9:E9**.

(e) In cells **F4:F7** we need to calculate the discounted sales. A discount is now given IF the actual sales (from the Sales Volume sheet) **FOR EITHER PRODUCT** are greater than or equal to the volume target for each customer – in cells B4:B7. So the sales for SuperCruise OR the sales for Windrush must be bigger than target – this will form your logical test.

(f) Copy the **totals** across in row 9.

(g) In **G4:G7** you need a formula to say 'Yes' if a discount has been given and 'No' if it has not. There are several ways to achieve this.

(h) Save the file as **Activity 12-6** in the **Solutions** folder and close it.

## Test your understanding 12-7

This is an example of a **VLOOKUP** requiring the use of **TRUE** rather than FALSE as the final argument, included for illustration purposes.

(a) **Open** the **Salary VLookup** file from the **Activities** folder.

(b) This workbook contains two worksheets:

**Lookup Table** – Shows a range of sales targets, along with the basic salaries, commission and bonus which would be paid at those levels.

**Salary Calculator** – based on the salary entered in cell D5, the basic wage, commission and bonus should be calculated using the information in **Lookup Table**.

(c) On the **Salary Calculator** worksheet, enter a test value for sales of **15000** in **D5**.

(d) We now need to populate the Basic Wage in **D9**. This requires the **Lookup Table**.

(e) We need a formula to 'find' the appropriate sales range (in this case 0-20000), and return the value in column C, the basic. This is done using **VLOOKUP**. Enter a **VLOOKUP** formula in cell **D9** on Salary Calculator. Note you will need to make the **Range_lookup TRUE** (see note at the end of the activity).

(f) With a correct formula you should get a basic wage of £1,000. Change the 15000 in D5 to 75000 and the basic should change to £1,100.

(g) We need a similar lookup for commission in **E9** on **Salary Calculator**. We need the lookup to calculate the value of the salary so remember to multiply the % by the monthly sales figure.

(h) Put a similar formula in to **F9** to calculate the bonus (as a percentage of monthly sales) and find the **total** in **G9**.

(i) Save the file in the **Solutions** folder as **Activity 12-7** and close it.

**Note**: If we had used FALSE instead of TRUE in this activity, the formula would 'look' down cells A1:A8 of the table to try and find 15,000, but it is not there, so a #N/A error would be shown.

TRUE finds the nearest match which is smaller than the lookup value, again working down the column. So A1='Sales' – this would be ignored as it is not a number. A2=0 – 15000 is bigger than zero, so try the next. A3=20,001 – this is bigger than 15000, so use the data in row 2, and give a Basic of 1000.

When we changed sales to 75000, the nearest match which is smaller than 75000 is 50000, so a basic of 1100 is given, as required.

## Test your understanding 12-8

This is the same example as Activity 12-7, but using **HLOOKUP**

(a) **Open** the **Salary HLookup** file from the **Activities** folder.

(b) Following the steps in **activity 12-7**, use **HLOOKUP** to find a Basic Wage, Commission and Bonus based on the Monthly Sales in cell D5, along with a total.

(c) Make sure the value in **D5** is **zero** – You should see **#N/A** errors:

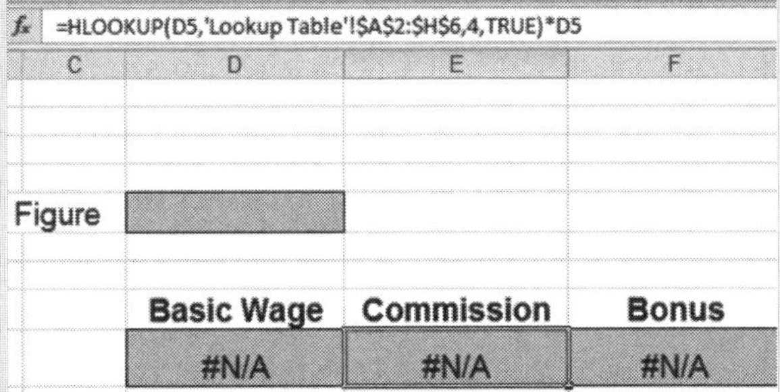

(d) This is because of the Lookup Table. Notice that the first salary is £1. The lookup looks for the nearest value less than or equal to zero – as there are no values less than or equal to zero, #N/A is returned. **Change the sales figure to 1**, and the lookups will work.

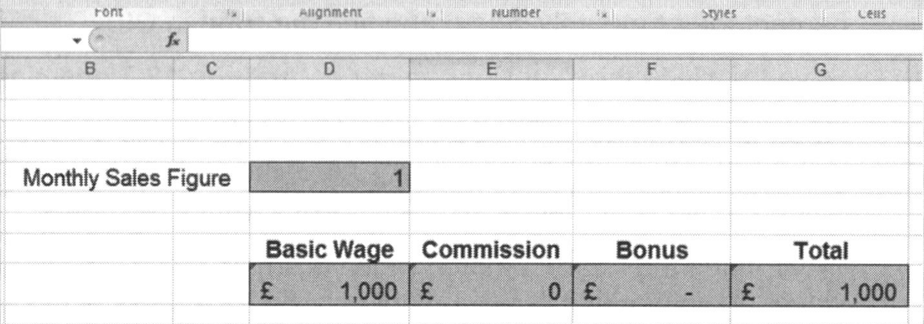

| B | C | D | E | F | G |
|---|---|---|---|---|---|
| Monthly Sales Figure | | 1 | | | |
| | | Basic Wage | Commission | Bonus | Total |
| | | £ 1,000 | £ 0 | £ - | £ 1,000 |

(e) #N/A errors do not look very professional. We could use an IF statement to remove them. The idea would be IF the value in D5 is zero, show zero, otherwise do the lookup.

Add IF statements to cells D9, E9 and F9 to remove the #N/A errors.

(f) Change the sales back to zero to check that the errors do not appear.

(g) Save the file as **Activity 12-8** in the **Solutions** folder and close it.

# Tracing errors in formulas

13

## Introduction

This chapter will help you to understand the types of errors that can occur and learn how to trace errors in formulas. It will also demonstrate how to use some of Excel's tools to find errors and some useful ways to track down any problems you may be having with your formulas.

### ASSESSMENT CRITERIA

Use appropriate tools to identify and resolve errors (4.1)

Protect integrity of data (4.3)

Report accounting information (5.2)

### CONTENTS

# 1 Types of error

## 1.1 Introduction

You need to be aware of a number of different types of error. The errors below will be displayed in the cell where the problem is.

| Error | Description |
|---|---|
| **#DIV/0!** | This occurs if we have tried to divide by zero or a blank cell. |
| **#N/A** | This occurs if data is not available. It is common in LOOKUP functions. |
| **#NAME?** | This occurs if we use a name that Excel doesn't recognise. This is common in incorrectly spelled function names. |
| **#NUM!** | This occurs if you place an invalid argument in a function. |
| **#REF!** | This occurs if a formula uses an invalid cell reference. |
| **#VALUE!** | This occurs if we attempt to use an incorrect data type. |

**Tip**

When you are editing a cell that contains a formula, Excel colour codes the formula and then places a coloured border around cells that make up the formula.

## 1.2 Formula AutoCorrect

When writing formulas sometimes parentheses (Brackets) get left out or placed in the wrong order, or you might enter the wrong number of arguments (syntax error). **Formula AutoCorrect** will pop up on screen and offer to correct the problem. Whilst Excel is very good at finding errors you do need to be careful as it sometimes guesses incorrectly.

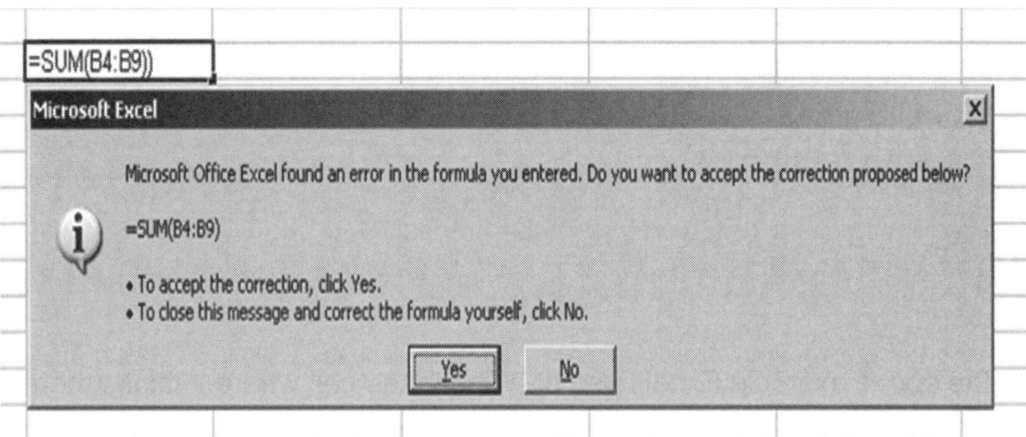


In the example above Excel has correctly determined that one too many brackets have been placed in the formula. In this instance you can accept the offered solution.

# 2 Identifying errors

## 2.1 Error checking

Excel can be set up to check for errors, and highlight problem cells. The settings can be found in the **File** tab, under **Options, Formulas.**

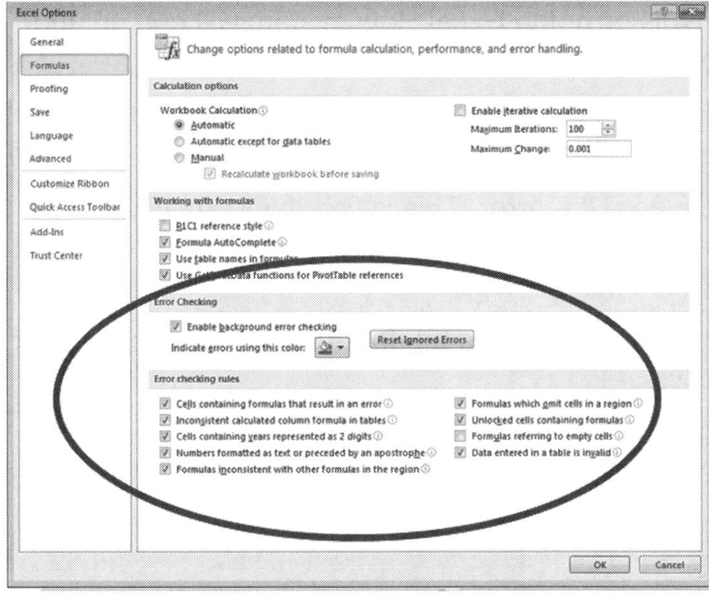


These options allow you to set your own rules for error checking. It is probably best left in its default setting.

If Error Checking is turned on, when a problem is found with a formula, Excel will place a green 'flag' in the cell.

Excel also has a more local error checking tool. When you enter a formula Excel will place a flag in a cell if it thinks you are making an error.

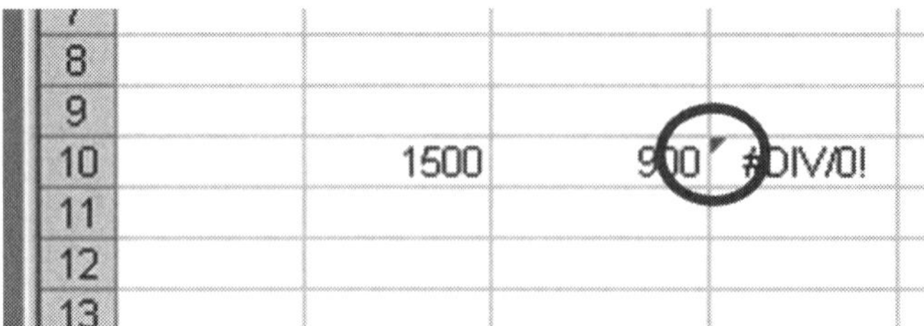


In the above example Excel has put a flag in the cell where it thinks there is an error. If you click into the error cell you will be given the option to review and deal with the error.

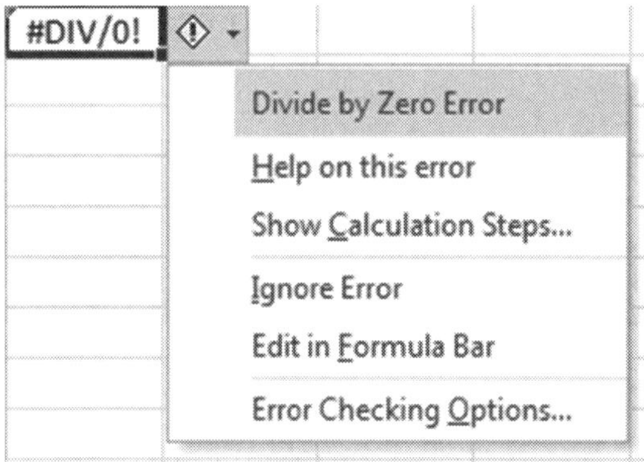


Above you can see a **Divide by zero error**. You now have the opportunity to get help from a number of sources, or ignore the error.

- If you click Help on this error the Excel Help system will pop up and you can ask questions and seek help from here.
- 'Show calculation steps' is dealt with later in the chapter under **Evaluate Formula**.
- You can choose to ignore the error. This is fine if you know what the problem is and can fix it, but you should not simply ignore the error as you will create problems elsewhere.
- Edit in formula bar puts the cursor in the formula bar, and you can fix your problem directly.
- Error checking options will bring up the menu shown in 2.1.

# 3 Formula Auditing Toolbar

## 3.1 Introduction

The **Formula Auditing Toolbar** is a very useful tool for finding and controlling errors in spreadsheets – especially complex ones. It is found in the **Formulas** tab.

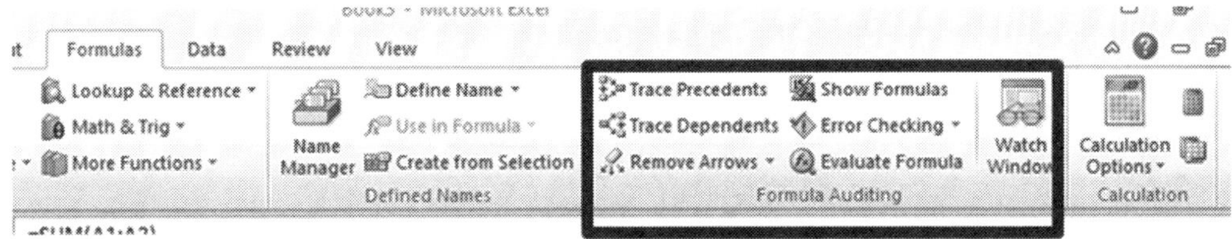


The different options will be explained in the rest of the chapter.

## 3.2 Trace precedents

This useful tool allows you to see which cells are used in the calculation of your selected cell. This is helpful if you are trying to work out why a formula is giving an unexpected value or error.

Function Library

C7 =B7*A$2

| | A | B | C | D |
|---|---|---|---|---|
| 1 | Labour rate: | Bonus % | | |
| 2 | £8.00 | 10% | | |
| 3 | | | | |
| 4 | Staff number | Hours worked | Basic pay | Bonus |
| 5 | F0254 | 35 | £280.00 | £28.00 |
| 6 | F0255 | 32 | £256.00 | £25.60 |
| 7 | F0256 | 34 | £272.00 | £27.20 |
| 8 | F0257 | 35 | £280.00 | £28.00 |

Clicking the 'Trace Precedents' button with C7 selected will show which cells are being used.

### 3.3 Trace dependents

Similar to trace precedents, clicking this button will show all the cells which are referring to this cell in a formula.

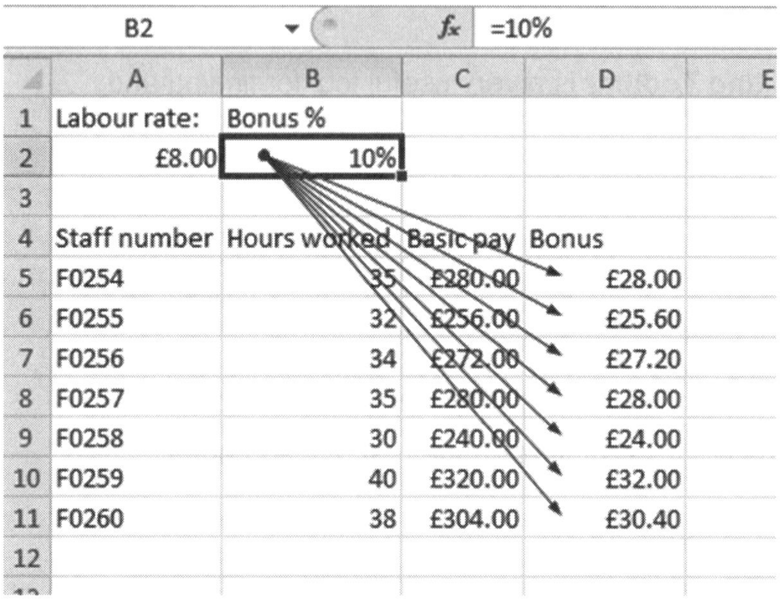

B2 =10%

| | A | B | C | D | E |
|---|---|---|---|---|---|
| 1 | Labour rate: | Bonus % | | | |
| 2 | £8.00 | 10% | | | |
| 3 | | | | | |
| 4 | Staff number | Hours worked | Basic pay | Bonus | |
| 5 | F0254 | 35 | £280.00 | £28.00 | |
| 6 | F0255 | 32 | £256.00 | £25.60 | |
| 7 | F0256 | 34 | £272.00 | £27.20 | |
| 8 | F0257 | 35 | £280.00 | £28.00 | |
| 9 | F0258 | 30 | £240.00 | £24.00 | |
| 10 | F0259 | 40 | £320.00 | £32.00 | |
| 11 | F0260 | 38 | £304.00 | £30.40 | |
| 12 | | | | | |

### 3.4 Remove arrows

If you have been using Trace Precedents/Dependents, this button will remove all of the arrows from the spreadsheet. There are two options within this button – to just remove precedent or dependent arrows.

### 3.5 Show formulas

This has already been seen in a previous chapter – this button toggles between showing the results of the formula in a cell, and showing the formula itself.

### 3.6 Evaluate formula

This may be the most useful function within the Formula Auditing toolbar – it allows you to work through a formula step by step to see how the result is being calculated. It is especially useful for more complicated formulas like **VLOOKUP** and **IF** statements.

To Evaluate a Formula, select the cell and click '**Evaluate Formula**'.

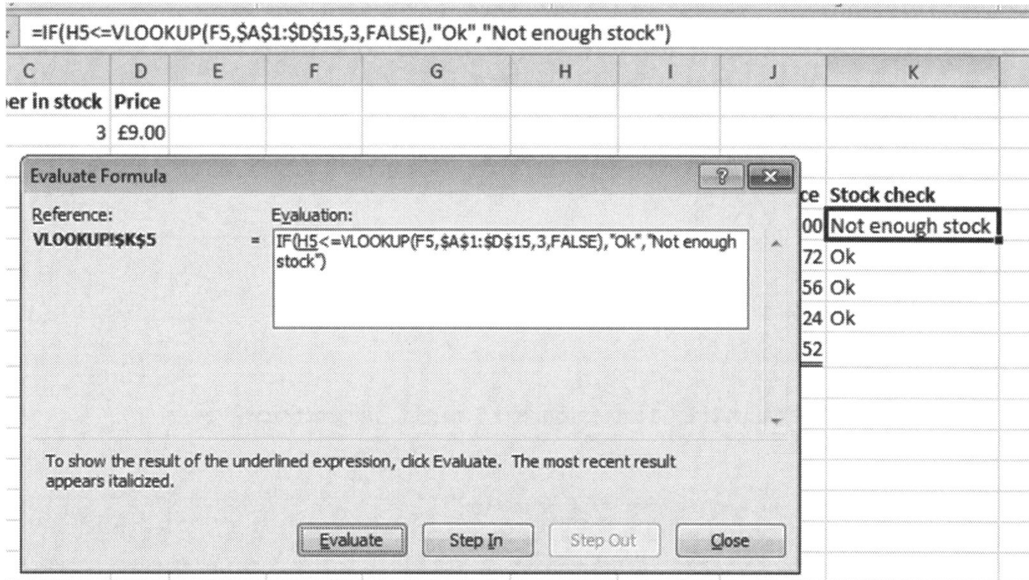


This is a fairly complicated formula using an **IF** statement and a **VLOOKUP** – explained in detail in Chapter 12. You can see that the '**H5**' in the formula is underlined – this means that Excel will calculate this part of the formula first. Click on '**Evaluate**' to move on to the next part of the calculation.

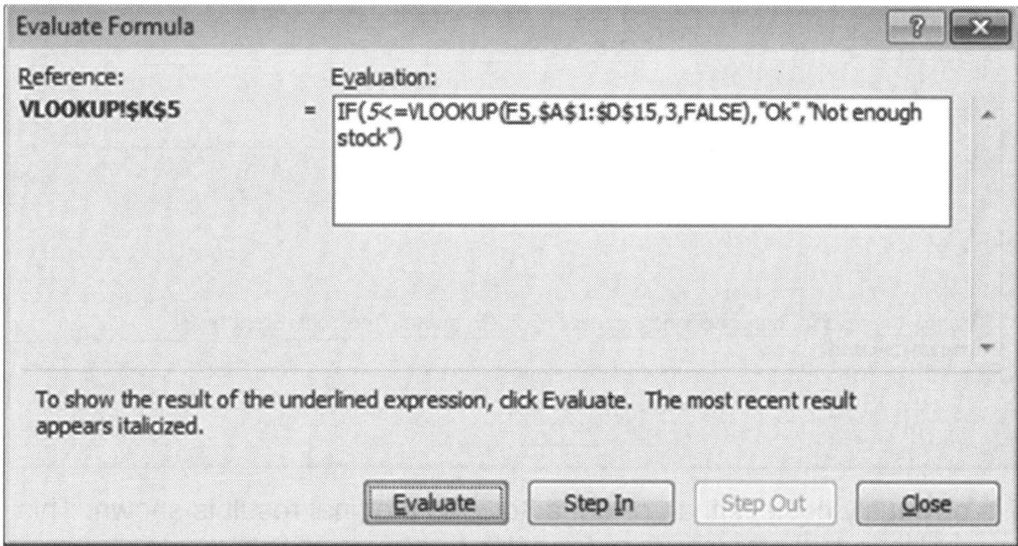


The value in cell H5 is 5. The next part of the evaluation is '**F5**'. Keep clicking '**Evaluate**' to see how the calculation works.

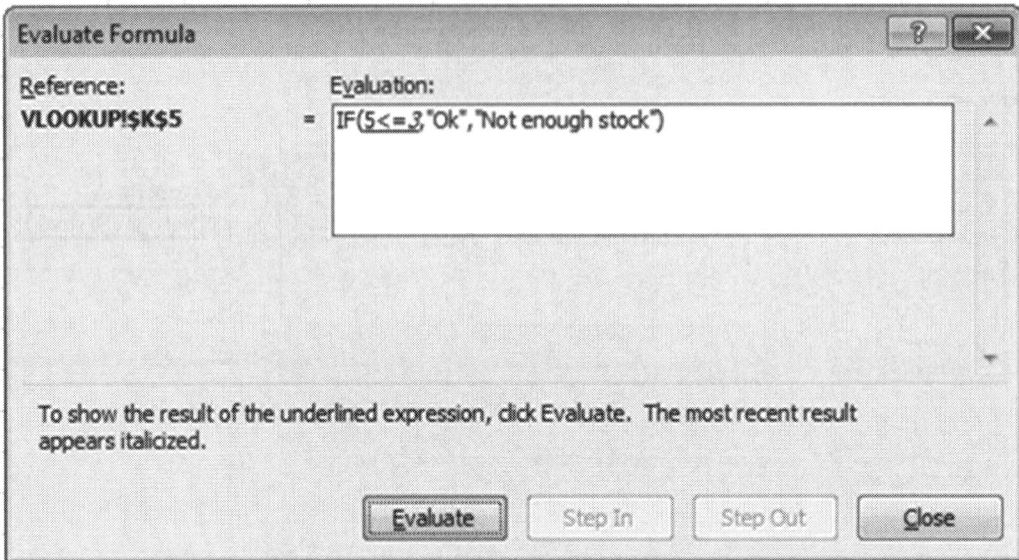


After a few clicks, we have the expression above. '3' is the value of the VLOOKUP part of the formula – this is now a simple IF function – IF 5 is less than or equal to 3, then put "Ok", otherwise put "Not enough stock".

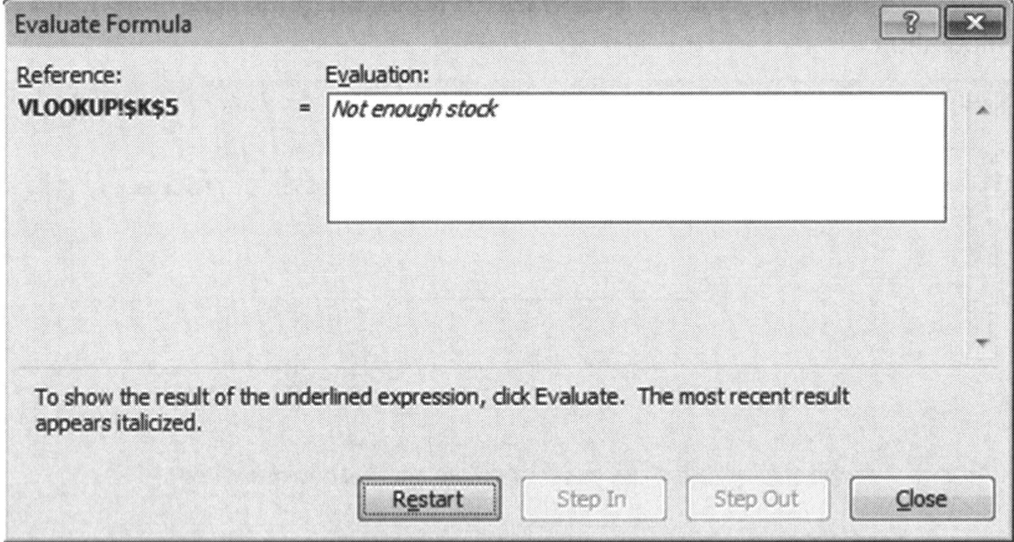


5 is obviously not less than or equal to 3, so the final result is shown. This can make finding errors in your formulas very easy to find.

## 3.7 Watch Window

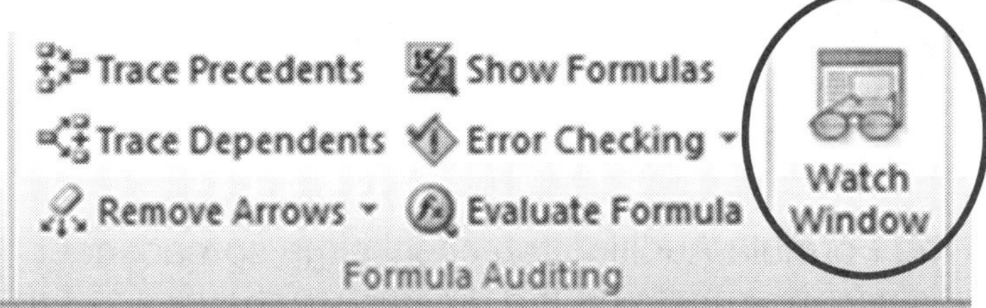


This tool is most useful when dealing with formulas that reference across multiple worksheets or workbooks. It allows you to 'watch' a cell or cells, without having to have that cell visible on your worksheet.

To select a cell to 'watch', click on the **'Watch Window**' button, then '**Add Watch**', and select the cell you wish to watch. The window will then show the cell's formula and value even if you don't have that sheet visible.

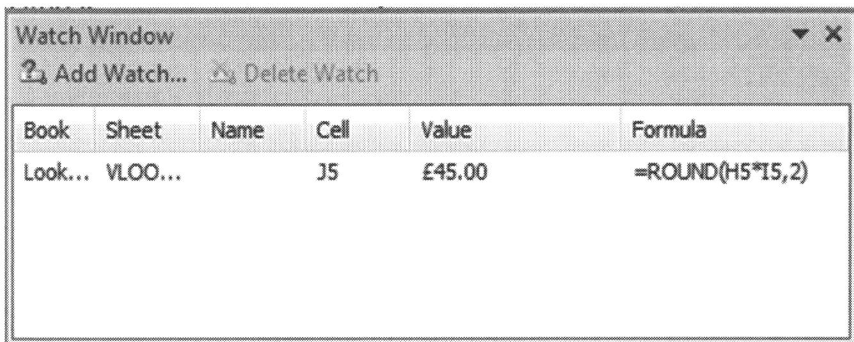


| | A | B | C | D |
|---|---|---|---|---|
| 1 | Labour rate: | Bonus % | | |
| 2 | 8 | =10% | | |
| 3 | | | | |
| 4 | Staff number | Hours worked | Basic pay | Bonus |
| 5 | F0254 | 35 | =B5*A$2 | =C5*B$2 |
| 6 | F0255 | 32 | =B6*A$2 | =C6*B$2 |
| 7 | F0256 | 34 | =B7*A$2 | =C7*B$2 |
| 8 | F0257 | 35 | =B8*A$2 | =C8*B$2 |
| 9 | F0258 | 30 | =B9*A$2 | =C9*B$2 |
| 10 | F0259 | 40 | =B10*A$2 | =C10*B$2 |
| 11 | F0260 | 38 | =B11*A$2 | =C11*B$2 |
| 12 | | | | |

# 4 Error checking

## 4.1 Introduction

This button, located on the Formula Auditing tab checks the spreadsheet for cells with errors, and gives more help on the options you have.

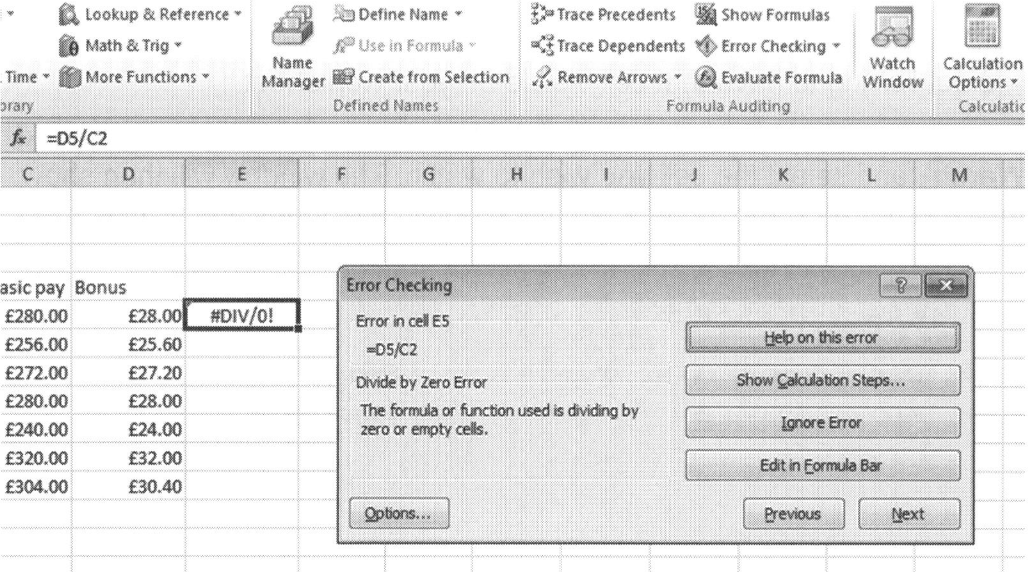


Here, we have a Divide by Zero error which has been highlighted. The options are:

- **Help on this error** – brings up the Help Function.
- **Show Calculation Steps** – performs the **Evaluate Formula** function (see below) on the cell.
- **Ignore Error** – moves on to the next error on the sheet.
- **Edit in Formula Bar** – allows you to correct the error.
- **Options** – brings up the menu shown in **Section 12.4**.
- **Previous** – move back to the last error found.
- **Next** – move on to the next error in the sheet (same as **Ignore**).

There are two other options available within the Error Checking button.

## 4.2 Trace error

This works in the same way as **Trace Precedents**, allowing you to see which cells are being used in order to help find where the error is coming from.

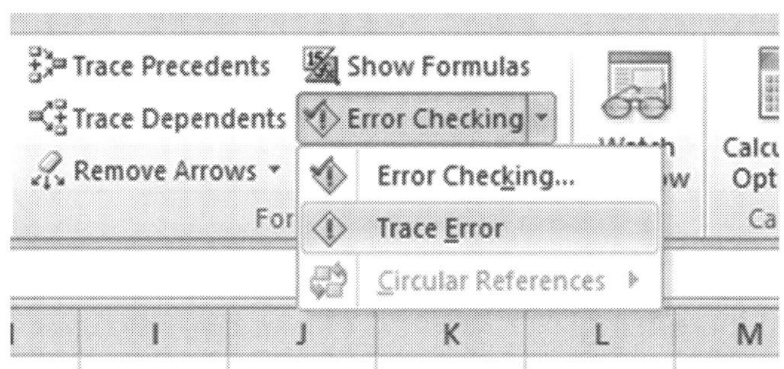


If the Active Cell contains an error, then clicking this will show the cells used in the formula.

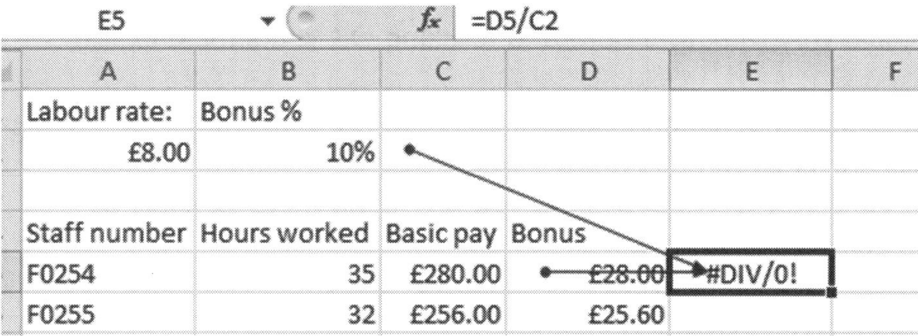


## 4.3 Circular references

If there are circular references in your workbook, this menu allows you to identify and navigate to them quickly. If there are no circular references it will be greyed out and unavailable for selection.

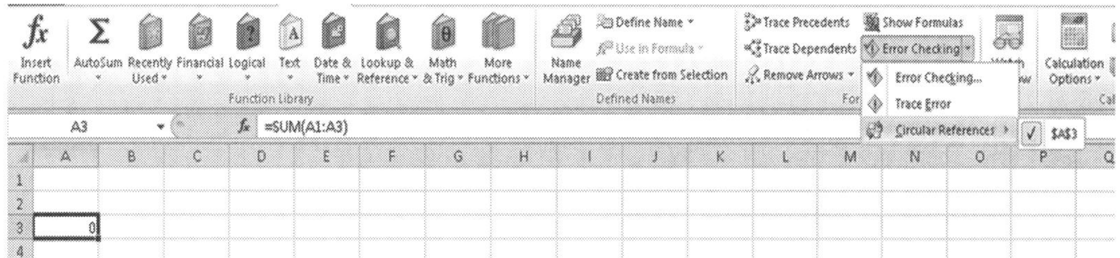


A circular reference is a common error and occurs when you try to include the cell that we are writing a formula in as part of the formula. For example:

If you typed the following formula into Cell A3, you would get a circular reference message.

**=SUM(A1:A3)**

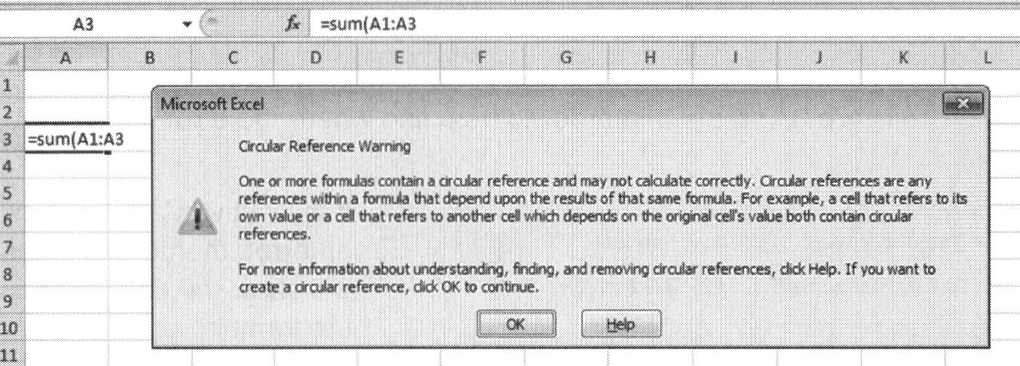


This is a circular reference, as you are telling Excel to add the value in cell A3 to cell A3 – it should keep increasing!

As the warning says, you can click on help to get more detail, or just click OK to continue. Although circular references can be required in some situations, it is very rare, therefore after clicking OK you should fix the formula.

Excel will allow you to continue with the circular reference in place, but the formula will not work and can cause strange results. To try and bring attention to this, the Status Bar at the bottom of the page displays a warning if a circular reference is in place.

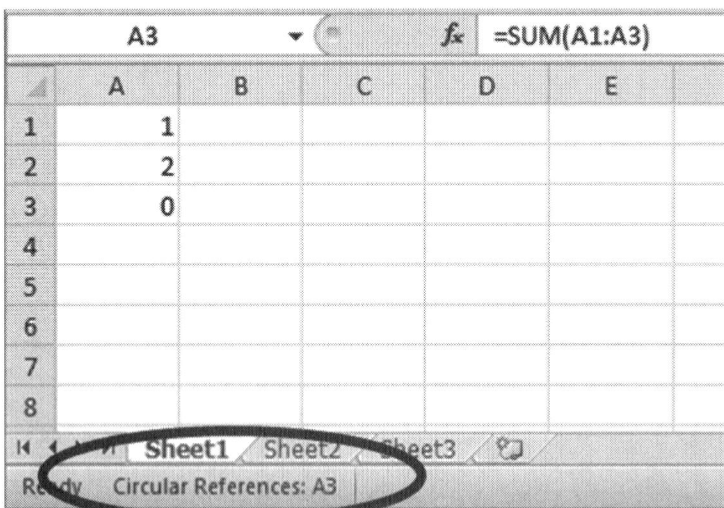

# 5 Formula Bar

## 5.1 Using the Formula Bar to Evaluate a Formula

A useful little trick is to use the formula bar to evaluate a section of a complicated formula. Using the same example, we might want to know what the value returned from the **VLOOKUP** would be. Highlight (left-click and drag) the part of the formula you wish to evaluate in the formula bar:

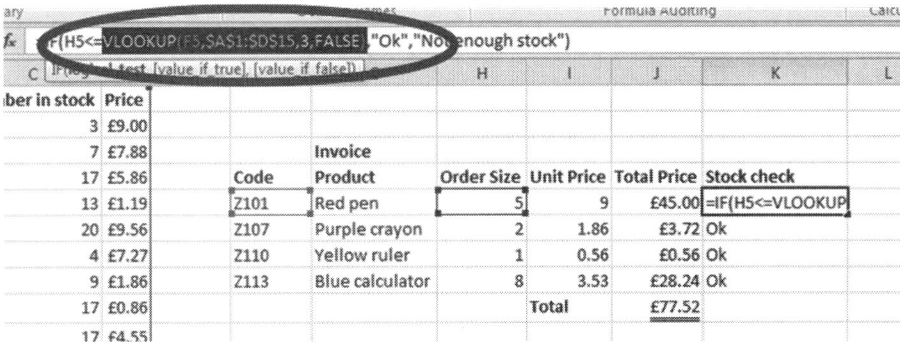

Press **F9** to evaluate this part of the Formula.

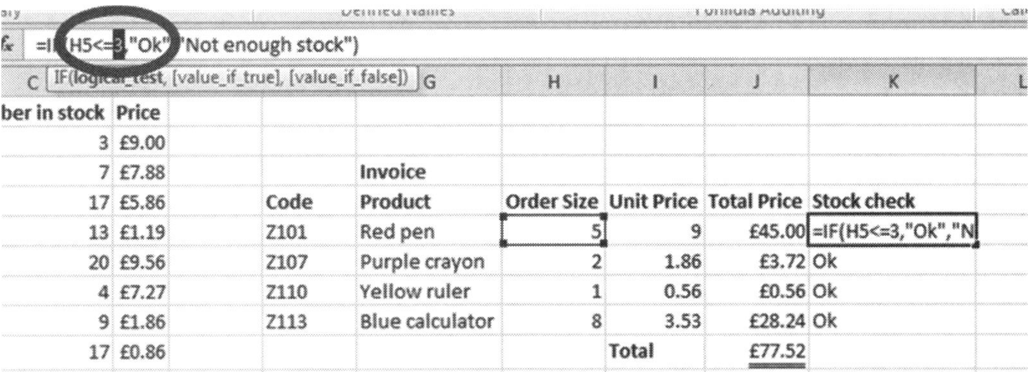

The value of the highlighted section is shown.

**Note:** press **ESCAPE** if you want to leave the formula as it was originally. If you press Enter then the formula will be shown as above, with the value in instead of the formula. Of course if you do this, pressing **Ctrl-Z** (undo) will correct the mistake.

## 6 Test your understanding

These techniques can be applied to any spreadsheet – try to use them wherever possible. Complicated formulas often don't work the first time you try them – use error checking techniques to try and find where the problem is.

# Charts and graphs

## Introduction

This chapter will guide you on how to create a number of different graphs and how to move and change these charts and graphs within the spreadsheet. We will be looking at several types of charts and their construction, formatting and location.

In essence there is very little difference between a chart and a graph and the term is interchangeable. One minor difference is that some charts do not have axes, whilst graphs always do.

### ASSESSMENT CRITERIA

Select and use appropriate tools to generate and format charts (3.3)

Edit and update data (3.4)

Assess that new data has been accurately added (4.2)

### CONTENTS

# 1 Terminology

## 1.1 Chart and graph terminology

Listed below are the more common charting terms:

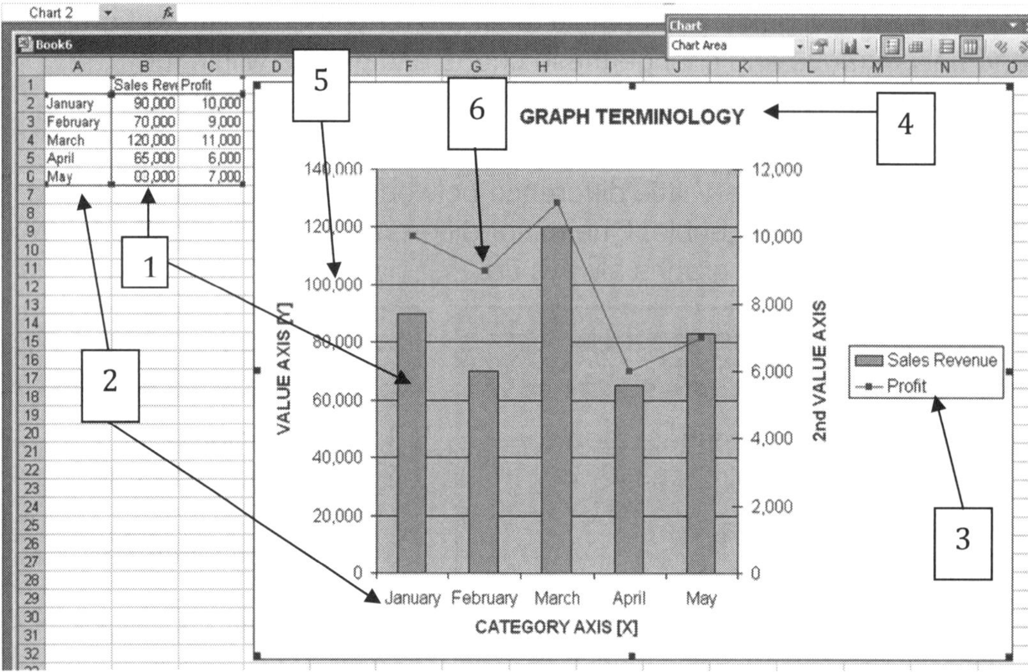


1 **Data Series** – these are the numbers **[values]** from which Excel is creating the graph. These are plotted on the **Value or 'Y' axis**.

2 **Category** – the information that identifies the data series. This is plotted along the **Category or 'X' axis**.

3 **Legend** – this identifies the different data series.

4 **Title** – gives meaning to the graph.

5 **Scale** – both the 'X' and the 'Y' axis (if numerical) can have a scale. These identify the range of values in the data series.

6 **Data Point** – this denotes the value of a particular data series. **Data Labels** can be placed next to data points to give greater meaning. Data Points have Data Markers. **Data Markers** are different shapes and colours for each data series.

### 1.2 Creating charts and graphs

Within Excel there are two basic ways to display charts and graphs. There is no right or wrong way; it is down to user preference. It is also a simple matter to switch between the two types.

1 **Chart Sheet** – here the chart or graph becomes the entire worksheet.

2 **Embedded** – here the chart or graph is located on the sheet that contains the data. The chart can be moved around to suit the user.

The easiest way to create a chart in Excel is to **Select** the **Data** you wish to chart, then go to the **Insert** tab, and select the **Chart** you wish to insert.

You can also highlight the data you want in your chart and **press F11**. Excel will create a default (column) chart on a chart sheet.

## 2 Types of charts and graphs

### 2.1 Types of charts and graphs

You need to be aware of the following types of graph:

- Bar and Column charts.
- Pie and Doughnut charts.
- Scatter graph.
- Bubble chart.
- Single and double line graphs.
- Multiple graph types on one chart.

### 2.2 Bar and Column charts

Bar and column charts are used to display and compare the number, frequency or other measure for different discrete categories of data. They are one of the most commonly used types of graph because they are simple to create and very easy to interpret. They are also a flexible chart type and there are several variations of the standard bar chart including component bar charts, and compound bar charts.

Bar charts are useful for displaying data that are classified into categories.

Bar charts are also useful for displaying data that include categories with negative values, because it is possible to position the bars below and above the x-axis.

The chart is constructed such that the lengths of the different bars are proportional to the size of the category they represent. The x-axis represents the different categories and so has no scale. In order to emphasise the fact that the categories are discrete, a gap is left between the bars on the x-axis. The y-axis does have a scale and this indicates the units of measurement.

A column chart has vertical columns to represent the data and bar charts have horizontal columns.

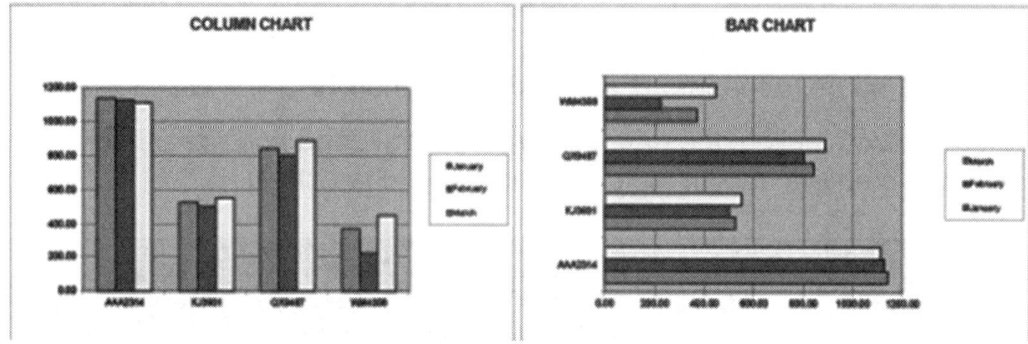


## 2.3 Pie and Doughnut charts

A pie chart is a circular graph that shows the relative contribution that different sub-groups contribute to an overall category. A wedge of the circle represents each sub-groups contribution. Every 1% contribution that a sub-group contributes to the total corresponds to an angle of 3.6 degrees.

Pie charts are generally used to show percentage or proportional data, but they can only represent one category split into its sub-groups. This makes it harder to draw any comparisons between either products or areas without producing multiple pie charts. It is also not possible to 'read off' the actual data unless data labels are added, which is possible with other forms of graphical representation.

Pie charts are good for displaying data for around 6 sub-groups or fewer. When there are more sub-groups it is difficult for the eye to distinguish between the relative sizes of the different sectors and so the chart becomes difficult to interpret.

Pie and Doughnut charts are very similar. They both represent proportions of a whole and neither of them have axes. The major difference between the two is that a Pie Chart can only have one data series whilst a Doughnut can have two or more.

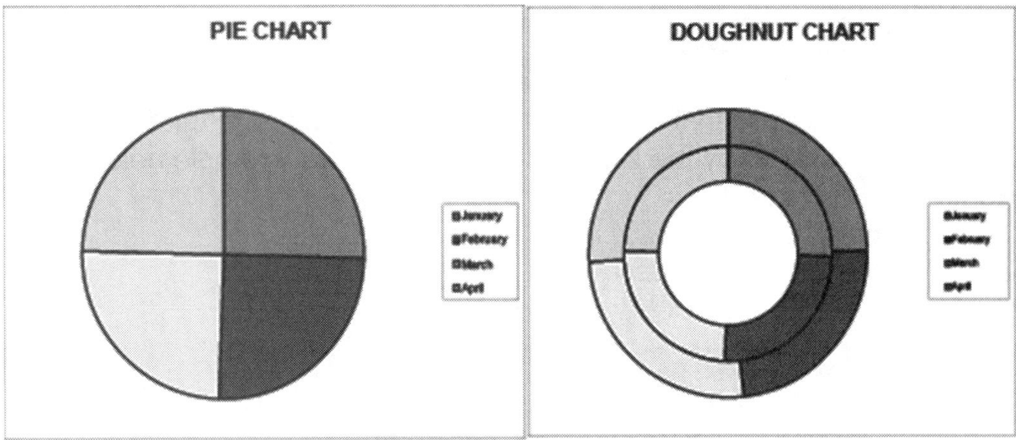


## 2.4 Scatter graph (XY)

Scatter diagrams are used to show the relationship between pairs of quantitative measurements made for the same object or individual. For example, a scatter diagram could be used to present information about production levels and costs.

In a scatter diagram a dot or cross represents each data set and is plotted on the graph with reference to the x-axis and y-axis, each of which represent one of the two measurements. On a scatter diagram both the x and y-axis have scales. By analysing the pattern of dots that make up a scatter diagram it is possible to identify whether there is any relationship (correlation) between the two measurements. Regression lines, lines of best fit, can also be added to the graph and used to decide whether the relationship between the two sets of measurements can be explained or if it is due to chance.

In the example below the relationship is of sales volume to sales revenue. The data points (represented by diamonds) show the intersection of the two sets of numbers.

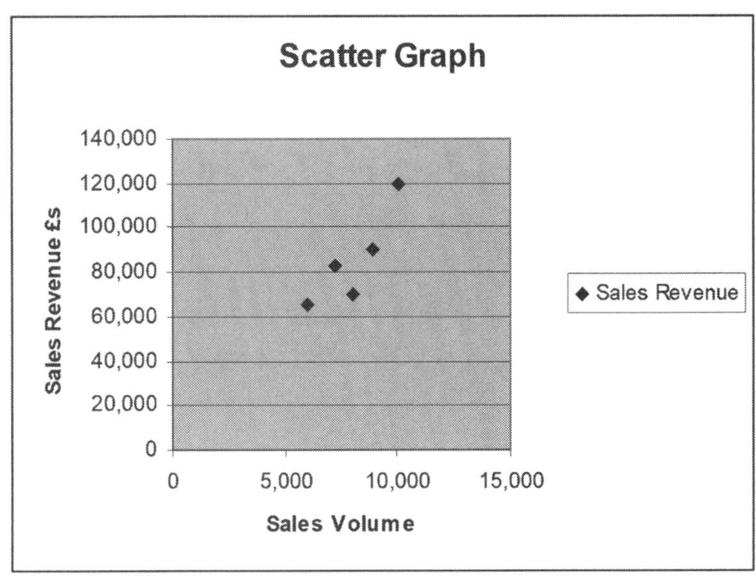

## 2.5 Bubble chart

A Bubble chart is very similar to a scatter graph in that it compares values. The difference here is that a third data series is added. The third data series is represented by the size of the bubble. In our example below the bubble represents profit.

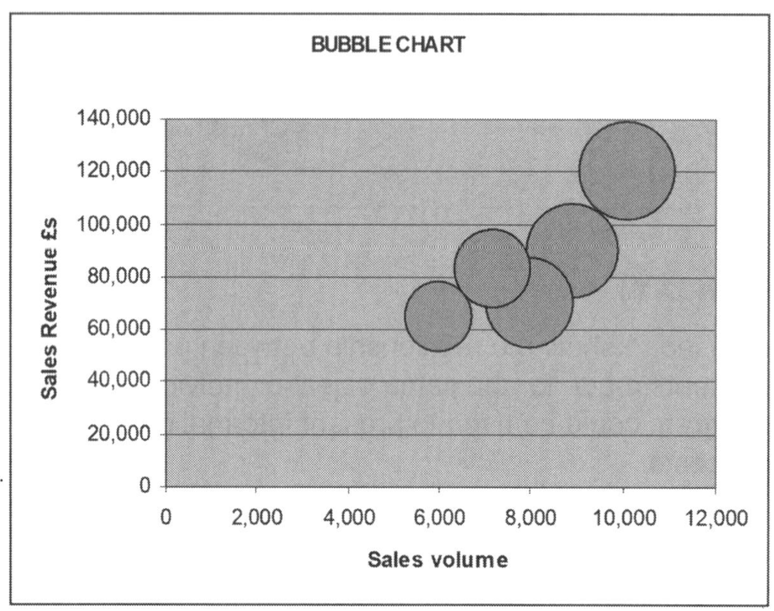


## 2.6 Single and double line graphs

Line charts are used to plot continuous data and are very useful for showing trends. The more **data series** there are the more lines you can have on your graph.

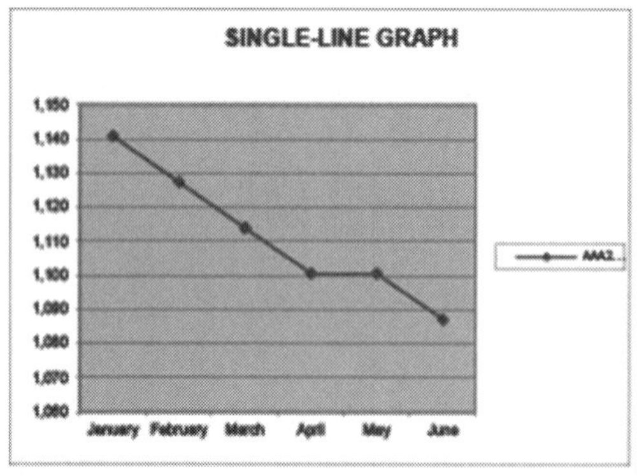


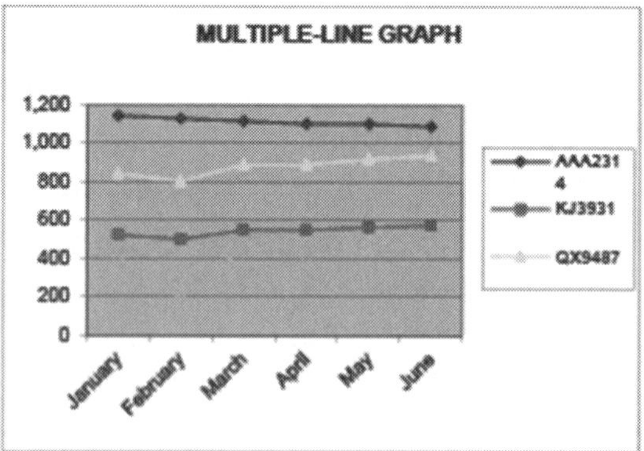

## 2.7 Multiple graph types on one chart

Also known as **Combination Charts** these charts must consist of at least two data series. With this chart type you can have either two graph types on **one** axis or insert a second **value** or **'Y'** axis.

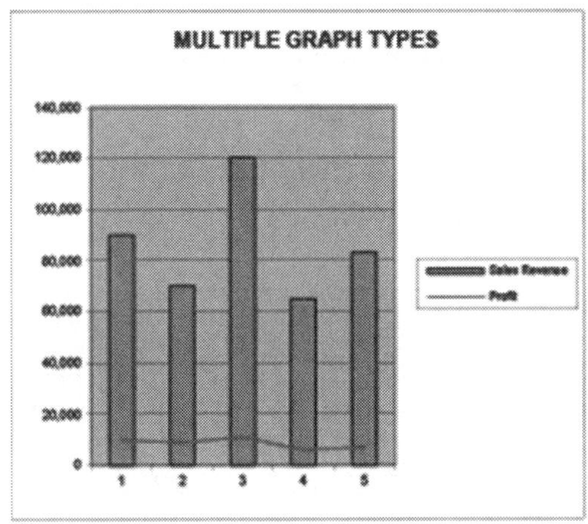


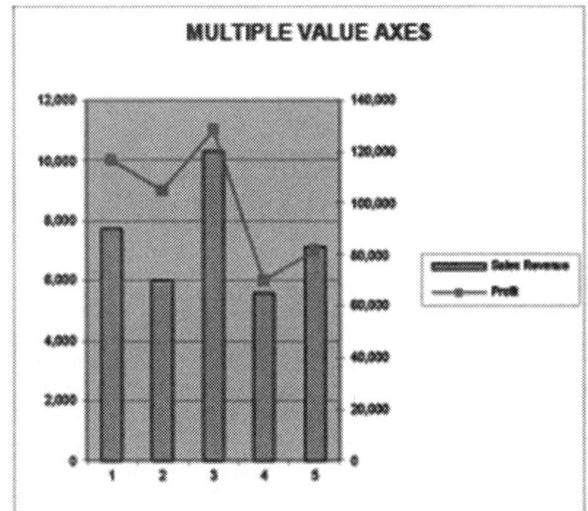


# 3 Creating a chart or graph

## 3.1 Creating a chart or graph

Select the data you wish to graph, and on the **Insert** tab, select the chart type you want.

B1 | *fx* Product

| | A | B | C | D | E |
|---|---|---|---|---|---|
| 1 | Code | Product | Number in stock | Price | |
| 2 | Z101 | Red pen | 3 | £9.00 | |
| 3 | Z102 | Yellow pen | 7 | £7.88 | |
| 4 | Z103 | Purple pen | 17 | £5.86 | |
| 5 | Z104 | Green pen | 13 | £1.19 | |
| 6 | Z105 | Red crayon | 20 | £9.56 | |
| 7 | Z105 | Yellow crayon | 4 | £7.27 | |
| 8 | Z107 | Purple crayon | 9 | £1.86 | |
| 9 | Z108 | Green crayon | 17 | £0.86 | |
| 10 | Z109 | Red ruler | 17 | £4.55 | |
| 11 | Z110 | Yellow ruler | 20 | £0.56 | |
| 12 | Z111 | Green ruler | 12 | £5.35 | |
| 13 | Z112 | Purple ruler | 4 | £4.88 | |
| 14 | Z113 | Blue calculator | 12 | £3.53 | |
| 15 | Z114 | Orange calculator | 6 | £7.16 | |
| 16 | | | | | |

Select the data, then find the chart type you are after.

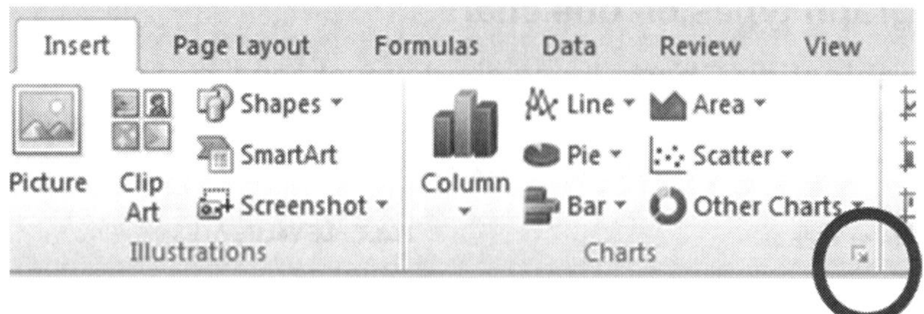


If you cannot see the chart you need, click the little arrow in the corner of the **Charts** menu, and all available charts will be shown.

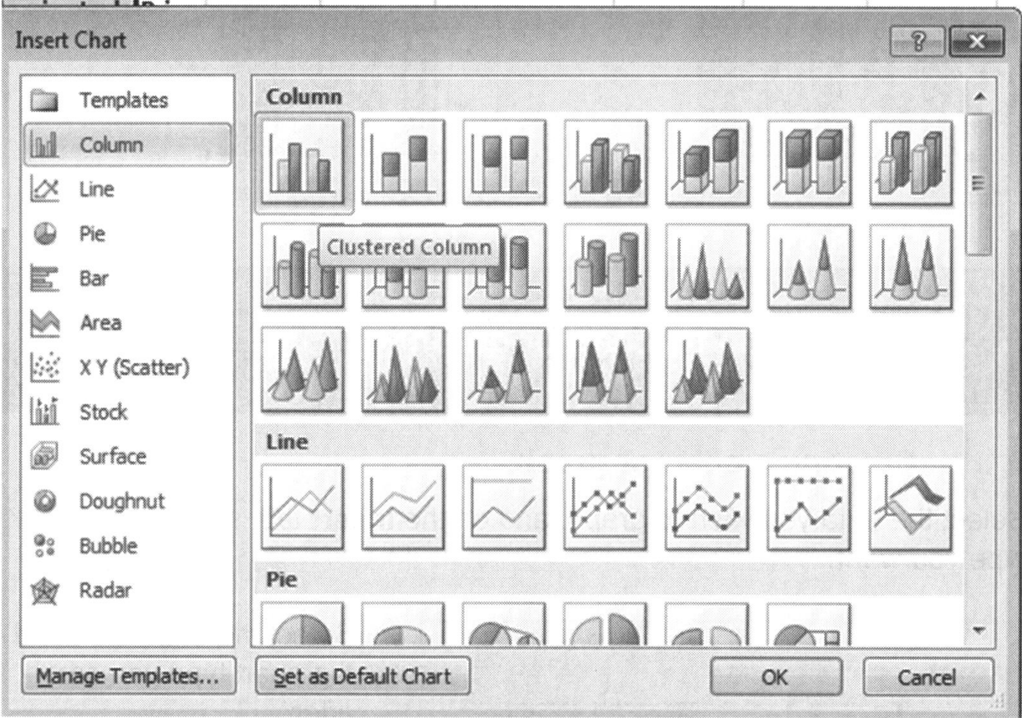


So, if you are asked for a **Clustered Column chart**, and do not know what it is – go into this menu and hover over the options to find what you need. Click **OK** once you have found what you need, and the chart will be shown.

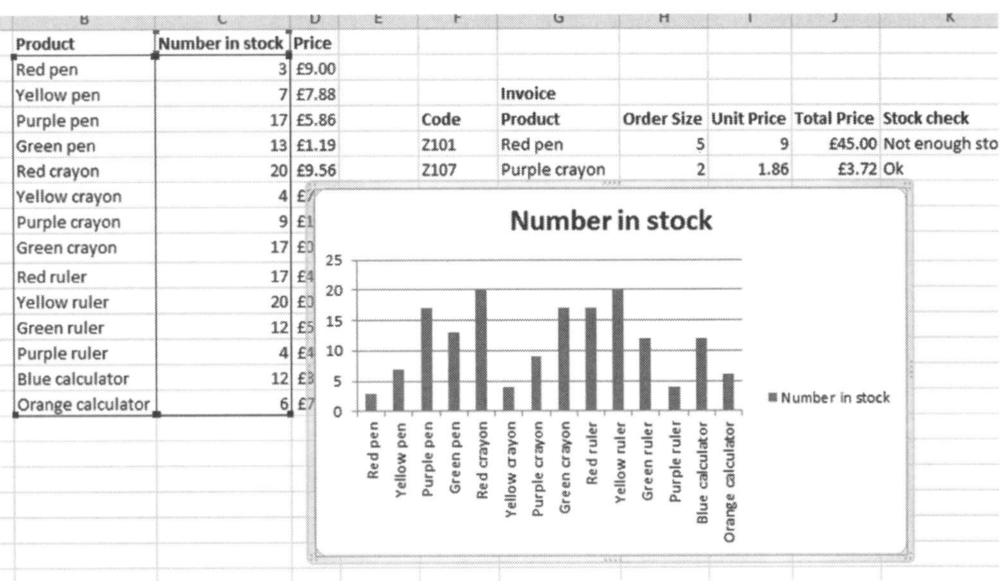


You can also see that the data being used is also highlighted.

As shown, creating a chart is not difficult – what may prove more difficult is getting it to look exactly how you want it to. There are many options available, and these will be dealt with in turn.

# 4 Formatting a chart or graph

## 4.1 The chart tools tabs

When you create a chart, or have one selected, the chart tools tabs will become available on the Ribbon. These will allow you to change the features of your chart.

There are 3 tabs within the Chart Tools menu, Design tab, Layout tab and Format tab.

## 4.2 Design Tab

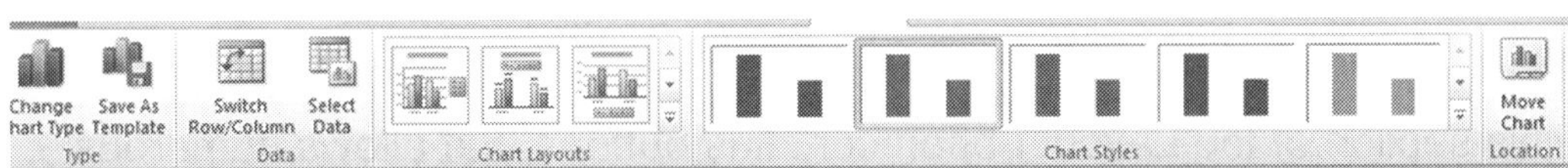


This is to do with the fundamental features of your chart – what sort of chart it is, the data used and where it is shown on your spreadsheet. The main options are:

- Type – This allows you to change the type of chart you are using. The menu showing all available charts is shown, and can be selected in the same way as a new chart.

- Data – This is a very important menu. It allows you to change the data being used, or add new **Series** (data sets) to the chart.

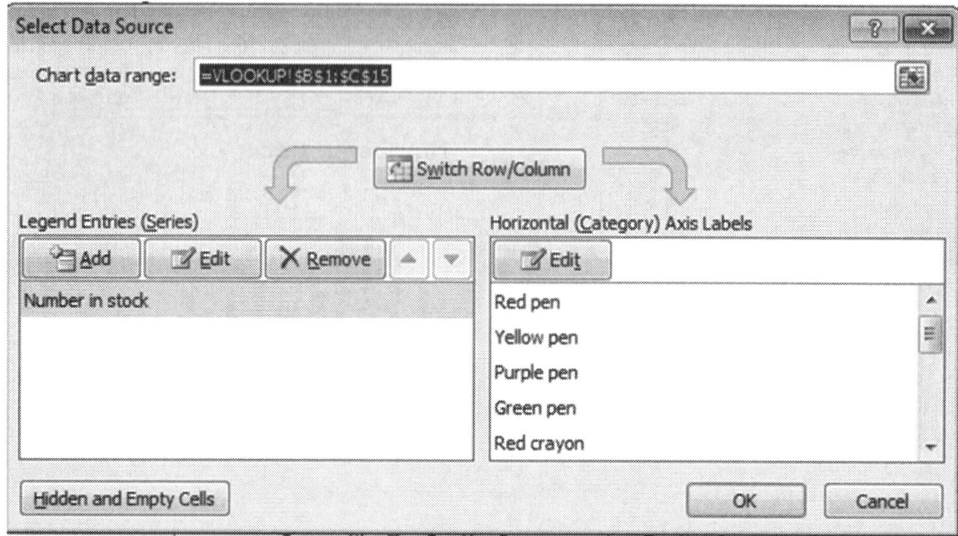


- The data range, as shown here, is the original data that was selected to draw the graph. This can be edited if more data is added, or if you wish to add another set of data to the graph.
- Layouts and Styles – This allows you to choose how the chart looks – the location of the title and legend and the colour scheme and general appearance of the chart.
- Move chart – This allows you to switch between an **embedded** chart and a **Chart Sheet**. Simply click on the **Move Chart** button to change the location of your chart.

## 4.3 Layout Tab

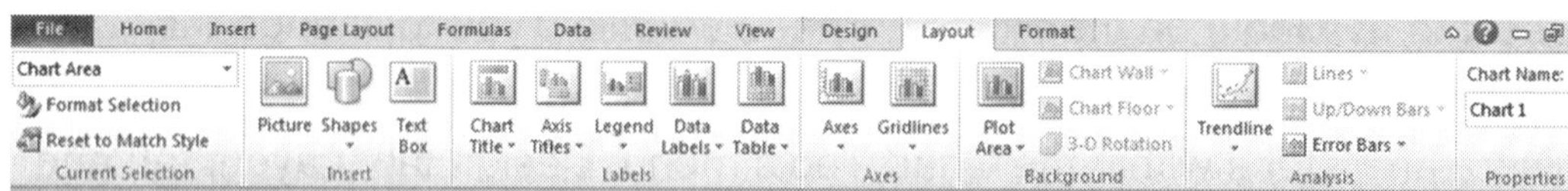


This is where you can change many of the key visual features of your chart, such as titles and legends.

## 4.4 Labels

This section of the Layout ribbon contains buttons that allows numerous aspects of the charts appearance to be amended:

- Chart title – this allows you to add or remove a main Title for your chart. There are also options as to where and how the title is displayed.
- Axis titles – enables you to add or remove titles for both axes.

- Legend – the **Legend** is the 'key' which explains what the different colours or bars on the graph correspond to. Use this button to add or remove a **Legend**, as well as change the location of the **Legend**.

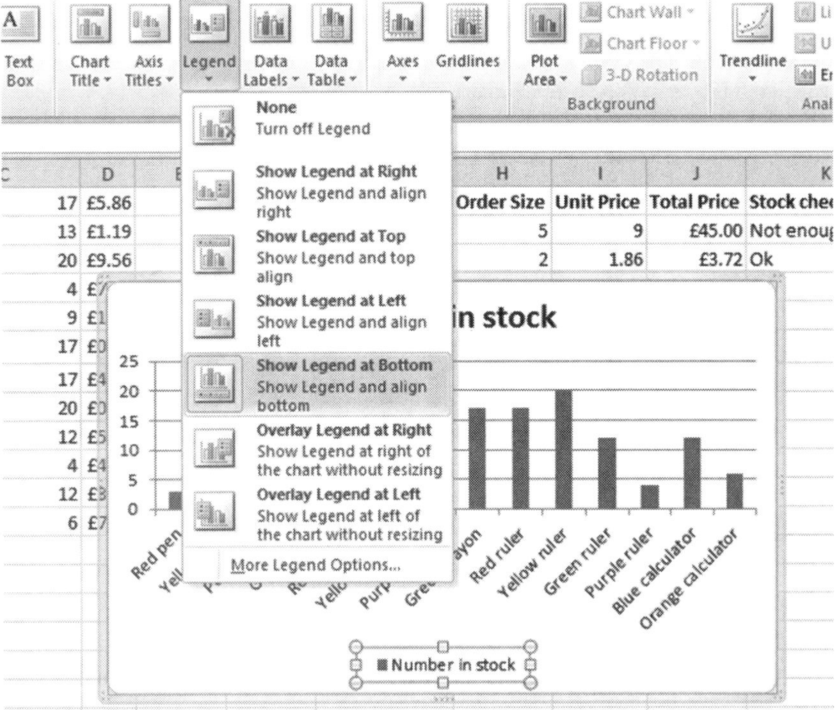

- Data labels – These show the actual values of the data points on the graph. You can turn them on or off, as well as where they appear on the chart.

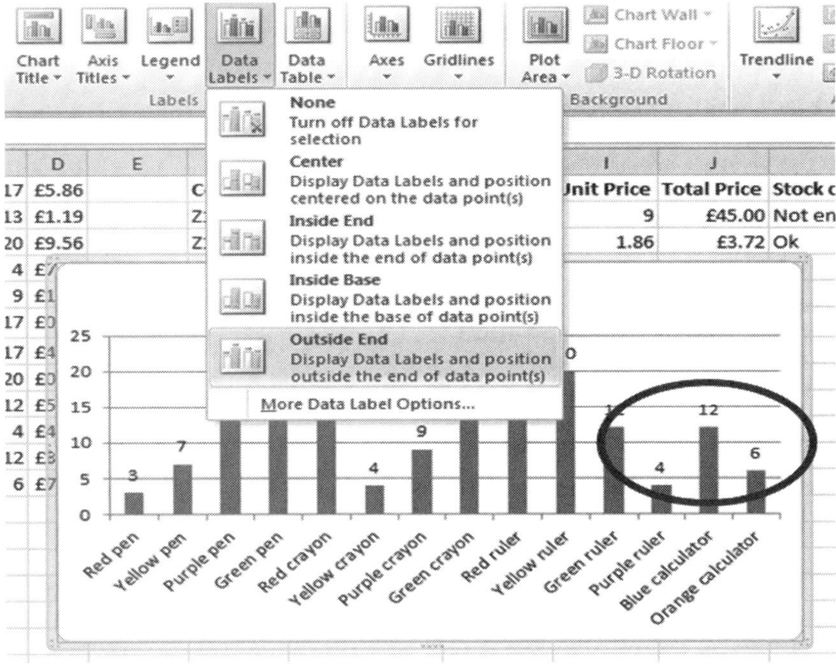

- Data table – A data table shows the actual data points being used to make the chart – like data labels but shown beneath the chart. Use this option to add/remove a data table, with or without a legend (key). The example below shows a data table with a legend key.

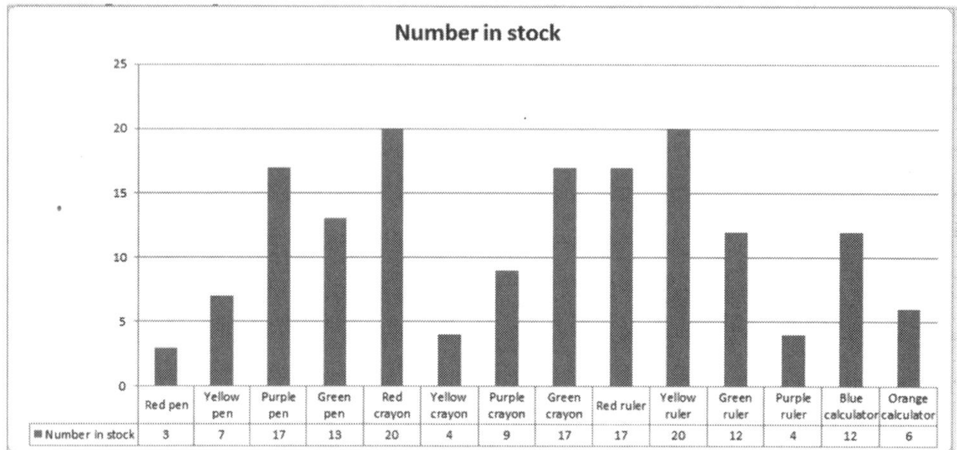


## 4.5 Trend lines

A trend line shows the general pattern of movement in your data set. Use the **Trend Line** button to do this. You will be presented with several options – normally you will choose **Linear Trendline**. The trendline will be added.

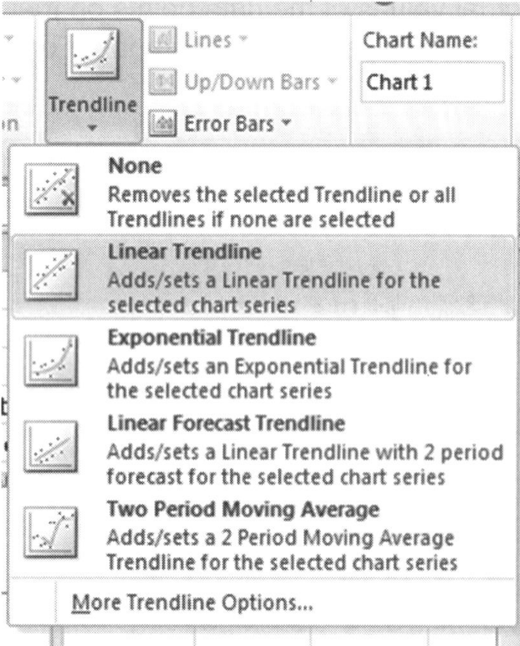

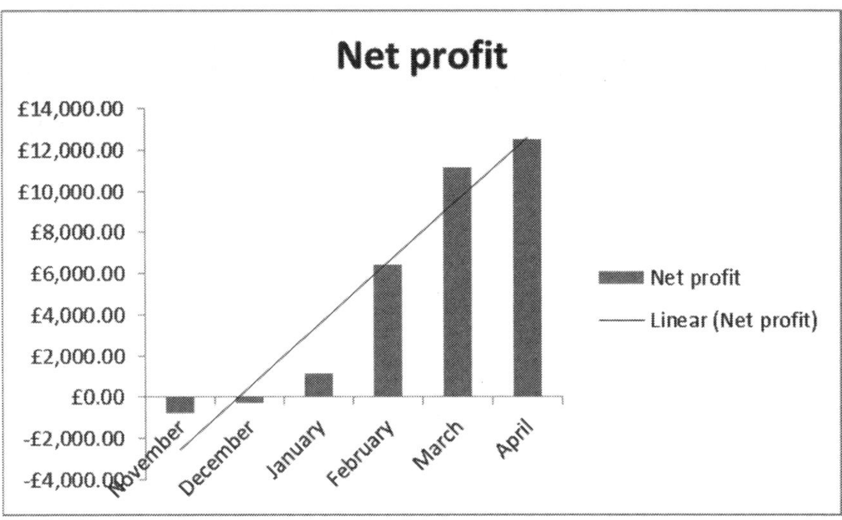


## 4.6 Format Tab

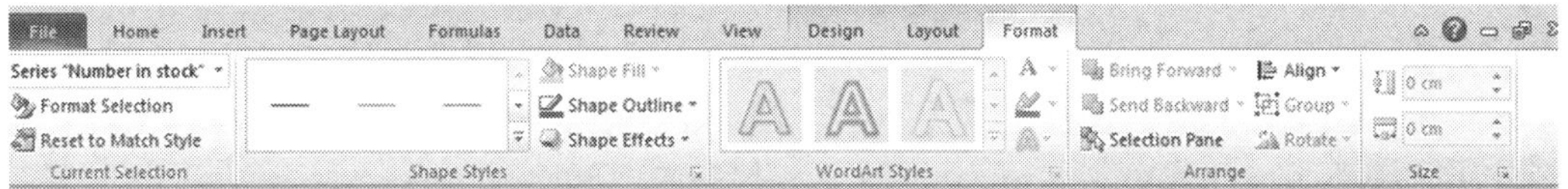


This tab allows you to change the format of any aspect of your graph – colours, thickness of lines and several other formatting options. Select (left-click on) the area of the graph you need to format and then select the option you need.

## 4.7 Just right click!

The Right Mouse button brings up many context-sensitive options within Excel. This is certainly true when dealing with charts. Right-clicking on the area of the graph you wish to manipulate is often the quickest way to achieve what you need to achieve.

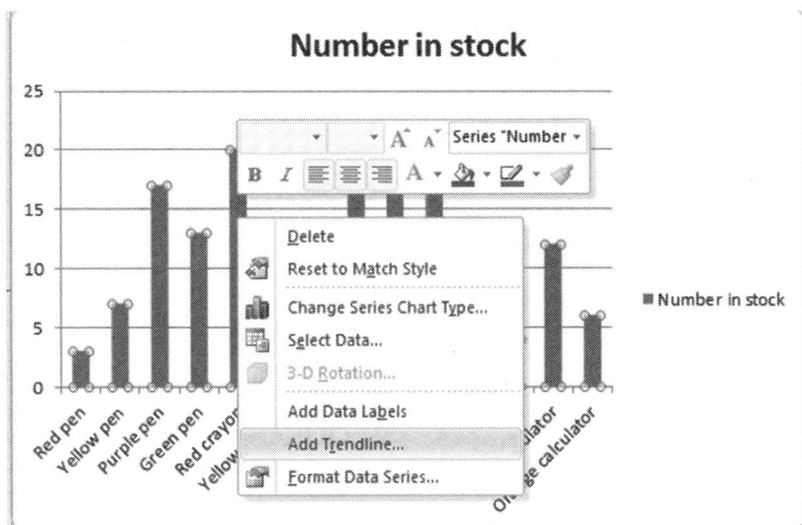


Here, right-clicking on a data point gives options to change the chart type, or add a trend line, as well as a few others.

# 5 Adding data

## 5.1 Adding another data set

As mentioned in **Section 4.2**, more data series can be added if you want to show more information on your graph. This is done within the **Select Data** option. Click **Add** to add more data.

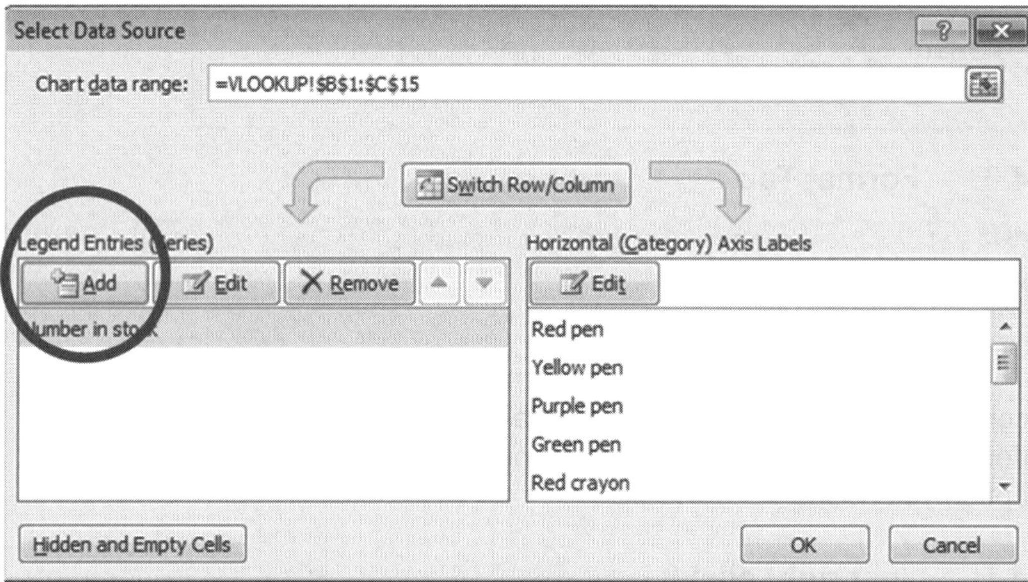

The **Series name** box allows you to select the name for your new data set – this can either be a cell reference or typed value.

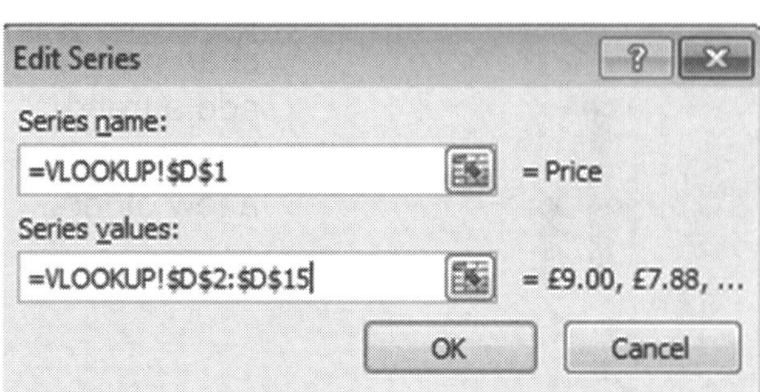


The **Series values** represent the actual data points, which can also be selected.

The sheet name – '**VLOOKUP**' is added automatically.

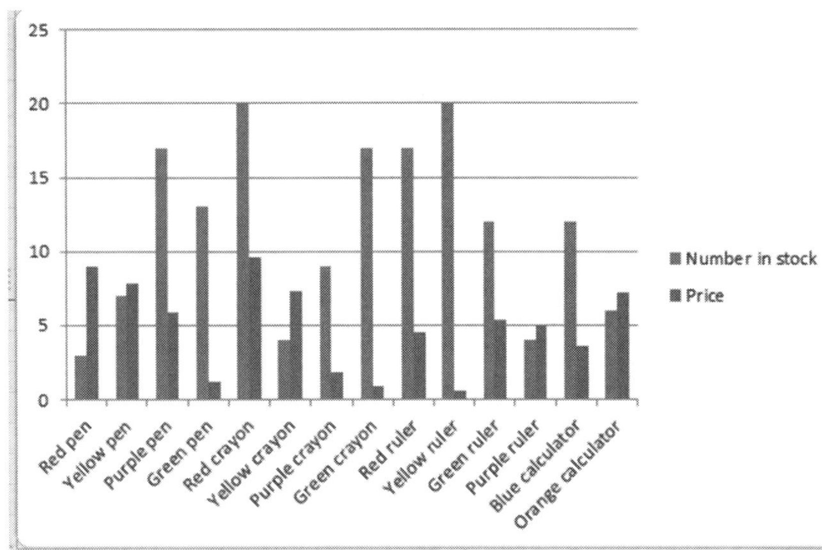


The new data series is shown on the graph. However, you may wish to show the second data series on an alternative scale – this is also possible. You need to **Format** the data series.

This can be done by either:

- **Right-Clicking** on the data series on the graph itself, and selecting **Format Data Series**.

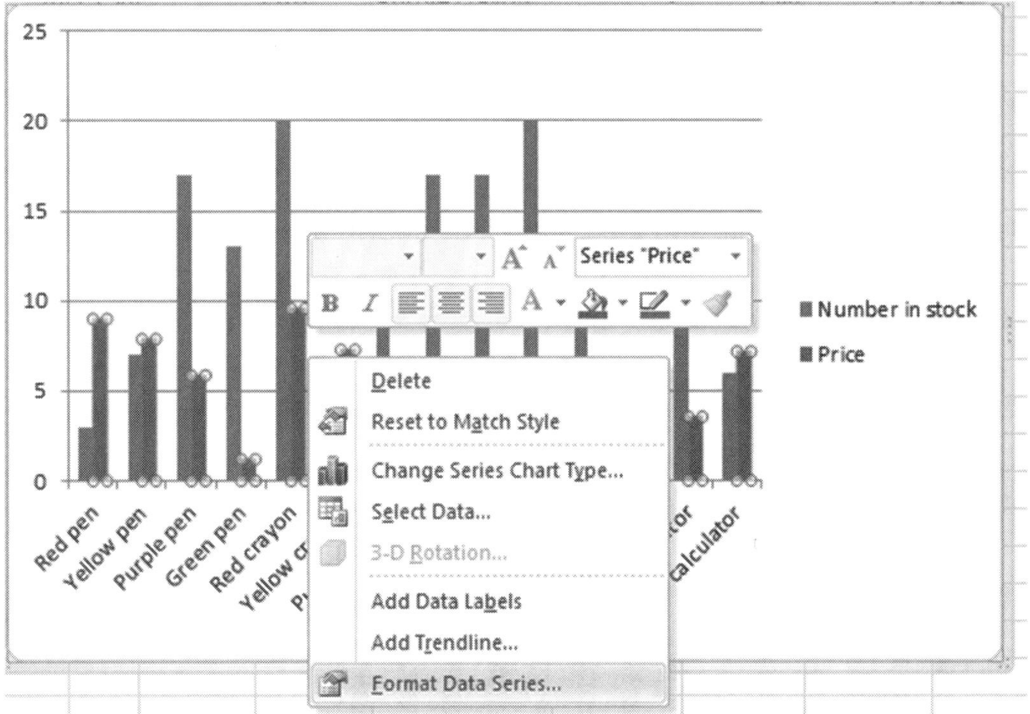


- Or select (left-click on) the data series, and in the **Layout** tab of Chart Tools, select **Format Selection**.

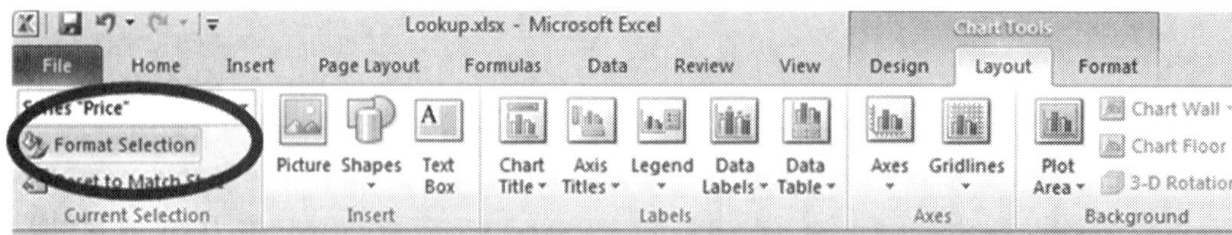


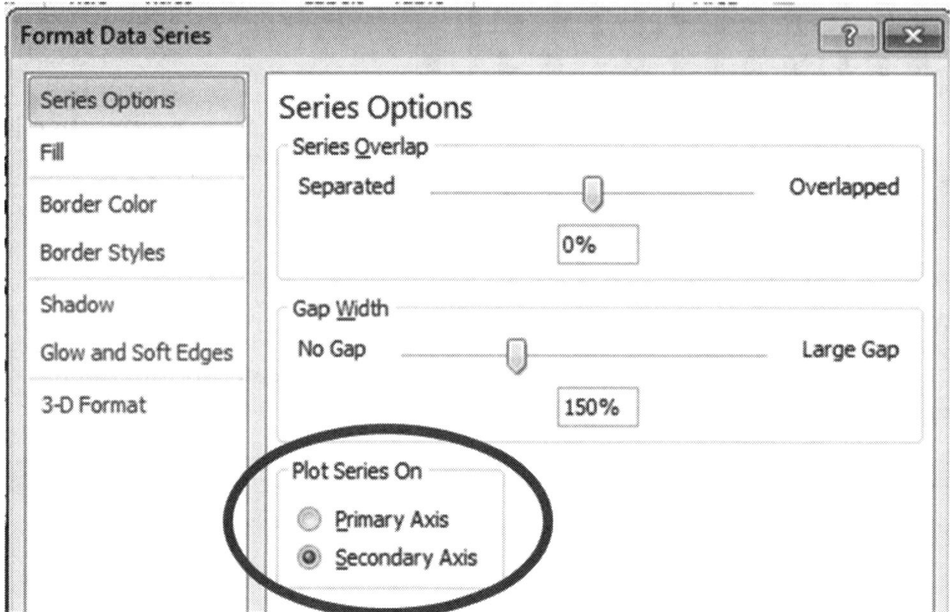


Select Secondary Axis, and the data will be shown as required.

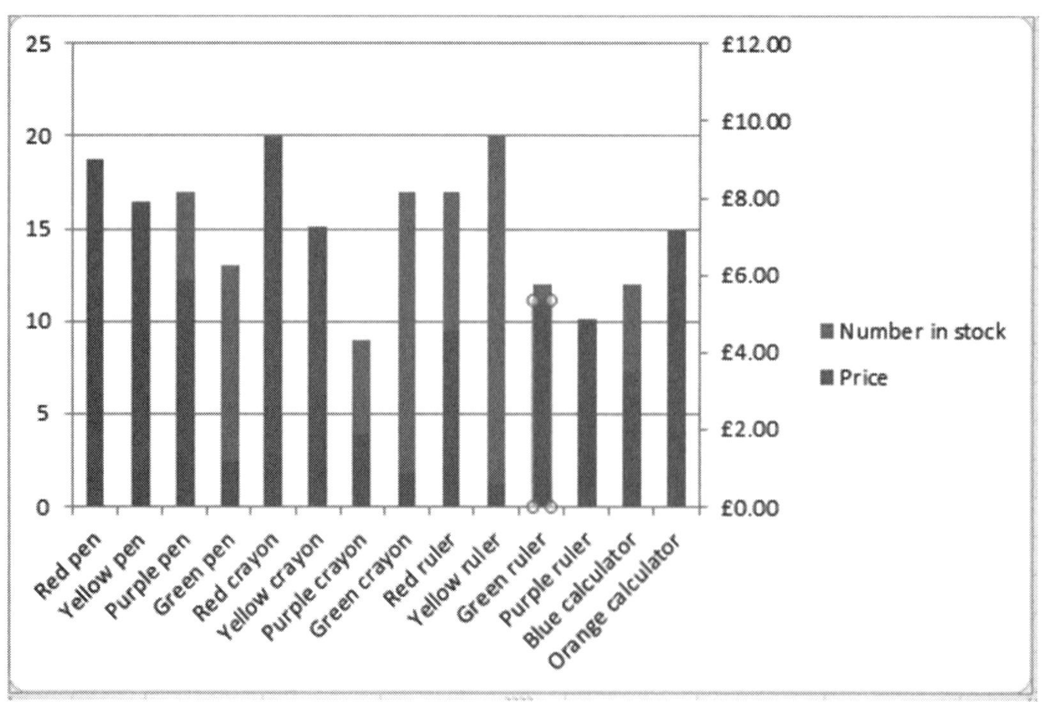

However, this may not be exactly what you want – remember that the chart function is very flexible. You could, for example, select the data set again and change the chart type to 'Line'.

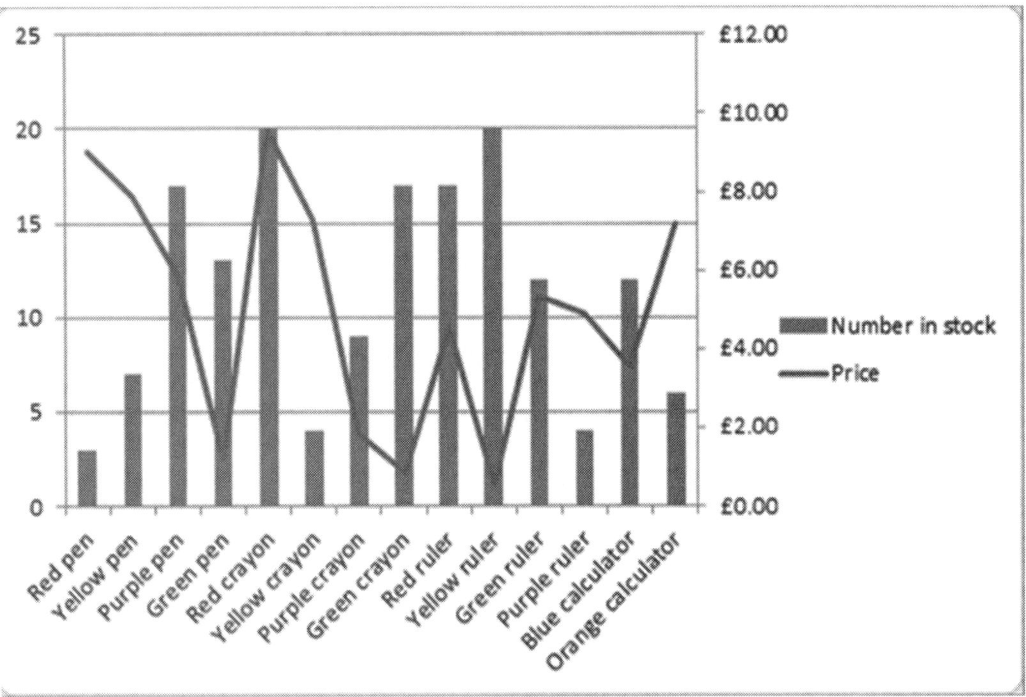


Remember, if you change the chart type and it doesn't appear as you would like, use the **undo** button.

# 6 Test your understanding

The activities in this guide are designed to test your knowledge on the techniques shown in this chapter. They may also use techniques used in previous chapters, to build up your knowledge. Suggested answers are available on MyKaplan, although it is better to refer to the notes and try to understand the methods than look straight at the answers.

## Test your understanding 14-1

This activity allows you to practice creating a simple chart.

(a) Open the **Graph Sales Data** in the **Activities** folder, and select **Sheet1**.

(b) You need to draw a **Clustered Column** chart showing the first 3 Quarters' results for each area. To do this, select all of the data – cells B13:E16, and insert the chart.

(c) Add a title to the chart – **Quarterly Sales 20X0**.

Add a title to the y-axis – **£000**.

Delete the Legend.

Add a data table to the graph – with a legend.

(d) Move the chart to the right of the data so everything is visible.

(e) Save the file as **Activity 14-1** in the **Solutions** folder.

## Test your understanding 14-2

This activity allows you to edit an existing chart. It follows directly on from **Activity 14-1**.

(a) If it is not already open, open **Activity 14-1** from the **Solutions** folder.

(b) The aim of this exercise is to add the Quarter 4 Forecast information to the chart. To do this, **Select** the chart, and use **Select Data** from the **Design** tab. Notice the Chart data range:

(c) We need to extend the data range to include the Quarter 4 forecast – F13:F16.

(d) Change the **Forecast Increase** figure in cell A2 to 100%. The Quarter 4 forecast is based on this – the figures, and the chart, will update. Change it back to 10%.

(e) **Move** the chart to a chart sheet.

(f) Save the workbook as **Activity 14-2** in the **Solutions** folder.

## Test your understanding 14-3

This activity allows you to change the chart type being used, add a trendline, and deal with formatting of chart items.

(a) Open the **Graph Sales Data** workbook from the **Activities** folder, and select **Sheet2**.

(b) This is a stacked column chart, showing sales, costs and gross profit. It is not a meaningful representation of the data. For example, the first bar, for January, shows a total of £20,000. This is the sum of sales, costs and profit. The individual coloured sections do indicate the size of each item, but it is hard to interpret.

The first thing to do is change the gross profit series to show as a line.

(c) **Select** the gross profit data series (click on any part of the chart coloured in cream).

(d) In the **Design** tab, select **Change Chart Type**, and select **Line.**

(e) **Delete** the costs data series, and change the title to **Sales and Profit comparison**.

(f) Add a secondary axis for the gross profit data series by using the **Format Data Series** menu.

(g) Add a **linear trendline** to the gross profit data series.

(h) **Select** the trendline. Change the format so that it is a thick line (3pt), coloured bright green.

(i) Save the file as **Activity 14-3** in the **Solutions** folder.

# Data validation

15

## Introduction

This chapter will explain how to restrict data within cells and give a brief introduction to named ranges.

**ASSESSMENT CRITERIA**

Select relevant data (2.1)

Protect integrity of data (4.3)

**CONTENTS**

# 1 Data validation

## 1.1 Introduction

Data validation allows a user to restrict what values can be entered into a cell. This can prevent incorrect data entry, or allow another user to select from a Dropdown list, making data entry easier.

## 1.2 Data validation

To add data validation, select the cell(s) required, then in the **Data** tab, select **Data Validation**.

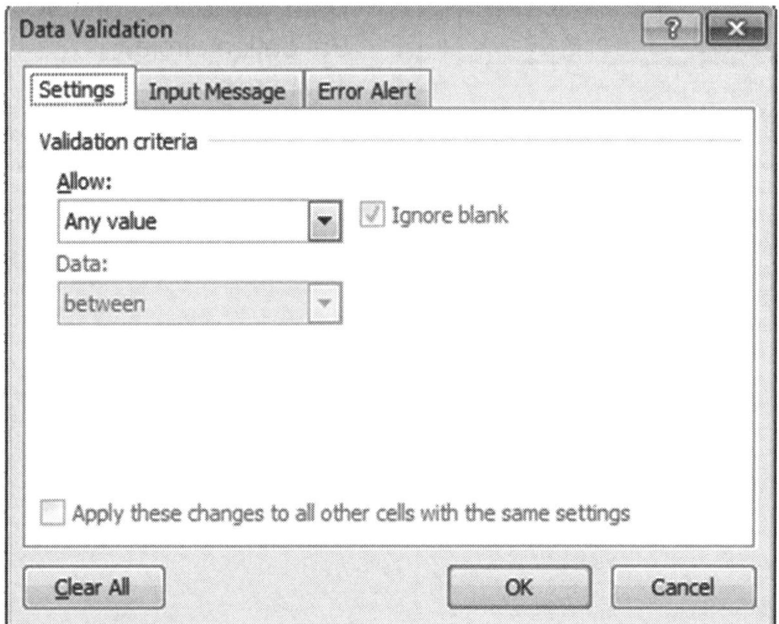


The Data Validation menu has three tabs – Settings, Input Message and Error Alert.

# 2 Data validation settings

## 2.1 Settings

This is where you define exactly how you would like to restrict your cell entry. The default is as shown above – **Allow any value**. Selecting this dropdown box shows the options available.

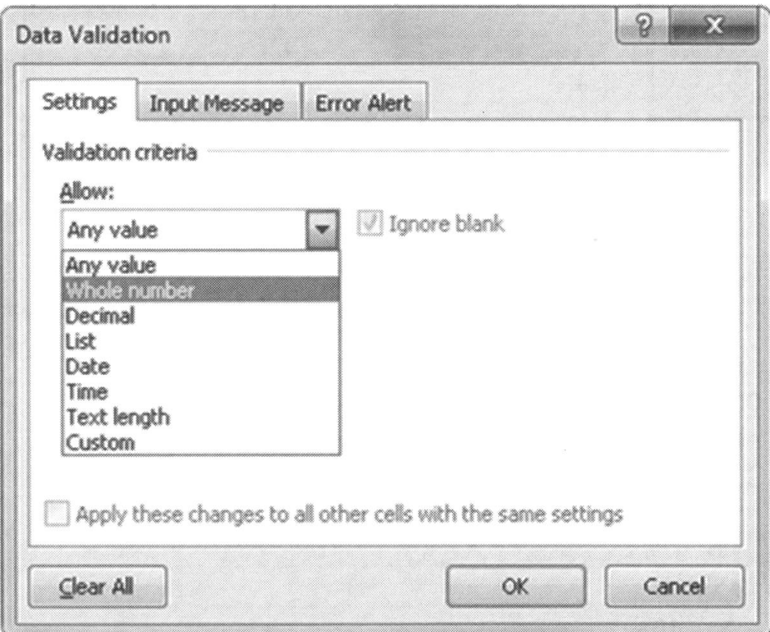


When an option is selected, more options become available. For example, whole number only allows whole numbers, but you can further restrict the range.

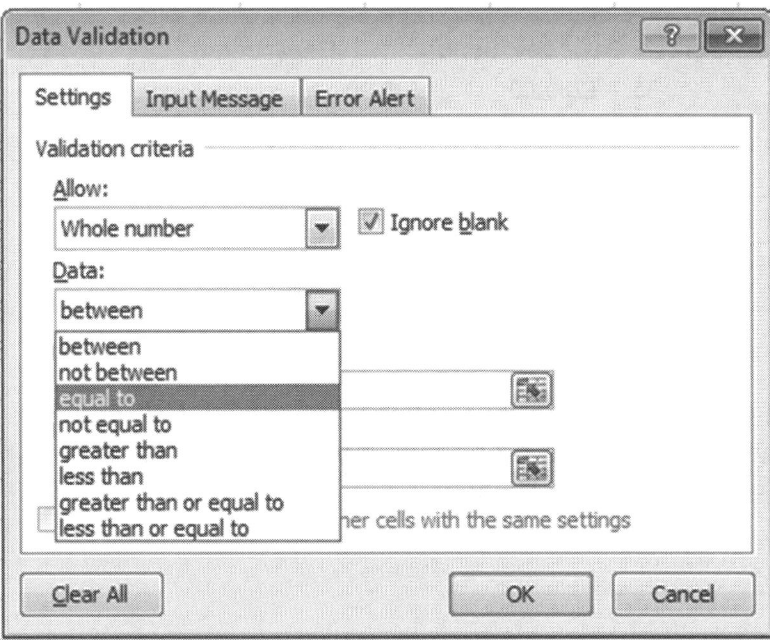


As on many other options, you can restrict to certain ranges, or above or below other numbers (which can be based on cell values).

You can also restrict to a list of options. This is very useful when a cell should only contain certain entries.

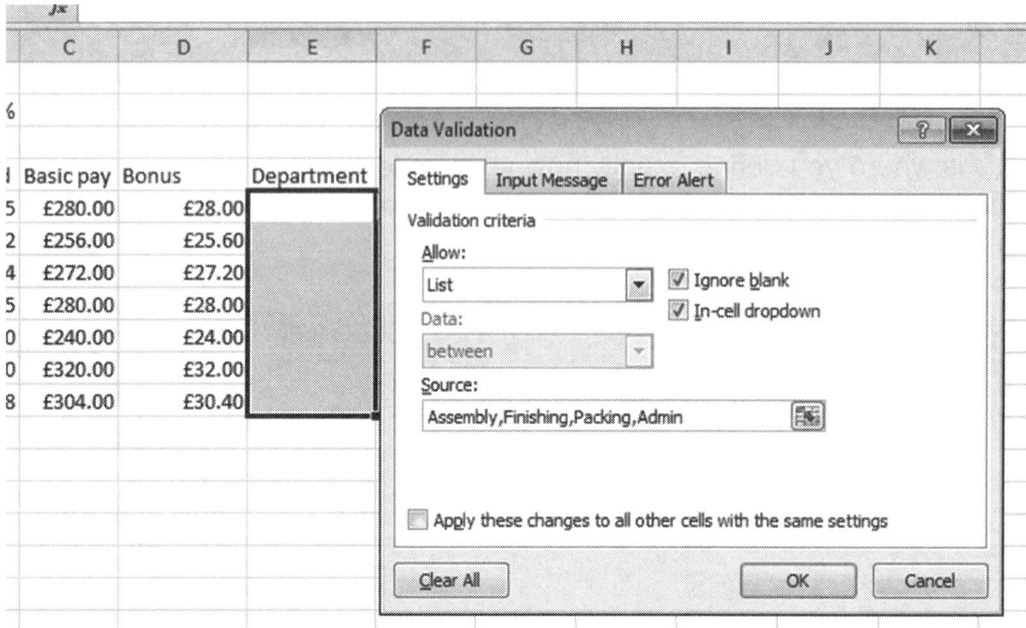


In the Data Validation menu, select Allow **List**, and type the possible options in the box, separated by a comma. Notice the **In-cell dropdown** option is checked. Click **OK**.

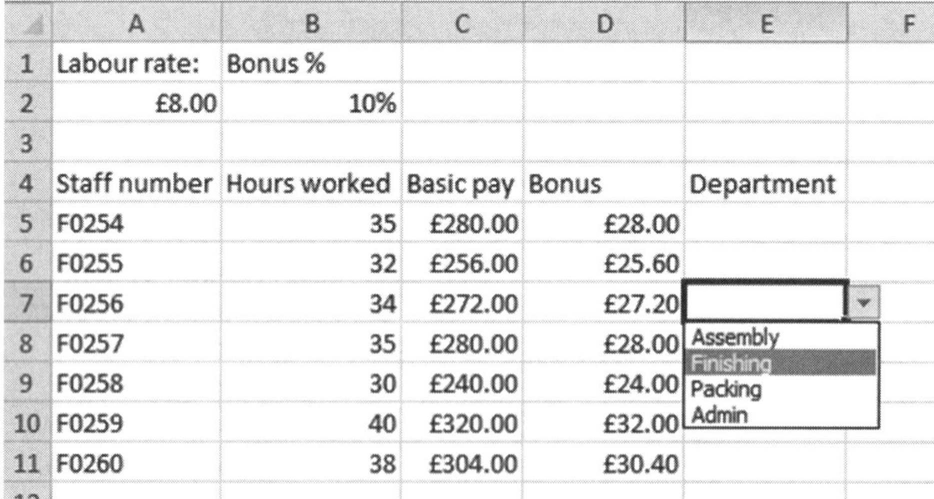

| | A | B | C | D | E |
|---|---|---|---|---|---|
| 1 | Labour rate: | Bonus % | | | |
| 2 | £8.00 | 10% | | | |
| 3 | | | | | |
| 4 | Staff number | Hours worked | Basic pay | Bonus | Department |
| 5 | F0254 | 35 | £280.00 | £28.00 | |
| 6 | F0255 | 32 | £256.00 | £25.60 | |
| 7 | F0256 | 34 | £272.00 | £27.20 | |
| 8 | F0257 | 35 | £280.00 | £28.00 | Assembly |
| 9 | F0258 | 30 | £240.00 | £24.00 | Finishing<br>Packing |
| 10 | F0259 | 40 | £320.00 | £32.00 | Admin |
| 11 | F0260 | 38 | £304.00 | £30.40 | |

Now, when the cell is clicked on, the four options are shown. You can still type in the cell, as well as using the dropdown. If you type something that is not in the list an error message will show.

Rather than typing the values in, you can also refer to a range of cells.

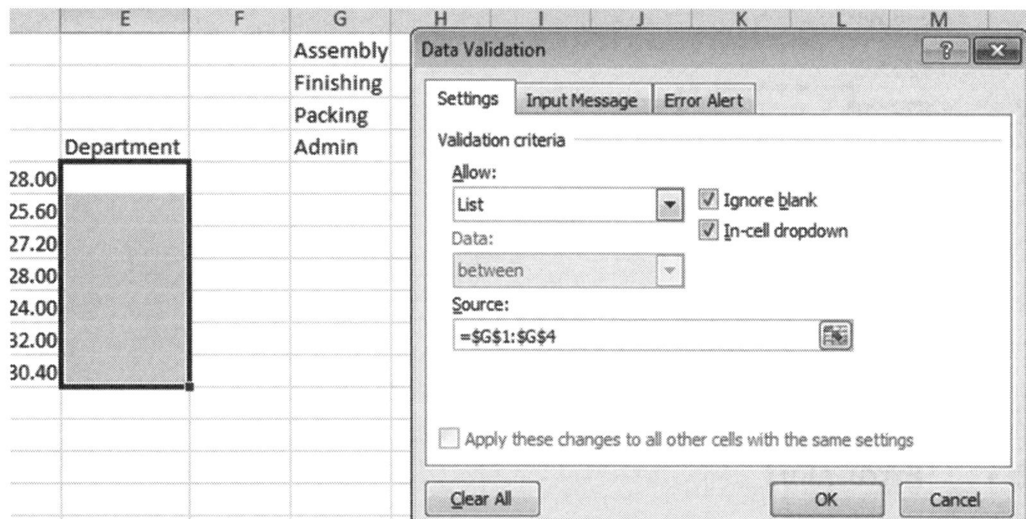


This will achieve the same effect.

## 2.2 Input message

This option is again useful for helping other users of the spreadsheet to enter the correct data. If activated, when the cell is selected a message will be displayed giving help on what can be entered.

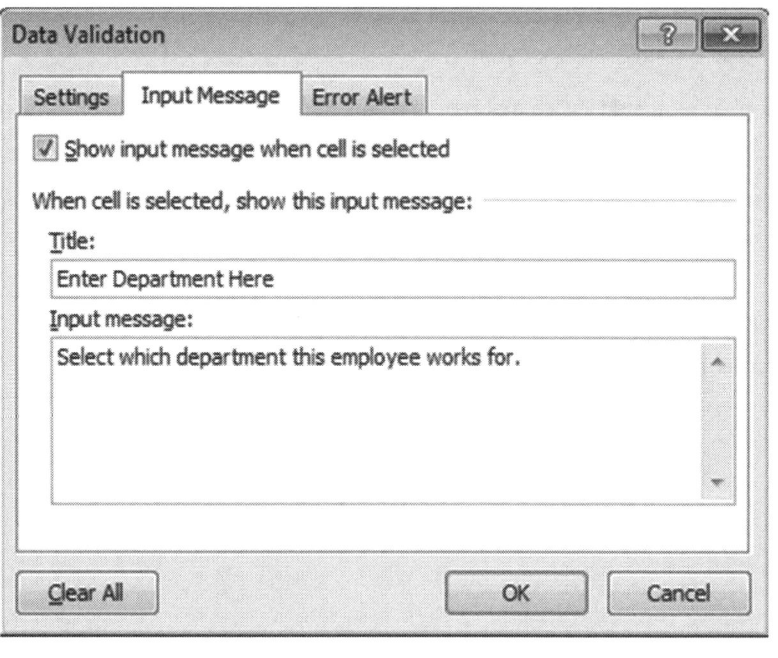


The message shown should provide useful information for the spreadsheet user.

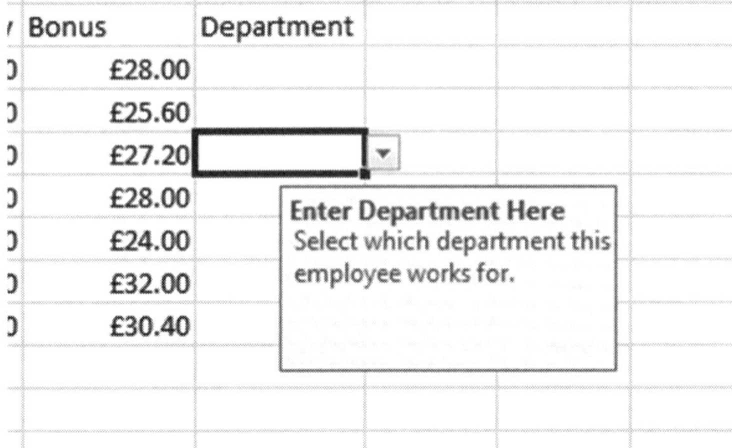


When the cell is selected, the message is shown.

### 2.3 Error alert

This tab allows you to select the error message that is shown if incorrect data is entered. By default, if the data validation restrictions are not met, the following error is shown:

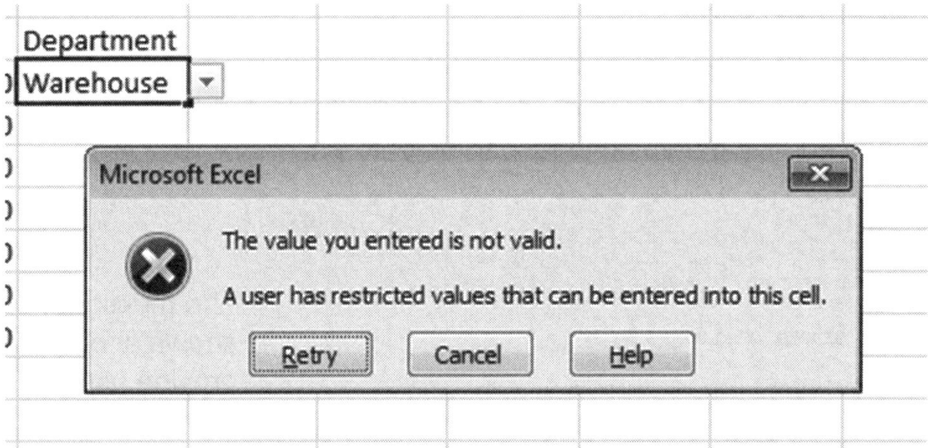


This is not particularly helpful to a user, as they may not know what they have done wrong. Use the Error Alert tab to change this message.

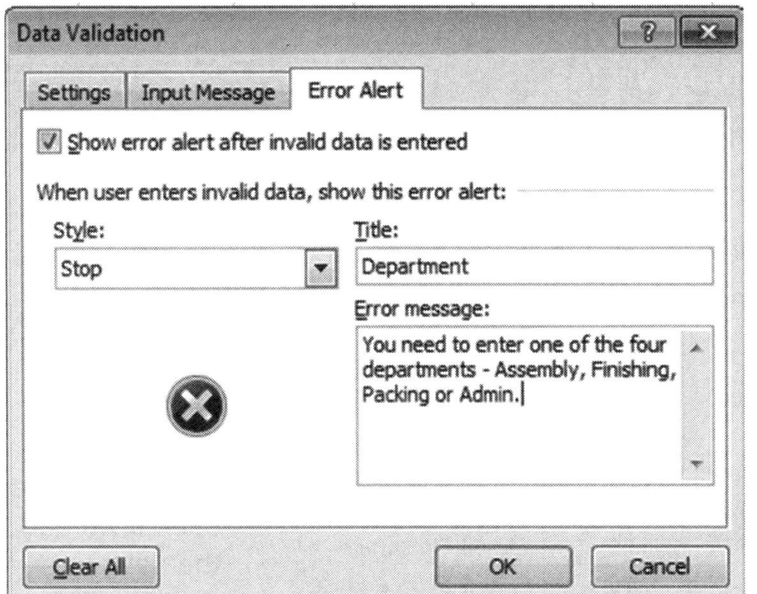


The 'Style' option selects what icon is shown – this is purely cosmetic.

The remaining message is up to you – the more descriptive the better.

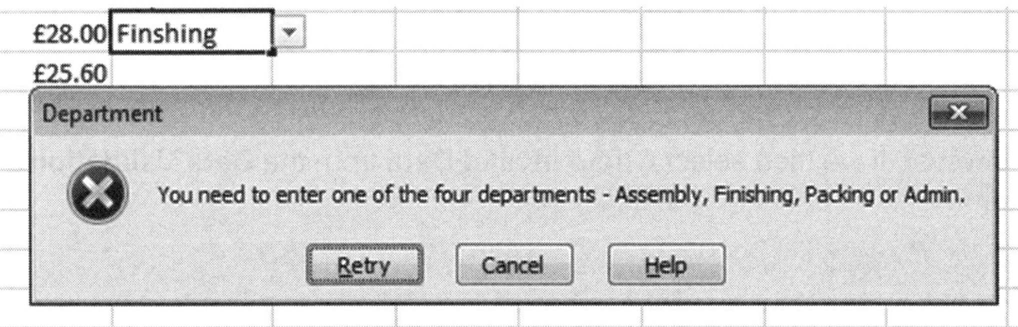


A more useful message is now shown.

# 3 Validation circles

## 3.1 Circles

Similar to Error Checking, invalid data can be 'Circled'. This is often useful if the data validation is added after the data has been entered.

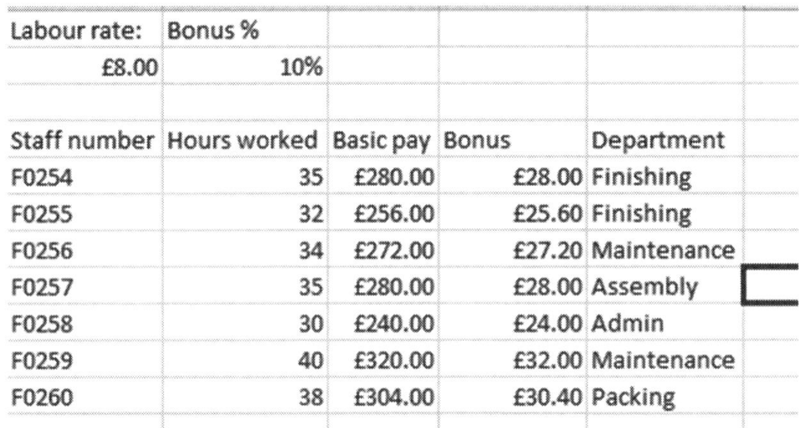

| Labour rate: | Bonus % | | | |
|---|---|---|---|---|
| £8.00 | 10% | | | |
| | | | | |
| Staff number | Hours worked | Basic pay | Bonus | Department |
| F0254 | 35 | £280.00 | £28.00 | Finishing |
| F0255 | 32 | £256.00 | £25.60 | Finishing |
| F0256 | 34 | £272.00 | £27.20 | Maintenance |
| F0257 | 35 | £280.00 | £28.00 | Assembly |
| F0258 | 30 | £240.00 | £24.00 | Admin |
| F0259 | 40 | £320.00 | £32.00 | Maintenance |
| F0260 | 38 | £304.00 | £30.40 | Packing |

This is the data set – if we add the data validation as before, no error is shown.

However, if we then select **Circle Invalid Data** from the **Data Validation** menu:

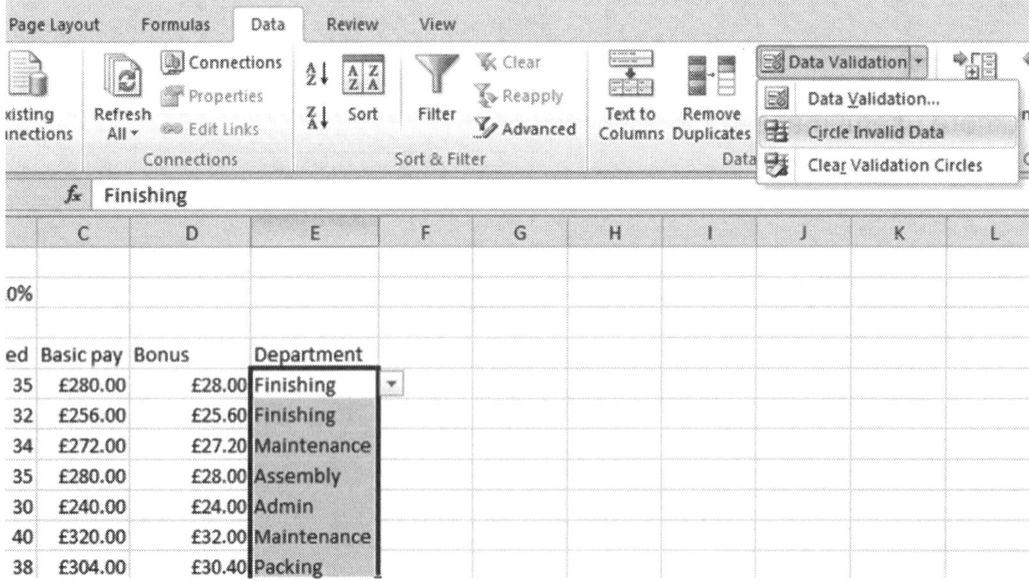

The invalid data will be circled.

| er | Hours worked | Basic pay | Bonus | Department |
|---|---|---|---|---|
| | 35 | £280.00 | £28.00 | Finishing |
| | 32 | £256.00 | £25.60 | Finishing |
| | 34 | £272.00 | £27.20 | Maintenance |
| | 35 | £280.00 | £28.00 | Assembly |
| | 30 | £240.00 | £24.00 | Admin |
| | 40 | £320.00 | £32.00 | Maintenance |
| | 38 | £304.00 | £30.40 | Packing |

This may indicate that we need to change the validation rules, or change the data.

# 4 Test your understanding

The activities in this guide are designed to test your knowledge on the techniques shown in this chapter. They may also use techniques used in previous chapters, to build up your knowledge. Suggested answers are available on MyKaplan, although it is better to refer to the notes and try to understand the methods than look straight at the answers.

## Test your understanding 15-1

This activity takes you through **Data Validation** techniques, as well as using **VLOOKUP** and **IF** functions, explained in Chapter 12.

(a) Open the **Product Order** workbook from the **Activities** folder, and look at the **Order Sheet** worksheet.

(b) This sheet can be used as an order form. The products available, and various details about them, are on the **Products** sheet.

(c) In cell A12, use **Data Validation** to restrict entry to the available product codes found on the Products Sheet.

**Note** – you could give a **Name** to this range (see Chapter 7), and use that in the **Data Validation**. This is not necessary in Excel 2010, but would be in previous versions.

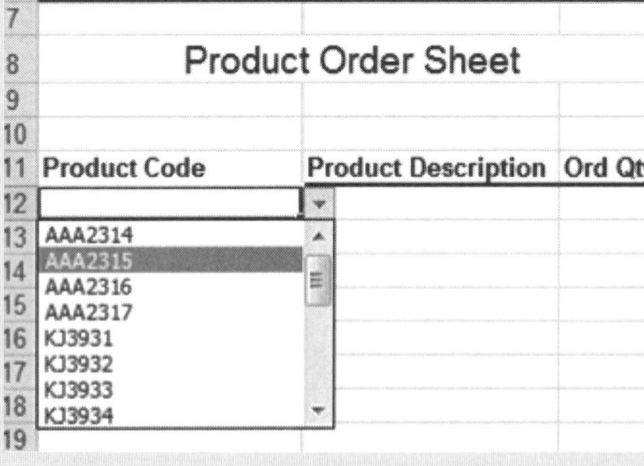


The products should be available as shown.

(d) Copy the Validation from cell A12 into cells A13:A40. This can be performed using **Paste Special**, and selecting **Validation**.

Select AAA2315 in Cell A12.

(e) In cell B12, use a **VLOOKUP** formula to return the description. Add an **IF** function to return a blank cell if the value in column A is also blank.

(f) Copy the formula down into cells B13:B40.

(g) In Cell C12, use data validation to restrict the order quantities to whole numbers greater than or equal to the minimum order quantity in cell B1 (consider cell referencing. Add an error alert explaining that the value in the cell must be greater than or equal to the minimum order quantity.

(h) Copy the validation into cells C13:C40.

(i) Enter 20 in cell C12. An error should appear. Click Cancel. Enter 25 in C12. The order value should update.

(j) Select product KJ3932 in A13, QX9489 in A14 and WM4361 in A15. Enter order quantities of 35, 28 and 40 respectively.

(k) Change the value in cell B1 to 30.

(l) In the **Data** tab, select **Data Validation,** and **Circle Invalid Data**.

(m) The values below 30 should be circled.

| Product Order Sheet | | | Date | |
|---|---|---|---|---|
| **Product Code** | **Product Description** | **Ord Qty** | **List Price** | **Order Value** |
| AAA2315 | Widget White | 25 | £6.00 | £150.00 |
| KJ3932 | Wotsit White | 35 | £3.00 | £105.00 |
| QX9489 | Thingy Blue | 28 | £10.00 | £280.00 |
| WM4361 | Youknow Orange | 40 | £6.00 | £240.00 |

Save the file as **Activity 15-1** in the **Solutions** folder. Note: when the spreadsheet is saved the validation circles will be cleared.

# Spreadsheet templates

16

## Introduction

This chapter will help you to understand what a template does, where to store it, and how to retrieve it.

### ASSESSMENT CRITERIA

Organise data in a timely manner (1.1)

Securely store and retrieve relevant information (1.2)

### CONTENTS

## 1 Templates

Templates are useful tools for creating and storing workbooks that are used constantly. The most used templates are the Excel workbooks that contain three sheets that we use all the time. There are also a number of templates readily available in Excel.

When you create a template you should save it to a special template folder.  Excel will add an .xlt or.xltx extension to the workbook.

The next time you want to open the template, you open it from the template folder and Excel will create the new workbook with the same name as the template – but it will add a number to it.

# 2 Test your understanding

This activity takes you through the steps required to create a template.

## Test your understanding 16-1

(a) Open the **Product Order** workbook in the **Activities** folder.

This spreadsheet could be used regularly as an order form.

(b) Choose **Save As** from the **File** tab.

(c) Select the **Excel Template** option in the **Save as type** dropdown menu.

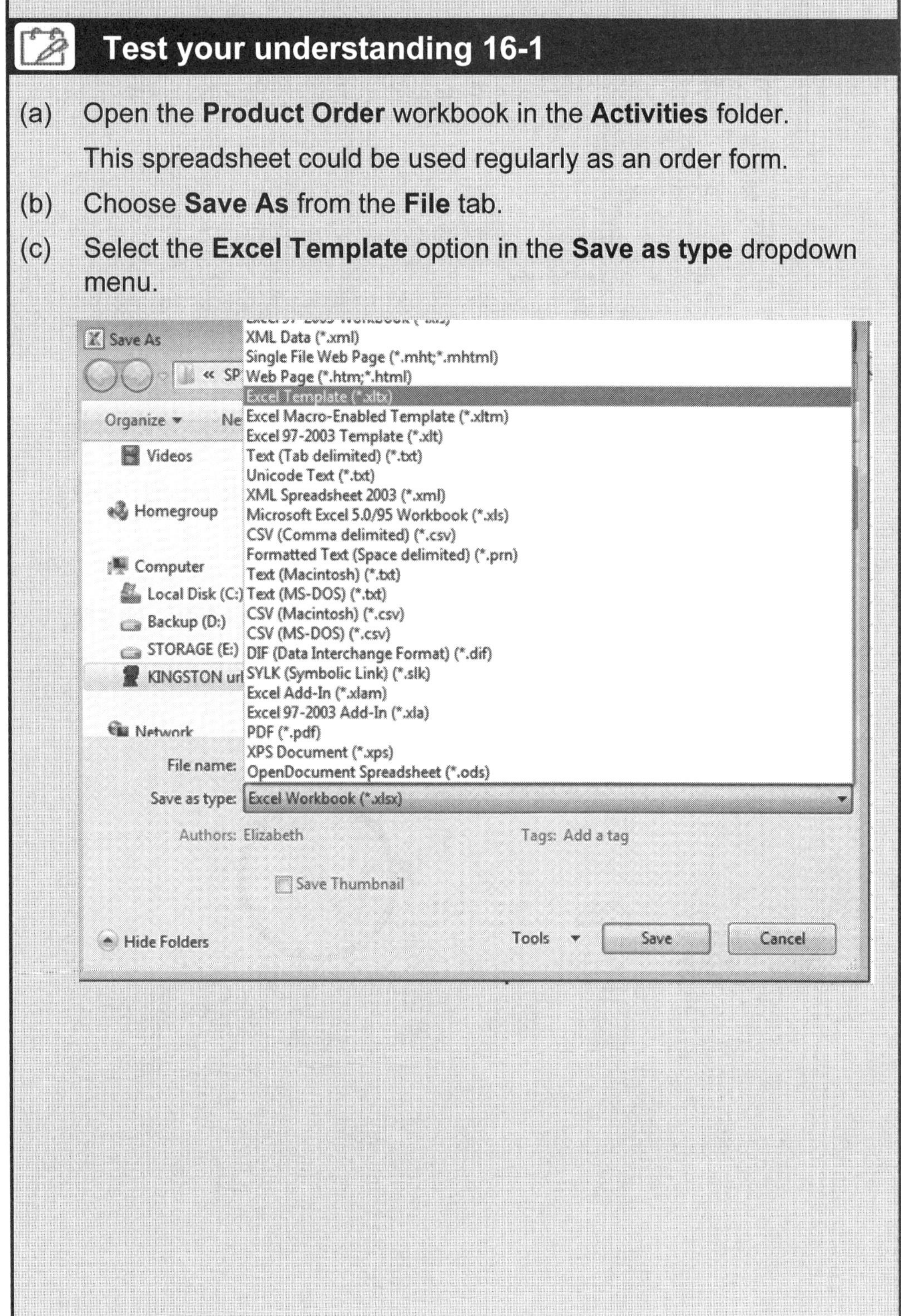

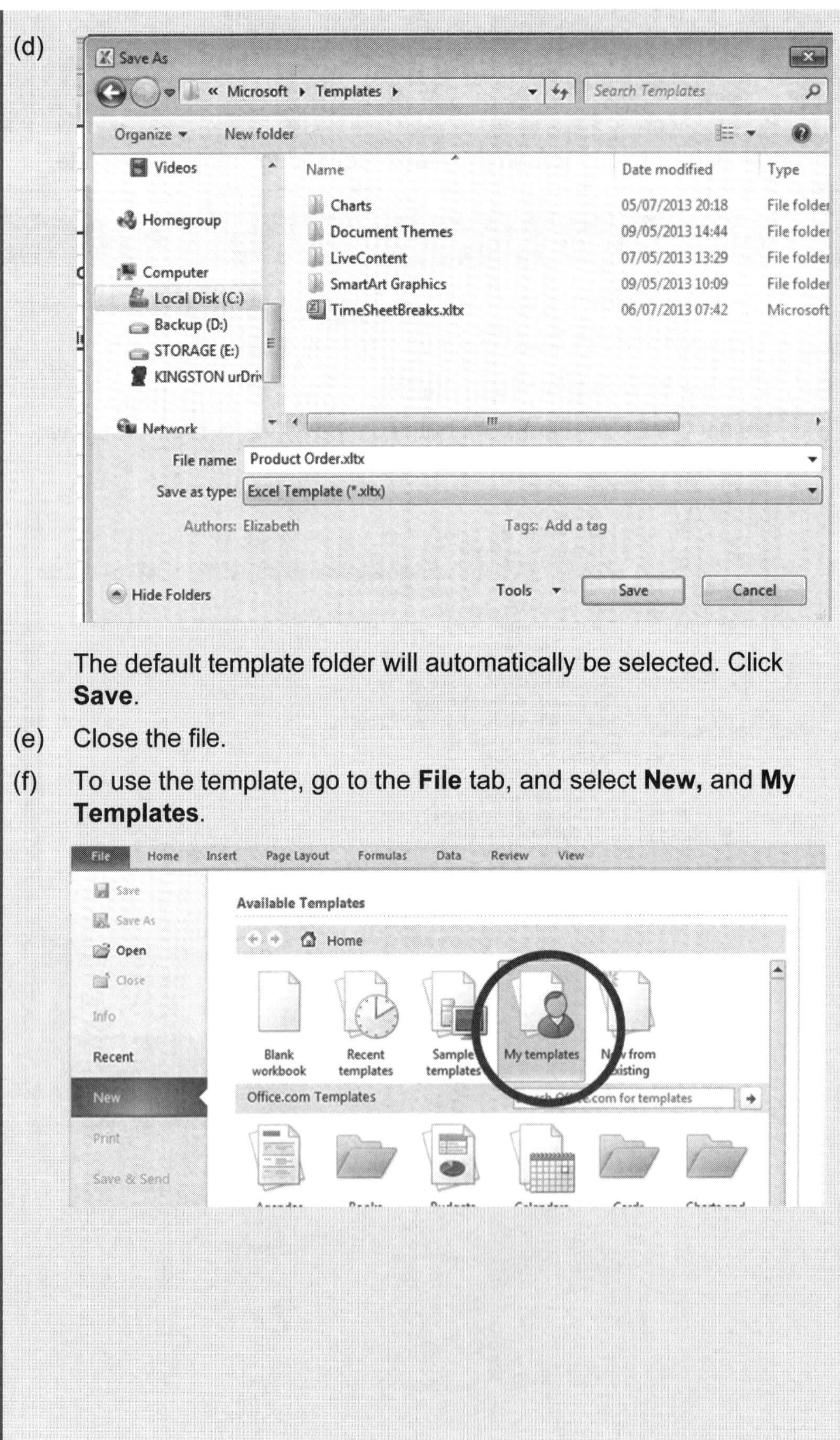


(d) The default template folder will automatically be selected. Click **Save**.

(e) Close the file.

(f) To use the template, go to the **File** tab, and select **New,** and **My Templates**.

(g) Select the appropriate template.

(h) The template is available for use:

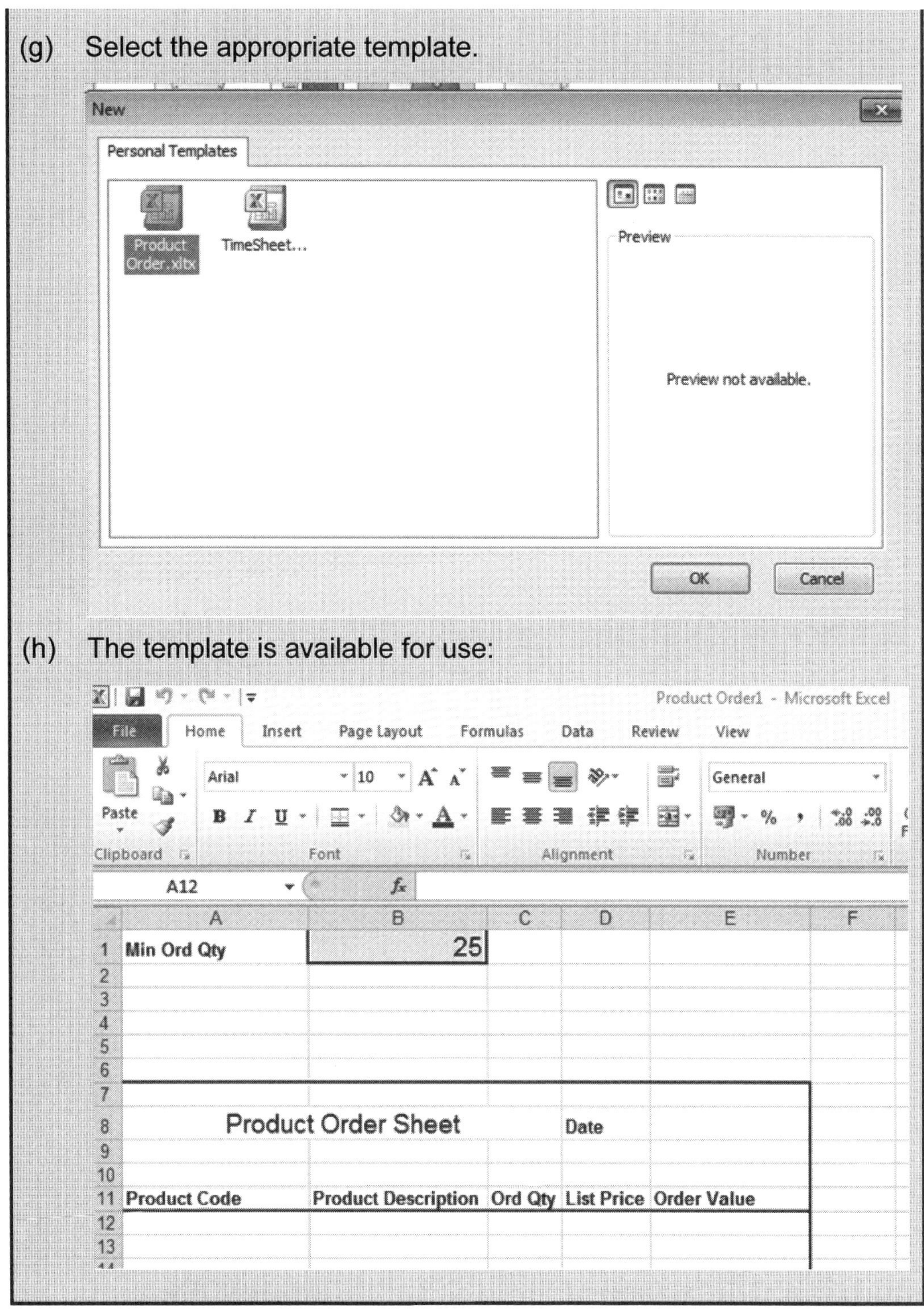

# Spreadsheet protection

## Introduction

This chapter will show you how to protect your spreadsheets so that no other user can change the content of the spreadsheet. In this chapter you will learn how to:

- How to hide formulas.
- How to lock cells.
- How to protect a worksheet.
- How to protect a workbook.

### ASSESSMENT CRITERIA

Securely store and retrieve relevant information (1.2)

Protect integrity of data (4.3)

### CONTENTS

# 1 Protecting your data

## 1.1 Worksheet protection

To prevent accidental/unauthorised changes to a worksheet, it must be protected. This is performed in the **Review** tab.

Click **Protect Sheet** to protect the sheet. You are then presented with a series of options giving you the power to restrict various activities.

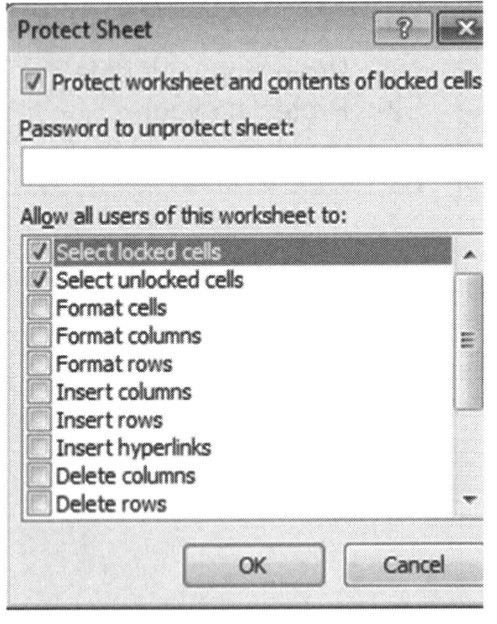


Check/uncheck the boxes as required, depending on what access you wish to give/remove.

You can also set a password if required. If you enter a password you will be required to confirm it. This password will then be required to unprotect the sheet.

Note the warning. If you forget the password to unprotect a worksheet, then it cannot be recovered.

If the password is forgotten then copy and paste the locked spreadsheet into a new, unlocked sheet.

When you protect a spreadsheet, only LOCKED cells will be affected.

If a sheet is protected, then use the **Unprotect Sheet** option to remove protection.

## 1.2 Cell protection

All cells in a workbook are locked by default. If you wish to protect one cell or a range of cells in a worksheet it may be necessary to unlock all the cells in the worksheet first and then lock the cells you want to protect.

This can be done in the **Format cells** menu.

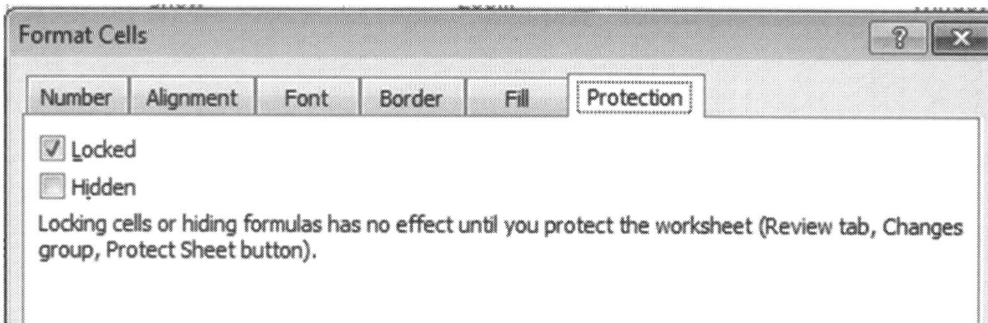


As explained in the menu – this will have no effect until the worksheet is protected using **Protect Sheet** on the Review tab.

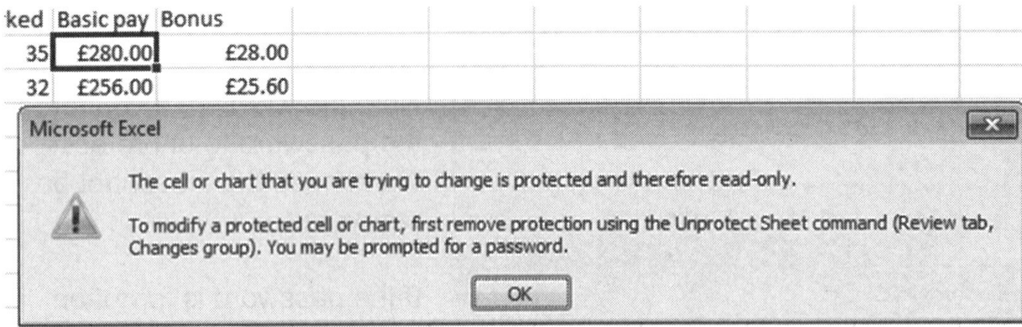


If you try to edit a locked cell, the above warning will be shown.

## 1.3 Hide formulas

Again, this is done in the **Format Cells** menu, under **Protection**. Check or uncheck the tickbox as required, and the formulas will be hidden.

To hide formulas you will need to go to the **Format Cells** dialogue box, open the protection tab and click **hidden**. It must be stressed that the formulas will only become hidden when the worksheet is protected.

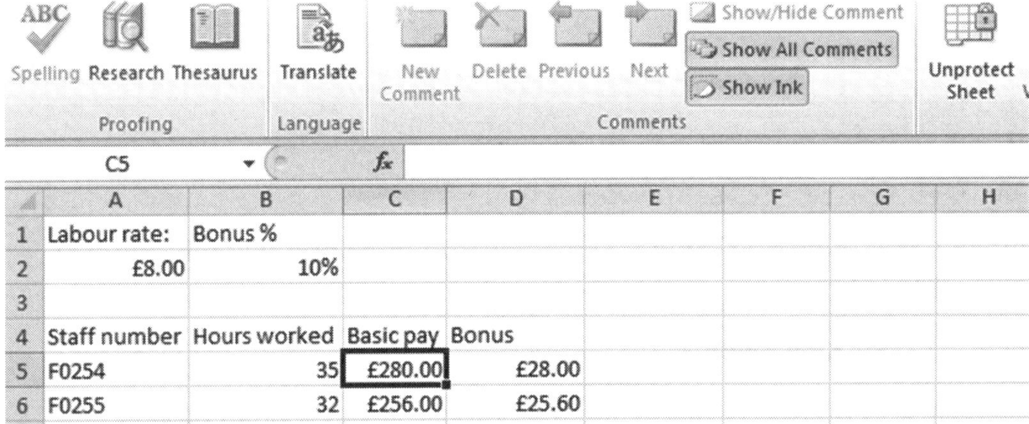


| | A | B | C | D |
|---|---|---|---|---|
| 1 | Labour rate: | Bonus % | | |
| 2 | £8.00 | 10% | | |
| 3 | | | | |
| 4 | Staff number | Hours worked | Basic pay | Bonus |
| 5 | F0254 | 35 | £280.00 | £28.00 |
| 6 | F0255 | 32 | £256.00 | £25.60 |

This worksheet is protected, and the formula in cell C5 is hidden – it is not shown in the Formula Bar.

# 2 Protecting your workbook

## 2.1 Workbook protection

There are two main options regarding workbook protection:

- To prevent unauthorised access/changes to the workbook itself.
- To prevent unauthorised changes to the structure of the workbook.

## 2.2 Adding a password to a workbook

You can add a password to a workbook when you save it. Choose the **Save As** option.

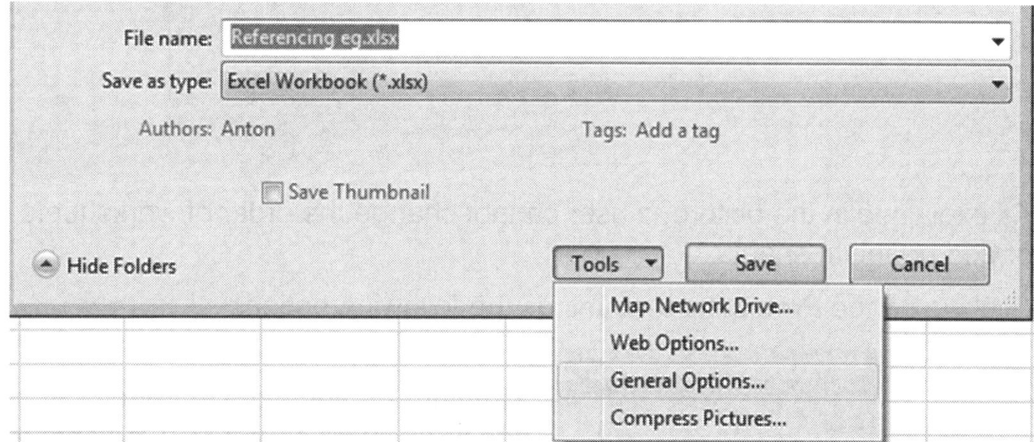


At the bottom of the window is the **Tools** option. Select **General Options**.

There are two main options – Password to open means a password is required to access the document.

Password to modify allows users to view the document, but requires a password to make any changes.

Any passwords used will require verification and must not be forgotten or lost.

## 2.3 Protecting the workbook structure

This is performed within the **Review** tab, in the **Changes menu.**

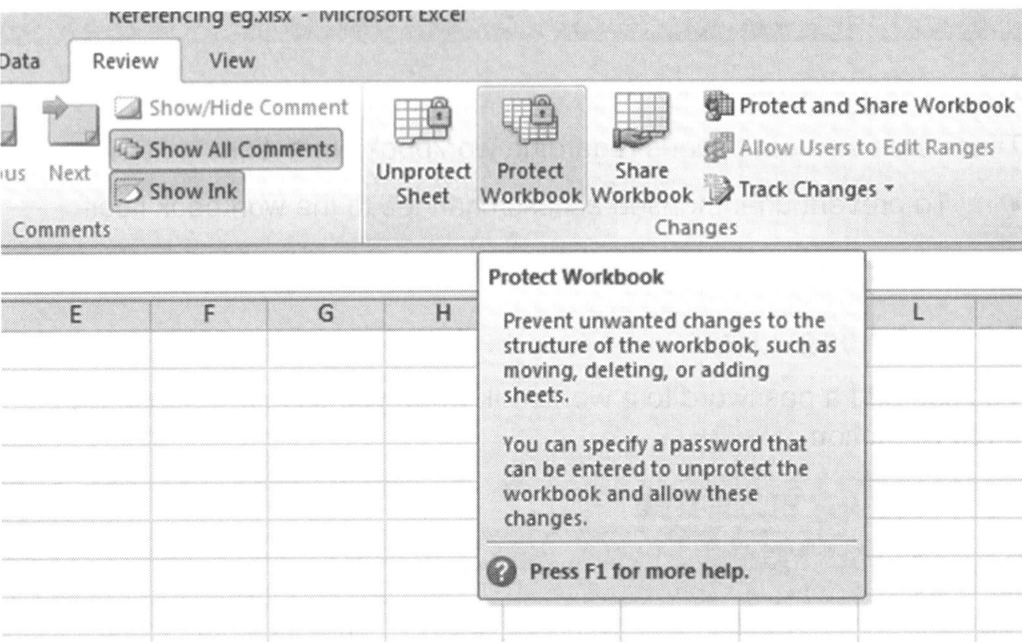


As explained in the picture, a user cannot change the order of worksheets, or add or delete sheets.

Clicking on the Protect buttons brings the following options:

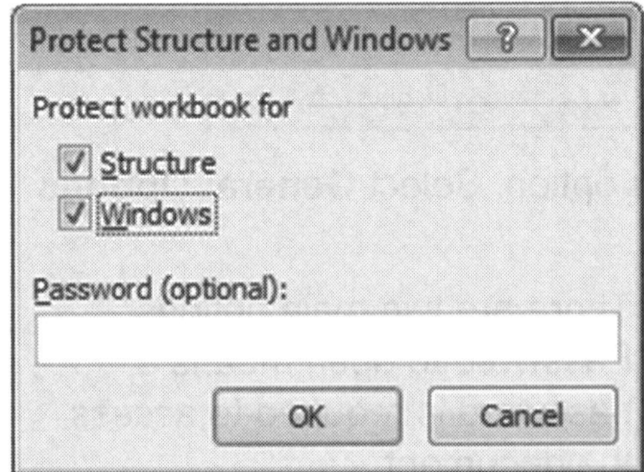


Structure prevents users from adding/deleting or moving worksheets within the workbook.

Windows prevents users from resizing windows in the workbook.

Again, if a password is used, it is essential not to forget/lose it.

# Sharing workbooks

18

## Introduction

This chapter will show you the function of 'read only' spreadsheets and how to share workbooks.

### ASSESSMENT CRITERIA

Securely store and retrieve relevant information (1.2)

Protect integrity of data (4.3)

### CONTENTS

# 1 Sharing a workbook

## 1.1 Sharing a workbook

Normally when a user tries to open a workbook that is in use already they are presented with the dialogue box below. Here they have three options.

1 They could open the file **Read-Only**. They can have access to the file, but they can only save changes they make if they use **Save-as** and give the file a new name.

2 They could open the file with the **Notify** button. Here they can view the file and when presented with another dialogue box informing them that the file is available for **read-write** they can make their changes.

3 They can click **Cancel** to close the dialogue box without opening the file.

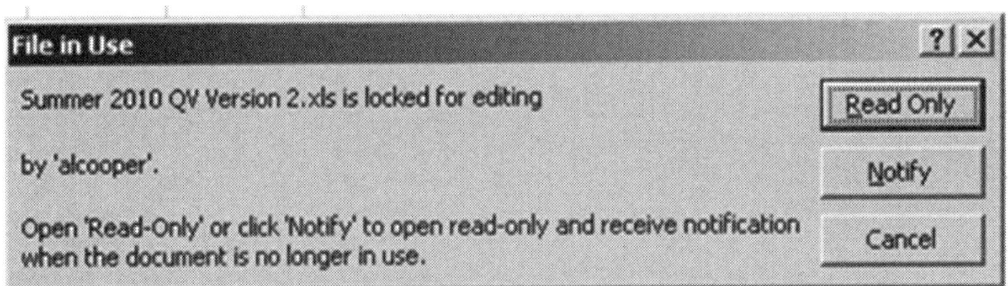


Excel cannot be considered a multi-user application. It does, however, have a feature called **Share Workbook** that does allow more than one user on a **network** to update a spreadsheet at the same time.

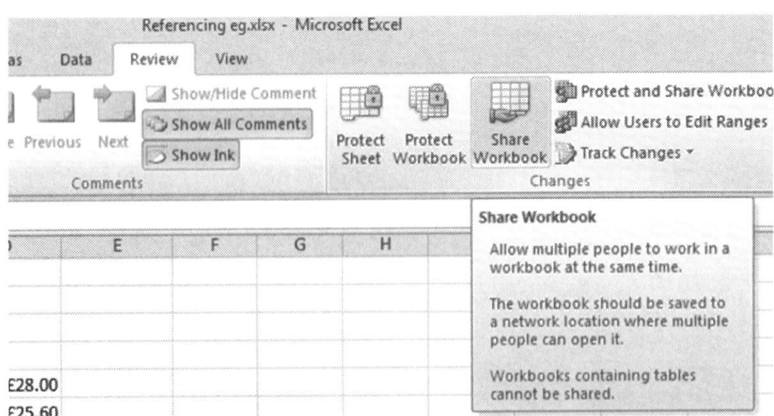


If the writer follows the path above they will be presented with the following dialogue box. If they tick the **Allow Changes** box the workbook will allow multiple users. When in this mode Excel keeps a track of the changes that have been made. Also the 2nd tab becomes available.

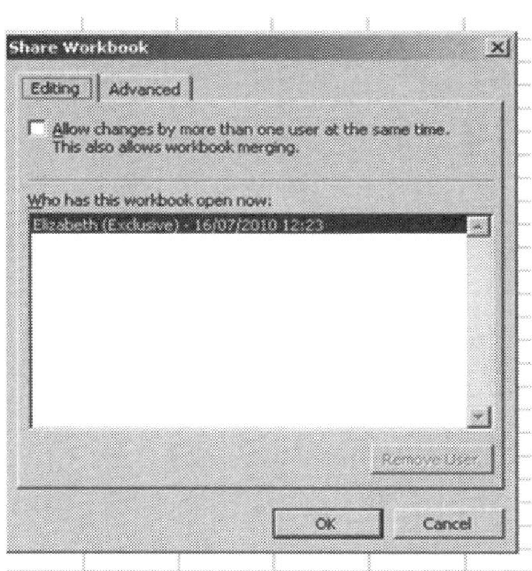


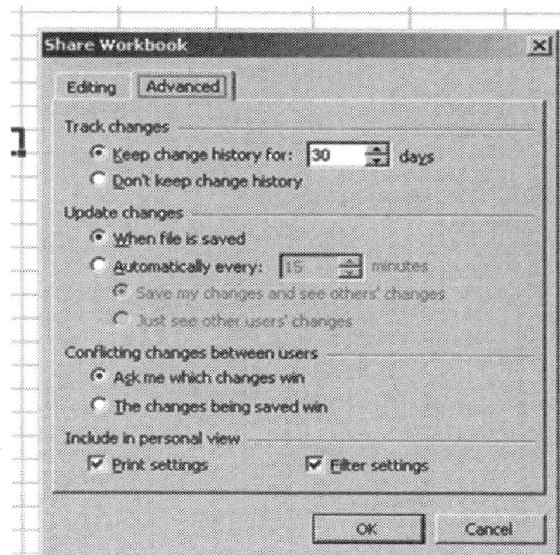


The writer can then stipulate:

- If changes should be recorded and for how long.
- When the changes will come into effect.
- That, when changes being made conflict – whose changes are actually made.

**Note**

When a workbook is shared most of the functionality of the spreadsheet is impaired. For instance: deleting; merging, insert charts and objects, conditional formats, data validation and subtotals, to name but a few. If any of these are required, sharing must be turned off, the task performed, sharing can then be resumed.

# Consolidating worksheets

## Introduction

This chapter will show you how to join one or more workbooks together using the consolidation tool and to understand the various aspects of this function.

### ASSESSMENT CRITERIA

Format data (2.3)

Select and use relevant tools to analyse and interpret data (3.2)

### CONTENTS

# 1 Consolidation

## 1.1 The consolidation tool

We have seen in Chapter 7 how to link two or more worksheets and or workbooks together to when referencing to cells and worksheets in calculations. Excel comes equipped with a **Consolidation** tool to aid us in this task.

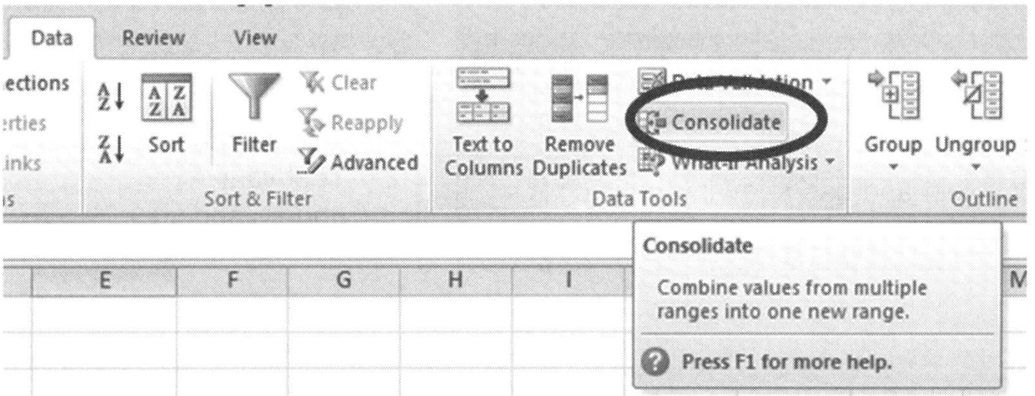


Consolidation can be done with or without creating links to the source data. With a link means any updates in the source data will also update the consolidation, without links and any updates in the source data will not show in the consolidation.

Links to source data can be set up without the source data being open but it is often easier if it is.

The consolidation tool is very useful as it allows you to use row and column headings to perform the consolidation. This is very effective as the row and column labels do not need to be in the same position in the worksheets. However, the row and column labels MUST be spelt exactly the same (they are not case sensitive).

The **Consolidation Tool** when opened presents you with the following dialogue box.

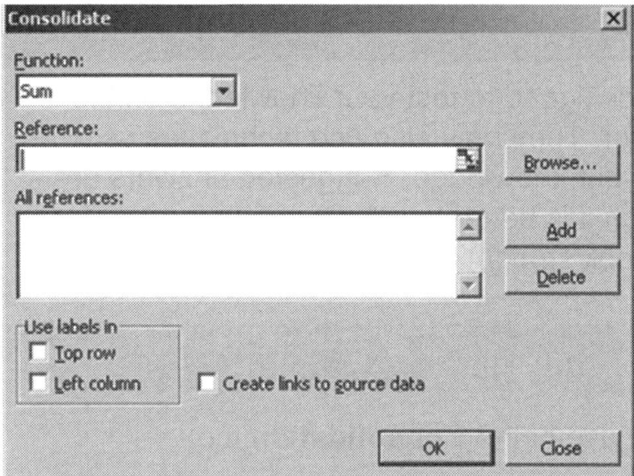


You select the data you wish to consolidate in the **Reference** box, and then click **Add**. Add all the data sources you wish to consolidate, and then click **OK**. The data will be consolidated.

You can also choose the function – **SUM**, **AVERAGE**, **MIN** or **MAX** – depending on what you want Excel to do.

# 2 Test your understanding

The activities in this guide are designed to test your knowledge on the techniques shown in this chapter. They may also use techniques used in previous chapters, to build up your knowledge. Suggested answers are available on MyKaplan, although it is better to refer to the notes and try to understand the methods than look straight at the answers.

## Test your understanding 19-1

This activity demonstrates the use of the **Consolidation** tool.

(a) Open the following workbooks from the **Activities** folder:

- NorthvSouth Consolidation
- Southern
- Northern.

(b) The aim is to consolidate the data on the Southern and Northern workbooks into the NorthvSouth Consolidation workbook.

(c) Select cell **B2** in the NorthvSouth Consolidation workbook. This is where we need to consolidate our data.

(d) Select the **Consolidation** tool from the **Data** tab.

(e) You need to add two references – one each from the Northern and Southern workbooks. Use the reference button at the end of the Reference box, select the required data, and click the reference button again:

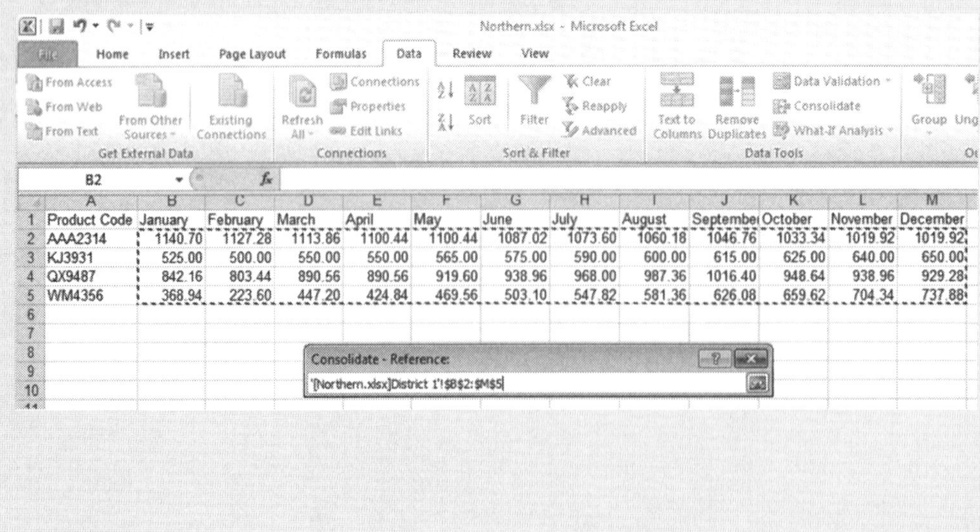

(f) Once the data is selected, click **Add** to add it to the consolidation.

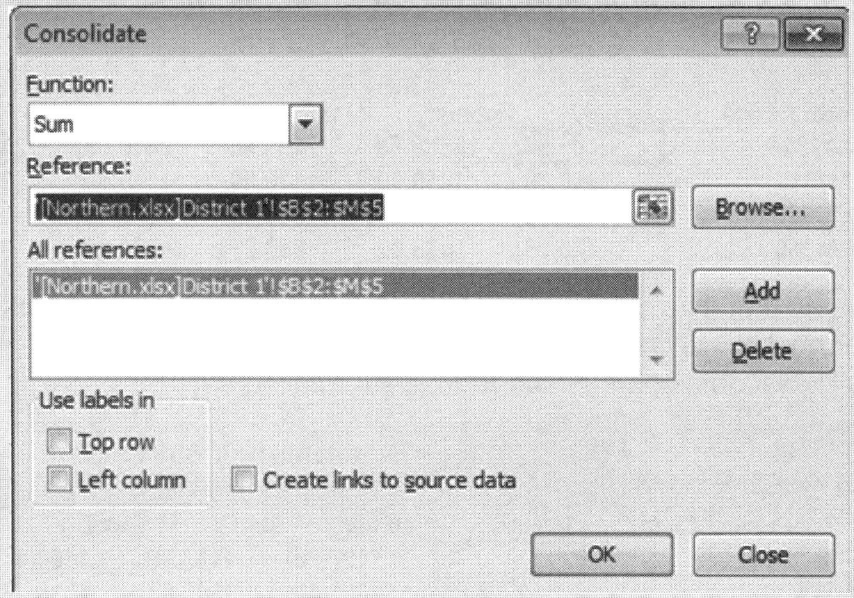

Consolidate

Function:
Sum
Reference:
'[Northern.xlsx]District 1'!$B$2:$M$5
Browse...
All references:
'[Northern.xlsx]District 1'!$B$2:$M$5
Add
Delete
Use labels in
Top row
Left column
Create links to source data
OK
Close

(g) Repeat for the other data set.

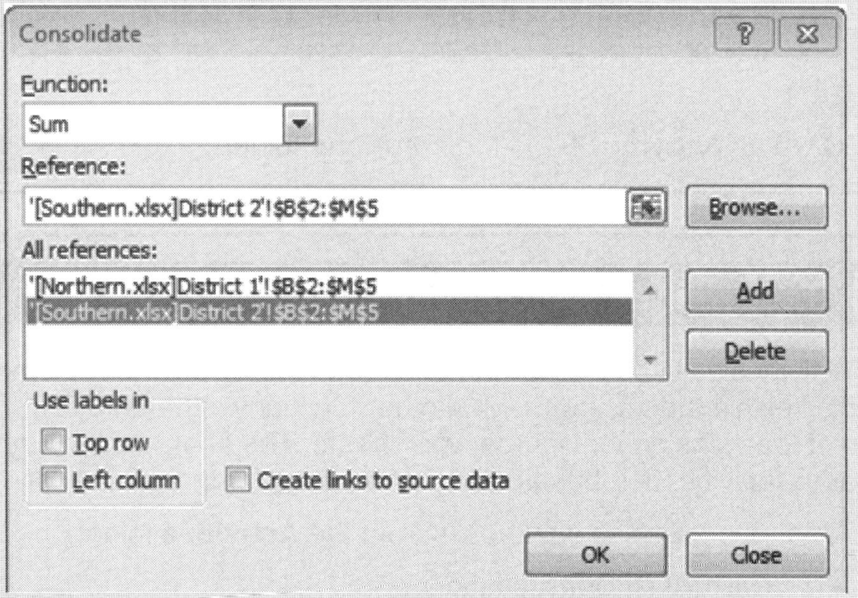

Consolidate

Function:
Sum
Reference:
'[Southern.xlsx]District 2'!$B$2:$M$5
Browse...
All references:
'[Northern.xlsx]District 1'!$B$2:$M$5
'[Southern.xlsx]District 2'!$B$2:$M$5
Add
Delete
Use labels in
Top row
Left column
Create links to source data
OK
Close

Note that you could select a different function, for example **AVERAGE** or **MAX**, but we need **SUM** here. Click **OK**.

(h) The data is consolidated (added up).

B2 | $f_x$ | 2509.54

| | A | B | C | D | E | F |
|---|---|---|---|---|---|---|
| 1 | Product Code | January | February | March | April | May |
| 2 | AAA2314 | 2509.54 | 2482.70 | 2455.86 | 2415.60 | 2415.60 |
| 3 | KJ3931 | 1060.00 | 1010.00 | 1110.00 | 1110.00 | 1140.00 |
| 4 | QX9487 | 1703.68 | 1626.24 | 1800.48 | 1800.48 | 1858.56 |
| 5 | WM4356 | 726.70 | 436.02 | 883.22 | 838.50 | 927.94 |

(i) Note that if you select the "Create links to source data" in part f, formulas are created so that the figures will be updated if the original data changes, as well as subtotals created.

B2 | $f_x$ | ='[Northern.xlsx]District 1'!$B$2

| 1 2 | | A | B | C | D | E | |
|---|---|---|---|---|---|---|---|
| | 1 | Product Code | January | February | March | April | May |
| · | 2 | | 1140.70 | 1127.28 | 1113.86 | 1100.44 | |
| · | 3 | | 1368.84 | 1355.42 | 1342.00 | 1315.16 | |
| − | 4 | AAA2314 | 2509.54 | 2482.70 | 2455.86 | 2415.60 | |
| + | 7 | KJ3931 | 1060.00 | 1010.00 | 1110.00 | 1110.00 | |
| + | 10 | QX9487 | 1703.68 | 1626.24 | 1800.48 | 1800.48 | |
| + | 13 | WM4356 | 726.70 | 436.02 | 883.22 | 838.50 | |
| | 14 | | | | | | |

(j) Save as **Activity 19-1** in the **solutions** folder.

## Test your understanding 19-2

This activity also uses the **consolidation** tool, but demonstrates how it is more flexible than using SUM or other functions if the data is in different locations on the source worksheets. The approach is very similar to Activity 19-1, but labels must be used for the consolidation.

(a) Open the following workbooks from the **Activities** folder:

- EastvWest Consolidation
- Eastern
- Western.

(b) As in Activity 19-1, we need to consolidate (**SUM**) the data on the two data workbooks – Eastern and Western. Notice though, that the data is laid out differently – the Months and products are in a different order on the two sheets.

(c) Select cell **A1** in the EastvWest Consolidation workbook, and select the Consolidation tool.

(d) Add the two references as before – except that the data **AND** row and column headings must be selected – i.e. from cell A1 to the corner of the data. Also select the options to use labels.

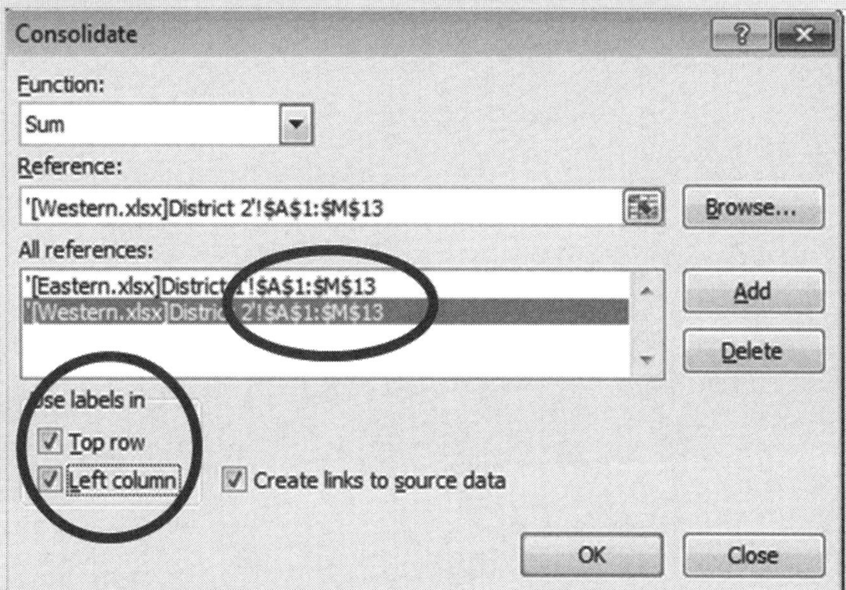


(e) When the consolidation is complete, the formulas will allow for the fact that the labels are in different places on each sheet.

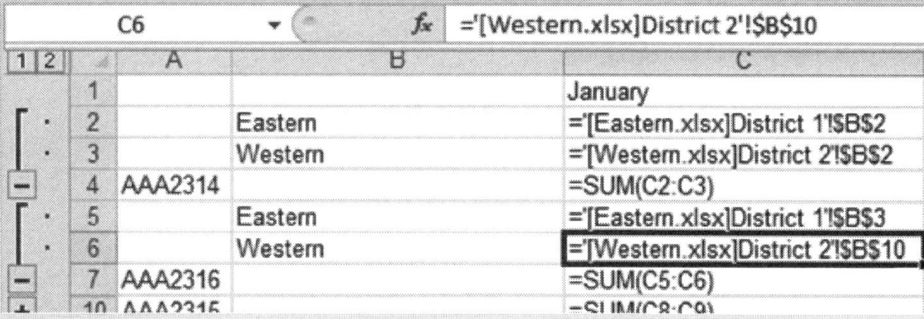


For example, product AAA2314 is in row 3 on the Eastern Spreadsheet, and row 10 on the Western, as shown here.

(f) Save as **Activity 19-2** in the **solutions** folder.

# Creating simple pivot tables

## Introduction

This chapter will show you how to use the function of pivot tables as a form of consolidation, how to insert formulas into these pivot tables, and how to create charts from pivot tables

## ASSESSMENT CRITERIA

Select and use relevant tools to analyse and interpret data (3.2)

Select and use appropriate tools to generate and format charts (3.3)

## CONTENTS

# 1 Important note

## 1.1 An important point about pivot tables

Pivot Tables may seem a bit confusing when you first use them – there are a lot of options to choose from and they might not do what you want them to first time. The important point is that **you cannot break a pivot table**! Aside from the ability to use Ctrl-Z to undo any mistakes, a pivot table **will never change the original data**. So if it all goes wrong, just delete the table and start again.

# 2 Creating a pivot table

## 2.1 Construction of pivot tables

A **Pivot Table** is a tool used for turning tables of data into meaningful reports. The tool can be used to create reports from external sources, multiple-workbooks (another consolidation tool) and workbooks.

In essence a **Pivot Table** is a means of taking raw data and presenting it so that the user can understand what they are looking at. It is often best to think in terms of 'what would I want a report on this data to look like?' You can then set your pivot table to look like this.

## 2.2 Creating a report

Pivot tables are particularly useful when there is a large amount of data to analyse.

We want to create a report showing total sales for each month, split by region. We can use the Pivot Table to show this very easily.

To create a pivot table, select the data (**including headers**) you wish to use, then in the **Insert** tab, select **Pivot Table**.

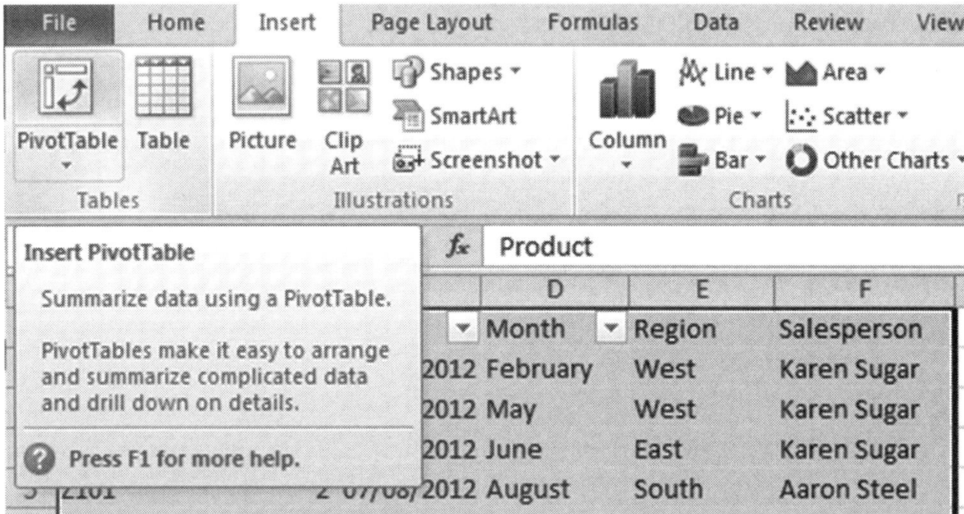


This opens the **PivotTable Wizard**.

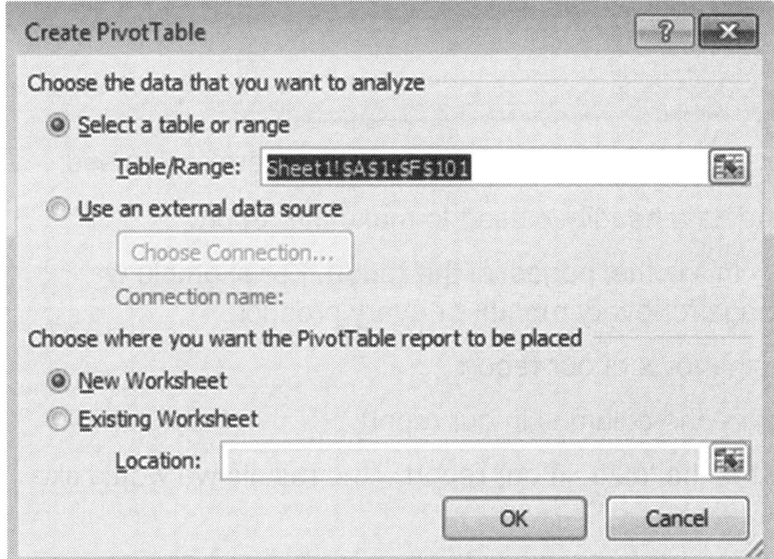


You can also choose whether to create the table in a new worksheet or place it somewhere on your existing sheet.

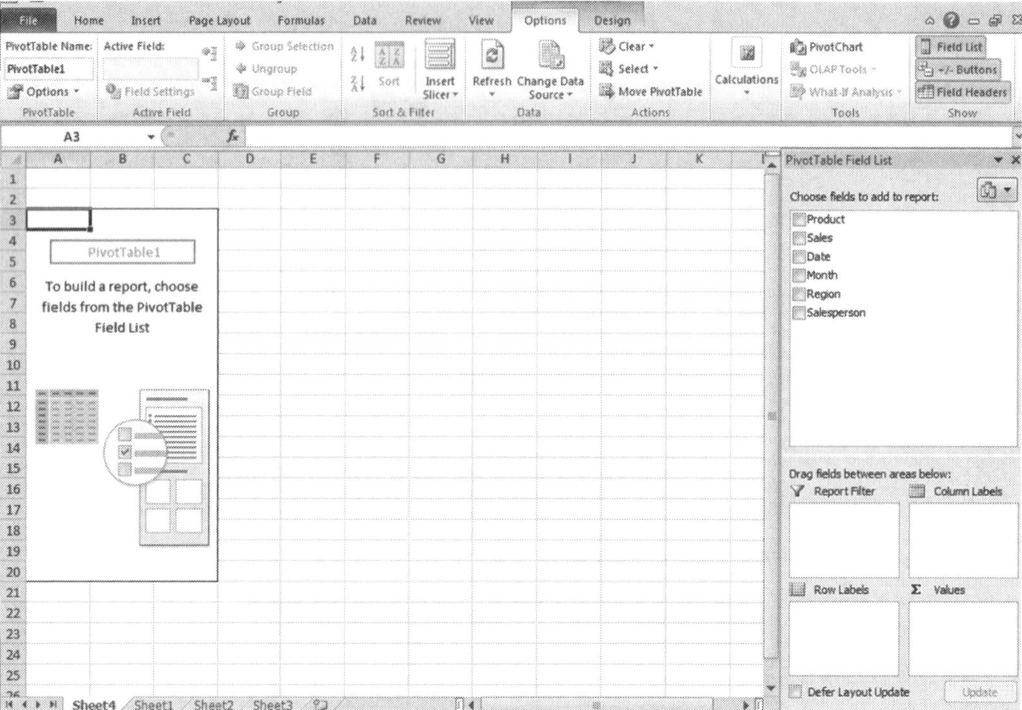


This view allows you to build your report. The following terms are used:

- **Fields** – are the data headings used to make the report.
- **Report Filter** – this is the 'pages' of the report. For example we might have a page for every month, or every product.
- **Row Labels** – the rows of our report.
- **Column Labels** – the columns in our report.
- ∑ **Values** – this is the 'data' in our report – the results we would like to show.

The box on the left of the sheet is where the report is shown. The idea is to 'drag' the fields into the required box – report filter, rows, columns and values.

Depending on preference we would then choose our column and row labels. If we want **Month** as the row labels, and **Region** as the column labels drag the field names into the appropriate box/area on the table.

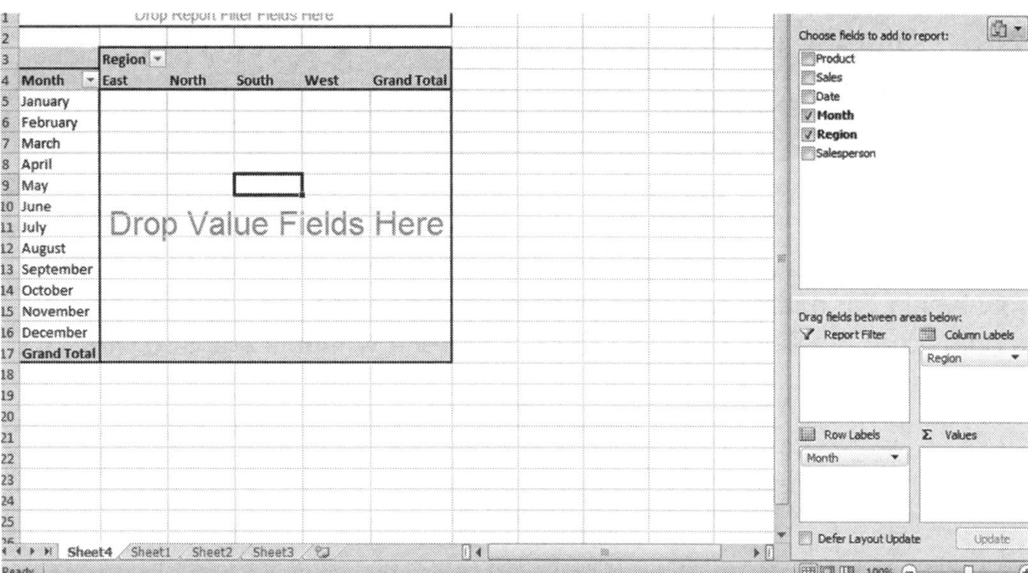


Our report is starting to take shape. We need some data though – that is the **value field.** We would like to know sales by month, so drag the sales field into the value area.

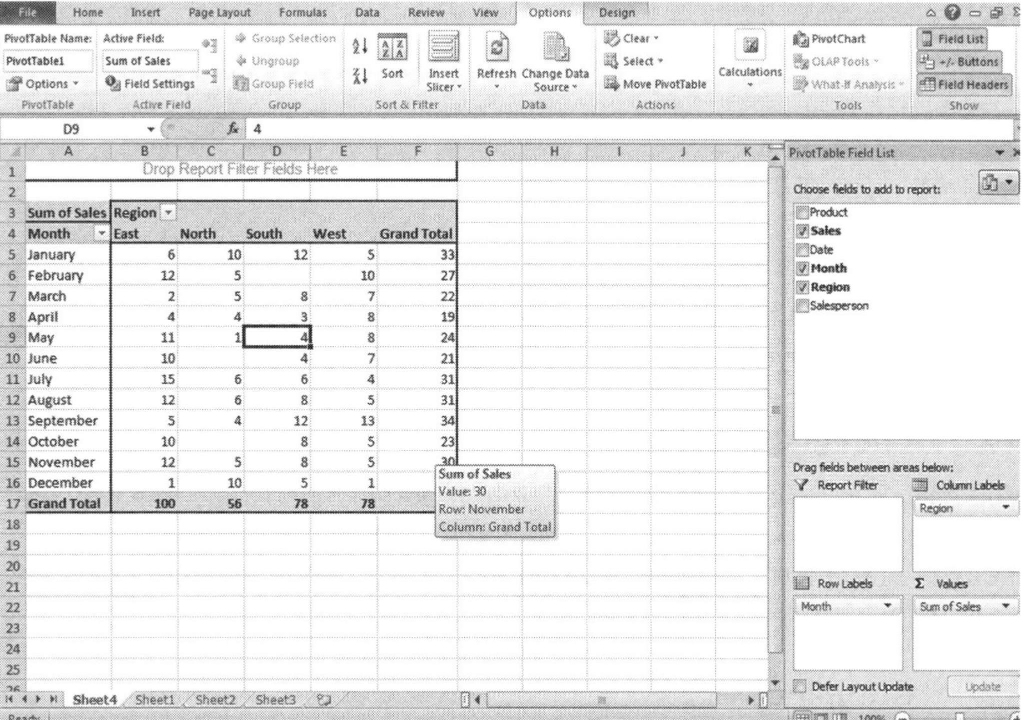


The report is now complete but may require some tidying up and formatting.

# 3 Further report options

## 3.1 Adding row labels

Pivot Tables are very versatile. You are not restricted to one field in the row labels, for example – if we wanted to show each individual's sales by month, drag the salesperson field over to the row labels and see what happens:

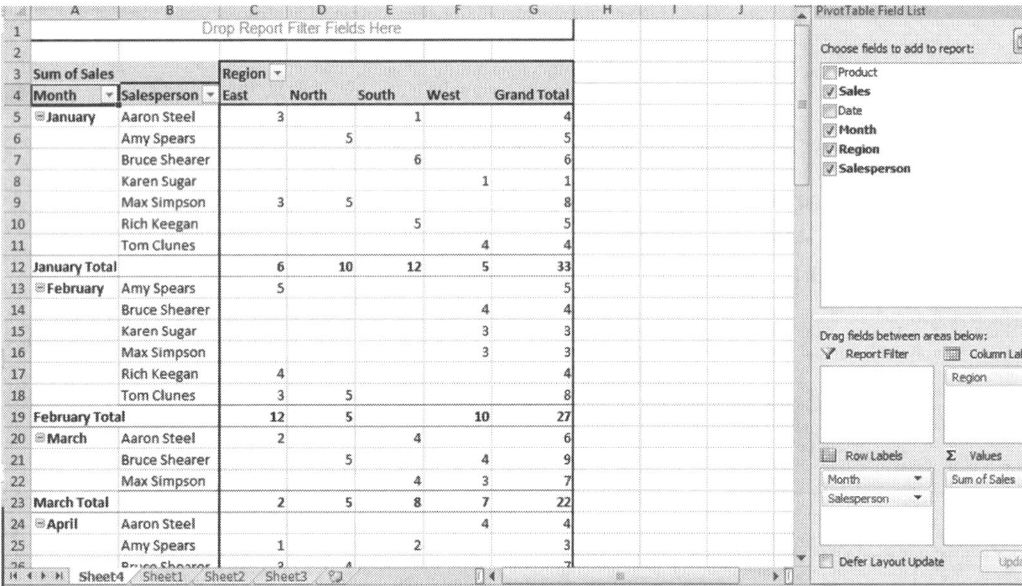

| Sum of Sales | | Region | | | | |
|---|---|---|---|---|---|---|
| Month | Salesperson | East | North | South | West | Grand Total |
| January | Aaron Steel | 3 | | 1 | | 4 |
| | Amy Spears | | 5 | | | 5 |
| | Bruce Shearer | | | 6 | | 6 |
| | Karen Sugar | | | | 1 | 1 |
| | Max Simpson | 3 | 5 | | | 8 |
| | Rich Keegan | | | 5 | | 5 |
| | Tom Clunes | | | | 4 | 4 |
| January Total | | 6 | 10 | 12 | 5 | 33 |
| February | Amy Spears | 5 | | | | 5 |
| | Bruce Shearer | | | | 4 | 4 |
| | Karen Sugar | | | | 3 | 3 |
| | Max Simpson | | | | 3 | 3 |
| | Rich Keegan | 4 | | | | 4 |
| | Tom Clunes | 3 | 5 | | | 8 |
| February Total | | 12 | 5 | | 10 | 27 |
| March | Aaron Steel | 2 | | 4 | | 6 |
| | Bruce Shearer | | 5 | | 4 | 9 |
| | Max Simpson | | | 4 | 3 | 7 |
| March Total | | 2 | 5 | 8 | 7 | 22 |
| April | Aaron Steel | | | | 4 | 4 |
| | Amy Spears | 1 | | 2 | | 3 |



We have now got the detail we wanted. The best thing to do is to play with all the different layouts and see what suits your needs the best.

## 3.2 Changing an existing layout

You can change the appearance of your report in much the same way as you create the report – drag the field names out of the report to remove them, or drag them to a new part of the table to change the appearance of your table.

## 3.3 Grouping

You can group individual items within a field to create a new data item. For example we might want to show our data quarterly rather than monthly – to do this we would need to group the months together by quarter. There are two ways to do this:

Select the items you wish to group, and click on **Group Selection** in the **PivotTable Tools/Options** tab.

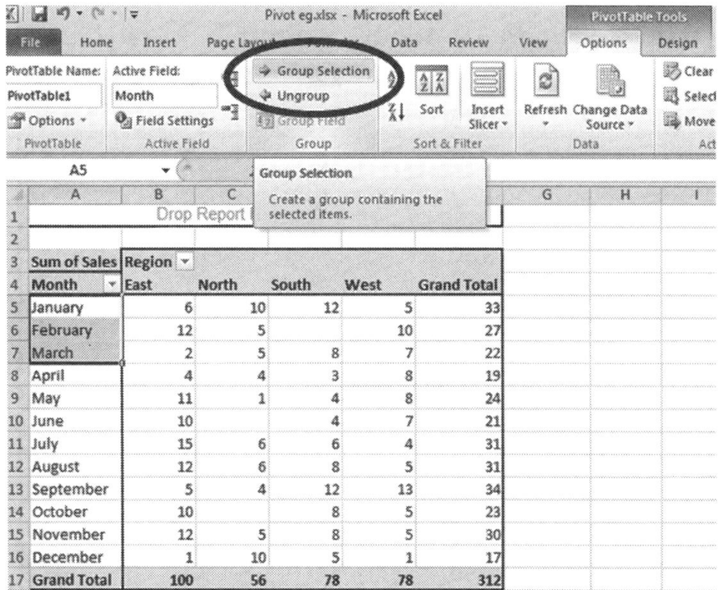


| Sum of Sales | Region | | | | |
|---|---|---|---|---|---|
| Month | East | North | South | West | Grand Total |
| January | 6 | 10 | 12 | 5 | 33 |
| February | 12 | 5 | | 10 | 27 |
| March | 2 | 5 | 8 | 7 | 22 |
| April | 4 | 4 | 3 | 8 | 19 |
| May | 11 | 1 | 4 | 8 | 24 |
| June | 10 | | 4 | 7 | 21 |
| July | 15 | 6 | 6 | 4 | 31 |
| August | 12 | 6 | 8 | 5 | 31 |
| September | 5 | 4 | 12 | 13 | 34 |
| October | 10 | | 8 | 5 | 23 |
| November | 12 | 5 | 8 | 5 | 30 |
| December | 1 | 10 | 5 | 1 | 17 |
| Grand Total | 100 | 56 | 78 | 78 | 312 |

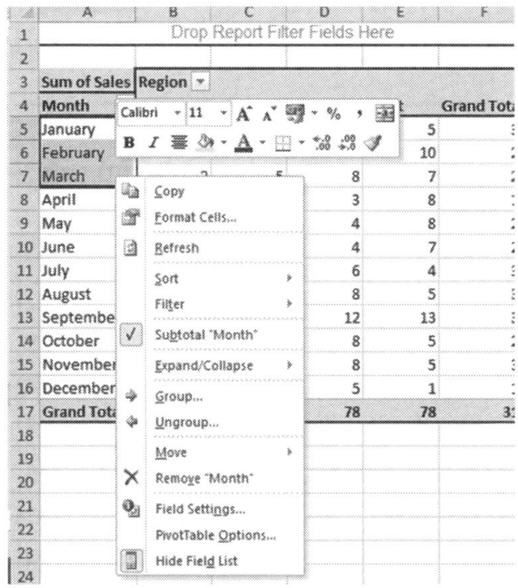


Or **Right-Click** on the selected items and select **Group**.

The field is split and the new group shown. This can be renamed by typing the new name in the cell.

| Sum of Sales | | Region | | | | |
|---|---|---|---|---|---|---|
| Month2 | Month | East | North | South | West | Grand Total |
| ⊟Group1 | January | 6 | 10 | 12 | 5 | 33 |
| | February | 12 | 5 | | 10 | 27 |
| | March | 2 | 5 | 8 | 7 | 22 |
| ⊟April | April | 4 | 4 | 3 | 8 | 19 |
| ⊟May | May | 11 | 1 | 4 | 8 | 24 |
| ⊟June | June | 10 | | 4 | 7 | 21 |
| ⊟July | July | 15 | 6 | 6 | 4 | 31 |
| ⊟August | August | 12 | 6 | 8 | 5 | 31 |
| ⊟September | September | 5 | 4 | 12 | 13 | 34 |
| ⊟October | October | 10 | | 8 | 5 | 23 |
| ⊟November | November | 12 | 5 | 8 | 5 | 30 |
| ⊟December | December | 1 | 10 | 5 | 1 | 17 |
| Grand Total | | 100 | 56 | 78 | 78 | 312 |

Drop Report Filter Fields Here

| Sum of Sales | | Region | | | | |
|---|---|---|---|---|---|---|
| Month2 | Month | East | North | South | West | Grand Total |
| ⊟Q1 | January | 6 | 10 | 12 | 5 | 33 |
| | February | 12 | 5 | | 10 | 27 |
| | March | 2 | 5 | 8 | 7 | 22 |
| ⊟Q2 | April | 4 | 4 | 3 | 8 | 19 |
| | May | 11 | 1 | 4 | 8 | 24 |
| | June | 10 | | 4 | 7 | 21 |
| ⊟Q3 | July | 15 | 6 | 6 | 4 | 31 |
| | August | 12 | 6 | 8 | 5 | 31 |
| | September | 5 | 4 | 12 | 13 | 34 |
| ⊟Q4 | October | 10 | | 8 | 5 | 23 |
| | November | 12 | 5 | 8 | 5 | 30 |
| | December | 1 | 10 | 5 | 1 | 17 |
| Grand Total | | 100 | 56 | 78 | 78 | 312 |

Clicking on the boxes next to the field items allows you to expand/contract the data, similar to subtotals.

We could remove the individual months' data by removing that field from the table:

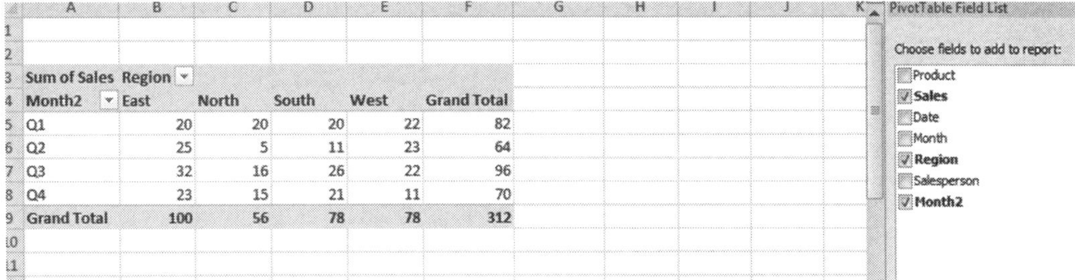

| Sum of Sales | Region | | | | |
|---|---|---|---|---|---|
| Month2 | East | North | South | West | Grand Total |
| Q1 | 20 | 20 | 20 | 22 | 82 |
| Q2 | 25 | 5 | 11 | 23 | 64 |
| Q3 | 32 | 16 | 26 | 22 | 96 |
| Q4 | 23 | 15 | 21 | 11 | 70 |
| Grand Total | 100 | 56 | 78 | 78 | 312 |

PivotTable Field List

Choose fields to add to report:

- Product
- Sales
- Date
- Month
- Region
- Salesperson
- Month2

To remove grouping(s), select the grouping(s), and click **Ungroup**.

## 4.1 Dealing with totals

Totals and subtotals can be added and removed from your **Pivot Table**. As is often the case, right-clicking on the subtotal you want to add/remove is often the easiest way, but here are the key methods.

## 4.2 Subtotals

You may require subtotals for individual fields. For example, we might want to see a subtotal for each exam. This would be the Month2 field.

Select the field by clicking anywhere within it. Then, in the **PivotTable Tools/Options** tab, choose **Field Settings**.

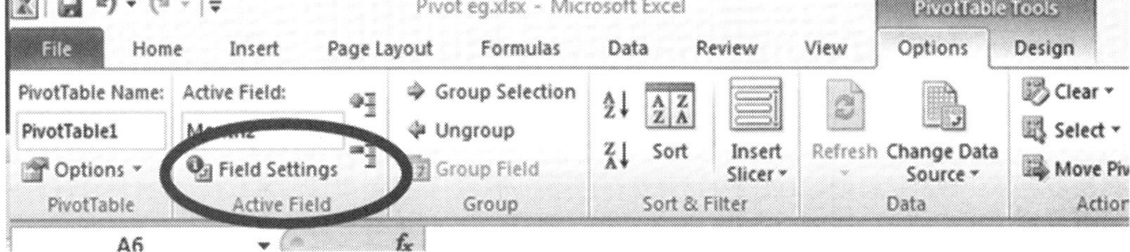

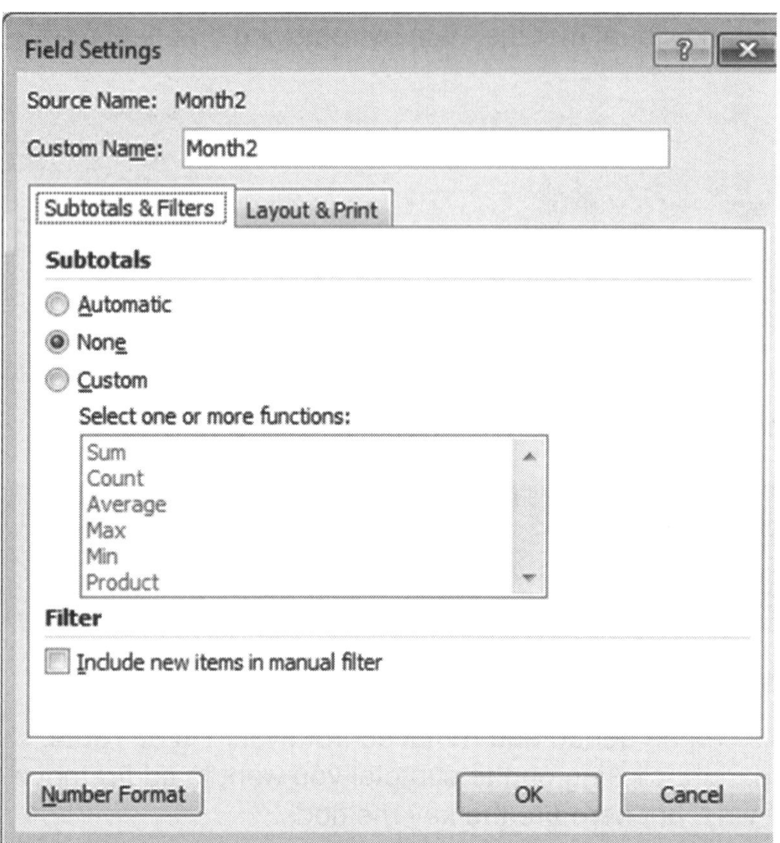


This will bring the appropriate menu up:

Select **Automatic** to add subtotals, or **None** to remove existing subtotals. You could use custom for more advanced subtotals using different functions.

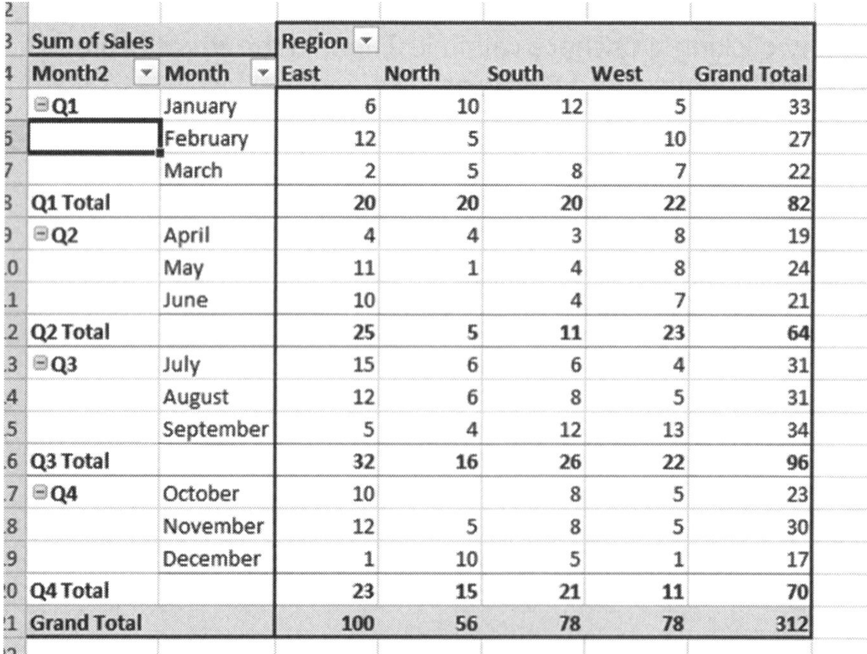

| Sum of Sales | | Region | | | | |
|---|---|---|---|---|---|---|
| Month2 | Month | East | North | South | West | Grand Total |
| Q1 | January | 6 | 10 | 12 | 5 | 33 |
| | February | 12 | 5 | | 10 | 27 |
| | March | 2 | 5 | 8 | 7 | 22 |
| **Q1 Total** | | **20** | **20** | **20** | **22** | **82** |
| Q2 | April | 4 | 4 | 3 | 8 | 19 |
| | May | 11 | 1 | 4 | 8 | 24 |
| | June | 10 | | 4 | 7 | 21 |
| **Q2 Total** | | **25** | **5** | **11** | **23** | **64** |
| Q3 | July | 15 | 6 | 6 | 4 | 31 |
| | August | 12 | 6 | 8 | 5 | 31 |
| | September | 5 | 4 | 12 | 13 | 34 |
| **Q3 Total** | | **32** | **16** | **26** | **22** | **96** |
| Q4 | October | 10 | | 8 | 5 | 23 |
| | November | 12 | 5 | 8 | 5 | 30 |
| | December | 1 | 10 | 5 | 1 | 17 |
| **Q4 Total** | | **23** | **15** | **21** | **11** | **70** |
| **Grand Total** | | **100** | **56** | **78** | **78** | **312** |

The subtotals are added. This could also be achieved by **right-clicking** in the field, and selecting '**Subtotal Month 2**'.

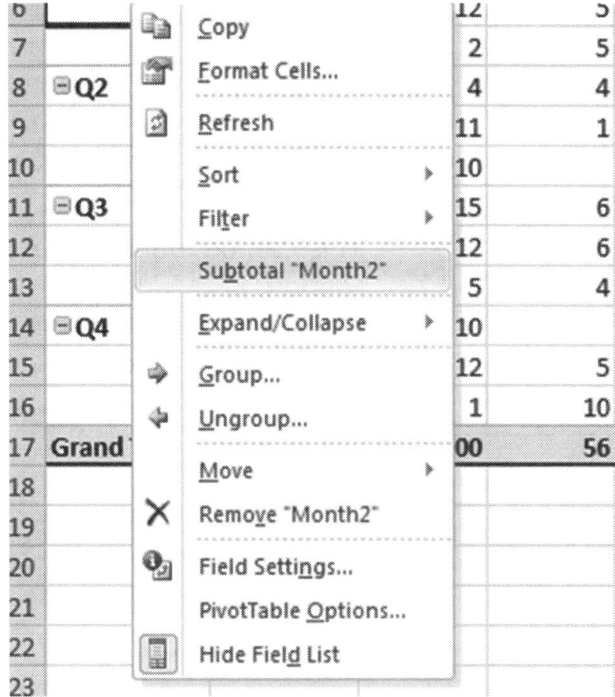


There are many useful options available by right-clicking. If in doubt, right-click!

## 4.3 Grand totals

Grand Totals at the bottom/end of your table can also be added or removed. To remove them right click on the total, and select **Remove Grand Total**.

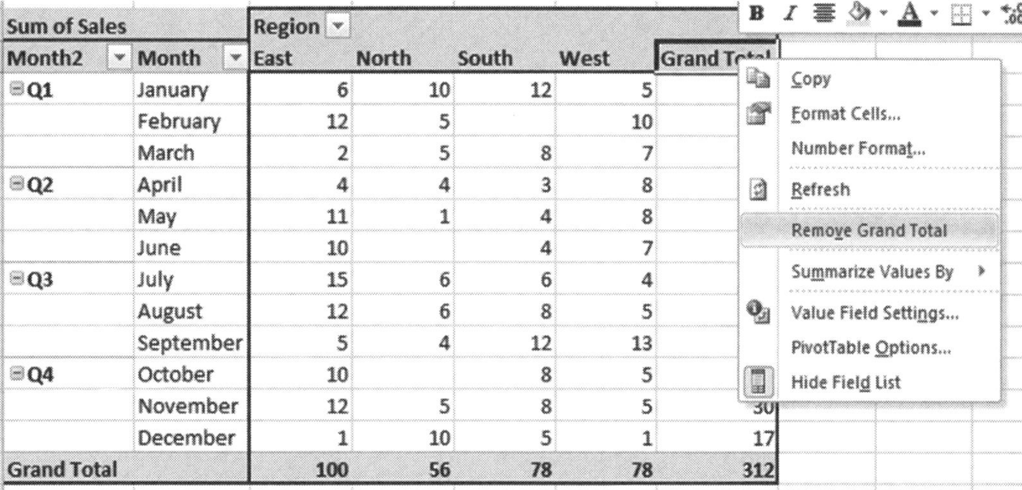

| Sum of Sales | | Region | | | | |
|---|---|---|---|---|---|---|
| Month2 | Month | East | North | South | West | Grand Total |
| Q1 | January | 6 | 10 | 12 | 5 | |
| | February | 12 | 5 | | 10 | |
| | March | 2 | 5 | 8 | 7 | |
| Q2 | April | 4 | 4 | 3 | 8 | |
| | May | 11 | 1 | 4 | 8 | |
| | June | 10 | | 4 | 7 | |
| Q3 | July | 15 | 6 | 6 | 4 | |
| | August | 12 | 6 | 8 | 5 | |
| | September | 5 | 4 | 12 | 13 | |
| Q4 | October | 10 | | 8 | 5 | |
| | November | 12 | 5 | 8 | 5 | 30 |
| | December | 1 | 10 | 5 | 1 | 17 |
| Grand Total | | 100 | 56 | 78 | 78 | 312 |

To add Grand Totals you need the **PivotTable Options** menu.

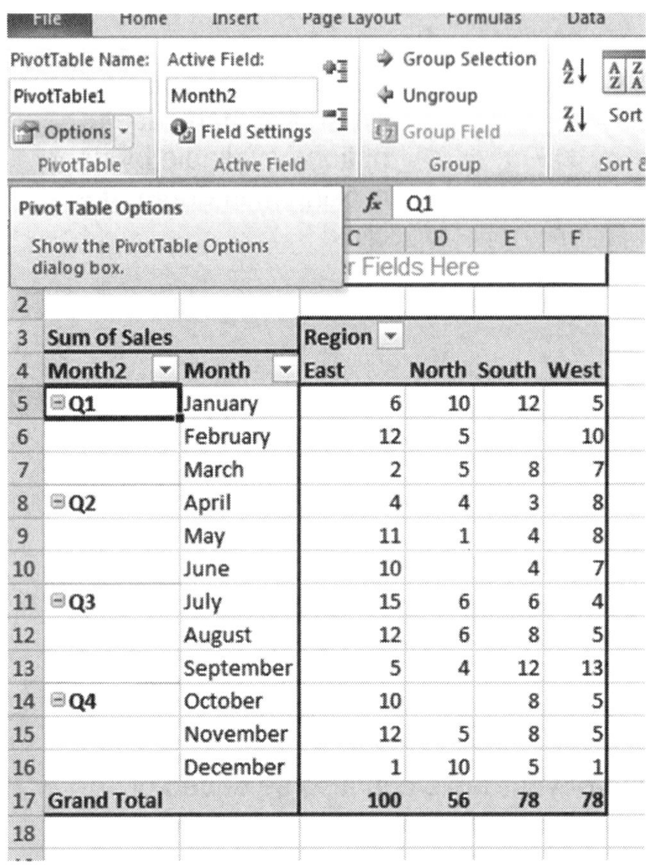


| Sum of Sales | | Region | | | |
|---|---|---|---|---|---|
| Month2 | Month | East | North | South | West |
| Q1 | January | 6 | 10 | 12 | 5 |
| | February | 12 | 5 | | 10 |
| | March | 2 | 5 | 8 | 7 |
| Q2 | April | 4 | 4 | 3 | 8 |
| | May | 11 | 1 | 4 | 8 |
| | June | 10 | | 4 | 7 |
| Q3 | July | 15 | 6 | 6 | 4 |
| | August | 12 | 6 | 8 | 5 |
| | September | 5 | 4 | 12 | 13 |
| Q4 | October | 10 | | 8 | 5 |
| | November | 12 | 5 | 8 | 5 |
| | December | 1 | 10 | 5 | 1 |
| Grand Total | | 100 | 56 | 78 | 78 |

This can be found in the Ribbon, or by right-clicking on the table and select **PivotTable Options**.

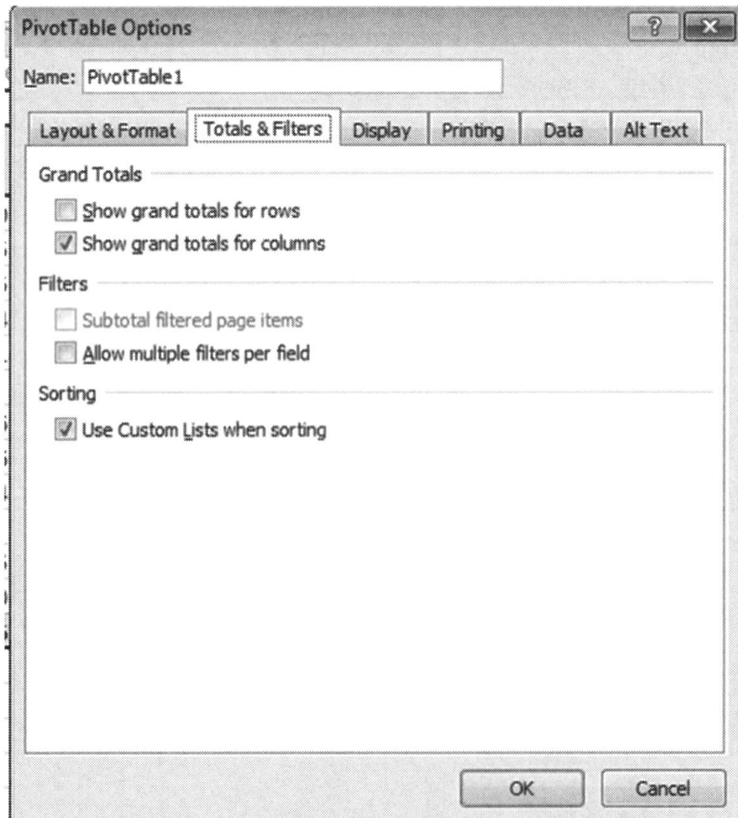


In Totals & Filters, select the Grand Totals required.

Both subtotals and grand totals can also be added or removed in the **PivotTable Tools/Design** tab.

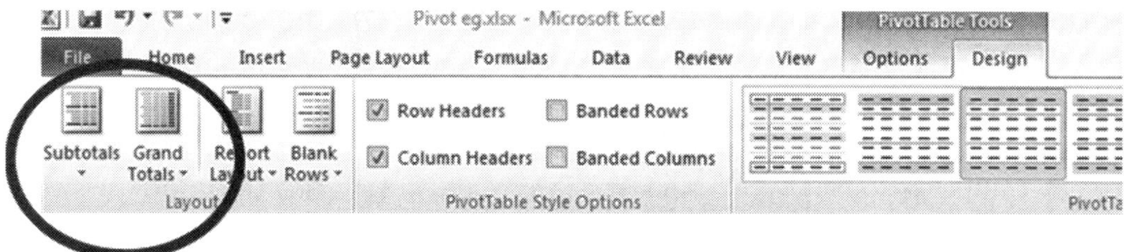


# 5 Filters

## 5.1 Filters

You may have already noticed the **filter** buttons on each field. This allows you to further customise your table to show what you want. These are used in the same way as AutoFilters, explained in **Chapter 4**. Click on the box to apply a filter.

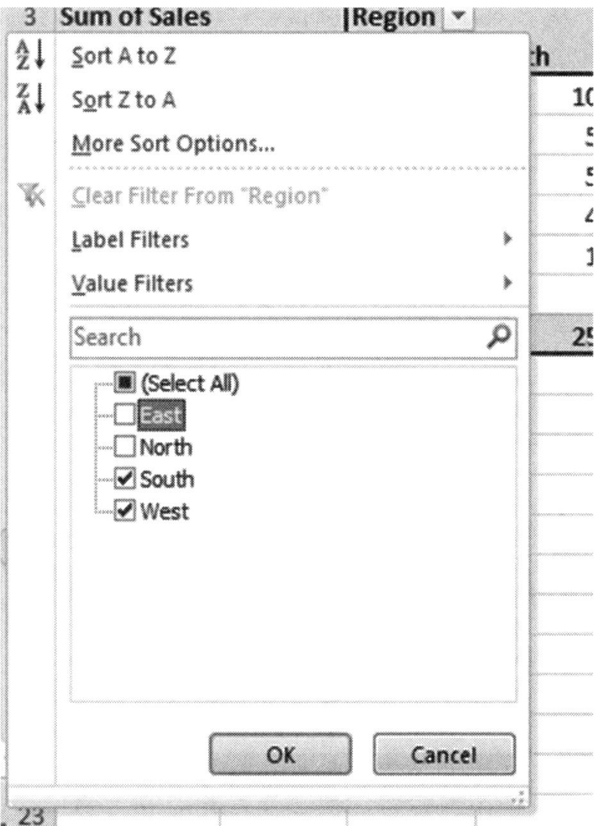


A filter has been applied to only show the South and West's results.

| Sum of Sales | | Region | | |
|---|---|---|---|---|
| Month2 | Month | South | West | Grand Total |
| ⊟Q1 | January | 12 | 5 | 17 |
| | February | | 10 | 10 |
| | March | 8 | 7 | 15 |
| ⊟Q2 | April | 3 | 8 | 11 |
| | May | 4 | 8 | 12 |
| | June | 4 | 7 | 11 |
| Grand Total | | 31 | 45 | 76 |

You can see from the icons that Month2 and Region both have filters applied. The totals are updated accordingly.

## 5.2 Report filter

This is just another part of the report – as explained earlier it acts as 'pages' of your report 'book'. We could use 'Salesperson' as our pages – drag the Salesperson field into the report filter box.

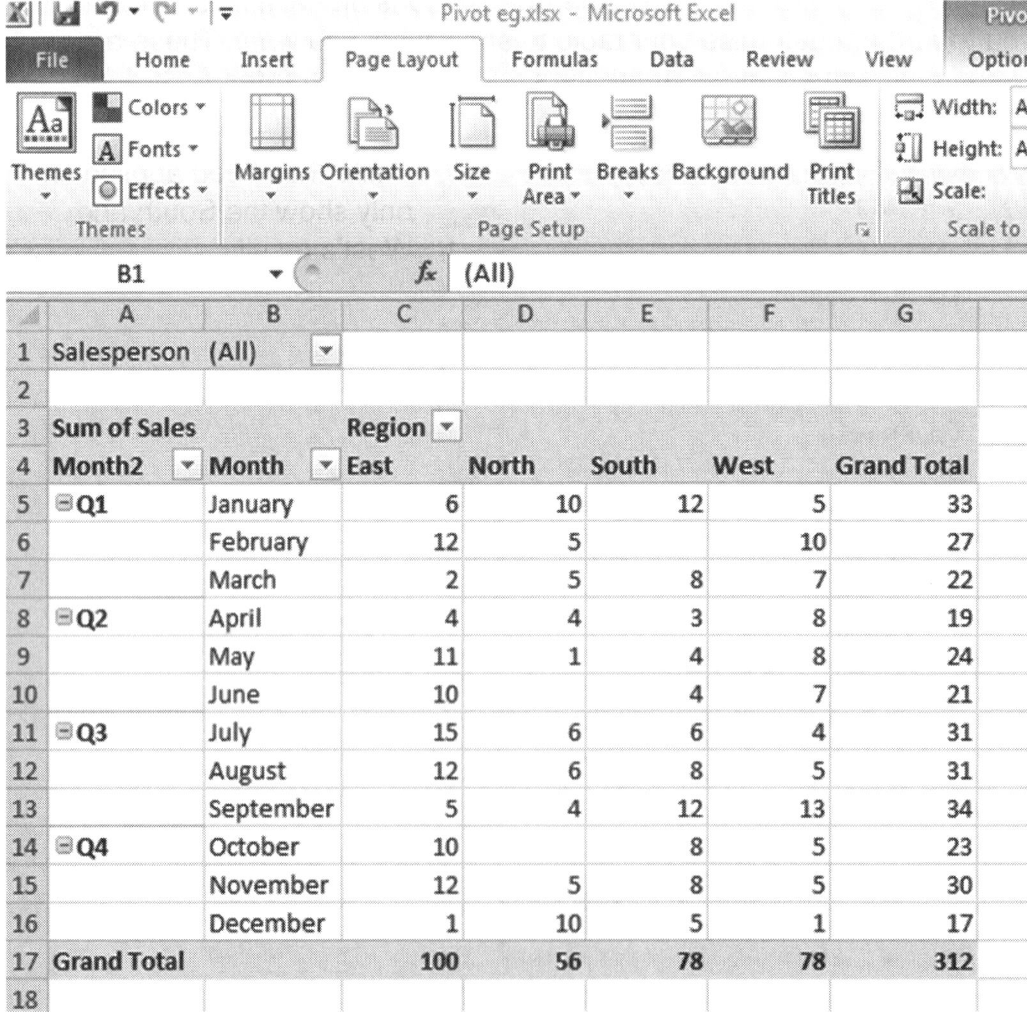

| | A | B | C | D | E | F | G |
|---|---|---|---|---|---|---|---|
| 1 | Salesperson | (All) | | | | | |
| 2 | | | | | | | |
| 3 | Sum of Sales | | Region | | | | |
| 4 | Month2 | Month | East | North | South | West | Grand Total |
| 5 | ⊟Q1 | January | 6 | 10 | 12 | 5 | 33 |
| 6 | | February | 12 | 5 | | 10 | 27 |
| 7 | | March | 2 | 5 | 8 | 7 | 22 |
| 8 | ⊟Q2 | April | 4 | 4 | 3 | 8 | 19 |
| 9 | | May | 11 | 1 | 4 | 8 | 24 |
| 10 | | June | 10 | | 4 | 7 | 21 |
| 11 | ⊟Q3 | July | 15 | 6 | 6 | 4 | 31 |
| 12 | | August | 12 | 6 | 8 | 5 | 31 |
| 13 | | September | 5 | 4 | 12 | 13 | 34 |
| 14 | ⊟Q4 | October | 10 | | 8 | 5 | 23 |
| 15 | | November | 12 | 5 | 8 | 5 | 30 |
| 16 | | December | 1 | 10 | 5 | 1 | 17 |
| 17 | Grand Total | | 100 | 56 | 78 | 78 | 312 |
| 18 | | | | | | | |

Nothing has changed, but we have the option to further summarise our data by using the filter on that field.

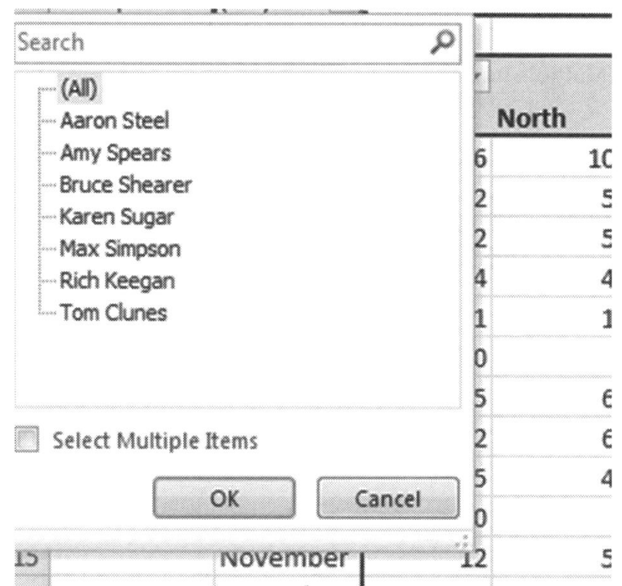


Clicking the **Filter** button allows us to select the salesperson we wish to view the data for.

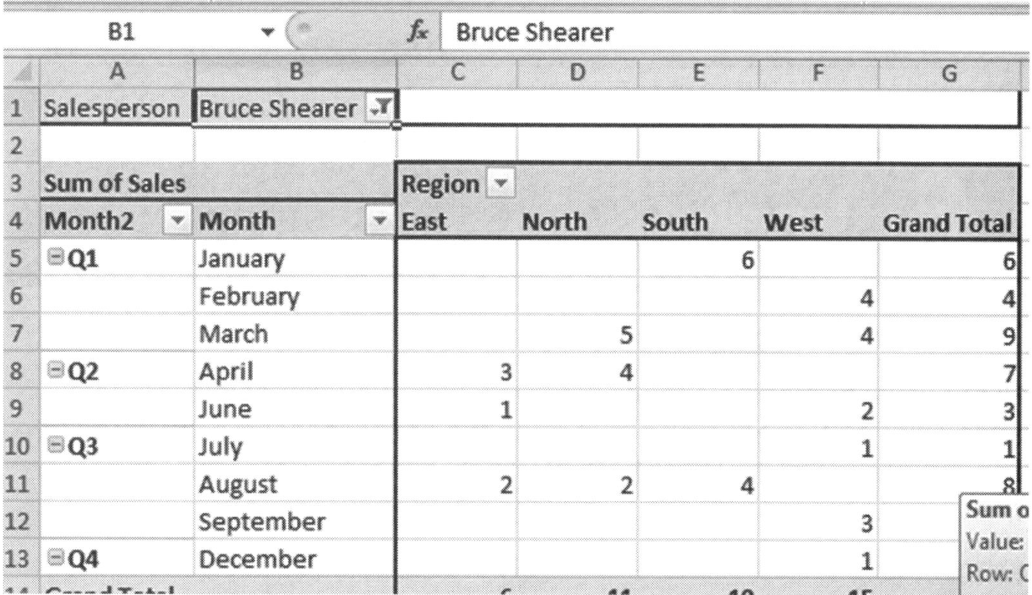


Selecting one field item just shows the information for that person. We could pick more than one.

Notice that the **Select Multiple Items** box needs to be ticked.

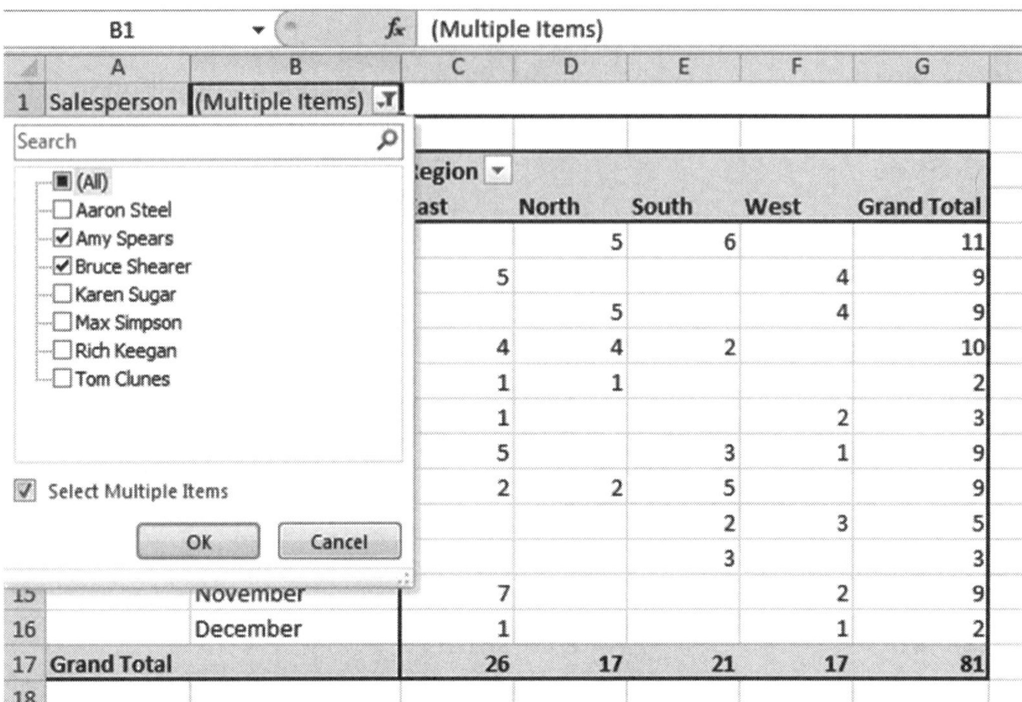


# 6 Formatting

## 6.1 Formatting options

All the usual formatting options are available – you can select the data items and use **Format Cells** to change the appearance of cells. There are also options in the **PivotTable Options** menu for how to deal with errors or zero values.

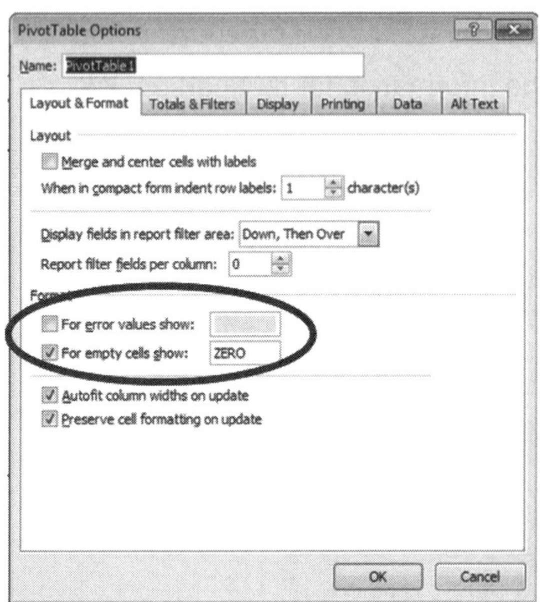


Here, I have selected that empty cells be filled with the text “ZERO” – to show the effect. You can also specify what to do if a cell contains an error.

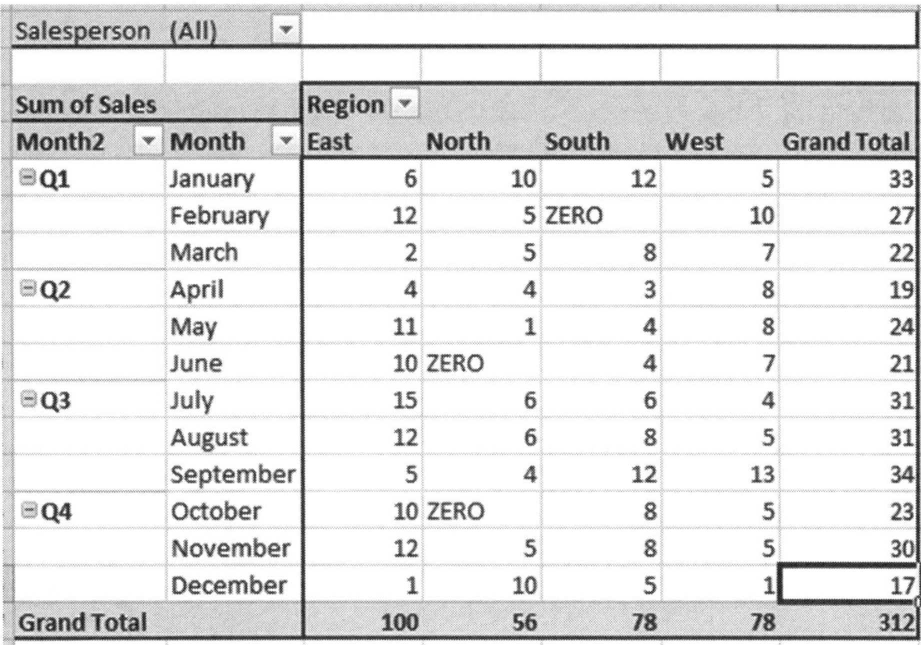

Salesperson (All)

| Sum of Sales | | Region | | | | |
|---|---|---|---|---|---|---|
| **Month2** | **Month** | **East** | **North** | **South** | **West** | **Grand Total** |
| ⊟Q1 | January | 6 | 10 | 12 | 5 | 33 |
| | February | 12 | 5 | ZERO | 10 | 27 |
| | March | 2 | 5 | 8 | 7 | 22 |
| ⊟Q2 | April | 4 | 4 | 3 | 8 | 19 |
| | May | 11 | 1 | 4 | 8 | 24 |
| | June | 10 | ZERO | 4 | 7 | 21 |
| ⊟Q3 | July | 15 | 6 | 6 | 4 | 31 |
| | August | 12 | 6 | 8 | 5 | 31 |
| | September | 5 | 4 | 12 | 13 | 34 |
| ⊟Q4 | October | 10 | ZERO | 8 | 5 | 23 |
| | November | 12 | 5 | 8 | 5 | 30 |
| | December | 1 | 10 | 5 | 1 | 17 |
| **Grand Total** | | **100** | **56** | **78** | **78** | **312** |

Note – usually a blank, hyphen or 0 would be used.

## 6.2 Changing the calculation function

Most of the time, **SUM** is the most appropriate function. However, you may wish to use **COUNT** – for example if you want to **COUNT** the number of times something occurs, or **MAX/MIN** to find the biggest or smallest amount in your data set.

To change the function you need the **Value Field Settings** menu. This can be found by either **Right-Clicking** in the pivot table, or by going to the **PivotTable Tools/Options** tab.

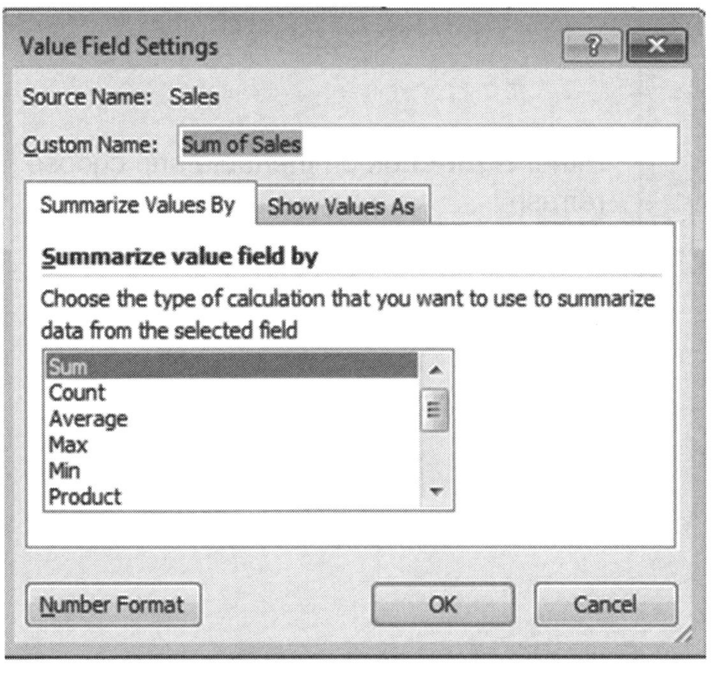


Select the function you want here. For example, **MAX**.

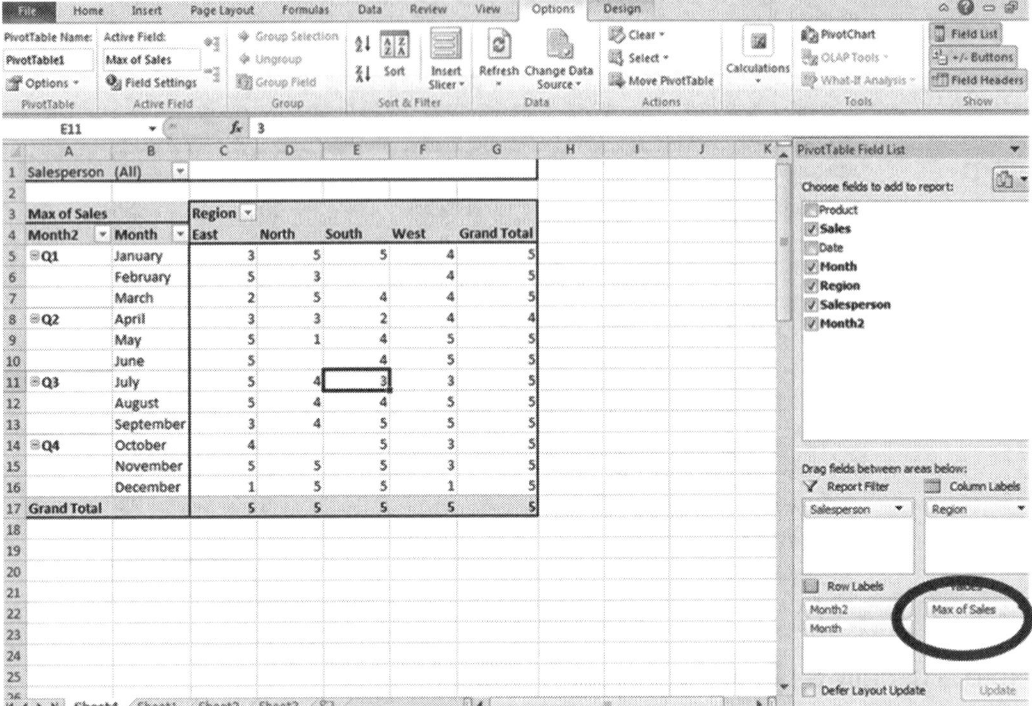

| Month2 | Month | East | North | South | West | Grand Total |
|---|---|---|---|---|---|---|
| Q1 | January | 3 | 5 | 5 | 4 | 5 |
| | February | 5 | 3 | | 4 | 5 |
| | March | 2 | 5 | 4 | 4 | 5 |
| Q2 | April | 3 | 3 | 2 | 4 | 4 |
| | May | 5 | 1 | 4 | 5 | 5 |
| | June | 5 | | 4 | 5 | 5 |
| Q3 | July | 5 | 4 | 3 | 3 | 5 |
| | August | 5 | 4 | 4 | 5 | 5 |
| | September | 3 | 4 | 5 | 5 | 5 |
| Q4 | October | 4 | | 5 | 3 | 5 |
| | November | 5 | 5 | 5 | 3 | 5 |
| | December | 1 | 5 | 5 | 1 | 5 |
| Grand Total | | 5 | 5 | 5 | 5 | 5 |

The table now shows the largest number of sales on a single day in each month. You should note too that in the Value field box, **Max of Sales** is shown.

## 6.3 Refreshing data

If there are any updates to the original data, the **Pivot Table** will need to be updated to reflect this change. Note that this **does not** happen automatically. It is a simple process –

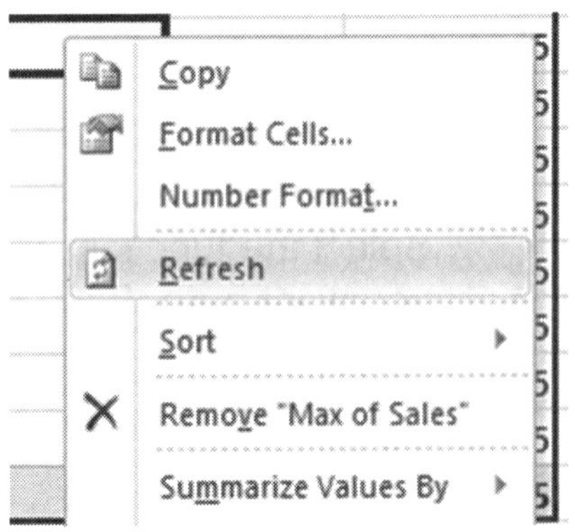


Either **right-click** on the table and choose refresh.

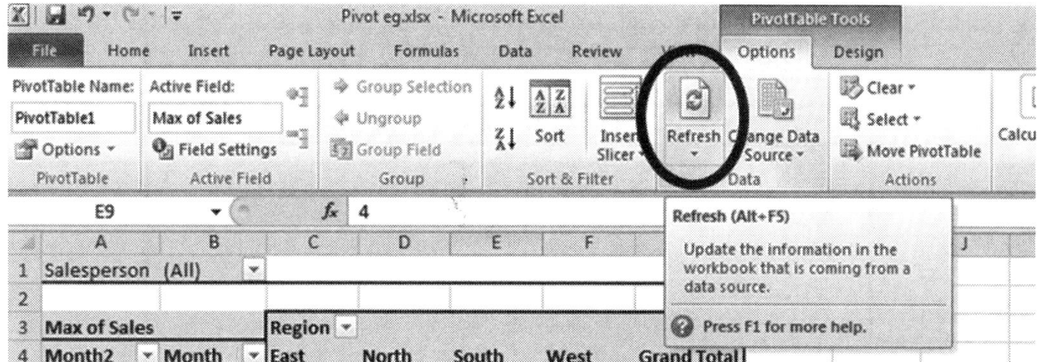


Or use the **Refresh** button in the **PivotTable Tools/Options** tab.

**Remember** – you cannot change the original data via the Pivot Table.

# 7 Classic view

## 7.1 Classic view

There is an alternative way to create a Pivot Table, which many people feel is more user-friendly. This may be displayed by default, but if your screen looks like the screenshot on the previous page, you could try Classic View, in the **Options** tab, select **Options**.

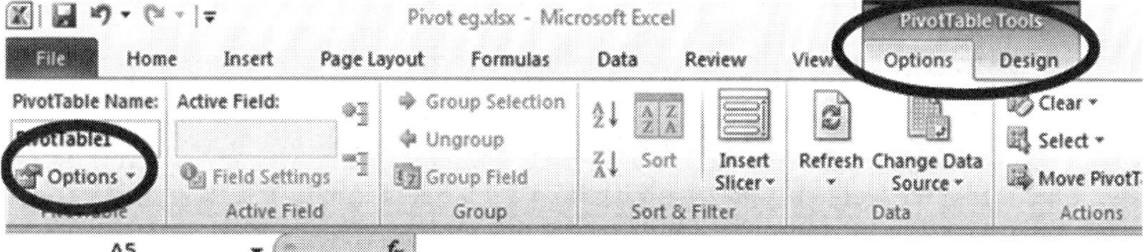


In the Display tab select Classic Layout for a more user-friendly method of creating the Table.

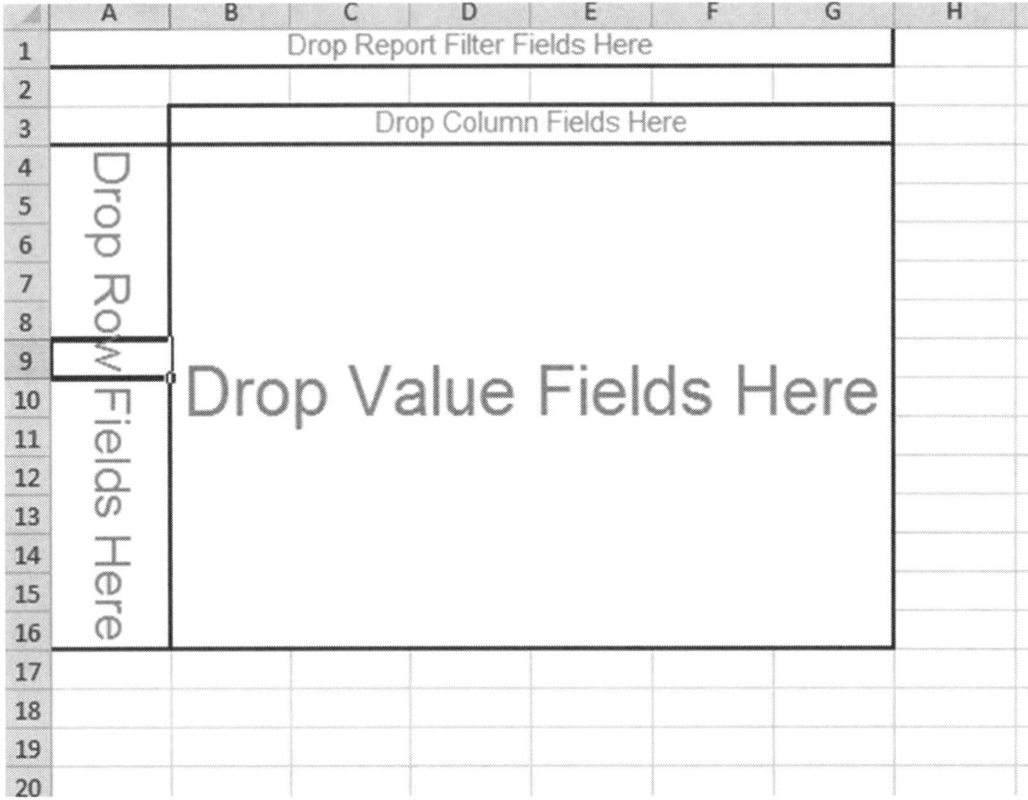


The appearance of the table changes – as it says, you can now 'drag and drop' the field names onto the table if you prefer. There is no difference in terms of the final appearance, but many people prefer this method.

# 8 Pivot charts

## 8.1 Pivot charts

A Pivot Chart is just a chart based on a pivot table. They work in exactly the same way as a normal chart. Pivot Charts change according to the filters applied to your PivotTable.

To insert a Pivot Chart, with the Pivot Table selected, click the **PivotChart** button in the **PivotTable Tools/Options** tab.

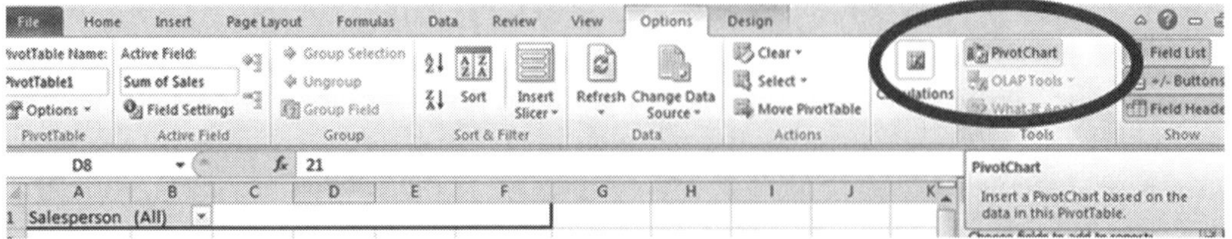

Alternatively, you can use the **Insert** tab, in exactly the same way as creating a normal chart (as long as the Pivot Table is selected). Exactly the same options and chart types are available. It will be created on the same sheet as your Pivot Table by default, although it can be moved to its own sheet in the usual way.

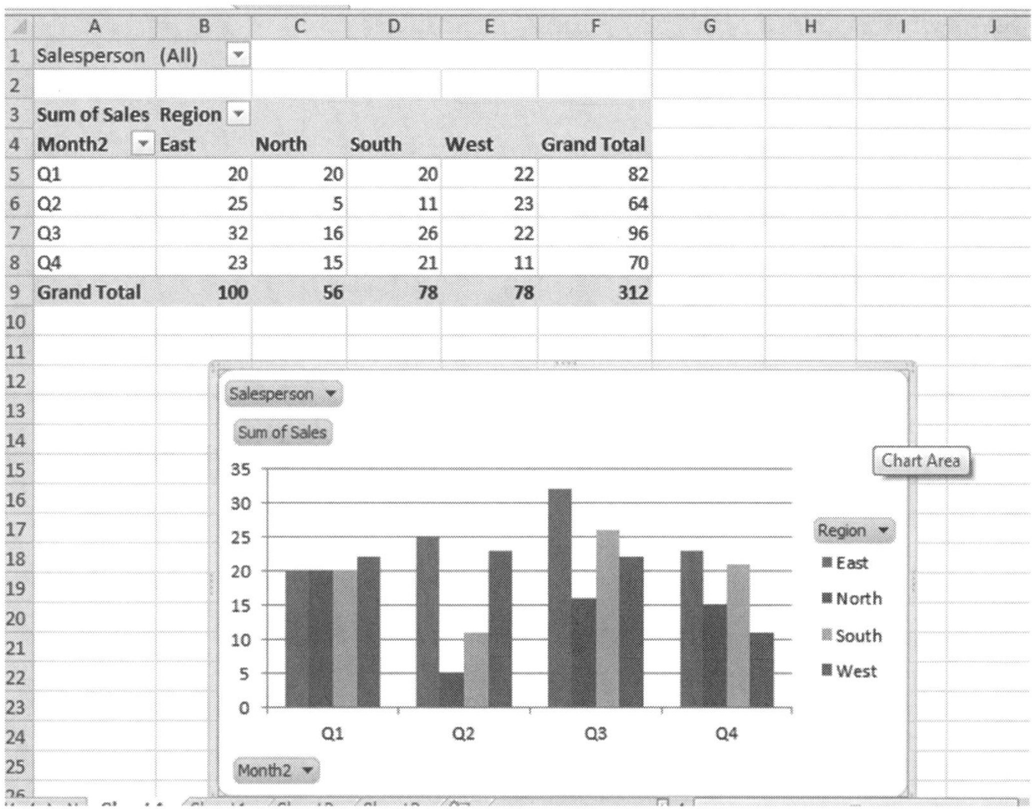

| Salesperson | (All) | | | | |
|---|---|---|---|---|---|
| | | | | | |
| **Sum of Sales** | **Region** | | | | |
| **Month2** | **East** | **North** | **South** | **West** | **Grand Total** |
| Q1 | 20 | 20 | 20 | 22 | 82 |
| Q2 | 25 | 5 | 11 | 23 | 64 |
| Q3 | 32 | 16 | 26 | 22 | 96 |
| Q4 | 23 | 15 | 21 | 11 | 70 |
| **Grand Total** | **100** | **56** | **78** | **78** | **312** |



Here, a column chart has been created based on the table. If the Filters are applied in the Table, the chart will be updated, and vice versa.

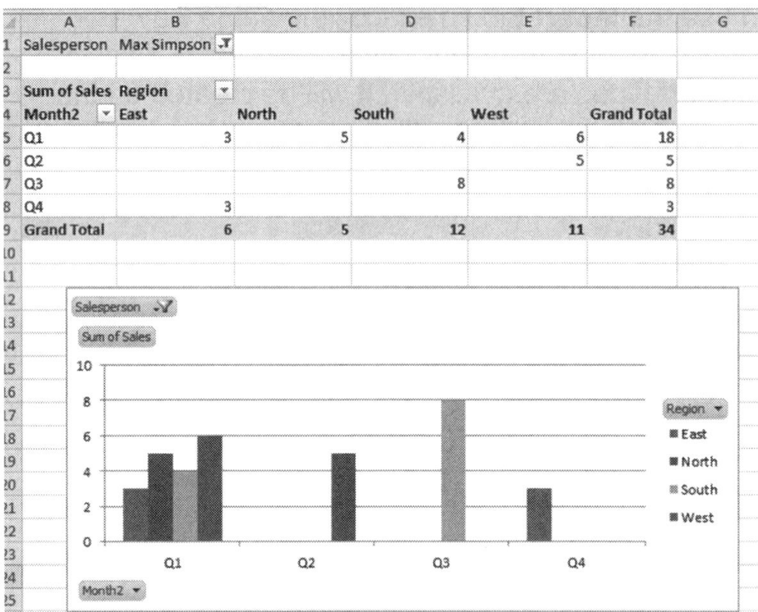

| Salesperson | Max Simpson | | | | |
|---|---|---|---|---|---|
| | | | | | |
| Sum of Sales | Region | | | | |
| Month2 | East | North | South | West | Grand Total |
| Q1 | 3 | 5 | 4 | 6 | 18 |
| Q2 | | | | 5 | 5 |
| Q3 | | | 8 | | 8 |
| Q4 | 3 | | | | 3 |
| Grand Total | 6 | 5 | 12 | 11 | 34 |



An example filter – note that the graph still shows the data in the Pivot Table.

# 9 Test your understanding

The activities in this guide are designed to test your knowledge on the techniques shown in this chapter. They may also use techniques used in previous chapters, to build up your knowledge. Suggested answers are available on MyKaplan, although it is better to refer to the notes and try to understand the methods than look straight at the answers.

## Test your understanding 20-1

This activity allows you to create a **Pivot Table**, and manipulate it as necessary.

(a) Open the **ResultsPivotData** workbook in the **Activities** folder. This only contains one sheet, which contains a data set of exam results.

(b) Create a Pivot Table on a new worksheet that enables us to know how many students were taught by each teacher and sat each exam. We will want to filter our report to show the results (pass or fail).

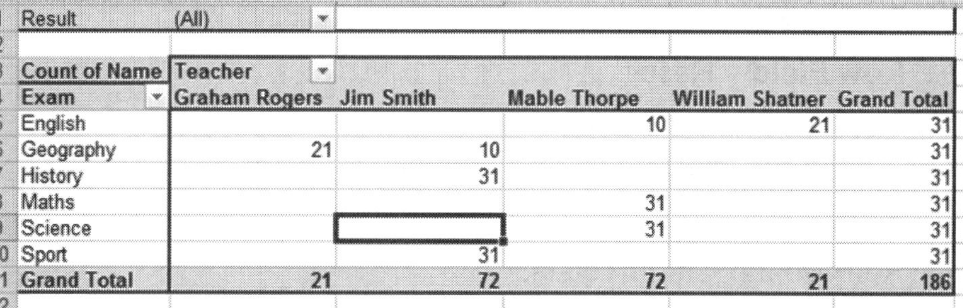

| Result | (All) | | | | |
|---|---|---|---|---|---|
| | | | | | |
| Count of Name | Teacher | | | | |
| Exam | Graham Rogers | Jim Smith | Mable Thorpe | William Shatner | Grand Total |
| English | | | 10 | 21 | 31 |
| Geography | 21 | 10 | | | 31 |
| History | | 31 | | | 31 |
| Maths | | | 31 | | 31 |
| Science | | | 31 | | 31 |
| Sport | | 31 | | | 31 |
| Grand Total | 21 | 72 | 72 | 21 | 186 |

(c) We now want to use the same Pivot Table to summarise the exam subjects as **Core** subjects (English, Maths and Science), and **Sundry** (everything else). We can **group** the data items to do this.

You will need to hold down **Ctrl** to select the cells as they are not adjacent.

**Group** these items using **Group Selection** from the **Options** tab.

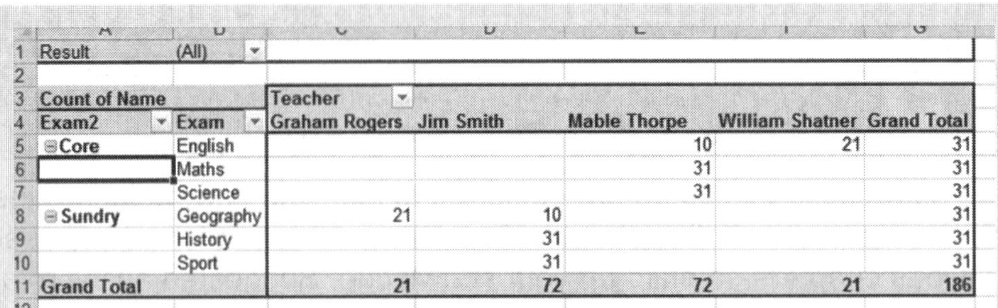

| Result | (All) | | | | | |
|---|---|---|---|---|---|---|
| | | | | | | |
| Count of Name | | Teacher | | | | |
| Exam2 | Exam | Graham Rogers | Jim Smith | Mable Thorpe | William Shatner | Grand Total |
| ⊟Core | English | | | 10 | 21 | 31 |
| | Maths | | | 31 | | 31 |
| | Science | | | 31 | | 31 |
| ⊟Sundry | Geography | 21 | 10 | | | 31 |
| | History | | 31 | | | 31 |
| | Sport | | 31 | | | 31 |
| Grand Total | | 21 | 72 | 72 | 21 | 186 |

(d) Move the **Exam 2** field into the **Report Filter** area. Move **Result** into the **Row Labels** (it should be to the right of Exam). You can now select to just see core subjects, sundry subjects, or both. Select **Core**.

(e) Save the file as **Activity 20-1** in the **solutions** folder.

## Test your understanding 20-2

This activity continues with the same PivotTable data, and talks you through the steps of creating a **PivotChart**.

(a) Open the **ResultsPivotData** workbook in the **Activities** folder.

(b) Create a **PivotTable** from the data. Use the following settings:

**Report Filter** = Name

**Row Field** = Result

**Column Field** = Exam

**Value Field** = Score (we want to show the highest percentage formatted to zero decimal places).

(c) Remove the Grand Totals.

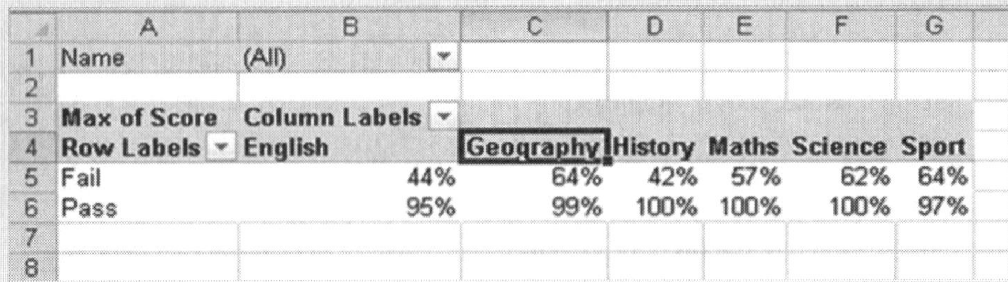

| Name | (All) | | | | | |
|---|---|---|---|---|---|---|
| | | | | | | |
| Max of Score | Column Labels | | | | | |
| Row Labels | English | Geography | History | Maths | Science | Sport |
| Fail | 44% | 64% | 42% | 57% | 62% | 64% |
| Pass | 95% | 99% | 100% | 100% | 100% | 97% |

(d) Now, create a **PivotChart**. Make a **clustered bar** chart. The graph will display the data shown in the table.

(e) Add a title to the chart – **Exam Results 2012**.

(f) Change the **Name** to select Gareth Jones and see how the chart changes to show their results.

(g) Save the workbook as **Activity 20-2** in the **Solutions** folder.

# Find and replace

## Introduction

This chapter will show you how to use a very useful function within Excel, ‘find and replace’

### ASSESSMENT CRITERIA

Accurately enter data (2.2)

Select and use a range of formulas and functions to perform calculations (3.1)

Select and use relevant tools to analyse and interpret data (3.2)

### CONTENTS

# 1 Find and replace

## 1.1 Find and replace

Sometimes you discover that data has been input into a spreadsheet that you need to find or change. This is a fairly simple routine using the **Find and Replace** tool, found in the **Home** tab under **Find & Select**.

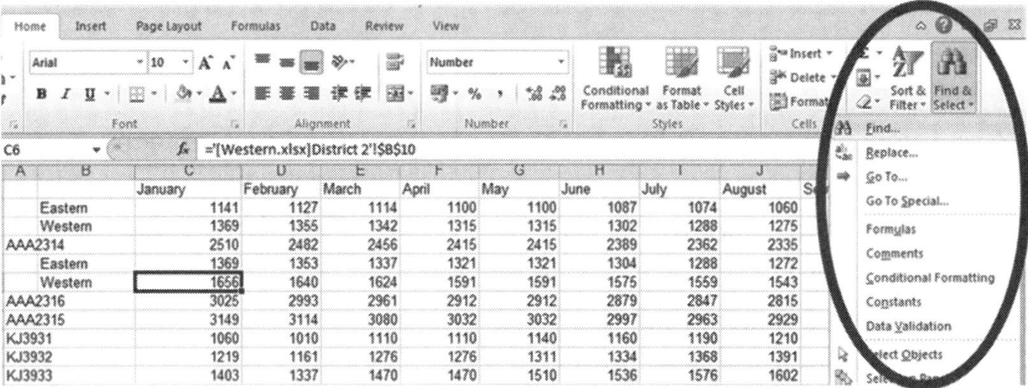


| | January | February | March | April | May | June | July | August |
|---|---|---|---|---|---|---|---|---|
| Eastern | 1141 | 1127 | 1114 | 1100 | 1100 | 1087 | 1074 | 1060 |
| Western | 1369 | 1355 | 1342 | 1315 | 1315 | 1302 | 1288 | 1275 |
| AAA2314 | 2510 | 2482 | 2456 | 2415 | 2415 | 2389 | 2362 | 2335 |
| Eastern | 1369 | 1353 | 1337 | 1321 | 1321 | 1304 | 1288 | 1272 |
| Western | 1656 | 1640 | 1624 | 1591 | 1591 | 1575 | 1559 | 1543 |
| AAA2316 | 3025 | 2993 | 2961 | 2912 | 2912 | 2879 | 2847 | 2815 |
| AAA2315 | 3149 | 3114 | 3080 | 3032 | 3032 | 2997 | 2963 | 2929 |
| KJ3931 | 1060 | 1010 | 1110 | 1110 | 1140 | 1160 | 1190 | 1210 |
| KJ3932 | 1219 | 1161 | 1276 | 1276 | 1311 | 1334 | 1368 | 1391 |
| KJ3933 | 1403 | 1337 | 1470 | 1470 | 1510 | 1536 | 1576 | 1602 |

**Shortcut**

The simplest and fastest way to launch this tool is

**Ctrl-f**

When the tool is launched the following dialogue box appears:

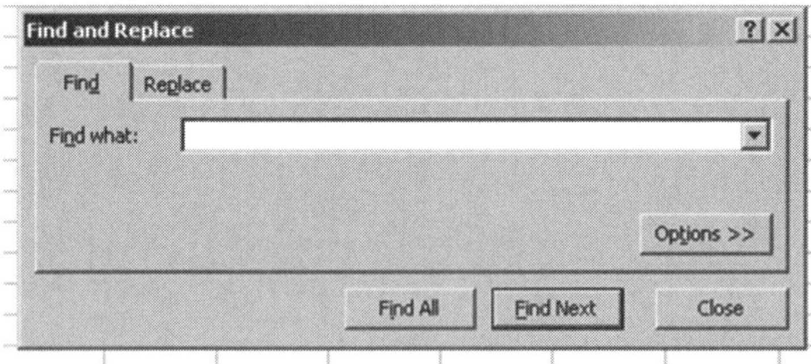


If you are trying to find a value you type it into the **Find what:** field. You can then choose to either find the next version of the value or find them all. If you opt to find them all Excel will present a list that you can scroll through.

There are also options that allow you to choose the case and position if you desire.

If your intention is to find and replace a value then you should select the **Replace** tab. You will then be faced with the following:

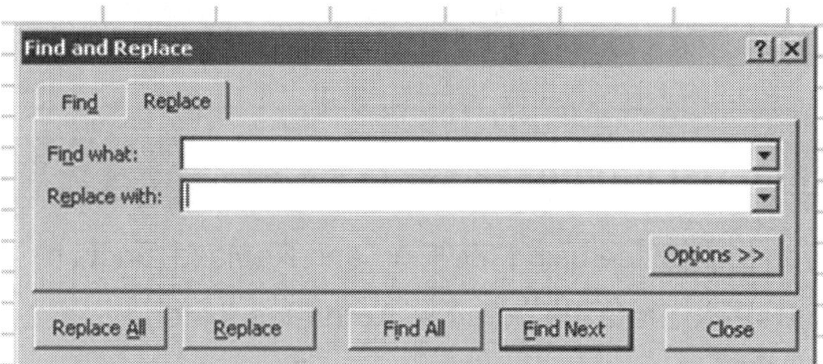


On this tab you again ask Excel to find the value and then type in a value to **Replace with**.

# 2 Test your understanding

## Test your understanding 21-1

This activity allows you to practice using the Find and Replace function.

(a) **Open** the **ResultsPivotData** file from the **Activities** folder.

(b) Use the **Find** and **Replace** function to replace all instances of the word **Science** and replace them with **Geology**.

(c) **Find** all instances of Lowther and **replace** them with Luther.

(d) Save the file as **Activity 21-1** in the **Solutions** folder and close it.

# 'What-if' analysis

## Introduction

This chapter will show you how to carry out the forecasting technique of 'what-if' analysis. What-If analysis involves creating a spreadsheet and then asking the question "what if this/these figures were to change". There are a number of tools to look at:

- Creating **Manual** what-if solutions.
- Data Tables.
- Scenario Manager.
- Goal Seek.

### ASSESSMENT CRITERIA

Select and use a range of formulas and functions to perform calculations (3.1)

### CONTENTS

# 1 What-if

## 1.1 Introduction

With the exception of manual solutions, the above tools can be found in the **Data** tab, in the **Data Tools** section, under What-If Analysis.

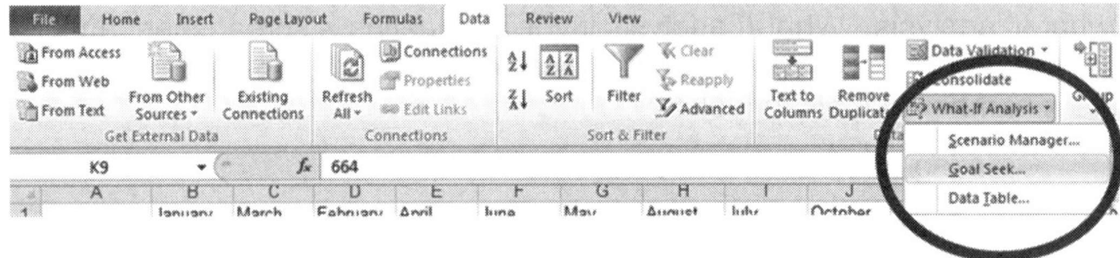


## 1.2 Creating manual 'What-If' solutions

In previous chapters you have created spreadsheets that used fixed cell references to get their data. These spreadsheets were manual 'what-if' solutions.

The overriding principle for 'what-if' solutions is do not 'hard code' variable data into formulas and functions. If you do this you will be unable to carry out 'what-if' without finding and replacing the hard coded data.

## 1.3 Data tables

A **Data Table**, as the name suggests, is a table showing how results will change if one or two variables are changed.

There are two types of **Data Table**:

1. **Single Input:** This table allows you to create a spreadsheet with multiple formulas and functions to create a **solution**. The spreadsheet itself can have many variables and you can use a single input **Data Table** to evaluate a change in **one** of these variables – this is its draw back. However, there is nothing to stop you changing any of the other numbers once the table is formed.
2. **Two-Input:** This table works in the same way as above but in this instance you can create a table that allows a change to **two** variables – but only two.

Once your spreadsheet **solution** is created you will be ready create the **Data Table**. Activate the tool as above and you will be presented with the following dialogue box.

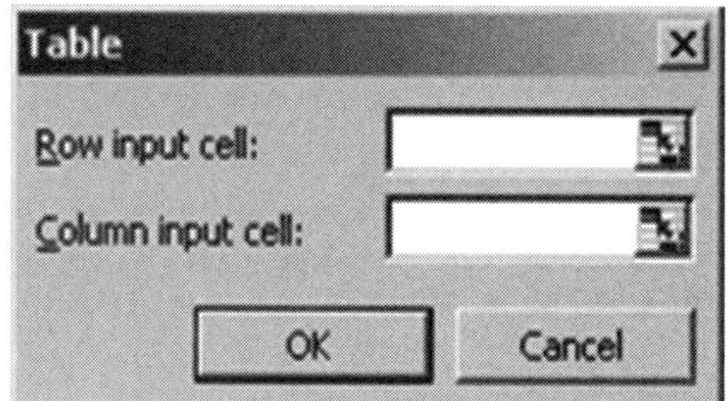


For a **single input** table you will need either a Row or Column input cell, not both. This is determined by the way in which the spreadsheet solution is constructed, either in a Row or a Column. In a single input data table the top-left cell of the table is not used.

For **two input** data tables you will need both Row and Column Inputs. In a two input data table the top-left is used to hold a formula that refers to the solution cell.

## 1.4 Scenario manager

Scenario manager is a tool that allows you to create scenarios of a particular solution. For example, you are trying to work out your product costs to calculate profits. However, you are uncertain as to the actual costs. You can use **Scenario Manager** to create versions of the potential outcome.

When you are using **Scenario Manager** it will be very useful to **Name** some of the cells to make the reports more understandable. **Naming** cells and ranges is explained in **Chapter 7**.

**Using scenario manager**

Scenario Manager is used to set up different possible outcomes – you choose which cells (variables) you wish to change, and for each Scenario you set up, you specify the value of these variables – for example you could look at a variety of different sales volumes or prices.

Once all of the different scenarios have been set up, you can run a report to summarise all of the results for your scenarios.

## 1.5 Goal seek

**Goal Seek** is 'what-if' in reverse. Here a tool is used to determine a change to a variable that will result in the solution that you want.

For example you may want to make a Net Profit of £10,000 but are unsure of how much a variable such as labour rate will have to change to create this profit.

When you launch **Goal Seek** you are faced with the following dialogue box:

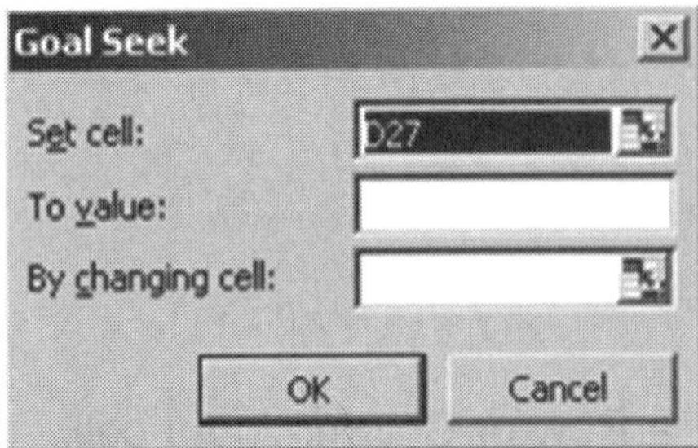


You are asked:

- to **set** a particular cell
- to a particular **value**
- by **changing** a particular cell.

Sometimes a solution cannot be found. If this is the case you will need to adjust the values you are asking **Goal Seek** to find till you get a correct answer.

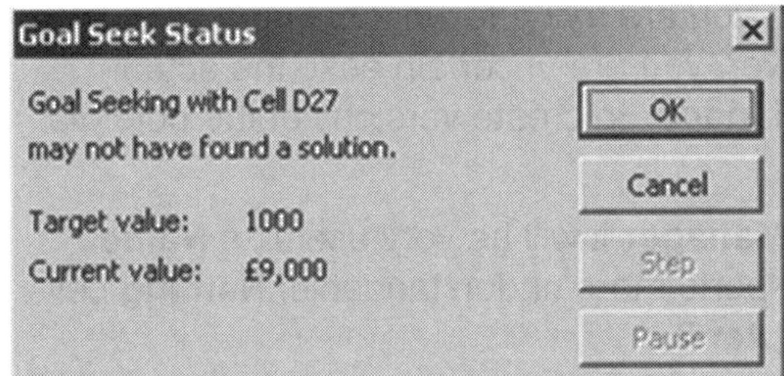


Don't forget to check that the variable is actually involved in the calculation.

# 2 Test your understanding

The following activities are step-by-step examples showing how the techniques described in this chapter work in practice. Suggested answers are available on MyKaplan, although it is better to refer to the notes and try to understand the methods than look straight at the answers.

## Test your understanding 22-1

This activity is to show the use of a single input Data Table.

(a) Open the **Data Table 1** file in the **Activities** folder.

(b) The aim is to set up a table which shows how total production costs will change with changing variables – for example if the material cost/kg changes.

(c) In cells D17:D20 we need to calculate full cost for labour, material, fixed costs and full cost. For example, labour will be volume*hourly rate*hours/unit.

**Note – for the data table to work, these formulas should use absolute referencing ($ signs).**

D17 | fx =$D$4*$D$5*$D$6

| | A | B | C | D |
|---|---|---|---|---|
| 1 | | | | |
| 2 | | | PRODUCT ALPHA | |
| 3 | | | | |
| 4 | | | Production Volume | 500 |
| 5 | | | Hourly Rate | £10.00 |
| 6 | | | Labour Hours/unit | 2.00 |
| 7 | | | Material Cost/kg | £12.00 |
| 8 | | | Material Used/unit | 3.50 |
| 9 | | | Fixed Cost | £38,000.00 |
| 10 | | | | |
| 11 | | | | |
| 12 | | | | |
| 13 | | | | |
| 14 | | | | |
| 15 | | | FULL PRODUCTION COST | |
| 16 | | | | |
| 17 | | | Labour Cost | £10,000.00 |
| 18 | | | Material Cost | £21,000.00 |
| 19 | | | Fixed Cost | £38,000.00 |
| 20 | | | Full Production Cost | £69,000.00 |

(d) We now need to set up the data table – this will go on the right of the sheet where the empty formatting is. The blue shaded part should contain the headings – labour cost, material cost, fixed cost and full cost. The simplest way to achieve this is to copy the headings in C17:C20, then **Paste-Special** in Cell G16 and select transpose.

We also need to put the values for our variable in cells F18:F24. As we will be changing the material cost, enter 10, 11, 12…16 in these cells.

| | Labour Cost | Material Cost | Fixed Cost | Full Production Cost |
|---|---|---|---|---|
| | | | | |
| £10 | | | | |
| £11 | | | | |
| £12 | | | | |
| £13 | | | | |
| £14 | | | | |
| £15 | | | | |
| £16 | | | | |

(e) In the top row of the 'table', underneath the headings, we need to refer to the existing calculations for the values. This is done by linking to the appropriate formula.

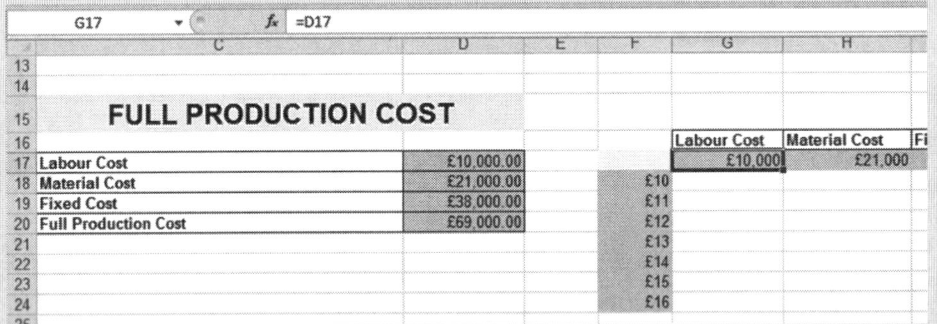

G17 =D17

| | C | D | E | F | G | H |
|---|---|---|---|---|---|---|
| 13 | | | | | | |
| 14 | | | | | | |
| 15 | FULL PRODUCTION COST | | | | | |
| 16 | | | | | Labour Cost | Material Cost |
| 17 | Labour Cost | £10,000.00 | | | £10,000 | £21,000 |
| 18 | Material Cost | £21,000.00 | | £10 | | |
| 19 | Fixed Cost | £38,000.00 | | £11 | | |
| 20 | Full Production Cost | £69,000.00 | | £12 | | |
| 21 | | | | £13 | | |
| 22 | | | | £14 | | |
| 23 | | | | £15 | | |
| 24 | | | | £16 | | |

The table is now set up. Select the cells from F17:J24 and the Data Table function from the What-If Analysis menu.

(f) The column input cell is D7 – this is the material cost per unit. If you wish to see how changing other variables will affect the result, select that cell instead. You will probably need to change the values in cells F18:D24 as a result.

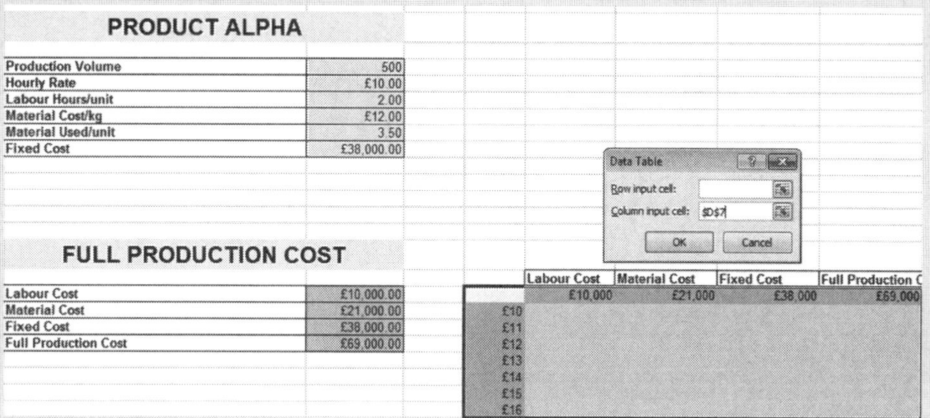

**PRODUCT ALPHA**

| | |
|---|---|
| Production Volume | 500 |
| Hourly Rate | £10.00 |
| Labour Hours/unit | 2.00 |
| Material Cost/kg | £12.00 |
| Material Used/unit | 3.50 |
| Fixed Cost | £38,000.00 |

**FULL PRODUCTION COST**

| | |
|---|---|
| Labour Cost | £10,000.00 |
| Material Cost | £21,000.00 |
| Fixed Cost | £38,000.00 |
| Full Production Cost | £69,000.00 |



| | Labour Cost | Material Cost | Fixed Cost | Full Production C |
|---|---|---|---|---|
| | £10,000 | £21,000 | £38,000 | £69,000 |
| £10 | | | | |
| £11 | | | | |
| £12 | | | | |
| £13 | | | | |
| £14 | | | | |
| £15 | | | | |
| £16 | | | | |

(g) The final table is populated – only the material costs and total costs change – this is because labour and fixed costs are unaffected by changes in material cost.

| | Labour Cost | Material Cost | Fixed Cost | Full Production Cost |
|---|---|---|---|---|
| | £10,000 | £21,000 | £38,000 | £69,000 |
| £10 | £10,000 | £17,500 | £38,000 | £65,500 |
| £11 | £10,000 | £19,250 | £38,000 | £67,250 |
| £12 | £10,000 | £21,000 | £38,000 | £69,000 |
| £13 | £10,000 | £22,750 | £38,000 | £70,750 |
| £14 | £10,000 | £24,500 | £38,000 | £72,500 |
| £15 | £10,000 | £26,250 | £38,000 | £74,250 |
| £16 | £10,000 | £28,000 | £38,000 | £76,000 |

(h) Save the file in the **Solutions** folder as **Activity 22-1** and close it.

## Test your understanding 22-2

This activity shows the use of a two-input **data table**, following on from activity 22-1.

(a) Open the **Data Table 2** file in the **Activities** folder.

(b) The spreadsheet is already set up – note the use of an **IF** formula in cell D25 to calculate a discounted material cost if necessary.

(c) There are going to be two variables for this table – volume and price. We need to specify what end result needs to be shown in the table – we want Net Profit. To do this, use the top corner of the table – G22, and refer to the calculation you need – **=D28**.

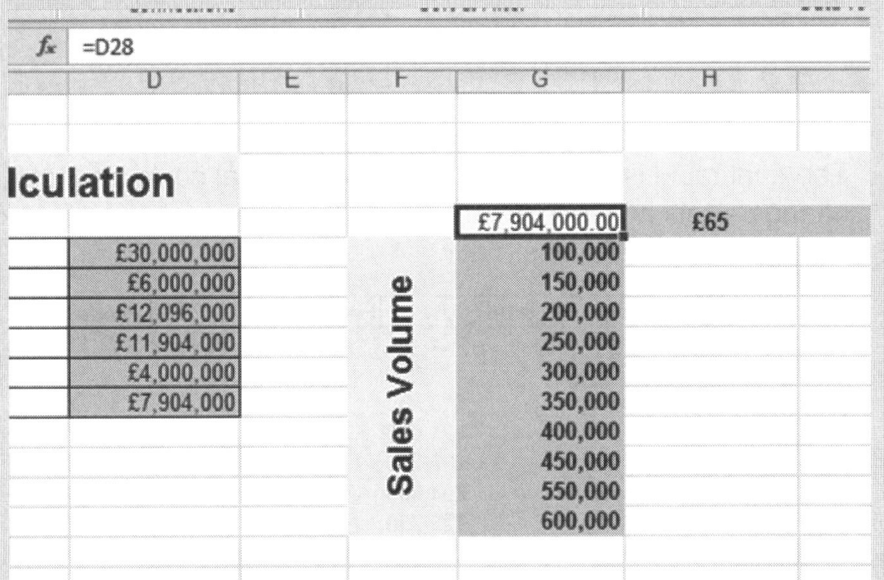


(d) Select the cells in the table (G22:L32), and select the Data Table function. The Row input is sales price – this is cell D5, the column is sales volume – D4.

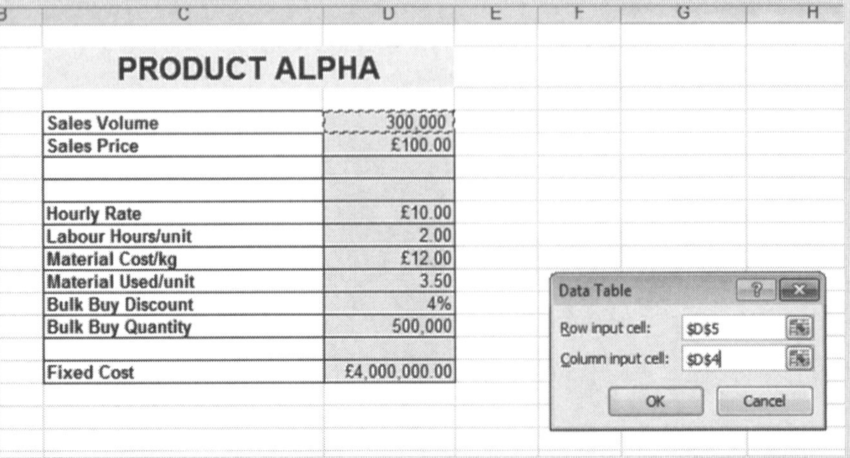

(e) The table is populated accordingly.

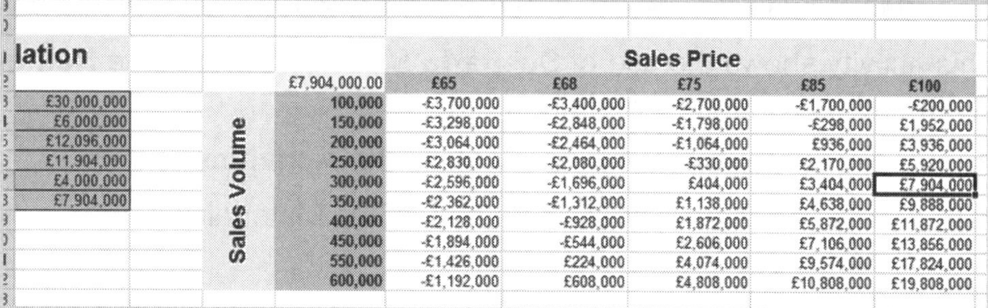

lation

| |
|---|
| £30,000,000 |
| £6,000,000 |
| £12,096,000 |
| £11,904,000 |
| £4,000,000 |
| £7,904,000 |

| | Sales Price | | | | |
|---|---|---|---|---|---|
| £7,904,000.00 | £65 | £68 | £75 | £85 | £100 |
| 100,000 | -£3,700,000 | -£3,400,000 | -£2,700,000 | -£1,700,000 | -£200,000 |
| 150,000 | -£3,298,000 | -£2,848,000 | -£1,798,000 | -£298,000 | £1,952,000 |
| 200,000 | -£3,064,000 | -£2,464,000 | -£1,064,000 | £936,000 | £3,936,000 |
| 250,000 | -£2,830,000 | -£2,080,000 | -£330,000 | £2,170,000 | £5,920,000 |
| 300,000 | -£2,596,000 | -£1,696,000 | £404,000 | £3,404,000 | £7,904,000 |
| 350,000 | -£2,362,000 | -£1,312,000 | £1,138,000 | £4,638,000 | £9,888,000 |
| 400,000 | -£2,128,000 | -£928,000 | £1,872,000 | £5,872,000 | £11,872,000 |
| 450,000 | -£1,894,000 | -£544,000 | £2,606,000 | £7,106,000 | £13,856,000 |
| 550,000 | -£1,426,000 | £224,000 | £4,074,000 | £9,574,000 | £17,824,000 |
| 600,000 | -£1,192,000 | £608,000 | £4,808,000 | £10,808,000 | £19,808,000 |

(Row labels: Sales Volume)

You should also see that the profit for the current variables – price of £100 and sales of 300,000, is the same value shown in Cell D28.

(f) If you want to see a different result, for example contribution, change cell G22 to refer to the contribution calculation instead:

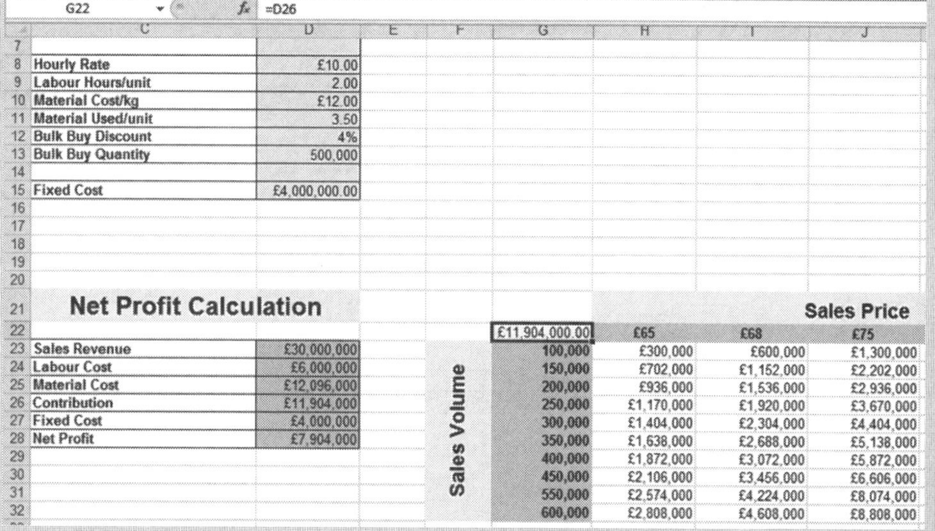

G22 =D26

| Row | C | D |
|---|---|---|
| 8 | Hourly Rate | £10.00 |
| 9 | Labour Hours/unit | 2.00 |
| 10 | Material Cost/kg | £12.00 |
| 11 | Material Used/unit | 3.50 |
| 12 | Bulk Buy Discount | 4% |
| 13 | Bulk Buy Quantity | 500,000 |
| 15 | Fixed Cost | £4,000,000.00 |
| 21 | **Net Profit Calculation** | |
| 23 | Sales Revenue | £30,000,000 |
| 24 | Labour Cost | £6,000,000 |
| 25 | Material Cost | £12,096,000 |
| 26 | Contribution | £11,904,000 |
| 27 | Fixed Cost | £4,000,000 |
| 28 | Net Profit | £7,904,000 |

| | Sales Price | | |
|---|---|---|---|
| £11,904,000.00 | £65 | £68 | £75 |
| 100,000 | £300,000 | £600,000 | £1,300,000 |
| 150,000 | £702,000 | £1,152,000 | £2,202,000 |
| 200,000 | £936,000 | £1,536,000 | £2,936,000 |
| 250,000 | £1,170,000 | £1,920,000 | £3,670,000 |
| 300,000 | £1,404,000 | £2,304,000 | £4,404,000 |
| 350,000 | £1,638,000 | £2,688,000 | £5,138,000 |
| 400,000 | £1,872,000 | £3,072,000 | £5,872,000 |
| 450,000 | £2,106,000 | £3,456,000 | £6,606,000 |
| 550,000 | £2,574,000 | £4,224,000 | £8,074,000 |
| 600,000 | £2,808,000 | £4,608,000 | £8,808,000 |

(Row labels: Sales Volume)

(g) If you look at the formulas in the table, they have curly brackets round them **{}** – these are called **array formulas**. They are very powerful, but not required as part of the SPSH syllabus.

(h) Save the file in the **Solutions** folder as **Activity 22-2** and close it.

##  Test your understanding 22-3

This activity shows the use of **Scenario Manager**, with some **Named Cells** and a few basic calculations.

(a) Open the **Scenario Manager** file in the **Activities** folder.

(b) **Name** cell D2 as LabourRate and D3 as MaterialCost (see chapter 7).

(c) The formulas for the green cells (other than total variable costs) need to be populated. These are the Labour Cost per Unit, Material Cost per Unit, Contribution Per Unit, Total Contribution and Net Profit.

Note: contribution=selling price-variable costs.

(d) **Name** the three net profit results **Alpha_NP**, **Bravo_NP** and **Charlie_NP** respectively (cells D27, E27 and F27).

Charlie_NP | fx =F22-F25

| | A | B | C | D | E | F | G |
|---|---|---|---|---|---|---|---|
| 1 | | | | | | | |
| 2 | | | Labour Rate per hour | £12 | | | |
| 3 | | | Material Cost per kg | £14 | | | |
| 4 | | | | | | | |
| 5 | | | | | | | |
| 6 | | | | | | | |
| 7 | | | | | | | |
| 8 | | | | | | | |
| 9 | | | | ALPHA | BRAVO | CHARLIE | TOTAL |
| 10 | | | Hours in Production | 2 | 3 | 4 | |
| 11 | | | Material Quantity per unit | 1 | 2 | 3 | |
| 12 | | | Labour Cost per Unit | £24 | £36 | £48 | |
| 13 | | | Material Cost per Unit | £14 | £28 | £42 | |
| 14 | | | **Total Variable Costs** | £38 | £64 | £90 | |
| 15 | | | | | | | |
| 16 | | | Selling Price | £77 | £199 | £143 | |
| 17 | | | | | | | |
| 18 | | | **Contribution per Unit** | £39 | £135 | £53 | |
| 19 | | | | | | | |
| 20 | | | Sales Volume | 1000 | 400 | 1299 | |
| 21 | | | | | | | |
| 22 | | | **Total Contribution** | £39,000 | £54,000 | £68,847 | £161,847 |
| 23 | | | | | | | |
| 24 | | | | | | | |
| 25 | | | Fixed Costs | 30000 | 45000 | 28000 | |
| 26 | | | | | | | |
| 27 | | | **Net Profit** | £9,000 | £9,000 | £40,847 | £58,847 |

(e) The Scenario is ready to be set up. The idea is that we can show how the net profit results will change if the labour rate and material cost change to certain specified values. We could do this manually, but the Scenario Manager handles the changes quickly and presents them in a user-friendly way.

Select **Scenario Manager** from the **What-if Analysis** menu.

(f) Add the first Scenario – called 'Preferred'. The changing cells will be D2 and D3.

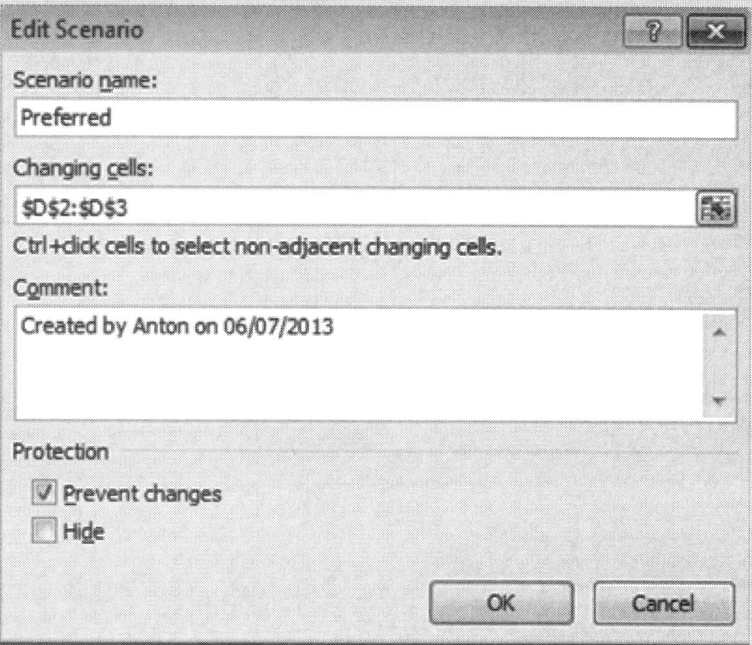


(g) After clicking **OK**, you will be asked to enter the values for the variables. Use 12 for the Labour Rate and 14 for the Material Cost. Notice that naming the cells makes this step easier – without the names you would be prompted for $D$2 and $D$3, and would have to work out what these meant.

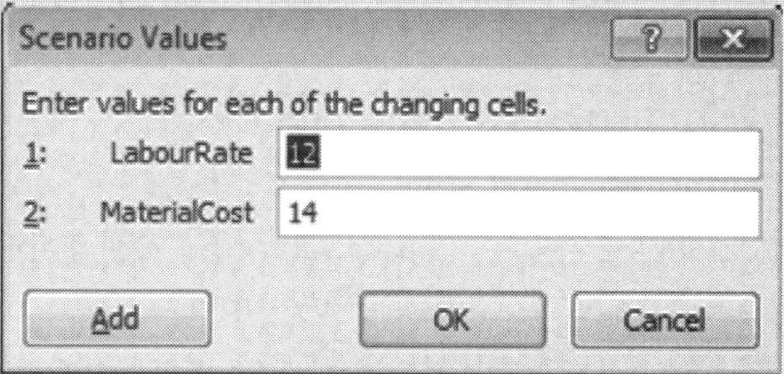


Click on **OK** – the first scenario has been entered.

(h) Add three more scenarios, as follows:

**Unlikely** – labour rate 13, material cost 15

**Moderate** – labour rate 16, material cost 18

**Extreme** – labour rate 20, material cost 18.

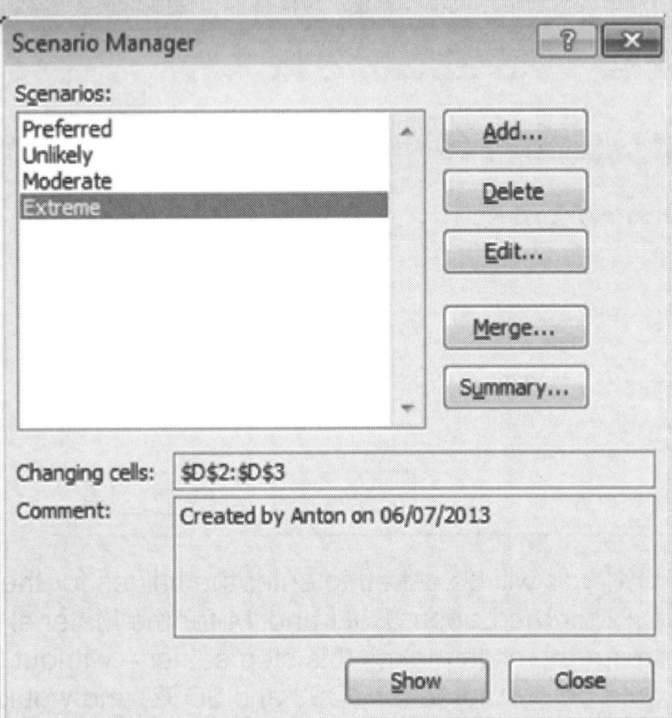


(i) Clicking **Show** will change the values in the two cells to match the scenario highlighted.

(j) Clicking **Summary** will produce a summary report.

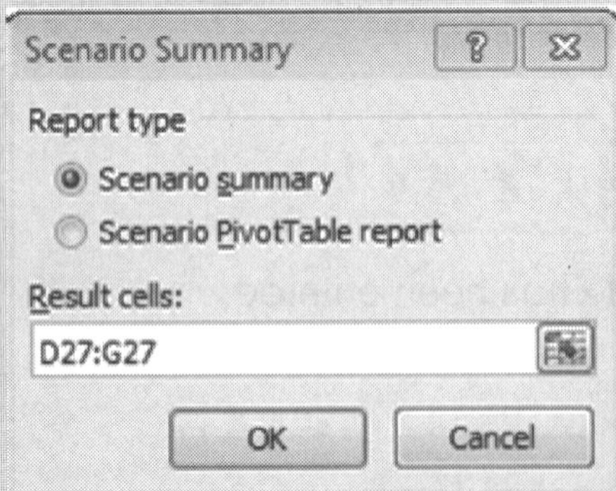


Select either a Pivot Table or summary report.

The result cells are the final results you wish to see – here the profit figures have been (correctly) selected by default.

(k) The final report is created on a new tab:

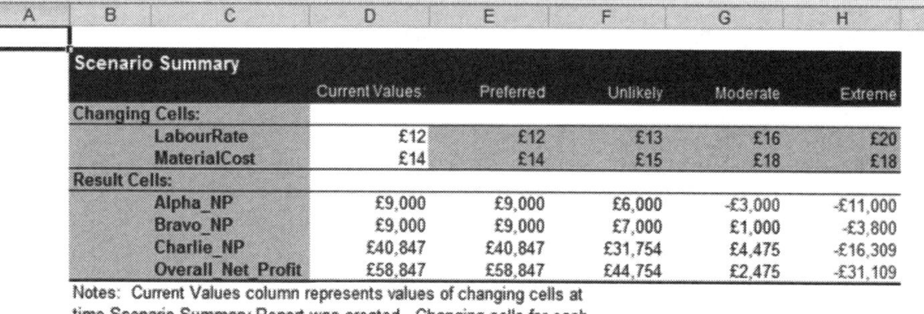

**Scenario Summary**

| | Current Values: | Preferred | Unlikely | Moderate | Extreme |
|---|---|---|---|---|---|
| **Changing Cells:** | | | | | |
| LabourRate | £12 | £12 | £13 | £16 | £20 |
| MaterialCost | £14 | £14 | £15 | £18 | £18 |
| **Result Cells:** | | | | | |
| Alpha_NP | £9,000 | £9,000 | £6,000 | -£3,000 | -£11,000 |
| Bravo_NP | £9,000 | £9,000 | £7,000 | £1,000 | -£3,800 |
| Charlie_NP | £40,847 | £40,847 | £31,754 | £4,475 | -£16,309 |
| Overall_Net_Profit | £58,847 | £58,847 | £44,754 | £2,475 | -£31,109 |

Notes: Current Values column represents values of changing cells at time Scenario Summary Report was created. Changing cells for each scenario are highlighted in gray.

Again, note that the changing cells and result cells are shown in a user friendly way as we named them – otherwise the cell reference would be shown here, which would not be very useful.

(l) Save the file in the **Solutions** folder as **Activity 22-3** and close it.

## Test your understanding 22-4

This activity shows the use of **Goal Seek** in What-If Analysis.

(a) Open the **Goal Seek** file in the **Activities** folder.

(b) We can use **Goal Seek** to find, for example, what material cost/kg would be required to give us a profit of £10,000 for a product.

(c) Select the Alpha Net Profit cell, D27, and launch Goal Seek.

(d) We wish to set cell D27 to a value of 10000 by changing D3.

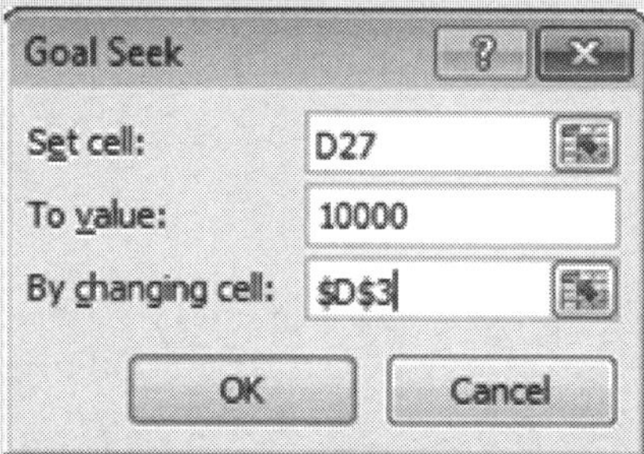

(e) A success message should be shown:

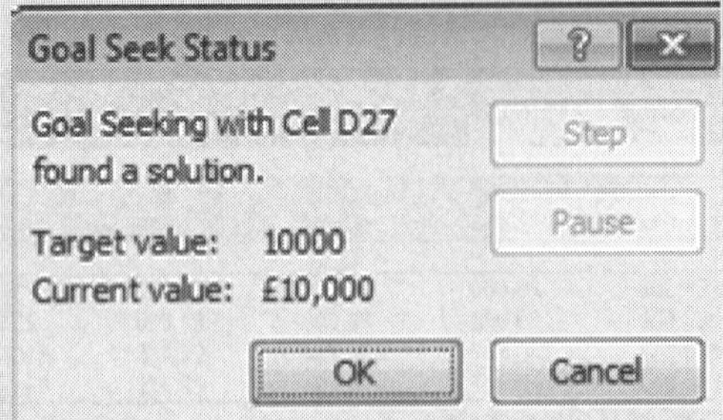


(f) Note that the material cost has been changed to give the required profit. Try other combinations. Remember, **Ctrl-Z** will still work after a Goal Seek, if you don't like the results.

(g) Save the file in the **Solutions** folder as **Activity 22-4** and close it.

# Analysis tools

## Introduction

This chapter will show you how launch an 'add-in' and to understand how to use analysis tools.

### ASSESSMENT CRITERIA

Select and use relevant tools to analyse and interpret data (3.2)

Use appropriate tools to identify and resolve errors (4.1)

### CONTENTS

# 1 Analysis tools

## 1.1 Installing analysis tools

Within Excel there is a selection of **Analysis Tools**. These tools do not come as standard on any menu and to use them you will need to activate an **Add-In.** These are found in the **Options** menu within the **File** tab.

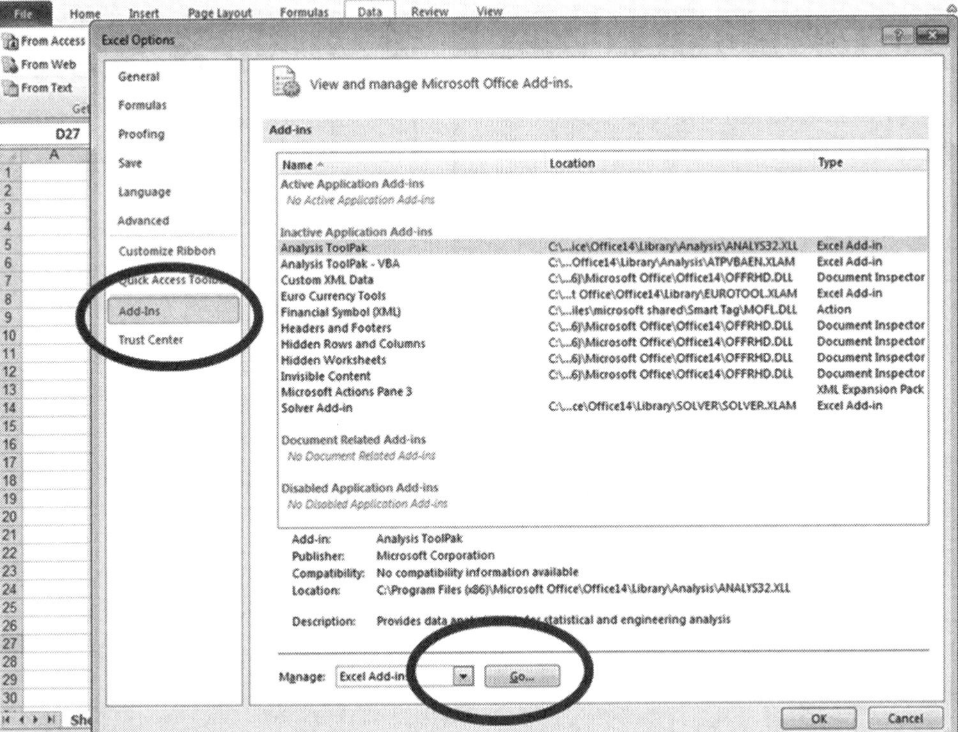


With **Manage Excel Add-ins** selected, click **Go**.

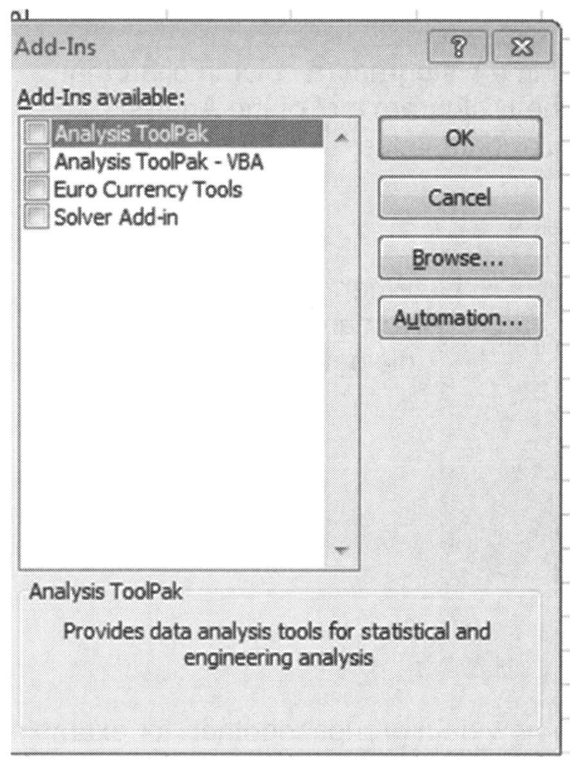


Select the Analysis ToolPak, and click OK.

## 1.2 Using analysis tools

There are lots of **Analysis Tools** but the ones you should be aware of are:

1 Histogram.

2 Moving Average.

3 Random Number.

4 Rank & Percentile.

5 Sampling.

Once the tools have been installed they can be accessed on the **Data** tab.

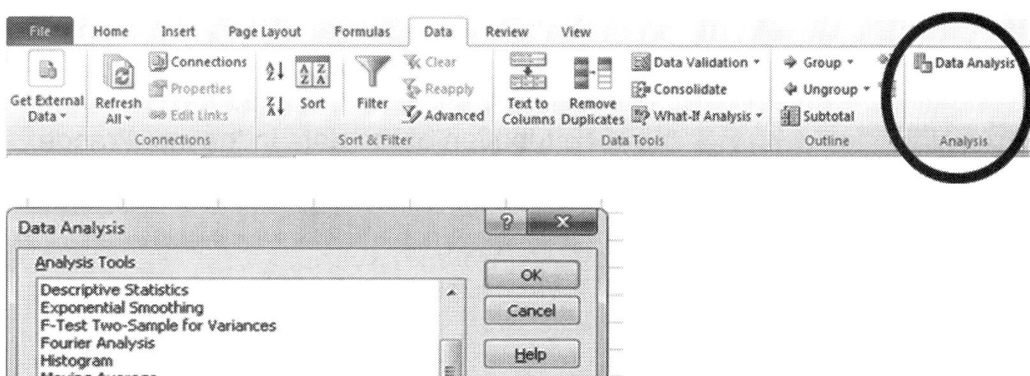

## 1.3 Histogram

You can analyse data and display it in a histogram (a column chart that displays frequency data) by using the Histogram tool of the Analysis ToolPak. The frequency of a particular data value is the number of times the data value occurs.

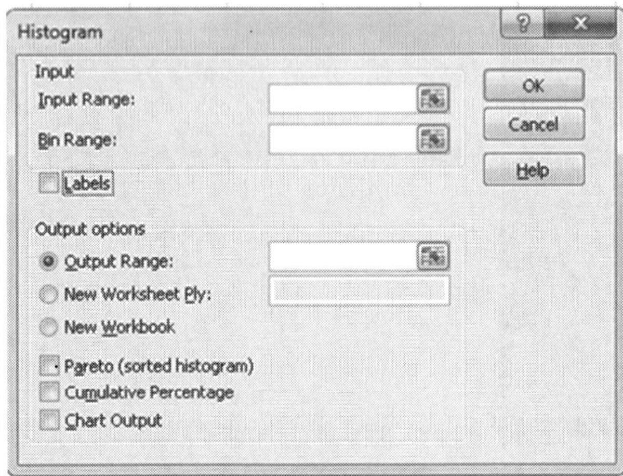


When the tool is launched you are presented with this dialogue box.

We can use a histogram to analyse how data groups together, for example the marks received from an exam.

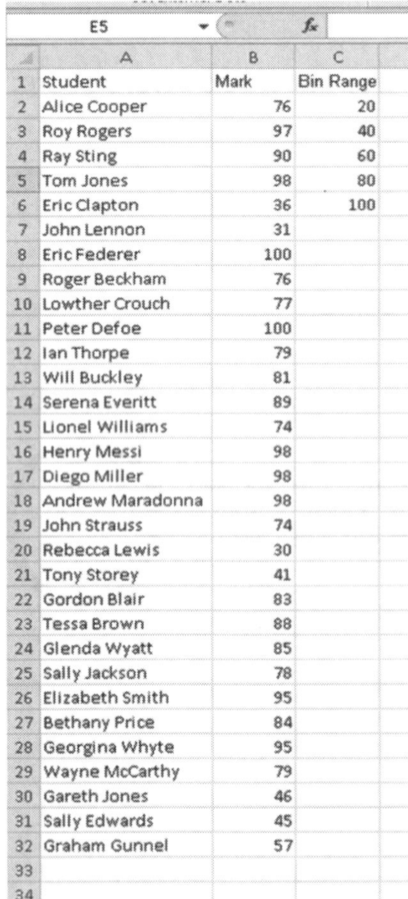

E5

| | A | B | C |
|---|---|---|---|
| 1 | Student | Mark | Bin Range |
| 2 | Alice Cooper | 76 | 20 |
| 3 | Roy Rogers | 97 | 40 |
| 4 | Ray Sting | 90 | 60 |
| 5 | Tom Jones | 98 | 80 |
| 6 | Eric Clapton | 36 | 100 |
| 7 | John Lennon | 31 | |
| 8 | Eric Federer | 100 | |
| 9 | Roger Beckham | 76 | |
| 10 | Lowther Crouch | 77 | |
| 11 | Peter Defoe | 100 | |
| 12 | Ian Thorpe | 79 | |
| 13 | Will Buckley | 81 | |
| 14 | Serena Everitt | 89 | |
| 15 | Lionel Williams | 74 | |
| 16 | Henry Messi | 98 | |
| 17 | Diego Miller | 98 | |
| 18 | Andrew Maradonna | 98 | |
| 19 | John Strauss | 74 | |
| 20 | Rebecca Lewis | 30 | |
| 21 | Tony Storey | 41 | |
| 22 | Gordon Blair | 83 | |
| 23 | Tessa Brown | 88 | |
| 24 | Glenda Wyatt | 85 | |
| 25 | Sally Jackson | 78 | |
| 26 | Elizabeth Smith | 95 | |
| 27 | Bethany Price | 84 | |
| 28 | Georgina Whyte | 95 | |
| 29 | Wayne McCarthy | 79 | |
| 30 | Gareth Jones | 46 | |
| 31 | Sally Edwards | 45 | |
| 32 | Graham Gunnel | 57 | |
| 33 | | | |
| 34 | | | |

**Input Range**: This is the data that you wish to include in the histogram, in this case the marks received. The data must be quantitative numeric data (such as item amounts or test scores).

**Bin Range**: In a histogram you can select a number of ranges or bins that you wish to group the data in. We want to see how many of the scores were between 0 and 20, 21 and 40, 41 and 60, 61 and 80 and finally between 81 and 100. If you do not create and select bins then Excel will create 10 bins for you based on an equal distribution of the data in the input range.

The completed dialogue box:

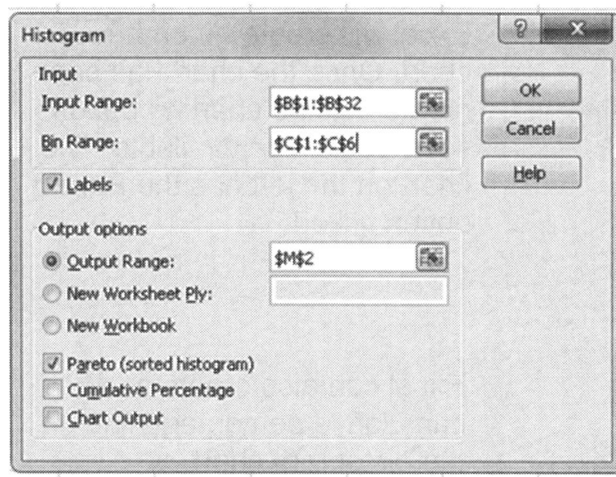


**Labels**: Excel will create suitable labels for the histogram; however, you should tick this box if the 1st row or column of your selected data contains labels.

**Output Range**: Select the cell where you would like the output table to be located.

**New Worksheet Ply**: If you wish for the output table to be in a new worksheet select it here.

**New Workbook**: If you wish for the output to be in a new workbook, select this option.

| M | N | O | P |
|---|---|---|---|
| *Bin Range* | *Frequency* | *Bin Range* | *Frequency* |
| 20 | 0 | 100 | 16 |
| 40 | 3 | 80 | 8 |
| 60 | 4 | 60 | 4 |
| 80 | 8 | 40 | 3 |
| 100 | 16 | 20 | 0 |
| More | 0 | More | 0 |

**Pareto (sorted histogram)**: Select this to present data in the output table in descending order of frequency i.e. the most frequently occurring event will be shown first (see column O and P). If this check box is cleared, Excel presents the data in ascending order and omits the two columns that contain the sorted data.

| *Bin Range* | *Frequency* | *Cumulative %* |
|---|---|---|
| 20 | 0 | 0.00% |
| 40 | 3 | 9.68% |
| 60 | 4 | 22.58% |
| 80 | 8 | 48.39% |
| 100 | 16 | 100.00% |
| More | 0 | 100.00% |

**Cumulative Percentage**: Select this if you want Excel to create a cumulative percentage column in the output table.

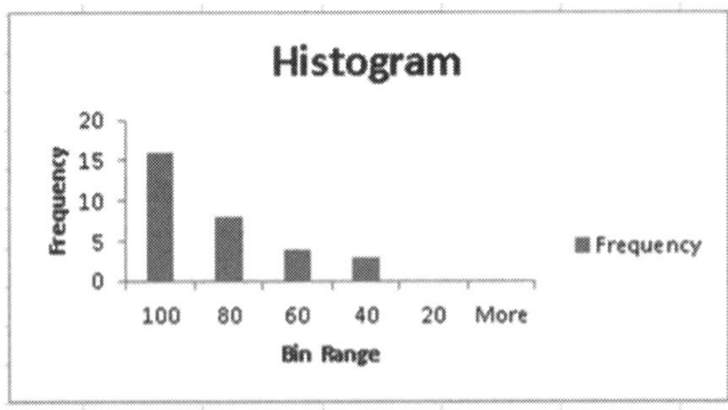


**Chart Output**: Select this if you wish Excel to create a chart. Excel will create an embedded chart. Once the chart has been created all the charting options seen earlier are available. The chart on the left has the Pareto option ticked.

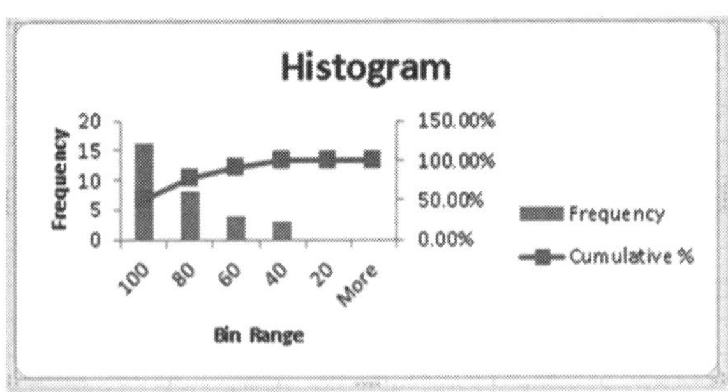


Excel can also create a cumulative percentage line on the histogram chart.

## 1.4 Moving average

A **Moving Average** is a series of averages calculated from time series data. By using moving averages, the variations in a time series can be eliminated leaving a 'smoothed' set of figures which is taken as the trend.

A moving average is used by accountants to smooth out fluctuations in numerical data over a time period, for example sales volumes over a year. It enables accountants to identify any trends in the data. When the tool is launched the following dialogue box appears:

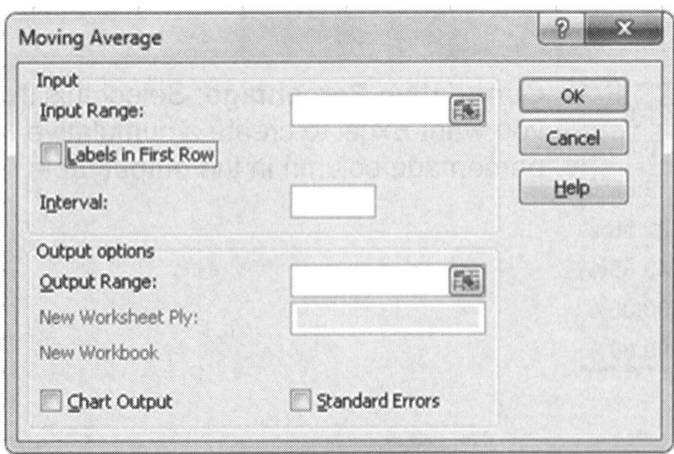

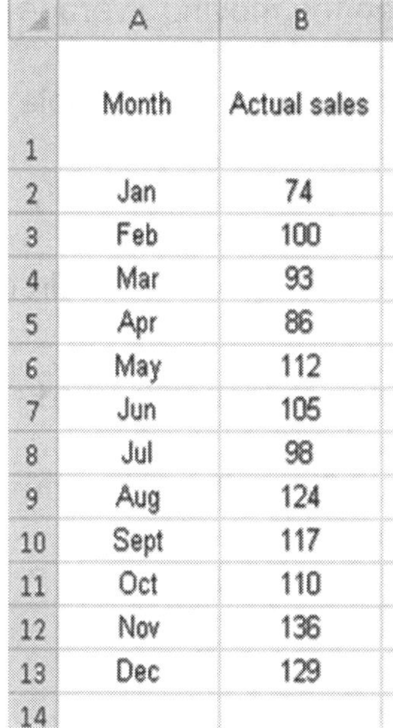

| | A | B |
|---|---|---|
| 1 | Month | Actual sales |
| 2 | Jan | 74 |
| 3 | Feb | 100 |
| 4 | Mar | 93 |
| 5 | Apr | 86 |
| 6 | May | 112 |
| 7 | Jun | 105 |
| 8 | Jul | 98 |
| 9 | Aug | 124 |
| 10 | Sept | 117 |
| 11 | Oct | 110 |
| 12 | Nov | 136 |
| 13 | Dec | 129 |
| 14 | | |

**Input Range:** This is the data that you wish to include in the **moving average**. It needs to be a single column of data for example the actual sales in the image.

**Labels:** Excel will create suitable labels for the moving average; however, you should tick this box if the 1st row of your data contains labels.

**Interval:** This refers to the grouping of the data. For example you might be grouping your data into quarters of a year, and therefore your interval would be three (three months in a quarter).

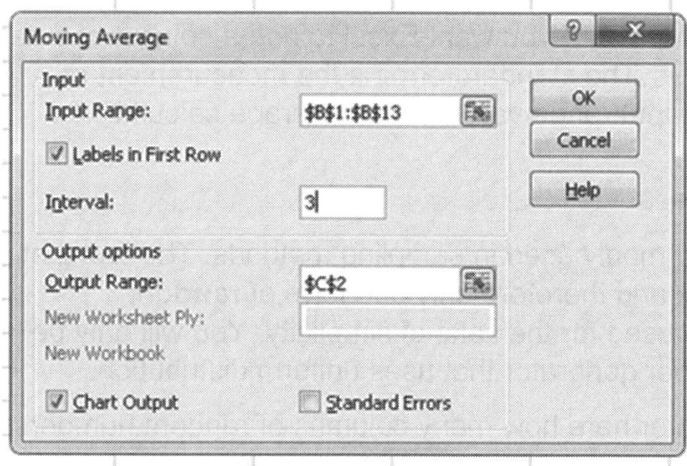


**Output Range:** Select the cell where you would like the output table to be. There is no option to put the output in a new workbook or worksheet.

| | A | B | C | D |
|---|---|---|---|---|
| 1 | Month | Actual sales | | |
| 2 | Jan | 74 | #N/A | |
| 3 | Feb | 100 | #N/A | 89 |
| 4 | Mar | 93 | 89 | 93 |
| 5 | Apr | 86 | 93 | 97 |
| 6 | May | 112 | 97 | 101 |
| 7 | Jun | 105 | 101 | 105 |
| 8 | Jul | 98 | 105 | 109 |
| 9 | Aug | 124 | 109 | 113 |
| 10 | Sept | 117 | 113 | 117 |
| 11 | Oct | 110 | 117 | 121 |
| 12 | Nov | 136 | 121 | 125 |
| 13 | Dec | 129 | 125 | |
| 14 | | | | |

**Note:** When the moving average is calculated the first 2 rows contain #N/A as it is not possible to calculate a moving average based on intervals of 3 with only 2 sets of data. The first value given is the average over the first 3 months.

When moving averages is used as a forecasting tool the first value is usually positioned in the middle of the period it is averaging – see column D.

**Chart Output:** Select this if you wish Excel to create a chart. Excel will create an embedded chart. Once the chart has been created all the charting options seen earlier are available.

**Standard Error:** Select this only if you want Excel to add a column of data showing the standard error. The standard error is the measurement of how far the values in the input range vary from an average calculation.

## 1.5 Random numbers

Random numbers are commonly used in sampling methods. The tool that Excel provides is complex and therefore only one form of **random number** generator will be used for the sake of simplicity. You will only be looking at a random number generator that uses uniform distribution.

**Number of Variables**: Enter here how many columns of random numbers you require.

**Number of Random Numbers**: Enter here how many random numbers you require in each column.

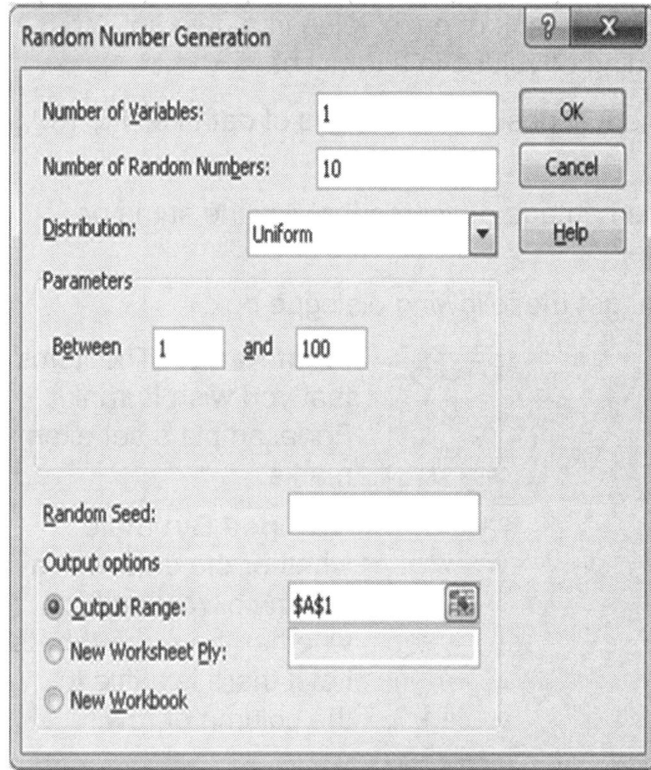


**Distribution**: This is the complex area of this tool. Different types of distribution are used for different purposes. We will use uniform distribution.

**Parameters**: Enter here a range between which you want the numbers generated.

**Random Seed**: A value can be entered from which the random numbers will be generated. This can be used to ensure that the same numbers are generated in the future.

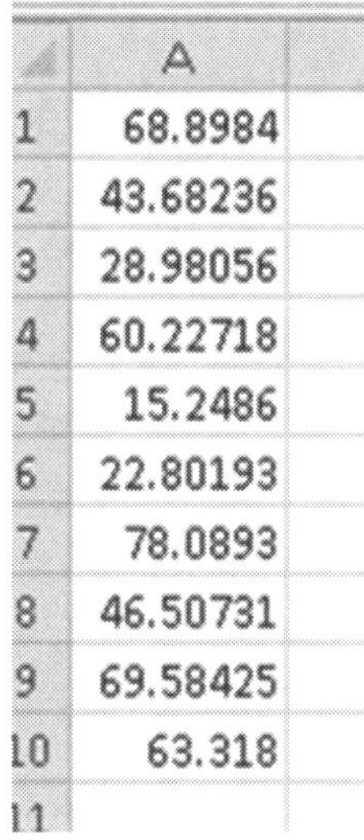

| | A |
|---|---|
| 1 | 68.8984 |
| 2 | 43.68236 |
| 3 | 28.98056 |
| 4 | 60.22718 |
| 5 | 15.2486 |
| 6 | 22.80193 |
| 7 | 78.0893 |
| 8 | 46.50731 |
| 9 | 69.58425 |
| 10 | 63.318 |
| 11 | |

Clicking ok on the above dialogue box has produced the random numbers to the left. If the same box was completed again different numbers would appear as the Random Seed box is blank.

**Output Range**: Select the cell where you would like the output table to be located.

**New Worksheet Ply**: If you wish for the output table to be in a new worksheet select it here.

**New Workbook**: If you wish for the output to be in a new workbook, select this option.

## 1.6 Rank and percentile

The Rank and Percentile analysis tool produces a four column table that contains the ordinal and percentile rank of each value in a data set. You can analyse the relative standing of values in a data set.

- **Ordinal rank:** The numerical position in a series of data i.e. 1st, 10th, 23rd.
- **Percentile rank:** The percentage of scores that are the same or lower than a given score.

When you launch the tool you get the following dialogue box.

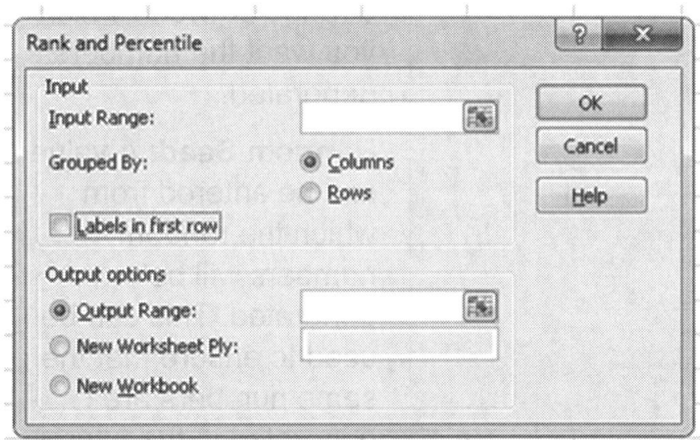


**Input Range:** The items that you wish to rank. For example a set exam marks.

**Grouped By:** State whether the data is in a column or row and whether there are **labels** i.e. if there is a title to the column or row.

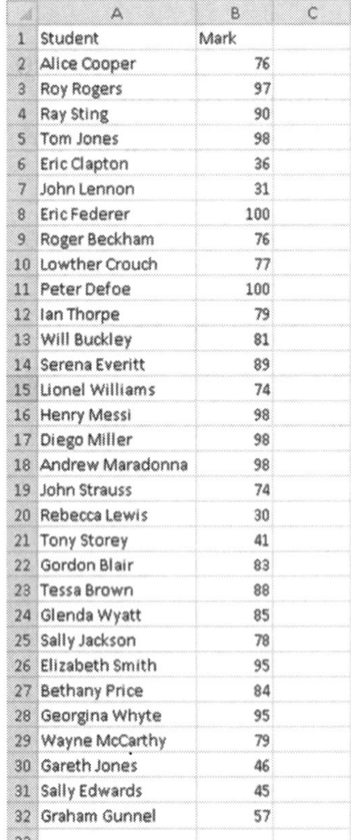

| | A | B | C |
|---|---|---|---|
| 1 | Student | Mark | |
| 2 | Alice Cooper | 76 | |
| 3 | Roy Rogers | 97 | |
| 4 | Ray Sting | 90 | |
| 5 | Tom Jones | 98 | |
| 6 | Eric Clapton | 36 | |
| 7 | John Lennon | 31 | |
| 8 | Eric Federer | 100 | |
| 9 | Roger Beckham | 76 | |
| 10 | Lowther Crouch | 77 | |
| 11 | Peter Defoe | 100 | |
| 12 | Ian Thorpe | 79 | |
| 13 | Will Buckley | 81 | |
| 14 | Serena Everitt | 89 | |
| 15 | Lionel Williams | 74 | |
| 16 | Henry Messi | 98 | |
| 17 | Diego Miller | 98 | |
| 18 | Andrew Maradonna | 98 | |
| 19 | John Strauss | 74 | |
| 20 | Rebecca Lewis | 30 | |
| 21 | Tony Storey | 41 | |
| 22 | Gordon Blair | 83 | |
| 23 | Tessa Brown | 88 | |
| 24 | Glenda Wyatt | 85 | |
| 25 | Sally Jackson | 78 | |
| 26 | Elizabeth Smith | 95 | |
| 27 | Bethany Price | 84 | |
| 28 | Georgina Whyte | 95 | |
| 29 | Wayne McCarthy | 79 | |
| 30 | Gareth Jones | 46 | |
| 31 | Sally Edwards | 45 | |
| 32 | Graham Gunnel | 57 | |

**Output Range**: Select the cell where you would like the output table to be located.

**New Worksheet Ply**: If you wish for the output table to be in a new worksheet select it here.

**New Workbook**: If you wish for the output to be in a new workbook, select this option.

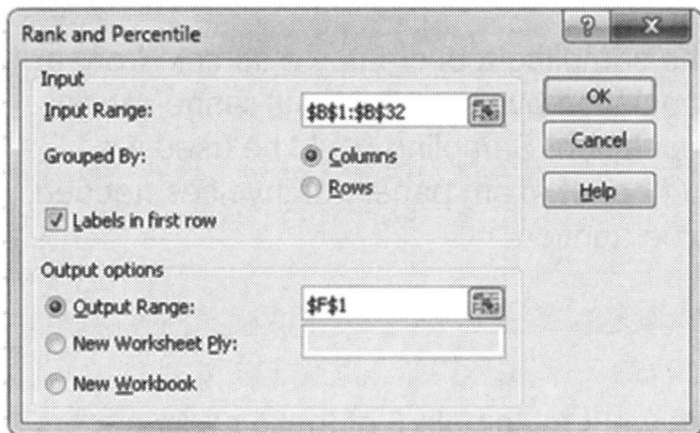


The information input into the dialogue box will produce the following results:

| F | G | H | I |
|---|---|---|---|
| *Point* | *Mark* | *Rank* | *Percent* |
| 7 | 100 | 1 | 97% |
| 10 | 100 | 1 | 97% |
| 15 | 98 | 3 | 87% |
| 16 | 98 | 3 | 87% |
| 17 | 98 | 3 | 87% |
| 4 | 98 | 6 | 83% |
| 2 | 97 | 7 | 80% |
| 25 | 95 | 8 | 73% |
| 27 | 95 | 8 | 73% |
| 3 | 90 | 10 | 70% |
| 13 | 89 | 11 | 67% |
| 22 | 88 | 12 | 63% |
| 23 | 85 | 13 | 60% |
| 26 | 84 | 14 | 57% |
| 21 | 83 | 15 | 53% |
| 12 | 81 | 16 | 50% |
| 11 | 79 | 17 | 43% |
| 28 | 79 | 17 | 43% |
| 24 | 78 | 19 | 40% |
| 9 | 77 | 20 | 37% |
| 1 | 76 | 21 | 30% |
| 8 | 76 | 21 | 30% |
| 14 | 74 | 23 | 23% |
| 18 | 74 | 23 | 23% |
| 31 | 57 | 25 | 20% |
| 29 | 46 | 26 | 17% |
| 30 | 45 | 27 | 13% |
| 20 | 41 | 28 | 10% |
| 5 | 36 | 29 | 7% |
| 6 | 31 | 30 | 3% |
| 19 | 30 | 31 | 0% |

The four columns represent:

**Point**: The location of the item in the original data.

**Mark**: The value of the data.

**Rank**: The numerical position in the series data.

**Percent**: the percentage of numbers in the data-set that are the same or below it.

## 1.7 Sampling

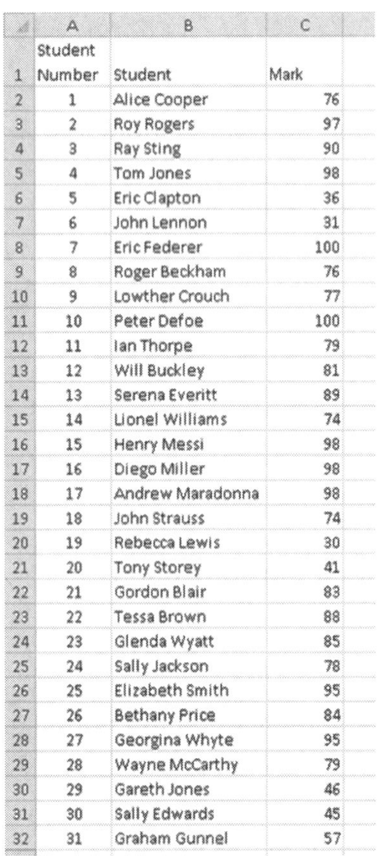

| | A | B | C |
|---|---|---|---|
| 1 | Student Number | Student | Mark |
| 2 | 1 | Alice Cooper | 76 |
| 3 | 2 | Roy Rogers | 97 |
| 4 | 3 | Ray Sting | 90 |
| 5 | 4 | Tom Jones | 98 |
| 6 | 5 | Eric Clapton | 36 |
| 7 | 6 | John Lennon | 31 |
| 8 | 7 | Eric Federer | 100 |
| 9 | 8 | Roger Beckham | 76 |
| 10 | 9 | Lowther Crouch | 77 |
| 11 | 10 | Peter Defoe | 100 |
| 12 | 11 | Ian Thorpe | 79 |
| 13 | 12 | Will Buckley | 81 |
| 14 | 13 | Serena Everitt | 89 |
| 15 | 14 | Lionel Williams | 74 |
| 16 | 15 | Henry Messi | 98 |
| 17 | 16 | Diego Miller | 98 |
| 18 | 17 | Andrew Maradonna | 98 |
| 19 | 18 | John Strauss | 74 |
| 20 | 19 | Rebecca Lewis | 30 |
| 21 | 20 | Tony Storey | 41 |
| 22 | 21 | Gordon Blair | 83 |
| 23 | 22 | Tessa Brown | 88 |
| 24 | 23 | Glenda Wyatt | 85 |
| 25 | 24 | Sally Jackson | 78 |
| 26 | 25 | Elizabeth Smith | 95 |
| 27 | 26 | Bethany Price | 84 |
| 28 | 27 | Georgina Whyte | 95 |
| 29 | 28 | Wayne McCarthy | 79 |
| 30 | 29 | Gareth Jones | 46 |
| 31 | 30 | Sally Edwards | 45 |
| 32 | 31 | Graham Gunnel | 57 |

The sampling tool creates a sample from a population by using the input range as the population. Sampling could be used if a number of exam papers or invoices needed to be audited.

We want to sample 5 of these exam papers randomly to check the assessment is correct.

When the tool is launched you get the following dialogue box:

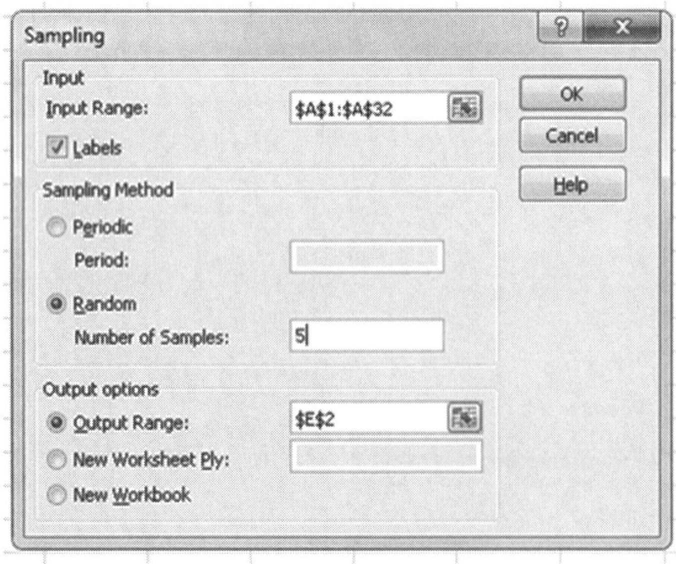


**Input Range:** The items in your population that you wish to pick your sample from. The input range should be numerical.

**Labels:** tick this box if your selected data has a heading.

**Sampling method:**

- **Periodic:** This is where you choose to select every n[th] value in your population, for example every 9[th] value.
- **Random:** This is where we allow Excel to choose our sample at random from the population.

**Number of samples:** How many items do you wish to choose from the population.

Clicking OK produces a list of student numbers to use to sample the exams:

| E |
|---|
| Sample |
| 22 |
| 29 |
| 10 |
| 20 |
| 4 |

# AAT Sample assessment 1 – Questions

## Introduction

This chapter contains the revised sample assessment 1 issued by the AAT in 2018.

You should work through this assessment both to familiarise yourself with the format and structure, but also as a practice exam, before looking at the walkthrough in the next chapter.

The spreadsheet files can be downloaded from your MyKaplan account.

# PART 1

Task 1.1 is based on a workplace scenario separate to the rest of the assessment.

Task 1.2 to 1.3 and 2.1 to 2.2 are based on the workplace scenario of BLM & Co, which is as follows:

| |
|---|
| You are Sam Jones, a part-qualified Accounting Technician. You work for BLM & Co, a business which manufactures and sells sinks.<br>BLM & Co is owned and run by Brian and Lakmani Moore in partnership. You cover all aspects of bookkeeping and accounting for the business. |

## Task 1.1 (15 marks)

This task is based on a workplace scenario separate to the rest of the assessment.

Wajid is an accountant who works for Laleham Ltd, a large organisation with many employees. Tara, a new accountant with Laleham Ltd, has made two statements to Wajid about how she believes the ethical code applies to her.

**(a) Are these statements true or false? (2 marks)**

| Statement | True | False |
|---|---|---|
| 'I have no duty to act in the public interest provided that I act in the interests of Laleham Ltd and the accountancy profession.' | | |
| 'The ethical code provides detailed rules on how I should act in every possible situation that I might encounter at work.' | | |

**(b) Show whether or not the ethical code specifically requires Tara to take each of the following actions in order to act in line with the principle of professional behaviour. (2 marks)**

∇ Drop down list for task 1.1 (b)

| |
|---|
| Required |
| Not required |

| Action | Required/not required |
|---|---|
| Comply with all regulations that affect Laleham Ltd. | ∇ |
| Promote the reputation of the profession at every opportunity. | ∇ |

Wajid has noticed that Tara does not conduct her work thoroughly and she often completes it late. He believes that, as a result of Tara's lack of diligence, she is in breach of one of the fundamental principles.

**(c) Which fundamental principle has Tara breached? (2 marks)**

| | |
|---|---|
| Integrity | |
| Professional competence and due care | |
| Objectivity | |

Tara has been told that she is facing disciplinary procedures because she has behaved unethically.

**(d) Show whether or not each organisation below may bring disciplinary procedures against Tara for her unethical behaviour. (3 marks)**

∇ Drop down list for task 1.1 (d)

| |
|---|
| May |
| May not |

| | | |
|---|---|---|
| AAT | ∇ | … bring disciplinary procedure against Tara |
| The National Crime Agency | ∇ | … bring disciplinary procedure against Tara |
| Laleham Ltd (Tara's employer | ∇ | … bring disciplinary procedure against Tara |

Employment regulations require employers to pay workers at least at the National Minimum Wage (NMW).

Laleham Ltd makes high levels of profits. The Chief Executive insists that managers should be paid at very high rate with regular bonuses, but workers should receive only the NMW, with no entitlement to bonuses.

**(e) Show whether the following statements are true or false.**

**(2 marks)**

| Statement | True | False |
|---|---|---|
| The Chief Executive's policy on employees pay raises doubts about the ethical nature of the leadership and culture of Laleham Ltd. | | |
| Because Laleham Ltd complies with the NMW regulations, it is automatically considered to be behaving ethically in relation to its employees. | | |

Ian is an accountant who has just started working for Penton Ltd, reporting to Hettie, who is also an accountant. Ian has discovered a material error in Penton Ltd's last corporation tax return.

**(f) What action must Ian now take? (2 marks)**

| | |
|---|---|
| Resign. | |
| Advise HMRC of the error without disclosing any information to Hettie or Penton Ltd. | |
| Tell Hettie about the error and recommend that Penton Ltd disclose the error to HMRC. | |

Hettie realises that she has inadvertently become involved in Penton Ltd's money laundering operation.

**(g) Complete the following statement. (2 marks)**

∇ Drop down list for task 1.1 (g)

| |
|---|
| A protected disclosure |
| An authorised disclosure |
| A prompt disclosure |

Hettie may have a defence against a money laundering charge if she makes

[ ∇ ]

to the relevant authority.

## Task 1.2 (15 marks)

This task is based on the workplace scenario of BLM & Co.

Today's date is 15 April 20X7.

BLM and Co's VAT control account at 31 March is as follows:

**VAT control account**

| | | £ | | | £ |
|---|---|---|---|---|---|
| 06/02 | Cash book | 60,880.98 | 01/01 | Balance b/d | 60,880.98 |
| 31/03 | Purchases day book | 99,120.25 | 31/03 | Sales day book | 161,728.27 |
| 31/03 | Sales returns day book | 3,529.57 | 31/03 | Purchases returns day book | 2,403.68 |
| 31/03 | Balance c/d | 61,482.13 | | | |
| | | 225,012.93 | | | 225,012.93 |

On reviewing BLM & Co's day books, you have found two errors:

- Output VAT of £2,983.50 on a sales invoice was wrongly recorded as sales on 29 March.
- A supplier had overstated input VAT by £50 on an invoice received and posted by BLM on 27 March.

You prepare journals to correct these errors.

**(a) Once the journals have been processed, what will be the revised balance carried down on the VAT account? (2 marks)**

| £ | |
|---|---|

**(b) Complete the following sentence by selecting ONE of the options below. (1 mark)**

This balance will appear on the ____________ side of the trial balance.

| Credit | |
|---|---|
| Debit | |

You discover that BLM & Co has been supplying sinks to Malone Ltd, a company owned and run by the brother of your fully qualified colleague, Jed Malone. When you look at the relevant invoices you realise that Jed has been misrecording VAT so that BLM & Co's sales to Malone Ltd are overstated. As a result, Malone Ltd qualifies for a 15% trade discount on its future purchases from BLM & Co.

**(c) Applying the conceptual framework from the ethical code, which ONE of the following describes the situation faced by Jed Malone when recording sales to his brother's company?** **(2 marks)**

| | |
|---|---|
| A self-review threat to professional competence and due care. | |
| A familiarity threat to objectivity. | |
| An intimidation threat to professional behaviour. | |

You conclude that the deliberate misrecording of VAT is unethical behaviour by Jed Malone.

**(d) What should be your next action?** **(1 mark)**

| | |
|---|---|
| Send a Suspicious Activity Report to the National Crime Agency. | |
| Tell Brian and Lakmani about your concerns. | |

On the morning of 16 April, Jed Malone is dismissed for misconduct by BLM & Co and leaves the office. You are temporarily BLM & Co's only accountant. A VAT officer will be coming to the office for a planned visit on the afternoon of 16 April. You are not prepared for this visit and do not believe you can answer any questions from the VAT officer effectively. Brian and Lakmani insist that you must be present and deal with the VAT officer without assistance.

**(e) Which of the following should be your next action?** **(2 marks)**

| | |
|---|---|
| Resign from BLM & Co. | |
| Request that the visit by the VAT officer is postponed. | |
| Agree to deal with the VAT officer in line with your employers' instructions. | |

As a result of Jed's misconduct, Brian and Lakmani have asked you to examine his recording of sales ledger transactions in the three months ended 31 March 20X7. You identify the following information:

Sales ledger control account balance at 1 January 20X7: £492,409.

From 1 January to 31 March:

- Receipts from credit customers: £934,076.
- Sales to credit customers, including VAT: £970,370.
- Returns from credit customers, include VAT: £21,177.
- Irrecoverable debts written off, including VAT: £4,330.

Amounts owed at 31 March 20X7, as confirmed by credit customers: £487,354.

**(f) drag each of the four options below to the appropriate column AND enter the totals to reconstruct the sales ledger control account for the three months ended 31 March 20X7. (2 marks)**

**Sales ledger control account**

| | £ | | £ |
|---|---|---|---|
| Balance b/d | 492,409 | | |
| | | | |
| | | | |
| | | | |
| | | Balance c/d | 487,354 |
| **Total** | | **Total** | |

**Options:**

| | |
|---|---|
| Cash book | 934,076 |
| Sales day book | 970,370 |
| Sales returns day book | 21,177 |
| Journal (irrecoverable debt) | 4,330 |

**(g) Calculate the missing figure in the sales ledger control account. (1 mark)**

| £ | |
|---|---|

**(h) Which of the following could the missing figure represent?**
**(2 marks)**

| | |
|---|---|
| Discounts allowed. | |
| Cheque from customer returned unpaid by the bank. | |
| Cash sales. | |

**(i) Complete the following statement about irrecoverable debts.**
**(2 marks)**

The amount of an irrecoverable debt_____________________________.

| | |
|---|---|
| … is calculated as a percentage of the total of trades receivables | |
| … always relates to a specified customer | |
| … increases the balance on the allowance for doubtful debts account | |

## Task 1.3 (15 marks)

This task is based on the workplace scenario of BLM & Co.

Today's date is 28 February 20X8.

Brian has asked you to prepare some financial statements urgently. These include a statement of cash flows and a cash budget. He needs to send these to the bank by the end of the week in support of a loan application. Brian tells you that obtaining the loan is very important for the survival of the business. The jobs of everyone in the business depend on this. Your studies so far have not covered statements of cash flows or cash budgets.

**(a) (i) Describe TWO threats to your ethical principles as a result of Brian's request. (2 marks)**

**(ii) What response should you give to Brian in order to remain ethical? (1 mark)**

**(iii) Give Brian ONE reason for your response to him. (1 mark)**

**In your answer you should refer to the guidance found in the ethical code for professional accountants.**

**(i) Threats**

**(ii) Response to Brian**

**(iii) Reason**

Your role at BLM & Co includes:

- supporting sustainability throughout the business
- measuring sustainability in the business.

**(b) State why you, as an accountant, have a professional duty to uphold sustainability in your work.** **(1 mark)**

You receive the following email from Lakmani Moore:

**To: Sam Jones <Sam.Jones@BLMCo.co.uk>**

**From: Lakmani Moore <Lakmani.Moore@BLMCo.co.uk>**

**Date: 28/2/X8**

**Subject: BLM & Co: change in structure**

Good morning Sam,

Brian and I are considering starting to operate the business as a limited company.

I would like you to tell me more about the implications of a partnership becoming a limited company.

Please include three sections in your response to me as follows:

1 A brief description of a limited company

2 A summary of our position as owners if the business becomes a limited company

3 Explanations of one key advantage and one key disadvantage of operating as a limited company.

Regards,

Lakmani

**(c) Prepare an email to Lakmani, addressing all her points.**

**(10 marks)**

**To:**

**Subject:**

**From:** Sam Jones <Sam.Jones@BLMCo.co.uk>

**Date:** 28/2/X8

# PART 2

Note: all the information for task 2 was contained within the excel files provided.

## Task 2.1 (25 marks)

**Download the assessment file**

The spreadsheet file includes all questions and data required for this task.

Download the spreadsheet file **"AVSY – Sample assessment 1 – assessment book and data – task 2.1"** from the assessment environment.

1. Save the spreadsheet file in the appropriate location and rename it in the following format: 'your initial-surname-AAT no-dd.mm.yy-Task2.1'. For example: J-Donnovan-123456-12.03.xx-Task2.1
2. Follow the instructions within, which provide the full details for each task
3. Before you proceed to the next task, **save close and upload your completed spreadsheet** using the upload files button.

**Complete the tasks in the assessment**

Below is a checklist for each task in this assessment. As you complete each task, tick it off the list to show your progress. Check boxes are provided for your assistance, using them does not constitute formal evidence that a task has been completed.

| | | Completed |
|---|---|---|
| **Part (a)**<br>Percentage, flexed budget and actual in 'Original Budget' worksheet | (9 marks) | |
| **Part (b)**<br>Variances, operating profit in 'Original Budget' worksheet | (9 marks) | |
| **Part (c)**<br>IF statement and freezing | (4 marks) | |
| **Part (d)**<br>Goal seek in the 'Goal Seek' worksheet | (3 marks) | |

**SUBMIT THE EVIDENCE REQUIRED**

## Task 2.2 (30 marks)

**Download the assessment file**

The spreadsheet file includes all questions and data required for this task.

Download the spreadsheet file **"AVSY – Sample assessment 1 – assessment book and data – task 2.2"** from the assessment environment.

1 Save the spreadsheet file in the appropriate location and rename it in the following format: 'your initial-surname-AAT no-dd.mm.yy-Task2.1'. For example: J-Donnovan-123456-12.03.xx-Task2.1

2 Follow the instructions within, which provide the full details for each task

3 Before you proceed to the next task, **save close and upload your completed spreadsheet** using the upload files button.

**Complete the tasks in the assessment**

Below is a checklist for each task in this assessment. As you complete each task, tick it off the list to show your progress. Check boxes are provided for your assistance, using them does not constitute formal evidence that a task has been completed.

| | | Completed |
|---|---|---|
| **Part (a)**<br>Lookup table and absolute referencing in 'Invoices worksheet | (4 marks) | |
| **Part (b)**<br>Removal of duplicate invoices in 'Invoices worksheet | (5 marks) | |
| **Part (c)**<br>Pivot chart and table in 'Diamond sinks sold' worksheet | (6 marks) | |
| **Part (d)**<br>Complete appropriation statement and current accounts | (15 marks) | |

**SUBMIT THE EVIDENCE REQUIRED**

# AAT Sample assessment 1 – Walkthrough and answers

## Introduction

This chapter walks through the (revised) AAT sample assessment 1 and discusses how to arrive at the model answer. You are advised to attempt the sample assessment in the previous chapter before reading this chapter.

# Task 1.1

## Introduction

In the sample assessment, task 1.1 correlates with assessment objective 1:

| Assessment objective 1 | Demonstrate an understanding of the relevance of the ethical code for accountants, the need to act ethically in a given situation, and the appropriate action to take in reporting questionable behaviour |
|---|---|

Task 1.1 is, therefore, primarily about ethics. In this task you should therefore expect to be given scenarios where you may have to

- indicate why you should act ethically,
- identify which ethical principles are threatened and
- what action is required as a result?

It is also worth noting that, as we shall see, other tasks also have ethical aspects to them.

In the exam you are provided with reference material covering the following:

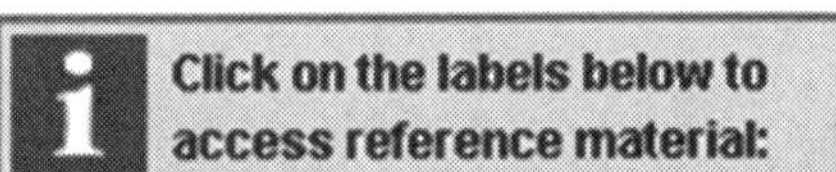

Click on the labels below to access reference material:


**Code of Professional Ethics - Part A**

Introduction - 100
Fundamental principles - 100.5
Conceptual framework approach - 100.6
Threats and safeguards - 100.12
Threats and safeguards - 100.13 to 100.16
Conflicts of interest - 100.17
Ethical conflict resolution - 100.19
Communicating with those charged with governance - 100.25
Integrity - 110
Objectivity - 120
Professional competence and due care - 130
Confidentiality - 140.1 to 140.6
Confidentiality - 140.7 to 140.8
Professional behaviour - 150

### Task 1.1(a)

You have to identify whether two statements are true or false:

| Statement | True | False |
|---|---|---|
| 'I have no duty to act in the public interest provided that I act in the interests of Laleham Ltd and the accountancy profession.' | | |
| 'The ethical code provides detailed rules on how I should act in every possible situation that I might encounter at work.' | | |

Key considerations:

- Read the statements carefully to make sure you don't get things back to front.
- A professional accountant's responsibility is not just to satisfy the needs of a client/employer but also be to act in the public interest.
- In acting in the public interest a professional accountant should observe and comply with the fundamental ethical requirements shown in the IFAC Code.
- The code adopts a principles-based approach. It does not attempt to cover every situation where a member may encounter professional ethical issues, prescribing the way in which he or she should respond. Instead, it adopts a value system, focusing on fundamental professional and ethical principles.

Given this, it can be seen that both statements are false:

| Statement | True | False |
|---|---|---|
| 'I have no duty to act in the public interest provided that I act in the interests of Laleham Ltd and the accountancy profession.' | | ✓ |
| 'The ethical code provides detailed rules on how I should act in every possible situation that I might encounter at work.' | | ✓ |

## Task 1.1(b)

Task 1.1(b) is also based on the mini scenario introduced above but focusses on the action Tara must take to act in line with the principle of professional behaviour.

| **Action** | **Required/not required** |
|---|---|
| Comply with all regulations that affect Laleham Ltd. | ∇ |
| Promote the reputation of the profession at every opportunity. | ∇ |

Key considerations:

- While all the actions may be advisable, here we are only interested in ones that correlate to the principle of professional behaviour.
- The principle of professional behaviour states that a professional accountant should comply with relevant laws and regulations and should avoid any action that discredits the profession.
- It does not state that accountants should seek to promote the profession at every opportunity, rather that they should avoid action that discredits the profession.

The required answers are thus:

| **Action** | **Required/not required** |
|---|---|
| Comply with all regulations that affect Laleham Ltd. | Required ∇ |
| Promote the reputation of the profession at every opportunity. | Not Required ∇ |

## Task 1.1(c)

We are then presented with further information concerning Laleham Ltd:

> Wajid has noticed that Tara does not conduct her work thoroughly and she often completes it late. He believes that, as a result of Tara's lack of diligence, she is in breach of one of the fundamental principles.

You then have to identify which principle has been breached:

| | |
|---|---|
| Integrity | |
| Professional competence and due care | |
| Objectivity | |

Key considerations:

- This is likely to be a very common aspect of task 1.1, so it is vital that you know the difference between the difference ethical principles.

  As mentioned before, if you need to check anything, remember that you can access elements of the AAT ethical code via the reference material in the exam.

- It would be advisable to commit at least the key aspects of the ethical principles to memory to save time having to look them up.
- The key emphasis of "integrity" is fair dealing and truthfulness, being straightforward and honest.
- "Professional competence" is more concerned with maintaining professional knowledge and skill at the level required. The "due care" aspect means a member must act diligently and in accordance with applicable standards when providing professional services.
- "Objectivity" means that a member must not allow bias, conflict of interest or undue influence of others to override professional or business judgements.

Tara's lack of diligence and thoroughness mean she is not exercising due care, so the required answer is.

| | |
|---|---|
| Integrity | |
| Professional competence and due care | ✓ |
| Objectivity | |

**Task 1.1(d)**

The story of Tara then continues with the following:

| |
|---|
| Tara has been told that she is facing disciplinary procedures because she has behaved unethically. |

You then have to identify which organisations may bring disciplinary procedures against Tara:

| | | |
|---|---|---|
| AAT | ∇ | … bring disciplinary procedure against Tara |
| The National Crime Agency | ∇ | … bring disciplinary procedure against Tara |
| Laleham Ltd (Tara's employer) | ∇ | … bring disciplinary procedure against Tara |

Key considerations:

- The AAT may discipline members who fail to meet required standards of ethical or professional behaviour.
- The NCA may bring prosecutions if someone has broken the law.
- Firms may discipline their employees if they have breached required standards of behaviour, terms in their contracts of employment or ethical codes, subject to following due process.

The required answers are thus:

| | | |
|---|---|---|
| AAT | **May** | … bring disciplinary procedure against Tara |
| The National Crime Agency | **May not** | … bring disciplinary procedure against Tara |
| Laleham Ltd (Tara's employer | **May** | … bring disciplinary procedure against Tara |

### Task 1.1(e)

The scenario then switches to Laleham Ltd's approach to remuneration:

> Employment regulations require employers to pay workers at least at the National Minimum Wage (NMW).
>
> Laleham Ltd makes high levels of profits. The Chief Executive insists that managers should be paid at very high rate with regular bonuses, but workers should receive only the NMW, with no entitlement to bonuses.

You then have to identify whether two statements are true or false:

| Statement | True | False |
|---|---|---|
| The Chief Executive's policy on employees pay raises doubts about the ethical nature of the leadership and culture of Laleham Ltd. | | |
| Because Laleham Ltd complies with the NMW regulations, it is automatically considered to be behaving ethically in relation to its employees. | | |

Key considerations:

- There is no suggestion here that Laleham Ltd is doing anything **illegal**. However, there may still be an **ethical** issue. Don't confuse illegal acts with unethical ones.
- To help assess these you can refer to CIMA ethical principles, your own sense of what is fair and whether one party is being disadvantaged in favour of another.
- With the first statement, it seems unfair that managers get bonuses whether or not they have done anything to deserve them, and that workers cannot gain rewards even if they excel in everything.
- The second statement focusses on the confusion between legal and ethical factors. Just because Laleham is acting within the law does not automatically mean it is also acting ethically.

The required answers are thus:

| Statement | True | False |
|---|---|---|
| The Chief Executive's policy on employees pay raises doubts about the ethical nature of the leadership and culture of Laleham Ltd. | ✓ | |
| Because Laleham Ltd complies with the NMW regulations, it is automatically considered to be behaving ethically in relation to its employees. | | ✓ |

## Task 1.1(f)

The scenario now switches to a completely different organisation altogether:

| Ian is an accountant who has just started working for Penton Ltd, reporting to Hettie, who is also an accountant. Ian has discovered a material error in Penton Ltd's last corporation tax return. |
|---|

You are then asked to advise what action Ian should take, the options being as follows:

| | |
|---|---|
| Resign. | |
| Advise HMRC of the error without disclosing any information to Hettie or Penton Ltd. | |
| Tell Hettie about the error and recommend that Penton Ltd disclose the error to HMRC. | |

Key considerations:

- There are very specific rules relating to ethics and taxation – many students may prefer to you can look these up in the exam within the reference material supplied.
- Clicking on "Taxation – 160.1 to 160.9" reveals the following:

> ***160.9***
>
> When a member learns of a material error or omission in a tax return of a prior year, or of a failure to file a required tax return, the member has a responsibility to advise promptly the client or employer of the error or omission and recommend that disclosure be made to HMRC. If the client or employer, after having had a reasonable time to reflect, does not correct the error, the member shall inform the client or employer in writing that it is not possible for the member to act for them in connection with that return or other related information submitted to the authorities. Funds dishonestly retained after discovery of an error or omission become criminal property and their retention amounts to money laundering by the client or employer. It is also a criminal offence in the UK for a person, including an accountant, to become concerned in an arrangement which he knows or suspects facilitates (by whatever means) the acquisition, retention, use or control of criminal property by or on behalf of another person...

- As before, you may feel that it would be simpler and take less time just to learn the key rules, or perhaps at least learn where to look!
- Resignation is usually a last resort, so is rarely the correct answer in questions unless other avenues have already been explored and found wanting.
- The error is last year's computations may have been accidental, based on inadequate information or deliberate. Unless Ian suspects Hettie of being involved in money laundering, then he should tell her about the error.
- Whenever a material error is found in tax computations then it is standard procedure to recommend to the parties concerned (employer or client) that **disclosure** be made to **HMRC**.
- If Penton Ltd, after having had a reasonable time to reflect, refuses to correct the error and make disclosure to HMRC, Ian should resign and report the refusal and the facts surrounding it to the MLRO (or NCA).

The required answers are thus:

| | |
|---|---|
| Resign. | |
| Advise HMRC of the error without disclosing any information to Hettie or Penton Ltd. | |
| Tell Hettie about the error and recommend that Penton Ltd disclose the error to HMRC. | ✓ |

### Task 1.1(g)

The situation then develops where money laundering is the issue:

| |
|---|
| Hettie realises that she has inadvertently become involved in Penton Ltd's money laundering operation. |

You are asked what Hettie needs to do to have a defence against a money laundering charge, with the options being:

| |
|---|
| A protected disclosure |
| An authorised disclosure |
| A prompt disclosure |

Key considerations:

- There are very specific rules relating to money laundering – make sure you know the detail.
- Any person who realises they may have engaged in or be about to engage in money laundering should make what is known as an **authorised disclosure** to the **NCA**.
- This may provide a defence against charges of money laundering provided the disclosure is made before the act is carried out (and NCA's consent to the act is obtained), or it is made as soon as possible after the act is done with good reason being shown for the delay.

The required answer is thus:

| |
|---|
| An authorised disclosure |

# Task 1.2

## Introduction

In the sample assessment, task 1.2 correlates with assessment objective 2:

| Assessment objective 2 | Prepare accounting records and respond to errors, omissions and other concerns, in accordance with accounting and ethical principles and relevant regulations |
|---|---|

This task is based on the workplace scenario of BLM & Co.

### Task 1.2(a and b)

To start with you are given a VAT control account and two errors to deal with:

> On reviewing BLM & Co's day books, you have found two errors:
>
> - Output VAT of £2,983.50 on a sales invoice was wrongly recorded as sales on 29 March.
> - A supplier had overstated input VAT by £50 on an invoice received and posted by BLM on 27 March.
>
> You prepare journals to correct these errors.

You are asked to determine, what the revised balance carried down on the VAT account will be once the journals have been processed.

Key considerations:

- This requires knowledge of how to correct errors using the VAT aspects of your financial accounting and bookkeeping knowledge.
- In part (d) we were looking at box 1 of the VAT return, so only interested in the sales side – here we need to consider the whole VAT account.
- The first error means that output VAT has been **understated** by £2,983.50.
- The second error means that input VAT has been **overstated** by £50.
- The net result is that the amount owed to HMRC will be **understated** by 2,983.50 **+** 50 = £3,033.50.
- This means the revised balance should be 61,482.13 + 3,033.50 = **64,515.63**.
- This will be brought down as a **credit** balance and represents the amount owed to HMRC.

### Task 1.2(c)

You are then given a scenario with an ethical dimension to the VAT:

| You discover that BLM & Co has been supplying sinks to Malone Ltd, a company owned and run by the brother of your fully qualified colleague, Jed Malone. When you look at the relevant invoices you realise that Jed has been misrecording VAT so that BLM & Co's sales to Malone Ltd are overstated. As a result, Malone Ltd qualifies for a 15% trade discount on its future purchases from BLM & Co. |
|---|

You are asked to identify which type of ethical threat is being faced by Jed Malone:

| | |
|---|---|
| A self-review threat to professional competence and due care. | |
| A familiarity threat to objectivity. | |
| An intimidation threat to professional behaviour. | |

Key considerations:

- If you cannot remember the detail, then you can look up the different types of ethical threat in the reference materials under "Threats and safeguards – 100.12".
- Remember that
  - a self-review threat may occur when previous judgement needs to be re-evaluated by the member responsible for that judgement
  - a familiarity threat may occur when, because of a close or personal relationship, a member becomes too sympathetic to the interests of others
  - an intimidation threat may occur when a member may be deterred from acting objectively by threats, whether real or perceived.
- Here, because of Jed's relationship with his brother, we have a familiarity threat.

| | |
|---|---|
| A self-review threat to professional competence and due care. | |
| A familiarity threat to objectivity. | ✓ |
| An intimidation threat to professional behaviour. | |

## Task 1.2(d)

The scenario is now updated as follows:

| You conclude that the deliberate misrecording of VAT is unethical behaviour by Jed Malone. |
|---|

You are asked what your next action should be from the following options:

| | |
|---|---|
| Send a Suspicious Activity Report to the National Crime Agency. | |
| Tell Brian and Lakmani about your concerns. | |

Key considerations:

- There is nothing here to suggest that money laundering is an issue, so sending a SAR to the NCA would be premature. The question specifically states the "next" action.
- It makes much more sense to report the issue to the partners, Brian and Lakmani so that they can investigate and take appropriate action.

| | |
|---|---|
| Send a Suspicious Activity Report to the National Crime Agency. | |
| Tell Brian and Lakmani about your concerns. | ✓ |

## Task 1.2(e)

The scenario moves forward in time to the following:

| On the morning of 16 April, Jed Malone is dismissed for misconduct by BLM & Co and leaves the office. You are temporarily BLM & Co's only accountant. A VAT officer will be coming to the office for a planned visit on the afternoon of 16 April. You are not prepared for this visit and do not believe you can answer any questions from the VAT officer effectively. Brian and Lakmani insist that you must be present and deal with the VAT officer without assistance. |
|---|

As before, you are asked for your "next" action from 3 options:

| | |
|---|---|
| Resign from BLM & Co. | |
| Request that the visit by the VAT officer is postponed. | |
| Agree to deal with the VAT officer in line with your employers' instructions. | |

Key considerations:

- As stated when looking at task 1.1(f), resignation is rarely the correct answer in questions unless other avenues have already been explored and found wanting.
- Agreeing to deal with the VAT officer would compromise the ethical principle of professional competence, so requesting that the visit be postponed is the best option.

| | |
|---|---|
| Resign from BLM & Co. | |
| Request that the visit by the VAT officer is postponed. | ✓ |
| Agree to deal with the VAT officer in line with your employers' instructions. | |

### Task 1.2(f)

You are now asked to insert four figures into a sales ledger control account (SLCA) using your bookkeeping knowledge.

Key considerations:

- It is worth considering the double entry required for each item:
- Receipts from credit customers:

  Dr Cash

  Cr SLCA
- Sales to credit customers:

  Dr SLCA

  Cr Sales
- Returns from credit customers:

  Dr Sales returns

  Cr SLCA
- Irrecoverable debts written off:

  Dr VAT (subject to various conditions being met)

  Cr SLCA

The updated SLCA thus looks like this:

| | £ | | £ |
|---|---|---|---|
| Balance b/d | 492,409 | Cash book | 934,076 |
| Sales day book | 970,370 | Sales returns day book | 21,177 |
| | | Journal (irrecoverable debt) | 4,330 |
| | | | |
| | | Balance c/d | 487,354 |
| **Total** | 1462779 | **Total** | 1446937 |

### Task 1.2(g)

This asks for the balancing figure for the above revised SLCA.

We need an additional (1462779 – 1446937) **15842** on the credit side.

| **£** | **15842** |
|---|---|

### Task 1.2(h)

Next you are asked what this difference could represent from three choices:

| | |
|---|---|
| Discounts allowed. | |
| Cheque from customer returned unpaid by the bank. | |
| Cash sales. | |

Key considerations:

- As before, it is worth considering the double entry required for each item:
- Discounts allowed – reduces the amount owed:

  Dr Discounts allowed (expense)

  Cr SLCA
- Returned cheque – reinstate the debt:

  Dr SLCA

  Cr Cash
- Cash sales do not go via the SLCA:

  Dr Cash

  Cr Sales

- Out of these the only option that generates a credit entry into the SLCA is the first:

| | |
|---|---|
| Discounts allowed. | ✓ |
| Cheque from customer returned unpaid by the bank. | |
| Cash sales. | |

### Task 1.2(i)

Next you are asked about irrecoverable debts. Remember that irrecoverable debts must relate to specific customers, whereas an allowance for doubtful debts can be related to specific customers or calculated in general terms as a percentage.

The correct answer is thus:

The amount of an irrecoverable debt **always relates to a specified customer.**

## Task 1.3

### Introduction

In the sample assessment, task 1.3 correlates with assessment objective 3:

| | |
|---|---|
| Assessment objective 3 | Apply ethical and accounting principles when preparing final accounts for different types of organisation, develop ethical courses of action and communicate relevant information effectively |

Task 1.3 is, therefore, primarily about ethics but in the context of preparing accounts.

Again this is based on the workplace scenario of BLM & Co.

### Task 1.3(a)(i) – 2 marks

The task starts by presenting you with an ethical dilemma:

| |
|---|
| Today's date is 28 February 20X8.<br>Brian has asked you to prepare some financial statements urgently. These include a statement of cash flows and a cash budget. He needs to send these to the bank by the end of the week in support of a loan application. Brian tells you that obtaining the loan is very important for the survival of the business. The jobs of everyone in the business depend on this. Your studies so far have not covered statements of cash flows or cash budgets. |

You are then asked to describe TWO threats to your ethical principles that you face as a result of Brian's request, referring to the conceptual framework of principles, threats and safeguards in the Code of Professional Ethics where relevant.

Key considerations:

- We saw similar scenarios in task 1.1. The difference is that, here, the scenario is slightly longer and, in this requirement you are not given options to choose between. Instead of identifying issues, you have to explain them.
- When you read through the scenario, ask yourself which of the 5 ethical principles are/is involved and don't be surprised if there is more than one.

  Professional competence and due care could be compromised as you don't have the required expertise.

  Integrity could be compromised if you feel pressure to undertake the work before you are ready, or to make the figures look more positive then then really are.

  Similarly objectivity could be compromised as you might be biased due to the implied threat to your own job security.
- Next see if you can identify which threats are involved:

  A self-interest threat due to the risk of losing your job

  An intimidation threat due to pressure from Brian

  Possibly even a familiarity threat as friends and colleagues may also lose their jobs.
- As with task 1.1 use the reference material if you get stuck here.

The final answer could thus look like the following.

| (i) I am facing familiarity, intimidation and self-interest threats **(1)** because the partners of BLM & Co are trying to appeal to my loyalty to colleagues and fear of losing my job **(1).** |
|---|

### Task 1.3(a)(ii) – 1 mark

Key considerations:

- You are not competent to do the task, so you could either recommend asking for training or/and asking that someone with more experience and expertise does it. If possible, suggest who that might be.

This would give an answer like the following:

| (ii) I would tell Brian that I can only complete the tasks they have requested if I have additional training/qualified support/supervision to do so (which will take time) **(1)** OR I would tell Brian that I cannot undertake the task competently so it should be given to someone else **(1).** |
|---|

### Task 1.3(a)(iii) – 1 mark

Here you have to explain your response.

Key considerations:

- You are not competent to do the task, so to do so would compromise your ethical principle of professional competence and due care.
- You would also compromise your integrity to continue while knowing you would not be able to do the job properly.

This would give an answer like the following:

| (iii) I do not have the experience, expertise (knowledge and skills), or time to complete the tasks properly. It would be a breach of the principles of professional competence and due care, and integrity, to attempt to do so immediately. **(1).** |
|---|

### Task 1.3(b) – 1 mark

Next you have to state why you have a professional duty to uphold sustainability at work.

Key considerations:

- The easiest way to argue this is to refer to the public interest. Sustainability is in the public interest and accountants have a duty to work in the public interest.

This would give an answer like the following:

| Ensuring sustainability is in the public interest, and accountants have a responsibility to work in the public interest **(1).** |
|---|

## Task 1.3(c) – 10 marks

A different style of task, where you are asked to respond to a letter requesting information.

> Good morning Sam,
>
> Brian and I are considering starting to operate the business as a limited company. I would like you to tell me more about the implications of a partnership becoming a limited company.
>
> Please include three sections in your response to me as follows:
>
> - A brief description of a limited company
> - A summary of our position as owners if the business becomes a limited company
> - Explanations of one key advantage and one key disadvantage of operating as a limited company.

Part (c) is worth 10 marks, so you would have 18 minutes in the real assessment to attempt something like this.

Key considerations:

- Given the assessment is computer based, then you can use the answer box for planning purposes. Set up headings for each requirement and briefly jot down some ideas under each heading.

  For example,

  > **Limited Company**
  >
  > Separate legal entity
  >
  > Needs to be registered
  >
  > Company accounts separate from owner
  >
  > **Position as owners**
  >
  > Shareholders and/or directors
  >
  > SH – implications – dividends, votes, other SH?
  >
  > Directors – implications – salary, control, other directors?
  >
  > **Advantages of being a limited co**
  >
  > Limited liability
  >
  > Raising finance
  >
  > **Disadvantages**
  >
  > Regulation – e.g. filing accounts, audit

- Check again that you are answering the question and then select which points to write up (e.g. the requirement asks for just one advantage). Try to add value to your answer by developing points, explaining issues, applying them to the specific circumstances, etc.

The suggested model answer to this is as follows:

Hello Lakamni

Thank you for your email of 28/2/X8

(1) A limited company is a business structure which is a separate legal entity distinct from its owners (known as shareholders).

It needs to be registered at Companies House.

A company's accounts and finances are separate from the personal finances of its owners.

(2) A company is owned by shareholders, who have equity shares in the company.

Persons acting as directors are responsible for running the company. A company must have at least one shareholder and at least one director.

You and Brian can remain as the only owners if you own all the shares in the company between you; your ownership will be diluted if you include more shareholders.

You can continue to run the company, acting as its only directors, or you may appoint additional directors.

Directors may be paid a salary by the company from its pre-tax profits. Shareholders may receive dividends paid from its after-tax profits.

Any after-tax profits that are not paid out as dividends are reinvested in the company on the shareholder's behalf.

(3) The key advantage of operating as a limited company is that of limited liability for the owners.

While you as partners in BLM & Co currently have unlimited liability for all the debts of the business, shareholders' liability for any unpaid debts of the company is limited and they only stand to lose their investments in shares. The company as a separate legal entity remains fully liable for its debts.

The key disadvantage of operating as a limited company is that companies are heavily regulated.

> There are a number of accounting regulations involved with running a limited company, and the statutory requirements of the Companies Act 2006 apple, as do accounting standards. This means that there is a much greater administrative burden than for a partnership. A company must file accounts each year before a certain date and it must file documents when it is set up. All this extra administration bears a cost.
>
> I hope this is useful to you. Please contact me if you have any questions.
>
> Kind regards, Sam

Marking guidance for this is shown as follows:

| Marks | Descriptor |
|---|---|
| 0 | No response worthy of credit |
| 1–3 | Limited coverage of the three sections of information requested by Lakmani. Response is basic, relevant information is not communicated effectively and email structure incomplete. To access higher marks in the band, the answer will show a minimal understanding of what a limited company is. |
| 4–7 | Broader coverage of the three sections of information requested by Lakmani. Response is generally well structured, information is relatively well communicated, explanations generally flow with ease. To access higher marks in the band, the answer will illustrate a range of technical knowledge about limited companies relevant to Lakmani's request. |
| 8–10 | Full coverage of the three sections of information requested by Lakmani. Information is communicated effectively throughout and the response is well structured. To access higher marks in the band, the answer will include a clear description of a limited company, a sound understanding of change in ownership if the business becomes a limited company, and a clear explanation of one advantage and one disadvantage of operating as a limited company. |

# PART 2

Part 2 consists of 2 tasks, each of which involves using spreadsheet skills to solve a variety of problems. Each is based on BLM & Co, a business which manufactures and sells sinks and each requires candidates to download a data file.

## Task 2.1

### Introduction

Task 2.1 continues the scenario as follows:

> Today's date is 20 April 20X8.
>
> BLM & Co had originally budgeted to make and sell 5,000 sinks in the quarter to 31 March 20X8. Due to a marketing campaign, however, it actually made and sold 6,000 sinks in the quarter.
>
> The original budget for the quarter to 31 March 20X8 is in the 'Original Budget' worksheet of the provided spreadsheet.

Here you are going to be flexing budgets and analysing variances.

### Task 2.1(a) – 9 marks

To start with you have to determine the growth % to use to flex the budget. This is based on sales volume, so simply involves comparing the 5000 budget with 6000 actual. A suitable formula for cell D1 could be

= (6000-5000)/5000

Don't forget to format this cell as a percentage to two decimal places (#.##%). This then gives 20.00% as the answer.

Next you need to flex the budget

Key considerations:

- Make sure you build absolute referencing when including the 20%. For example, in cell D5

  =C5*$D$1+C5

- Make sure you do not increase fixed costs when flexing.
- Actual results then need to be copied across.

This gives (with a little tidying up) the following:

| | A | B | C | D | E |
|---|---|---|---|---|---|
| 1 | | | | 20.00% | |
| 2 | | | | | |
| 3 | **BLM & Co: original budget for quarter ended 31 March 20X8** | | | | |
| 4 | **Item** | | **Original Budget £** | **Flexed budget £** | **Actual Results £** |
| 5 | Revenue | | 800,000 | 960,000 | 975,000 |
| 6 | Materials: | Direct materials 1 | 90,000 | 108,000 | 105,000 |
| 7 | Materials: | Direct materails 2 | 110,000 | 132,000 | 125,000 |
| 8 | Materials: | Direct materials 3 | 140,000 | 168,000 | 164,700 |
| 9 | Direct labour: | Skilled | 30,000 | 36,000 | 35,000 |
| 10 | Direct labour: | Unskilled | 70,000 | 84,000 | 81,500 |
| 11 | Variable overheads: | Supervision | 42,000 | 50,400 | 49,000 |
| 12 | Variable overheads: | Quality Control | 60,000 | 72,000 | 70,000 |
| 13 | Variable overheads: | Production planning | 55,000 | 66,000 | 60,000 |
| 14 | Fixed overheads: | Administration | 80,000 | 80,000 | 85,000 |
| 15 | Fixed overheads: | Selling and distribution | 90,000 | 90,000 | 110,000 |
| 16 | Operating Profit | | | | |

## Task 2.2(b) – 9 marks

Here we have to show the operating profit and set up another column and calculate variances.

To get the profit figures we need to deduct costs from revenue. So for the original budget the formula in cell C16 would be

=C5-SUM(C6:C15) or similar

For the variances key considerations are as follows:

- Variances are simply the difference between actual and flexed budget.
- However, make sure you set up formulae so that favourable variances are positive. This means that will revenue you want (Actual – flexed budget) but with costs it should be the other way round.

  So for revenue, cell F5 would contain

  =E5-D5

  But costs such as F6 would have

  =D6-E6
- Make sure cell F16 is just the sum of the variances above.

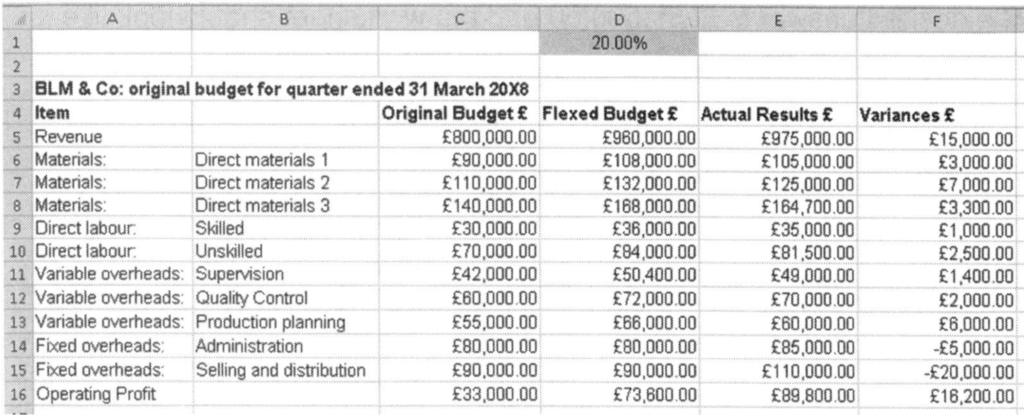

| | A | B | C | D | E | F |
|---|---|---|---|---|---|---|
| 1 | | | | 20.00% | | |
| 2 | | | | | | |
| 3 | BLM & Co: original budget for quarter ended 31 March 20X8 | | | | | |
| 4 | Item | | Original Budget £ | Flexed Budget £ | Actual Results £ | Variances £ |
| 5 | Revenue | | £800,000.00 | £960,000.00 | £975,000.00 | £15,000.00 |
| 6 | Materials: | Direct materials 1 | £90,000.00 | £108,000.00 | £105,000.00 | £3,000.00 |
| 7 | Materials: | Direct materials 2 | £110,000.00 | £132,000.00 | £125,000.00 | £7,000.00 |
| 8 | Materials: | Direct materials 3 | £140,000.00 | £168,000.00 | £164,700.00 | £3,300.00 |
| 9 | Direct labour: | Skilled | £30,000.00 | £36,000.00 | £35,000.00 | £1,000.00 |
| 10 | Direct labour: | Unskilled | £70,000.00 | £84,000.00 | £81,500.00 | £2,500.00 |
| 11 | Variable overheads: | Supervision | £42,000.00 | £50,400.00 | £49,000.00 | £1,400.00 |
| 12 | Variable overheads: | Quality Control | £60,000.00 | £72,000.00 | £70,000.00 | £2,000.00 |
| 13 | Variable overheads: | Production planning | £55,000.00 | £66,000.00 | £60,000.00 | £6,000.00 |
| 14 | Fixed overheads: | Administration | £80,000.00 | £80,000.00 | £85,000.00 | -£5,000.00 |
| 15 | Fixed overheads: | Selling and distribution | £90,000.00 | £90,000.00 | £110,000.00 | -£20,000.00 |
| 16 | Operating Profit | | £33,000.00 | £73,600.00 | £89,800.00 | £16,200.00 |

## Task 2.2(c) – 4 marks

This task gets you to check that the total of the variances in F16 equates to the difference between actual profit and the flexed budget (E16-D16).

One way of doing this is to enter the formula in cell F18:

=IF(F16=E16-D16,"Agreed","Check")

If you have any variances the wrong way round, then it will be revealed at this stage.

You are also asked to freeze so that the range A1:B16 always remains visible during scrolling.

## Task 2.2(d) – 3 marks

We now have to use the Goal Seek function to investigate what change in the actual Direct materials 3 cost figure (cell E8) would be required to generate an actual operating profit of £95,000 in cell E16.

Be careful to take the screen grab when requested otherwise your answer will be incomplete.

Using the goal seek function:

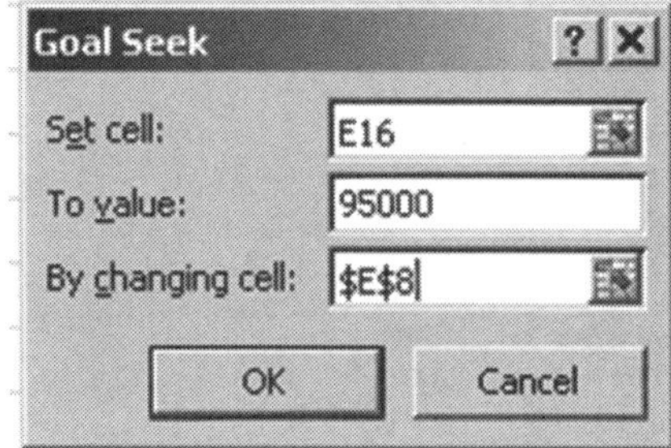

The desired answer is £159,500.00 and the worksheet should look like this:

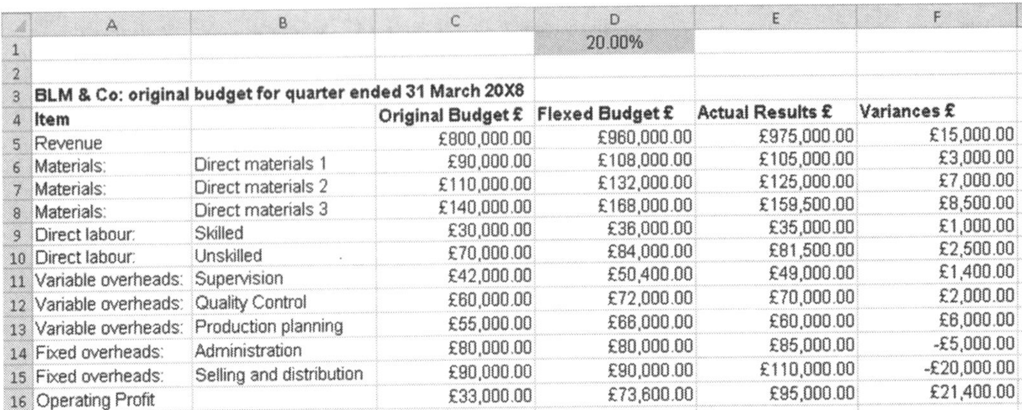

| | A | B | C | D | E | F |
|---|---|---|---|---|---|---|
| 1 | | | | 20.00% | | |
| 2 | | | | | | |
| 3 | **BLM & Co: original budget for quarter ended 31 March 20X8** | | | | | |
| 4 | **Item** | | **Original Budget £** | **Flexed Budget £** | **Actual Results £** | **Variances £** |
| 5 | Revenue | | £800,000.00 | £960,000.00 | £975,000.00 | £15,000.00 |
| 6 | Materials: | Direct materials 1 | £90,000.00 | £108,000.00 | £105,000.00 | £3,000.00 |
| 7 | Materials: | Direct materials 2 | £110,000.00 | £132,000.00 | £125,000.00 | £7,000.00 |
| 8 | Materials: | Direct materials 3 | £140,000.00 | £168,000.00 | £159,500.00 | £8,500.00 |
| 9 | Direct labour: | Skilled | £30,000.00 | £36,000.00 | £35,000.00 | £1,000.00 |
| 10 | Direct labour: | Unskilled | £70,000.00 | £84,000.00 | £81,500.00 | £2,500.00 |
| 11 | Variable overheads: | Supervision | £42,000.00 | £50,400.00 | £49,000.00 | £1,400.00 |
| 12 | Variable overheads: | Quality Control | £60,000.00 | £72,000.00 | £70,000.00 | £2,000.00 |
| 13 | Variable overheads: | Production planning | £55,000.00 | £66,000.00 | £60,000.00 | £6,000.00 |
| 14 | Fixed overheads: | Administration | £80,000.00 | £80,000.00 | £85,000.00 | -£5,000.00 |
| 15 | Fixed overheads: | Selling and distribution | £90,000.00 | £90,000.00 | £110,000.00 | -£20,000.00 |
| 16 | Operating Profit | | £33,000.00 | £73,600.00 | £95,000.00 | £21,400.00 |

## Task 2.2

For task 2.2 the scenario is updated as follows:

BLM & Co has suffered a computer crash. You have been asked to complete the half year sales spreadsheet for the six months ended 31 December 20X7 which was extracted immediately before the crash.

You have been given this spreadsheet which contains information relating to sales in the last six months of 20X7. In addition to the assessment tasks, this spreadsheet contains four worksheets: 'Invoices', 'Price list', 'Screen print' and 'BLM 1'.

The sales information contains nearly 400 invoices with the following headings:

| | A | B | C | D | E | F | G | H | I |
|---|---|---|---|---|---|---|---|---|---|
| 1 | | | | | | | | | |
| 2 | BLM & Co | | | | | | | VAT | 20% |
| 3 | | | | | | | | Average Gross Invoice Value | |
| 4 | | 20X7 sales of sinks for the last 6 months of trading through various outlets | | | | | | | |
| 5 | | | | | | | | | |
| 6 | **Type** | **Description** | **Item No** | **Quantity Sold** | **When** | **Where** | **Invoice No** | **Net Sales** | **Gross Sales** |
| 7 | Jade | 1 Bowl & drainer | 35698 | 46 | July | Internet | 281762 | | |
| 8 | Jade | 1 Bowl & drainer | 35698 | 47 | July | Direct | 281763 | | |
| 9 | Jade | 1 Bowl & drainer | 35698 | 34 | July | Jones & Co | 281764 | | |
| 10 | Jade | 1 Bowl & drainer | 35698 | 42 | July | Elders | 281765 | | |
| 11 | Jade | 1 Bowl & drainer | 35698 | 11 | July | Brinks | 281766 | | |
| 12 | Jade | 1 Bowl & drainer | 35698 | 44 | July | Ables | 281767 | | |
| 13 | Jade | 1 Bowl & drainer | 35698 | 39 | July | Elways | 281768 | | |
| 14 | Jade | 1 Bowl & drainer | 35698 | 43 | July | Zeebras | 281769 | | |
| 15 | Emerald | 1 Bowl reversible drainer | 28654 | 13 | July | Internet | 281722 | | |
| 16 | Emerald | 1 Bowl reversible drainer | 28654 | 12 | July | Direct | 281723 | | |
| 17 | Emerald | 1 Bowl reversible drainer | 28654 | 6 | July | Jones & Co | 281724 | | |
| 18 | Emerald | 1 Bowl reversible drainer | 28654 | 49 | July | Elders | 281725 | | |
| 19 | Emerald | 1 Bowl reversible drainer | 28654 | 12 | July | Brinks | 281726 | | |
| 20 | Emerald | 1 Bowl reversible drainer | 28654 | 11 | July | Ables | 281727 | | |

The price list is shown as

| | A | B | C | D | E |
|---|---|---|---|---|---|
| 1 | | | | | |
| 2 | | | ONLY Marketing are allowed to alter these prices | | |
| 3 | | | | | |
| 4 | Item No | Type | Description | Price | |
| 5 | 28654 | Emerald | 1 Bowl reversible drainer | £ 124.00 | |
| 6 | 35698 | Jade | 1 Bowl & drainer | £ 127.00 | |
| 7 | 15874 | Quartz | 1.5 square reversible | £ 128.00 | |
| 8 | 28791 | Quartz | 1 square reversible | £ 136.00 | |
| 9 | 26221 | Jade | 1.5 Bowl & drainer | £ 145.00 | |
| 10 | 28457 | Diamond | 1 cubic bowl & drainer | £ 165.00 | |
| 11 | 27894 | Emerald | 1.5 Bowl reversible drainer | £ 180.00 | |
| 12 | 35789 | Pearl | 1.5 reversible oval | £ 198.00 | |
| 13 | | | | | |

### Task 2.2(a) – 4 marks

The first task is to use a lookup function on the 'Item No' data to calculate the net sales using information from the Price List worksheet.

Key considerations:

- Sales will be volume (column D) × price
- To get the price you need to use the VLOOKUP function taking the data from the price list sheet. Make sure you use absolute referencing so you can copy the formulae.
- For example, the formula for cell H7 would be

  =D7*VLOOKUP(C7,'Price list'!$A$4:$D$12,4,FALSE)

Next you need to get gross sales value using the VAT figure in cell I2. Here you are told to use absolute referencing but only do so for the I2 reference.

Alternative ways of doing this in cell I7 would be

=H7*(1+$I$2)

=H7*$I$2 + H7

## Task 2.2(b) – 5 marks

Next you are asked to remove duplicates. There are a number of ways of doing this but the task specifies the use of the "remove duplicates" function.

Highlight the whole table of data and select Data > Remove Duplicates. Before you apply this you have to take a screen shot:

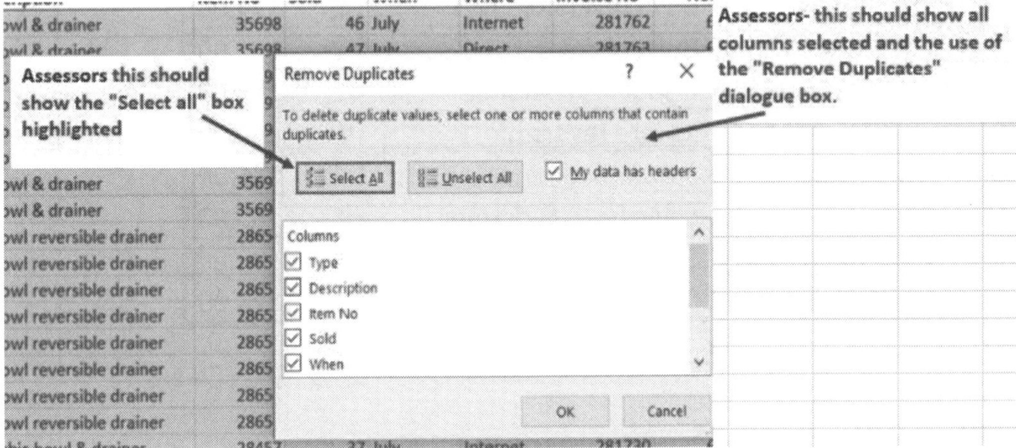


After you click "OK", you see the following popup

We therefore need to enter "2" into cell J2

Finally for this section you are asked to determine the average value of their invoices were for the year and complete some formatting. Gross sales are in column I so the easiest way to calculate the average is to use the average formula:

=AVERAGE(I7:I390)

### Task 2.2(c) – 6 marks

Part (c) involves using pivot tables to analyse sales of 'Diamond' type sinks.

There are a number of ways of doing this but make sure you select by type (Diamond) and set up the table to show months and numbers sold, giving:

| | |
|---|---|
| July | 227 |
| August | 197 |
| September | 253 |
| October | 243 |
| November | 220 |
| December | 219 |
| Grand Total | 1359 |

Applying a simple column bar chart gives:

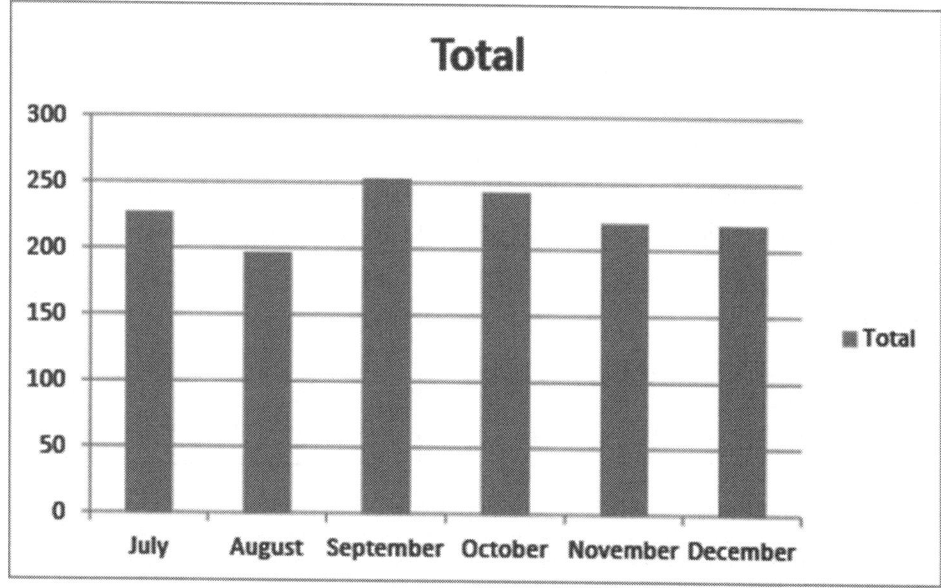


You are also asked to format the chart series to show highest sales for the period in black and lowest sales in red.

## Task 2.2(d) – 15 marks

Task 2.2(d) continues the scenario as follows:

> You are now preparing the final accounts for BLM & Co for the year ended 31 December 20X7.
>
> The statement of profit or loss for BLM & Co shows a profit for the year ended 31 December 20X7 of £250,000.
>
> The business is still operated as a partnership.
>
> You are given the following information arising from the partnership agreement:
>
> - Lakmani is entitled to a salary of £25,000 per annum.
> - Over the year, Brian has earned commission of £8,586 and Lakmani has earned commission of £8,500.
> - Brian has taken drawings of £91,200 over the year, and Lakmani has taken £84,400.
> - Interest on drawings has been calculated at £300 for Brian and £180 for Lakmani for the year ended 31 December 20X7.
> - The residual profit after adjustments is shared between Brian and Lakmani in the ratio 3:2.

This is simply a matter of inputting data into the correct cells and setting up formulae to determine totals, carry forward balances and to ensure the partnership rules are applied correctly, giving the following:

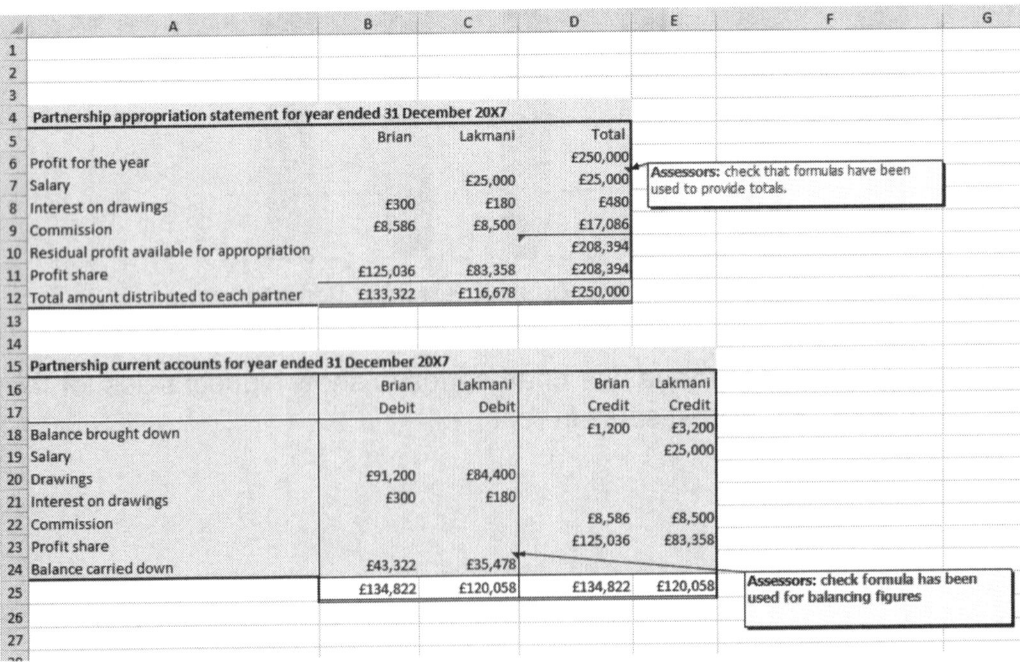

**Partnership appropriation statement for year ended 31 December 20X7**

| | Brian | Lakmani | Total |
|---|---|---|---|
| Profit for the year | | | £250,000 |
| Salary | | £25,000 | £25,000 |
| Interest on drawings | £300 | £180 | £480 |
| Commission | £8,586 | £8,500 | £17,086 |
| Residual profit available for appropriation | | | £208,394 |
| Profit share | £125,036 | £83,358 | £208,394 |
| Total amount distributed to each partner | £133,322 | £116,678 | £250,000 |

Assessors: check that formulas have been used to provide totals.

**Partnership current accounts for year ended 31 December 20X7**

| | Brian Debit | Lakmani Debit | Brian Credit | Lakmani Credit |
|---|---|---|---|---|
| Balance brought down | | | £1,200 | £3,200 |
| Salary | | | | £25,000 |
| Drawings | £91,200 | £84,400 | | |
| Interest on drawings | £300 | £180 | | |
| Commission | | | £8,586 | £8,500 |
| Profit share | | | £125,036 | £83,358 |
| Balance carried down | £43,322 | £35,478 | | |
| | £134,822 | £120,058 | £134,822 | £120,058 |

Assessors: check formula has been used for balancing figures

This completes the walk-through.

# Mock assessment – Questions

## Introduction

The spreadsheets files needed for part 2 of this assessment can be found within your MyKaplan account.

# PART 1

## Task 1.1

This task is based on the workplace scenario of HVN & Co, a business that manufactures guitar effects pedals. HVN & Co is owned and run by Helen and Vincent Ng in partnership.

You are Steve Jones, a part-qualified accounting technician, working in the accounts department of HVN & Co. You report to Sally Chan, the chief accountant.

Sarah Vin, a new trainee accountant with HVN & Co, has made two statements to you about how she believes the ethical code applies to her.

**(a) Are these statements true or false? (2 marks)**

| Statement | True | False |
|---|---|---|
| 'I do not have to follow the ethical code as I am not a fully qualified AAT member.' | | |
| 'As long as I make sure I don't break any laws, then I don't have to worry about ethical codes.' | | |

**(b) Show whether or not the ethical code specifically requires Sarah to take each of the following actions in order to act in line with the principle of professional competence. (2 marks)**

∇ Drop down list for task 1.1(b)

| Required |
|---|
| Not required |

| Action | Required/not required |
|---|---|
| Pass all her AAT exams first time. | ∇ |
| Decline from undertaking any tasks that she does not have the required skills to perform. | ∇ |

You are a friend of Sarah on a popular social media site and have noticed that she often talks about projects that she is involved in at work, sometimes in considerable detail.

**(c) Which fundamental principle has Sarah breached? (2 marks)**

| | |
|---|---|
| Integrity | |
| Professional competence and due care | |
| Confidentiality | |

Sarah has been given a warning about her behaviour and additional training by Helen and Vincent Ng to help her understand confidentiality better.

However, she is still unsure and asks you when it is 'permissible' to share confidential information and when it may be 'required'.

**(d) Show whether in each case disclosure of confidential information is permissible or required. (3 marks)**

∇ Drop down list for task 1.1(d)

| |
|---|
| Permissible but not required |
| Required |

| | |
|---|---|
| Asked by the police to produce documents required as evidence in legal proceedings. | ∇ |
| Disclosure of money laundering. | ∇ |
| Where authorised by the company in connection with a new product launch. | ∇ |

In the market for guitar effects pedals, many potential customers are influenced by product reviews on websites and online forums. Because of this, Vincent Ng encourages all staff members to set up spoof online identities so they can post glowing reviews of HVN & Co products. Sarah has voiced concerns over doing this.

**(e) Show whether the following statements are true or false.**

**(2 marks)**

| **Statement** | **True** | **False** |
|---|---|---|
| Vincent's approach to online reviews raises doubts about the ethical nature of the leadership and culture of HVN & Co. | | |
| Posting spoof online reviews would breach the fundamental ethical principle of objectivity. | | |

You have been assisting with the preparation of this year's tax return and have found a letter from HMRC asking for further details on certain issues. You have seen the draft response but do not believe that this fairly represents the situation and might mislead the tax authorities.

**(f) What action should you now take? (2 marks)**

| | |
|---|---|
| Advise HMRC of the potential problem without talking to anyone at HVN & Co about it. | |
| Raise your concerns with Sally Chan (chief accountant). | |
| Resign. | |

Sally Chan, the chief accountant, has told you not to worry about correspondence with HMRC and that it is none of your business. Furthermore, she tells you that she suspects Helen and Vincent of money laundering and has alerted the authorities. You are not sure whether to believe her.

**(g) What action should you now take? (2 marks)**

| | |
|---|---|
| Go and discuss it with Helen and Vincent. | |
| Contact the NCA with your concerns. | |
| Resign. | |

**(Total: 15 marks)**

## Task 1.2

HVN &Co. buys some rare vintage transistors and other "new old stock" components from NOS Electronics. You happened to be looking at an August invoice from NOS Electronics and noticed that it overstated the VAT, thus increasing the amount HVN & Co. owed them.

Your colleague Carly Kale, a junior accounts assistant, is supposed to check this type of detail on invoices received when entering them into the purchases day book.

When you ask her about it, she starts crying and tells you that her boyfriend owns NOS electronics and that he told her she would "be in trouble" if she said anything. It appears that NOS electronics were recording the smaller, correct VAT amount within their books and keeping the difference when additional cash was received.

**(a) Applying the conceptual framework from the ethical code, which of the following describes the situation faced by Carly Kale when ignoring the VAT error? Choose ONE option. (2 marks)**

| | |
|---|---|
| A self-review threat to professional competence and due care. | |
| An advocacy threat to objectivity. | |
| An intimidation threat to professional behaviour. | |

In response to this you decide to call the AAT ethics helpline and discuss the invoices concerned for advice.

**(b) Complete the following statement by selecting ONE of the options below. (2 marks)**

In relation to the evidence and documents, the accountant must be particularly careful to ensure the fundamental principle of ____________________ is not breached when seeking guidance.

| | |
|---|---|
| confidentiality | |
| professional competence and due care | |
| professional behaviour | |

You conclude that the deliberate ignoring of the mis-recording of VAT is unethical behaviour by Carly Kale and that you should do something about it.

**(c) What should be your next action?** **(2 marks)**

| | |
|---|---|
| Send a Suspicious Activity Report to the National Crime Agency. | |
| Tell Sally Chan (chief accountant).about your concerns. | |
| Resign. | |

It is now 5 October 20X6.

Helen and Vincent Ng are worried whether there are other issues relating to the recording of purchases and amounts owed to suppliers. As a result of this, they ask you to perform a logic check of purchase ledger transactions for the month of September 20X7.

You identify the following information:

Corrected purchase ledger control account balance at 1 September 20X7: £254,875.

For September 20X6:

- Payments made to credit customers: £154,856.
- Purchases made on credit, including VAT: £160,487.
- Returns to credit suppliers, including VAT: £5,256.
- Contra with sales ledger control account: £2,500.

Amounts owed at 30 September 20X6, as confirmed by credit suppliers: £250,977.

**(d) Place each of the four options below into the appropriate column and enter the totals to reconstruct the purchases ledger control account for September 20X6.** **(2 marks)**

**Options:**

| | |
|---|---:|
| Cash book | 154,856 |
| Purchases day book | 160,487 |
| Purchases returns day book | 5,256 |
| Journal (contra) | 2,500 |

**Purchases ledger control account**

| | £ | | £ |
|---|---|---|---|
| | | Balance b/d | 254,875 |
| | | | |
| | | | |
| | | | |
| Balance c/d | 250,977 | | |
| **Total** | | **Total** | |

(e) **Calculate the missing figure in the purchases ledger control account.** **(1 mark)**

| £ | |
|---|---|

(f) **Which of the following could the missing figure represent?** **(2 marks)**

| | |
|---|---|
| Discounts received. | |
| Lost purchases invoices that never got recorded in the purchases day book. | |
| Cash purchases. | |

Having looked through the invoices you notice that some involve buying component containing rare metals. This makes you worry that the company is not focussing sufficiently on sustainability in its operations.

(g) **Complete the following definition of sustainability by selecting ONE of the options below.** **(2 marks)**

Sustainable development is development that meets the needs of ____________________without compromising the ability of future generations to meet their own needs.

| | |
|---|---|
| the world | |
| stakeholders | |
| the present | |

Sally Chan suggests that the company could start setting targets for energy usage in the factory.

**(h) Which of the three Ps of triple bottom line reporting (TBL) does this target relate to? (2 marks)**

| | |
|---|---|
| People | |
| Planet | |
| Profit | |

## Task 1.3

Today's date is 31 January 20X7.

HVN & Co sell some pedals via adverts in guitar magazines. Here, customers pay a deposit up front and then settle the balance when the pedals are sent out. You recently discovered that Sally Chan, the chief accountant has been mistreating customer deposits by recognising them as sales revenue as soon as customers paid their deposit rather than treating it as prepaid income (the correct treatment under company policy).

You discussed this with her to ascertain the reason why this occurred and she admitted that, whilst knowing that this was wrong she had agreed to do it as a result of a personal relationship that she was having with one of the sales team, who stood to win a bonus if sales targets were hit and, as Sally and the sales executive were planning to move in together soon, they needed the money for a house deposit.

**(a) Explain the ethical issues that Sally faced in this case. In your answer refer to ethical principles and threats in the Code of Professional Ethics where relevant. (8 marks)**

You have received the following email from Vincent Ng:

**To: Steve Jones**

**From: Vincent Ng**

**Date: 28/2/X7**

**Subject: HVN & Co: change in structure**

Good morning Steve,

Helen and I are considering starting to operate the business as a limited company. I would like you to tell me more about the implications of a partnership becoming a limited company.

Please include a brief description of a limited company and explanations of two key advantages and two key disadvantages of operating as a limited company.

Thanks

Vincent

**(b) Reply to Vincent, addressing all the points that have been raised. (7 marks)**

**To:**

**Subject:**

**From:** Steve Jones

**Date:** 28/2/X7

**(Total: 15 marks)**

# PART 2

## Task 2.1 (30 marks)

You are Steve Jones, a part-qualified accounting technician. You work for HVN & Co, a business which manufactures and sells guitar effects pedals. HVN & Co is owned and run by Helen and Vincent Ng in partnership.

You cover all aspects of bookkeeping and accountant for the business.

Today's date is 1 February 20X8.

You are preparing the final accounts for HVN & Co for the year ended 31 December 20X7 and helping determine variances.

To assist you with these you have been provided with the spreadsheet Text Mock – Task 2.1 Data file.

The statement of profit or loss for HVN & Co shows a profit for the year ended 31 December 20X7 of £550,000. The business is still operating as a partnership.

You are given the following information arising from the partnership agreement:

- Helen and Vincent are entitled to salaries of £50,000 and £45,000 per annum respectively.
- Vincent has lent the business £500,000 as a long term loan and gets paid interest at 6% per annum.
- Partners may take drawings out of the business but get charged interest at 1% per month once the cumulative drawings figure exceeds £25,000. This is then calculated on the month-end cumulative balance.
- The residual profit after adjustments is shared between Helen and Vincent in the ratio 2:1.

Details of the partners' monthly drawings are in a separate spreadsheet.

**You are required to prepare the appropriation account for HVN & Co for the year ended 31 December 20X7.**

**(a) Use the partnership data supplied in the table in the spreadsheet in the following manner:**

- **Format all headings to have bold size 12 font.**
- **Merge and centre the partners' names over their respective columns. Align the month column, including the heading, to the left. Align the other columns, including the category headers, to the right.**
- **Calculate the cumulative position of each partner for each month.**
- **Use an IF statement to calculate the interest on drawings for each partner for each month.**
- **Total each of the columns D and G.**
- **Custom Format the range of figures in GBP currency with the thousand separator and two decimal places (e.g. £3,200.00).** **(4 marks)**

**(b) (i) On a new sheet, design a partnership appropriation statement in the spreadsheet to appropriate the profit for the year ended 31 December 20X7 between the two partners in accordance with the partnership agreement. Start with the profit for the year, and show clearly:**

- **Separate lines for each of the entitlements or charges adjusting this profit. Provide direct references from your answer to (a) where possible.**
- **The residual profit available for appropriation.**
- **Each partner's share of that residual profit.**
- **The total amount distributed to each partner for the year.**

**(ii) Custom format your statement to show GBP currency with the thousand separator, no decimals, and black font for positive. Ensure that any negative figures are Custom Formatted to red with a minus sign.** **(8 marks)**

Helen now asks you what figure the profit for the year would need to be if she were to have a total amount distributed to her of £350,000. Assume all other data is uncharged.

**(c) Amend your spreadsheet to show this:**

- **Open a new worksheet and name it 'Goal Seek'.**
- **Return to the original worksheet. In your partnership appropriation statement, use What if Goal Seek analysis to amend your data.**
- **When the completed Goal Seek dialogue box is showing – but BEFORE you click the OK button – take a screenshot (without pasting). The complete the Goal Seek analysis.**
- **Return to the 'Goal Seek' worksheet and paste the screenshot. (4 marks)**

On 1 September 20X7 HVN & Co started selling a new 'chorus' pedal.

The original budget for the quarter to 31 December 20X7 is in the 'Original Budget' worksheet of the provided spreadsheet. The original plan was to sell 150 per month at a price of £120 each, but actual sales for the period amounted to 165 units at the lower price of £118.

Download this spreadsheet file from the assessment environment.

**(d) In the worksheet called 'Original Budget', calculate the percentage to flex this budget in line with the information above and insert this percentage (%) figure into cell D1.**

- **In cell D4 enter the title 'Flexed budget'. Calculate the flexed budget for the relevant entries using absolute referencing where appropriate.**
- **In cell E4 enter the title 'Actual Results'. The actual revenue and costs for the quarter are shown in the worksheet headed 'Actual results'. Use 'copy' and 'paste link' to insert these from the source worksheet into the correct positions in column E of the 'Original Budget' worksheet. (2 marks)**

(e) In cell F4 insert the title 'Variances'. Calculate the variances for the revenue and each cost. Show these in column F so that favourable variances are positive and adverse variances negative.

- Calculate the operating profit for the original, flexed budget, and actual results.
- Calculate the total overall variance in cell F15.
- Use IF statements in column G to show whether variances are "Favourable" or "Adverse". (4 marks)

(f) Put an IF statement in F18 that will show 'Balanced' if the column totals balanced, and 'Check' if they do not.

- Colour cell F18 with a yellow background and a black border.
- Make sure all column headings are in bold, and adjust all cells so that the contents can be seen. (2 marks)

(g) The partners are wondering what increase in sales volume over the original budget would have given a profit of £10,000.

- Format cell D1 to show percentages to 1 decimal place.
- In cell A20 add the text 'Increase in sales over budget to give a profit of £10,000'.
- Using the goal seek function determine what increase in sales volume over budget (cell D1) would have resulted in a flexed budget profit of £10,000.
- Type this amount into cell D20. (4 marks)

(h) Next you need to identify the two largest variances.

- From the variances in cells F5 to F15, identify the two most significant variances. Insert appropriate text in column H adjacent to each variance, e.g. 'Most significant variance' and 'Second most significant variance'. (2 marks)

## Task 2.2 (25 marks)

You are Steve Jones, a part-qualified accounting technician. You work for HVN & Co, a business which manufactures and sells guitar effects pedals. HVN & Co is owned and run by Helen and Vincent Ng in partnership.

You cover all aspects of bookkeeping and accountant for the business.

Today's date is 15 April 20X7.

HVN & Co have introduced a new accounting system and are currently running both systems in parallel as part of the changeover process. Unfortunately the two systems are showing different sales figures, which is causing some alarm. You have been asked to complete the quarterly sales spreadsheet for the three months ended 31 March 20X7 which has been produced by going back to copies of the original sales invoices.

You have been given a spreadsheet which contains information relating to sales in the first three months of 20X7. It contains three worksheets: 'invoices', 'Price list' and 'Forecast'.

Download this spreadsheet file from the assessment environment and rename it.

(a) **Open this renamed file. In the worksheet called 'Invoices' use a lookup function on the 'Item No' data to calculate the net sales using information from the Price List worksheet. (2 marks)**

(b) **Use absolute referencing to calculate the gross sales value of each invoice using the VAT figure provided in cell H2. (2 marks)**

(c) **Check for and remove any duplicates in the invoices.**

- **Use conditional formatting to highlight duplicate invoice numbers.**
- **Remove duplicates.**
- **If there were any duplicates, enter the number found in I2.**
- **Make sure all the contents of every cell can be seen.**
- **Format the sales columns to 2 dp. (5 marks)**

(d) Insert a pivot chart and pivot table into a new worksheet of the net sales in each of the three months from January to March through the Amazon channel.

- Ensure the pivot table is sorted in chronological month order.
- Format the chart series to show best sales for the period in black and worst sales in red.
- Add a chart title 'Amazon Sales'.
- Enlarge the chart so that the whole legend is clearly seen.
- Produce a trend line, making it dashed and colour it red.
- Name this worksheet 'Amazon Sales'. (6 marks)

(e) Use your pivot table to determine the total sales for each month through all channels. Copy the values of these into the relevant cells in the worksheet 'Forecast'. (Note: make sure you set your pivot table back to just Amazon sales before saving).

Use the FORECAST function to predict the sales for the next three months. (4 marks)

(f) Return to the 'Invoices' worksheet and filter the whole table by net sales to show the bottom ten net sales.

- Insert a subtotal formula in the net sales column to work out the average of the bottom ten sales.
- Insert a subtotal formula in the net sales column to count how many items are listed in the "bottom ten".
- Format this column as GBP currency (£).
- Use the filters to show how many of the bottom ten sales were to Bob's music shop. (6 marks)

(Total: 25 marks)

# Mock assessment – Answers

# Task 1.1

## Task 1.1(a)

| Statement | True | False |
|---|---|---|
| 'I do not have to follow the ethical code as I am not a fully qualified AAT member.' | | ✓ |
| 'As long as I make sure I don't break any laws, then I don't have to worry about ethical codes.' | | ✓ |

## Task 1.1(b)

| | |
|---|---|
| Pass all her AAT exams first time. | **Not Required** |
| Decline from undertaking any tasks that she does not have the required skills to perform. | **Required** |

## Task 1.1(c)

| | |
|---|---|
| Integrity | |
| Professional competence and due care | |
| Confidentiality | ✓ |

## Task 1.1(d)

| | |
|---|---|
| Asked by the police to produce documents required as evidence in legal proceedings. | **Required** |
| Disclosure of money laundering. | **Required** |
| Where authorised by the company in connection with a new product launch. | **Permissible** |

## Task 1.1(e)

| Statement | True | False |
|---|---|---|
| Vincent's approach to online reviews raises doubts about the ethical nature of the leadership and culture of HVN & Co. | ✓ | |
| Posting spoof online reviews would breach the fundamental ethical principle of objectivity. | | ✓ |

Note: with the second statement, the principle breached would be integrity, not objectivity.

### Task 1.1(f)

| | |
|---|---|
| Advise HMRC of the potential problem without talking to anyone at work about it. | |
| Raise your concerns with Sally Chan, the chief accountant. | ✓ |
| Resign. | |

### Task 1.1(g)

| | |
|---|---|
| Go and discuss it with Helen and Vincent. | |
| Contact the NCA with your concerns. | ✓ |
| Resign. | |

Note: If you talk to Helen and Vincent, then you may be guilty of "tipping off" if they are involved in money laundering.

## Task 1.2

### Task 1.2(a)

| | |
|---|---|
| A self-review threat to professional competence and due care. | |
| An advocacy threat to objectivity. | |
| An intimidation threat to professional behaviour. | ✓ |

### Task 1.2(b)

| | |
|---|---|
| Confidentiality | ✓ |
| Professional competence and due care | |
| Professional behaviour | |

### Task 1.2(c)

| | |
|---|---|
| Send a Suspicious Activity Report to the National Crime Agency. | |
| Tell Sally Chan (chief accountant).about your concerns. | ✓ |
| Resign. | |

## Task 1.2(d)

**Purchases ledger control account**

| | £ | | £ |
|---|---|---|---|
| | | Balance b/d | 254,875 |
| Bank payments | 154,856 | Purchases (PDB) | 160,487 |
| Purchase returns | 5,256 | | |
| Contra with SLCA | 2,500 | | |
| Balance c/d | 250,977 | | |
| **Total** | **413,589** | **Total** | **415,362** |

## Task 1.2(e)

We need an additional (415,362 – 413,589) **1,773** on the debit side.

| **£** | **1,773** |
|---|---|

## Task 1.2(f)

| | |
|---|---|
| Discounts received. | ✓ |
| Lost purchases invoices that never got recorded in the purchases day book. | |
| Cash purchases. | |

**(g) Complete the following definition of sustainability by selecting ONE of the options below.** **(2 marks)**

Sustainable development is development that meets the needs of ______________________ without compromising the ability of future generations to meet their own needs.

| | |
|---|---|
| the world | |
| stakeholders | |
| the present | ✓ |

**(h) Which of the three Ps of triple bottom line reporting (TBL) does this target relate to?** **(2 marks)**

| | |
|---|---|
| People | |
| Planet | ✓ |
| Profit | |

# Task 1.3

## Task 1.3(a) – 8 marks

Sally has potentially breached the following ethical guidelines.

**Integrity** – It would appear that Sally and the sales executive have broken this principle by allowing the sales of HVN to be over stated to be paid a higher bonus, which is clearly unacceptable.

**Objectivity** – It would seem that Sally has allowed her relationship with the sales executive to cloud her judgement as to the treatment of the customer's deposits. She was motivated either as a result of wanting to help the sales executive to achieve targets, or as a result of personally benefiting from the bonus that the sales executive would earn.

**Professional Behaviour** – Sally has not followed the correct company procedure and has contravened relevant accounting standards.

Sally was facing the following ethical threats.

**Familiarity Threat** – Sally may have agreed to mis-record the sales revenue due to the pressure that the sales executive was under to achieve the sales target. It is unlikely that she would have been this sympathetic had she not been in a relationship with the sales executive.

**Self Interest Threat** – Here, due to the personal relationship that exists between Sally and the sales executive and their need to raise a deposit for a house, it could be argued that Sally would be a direct beneficiary of the sales executive's bonus which has resulted in a temptation to engage in this action.

## Task 1.3(b)

Hello Vincent

Thank you for your email of 28/2/X8

(1) A limited company is a business structure which is a separate legal entity distinct from its owners (known as shareholders).

It needs to be registered at Companies House.

A company's accounts and finances are separate from the personal finances of its owners.

(2) The key advantage of operating as a limited company is that of limited liability for the owners.

While you as partners in HVN & Co currently have unlimited liability for all the debts of the business, shareholders' liability for any unpaid debts of the company is limited and they only stand to lose their investments in shares. The company as a separate legal entity remains fully liable for its debts.

Another advantage of becoming a limited company is the ability to introduce additional owners through share issues, making raising finance easier.

The key disadvantage of operating as a limited company is that companies are heavily regulated.

There are a number of accounting regulations involved with running a limited company, and the statutory requirements of the Companies Act 2006 apply, as do accounting standards. This means that there is a much greater administrative burden than for a partnership. A company must file accounts each year before a certain date and it must file documents when it is set up. All this extra administration bears a cost.

Another key disadvantage of becoming a company is the need for an annual audit, involving both cost and inconvenience.

I hope this is useful to you. Please contact me if you have any questions.

Kind regards

Steve

## Task 2.1

### Task 2.1(a) – 4 marks

To get the cumulative balance there are a number of methods. One of the simplest would be for cell C7:

=C6+B7

You then need to apply the interest rule. To do this you need to use an IF statement.

For example, in cell D6 you could have

=IF(C6>25000,C6*0.01,0)

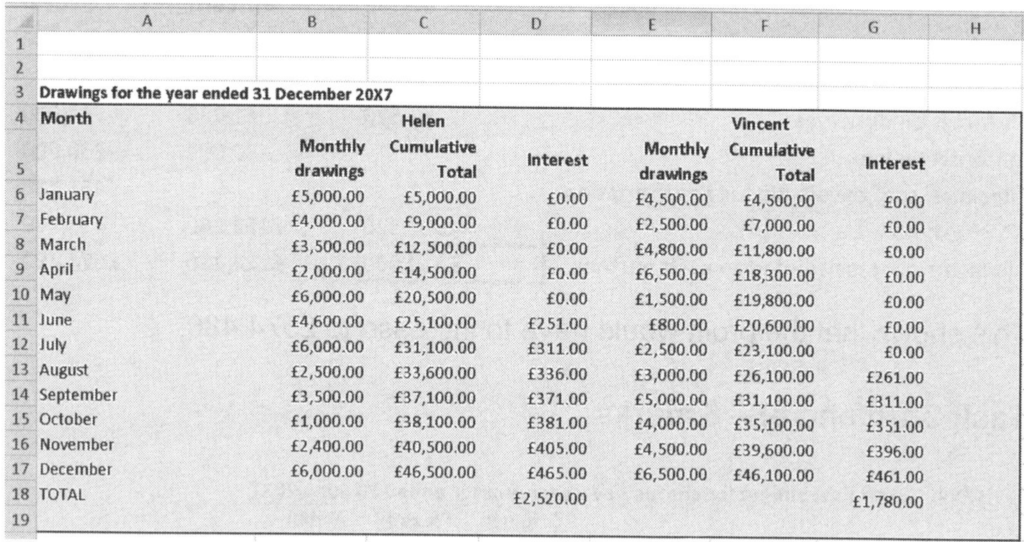

**Drawings for the year ended 31 December 20X7**

| Month | Helen Monthly drawings | Helen Cumulative Total | Helen Interest | Vincent Monthly drawings | Vincent Cumulative Total | Vincent Interest |
|---|---|---|---|---|---|---|
| January | £5,000.00 | £5,000.00 | £0.00 | £4,500.00 | £4,500.00 | £0.00 |
| February | £4,000.00 | £9,000.00 | £0.00 | £2,500.00 | £7,000.00 | £0.00 |
| March | £3,500.00 | £12,500.00 | £0.00 | £4,800.00 | £11,800.00 | £0.00 |
| April | £2,000.00 | £14,500.00 | £0.00 | £6,500.00 | £18,300.00 | £0.00 |
| May | £6,000.00 | £20,500.00 | £0.00 | £1,500.00 | £19,800.00 | £0.00 |
| June | £4,600.00 | £25,100.00 | £251.00 | £800.00 | £20,600.00 | £0.00 |
| July | £6,000.00 | £31,100.00 | £311.00 | £2,500.00 | £23,100.00 | £0.00 |
| August | £2,500.00 | £33,600.00 | £336.00 | £3,000.00 | £26,100.00 | £261.00 |
| September | £3,500.00 | £37,100.00 | £371.00 | £5,000.00 | £31,100.00 | £311.00 |
| October | £1,000.00 | £38,100.00 | £381.00 | £4,000.00 | £35,100.00 | £351.00 |
| November | £2,400.00 | £40,500.00 | £405.00 | £4,500.00 | £39,600.00 | £396.00 |
| December | £6,000.00 | £46,500.00 | £465.00 | £6,500.00 | £46,100.00 | £461.00 |
| TOTAL | | | £2,520.00 | | | £1,780.00 |

### Task 2.1(b) – 8 marks

| Partner's appropriation statement for year ended 31 December 20X8 | | | |
|---|---|---|---|
| | **Helen** | **Vincent** | **Total** |
| Profit for the year | | | £550,000 |
| Salary | £50,000 | £45,000 | -£95,000 |
| Interest on drawings | -£2,520 | -£1,780 | £4,300 |
| Interest on loan | | £30,000 | -£30,000 |
| Residual profit available for appropriation | | | £429,300 |
| Profit share | £286,200 | £143,100 | -£429,300 |
| Total amount distributed to each partner | £333,680 | £216,320 | £550,000 |

### Task 2.1(c) – 4 marks

Using the goal seek function:

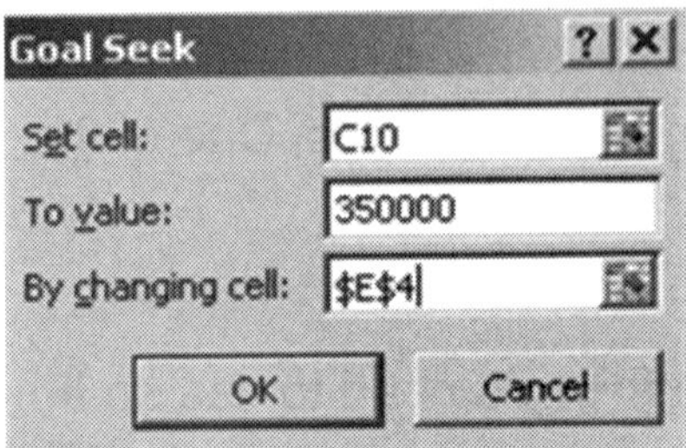


You get the following table:

| Partner's appropriation statement for year ended 31 December 20X8 | | | |
|---|---|---|---|
| | Helen | Vincent | Total |
| Profit for the year | | | £574,480 |
| Salary | £50,000 | £45,000 | -£95,000 |
| Interest on drawings | -£2,520 | -£1,780 | £4,300 |
| Interest on loan | | £30,000 | -£30,000 |
| Residual profit available for appropriation | | | £453,780 |
| Profit share | £302,520 | £151,260 | -£453,780 |
| Total amount distributed to each partner | £350,000 | £224,480 | £574,480 |

This shows that the profit would have to increase to £574,480.

### Task 2.1(d and e) – 6 marks

| 3 | HVN & Co: original budget for chorus pedals for quarter ended 30 June 20X7 | | | | | | |
|---|---|---|---|---|---|---|---|
| 4 | Item | | Original Budget | Flexed Budget | Actual Results | Variances | |
| 5 | Revenue | | 18000 | 19800 | 19470 | -330 | Adverse |
| 6 | Materials: | Case | 750 | 825 | 850 | -25 | Adverse |
| 7 | Materials: | Electrical Components | 2250 | 2475 | 2500 | -25 | Adverse |
| 8 | Materials: | Switches | 600 | 660 | 675 | -15 | Adverse |
| 9 | Direct labour: | Skilled | 3000 | 3300 | 3100 | 200 | Favourable |
| 10 | Direct labour: | Unskilled | 1500 | 1650 | 1620 | 30 | Favourable |
| 11 | Variable overheads: | Electricity, solder, etc | 450 | 495 | 510 | -15 | Adverse |
| 12 | Fixed overheads: | Production | 450 | 450 | 455 | -5 | Adverse |
| 13 | Fixed overheads: | Administration | 300 | 300 | 290 | 10 | Favourable |
| 14 | Fixed overheads: | Selling and distribution | 150 | 150 | 160 | -10 | Adverse |
| 15 | Operating Profit | | 8550 | 9495 | 9310 | -185 | Adverse |

Example of formula for column G – cell G5 has =IF(F5>0,"Favourable","Adverse")

### Task 2.1(f) – 2 marks

One way of doing this is to enter the formula in cell F18:

=IF(D15+F15=E15,"Balanced","Check")

## Task 2.1(g) – 4 marks

Using

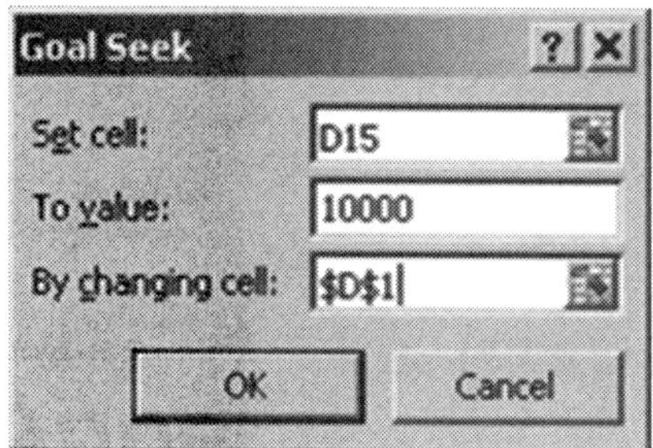


Gives a result of 15.3%.

## Task 2.1(h) – 2 marks

| | A | B | C | D | E | F | G | H |
|---|---|---|---|---|---|---|---|---|
| 1 | | | | 10.0% | | | | |
| 2 | | | | | | | | |
| 3 | **HVN & Co: original budget for chorus pedals for quarter ended 30 June 20X7** | | | | | | | |
| 4 | **Item** | | **Original Budget** | **Flexed Budget** | **Actual Results** | **Variances** | | |
| 5 | Revenue | | 18000 | 19800 | 19470 | -330 | Adverse | Most significant variance |
| 6 | Materials: | Case | 750 | 825 | 850 | -25 | Adverse | |
| 7 | Materials: | Electrical Components | 2250 | 2475 | 2500 | -25 | Adverse | |
| 8 | Materials: | Switches | 600 | 660 | 675 | -15 | Adverse | |
| 9 | Direct labour: | Skilled | 3000 | 3300 | 3100 | 200 | Favourable | Second most significant variance |
| 10 | Direct labour: | Unskilled | 1500 | 1650 | 1620 | 30 | Favourable | |
| 11 | Variable overheads: | Electricity, solder, etc | 450 | 495 | 510 | -15 | Adverse | |
| 12 | Fixed overheads: | Production | 450 | 450 | 455 | -5 | Adverse | |
| 13 | Fixed overheads: | Administration | 300 | 300 | 290 | 10 | Favourable | |
| 14 | Fixed overheads: | Selling and distribution | 150 | 150 | 160 | -10 | Adverse | |
| 15 | Operating Profit | | 8550 | 9495 | 9310 | -185 | Adverse | |
| 16 | | | | | | | | |
| 17 | | | | | | | | |
| 18 | Made and sold in quarter: 150 chorus pedals | | | | | Balanced | | |
| 19 | | | | | | | | |
| 20 | Increase in sales over budget to give a profit of £10,000 | | | 15.3% | | | | |

# Task 2.2

## Task 2.2(a) – 2 marks

- Sales will be volume (column C) × price, where the price must be looked up.
- For example, the formula for cell G7 could be

  =C7*VLOOKUP(B7,'Price list'!$A$4:$D$12,4,FALSE)

## Task 2.2(b) – 2 marks

Alternative ways of doing this in cell H7 would be

=G7*(1 + $H$2)

=G7*$H$2 + G7

## Task 2.2(c) – 5 marks

You are also asked to remove duplicates using conditional formatting. Note that this is a different approach from that specified in first sample assessment.

To do this you need to highlight column F (invoice numbers), select (on the home tab)

conditional formatting > highlight cells rules > duplicate values.

The invoices 81770, 81754, 81876 and 81907 have been repeated, so we need to enter "4" into cell J2 and delete one row of each double.

## Task 2.2(d) – 6 marks

Highlight the table of data and add the pivot table using the following fields.

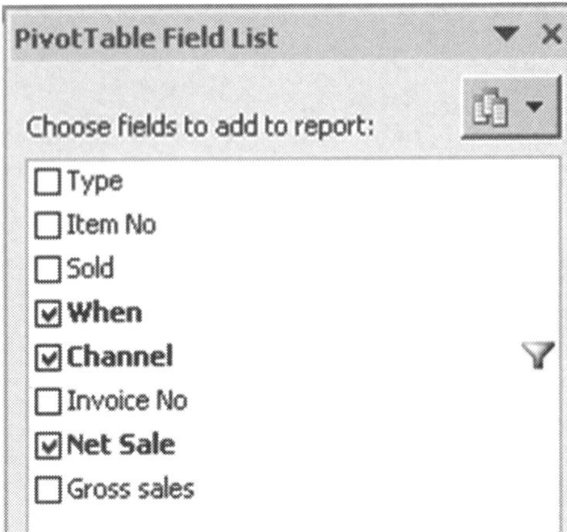

Filtering by channel > Amazon gives the following

| Sum of Net Sale | When | | | |
|---|---|---|---|---|
| Channel | January | February | March | Grand Total |
| Amazon | 16831 | 16808 | 16813 | 50452 |
| Grand Total | 16831 | 16808 | 16813 | 50452 |

**Chart**

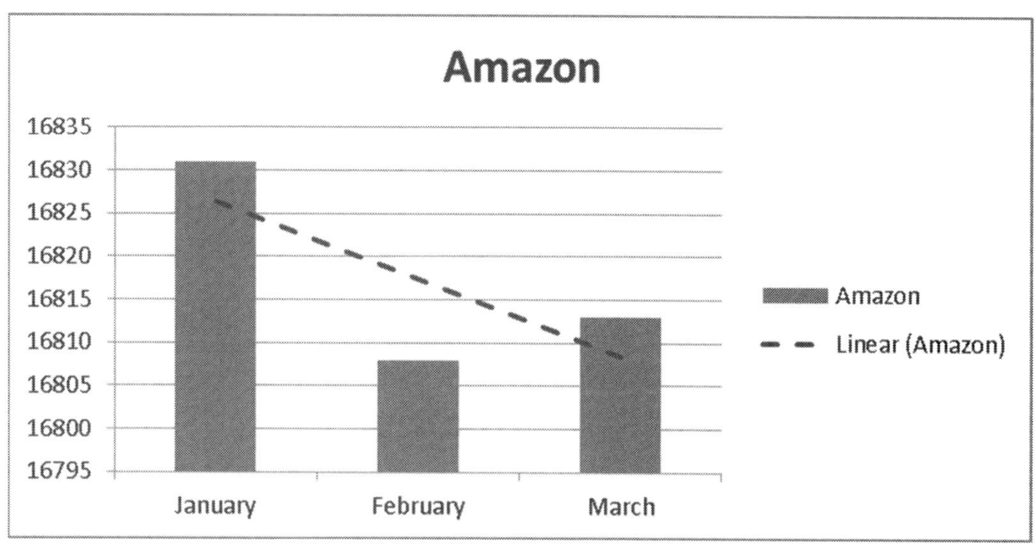


### Task 2.2(e) – 4 marks

In cell C12 we would enter =FORECAST(B8,$C$5:$C$7,$B$5:$B$7)

- The first aspect, A12, gives the "x" value of the month for which we need a forecast (month 10)
- The second, $C$5:$C$7, gives the range of sales figures ("y" values) we know (C5 to C7)
- Finally, $B$5:$B$7 gives the range of months ("x" values) for which we know sales figures (B5 to B7)

This gives the following forecasts:

| | A | B | C |
|---|---|---|---|
| 1 | Forecasts | | |
| 2 | | | |
| 3 | **Month** | **Month value** | **Monthly Sales** |
| 4 | | | |
| 5 | January | 1 | 76,425 |
| 6 | February | 2 | 71,410 |
| 7 | March | 3 | 73,335 |
| 8 | April | 4 | 70,633 |
| 9 | May | 5 | 69,088 |
| 10 | June | 6 | 67,543 |
| 11 | | | |

## Task 2.2(f) – 6 marks

Bottom ten actually delivers 11 results with an average of £208.27

Formula for average is =SUBTOTAL(1,G36:G358)

Formula for number is =SUBTOTAL(2,G36:G358)

Note: remember that with the SUBTOTAL formula the first number gives the type of function you want ("1" = average, "2" = the number, "9" = SUM, etc)

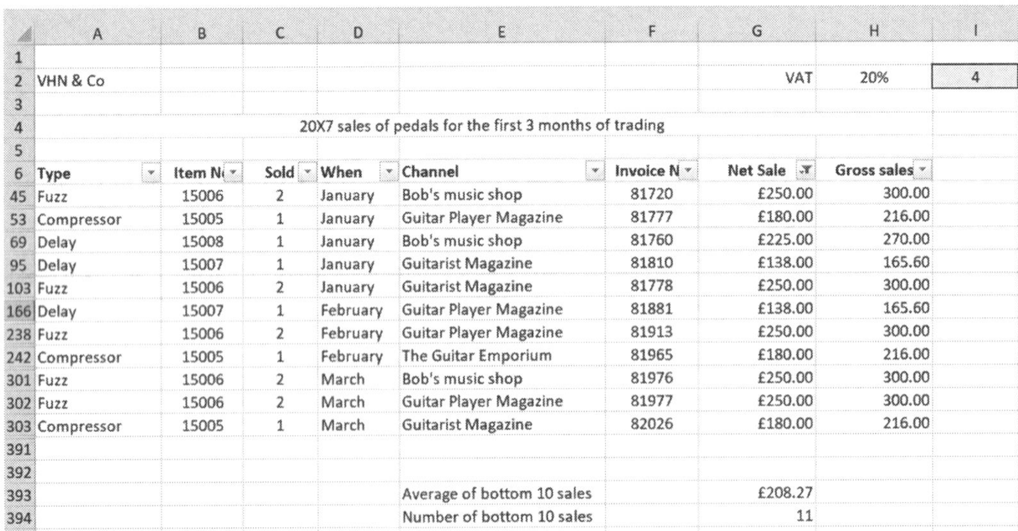

| | A | B | C | D | E | F | G | H | I |
|---|---|---|---|---|---|---|---|---|---|
| 1 | | | | | | | | | |
| 2 | VHN & Co | | | | | | VAT | 20% | 4 |
| 3 | | | | | | | | | |
| 4 | | | | | 20X7 sales of pedals for the first 3 months of trading | | | | |
| 5 | | | | | | | | | |
| 6 | Type | Item N | Sold | When | Channel | Invoice N | Net Sale | Gross sales | |
| 45 | Fuzz | 15006 | 2 | January | Bob's music shop | 81720 | £250.00 | 300.00 | |
| 53 | Compressor | 15005 | 1 | January | Guitar Player Magazine | 81777 | £180.00 | 216.00 | |
| 69 | Delay | 15008 | 1 | January | Bob's music shop | 81760 | £225.00 | 270.00 | |
| 95 | Delay | 15007 | 1 | January | Guitarist Magazine | 81810 | £138.00 | 165.60 | |
| 103 | Fuzz | 15006 | 2 | January | Guitarist Magazine | 81778 | £250.00 | 300.00 | |
| 166 | Delay | 15007 | 1 | February | Guitar Player Magazine | 81881 | £138.00 | 165.60 | |
| 238 | Fuzz | 15006 | 2 | February | Guitar Player Magazine | 81913 | £250.00 | 300.00 | |
| 242 | Compressor | 15005 | 1 | February | The Guitar Emporium | 81965 | £180.00 | 216.00 | |
| 301 | Fuzz | 15006 | 2 | March | Bob's music shop | 81976 | £250.00 | 300.00 | |
| 302 | Fuzz | 15006 | 2 | March | Guitar Player Magazine | 81977 | £250.00 | 300.00 | |
| 303 | Compressor | 15005 | 1 | March | Guitarist Magazine | 82026 | £180.00 | 216.00 | |
| 391 | | | | | | | | | |
| 392 | | | | | | | | | |
| 393 | | | | | Average of bottom 10 sales | | £208.27 | | |
| 394 | | | | | Number of bottom 10 sales | | 11 | | |

Filtering by Bob's Music Shop as well shows 3 results:

| | A | B | C | D | E | F | G | H | I |
|---|---|---|---|---|---|---|---|---|---|
| 1 | | | | | | | | | |
| 2 | VHN & Co | | | | | | VAT | 20% | 4 |
| 3 | | | | | | | | | |
| 4 | | | | | 20X7 sales of pedals for the first 3 months of trading | | | | |
| 5 | | | | | | | | | |
| 6 | Type | Item N | Sold | When | Channel | Invoice N | Net Sale | Gross sales | |
| 45 | Fuzz | 15006 | 2 | January | Bob's music shop | 81720 | £250.00 | 300.00 | |
| 69 | Delay | 15008 | 1 | January | Bob's music shop | 81760 | £225.00 | 270.00 | |
| 301 | Fuzz | 15006 | 2 | March | Bob's music shop | 81976 | £250.00 | 300.00 | |
| 391 | | | | | | | | | |
| 392 | | | | | | | | | |
| 393 | | | | | Average of bottom 10 sales | | £241.67 | | |
| 394 | | | | | Number of bottom 10 sales | | 3 | | |

# Appendix 1: Advanced Bookkeeping

## Introduction

This chapter recaps the key aspects of the underlying Advanced Bookkeeping Unit.

| UNIT LEARNING OBJECTIVES STILL RELEVANT FOR THE SYNOPTIC ASSESSMENT | |
|---|---|
| LO1 | Apply the principles of advanced double-entry bookkeeping |
| LO2 | Implement procedures for the acquisition and disposal of non-current assets |
| LO3 | Prepare and record depreciation calculations |
| LO4 | Record period end adjustments |
| LO5 | Produce and extend the trial balance |

# LO1 Apply the principles of advanced double-entry bookkeeping

## 1.1 Demonstrate the accounting equation

- Assets – Liabilities = Capital + Profit – Drawings

## 1.2 Classify assets, liabilities and equity in an accounting context

- Assets include non-current (tangible and intangible) and current (inventory, receivables, etc) – would expect these to have a debit balance
- Liabilities include non-current (e.g. bank loans) and current (e.g. payables, etc) – would expect these to have a credit balance
- Cash at bank – would expect to have a debit balance unless overdrawn
- Capital – would expect to have a credit balance
- Drawings – would expect to have a debit balance.

## 1.3 Demonstrate the purpose and use of books of prime entry and ledger accounting

**Double entry**

| Ledger account | |
|---|---|
| DR entries increase: | CR entries increase |
| Expenses | Liabilities |
| Assets | Income |
| Drawings | Capital |

**Balancing a ledger account**

- Total each side, inserting highest amount to the bottom of both side.
- On the lower side insert the balancing figure as 'bal c/d'.
- On the opposite side below the total, insert that same balancing figure as 'bal b/d.

## 1.4 Apply ethical principles when recording transactions

- Integrity – e.g. not using information for your own gain
- Objectivity – e.g. having a close relationship with a client
- Professional competence and due care – e.g. asking for help if needed
- Confidentiality – e.g. not discussing client information in public
- Professional behaviour – e.g. complying with the law re VAT.

## 1.5 Carry out financial period end routines

### Control account reconciliations

- The general ledger – a complete record of financial transactions. It holds all the account information needed to prepare financial statements.
- The subsidiary ledger contains separate accounts for individual receivables (the subsidiary sales ledger) and individual payables (the subsidiary purchases ledger). The subsidiary ledger is compared to the control accounts in the general ledger.
- Performing a control account reconciliation
  - Balance the control account
  - Strike a balance on the subsidiary ledger accounts
  - Compare the balances.
- Omissions and errors – the total balance of the subsidiary ledger accounts should agree to the total balance on the control account. If there is a difference this should be investigated and corrected.

### Bank reconciliations

| | |
|---|---|
| Balance as per bank statement | X |
| Add: uncleared lodgements | X |
| Less: unpresented cheques | (X) |
| | —— |
| Balance as per updated cash book | X |
| | —— |

# LO2 Implement procedures for the acquisition and disposal of non-current assets

## 2.1 Demonstrate the importance of prior authority for capital expenditure

- Authorisation required as (1) NCAs may be expensive (2) Funding issues.

## 2.2 Identify capital expenditure

- **Non-current assets**

  Assets that are purchased with the intention of long term use within the business e.g. property, machinery and vehicles.

- **Capital expenditure**

  Expenditure on non-current assets or on the improvement of non-current assets.

  Capital purchases are recorded as assets on the statement of financial position.

  The **initial cost** should include the cost of the asset and the cost of getting the asset to its current location and into working condition (e.g. delivery costs, legal and professional fees, installation costs and test runs).

  IAS 16 Property, Plant and Equipment states that **subsequent expenditure** on assets should only be capitalised in three circumstances:

  1. Where it enhances the value of the asset.
  2. Where a major component of the asset is replaced or restored.
  3. Where it is a major inspection or overhaul of the asset.

- **Revenue expenditure**

  All other expenditure within the business that is not of a capital nature.

  This may include further expenditure incurred on a non-current asset during its life, repairs and maintenance for example.

## 2.3 Differentiate between funding methods for acquisition of non-current assets

- Bank/cash
- Loan
- Hire purchase
- Lease – finance/operating
- Part exchange

## 2.4 Record acquisitions and disposals of non-current assets

**Acquisition**

Dr Non-current asset

Dr VAT control account (if applicable)

Cr Bank/payables

**Disposal**

Step 1 – Remove the original cost of the disposed asset from the asset account

Dr Disposals

Cr Non-current asset cost

Step 2 – Remove the accumulated depreciation of the disposed asset from the accumulated depreciation account

Dr Non-current asset accumulated depreciation

Cr Disposals

Step 3 – Enter the sale proceeds received/receivable for the disposed asset

Dr Bank/receivable

Cr Disposals

Step 4 – Balance off the ledger accounts and calculate whether a profit or loss has been made on disposal

# LO3 Prepare and record depreciation calculations

## 3.1 Calculate depreciation

- The measurement of the cost of the NCA consumed in a period.
- Straight line method

  $$\text{Charge} = \frac{\text{Initial cost} - \text{residual value}}{\text{Useful economic life}}$$

  OR, charge = cost × %
- Diminishing (reducing) balance method

  Charge = Carrying amount (NBV) × %
- Units of production method

  $$\text{Charge} = (\text{Cost} - \text{residual value}) \times \frac{\text{current year's activity}}{\text{expected activity in useful life}}$$

## 3.2 Record depreciation

Dr Depreciation charges (SPL)

Cr Accumulated depreciation (SFP)

# LO4 Record period end adjustments

## 4.1 Record accruals and prepayments in income and expense accounts

**The accruals concept**

- Income and expense should be recognised as and when it is earned or incurred not when the cash is received or paid.

**Accrued expenses**

- Expense that has been incurred but has not been paid for at the period end

  Dr Expense (SPL)

  Cr Accrual (SFP)

**Prepaid expenses**

- Expense that has been paid before the period it has been incurred

  Dr Prepayments (SFP)

  Cr Expense (SPL)

**Income**

- Accrued income – income earned but not received

  Dr Accrued income (current asset SFP)

  Cr Sundry income (e.g. rent – SPL)

- Prepaid income – income received but not earned

  Dr Sundry income (e.g. rent – SPL)

  Cr Prepaid income (current liability SFP)

## 4.2 Record irrecoverable debts and allowances for doubtful debts

**The prudence concept**

- The prudence concept requires an organisation to recognise future losses as soon as it becomes aware of their existence.

**Irrecoverable debts**

- The business believes the debt will NOT be recovered. Must be removed from the receivables ledger and expensed to the SPL.

  Dr Irrecoverable debts expense (SPL)

  Cr Receivables (SFP)

**Doubtful debts**

- There is some question as to whether or not the amount will be settled.

  Dr Allowance for doubtful debts adjustment (SPL)

  Cr Allowance for doubtful debts (SFP)

**Types of allowances for doubtful debts**

- Specific – against a particular receivable or invoice.
- General – % of overall receivables after irrecoverable and specific provision.

## 4.3 Record inventory

**Purchases**

- When inventory is purchased we account for it within purchases, no adjustment is made to the inventory account until the year end:

  Dr Purchases

  Cr Bank/trade payables

**IAS 2 and the calculation of inventory**

- Inventory should be valued at the lower of cost and net realisable value.
- Cost – expenditure incurred in the normal course of business in bringing a product to its present location and condition.
- Net realisable value – the actual or estimated selling price less all further costs to complete the item, less marketing, selling and distribution costs.

**Accounting for closing inventory**

Dr Inventory SFP (asset, hence DR)

Cr Inventory SPL (reduces cost of sales, hence CR)

**Accounting for opening inventory**

- The opening inventory balance in the inventory account is transferred to the statement of profit or loss as part of cost of sales

  Dr Inventory SPL (increases cost of sales, hence DR)

  Cr Inventory SFP (removing asset balance, hence CR)

**Impact on the financial statements**

| **SFP** | £ | £ |
|---|---|---|
| Current assets | | |
| **Closing inventory** | | X |

| **SPL** | £ | £ |
|---|---|---|
| Sales | | X |
| Less: cost of sales | | |
| **Opening inventory** | X | |
| Plus: purchases | X | |
| | X | |
| Less: **closing inventory** | (X) | |
| | | (X) |
| Gross profit | | X |

## 4.4 Record period end adjustments

- Period end adjustments can significantly affect the reported results of the organisation.
- Including misleading or inaccurate period end adjustments can result in non-compliance with regulations and misinformed decision making by users of the final accounts).
- Ethical issues include responding appropriately to period end pressures (e.g. time pressure, pressure to report favourable results, pressure from authority).

# LO5 Produce and extend the trial balance

## 5.1 Prepare a trial balance

**Enter trial balance into the working paper**

| | Trial balance | | Adjustments | | Statement of profit or loss | | Statement of financial position | |
|---|---|---|---|---|---|---|---|---|
| Ledger Account | Dr | Cr | Dr | Cr | Dr | Cr | Dr | Cr |

| Errors that cause an imbalance to the trial balance | Errors that do not cause an imbalance to the trial balance |
|---|---|
| Single entry | Original entry |
| Casting error | Errors of omission and commission |
| Transposition error | Error of principle |
| Extraction error | Reversal of entries |
| Omission | |
| Two entries on one side | |

**The suspense account**

- The suspense account is temporarily used to balance the trial balance when either one side of the accounting entry is unknown or there is an error to be investigated.

**Steps to correcting errors**

1 Determine the incorrect double entries.

2 Determine the entries that should have been made.

3 Produce a journal entry that cancels the error and results in the correct entries.

### 5.2 Carry out adjustments to the trial balance

- Accruals/prepayments
- Closing inventory
- Irrecoverable and doubtful debts
- Depreciation/disposals/additions re non-current assets
- Errors
- Clear any balance on the suspense account

### 5.3 Complete the extended trial balance

- Cross cast the information to the statement of profit or loss columns and the statement of financial position columns as appropriate.
- The figure required to make the totals of the statement of profit or loss Dr and Cr columns equal is entered on the extended trial balance as the profit or loss for the period. The other half of the double entry is in one of the statement of financial position columns, to make their totals equal.
- If the P&L credits exceed the debits, it will be a profit, if the P&L debits exceeds the credits it will be a loss.

# Appendix 2: Final Accounts Preparation

## Introduction

This chapter recaps the key aspects of the underlying Final Accounts Preparation Unit.

**UNIT LEARNING OBJECTIVES STILL RELEVANT FOR THE SYNOPTIC ASSESSMENT**

| | |
|---|---|
| LO1 | Distinguish between the financial recording and reporting requirements of different types of organisation |
| LO2 | Explain the need for final accounts and the accounting and ethical principles underlying their preparation |
| LO3 | Prepare accounting records from incomplete information |
| LO4 | Produce accounts for sole traders |
| LO5 | Produce accounts for partnerships |
| LO6 | Recognise the key differences between preparing accounts for a limited company and a sole trader |

# LO1 Distinguish between the financial recording and reporting requirements of different types of organisation

## 1.1 Describe the types of organisation that need to prepare final accounts

- Types of organisations that prepare final accounts
  - Sole traders
  - Partnerships
  - Limited companies
  - LLPs
  - Charities
- Differences
  - Profit v not-for-profit
  - Ownership
  - Management
  - Liability
  - Reporting regulations
  - Tax

## 1.2 Recognise the regulations applying to different types of organisation

- Limited companies must prepare their accounts in accordance with The Companies Act 2006 and relevant accounting standards.
- Charities must meet the definition of a charity, set out in the Charities Act 2011. Charities must prepare a statement of financial position at the end of each reporting period.
- Partnerships need to abide by the Partnership Act 1890.

# LO2 Explain the need for final accounts and the accounting and ethical principles underlying their preparation

## 2.1 Describe the primary users of final accounts and their needs

| User | Needs |
|---|---|
| Shareholders (investors) | To assess the ability of a business to pay dividends and manage resources. |
| Lenders such as banks | Interested in the ability of the business to pay interest and repay loans. |
| Employees | Need to know if their employer can offer secure employment and possible pay rises. |
| Other creditors | Use final accounts to decide whether to supply goods on credit and the terms of such credit. |
| Government agencies, such as HMRC | Use financial statements as a basis for assessing the amount of tax payable by a business. |
| Management | Use financial statements to compare information of the business they work for to other organisations in the same business sector. |

## 2.2 Describe the accounting principles underlying the preparation of final accounts

**The legal and regulatory framework**

- Accounting standards provide rules and guidance for specific accounting transactions.

**Underlying assumptions (The Conceptual Framework)**

| | |
|---|---|
| Going concern basis | Assumes that the entity will continue in operation for the foreseeable future. |
| Accruals basis | Transactions should be reflected in the financial statements for the period in which they occur. |

**Two fundamental qualitative characteristics of useful information**

| | |
|---|---|
| Relevance | Capable of influencing the decisions of users. |
| Faithful representation | Complete, neutral and free from error. |

**Four enhancing qualitative characteristics of useful information**

| | |
|---|---|
| Comparability | It should be possible to compare an entity over time and with similar information about other entities. |
| Verifiability | If information can be verified, this provides assurance to the users that it is both credible and reliable. |
| Timeliness | Information should be provided to users within a timescale suitable for their decision-making purposes. |
| Understandability | Information should be understandable to those who may want to review and use it. This can be facilitated through appropriate classification, characterisation and presentation of information. |

## 2.3 Apply ethical principles when preparing final accounts

- When preparing final accounts, it is important that accountants act professionally and with integrity.
- They must be technically competent and have an awareness of the potential for conflicts of interest and bias.

# LO3 Prepare accounting records from incomplete information

## 3.1 Recognise circumstances where there are incomplete records

- Manual records may have been destroyed – e.g. fire.
- Computer records may have been compromised – e.g. hacking.
- Problems with data entry – e.g. staff off sick, staff not qualified.

## 3.2 Prepare ledger accounts, using these to estimate missing figures

**Net assets approach**

- This requires the use of the accounting equation.
- All the known figures are compiled into the accounting equation and then the missing figure can be found.
- Typically calculate OAR using direct labour hours or machine hours.

Accounting equation

| | | |
|---|---|---|
| Assets – liabilities | = | Capital |
| Net assets | = | Opening capital + profit (–loss) + capital – drawings |
| Increase in net assets | = | Capital introduced + profit (–loss) – drawings |
| Closing net assets – opening net assets | = | Capital introduced + profit (–loss) – drawings |

**The working control account approach**

- This may include the construction of the sales ledger and/or purchase ledger control accounts to find missing figures, as well as, finding closing balances on the VAT and/or capital account.

**Templates**

| Purchase ledger control account (PLCA) | | | |
|---|---|---|---|
| | £ | | £ |
| Bank payments | X | Opening balance | X |
| Purchase returns (PRDB) | X | Purchases (PDB) | X |
| Discounts received | X | | |
| Contra with SLCA | X | | |
| Closing balance | X | | |
| | X | | X |

| Sales ledger control account (SLCA) | | | |
|---|---|---|---|
| | £ | | £ |
| Opening balance | X | Bank receipts | X |
| Sales (SDB) | X | Discount allowed | X |
| | | Sales returns (SRDB) | X |
| | | Irrecoverable debts | X |
| | | Contra with PLCA | X |
| | | Closing balance | X |
| | X | | X |

| Sales tax (VAT) | | | |
|---|---|---|---|
| | £ | | £ |
| | | Opening balance | X |
| Sales returns day book | X | Sales day book | X |
| Purchase day book | X | Purchase returns day book | X |
| Bank – HMRC | X | | |
| Expenses | X | | |
| Irrecoverable debts | X | | |
| Closing balance | X | | |
| | X | | X |

### 3.3 Calculate figures using mark-up and margin

- Mark-up and margin are used to express the gross profit as a percentage.

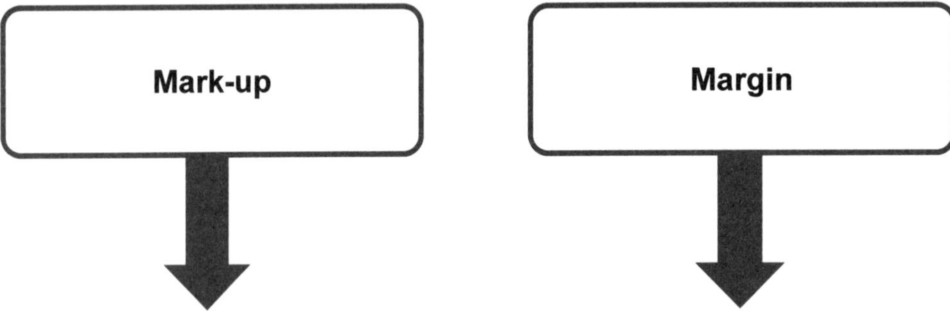


The % is added to cost to find the selling price.

The gross profit is a % of the selling price.

- You may be given the mark-up or margin percentage and asked to calculate one of the figures which makes up cost of goods sold.

### 3.4 Assess the reasonableness of given figures within a particular context

- Exercise professional scepticism.

## LO4 Produce accounts for sole traders

### 4.1 Calculate opening and/or closing capital for a sole trader

- Closing capital = opening capital + profit – drawings

### 4.2 Describe the components of a set of final accounts for a sole trader

- The statement of profit or loss is a summary of income and expenditure for a period to calculate the profit or loss made.
- The trading account calculates the gross profit or loss that has been made from trading activities.
- The net profit or loss is arrived at by deducting all expenses of the business from the gross profit.

## 4.3 Prepare a statement of profit or loss for a sole trader in the given format

**Statement of profit or loss for the year ended 31 December 20X1**

| | £ | £ |
|---|---|---|
| Sales revenue | | X |
| Less: Sales returns | | (X) |
| | | X |
| Opening inventory | X | |
| Purchases | X | |
| Purchase returns | (X) | |
| Carriage inwards | X | |
| Closing inventory | (X) | |
| Cost of goods sold | | (X) |
| Gross profit | | X |
| Add: Sundry income: | | |
| Discount received | | X |
| Interest received | | X |
| Profit on disposal of non-current asset | | X |
| Expenses: | | |
| Discounts allowed | X | |
| Rent | X | |
| Carriage outwards | X | |
| Electricity | X | |
| Depreciation | X | |
| Irrecoverable debt | X | |
| Allowance for doubtful debts adjustment | X | |
| Stationery | X | |
| Telephone | X | |
| Total expenses | | (X) |
| Net profit (loss) for the year | | X |

## 4.4 Prepare a statement of financial position for a sole trader in the given format

**Statement of financial position as at 31 December 20X1**

| | *Cost* | *Accumulated depreciation* | *Carrying amount* |
|---|---|---|---|
| | £ | £ | £ |
| Non-current assets: | | | |
| e.g. land and buildings | X | X | X |
| Current assets: | | | |
| Inventory | | X | |
| Trade receivables | X | | |
| Less allowance for doubtful debts | (X) | X | |
| | | X | |
| Prepayments | | X | |
| Bank | | X | |
| Total current assets | | X | |
| Current liabilities: | | | |
| Trade payables | (X) | | |
| VAT (Sales tax) | (X) | | |
| Accruals | (X) | | |
| Total current liabilities | | (X) | |
| Net current assets/(liabilities) | | | X/(X) |
| Non-current liabilities: | | | |
| Bank loan 20X5 | | | (X) |
| Net assets | | | X |
| Capital: | | | |
| Opening capital | | | X |
| Add: Profit/(Loss) for the year | | | X/(X) |
| Less: Drawings | | | (X) |
| Closing capital | | | X |

# LO5 Produce accounts for partnerships

## 5.1 Describe the key components of a partnership agreement

- The partnership agreement may include salaries, sales commission, interest on capital, interest on drawings and allocation of the residual profit or loss.
- Partnership Act 1890 is used where there is no formal partnership agreement in place.

## 5.2 Describe the accounting procedures for a change in partners

**Step by step instructions for admission of a partner**

- Step 1: Recognise existing goodwill in the accounts

  Dr: Goodwill

  Cr: Old partners' capital accounts in old profit-sharing ratio
- Step 2: Introduce new capital

  Dr: Cash/Assets

  Cr: Partner capital account
- Step 3: Eliminate goodwill from the accounts

  Dr: New partners' capital accounts in new profit-sharing ratio

  Cr: Goodwill
- In effect, goodwill has been introduced and then immediately eliminated from the partnership accounts; the consequence is that there is an adjustment to the capital account balances of those partners who remain in the business.

**Step by step instructions for retirement of a partner**

Need to calculate everything that belongs to the outgoing partner – current a/c, capital a/c and share of goodwill.

- Step 1: Transfer the retiring partner's current account balance to their capital account

  Dr: Partner current account (assuming CR bal on the capital a/c)

  Cr: Partner capital account

- Step 2: Recognise goodwill in the accounts

  Dr: Goodwill

  Cr: Old partners' capital accounts in old profit-sharing ratio

- Step 3: Pay off the retiring partner

  Dr: Partner capital account

  Cr: Cash and/or loan account

- Step 4: Eliminate goodwill from the accounts

  Dr: New partners' capital accounts in new profit-sharing ratio

  Cr: Goodwill

## 5.3 Describe the key components of partnership accounts

- Statement of profit or loss
- Appropriation account
- Statement of financial position
- Capital and current accounts.

## 5.4 Prepare a statement of profit or loss for a partnership, in the given format

- Same as for sole trader.
- Note: salaries, interest on capital and drawings are not expenses.

## 5.5 Prepare a partnership appropriation account, in compliance with the partnership agreement and in the given format

**Appropriation account template – horizontal format**

| | *Total* | *Partners* *A* | *B* |
|---|---|---|---|
| **Net profit** from statement of profit or loss account | X | | |
| Salary | (X) | X | X |
| Sales commission | (X) | X | X |
| Interest on capital | (X) | X | X |
| Interest charged on drawings | X | (X) | (X) |
| Residual profit | X | | |
| Residual profit allocation | (X) | X | X |
| Total to current account | | X | X |

## 5.6 Prepare the current accounts for each partner

**Current account template**

| Current accounts | | | | | |
|---|---|---|---|---|---|
| *Detail* | *A* £ | *B* £ | *Detail* | *A* £ | *B* £ |
| Drawings | | | Balance b/d | | |
| Int on drawings | | | Salary | | |
| | | | Sales commission | | |
| Balance c/d | | | Int on capital | | |
| Residual loss | | | Residual profit | | |
| | ____ | ____ | | ____ | ____ |
| | ____ | ____ | | ____ | ____ |

### 5.7 Prepare a statement of financial position for a partnership, in compliance with the partnership agreement and in the given format

- Top half same as for sole trader.
- Bottom half more complex due to capital and current accounts

| **Capital and current accounts:** | *A* | *B* | £ |
|---|---|---|---|
| Capital accounts | 45,000 | 25,000 | 70,000 |
| Current accounts | (2,050) | 3,550 | 1,500 |
| | 42,950 | 28,550 | 71,500 |

## LO6 Recognise the key differences between preparing accounts for a limited company and a sole trader

### 6.1 Describe the main sources of regulation governing company accounts

- The Companies Act 2006 which applies to all UK companies regardless of whether they follow UK or international accounting rules.
- The International Accounting Standards Board (IASB) and its associated bodies who are responsible for issuing International Financial Reporting Standards (IFRS Standards).
- IAS 1 sets out the overall requirements for financial statements for organisations adopting IFRS Standards, including how they should be structured and the minimum requirements for their content.
- IAS 2 requires inventory to be valued at the lower of cost and net realisable value.
- IAS 16 outlines the accounting treatment for most types of property, plant and equipment.

## 6.2 Describe the more detailed reporting arising from these regulations

**Key differences**

- the requirement to prepare financial statements at least annually and file them publicly
- the selection and application of accounting policies is regulated, and the objectives that should be met when developing them
- limited company financial statements need to follow statutory formats, with prescribed headings and terminology
- cost of sales and other expenses must be classified according to rules
- taxation is charged in the statement of profit or loss of a company
- only the carrying value of non-current assets appears on the statement of financial position of a company
- detailed notes must be provided as part of the financial statements of a company.

# Appendix 3: Management Accounting: Costing

## Introduction

This chapter recaps the key aspects of the underlying Management Accounting: Costing unit.

**UNIT LEARNING OBJECTIVES STILL RELEVANT FOR THE SYNOPTIC ASSESSMENT**

| | |
|---|---|
| LO1 | Understand the purpose and use of management accounting within an organisation |
| LO2 | Apply techniques required for dealing with costs |
| LO3 | Apportion costs according to organisational requirements |
| LO4 | Analyse and review deviations from budget and report these to management |
| LO5 | Apply management accounting techniques to support decision making |

# LO1 Understand the purpose and use of management accounting within an organisation

## 1.1 Demonstrate an understanding of internal reporting

- Management accounting provides information for **planning**, **controlling** and **decision making**.
- Management information can be produced in **any format** that is useful to the business and tends to be produced frequently, for instance **every month**.

## 1.2 Demonstrate an understanding of ethical principles in management accounting

- Key ethical principle = **integrity**.
- Integrity means to be straightforward and honest in all professional and business relationships.
- Integrity also implies fair dealing and truthfulness.

## 1.3 Critically compare different types of responsibility centres

- Responsibility centres
  - **Cost centre** – manager controls costs
  - **Profit centre** – manager controls costs and revenue
  - **Investment centre** – manager controls costs, revenue and investment.

Note: other terminology

- **Cost units** – an individual unit of product or service for which costs can be separately ascertained.
- Product and period costs
  - A **product** cost relates to the product being produced
  - A **period** cost relates to a time period.

## 1.4 Explain and demonstrate the differences between marginal and absorption costing

- **Key difference – inventory valuation**

| *Absorption costing* | *Marginal costing* |
|---|---|
| Inventory is valued at the full production cost (fixed and variable production costs) | Inventory is valued at the variable production cost only |

| Note: Differences in profit | |
|---|---|
| | £ |
| Absorption costing profit | X |
| Less: Change in inventory × OAR | +/–X |
| Marginal costing profit | X |

- **Format of income statement/profit and loss**

| *Absorption costing* | *Marginal costing* |
|---|---|
| Sales – cost of sales = gross profit | Sales – all variable costs = contribution |
| Costs are split based on function – production or non-production | Costs are split based on behaviour – variable or fixed |
| Non-production overheads are deducted after gross profit | Variable non-production overheads are excluded from the valuation of inventory but are deducted before contribution |
| | All fixed cost are period costs |

- **Usefulness**

| *Absorption costing* | *Marginal costing* |
|---|---|
| Financial reporting | Decision making – focus on contribution |

- **Ethical issue** – if using absorption costing then can boost profit just by making more than you can sell as OH get carried forward in closing inventory.

# LO2 Apply techniques required for dealing with costs

## 2.1 Record and calculate materials, labour and overhead costs

**Materials – pricing issues of raw materials**

- **FIFO** (First in, first out) – assumes that issues will be made based on the oldest prices leaving the more recent prices in stores.

  FIFO is acceptable by HMRC and adheres to IAS2 Inventories.

  If prices are rising, FIFO profit > LIFO

- **LIFO** (Last in, first out) – assumes that issues will be made based on the newest prices leaving the oldest prices in stores.

  LIFO should only be used within an organisation as it does not adhere to IAS2.

  If prices are declining, LIFO profit > FIFO

- **AVCO** (weighted average) – assumes that issues will be made based on the average cost per unit of the items in stores.

| Method | Advantages | Disadvantages |
|---|---|---|
| **FIFO** | Up to date closing inventory value as the recent priced items remain in inventory | Out of date valuation on issues to production as old prices are used to value issues to production<br><br>Identical jobs may have different costs |
| **LIFO** | Up to date valuation on issues as the recent priced items are used to value issues to production | Out of date closing inventory value as old prices as used to value inventory |
| **AVCO** | A compromise on inventory valuation and issues | The average price rarely reflects the actual purchase price of the material |

**Labour**

- **Remuneration systems**
  - Annual salary
  - Hourly rates
  - Piecework
  - Guaranteed minimum
  - Bonus schemes
- **Overtime**
  - Payment – the total amount paid for the hours worked above the normal number of hours.
  - Premium – the extra paid above the normal rate for the overtime hours.

## 2.2 Analyse and use appropriate cost information

- **Overtime premium**
  - Direct cost if overtime due to specific request of a customer.
  - Indirect cost if overtime due to general work pressures.

## 2.3 Apply inventory control methods

- **Re-order level**

  Re-order level = (maximum usage × maximum lead time) + buffer

- **Economic order level**

  $$EOQ = \sqrt{\frac{2 \times C_o \times D}{C_h}}$$

- **Maximum inventory**

  Maximum level = Re-order level + re-order quantity – (minimum usage × minimum lead time)

- **Minimum inventory**

  Minimum level = Re-order level – (average usage × average lead time)

## 2.4 Differentiate between cost classifications for different purposes

| Purpose | Classification |
|---|---|
| Financial accounts | By function – Cost of sales, distribution costs, administrative expenses |
| Cost control | By element – materials, labour, other expenses |
| Cost accounting | By relationship to cost units – direct, indirect |
| Budgeting, decision making | By behaviour – fixed, variable |

## 2.5 Differentiate between and apply different costing systems

**Job costing**

- Specific order costing
- Each job is the cost unit

**Batch costing**

- Specific order costing
- One batch will contain a number of units

**Service costing**

- Intangibility
- Heterogeneity
- Simultaneous production and consumption
- Perishability

**Process costing**

- Applicable where goods or services result from a sequence of repetitive processes.
- Example of continuous operation costing.
- If have losses, distinguish normal and abnormal

$$\text{Cost per unit} = \frac{\text{(Expected costs – scrap on normal losses)}}{\text{Expected good output}}$$

- Value good output, abnormal losses and abnormal gains at full cost per unit.
- If WIP, then work in EU = Number of physical units × % completion.
- If opening WIP then choice AVCO or FIFO.

# LO3 Apportion costs according to organisational requirements

## 3.1 Calculate and use overhead costs

**Budgeted overheads**

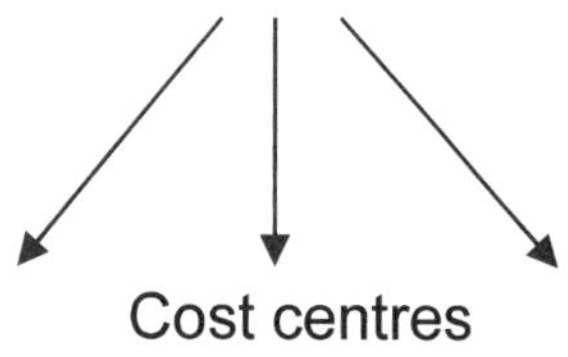

**Step 1:** Allocation or Apportionment

(Use sensible basis)

Cost centres

| **A** | **B** | **C** |
|---|---|---|
| (Prod$^n$) | (Prod$^n$) | (Service) |

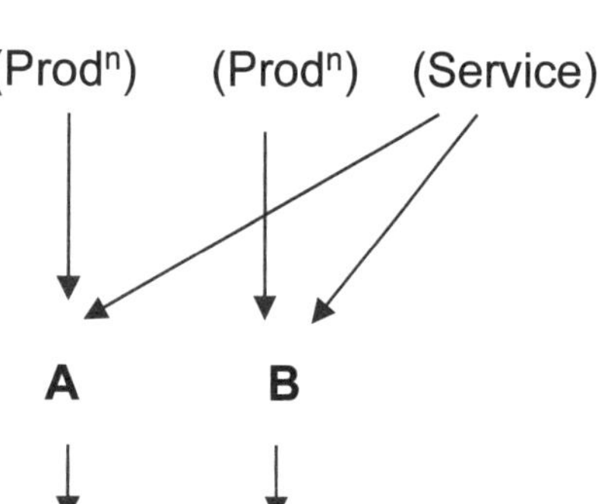

**Step 2:** Reapportion – direct or step down

**A** **B**

**Step 3:** Absorb – e.g. rate per hour

**Production output**

### 3.2 Calculate overhead recovery rates using traditional methods

- OAR = Budgeted overhead ÷ Budgeted activity.
- Typically calculate OAR using direct labour hours or machine hours.

### 3.3 Calculate overhead recovery rates using ABC

1. Group production overheads into activities, according to how they are driven.
2. Identify cost drivers for each activity.
3. Calculate a cost driver rate for each activity.
4. Absorb the activity costs into the product.
5. Calculate the overhead cost per unit of product.

### 3.4 Demonstrate understanding of the under or over recovery of overheads

1. Calculate the OAR = Budgeted overhead ÷ Budgeted activity
2. Calculate how much overhead has been absorbed by actual activity

   Absorbed = OAR × Actual activity
3. Compare the actual overhead cost with the absorbed overhead
4. Absorbed > Actual = over absorbed  
   Absorbed < Actual = under absorbed

**Journal entries**

| Production overhead control account | | | |
|---|---|---|---|
| | £ | | £ |
| Bank | (1) | Production | (2) |
| Statement of profit or loss | (3) | Statement of profit or loss | (4) |

(1) = actual costs

(2) = actual OH absorbed into production

(3) = over absorption adjustment

(4) = under absorption adjustment

# LO4 Analyse and review deviations from budget and report these to management

## 4.1 Calculate variances

- Compare actual v flexed budget.
- Can be sub-divided – e.g. into price and efficiency aspects.

## 4.2 Analyse and investigate variances

- Causes

| *Variance* | *Possible cause* |
|---|---|
| Sales | Price higher or lower than budgeted<br>Sales volume higher or lower than budgeted |
| Materials | Price higher or lower than budgeted<br>Used more/less than we should have done – e.g. wastage |
| Labour | Rate higher or lower than budgeted – e.g. overtime<br>Took longer (quicker) than we should have done – e.g. problems with poor materials |

## 4.3 Report on variances

- Look for factors in the scenario to explain.
- Look for linkages – e.g. inferior materials may be cheaper but result in higher waste.

# LO5 Apply management accounting techniques to support decision making

## 5.1 Estimate and use short-term future income and costs

**Ethical issue**

- Professional competence

**Relevant costing**

- Look at future incremental cash flows

**CVP analysis**

- Focus on contribution
- Breakeven point (units) = $\frac{\text{fixed costs}}{\text{contribution per unit}}$
- Margin of safety = (budgeted sales – BEP), usually given as a %
- Sales required to hit target profit (units) = $\frac{\text{fixed costs + target profit}}{\text{contribution per unit}}$
- Profit/volume ratio = C/S ratio = $\frac{\text{contribution}}{\text{selling price}}$
- Breakeven point (£) = $\frac{\text{fixed costs}}{\text{C/S ratio}}$

**Limiting factor analysis**

- Identify scarce resource
- Calculate contribution per unit
- Calculate contribution per scarce resource
- Rank options
- Allocate scarce resource based on ranking

## 5.2 Assess and estimate the effects of changing activity levels

- Separate out fixed and variable costs
- Use high-low analysis if necessary
- Watch out for stepped fixed costs

## 5.3 Use long-term future income and costs

**Payback**

- Payback = time to recoup initial investment
- For constant annual inflows, payback = $\frac{\text{initial investment}}{\text{annual inflow}}$
- Otherwise, work out cumulative cash position each year

**NPV**

- Money has a time value (due to inflation, cost of capital, investment opportunities and risk)
- PV = future CF × discount factor
- NPV = sum of PVs of inflows – outflows
- Accept project if NPV > 0 as should increase shareholder wealth

| Advantages of NPV | Disadvantages of NPV |
|---|---|
| • It considers the time value of money.<br>• It uses cash flows which are less subjective than profits.<br>• It considers the whole life of the project.<br>• It provides a monetary value for the return from an investment. | • Cash flows are future predictions and we are unable to predict the future with accuracy.<br>• Discounted cash flow as a concept is more difficult for a non-financial manager to understand.<br>• It may be difficult to decide on which discount rate to use. |

**IRR**

- IRR = breakeven discount rate where NPV = 0

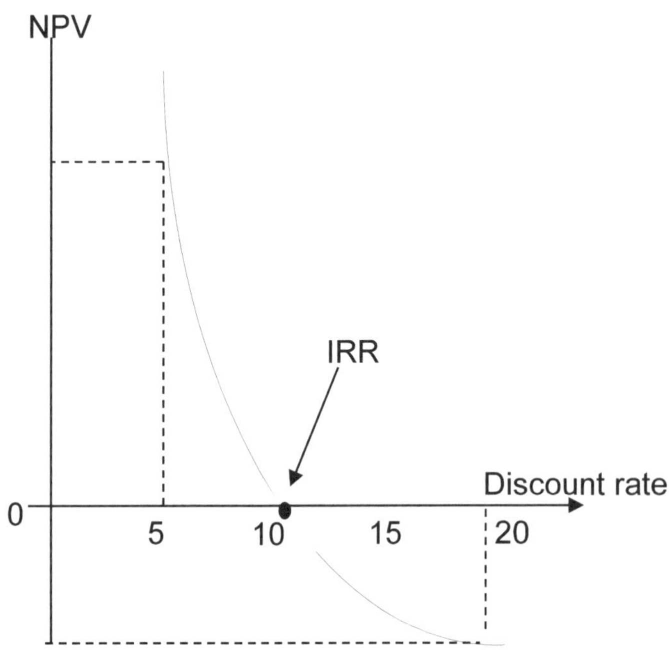


- IRR (%) = L + [$N_L$ ÷ ($N_L$ – $N_H$)] × (H – L)
- Accept project if cost of capital < IRR

| Advantages of IRR | Disadvantages of IRR |
|---|---|
| • It considers the time value of money.<br>• It uses cash flows which are less subjective than profits.<br>• It considers the whole life of the project.<br>• It provides a percentage return that is easier for non-financial managers to understand.<br>• It can be calculated without deciding on the desired cost of capital. | • Cash flows are future predictions and we are unable to predict the future with accuracy.<br>• Discounted cash flow as a concept is more difficult for a non-financial manager to understand.<br>• It does not provide a monetary value for the return available from the investment. |

- If NPV and IRR conflict, then use NPV.

# INDEX

**W**



**Y**



**#**